PAULO FREIRE

Studies in the
Postmodern Theory of Education

Shirley R. Steinberg
General Editor

Vol. 500

The Counterpoints series is part of the Peter Lang Education list.
Every volume is peer reviewed and meets
the highest quality standards for content and production.

PETER LANG
New York • Bern • Frankfurt • Berlin
Brussels • Vienna • Oxford • Warsaw

PAULO FREIRE

The Global Legacy

EDITED BY MICHAEL A. PETERS AND TINA BESLEY
Foreword by Ana María (Nita) Araújo Freire

PETER LANG
New York • Bern • Frankfurt • Berlin
Brussels • Vienna • Oxford • Warsaw

Library of Congress Cataloging-in-Publication Data
Paulo Freire: the global legacy / edited by Michael A. Peters, Tina Besley.
pages cm. — (Counterpoints: studies in the postmodern theory of education; v. 500)
Includes bibliographical references and index.
1. Freire, Paulo, 1921–1997. 2. Education—Philosophy. I. Peters, Michael A.
II. Besley, Tina, author, editor of compilation.
LB880.F732P378   370.11'5—dc23   2014025302
ISBN 978-1-4331-2532-4 (hardcover)
ISBN 978-1-4331-2531-7 (paperback)
ISBN 978-1-4539-1408-3 (e-book)
ISSN 1058-1634

Bibliographic information published by **Die Deutsche Nationalbibliothek.**
Die Deutsche Nationalbibliothek lists this publication in the "Deutsche
Nationalbibliografie"; detailed bibliographic data are available
on the Internet at http://dnb.d-nb.de/.

Cover depicts Te Whare Wānanga o Awanuiārangi.
Te Whare Wānanga o Awanuiārangi was established in 1991 by Te Rūnanga o Ngāti Awa and
officially became a Wānanga in 1997. It is one of only three institutions designated as Wānanga
under the New Zealand Education Act 1989. The establishment of Awanuiārangi was an
important step that recognized the role of education in providing positive pathways for Māori
development, offering a range of qualifications, from community education programs to doctoral
degrees. Awanuiārangi recognizes that their aspirations are linked to and expressed by other
indigenous people throughout the world. Awanuiārangi provides educational opportunities to all
Māori, New Zealanders, and indigenous students through campuses based in Whakatāne,
Auckland (Tāmaki) and Northland (Te Tai Tokerau), as well as through marae and community
networks across the country. See http://www.wananga.ac.nz/about.

The paper in this book meets the guidelines for permanence and durability
of the Committee on Production Guidelines for Book Longevity
of the Council of Library Resources.

© 2015 Peter Lang Publishing, Inc., New York
29 Broadway, 18th floor, New York, NY 10006
www.peterlang.com

Printed in the United States of America

To Paulo Freire, the great teacher, educator, and activist who continues to inspire so many people throughout the world.

Table of Contents

Section 2: Reading the World

Section 3: Education as the Practice of Freedom

Acknowledgments

Thanks to the Administrators at the Centre for Global Studies in Education, University of Waikato, Courtney White, Sabrina Van Saarloos and Maggie Lyall for editorial assistance in preparing this manuscript.

We are grateful for the continued excellent support from the Peter Lang team.

Thank you to the Philosophy of Education Society of Australasia for sponsorship funding assistance for the conference 'Paulo Freire: The Global Legacy,' from which this work is derived.

Foreword

The Understanding of Paulo Freire's Education: Ethics, Hope, and Human Rights

ANA MARIA (NITA) ARAÚJO FREIRE

INTRODUCTION

It is an honour being here for the first time in New Zealand, in Oceania, invited by the University of Waikato, to receive this tribute to my husband Paulo Freire for the legacy he left to the world, and to speak about this legacy. It is a joy which I will never forget.

Before I begin, I want to thank the Philosophy of Education Society of Australasia and the Centre for Global Studies in Education of Waikato University for organising the event and for the invitation. In addition, I would like to thank the support from the Faculty of Education, Waikato University, and Peter Lang Publishing, New York. Furthermore, I want to express nominally my gratitude to Professor Tina Besley and Professor Michael Peters of Waikato University.

I want to thank all of you who have come from different parts of the world to honour my husband. I regret that Donaldo Macedo cannot be with us. He is Paulo's and my great friend, and undoubtedly an authority when it comes to my husband's ideas.

MOMENT 1: A LITTLE ABOUT PAULO AND HIS LIFE

My subjectivity as a living partner has never allowed me to escape from the rigorous objectivity of the facts. Speaking of Paulo's grandeur and integrity, his personal virtues in his subjectivity, we will find the explanation of his theoretical comprehension. His virtues are evident in his knowledge of education and in his fundamental theoretical concepts.

Therefore, I must begin by speaking of the congruence[1] between Paulo's feelings, his thinking, his behaviour, and his writing. Then, I will continue addressing his prudence in his boldness, his tolerance in respecting the different, and even his antagonists. Yet, it is important to speak of his perennial good humour even in the face of difficulties and adversities, of his enormous patience in his immense impatience, of his almost limitless generosity in giving himself to his peers, of his strength in resisting the irresponsible and those who practised misdoings, and of his humility in not whining or complaining or indulging in self-pity.

I acknowledge his childlike and spontaneous curiosity. He never gave up in the face of discouragements. He was never satisfied to conform to those intellectuals who said, "It must be so…this and only this truth forever." His common sense always challenged the nonsense of those continually repeating, "It must be so, because it has always been thus." I acknowledge his moral force that enabled him to understand the fragility of men and women without condemning them. I acknowledge his deliberate decisions and readiness to love, and to be in solidarity with people of all nations, colours, religions, ages, and sexual orientations.

He displayed intense passion in all events and circumstances of his daily living, and demonstrated above all his faithful communion with those who suffer because they are dehumanised. He firmly believed that from the oppressed one could build a better world. The values he lived were true, whole, and complete, born out of compassion for those marginalised, excluded, and oppressed.

Paulo was totally lacking in prejudice, anger, and desire for revenge or vindictiveness. He devoted his life to practising the awareness that enables men and women to transform themselves from being oppressed objects of elitist and authoritarian societies, into those who are indeed the subjects of history, thus enabling them to pronounce their world. They have studied and reflected, and therefore have the possibility of positioning themselves as critical subjects in society. As they become more and more critical, and engage more authentically in ethical and political struggles, they can ultimately transform the society where they live, which has previously oppressed them.

Paulo's many values and beliefs are grounded in the principles of human rights.

I met Paulo when I was only four years old, and he had just received a scholarship donated by my parents[2] so that he could enroll in high school. He had lost his father, and his family had lost almost all their belongings. They moved from Recife[3] to Jaboatão,[4] where Paulo encountered many of his greatest sufferings, but where he also learned to fight for life and take an interest in social injustices that afflicted the majority of Brazil's population. He studied hard, and earned a law degree.

He was a teacher of the Portuguese language before becoming the major educator of our country. Today, Paulo is the Patron of Brazilian Education. With this title, the greatest and most important among hundreds of others that Paulo received in life, or after his death, the country of Brazil recognises him as the greatest educator in all our history. Further, our educators, in acknowledging him as Patron, have benefited immeasurably themselves, as has the quality of the education they provide. We all win. The Brazilian Nation wins!

My relationship with Paulo lasted many years and had various nuances. I was his student, his friend, his student again in my master's degree, and finally, "when we changed the nature of our relations," his wife. We shared together ten years of affectionate, sexual, and intellectual maturity. Ten years of unlimited confidence in each other; of deep friendship; of unending fascination; of untainted admiration; of total openness and honesty of one towards the other. We never hid from one another our dreams, desires, doubts, sorrows, joys, frustrations, and disappointments.

We experienced wonderful things, and we experienced difficult things. All of these taught us to love above everything else and in all circumstances. We loved each other deeply. We gave ourselves to each other, to the full realisation of our lives.

MOMENT 2: THE WORLD'S READING OF PAULO WITH A FOCUS ON THE READING OF CONCRETE CONTEXT

Paulo understood that in order to become a good educator, we must cultivate and nurture our virtues. We are not born with them, but we are born with tendencies toward good or evil.

Our genetic heritage, our family environment, our school environment, and other opportunities that our society gives or denies us are what enable us to be what we are, and what we will become. We are not born *determined* to be this or that, but we become *conditioned* for this or that. It is up to us, within our freedom, and our autonomy as subjects, to make our own choices and educate ourselves about the virtues, and to perfect them or not. Paulo took the ontological path to fight for ethical behaviour, guided by virtues. He educated himself according to the principles of *Greek arête*.

Paulo's coherent legacy was that of a humanist educator. He understood that the act of knowing does not originate only in the brain, where it is said the intelligence of the world is processed—the "house" or the place of the logic of discernment. He used to say, "I do not know only by using my head, or only by using my intelligence. My knowledge comes from the confluence of things emanating from my whole body, without compartmentalisation. Knowledge comes from the emotions, feelings, and other sentiments that go through my body, and because of my body, and also because of my mind. It is my body that tells me about what I must reflect. It is my body that becomes restless, that mobilises me for the *search of knowledge.* When I look repeatedly at the same thing, when my skin gets the chills, when my breast beats frenetically, my heart almost tells me, 'pay attention to it.'"

It is my body that tells me there is something that needs to be unveiled, to be made known, and to be shared socially. Indeed, there are signs in my body that warn me. "Paulo, focus your reflection on what makes you restless and uneasy." Thus, it is the conscious body that when instigated, provoked, and unsettled, leads to reflections that enable the establishment of an immaterial field of receptivity, where new knowledge can be "housed."

This new knowledge is still intuitive. It becomes possible then, in the light of reflexive reason, to sort out and systematise this *new knowledge.* This is how one produces knowledge—new knowledge. We do not discern only with the head, but with the whole body and everything it has, everything it processes, and everything it produces—emotions, feelings, experiences, intuitions, fears, terrors, joys, questions, myths, doubts, certainties, uncertainties....

Nobody acquires new knowledge because one has read, repeated, and memorised what was read. In order to know, we have in ourselves our primary and own condition of *human existence*, the knowability, i.e., the possibility created by us across thousands of years.

Starting from the gesture, the grunt, the cry, we stand up, walk, and the brain says, "I do, because I want to, intentionally." The very act of doing-thinking-doing has made available to us the conscience of the world, and the spoken languages, and then the written languages, through which we *communicate today.* In other words, with this millennia-long process, we have created in ourselves the *knowability*, we have created the ability to understand the reality, and thus we are able to create the romance, the poetry, the arts, the religions, the sciences, and the philosophies.

We have created the capacity to act on them, change them, and improve them. With *knowability*, we have the power to organise ourselves for social life that made, for example, this event possible, so that we can pay tribute to men like Paulo Freire.

We have turned ourselves into *cognisant beings*, beings capable of *knowing*, who constantly seek to know more, from the necessity and the curiosity to learn more. True knowledge implies *apprehending* the fact, the phenomenon, the object, so that we *appropriate* what we need to know, what we wish to know.

Another important understanding is the presence of one of many *subjectivities* open to what is new, stripped of the *prior "givens,"* and open to the authentic and true act of knowing. We do not learn alone, but *in communion* with others. This original knowledge, being historical, is always being replaced by new knowledge, through the dynamism of all sorts of technologies, and the human desires to continually improve.

The act of knowledge, according to Paulo's theorising, requires, therefore, these three elements: the *subject or cognisant subjects*; the *cognisable objects*; and the *dialectical and dialogical relationship between* these *two elements*.

It is our cognisability, or knowability, built up by us, and within us, across the millennia, that allows us to *apprehend* the fact, the event, and/or the phenomenon or thing. Then, we *appropriate to ourselves* the object that was unveiled. Then, and only then, do we learn what was previously sought.

For Paulo, the dialogue is founded in the loving relationship established between *cognisant* subjects, and the objective possibility of knowing through questions: Why? For what purpose? What? And for whom? Against what? Against whom? How? Where? When? These questions and answers successively generate *awareness*, and new questions and unveilings. It is a process similar to Socratic maieutic, but differing from it because, in the Freirean dialogue, one does not seek only the ready-knowledge that needs only to be "discovered." The Socratic maieutic is idealistic, and the dialogue denies the Freiran reading of the world.

The knowledge that can be given only objectively between subjectivities in the reading of the world of concrete things, while it provokes and establishes inside us a relationship of dialogue between one another, is, at the same time, and conversely, an act in which knowledge is absolutely individual and subjective. It occurs in introspection.

Understanding the *process of acquisition of knowledge*, Paulo denounced the *"banking" model education*, in which the educator tries to deposit content in the students' empty minds, an act that precludes objectivity/subjectivity. Instead of theorising education as "banking", Paulo proposes the concept of *critical education*—education that is *problematical, inquisitive, transformative, dialogic, dialectic, and liberating*.

Furthermore, according to Paulo, our *critical awareness of the world* tells us that we *know*, and can *know more*. In the continuous dynamic of departing from the practice of what is known, and seeking the theory that explains it, and practising again, brings with it the learning, the common sense, the institutions, and the emotions. This is what Paulo called *"the right thinking*, the need to think the practice, to practice better, and *to learn more*, and to learn better."

If for Paulo, all *true knowledge* derives from thinking the practice of everyday life, lived in common sense and in intuitive sense, and if true knowledge derives also from the *critical reading of the world*, then we are speaking of the concrete social, political, anthropological, and religious contexts in which one lives, practises, and thinks. Thus there is no way to escape the fact that Freirean theory embodies a policity, an "anthropolicity," and an ethnicity, and consequently an "aestheticity" in understanding the act of seeking knowledge, *of reading the world, and of acting in it.*

And so, education for Paulo is a critical-ethical-political-educational activity, which involves an *awareness* that enables engagement in the struggle for political and social participation, and in the *critical reading of the world*, for the transformation of the world.

MOMENT 3: POLITICITY, DIALOGICITY, AND HOPEFUL PRAXIS: THE ETHICAL NATURE OF PAULO FREIRE'S THEORY

In the era of *neoliberalism*, it is customary to honor intellectuals who are exclusively rational, rationalist, or pragmatic. Pragmatics is beholden to a capitalist market economy. However, Paulo was truly a humanist intellectual, an educator with ideas absolutely connected to his "Northeastern Brazilianity," influenced by aspects of phenomenology, Marxism, and personalism. He was a humanist critic who never feared acknowledging that his knowledge came from his emotions, from his feelings, and from his commonsense intuitions. This motivated him *to seek the 'raison d'être'* or *'reason for being' of objects* that could be known through reflection. Unlike the neoliberals, Paulo maintained that there is no such thing as *neutrality* in the choices, of options and actions, or in ideologies and practices, be they from the right or from the left. Paulo was a humanist critic who embraced the *ethics of life* because he was *in favor* of the destitute, the restricted, and the oppressed.

He was *against* the oppressors, oppressive *conditions*, and oppressive *relations*, which were the focus of his *denunciations*, and replaced with the *announcement* of a new man and a new woman living in a new society, more just, more fraternal, and more ethical, a society that respects human rights and upholds democracy.

In the era of economic globalization, which is supported by postmodern philosophies and by the most profound and rapid technological changes that history has known, a new "ethics" was established, the ethics of the market. According to the principles of this ethics, "human values" are dictated by market needs, and, as we know, this adopts values that serve the interests of those who have the capital and not the values inherent in more authentic human needs.

Today's ethics have become corrupted by a new and imperative paradigm of a highly technologised world that destroys, dehumanises living conditions and social relations. This "ethics," the "ethics of the market," is wrong. It is an ethic that is responsible for the concentration of income with the few, while the majority experience unemployment, hunger, and all different sorts of miseries that are "globalised" by the ease with which one corrupts and is corrupted, and by the lack of solidarity with and respect for others. This ethic is responsible for the disparities that increase every day between those who have, know, want, can, desire, aspire, and achieve their wishes and those who cannot (or *are not able to*) achieve any of these things, and those who cannot even have the right *to dream.*

The ethics of life embedded in Paulo's understanding of the world counteracts the ethics of the market because it has as its ultimate principle the respect for life and aims to dignify life. It is a fundamental requirement of democracy. The "ethics of the market," which denies the ethics of life, is essentially an unethical positioning. It hurts, mistreats, ages the youth, kills children, and steals the humanity of millions of men and women. It promotes death and not life. It is the "ethics" that despises values and virtues that characterise the humanity of men and women.

Ultimately, the "ethics of the market" in which money becomes a god prohibits others from accessing and maintaining material goods. It commands, trains, oppresses, and forces people to exploit their brothers and sisters. It supports imperialist countries, and those who forged them, or joined them. Its "agenda" is conquest, cultural invasion, manipulation, and division, all of which are opposed to a dialogical action theory (Freire, 2011).

So, we must ask ourselves: Do we, or do we not, need to create a new social organisation from the *ethics of life,* which could establish the humanism that enables people to be truly alive and who actively care for each other? Do we want an ethics of life that can inhibit and dismantle what is destroying the environment, and can promote the being concerned for the planet and all human beings, especially those who, across the millennia, have strived to construct a social life characterized by tolerance, fraternity, and solidarity? "Is the dream over?"

Did neoliberalism, by declaring the end of history and the class struggle, ever consider, along its destructive pathway, the possibilities of reinventing a new society more ethical, or better yet, truly ethical? Has Paulo's *possible dream* been definitively erased by the cynical pragmatism, the selfish, usurpation, devastation, (and misrepresentation of truths by those who command, order, enact, oppress, marginalise, and exclude the historical and ontological destiny of the great majority of the world's population?

The growing interest in and adherence to Freirean's praxis by numbers of Christians, Muslims, Jews, and Maoists, and their motivation to build a new world in which the *ethics of life,* dedicated to *liberation,* are guiding the world toward to new social behavior of their citizens.

The "philosopher of liberation," Enrique Dussel (2000), believes that the ethical-political-anthropological comprehension of Paulo's education embodies the essence of the ethics of liberation because in it "human life is the content of ethics."

"Freire is not just a pedagogue, in the specific sense of the term, he is more. He is an educator of 'ethical-critical consciousness' of the victims, the oppressed, the condemned of the earth, in the community" (Dussel, 2000, p. 427). Paulo Freire is "the pedagogue of an **ethical-critical conscience**" (Dussel, 2000, p. 487, footnote 161, emphasis mine).

We have no doubt that Paulo's understanding of education, enshrined in the essence of the ethics of life, has enabled the comprehension of what Dussel calls the "Ethics of Liberation", Paulo Freire's understanding of the impossibility of separating the concrete contexts of education as a practice for freedom and the process of liberation and transformation and life itself, as proposed by the "Ethics of Discourse." This ethic, in contrast with the ethics of life, understands education from a subjectivist view, which positions education as formation or as training or recycling of knowledge within a formal and universalist ethics that serves to maintain the *status quo*.

The issue of ethics always worried Paulo. In the last years of his life, he was devoted to thinking about it, and he intended to write, systematising his worries in the face of the calamities within an unethical world. His writing would have announced the redeeming of our humanity as a contribution from our presence in the world. I believe he would have been speaking of ethics that underlie the true *human rights* present in all his work, and implicitly or explicitly built in each of his words. In Paulo's view, *the word is like "palavração" (word + action): Word is already action.*

Therefore, Paulo's theory of knowledge is neither simply a progressive ideology nor a simple literacy methodology, as many claim. Paulo's theory is a theory of knowledge that incorporates an ethic that denies the ethics of discourse, but especially the ethics of the market. On the contrary, there is within Paulo's work an *ethics of life* that proposes a *liberating* education, an *emancipatory* education that allows the *autonomy of subjectivities*, grounded in respect for human rights.

I think I should say a few things about three premises of Paulo's theory. I have chosen: the Politicity, Dialogicity, and hopeful Praxis that are related dialectically. I see them as representing the unity in his theory and representing the constitutive ethical nature of his theory.

a. We find the Politicity or the political nature of education (and not the neutrality) evident in Paulo's work and praxis in the relationship between awareness, commitment and solidarity—acting together to transform education.

People need to become aware of dehumanising facts that "limit" their lives. The educator or the militant should and must challenge these "limit situations," and act in ways that respect the dignity of all people. This implies educators should become committed to overcoming social injustices of all sorts and act in solidarity with the oppressed who are excluded from the educational process, and from the opportunities to participate in the destiny of their country. The educator should share in taking risks with the oppressed and excluded so that they can abandon the *magic, mythic, or ingenuous understanding* of their *world* to appropriate a *critical awareness which Paulo Freire's dialogical action theory* provides. This critical consciousness allows the voiceless to *pronounce their world,* thus creating the possibility to restore the ontological humanity denied to the oppressed.

    b.   We find the Dialogicity between subjectivity and objectivity in comprehension of the educational act in Paulo's work and praxis requires educators to be curious (epistemological curiosity),[5] to authenticate themselves before others with respect, to be generous and to participate, to be tolerant of the different, to be tolerant of the multiplicity of ways that others read the world, and to open themselves up to revealing the knowledge with love and care. In other words, one must be curious, seeking to know more scientifically. One must respect the ethnic, racial, gender, religious, language, and cultural diversities; one must be generous and love others. One must be generous when showing solidarity toward all pains, distresses, and hardships of those vilipended and oppressed.

Educators should create an affective and restless atmosphere in their classrooms that helps students collaboratively and joyfully search for, create, and re-create knowledge with epistemological curiosity and scientific rigor. Educators also need to love the act of teaching and the school's curriculum. However, they are not obliged to love all pupils equally, but to respect and take care for them with equity.

The lovingness, as understood by Paulo in the pedagogical context, is a fundamental component of human rights, because it points to the need not only of respect and tolerance for differences, but also to exercise loving care and generosity toward the dignity of all participants.

    c.   Hopeful Praxis can be understood as a lifelong and positive outlook on enhancing the quality of life, and achieving personal fulfillment, but realising that complete achievement of these things is difficult, but possible, which Paulo repeated without tiring over the last years of his life. In engaging in life's struggle, one must trust and have faith in oneself and others; one must be humble and understand human striving to do better and to become more.

Hope for Paulo is more than a state of mind or one of the theological virtues. To him, hope reaches beyond these conceptions. Hope is a result of the incompleteness of *human existence.* It belongs, therefore, to our ontological nature. From that incompleteness comes the possibility of education. Or, putting it another way, education allows us to constitute ourselves as *human* beings of *human existence,* which is much more than simple animal life. Hope is, therefore, an ontological human quality that justifies education. Hopelessness is the contradictory moment of hope.

Authentic humility that has no relationship with humiliation is the virtue that reinforces and reaffirms tolerance and caring. Acceptance without complaint of life's difficulties as well as its successes is authentic humility. The arrogance of many educators lacking in humility could be overcome if the reductionist dichotomies between teacher and learner, and between the all-knowing and the ignorant, could be rejected. Paulo's humble understanding informs us that people learn in communion with others.

Paulo's humility is evident in his book *Pedagogy of the Oppressed*. More and more people from all over the world came to tell him: "Professor, your work is brilliant, masterful…. It has changed my life." When he said this to me, Paulo commented: "If I had not focused on my humbleness I would have lost myself…. I would have lost my ontological positioning, the purpose for which I had written this book."

Paulo's greatest example of humility was to insist that people should not repeat or follow him, or try to re-create him. They could have him as a reference, if they wanted, but they needed to appreciate that he never thought he had said nor done everything.

Paulo and his theory of knowledge, which he preferred to call, humbly, "a certain critical understanding of education" is characterised by an attitude toward respecting and dignifying life, through enabling the liberation and empowering of historical subjectivities. His theory of knowledge has always been at the service of the oppressed and excluded. His theory was constructed from his feelings, emotions, intuitions, wariness of truisms, and his "recifenses"[6] experiences, and reflections on the works of philosophers, sociologists, anthropologists, and educators from the ancient Greeks to the modern and postmodern eras.

In conclusion, Paulo's *words that pronounce the world* have within themselves their own liberating ethical force. They are deliberately imbued to the very core with Paulo's humanistic ethics. *The word* to him is liberative praxis, because in them, in his words, lead toward truth, understood as the dynamics of ethical praxis. Ethics for Paulo is truth. Paulo's understanding, education, and his epistemology based on his more radical ethics have permeated his studies of pedagogical, political, anthropological, philosophical, and sociological theories since his childhood and adolescence. All these understandings have equipped Paulo to propose his ethical paradigm *for liberatory education that enables us to transform our societies for the better*.

If today the world tries to understand its violence, lack of ethical decency, and naturalness with which it behaves toward a large measure of people facing hunger, disease, illiteracy, and wars, I would say that many people are looking to Paulo for his humanist understanding, soaked in rebellion and sweetness. They are looking to Paulo and his ethics of life, the ethics of liberation that sees in all people dignity, happiness, and justice.

That is what, I believe, we gathered here have sought, in the legacy of my husband Paulo Freire.

Thank you.
São Paulo, October 27, 2012.
Hamilton, Waikato University, November 26, 2012.

Ana Maria Araujo Freire, PhD in Education by Pontifical Catholic University of São Paulo, is the widow and the legal successor of the educator Paulo Freire's work, Patron of the Brazilian Education.

NOTES

1. Words in italics are from the original text in Portuguese. Translator's note.
2. Aluízio e Genove Araújo, the owners of Oswaldo Cruz School in Recife.
3. Recife is the capital and largest city of the state of Pernambuco, in the Northeast of Brazil. Currently the population of the city is 1,536,934 (Brazilian Institute of Geography and Statics —IBGE—IBGE, 2010). Translator's note.
4. Jaboatão is a part of the Recife metro area. Currently the population of the city is 650,000 (Brazilian Institute of Geography and Statics—IBGE—Census IBGE, 2010). Translator's note.
5. Paulo Freire valued the spontaneous curiosity that may become epistemological curiosity based on critical thinking.
6. Things or people that come from Recife, the birthplace of Paulo Freire. Translator's note.

REFERENCES

Freire, P. (2011). *Pedagogia do oprimido*. Rio de Janeiro, Brazil: Paz e Terra.
Dussel, E. (2000). Ética da Libertação na Idade da Globalização e da Exclusão. Petrópolis, Brazil: Editora Vozes.

Translators of Nita Freire's keynote presentation and this foreword
Ana Lúcia S. Ratto
Débora B. Agra Junker

REVIEWERS

Vin and Ted Glynn

Introduction

Paulo Freire: The Global Legacy

MICHAEL A. PETERS AND TINA BESLEY

Education either functions as an instrument which is used to facilitate integration of the younger generation into the logic of the present system and bring about conformity or it becomes the practice of freedom, the means by which men and women deal critically and creatively with reality and discover how to participate in the transformation of their world.

(PAULO FREIRE, *Pedagogy of the Oppressed*)

Paulo Freire, one of the greatest educators of all time, was born in Recife, Brazil, on September 19, 1921 and died of heart failure in Sao Paulo, Brazil on May 2, 1997. Freire taught Portuguese in secondary schools from 1941–1947 before becoming active in adult education and workers' training. He was the first Director of the Department of Cultural Extension of the University of Recife (1961–1964). Freire's *Pedagogy of the Oppressed* (1970) is an argument for a system of education that emphasizes learning as an act of culture and freedom. His works became justly famous as he gained an international reputation for his program of literacy education especially for the rural and dispossessed in Northeastern Brazil. He was jailed by the new government after 1964 and was forced into a political exile that lasted fifteen-years, eventually returning to Brazil in 1979. As a living testimony, his many works have been translated into many languages, and have inspired the tradition of critical pedagogy. (http://paulotgl.blogspot.co.nz/)

This paragraph was the basis of a notice to advertize the international conference Paulo Freire: The Global Legacy, held by the Centre for Global Studies in Education, University of Waikato, Te Whare Wananga o Waikato, Aotearoa/New Zealand, November 26–28, 2012. The conference aimed to involve experienced and new researchers, policy makers and practitioners from around the world who engage with Freire's work and it was organized into four broad themes that structured papers and presentations: Globalization; Decolonization; Indigenous Cultures; Cultural Studies.[1] The four themes were designed to capture the global reception of Freire's work alongside the use made of his philosophy in specific contexts and especially by indigenous peoples. This coupling of "global reception/indigenous use" is developed as a means for theorizing Paulo Freire's legacy. We were very fortunate indeed to have Ana Maria Araújo Freire, Paulo's widow and an academic in her own right, to open the conference with some personal remarks and reflections on Freire's enduring legacy. Her warmth, friendliness, and participation in the whole conference were much appreciated and her speech provided the foreword for this collection. The keynote speakers also included Peter McLaren (see Chapter 1), Antonia Darder (see Chapter 2), and a number of New Zealand and Maori speakers who had modeled their own work, educational practice, and lifetime commitment on developing Freire's ideas: Graham Hingangaroa Smith (see Chapter 3), Russell Bishop (see Chapter 5), Linda Tuhiwai Smith and Peter Roberts (see Chapter 4)—all scholars with strong international profiles who have been responsible for keeping the Freire legacy alive.[2] In addition, the conference was notable for the large number of visiting scholars from Freire's home country, Brazil, and from many other countries around the world. We were fortunate to have Dr. Ana Ratto, from Universidade Federal do Paraná, Curitiba, Brazil, as Visiting Scholar at the University of Waikato, who assisted Portuguese-speaking visitors. Débora Junker, Assistant Professor of Christian Education, Christian Theological Seminary, Indianapolis, Indiana, and Dante Romanó assisted with the translation of Nita Freire's presentation at the conference. The world premiere of the film *Finding Freire* directed by Julio Wainer and Dave Olive was also shown at the conference (see an excerpt from the film and commentary about the making of the film at http://paulotgl.blogspot.co.nz/ or http://www.youtube.com/watch?v=U8aExMg8foA).

In the New Zealand/Aotearoa context, the contributions to Maori education by three of the keynote speakers who have harnessed Freirean ideas are very important and highly significant for Maori and for all of New Zealand/Aotearoa. Graham Hingangaroa Smith (Ngati Apa, Ngati Kahungunu, Kai Tahu, and Ngati Porou) has been instrumental in developing the indigenous tertiary institution, Te Whare Wānanga o Awanuiārangi (http://www.wananga.ac.nz/). Along with Linda Tuhiwai Smith (Ngāti Awa, Ngāti Porou), who is the University of Waikato Pro-Vice Chancellor Maori, both have been leaders in establishing the state schooling system of Kura Kaupapa Māori, which positions the Māori language as the principal medium of instruction (see http://www.teara.govt.nz/en/maori-education-matauranga/page-5). Russell Bishop, a descendent of the Tainui and Ngati Pukeko iwi (tribes) of New Zealand and Scots and Irish peoples of Europe, was foundation Professor for Maori Education in the Faculty of Education at the University of Waikato. He was Director of Te Kotahitanga, a "research/professional development project that seeks to improve the educational achievement of Maori students in mainstream classrooms through the implementation of a culturally responsive pedagogy of relations and culturally responsive leadership" (see http://tekotahitanga.tki.org.nz/). By including three of the foremost scholar-researchers and innovators in the Freirean tradition who have devoted themselves to the cause of Maori education, together with Peter Roberts, Professor of Education at the University of Canterbury, an international scholar on Freire, this conference promised a great deal as evidenced by their work in the current volume. They demonstrate the currency and continuing legacy of Freire's work in contemporary neoliberal New Zealand.

Paulo Freire was an educator whose global legacy is of much the same stature as Nelson Mandela's; motivated by many of the same political sources; elevated by similar political ideas of freedom, equality, and emancipation; and shaped by the same decades of radical activity during the 1960s and 1970s. This is a very rare profile and reputation for an educator. It is often forgotten that during his university studies he taught Portuguese at the high school level, and while finishing his degree he began working with working-class people in Northeast Brazil, eventually becoming the director of education for an industrial service organization borne out of labor protests. In the ten years working for this organization, he became concerned with the "dehumanization of labor" and the effects of industrialization. In this phase, he was to be distinguished by his Christian (rather than communist) methods based on dialogue, and it was not long before he was appointed to Recife's Consultative Education Council (Kirkendall, 2010), partly on the strength of his participatory experiments with working-class literacy circles. During this period leading up the 1960s, Freire was influenced by a group of local thinkers dubbed "developmental nationalists" and by the generation of post-war existentialist and Catholic humanist thinkers such as Jean-Paul Sartre and Jacques Maritain. From the beginning of the evolution of his thought, it contained both the local and the global, an as-yet rudimentary notion of dialogue with the "Other", an emphasis on humanization together with an ontological commitment to "becoming" subjects of history, or author of one's own life and a notion of authenticity. One might speculate that this theoretical tool kit was a blend of Christian existential thought that focused on the collective dimension of existence in the concept of "class" (a notion still not theoretically realized in the early Freire).

Roberto Domingo Toledo in his "Existentialism and Latin America" (2014) indicates that the generative current of existentialism in Latin America considerably predated European and American sibling traditions, being forged in the crisis of identity of postcolonialism after the collapse of the Spanish empire. In terms of the Latin American tradition, Toledo mentions José Ortega y Gasset, Antonio

Caso, and Miguel de Unamuno who was influenced by Søren Kierkegaard and Friedrich Nietzsche. He goes on to claim: "Ibero-American existentialism's precocious intersubjective focus has two historically intertwined roots: Ibero-American marginality and Ibero-American Catholicism" (p. 216) and to indicate that its roots lie in Miguel de Cervantes's novel *Don Quixote*, first published in the seventeenth century (1605, 1615). He also points out how Latin American existentialism has Catholic roots: not only Maritain as we have mentioned but also Max Scheler, Gabriel Marcel, and Maurice Blondel. (Freire is not mentioned in this survey).

We mention this historical element to illustrate the cultural complexities of the crafting and reception of Freire's work. Ibero-American Christian existentialism was already well established as a potent philosophical mix well before Freire became its heir and it became the basis for integrating a labor and popular cultural movement in Recife and part of Freire's thinking and opus on the eve of his gaining a university chair in the history and philosophy of education. Kirkendall (2010, p. 21) mentions that Freire was strongly influenced by Simone Weil and the Romanian psychologist Zevedei Barbu (on dictatorship and democracy). One might argue that Freire's innovation was to apply these ideas to adult and community education for illiterate working class people in the Brazilian Northeast. His ideas really caught fire in the English-speaking world with the publication of *Pedagogy of the Oppressed* in 1970 and yet the popularization of his life and work, now narrated and discussed many times, really started as a trickle with contributions from scholars such as Joel Spring, Henry Giroux, and Ira Shor in the late 1970s and early 1980s. Already with a home in Brazil and Latin America, Freire's classic was popularized in the English-speaking world and his place in the tradition of educational praxis was solidified in a number of collaborations with U.S.-based critical educators including Ira Shor, Donaldo Macedo, Antonia Faundez, Henry Giroux, and others during the late 1980s and early 1990s. It gathered momentum with authoritative interpretations in the 1990s (e.g., Gadotti, 1994; McLaren & Lankshear, 1994; McLaren & Leonard, 1993; Taylor, 1993), and a kind of literary canonization and globalization in the 2000s, especially after the initiation and flowering of the critical pedagogy project in the United States with Henry Giroux, Michael Apple, Ira Shor, Joe Kincheloe, Peter McLaren, Colin Lankshear, Patti Lather, bell hooks, and many others. From the first publication as *Pedagogia do Oprimido* (in Portuguese) in 1968 to its English translation by Myra Ramos, it has sold more than one million copies. It quickly became one of the foundational texts of critical pedagogy and is one of the most cited books in the field of education, regularly appearing on the reading list of most teacher education institutions.

The cultural reception of a text including its translation is a complex affair, especially when it reaches iconic status as a classic and its influence continues to grow across both the decades and different political eras. Freire's revolutionary text received its thirtieth anniversary edition in 2000 by Bloomsbury Academic and

Continuum and a website was created to celebrate the book's fortieth anniversary at http://www.pedagogyoftheoppressed.com/. The website carries the section About the Book, an introduction by Donaldo Macedo, a bibliography of Freire's works (a list of some twenty-two works), a brief biography of Freire, resources for educators and students, praise and reviews, plus a new critical pedagogy series under the editorship of Shirley Steinberg and Ana Maria Araújo Freire, links (to four Freire Institutes), news and contacts.[3] The biography starts:

> Paulo Freire was born in 1921 in Recife, Brazil. He became familiar with poverty and hunger during the 1929 Great Depression. In school he fell behind and his social life revolved around playing pick up football with poorer kids, from whom he learned a great deal. These experiences would shape his concerns for the poor and would help to construct his particular educational viewpoint.

In another paragraph, the biography details Freire's revolutionary literacy methods and his exile after a U.S.-sponsored coup:

> In 1961, he was appointed director of the Department of Cultural Extension of Recife University, and in 1962 he had the first opportunity for significant application of his theories, when 300 sugarcane workers were taught to read and write in just 45 days. In response to this experiment, the Brazilian government approved the creation of thousands of cultural circles across the country. In 1964, a military coup put an end to that effort. Freire was imprisoned as a traitor for 70 days. After a brief exile in Bolivia, he worked in Chile for five years for the Christian Democratic Agrarian Reform Movement and the Food and Agriculture Organization of the United Nations. In 1967, he published his first book, *Education as the Practice of Freedom*. He followed this with his most famous book, *Pedagogy of the Oppressed*, first published in Portuguese in 1968.

The website biography provides a glimpse of the application of his work in other countries during Freire's lifetime:

> Freire was offered a visiting professorship at Harvard University in 1969. The next year, *Pedagogy of the Oppressed* was published in both Spanish and English, vastly expanding its reach. Because of the political feud between Freire, a Christian socialist, and the successive authoritarian military dictatorships, it wasn't published in his own country of Brazil until 1974. After a year in the United States, Freire moved to Switzerland to work as a special education advisor to the World Council of Churches. During this time he acted as an advisor on education reform in former Portuguese colonies in Africa, particularly Guinea-Bissau and Mozambique.

And finally, the last chapter of his life, so to speak:

> Freire moved back to Brazil in 1980. He joined the Workers' Party in the city of São Paulo, and acted as a supervisor for its adult literacy project from 1980 to 1986. When the Party prevailed in the municipal elections in 1988, Freire was appointed Secretary of Education for São Paulo. In 1986, his wife Elza died. Freire married Ana Maria Araújo Freire, who

continues with her own educational work. Paulo Freire died in 1997. (http://www.pedago gyoftheoppressed.com/author/)

In this encapsulated biography, we see a pressing lifetime of engagement with poverty, literacy, and empowerment, a preparedness to work in dialogue with others, a deep respect for the poor, illiterate, and the working class, and a profound spiritual philosophy of compassion and love that inspired Freire's praxis.[4]

The *Pedagogy of the Oppressed* is now undoubtedly a classic that joins the ranks of works by Plato, Kant, Rousseau, Piaget, Vygotsky, Dewey, Montessori, and A.S. Neil. It also occupies a special place in the canon of critical thought. It was forged as a synthesis of Latin American existentialism and liberation theology, and a range of contemporary global sources that inspired the radical decade of the sixties. It was the decade in which many countries gained independence from their European colonial powers, when widespread protests in the African American civil rights movement finally achieved national changes in racially discriminatory practices in a series of vital legislative changes, including the 1964 Civil Rights Act, the Voting Rights Act of 1965, the Immigration and Nationality Services Act of 1965, and the Fair Housing Act of 1968. The year 1968 was a momentous one, with Martin Luther King Jr. assassinated in April, and Andy Warhol shot and Robert Kennedy assassinated in June. It was the year that the "Prague Spring" in Czechoslovakia was crushed by the Soviet invasion and when the student riots in May in Paris sparked civil unrest, strikes, and fear of revolution. The sixties saw students around the globe protesting against the Vietnam War and for peace. It was a time when the "New Left" consolidated a range of freedom movements in gay, Hispanic, African American, second-wave feminist, and free speech rights and sparked a broad countercultural social revolution. This was an age when political protest and awareness became a civic duty for the postwar cohort called the "baby boomers".

The "New Left" was a term that was used to refer to activists and educators who sought reform on a broad front and was inspired by a range of continental thinkers who helped shape the student movement and the events of 1968: Albert Camus, Jean-Paul Sartre, Simone de Beauvoir, Frantz Fanon, Aimé Césaire, Emma Goldman, Guy Debord, Hannah Arendt, Henri Lefebvre, Mao Zedong, R.D. Laing, David Cooper, Ivan Illich, Rosa Luxemburg, Leon Trotsky, Bertrand Russell, Ernst Bloch, C. Wright Mills, Herbert Marcuse, André Gorz, Louis Althusser, Raymond Williams, Stuart Hall, and others. These thinkers and activists helped to mold a new generation of activists: Angela Davis, Daniel Cohn-Bendit, Abbie Hoffman, Malcolm X, Tom Nairn, Jerry Rubin, and Bill Ayers. To some extent, this loose confederation of thinkers and activists were united in their move away from the traditional "Old Left's" emphasis on labor as the vanguard of revolution to new student intellectuals (Cohen & Hale, 1966; Morgan, 1999). The New

Left rearticulated a democratic vision of socialism based on grassroots movements across the board and departed from Stalinism to embrace the idea of a socialist humanism liberated from the domination of capitalism and the consumer society and much more oriented to questions of subjectivity, participation, and dialogue.

In the first footnote to Chapter 1 of *Pedagogy of the Oppressed*, Freire acknowledges the then contemporary reality, the political significance of youth and what he calls "the style of the age":

> The current movements of rebellion, especially those of youth, while they necessarily reflect the peculiarities of their respective settings, manifest in their essence this preoccupation with people as beings in the world and with the world— preoccupation with what and how they are "being." As they place consumer civilization in judgment, denounce bureaucracies of all types, demand the transformation of the universities (changing the rigid nature of the teacher-student relationship and placing that relationship within the context of reality), propose the transformation of reality itself so that universities can be renewed, attack old orders and established institutions in the attempt to affirm human beings as the Subjects of decision, all these movements reflect the style of our age, which is more anthropological than anthropocentric. (Freire, 1970, fn 1, p. 43)

Freire's *Pedagogy of the Oppressed* reflected this new thinking. It is larded with references and footnotes (in order) to Hegel (2), Rosa Luxemburg, C. Wright Mills, Jose Luis Fiori, Karl Marx and Friedrich Engels (3), Georg Lukacs (2), Mao Tse-Tung (4), Erich Fromm (8), Herbert Marcuse, Candido Mendes, Frantz Fanon (2), Regis Debray, Alvaro Vieira Pinto (2), Simone de Beauvoir, Reinhold Niebuhr (3), Jean-Paul Sartre, Edmund Husserl, Ernani MariaJose-Luis Fiori, Che Guevara (5), Pierre Furter (2), Karl Marx (2), Karel Kosik, Hans Freyer, Maria Edy Ferreira, João Guimaraes Rosa, Lucien Goldman, Andre Nicolai, Patricio Lopes, Vladimir Lenin (2), Fidel Castro, Emma Goldman, Fernando Garcia, Gajo Petrovic, Pope John XXIII, Albert Memmi, Bishop Franic Split, Francisco Weffert, Getulio Varga, Mary Cole, Louis Althusser (3), Martin Buber, Mikel Dufrenne, M.D. Chenu, and Orlando Aguirre Ortiz.[5]

Eric Fromm, a psychoanalyst associated with the Frankfurt School, was a founding father of political psychology with path-breaking work such as *Escape From Freedom* (1941) and a humanism emphasizing relatedness, rootedness, sense of identity, transcendence, frame of reference, and other basic needs. It is clear why Freire also referred to Che Guevara, the Argentinian Marxist revolutionary who demonstrated an affinity with the poor and played a key role in the Cuban revolution. Among the luminaries that he referred to was a group of Latin American scholars and also, of course, the tradition of Marxist humanism, especially as it held hands with liberation theology.

There is one footnote that one of us (Michael Peters) learned a great deal from: "Having completed a BA Hons degree in Geography with Keith Buchanan at Victoria University of Wellington on the transformation of the Chinese land-scape, I was particularly interested in Freire's use of Mao when I came to read him first in the early 1970s while a school teacher and then again as a scholar in the field of education in the late 1970s." Freire makes the following footnote to Mao that acknowledges the radical character of Mao's thought in relation to the trans-formative power of dialogue based on the lived experience of the so-called masses and the relation of the philosopher-teacher whose job is not one of correction or banking education but rather of clarification and "feedback":

> In a long conversation with Malraux, Mao-Tse-Tung declared, "You know I've proclaimed for a long time: we must teach the masses clearly what we have received from them con-fusedly." Andre Malraux, *Anti-Memoirs* (New York, 1968), pp. 361–362. This affirmation contains an entire dialogical theory of how to construct the program content of education, which cannot be elaborated according to what the educator thinks best for the students. (fn 7, p. 93)

Given this scene, the flowering of the New Left, Freire's own experiences, and the struggles for self-determination that characterized the spirit of the age, it is not surprising how Freire's elegant Hegelian work captured and synthesized the kind of political humanization that recognized the agency of subjects working together to effect change for the better. One can only wonder why *Pedagogy of the Oppressed* has increased its readership during the neoliberal era.

On May 1, 2013, the Askwith Forum commemorated the forty-fifth anni-versary of the publication of Paulo Freire's *Pedagogy of the Oppressed* with a discus-sion among Noam Chomsky, Howard Gardner, and Bruno della Chiesa about the book's impact and its relevance to education today. The discussion was published on YouTube on May 29, 2013.[6] Chomsky begins by talking about the exile of Freire from a "nasty" dictatorship in 1968 before being offered a professorship at Harvard and publishing his book in English. The discussion focuses on the concept of lib-eration theology that attempted to bring back the Gospels, with its concern for the treatment of the poor, back to the center of Catholic teachings. Bruno della Chiesa mentions a number of the most prominent liberation theologists in Latin America popular at the time Freire was writing and Chomsky examines the United States' "vicious war against the church" to silence Jesuit scholars who supported this "her-esy." Gardner mentions the international web of thought—German phenome-nology, French existentialism, and German critical theory—that Freire drew on. Gardner suggests that "the fall of communism" in 1989 gave people the warrant to dismiss the significance and relevance of the 1960s counterculture.

But Freire himself was actively involved politically throughout his life. He was an acute observer and he theorized and analyzed the neoliberal era that began with the ascendency of Margaret Thatcher in 1979 and Ronald Reagan in 1980 that followed hard on the heels of the New Left and two decades of radical politics and social transformation. In a review essay, Peter Roberts (2003) reflects on Freire's engagement with postmodernism and neoliberalism, indicating that in the decade from 1987 to 1997 (the year of his death) Freire was actively willing to accept aspects of "progressive postmodernism" but absolutely opposed to the doctrine of neoliberalism.

If the reception of a text is a complex matter, then the reception of a dynamic and prolific author-activist such as Freire is even more complex. In terms of his readers and audiences, there has been almost fifty years separating his first readers from those who make up his audience today, many of whom are not a product of the radical sixties but have been born into the neoliberal era that is the dominant policy narrative for education (Peters, 2011). In essence, today, education as a form of human capital investment either by the state or the individual effectively recasts questions of agency, autonomy, and the subject in terms of market relations and robs Freire's political culture of its power of grassroots participation and democratic social action. Increasingly, as the State "responsibilizes" the individual for making investments in themselves, what Michel Foucault calls "entrepreneurs of themselves," the public dimension of education is eroded.

Much has changed since Paulo Freire's demise in 1997. While his work changed in response to the political environment and in particular the advent of neoliberalism, his classic work *Pedagogy of the Oppressed* that spelled out principles of public engagement, dialogue, and political action has a timeless quality because there are many different forms of oppression, and oppression is always with us as an inherent structural aspect of various economic and political systems that privilege elite groups over the majority. Witness the late twentieth-century and early twenty-first-century growth of inequalities under neoliberalism and the huge increase in poverty and youth unemployment in the so-called advanced economies of America and Western Europe, even though there has been some progress in reducing people in poverty in developing countries such as Brazil and China. Yet globalization brings new dangers and new forms of oppression or a new global awareness of old, entrenched problems such as the violence against women and girls by fundamentalist political, cultural, and religious movements that actively try to prevent the agency and education of girls. The core philosophy of Freire's classic, therefore, remains a critical part of a philosophy of engagement. It has strong significance and relevance in the contemporary world and its message is as vital as it was when Freire first drafted *Pedagogy of the Oppressed* nearly fifty years ago. It is a manual for organizing and educating, of providing the political education that returns to the ancient basis of people living together, of encountering each other, an inescapable encounter with the Other.

In one sense, with the failure of neoliberalism, especially since 2008 with the global financial crisis, the Great Recession, the Arab Spring, and the movements for democracy in Eastern Europe, some scholars suggest we are entering a new era of political activism, of people power, enhanced by greater world interconnectedness, by new forms of citizen engagement and journalism, and by a greater realization that world environmental problems threaten the very survival of humanity. There are some signs that a new era of political activism and grassroots movements is emerging, but this is different in some respects from the 1960s. In the Arab world, youth engage in the so-called Facebook and Twitter revolutions using new mobile technologies, especially smartphones, as tools for political protest, record, and coordination. In contrast, the burden of student debt in the United States, climbing above the $1 trillion mark as the largest form of mortgage after housing, has saddled students with financial commitments such that it has the effect of quieting their political behavior—of becoming docile bodies so they can compete in a highly selective job market. Even so, the Occupy movement that began in Zuccotti Park, Wall Street, in September 2011, and eventually spread globally, demonstrated a form of international solidarity against the corruption of the banking culture and the huge social and economic inequalities that finance capitalism had caused. Occupy went viral with protests in more than nine hundred cities in sixty-two countries, demonstrating a new level of awareness of the global stakes of the financial crisis (see http://en.wikipedia.org/wiki/Occupy_move ment). Young people in Europe and especially in the Mediterranean economies are facing the highest unemployment rate in the postwar era and have been in the vanguard of mass protests in Greece, Spain, Cyprus, France, and Britain. It may be that in the West new forms of oppression have emerged alongside a greater global awareness of and resistance to the different faces of oppression associated with alienation, marginalization, sexual exploitation, and social exclusion. Meanwhile, elsewhere in the world there is a growing political movement that recognises and resists all forms of violence against women and girls, against domestic violence, against sex-trade trafficking, against practices such as female genital mutilation, and against fundamentalist religio-cultural practices promoted by Islamist extremist groups such as the Taliban, Boko Haram, and others opposed to girls' education, for example, in some parts of developing countries such as Pakistan, Afghanistan, and northern Nigeria.

In the 1960s, Freire's embrace of the Hegelian dialectics rendered the simple opposition between the oppressor and the oppressed based around the poor, the dispossessed, and the illiterate. Traditional class-based forms of organizing and mobilizing might be in decline but new forms of mass protest, including the Arab Spring, indigenous mobilization in Latin America, the anti-globalization and global justice movements, the movement against violence to women and girls, environmental and green movements, indigenous peoples' movements, children's rights movements, indicate the myriad forms of oppression and new forms of protest. Freire's political philosophy, his methodology for reading the world, his deep project of humanization based on love, and the ontological vocation to become more fully human all appear to bear witness to a universal message concerning freedom and emancipation.

Following the foreword by Nita Freire and this introduction, the thirty-seven chapters that make up this collection are divided into three sections: Section 1: Theoretical Perspectives—Reclaiming the Legacy, Section 2: Reading the World, and Section 3: Education as the Practice of Freedom. Section 1, with nine chapters, has a more theoretical focus and includes contributions by keynote speakers and others. Section 2, with fourteen chapters, shifts to a global focus in relation to Freirean approaches used throughout the world—in Australia, sub-Saharan Africa, the UK, Brazil, Democratic Republic of the Congo, New Zealand, Pakistan, Sri Lanka, Japan, and the United Arab Emirates. Section 3, also with fourteen chapters, combines many aspects of the first two sections as it looks at education and pedagogies as practices of freedom as they operate in many locations and take different forms. These include higher education, dialogue, Steiner education, bilingual education, social justice, decolonization, social inclusion, behaviorism, early childhood education, performance, music education, embodied pedagogy, culturally responsive pedagogy, and adult education.

As organizers of this conference and editors of this collection, we believe that the authors of these chapters clearly present a rich, deep, and valuable portrait of the extent of the spheres of influence in education in its broadest sense, of the contemporary state of Freire's global legacy over the decades since he published *Pedagogy of the Oppressed.* We believe this volume is a worthy addition to the Freire literature and will be useful to educators around the world. We have been working with Brazilian colleagues in anticipation of another conference on Freire's global legacy that will be held in Brazil in the future, in a continuation of the legacy he has given the world.

NOTES

1. See Centre for Global Studies in Education website, http://www.waikato.ac.nz/globalstudies/home and the conference website at http://paulotgl.blogspot.co.nz/.
2. See the biographies of the keynote speakers at http://paulotgl.blogspot.co.nz/2012/03/keynote-speakers.html.
3. The full text of *Pedagogy of the Oppressed* is available at http://www.users.humboldt.edu/jwpowell/edreformFreire_pedagogy.pdf.
4. For other (auto)biographies, see Freire's (1995) *Letters to Christina: Reflections on My Life and Work*; see also his interviews listed under his Wikipedia entry at http://en.wikipedia.org/wiki/Paulo_Freire; and see his chronology at http://www.paulofreireinstitute.org/.
5. Recorded from the thirtieth anniversary edition, http://www.users.humboldt.edu/jwpowell/edreformFriere_pedagogy.pdf.
6. Available at http://www.youtube.com/watch?v=-SOw55BU7yg.

REFERENCES

Castells, M., Flecha, R., Freire, P., Giroux, H.A., Macedo, D., & Willis, P. (1999). *Critical education in the new information age*. Lanham, MD: Rowman & Littlefield.
Cohen, M., & Hale, D. (Eds.). (1966). *The new student left*. Boston, MA: Beacon Press.
Collins, D.E. (1977). *Paulo Freire: His life, works and thought*. New York, NY: Paulist Press.
Escobar, M., Fernandez, A.L., Freire, P., & Guervara-Niebla, G. (1994). *Paulo Freire on higher education*. Albany, NY: SUNY Press.
Faundez, A., & Freire, P. (1972). *Learning to question: A pedagogy of liberation* (T. Coates, Trans.). New York, NY: Continuum.
Gadotti, M. (1994). *Reading Paulo Freire: His life and work*. Albany, NY: SUNY Press.
Giroux, H.A. (1982). Paulo Freire and the concept of critical literacy. In *Radical pedagogy* (pp. 77–82). Philadelphia, PA: Temple University Press.
Kirkendall, A.J. (2010). *Paulo Freire and the cold war politics of literacy*. Chapel Hill: University of North Carolina Press.
Mayo, P. (1994). Synthesizing Gramsci and Freire: Possibilities for a theory of radical adult education. *International Journal of Lifelong Education, 13*(2), 125–148.
McLaren, P., & Lankshear, C. (Eds.). (1994). *Politics of liberation. Paths from Freire*. London, England: Routledge.
McLaren, P., & Leonard, P. (Eds.). (1993). *Paulo Freire: A critical encounter*. London, England: Routledge.
Morgan, E. (1999). *The 60s experience: Hard lessons about modern America*. Philadelphia, PA: Temple University Press.
Peters, M.A. (1999). Freire and postmodernism. In P. Roberts (Ed.), *Paulo Freire, politics and pedagogy: Reflections from Aotearoa–New Zealand* (pp. 113–122). Palmerston North, New Zealand: Dunmore Press.
Peters, M.A. (2011). *Neoliberalism and After? Education, Social Policy and the Crisis of Western Capitalism*. New York: Peter Lang.
Roberts, P. (2003). Pedagogy, neoliberalism and postmodernity: Reflections on Freire's later work. *Educational Philosophy and Theory, 35*(4), 451–465.
Shor, I. (Ed.). (1987). *Freire for the classroom: A sourcebook for liberatory teaching*. Portsmouth, NH: Boynton/Cook.
Shor, I., & Freire, P. (1987). *A pedagogy for liberation: Dialogues on transforming education*. South Hadley, MA: Bergin & Garvey.
Spring, J. (1975). The growth of consciousness: Marx to Freire. In J. Spring, *A primer of libertarian education* (pp. 61–79). Montreal, Quebec, Canada: Black Rose Books.
Taylor, P. (1993). *The texts of Paulo Freire*. Buckingham, England: Open University Press.
Toledo, R.D. (2014). Existentialism and Latin America. In F. Joseph, J. Reynolds, & A. Woodward, *The Bloomsbury companion to existentialism*, (pp. 215–237). London: Bloomsbury.

WORKS BY PAULO FREIRE, LISTED BY PUBLICATION DATE

Freire, P. (1970). *Pedagogy of the oppressed*. New York, NY: Herder & Herder.
Freire, P. (1972). *Cultural action for freedom*. Harmondsworth, England: Penguin.

Freire, P. (1973). *Education for critical consciousness*. New York, NY: Seabury Press.

Freire, P. (1976). *Education, the practice of freedom*. London, England: Writers and Readers.

Freire, P. (1978). *Pedagogy in process: The letters to Guinea-Bissau*. New York, NY: Seabury Press.

Freire, P. (1980). *A day with Paulo Freire*. Delhi, India: I.S.P.C.K.

Freire, P. (1983). *Pedagogy in process: The letters to Guinea-Bissau*. New York, NY: Continuum.

Freire, P. (1985). *The politics of education: Culture, power, and liberation*. South Hadley, MA: Bergin & Garvey.

Freire, P., & Macedo, D. P. (1987). *Literacy: Reading the word & the world*. Critical Studies in Education series. South Hadley, MA: Bergin & Garvey.

Freire, P., & Faundez, A. (1989). *Learning to question: A pedagogy of liberation*. New York, NY: Continuum.

Freire, P. (1993). *Pedagogy of the city*. New York, NY: Continuum.

Freire, P. (1993). *Pedagogy of the oppressed, 20th anniversary edition*. New York, NY: Continuum.

Freire, P., & Freire, A. M. A. (1994). *Pedagogy of hope: Reliving 'Pedagogy of the oppressed.'* New York, NY: Continuum.

Freire, P., & Macedo, D.P. (1996). *Letters to Cristina: Reflections on my life and work*. New York, NY: Routledge.

Freire, P. (1997). *Mentoring the mentor: A critical dialogue with Paulo Freire*. New York, NY: Peter Lang.

Freire, P., & Ana Maria Araújo Freire, A. P. A. (1997). *Pedagogy of the heart*. New York, NY: Continuum.

Freire, P. (1998). *Teachers as cultural workers: Letters to those who dare*. Boulder, CO: Westview Press.

Freire, P., Freire, A. M. A., & Macedo, D. P. (1998). *The Paulo Freire reader*. New York, NY: Continuum.

Freire, P. (1998). *Pedagogy of freedom: Ethics, democracy, and civic courage*. Lanham, MD: Rowman & Littlefield.

Section 1:
Theoretical Perspectives—
Reclaiming the Legacy

Reflections on Paulo Freire, Critical Pedagogy, and the Current Crisis of Capitalism

PETER McLAREN

It surely is the case that the age in which we inhabit so precariously demands manifestos, not desiderata or credos. Unless, of course, those creeds can become manifest as a rallying cry, a canticle for the undead slaves toiling in capitalism's grim hostelry, forceful enough to be heard beyond the sepulchers and catacombs where schooling, as a proprietary field entombed by its own unforgiving success, has been consigned for all eternity for desecrating the very heart of what it means to live and to learn. It is my wager that words can howl and on this brittle quiver of hope I set mine into print.

I am in sympathy with many of the youth of today, whose full-throated screams meet the immemorial silence of the pedagogical tradition—an ear-shattering silence that compelled me as a youngster, in baggy denims stained with grease and oil and sporting a jaunty oversized newsboy cap, to keep my eyes squarely focused ahead and my hands folded together on top of my desk as neat as a crisply starched handkerchief. My experiences of those times are housed in the cold chambers of memory. The earliest recollections I have of being schooled are felt in the sockets and joints of monumental time and while they do not bear the fleshiness of a living presence, they seem much more real. As one of the first students among my primary school classmates to enter the room each day, I was welcomed by row upon row of chairs stacked upside down on desks, what looked to me like varnished, wind-worn bones of long-vanished creatures. In the fog-bound reaches of my mind I can still recall the pungent stench of the cleaning fluid used to wipe away the undeviating anxiety of the school day, but I cannot recall the face of a single teacher prior to my junior high years, save one industrial arts teacher with a jack-o-lantern rictus who struck me repeatedly on top of my hand with the sharp edge of a metal ruler, swift strokes that left deep bruises. The bleak archeology of the setting and the threat of violence kept me uncomfortably attentive, which was its purpose. I came to understand the meaning of tradition as the repetition of misery, tragically prolonged. All I recall are charts, tables and formulae, wall diagrams and lists—dead letters for the living dead. I had little sympathy in 1959 for teachers. That came much later, in 1965. The countercultural zeitgeist had enervated me and I felt alive for the first time inside the walls of the academic prison house, beginning with readings of *Beowulf,* Chaucer, and Shakespeare, in that historical order.

After years of being victimized by the bloviating gasbags of the corporate media who served as little more than capitalist cheerleaders, I realized that my fate as a student in the academy was not as in peril as much as those who took the brunt of capitalism's brutal neoliberal assault—reserve armies of low wage earners and the unemployed. Capitalism is a colossus that bestrides the world, wreaking havoc. As a self-validating and self-perpetuating discourse and social relation, capitalism works as a self-fueling engine whose capacity to travel around the globe and devour everything in its path is expanding exponentially. For those communities who have harrowed the hell of this world-eater, some explanation is necessary, especially since many of these communities are searching for a role that education can play to free them and their children from the death grip of this seemingly unstoppable and imperishable leviathan. As a discourse and social practice that in its current neoliberal incarnation is shorn of neither self-enrapture nor fanatical adherence by most business leaders and guardians of commerce, capitalism shatters collective experience into monadic bits and pieces, bifurcating students' relationship to their bodies, brutally taxonomizing human behavior into mind and body, into manual and mental labor. Capitalism is so powerful it possesses the ability to commodify our souls (by commodity I here refer to something created expressly for market exchange). It possesses a terrible power of psychologizing entrenched and dependent hierarchies of power and privilege and reformulating them into homogeneous and private individual experiences. The upshot is that 99% of the world are made to feel solely responsible for their own plight.

When we talk of the working class, it is easy to fall into the trap of seeing class solely or mainly in terms of culture, i.e., working class culture. But I want to emphasize that it is the social relations of labor that determine a person's class location, not the opportunities for engorging your powers of acquisition through deregulated consumptive practices. With gold-filled pockets as large as the pouched cheeks of Dizzy Gillespie playing his trumpet, the rich and famous have set the standard for success as measured by human greed and a thirst for power as unfillable as the

Sistine Chapel. But for those who sell their labor power to earn a living (i.e., those who produce the profit for the capitalist) life is being enslaved to those who purchase human labor and take away the profits. While, for instance, the stock market may seem to produce wealth, it is really just redistributing the wealth produced by the labor of the workers. Profit does not come from market relations (buying low and selling high), but from human labor power. In this, I follow Marx's focus on the development of human productive forces—a very complex process that is historically related to the material conditions of production and the class struggle. The profound incompatibility between the forces and relations of production produces tremendous social conflict.

In the field of education, I want to draw attention to an irresoluble tension that exists between the possibilities of education and economic efficiency, threatening the professional autonomy and working conditions of educators and the very purpose of education itself. Marxism's protean focus on proletarian self-activity and the self-organization of the popular majorities are anathema to much of the work that falls under the dubious classification of social justice education. Although well-meaning progressive educators might be willing to criticize the manner in which humans are turned into dead objects (i.e., what Marxists refer to as fetishized commodities), they are often loathe to consider the fact that within capitalist society, all value originates in the sphere of production and a main role of schools is to serve as agents or functionaries of capital and its masters—the military industrial complex, the surveillance state and the transnational capitalist class. Furthermore, these educators fail to understand that education is more reproductive of an exploitative social order than a constitutive challenge to it precisely because it rests on the foundations of capitalist exchange value.

Taxpayer bailouts of the financial sector in 2009 have made billionaires of hedge fund managers, further widening the gap between the rich and poor, making the United States one of the most unequal countries in the so-called developed world. Faced with gargantuan cuts to school aid and an evisceration of programs designed to serve working-class communities, assaults on teachers and teacher unions, and a push for the privatization of schooling and test-based accountability, public schools are under siege, fighting for their very existence against the onslaught of the new Daddy Warbucks in postmodern corporate clothing—the Bill & Melinda Gates Foundations, the Eli & Edythe Broad Foundation, the Walton Family Foundation, the Laura and John Arnold Foundation, the Michael & Susan Dell Foundation, the Bradley Foundation, the Robertson Foundation, the Fisher Foundation and the Anschutz Foundation. And, as Diane Ravitch (2014) has pointed out, organizations that support privately-run school organizations with progressive sounding names such as "the American Federation for Children, the American Legislative Exchange Council (ALEC), Better Education for Kids (B$K), Black Alliance for Educational Options, the education program at the Brookings Institution, the Centre for Education Reforms, Chiefs for Change, ConnCAN (and its spin-off, 50CAN, as well as state-specific groups like Minn-CAN, NYCAN, RI-CAN), Democrats for Education Reform, the Education Equality Project, Education Reform Now, Educators 4 Excellence, EdVoice, the Foundation for Excellence in Education, the National Council on Teacher Quality, New Leaders for New Schools, NewSchools Venture Fund, Parent Revolution, Stand for Children, Students for Education Reform, StudentsFirst, Teach for America, Teach Plus" and others. Under the rallying cry of accountability through test-based evaluations of teachers, wealthy entrepreneurs and hedge fund speculators who have never attended public schools or taught in a classroom have partnered with billionaires to advance a corporate reform agenda in our nation's schools. These new 'reformers' span the ideological spectrum from Bill Gates to the Koch brothers. In fact, among some of the very persons responsible for championing the neoliberal economic policies that led to the current recession are those who are now anointing themselves as leading educational reformers.

Savvy members of the business community fresh from power lunches with insider beltway lobbyists and underwritten by private education management firms cravenly cement their agendas to the desperate cries for help from aggrieved communities, despoiling education by turning sites of learning into deregulated enterprise zones such that the rhetoric of democracy and education has now become oxymoronic. This is not to say that all attempts to create community and business partnerships for the improvement of education are merely cynical attempts to use market-driven reforms to create an unstable and de-unionized teaching force. But it is no coincidence that the push to privatize education has in many instances had the tragic effect of intensifying inequality through reproducing a government-subsidized class-tiered system of education, leaving many schools in working-class communities with inadequate resources and languishing in despair.

To overcome this juggernaut of capitalist cruelty that would profit from the tears of the poor if it knew how to market them effectively, critical revolutionary pedagogy flouts the frontier between scholarship and activism in order to outflank consensus and, in this way, works to create a counter-public sphere. We are askew to traditional academia and are not enmortgaged to its status and do not represent the ivory tower. In fact, we are often marginalized in and excoriated by various and sundry academic organizations. We want to mediate human needs and social relations in publicly discussable form to create a transnational social movement of aggressively oppositional power. However, critical pedagogy is not yet in a position to play a substantial role in the struggle for a socialist future. A more productive role for critical pedagogy needs to be discovered so that educators can become more effective agents of revolutionary transformation.

Immiseration, capitalism's ferocity, leaves no semblance today of the unsundered world of the 1950s suburbia, as it haunts the world like a fallen Tharmas, the bellowing beast with sea jelly eyes and filament-riven skin that haunts Blake's Apocalype. Schooling in the United States has been successful to the extent that it has refused to examine itself outside of the hive of capitalist ideology and its cloistered elitism—its precepts, concepts, its epistemicides and its various literacies of power through which ideas become slurred over time and actions on their behalf are guaranteed to remain as inactive as a drunken fisherman lost at sea. It has accepted the fact that answers will remain predesigned before questions can even be formulated. The vision of democracy is inevitably preformed and must be engraved on the minds of its citizens through ideological state apparatuses such as schools. As long as the ideas of the ruling class rule us, and they can certainly rule us with the help of new information technologies, we will be apprentices to the anguish of the oppressed, and ideas will be guaranteed to remain vacant, hidden in a thicket of "feel-good" bourgeois aesthetics whose complicity with inequality bulks as large as its opposition to it, making it an appropriate ideological form for late capitalist society. Such ideas will be guaranteed not to transgress the 'comfort zone' of those who tenaciously cling to the belief that with hard work and a steeled will, we will reap the rewards of the American Dream.

We fight to make available those vernaculars that have been deemed oppositional and counter-hegemonic/contestatory/revolutionary. With a critical lexicon, borne in blood-soaked struggles by those who have over centuries fought against the forces of domination and exploitation through poetry, art, philosophy, literature, politics, science, technology and a search for justice and equality, we can envision and create a new world. And finally, we can see those things that interdict a learner's ability to read the word and the world critically.

Zygmunt Bauman and others have argued that vulnerability and uncertainty are the foundation of all political power. The protective functions of the state that were once directed toward mitigating the extent to which citizens were at the mercy of the vulnerability and uncertainty of the market were brutally rescinded by Thatcher and Reagan as the welfare state was systematically dismantled. Government restraints upon market forces and business activities were removed. The market regained its omniscience. Market-generated insecurity against which the state could no longer shield its citizens had to be replaced by something more ominous—the zombies of the underclass, those who were not able or forbidden to participate in the market. Entrenched and indomitable structures of privilege and power were no longer acknowledged as the poor and powerless were now held responsible for their own immiseration. They were no longer to be protected, but instead had to be criminalized for the sake of order-building. Those who were unable to participate successfully in the market were held responsible for their own failure instead of being benevolently assisted as personalized solutions were now expected to challenge the systemic contradictions of the capitalist marketplace. The uncomplaisant and increasingly belligerent state had to augment the insecurity of the market by intensifying it, transferring its legitimacy to its ability to protect the public from terrorists through preemptive wars and drone assassinations and so on and a profligacy of heinous acts justified as protecting its citizenry and its interests. This was facilitated by the construction of a national identity via the corporate media that was a toxic admixture of statecraft and garage sale apocalyptic mysticism: America must carry the torch of democracy to the far corners of the globe as our God-given duty, a providential version of manifest destiny, if it means preemptive military strikes and, as George W. Bush put it, "kicking some ass." The current crisis of neoliberal globalization is re-patterning not only the objective world, but the subjective world as well, constantly breaking down cultures of political solidarity by trying to create a post-ideological universe of human experiences and selfhood consisting of commodified subjects whose affinity for any type of political solidarity has been replaced by participation in orgies of capitalist consumption and the creation of self-gratifying designer identities. A new imperialist vision of manifest destiny (Harvey, 2003) has shaped the foreign policy of the United States, giving a grotesque new meaning to the phrase "military-industrialist complex." That we live in a democracy is largely an ideological fabrication or illusion that lends legitimacy to the reproduction of this complex. In the language of the transnational capitalist class, this might be called a "beneficial untruth."

In the present theater of class warfare there remains a profound confusion as to how to wage our fight against the global contagion unleashed by the Great Recession. The seriousness of this crisis extends beyond developing isolated tactics for deployment in the struggle against state repression, imperialist wars, climate change, geopolitical insecurity and forms of abstract labor that are crippling workers and their families with a cruel malignity. Some of our best-intentioned fighters who are putting themselves most at risk in the struggle for social justice are operating under ideological assumptions that are squarely encapsulated to serve the needs of capital, thereby recuperating the very conditions they are struggling against. What's missing is a well-defined *strategic* sense of how capital as a monstrous entity can neither be placated nor reformed—but must be utterly destroyed. When we plea to the behemoth for compassion, it curls its hands, pulls back its rictus to reveal a wickedly jeering skull beneath its corporate skin, and retreats across a field of dried bones only to return again with an even larger club with which to pound us laughingly into dust.

Any state devoted to abolishing terror must itself inspire terror and in fact become more terrifying than the terrorists whom it purports to be fighting. However, this crisis has been able to demonstrate to many that egalitarian justice can only be achieved against capitalism, that justice for all cannot be achieved within the framework of a capitalist market economy that relies on wars, the arms industry, and ecocide to slake its endless thirst.

One of the foundational social relations that interdicts a student's access to resources necessary to see the world critically is, I believe, class exploitation—an exploitation that despoils communities and dispossesses workers of their humanity. Education opposes schooling. Education is that which intrudes upon our instincts and instruments of mind and augments them; it pushes us along the arcs of the stars where our thoughts can give rise to new vistas of being and becoming and to new solidarities with our fellow humans. Our responsibilities for creating critical citizens should be proportional to our privilege. Today a good education is no longer seen as a social responsibility but as picking carefully from an array of consumer choices provided by a number of gluttonous new companies and corporations.

In the main, I would say that we need to strive for cooperative, freely associated labour that is not value-producing. We need to look to the new social movements and uprisings throughout the world for new organizational forms, including those of non-Western peoples. Socialism is not an inevitability, despite what teleologically driven Marxists might tell you. Right now capitalism is reorganizing itself and attempting to reconstitute the working class by criminalizing it and disaggregating its revolutionary potential through new information technologies. Can democracy survive this historical self-immolation? I would say, no, not without the rise of social fascism. And then what kind of democracy would that be? A democracy in name only—which is not far from what we already have in the United States at the moment.

As we fall prey to the all-pervasive influence of corporations and their attempts to re-create us as desiring-machines (desiring what the corporations have to sell us), we have become a less mindful, less vigilant citizenry, watching passively as civil life becomes swallowed up by the logic of capital, consumption, and corporatism. People no longer want to become actors—they want to become celebrities. Our rhizomatous culture has become corralled by capital, so that it appears as if we are autonomous and in a constant state of self-actualization but in reality we are making ourselves more vulnerable to the crippling control of Big Brother. But of course it is easy to sink into a dystopian malaise and to be so fearful of the future that we end up in the thrall of paralysis.

In our pedagogies, in our public pedagogies more specifically (this term was developed first by Henry Giroux), I follow the tradition of popular education, liberation theology, and Freirean-based education. Freire's standing within the lineage of critical pedagogy is that of a global advocate for praxis. Freire's work demonstrates the possibility of what I would call a transformative volition, or protagonistic intent, that is, a movement of the human spirit (that resides in the flesh of our bodies and of our dreams) in and on the world designed to transform the material and social conditions that shape us and are shaped by us so that our capacities are enhanced and our humanity enlarged. Here I would draw attention to the enfleshment of Freire's concept of praxis in which he weaves the human body into his materialist dialectics of consciousness and praxis. For Freire, reality was a concrete totality, a reality that is already a structured, self-forming dialectical whole in the process of coming into existence. As subjects, Freire believes we can break out of the prison house of discourse and its attendant subjectivism by changing the material conditions that shape us in our practical activity. Through a method of analysis and a conception of the world that involves a dialectical analysis of reality and a dialectical unity with the oppressed, Freire is able to avoid solipsism and idealism. In other words, Freire was concerned with interrogating the causal relationships that inform our material consciousness and subjective volition and intentionality. In the process of understanding the world, we deepen our consciousness precisely through our actions in and on the world that enable us not only to grasp our positionality in the world but also to transform the totality of social relations that constitute the contradictory character of our existence. Freire was committed to freeing ourselves and others from the relations bound up in the dialectical contradictions of everyday life. His work was thus connected to Marx's negative conception of ideology—to actions and symbols that are really only partial and fragmented and therefore distorted. Here Freire admonishes us not to free people from their chains but to prepare them to free themselves through a dialogical praxis linked to a materialist dialectics of consciousness (see Au, 2007). Freire believes that the forms of action people take is a function of how they perceive themselves in the world. The critical action for freedom that Freire advocates stems fundamentally from our dialogical relations with other human beings and leads to a critical consciousness embedded relationally in the word and the world as a form of praxis, an act of knowing through problem-posing/coding/decoding and reconstruction.

Critical pedagogy invites students to understand everyday life from the perspective of those who are the most powerless in our society so that society can be transformed in the interests of a more humane and just existence for all. Understanding social life from the perspective of the oppressed goes beyond mere empathy. Here I would draw upon the insights of Augusto Boal, in particular his important concept of metaxis as a pedagogical process. Boal, like Bertolt Brecht before him, was suspicious of the use of empathy and catharsis in theater, since empathy and catharsis can destroy the audience's capacity for critique. Brecht developed the concept of *Verfremdung*, or "alienation-effect," which helped to create a distance between the audience and the character, and the actor and the person portrayed. Boal's notion of metaxis replaced the Aristotelean mimetic relationship between the theater and reality, so that both "the real and the fictional could be experienced simultaneously" (O'Connor, 2013, p. 11), a process that Vygotsky described as a "dual affect" "whereby the person is directly engaged with what is happening in the drama, and at the same time is distanced from it, as he or she watches his or her own engagement with the drama" (as cited in O'Connor, 2013, p. 13). Gavin Bolton sees this dual affect as "the tension which exists between the concrete world and the 'as if' world, sometimes leading to contradictory emotions" (as cited in O'Connor, 2013, p. 11). This process is reflected in Freirean critical consciousness as participants remain distanced from problems that others are facing in the contexts of everyday life yet at the same time are open to an empathetic response to those facing problems. Critical consciousness demands acting "as if" you were experiencing a problem situation experienced by others and yet remaining at a critical distance as a percipient of your own actions. Here empathy toward the other is not uncritical and removed from critical reflection necessary to transform the conditions responsible for the problems.

A critical approach to education needs to expand the issue of pedagogy beyond questions of management and governance to that of reclaiming the world for humanity. Technological revolution and the market will not be enough to solve the growing environmental challenge and alleviate the problem of ecological decline and overcome necessity. Educational inquiry, as well as pedagogy as a social practice, must be rethought from the standpoint of those who exist at the bottom of the global capitalist hierarchy if we are to prevail in the continuing wars over scarce resources. Whether we support models of eco-communalism, eco-socialism or the new sustainability paradigm, it is clear that critical educational studies underwritten by a social justice agenda will require more than lifestyle change; they will require a concerted critique and transformation of the unbridled barbarism of capitalist social relations.

In order that our social amnesia remains, resolutely unacknowledged, we hide behind an almost puritanical fear of any pedagogy that insists on opening the door to doubt, to recognizing our entanglement in the larger conflictual arena of political and social relations and how such an entanglement is itself deeply ensconced in merging religiosity into political ends. If we wonder how it is that here in the twenty-first century we are witnessing the steady erosion of human rights and civil liberties, we only have to examine the extent of our political denial and its implication for mis-educating our citizenry.

At this moment in history, the work of Paulo Freire threatens the culture of silence that informs our everyday life as educators in the world's greatest capitalist democracy, one overarching saga of which has been the successful dismantling of public schooling by the juggernaut of neoliberal privatization and the corporatization of the public sphere.

I met Paulo for the first time at an AERA conference in Chicago in 1985. In 1986, his beloved wife Elza died. Shortly after Elza's death, Paulo wrote me a letter expressing the great sadness that had enveloped him completely. I was surprised to receive a letter from Paulo, and especially such a personal letter, having at the time met him only once. Years later, I came across the letter in my office at UCLA and I remember thinking to myself that I wish the letter would be lost, as I no longer wanted the temptation to show a letter of such intimacy to friends or to colleagues. Within days of finding the letter, I lost it, and have never been able to recover it. I also remember the unmitigated joy Paulo felt when he married Maria Araújo Freire, and became a devoted husband to "Nita" who blessed his life with a reciprocal devotion, a fierce intelligence, and a relentless dedication to social justice. Nita became an inspiration for Paulo; their mutual love saturated both their lives and their work. One might be tempted to compare Paulo and Nita with Sartre and De Beauvoir, Luxemburg and Kautsky or Karl and Jenny Marx, but that would be romanticizing a relationship that needs no comparison with other historical couples. They were simply Nita and Paulo, lovers and intellectuals who combined both dimensions in their protagonistic actions in the service of the people and their needs. And in so doing, they created a moral affinity that constituted the conditions for the possibility of love. This is the true meaning of revolutionary love, recognizing that love can only exist between free and equal people who share similar ideals and a commitment to serving the poor and the oppressed. The revolutionary love of Nita and Paulo thrived in such conditions.

I remember meeting Nita in an airplane in Rio, quite accidently, and asking her what she thought of my idea about writing a book about Paulo and Ernesto Che Guevara. Nita replied that she thought Paulo would approve of such an idea, and Nita's enthusiastic support helped to give me the confidence I needed to complete the book. Eventually, Nita wrote the preface to *Che Guevara, Paulo Freire and the Pedagogy of Revolution* in an emotionally riveting style that set a beautiful tone for the work that followed.

During the decade that I came to know Paulo professionally and as a friend, I was particularly impacted by Freire's discussion of university professors, since at the time I was frustrated with finding a place for myself in the academy. Freire, I noted, directed some harsh criticism toward university professors who maintained a willful ignorance about the dialectical relationship between pedagogy and politics:

> I feel so sad concerning the future of these people who teach at universities and think that they are just professors. They don't put their hands into politics because they think that it is dirty. It's precisely in escaping from politics that you have to know that you are a politician, and that your tactics are not merely pedagogical ones. But we cannot escape from this fact that politics and education are interwoven. You must develop your tactics there in response to the situation you confront in the field, not here, in the university, unless you wish to stop the project. In that case you don't need tactics. You could just come back home and leave the project. (1985, p. 19)

Freire was especially disdainful of those professors who chose to remain isolated from the social contradictions of the day, and who ignored the historical conditions that helped to exacerbate those contradictions. To such professors, modes of inquiry and concepts are generally irrelevant to the pedagogical process. What matters most is how the teachers and students feel—not what they think or do—but whether or not they are enjoying what they do. Consequently and tragically, such professors exercise a "post" class pedagogy based on lifestyle, and irony, in which it is difficult—if not impossible—for students to confront the reality of others whose misery is the condition of their prosperity. At the very most, these professors muster their energy in order to free teachers and students from emotional distress rather than teach them about the social totality and its fatal entanglement in capitalist social relations. Such a pedagogy of domestication enforces anti-intellectual and trans-social individualism based on sharing one's lived experiences. Both Paulo and Nita recognize that a critical pedagogy needs to accomplish more than to facilitate the sharing of lived experiences with one another. What is needed is a concrete and critical analysis of experience, of experience effects, an analysis that, in fact, goes beyond experience, that teaches us something that we don't already know. This requires a language or languages to interpret experience, languages that can help us unpack the material conditions of experiences. Knowledge from our lived experiences cannot simply be read on their own terms; rather, critical educators must help students relate these experiences to their outside historical and social conditions. But also, we need to understand the loss of experience, including inner experience, as Walter Benjamin has distinguished this. Modernity has helped to replace remembering with memory, that is, collective memory (a magic disclosure of the world often accompanied by synaesthetic experience and self-forgetfulness) with memory in the service of the intellect (a purely instrumental form of lived experience expressed in corporeally established habits and mechanical and purposive rationality). Like Benjamin, Paulo understood the need for political and moral redemption as a step in restructuring our modes of experiencing a world that has been shattered by modernity. It was this lesson that stood out early in my university work and my task was to provide students with the most powerful theoretical tools to use to understand their own self and social formation in relation to larger social relations of capitalist production, relations created within a brutal and systematic extraction of surplus value from proletarianized regions of the world (usually festering in a climate of bourgeois-comprador nationalism) culminating in an condition of substantive inequality and an egregiously unequal division of labor. In my early work I would deploy contrapuntally critical pedagogy, neo-Marxist critique, and cultural analysis, and in my later work I utilize a revolutionary Marxist humanist perspective with a focus on the role of finance capitalism and the social relations of production and their ecocidal effects on the biosphere and planetary sustainability.

Paulo graciously wrote a preface for my 1995 book, *Critical Pedagogy and Predatory Culture*. In his preface he reflected on our "intellectual kinship" and our relationship as intellectual "cousins" while at the same time he lamented the preoccupation of so many academics and politicians with fighting among themselves when they should be uniting against their antagonists:

> If someone should ask if intellectual kinship is a sine qua non to our ability to influence or be influenced, to work together, to exchange points of view, build each other's knowledge, I say no. When such a kinship develops we need to cultivate within ourselves the virtue of tolerance, which "teaches" us to live with that which is different; it is imperative that we learn from and that we teach our "intellectual relative," so that in the end we can unite in our fight against antagonistic forces. Unfortunately, as a group, we academics and politicians alike expend much of our energy on unjustifiable "fights" among ourselves, provoked by adjectival or, even worse, by purely adverbial differences. While we wear ourselves thin in petty "harangues," in which personal vanities are displayed and egos are scratched and bruised, we weaken ourselves for the real battle: the struggle against our antagonists. (1995, p. x)

Freire was able to break free from such "petty harangues" and the contemporary postmodern discourses that domesticate both the heart and mind, so that he could remain focused on his efforts to help students unlearn those myths produced by the dominant ideology that deform humanity.

It is surely striking the extent to which Freire's eviscerating pedagogical commentary, by planting the seed of catharsis and thereby placing in our hands the responsibility to overcome the political amnesia that has become the hallmark of teaching, cannot be welcomed into the classrooms of our nation by the guardians of the state. They have witnessed the unnerving intimacy and camaraderie he was able to forge among his admirers worldwide and how they were challenged by the disseminating force of his liberatory language of hope and possibility. And while they have not been able to root him out of the philosophy of teaching, they have managed to domesticate his presence. They have done this by transforming the political revolutionary with Marxist ideas into a friendly old man who advocates a love of dialogue, separating this notion from that of a dialogue of love—hence, the importance of reclaiming Paulo Freire for these times.

What Freire teaches us is that truth is never about unmediated reflections of a real object—something resolutely immutable and transparent. Rather, it is always dialogical, always about the self/other. Instead of heeding a Freirean call for a multi-vocal public and international dialogue on our responsibility as the world's sole superpower, one that acknowledges that we as a nation are also changed by our relationship to the way we treat others, we in the United States have let a fanatical cabal of politicians convince us that dialogue is weakness, is an obstacle to peace.

Freire's dialectics of the concrete (to borrow a phrase from Karel Kosik) is very unlike that of the postmodernists who, in their artful counterposing of the familiar and the strange in order to deconstruct the unified subject of bourgeois humanism, mock the pieties of monologic authoritarianism with sportive saber slashes across the horizon of familiarity and consensus. Whereas postmodern "resistance" results in a playful hemorrhaging of certainty, a spilling forth of fixed meanings into the submerged grammars of bourgeois society, remixed in the sewers of the social as 'resistance' and rematerialized in the art house jargon of fashionable apostasy, Freire's work retains an unshakable modernist faith in human agency consequent upon language's ineradicable sociality and dialogical embedment. What Freire has in common with the postmodernists is a desire to break free of contemporary discourses that domesticate both the heart and mind, but he is not content to remain in the nocturnal world of the subconscious; rather, he is compelled to take his critical pedagogy to the streets of the real.

Paulo Freire's legacy in the field of popular education and critical pedagogy is one characterized by an ontological commitment to deploying literacy and learning as a matrix of critical mediation, of humanization. The corpus of works left by Freire are like the rings of a tree; they cover every aspect of pedagogy, reflecting the history of meaning-making in both historical and mythical time.

Freire was one of the first educational philosophers to underscore repeatedly the concept of "knowing" as a political act. One way of examining knowledge that is highly indebted to the ideas of Freire is to see educators as working within the intersection of temporality and narrative as a dialectical event. Here, experience, temporality, reflection, and social action come together in what is commonly referred to in Freirean discourse as "praxis." In the field of anthropology, profane or historical time of contemporary social groups (involving the concreteness, linearity and irreversibility of time) is often juxtaposed with the mythical time of so-called archaic societies (time that repeats paradigmatic or archetypal gestures that are filled with deep meaning for the participants who use such recurrent mythical forms as a prism for personhood). Freire's notion of praxis, however, brings both conceptions of time into the narrative fabric of the emergent self. The act of knowing is grounded in a type of mythopoetic desire (a desire to raise our own existence to a level of greater meaningfulness; see Freeman, 1998) linked to community, to a new level of sacred authenticity, to organizing life in imaginatively new ways that refuse to reproduce the alienation and objectification necessarily found in the world of abstract labor. Here, revolutionary praxis folds historical and mythical time into an act of negating what is, in anticipation of what could be. Schematically put, the line (the perpetual reappearance of the present in historical time) is folded into the circle (the primordial horizon of the irredeemably configured past).

One of Freire's goals is becoming conscious of and transcending the limits in which we can make ourselves. We achieve this through externalizing, historicizing and objectifying our vision of liberation, in treating theory as a form of practice and practice as a form of theory as we contest the psychopathology of everyday life incarnate in capitalism's social division of labor. We do this with the intention of never separating the production of knowledge from praxis, from reading the world and the world dialectically (Stetsenko, 2002). In so doing we maintain that practice serves as the ultimate ground for advancing and verifying theories as well as for providing warrants for knowledge claims. These warrants are not connected to some fixed principles that exist outside of the knowledge claims themselves, but are derived by identifying and laying bare the ideological and ethical potentialities of a given theory as a form of practice (Stetsenko, 2002). Critical educators seek to uncover what at first blush may appear as the ordinary, transparent relations and practices that make up our quotidian existence—what we might even call mundane social realities. We take these relationships and practices and try to examine their contractions when seen in relation to the totality of social relations in which those particular relations and practices unfold. Such an examination takes place against a transdisciplinary backdrop that reads the world and the world historically.

Freire does not use literacy to impose a matrix of reality upon the educand like some abstract desideratum to be followed, but to interrupt the continuity of everyday life and seize opportunities at the intersection of historical and mythical time so that life can be grasped and lived within the horizon of the configured past and the anticipated future. The educand learns to live in the historical moment as a subject of history, but history is simultaneously re-animated and re-narrativized such that it is linked to the struggles of oppressed groups in various geopolitical contexts throughout the course of history and into the future..

Freire was one of the first educators to affirm that the process of understanding cannot be reduced to the formal properties of language alone but has to take into account its relationship to extra-linguistic forms of knowing, other forms of corporeal and praxiological meanings that are all bound up with the production of ideology. Meaningful knowledge is not solely nor mainly the property of the formal properties of language but is enfleshed. It is neither ultra-cognitivist nor traditionally intellectualist. It cannot be abstracted "from all the concrete, particular, embodied, erotic, and expressive features of language in order to invest emancipatory possibilities from its formal properties" (McNally, 2001, p. 109). Knowledge, in other words, is embodied in the way we read the world and the word simultaneously in our actions with, against, and alongside other human beings. Of course, as Freire made clear, only the pre-Hegelian philosophers could think of transforming history in the head alone.

Freire writes that it is "impossible to think of transformation without thinking of getting power to transform" (1987, p. 226). He goes on to say that "education means a kind of action which on the one hand is explained by the power which constitutes it, on the other hand it works in the direction of preserving the power which constituted it or works against the power which constituted it" (Freire, 1987, p. 226). But Freire did not wish simply to organize political power in order to transform the world; he wished to reinvent power. Political power, of course, is based on economic power. Freire believed that resources for a dignified survival should be socially available and not individually owned.

According to Freire, there are distinct ways of thinking practiced by the rich or the "non-poor" that lead to ways of defending the interests and privilege of the ruling class and preserving and immortalizing their history (Freire, 1987, p. 221). It is a fatalistic way of thinking about the poor that rationalizes poverty as a constituent condition of living in a class-divided society. Such a fatalism also leads to political immobilization as teachers focus on "techniques, on psychological, behavioral explanations, instead of trying or acting, of doing something, of understanding the situation globally, of thinking dialectically, dynamically" (1987, p. 223). Freire asserts that the non-poor are often very liberal and progressive in their politics, yet when it comes time for them to confront the possibility of the poor becoming better off economically, they become reactionary. In addition to a failure to grasp critically the significance of class struggle, what the non-poor lack is an understanding of the role of dialogue in the process of knowing, which admits a social, historical, and cultural relationship to knowledge production.

For Freire, dialectical inquiry should be at the heart of "the act of knowing," which is fundamentally an act of transformation that goes well beyond the epistemological domain. As Freire writes:

> The act of knowing, which education implies, must be understood in connection with organization for changing, for transforming. The transformation, for example, about which we talk, constantly, has to go beyond the understanding that we have sometimes of transformation as something which happens inside of us. We have the tendency to stop the understanding of transformation at the level of some change in our way of thinking, in our way of speaking, for example, and it is not enough. The individual dimension of transformation has to be completed by the objective transformation, or the transformation of the objectivity, of reality, and it is a question again of politics. (1987, p. 223)

But in order to understand the process of knowing as a political act, and to complete the transformation of objective reality, we need to see this process in terms of the creation of historical, cultural, and material spaces where the dialogical nature of knowing is acknowledged and respected. As we begin to grasp its internal movement, it becomes clear that it can never be neutral. Part of Freire's task of dialogical education is to provide opportunities for students to recognize the unspoken ideological dimension of their everyday understanding and to encourage themselves to become part of the political process of transformation of structures of oppression to pathways to emancipation.

Recognizing that we live in a pluricentric world, Freire's approach to critical pedagogy is undertaken with a certain directiveness, not manipulation, with authority, not authoritarianism. While speaking with authority, it is important always to understand the place from which you speak, and from which you are being heard or ignored. On this note, Freire specifically urged U.S. educators to understand the role of their own country, especially in the context of the suffering masses of Latin America and other parts of the world. He warned:

> You must discover that you cannot stop history. You have to know that your country (the US) is one of the greatest problems for the world. You have to discover that you have all these things because of the rest of the world. You must think of these things. (1985, p. 22)

For Freire, an important task for critical educators is to grasp, comprehend, and generalize forms of resistance to oppression on the part of the oppressed (that is, resistance on the plane of immanence) and give some direction in challenging capitalism at its very roots with the purpose of offering an alternative social universe outside of capitalism's value form (that is, creating a concrete utopia). Critical educators should not take a passive role when it comes to spontaneous struggles; instead, they should elicit from the workers an understanding of the meaning of their own everyday struggles. Peter Hudis (2010) notes that this follows Marx's concept of the task of the revolutionary: "not to imbue or impart consciousness to the masses but rather to generalize and develop the social consciousness that is generated from their actual struggles." This requires that critical educators not regard its constituents as blank slates that need to be filled with revolutionary knowledge and strongly endorses Freire's critique of banking education. Critical educators who utilize the banking form of education believe that socialist consciousness cannot arise spontaneously from the masses; in fact, they vehemently oppose the (Platonic) notion that the critical educator is the "midwife" of knowledge (Hudis, 2010) and claim that the masses should be given the "correct" knowledge by an elite cadre of intellectuals. I share Freire's position that workers who are struggling against the alienation wrought by capitalism (at the attendant antagonisms of racism, sexism, ableism, homophobia), have themselves already acquired a sense of what kind of new society they want and that critical educators should not bring this knowledge to them from the outside. Rather, the idea of this new society is already implicit in the dialectic of negativity that characterizes the struggle of workers from practice to theory, and from theory back to practice. In other words, such knowledge is immanent in the workers' drive for total freedom (Hudis, 2010). Freire believed that it wasn't a prerequisite to acquire a critical consciousness in order to struggle for social justice. Quite the contrary. Critical consciousness was the outcome—not the precondition—of struggle. It is in the act of struggling that educands become critically conscious. Indeed, if Freire is right on this issue, and I believe that he is, what then is the role of the critical educator in the struggle to transform the world? Critical educators need in my view to make what is implicit in the educands' experiences explicit by linking their spontaneous development of a critical or socialist consciousness to a larger, more comprehensive theory and philosophy of revolution (Hudis, 2010). In other words, critical educators can hasten the outcome of mass struggle. This, in my view, is the real meaning of critical pedagogy.

I would like to share a description that I made of Paulo for a book edited by Tom Wilson, Peter Park, and Anaida Colon-Muniz called *Memories of Paulo*:

> He was a picaresque pedagogical wanderer, a timeless vagabond linked symbolically to Coal Yard Alley, to Rio's City of God, to the projects of Detroit and any and every neighborhood where working men and women have toiled throughout the centuries, a flaneur of the boulevards littered with fruiterers and fish vendors and tobacco and candy stalls, the hardscrabble causeways packed with migrant workers and the steampunk always of dystopian dreams. This man of the people was as much at home in the favelas as he was in the mango groves, a maestro who would cobble together the word and the world from the debris of everyday life, from its fury of dislocation, from the hoary senselessness of its cruelty, from its beautiful and frozen emptiness and wrathfulness of its violence. And in the midst of all of this he was able to fashion revolutionary hope from the tatters of humanity's fallen grace. This was Paulo Freire. (2010, p. 177)

It is impossible for me to think of Paulo in a strictly prosaic way. This is because Paulo is very much a poetic figure. This is not tantamount to saying that Paulo is larger than life, that he strides the world like some unmatchable pedagogical colossus, or that he is immune to critique. It simply means that I carry Paulo in my heart and memories of Paulo are stored by me in the language of poetry, not only to be emotionally caressed but to be unpacked, interrogated, analyzed, and understood with whatever theoretical tools I have available and under the historical conditions in which I am working. I learned to understand Freire differently while working in Venezuela than I did while working in Colombia, differently while working in Mexico than while working in Argentina, differently while working in Brazil than while working in Turkey, differently while working in Canada than while working in Greece.

If there is a spark of light in these very dark times, it can be found in the practices of resistance of which Paulo and Nita Freire speak, a resistance that I maintain is tethered to the fusty iron chassis of socialism. Too often, the term socialism evokes an image of spindle-shanked gangrels working the shop floor and agitating for better wages and improved working conditions, watched over in the panopticon of the factory by grim-faced men in dark frockcoats who report any infractions to the factory owners. Today, we have an example of the "electronic whip"—giant flat screen monitors that hang in the laundry rooms in the basements of the Disneyland hotels in Anaheim that serve to keep track of the fastest and slowest workers. But socialism is not something that can only or mainly be found in the European tradition. It is alive and well in indigenous communities throughout las Americas. I believe that a socialism for the twenty-first century will need to look to indigenous communities for ways to fight what Anibal Quijano calls "the coloniality of power" and to secure an ecologically sustainable socialist alternative to the barbarism of capitalism.

For those who believe that it is human nature for some groups to dominate and control others, the goal of liberation is to make both the despot and despotic regime more benign. For Freire, such a solution is tantamount to cutting off our legs in the hope that one day we shall grow wings. If we make the road to emancipation by walking, then we need to know at some point whether we are on the right path in freeing ourselves from the many antagonisms that beset us. For Freire, being on the right path is to have a coherent and consistent vision toward which progress is directed and that can serve as a template for living fearlessly, knowing that moving forward implies overcoming many obstacles. It is to be guided by a vision that ultimately and irrevocably can bring justice to a world in perilous imbalance. Grave changes are warranted in our political civilization—not only the abolition of the commercial helotry of the factories and sweatshops but also unclenching the fists we call our hearts, freeing us to reclaim our stolen humanity. Freire's struggle was to be humble enough to wonder yet courageous enough to defy, to be sufficiently self-assured to rebel yet possess enough self-doubt to keep from backsliding, to have the audacity to be creative yet remain unburdened by socio-cultural dogma, to be vigilant against the new faces of tyranny yet ever conscious of the flaws and insufficiencies of our own struggles. Freire worked with the generic potential to posit a world that does not make capitulation and defeat inevitable. Those liberals and conservatives alike who preach the virtues of democracy without recognizing that their vision remains beyond the recuperative powers of the prevailing capitalist system are laying the foundation for plutocracy, and in so doing sawing from the tree the branch upon which they are perched: wizened old vultures masquerading as feathery companions of Minerva. For Freire, understanding the alienation of human labor is the skeleton key that unlocks the bone yard of capitalism and makes it vulnerable for transformation into its opposite—a world of economic, social, cultural, racial, sexual, and gender equality. Freire's pedagogy is connected to the utopian impulse, freed from utopia's instrumental and petrified systematizing and idealist, totalizing form. It is a pedagogy committed to the historical, material and situationally specific needs of humanity. It is a pedagogy of and for our times.

The theogony of Freire's works is not derived from biblical scholarship and the hamartia of Adam nor does he reject this root and branch; rather, it can be linked at least implicitly to the pantheon of indigenous saints that stretch thousands of years into the past and that refuse to be whitened. This could be seen as anathema to those ensepulchred within the dogma of capitalist modernity for whom politics and spirituality are two fundamentally separable spheres, each of which somehow loses its integrity insofar as it loses autonomy to the other. However, Freire sees no contradiction in a pedagogy informed by both practical consciousness and spiritual conviction (see Rivage-Seul, 2006).

It was my privilege to have witnessed Freire walking among us, laughing and lightfooted, his tiny shoulders heaving like twin turbines beneath his crisp, freshly starched shirt, his slender legs gliding with a carefree, insouciant lilt, as if he were being helped along by a puckish breeze that served as a counterpoint to his steady, almost relentless gaze. To me it seemed as though he was always peering into the present somewhere from the future, in some future anterior where dreams are on a collision course with what is occurring in the laboratories of everyday life we call reality, where light breaks through dark chambers that cannot be illuminated without love. To understand that collision is to understand the essence of Freire's work. Without a careful reading of Freire's intellectual roots, one can only witness the collision without understanding the systems of intelligibility that make such a collision inevitable and without understanding the possibilities of sublating such a collision in order to bring about alternative futures linked to the sustainability of the planet and humanity as a whole. This is the grand mysterium of Freire's work.

The field of educational reform has been over-grazed, emerging as a multitude of conflicting opinions, varying according to the disposition of the reformer and the facts he or she has selected. The topsoil has worn thin as the sun withers and scorches seeds without roots. It is time to enrich the soil of our education reform if we are to once again grow roots. Until now, the socialist imaginary has lain buried deep within our pedagogical unconscious awaiting this historic moment to be revealed once again. We can begin by affirming our commitment to a communal self, one that implies a continuum between mind and spirit. We must fight for free expression of our productive capacities and free association with other workers in productive works. We need to learn how we can use our labor capacity outside and beyond capitalist production relations. This is what critical pedagogy is all about.

My goal is to develop transnational interactions from below—from the exploited and the excluded—and this may be called a counter-hegemonic globalization process if you want. These are local struggles that need to be globalized—and we know what they are. Boaventura de Sousa Santos has listed some of these as transnational solidarity networks, new labor internationalism, international networks of alternative legal aid, transnational human rights organizations, feminist movements, indigenous movements, ecological movements, alternative development movements and associations, literary, artistic and scientific movements on the periphery of the world system in search for non-imperialist, anti-hegemonic cultural and educational values.

Critical pedagogy needs to become activated through new social moments. The movements that I have witnessed of late—the Occupy Movement, the uprising in Greece, protests of university students in Mexico, the Indignados—are making more than minor demands; they are struggling for an entirely different kind of future and the originality and creativity of their protests speak to that future. They are not just about negating the present but also about reclaiming space—parks, public squares, university buildings, and other spaces where they can enact a new, more horizontal form of governance and decision making. They are moving beyond narrow sectarian interests and seeking to put participatory democracy into practice as an alternative to vertical forms of organization favored by liberal, representative democracy. And, of course, they are fighting state authoritarianism and a growing transnational fascism. They are seeking to challenge consumer citizens to become critical citizens again, as many citizens strove to become before the era of asset capitalism, or neoliberal capitalism. But the movement goes beyond nostalgia for the past, since most of the youth have known only neoliberal capitalism all of their lives. The youth have also figured out that parliamentary forms of representation can no longer suffice in creating democracy in a social universe of asset or finance capitalism that requires a neo-fascist reorganization of the state in order to preserve massive profits for the transnational capitalist class. Youth protesters today are struggling for participatory forms of association using new social media and new convergent media production as digital tools, as technological literacies to educate themselves and their comrades to link their experiences of struggle to goal-directed actions. They are struggling for different forms of social life. Here the digital media do not become ends in themselves but augment or supplement real-world experiences of struggle for popular sovereignty—and in the case of the Zapatistas in Chiapas or the Purepecha nation in Cheran, Mexico, an autonomous community within the state. As a result of these struggles, these tools become more integrated as part of an effort to create a collective intelligence with multiple visions of a socially just, fairer world.

The educational left needs to be more proactive in helping to transform such movements from spontaneous uprisings to historical blocs in the Gramscian sense. That said, I do believe there is an ongoing danger of communitarian popular fronts. Popular frontism could become reified as the "lost generation" versus the bankers and hedge fund profiteers. We have to be wary of the struggle becoming reduced to the "good capitalists" who are against monopolies, etc., versus the unproductive parasites in the finance sector who accumulate their fortunes on the sloping shoulders of others who are forced to sell their labor power for a wage. We must begin to wage a struggle for an alternative to capitalism based on the creation of real wealth rather than the value form of labor. Following Freire's pedagogically impassioned argument that freedom and education should never be separated, we cannot simply ride the crest of some cosmogenetic wave, merely going along for the ride, the winding sheet of humanity serving as our topsail. We cannot afford to rest our hope on the appearance of some galactic supernova of the soul, some parabolic flow into and out of historical time, as if merely a spectator in some arcane sideshow. We must liberate ourselves from the liberal indecisiveness that prevents us from escaping a sullied world. We must forge our vision on the anvil of class struggle, of revolutionary transformation, through a self-giving, interabiding collectivity of self-community grounded in an ethics of solidarity and love. We, as historical agents, are inseparable from the motion of praxis, entrusted to Marx but pluriversal in scope.

The battle is one that must be multipronged and coordinated with numerous interconnected struggles. One such struggle, while never independent from the struggle against capital, is the struggle over the production of knowledge and the meaning and purpose of teaching—in other words, the struggle over education. Popular education is a tree that throughout history has found a way to burst through the blood-soaked pitch of the battlefield, its roots firmly planted in the restitution of our planetary soul, its leaves finding shafts of sunlight slashing their way through the carnage.

NOTE

This chapter includes material published in Peter McLaren, Contemporary Youth Resistance Culture and the Class Struggle, *Critical Arts: South-North Cultural and Media Studies*, Vol. 28, no. 1 (February), 2014, pp. 152–160; Peter McLaren, Reflections on Love and Revolution. *The International Journal of Critical Pedagogy*, Volume 5, no. 1., 2013, pp. 60–68; the afterword in *Memories of Paulo* (pp. 173–178), edited by Tom Wilson, Peter Park, and Anaida Colon-Muniz, Rotterdam, The Netherlands: Sense, 2010; Peter McLaren, the afterword in *Paulo Freire's Intellectual Roots: Towards Historicity in Praxis* (pp. 231–236), edited by Robert Lake and Tricia Kress, London, England: Bloomsbury, 2013; and Peter McLaren, the afterword in *Paulo Freire: The Man From Recife* (pp. 305–320), by James D. Kirlyo, New York, NY: Peter Lang, 2011.

REFERENCES

Au, Wayne. (2007). Epistemology of the Oppressed: The Dialectics of Paulo Freire's Theory of Knowledge. *Journal for Critical Education Policy Studies*, volume 5, no. 2. Retrieved from http://. jeeps.com/imdex.php?pageID=article&articleID=100

Bauman, Z. (2010). *Living on borrowed time: Conversations with Citlali Rovirsoa-Madrazo*. Cambridge, England: Polity Press.

Boal, A. (1979). *Theater of the oppressed*. New York, NY: Urizen Books.

Brecht, B. (1964). *Brecht on theater: The development of an aesthetic* (J. Willett, Trans.). London, England: Methuen Drama.

Freeman, M. (1998). Mythical Time, Historical Time, and The Narrative Fabric of the Self. *Narrative Inquiry*, Vol. 8, Number 1: 27–50.

Freire, P. (1985). *Dialogue is not a chaste event.* Compiled by Paul Jurmo. The Center for International Education, School of Education. Hills House South. University of Massachusetts, Amherst.

Freire, P. (1987). Conversations with Paulo Freire on *Pedagogies for the non-poor.* In A. Frazer Evans, R. A. Evans, & W. B. Kennedy (Eds.), *Pedagogies for the non-poor* (pp. 219–231). Maryknoll, NY: Orbis Books.

Freire, P. (1995). Preface. In P. McLaren (Ed.), *Critical pedagogy and predatory culture: Oppositional politics in a postmodern era* (pp. ix–xi). New York, NY: Routledge.

Freire, P., & Macedo, D. (1987). *Literacy: Reading the word and the world.* Hove, England: Psychology Press.

Harvey, D. (2003). *The new imperialism.* Oxford, England: Oxford University Press.

Hudis, P. (2010, December). *The critical pedagogy of Rosa Luxemburg.* Paper presented at the Encuentro Internacional del Pensamiento Critico: Marxismo y Educacion Popular, Morelia, Michoacan, Mexico.

McLaren, Peter. (2010). Afterword. A *Fado for Freire.* In Tom Wilson, Peter Park, and Anaida Colon-Muniz (Eds.), *Memories of Paulo.* (pp. 173–178). Tapei and Rotterdam: Sense Publishers.

McNally, David. (2001). *Bodies of Meaning: Studies on Language, Labor, and Liberation.* Albany, New York: State University of New York Press.

O'Connor, P. (2013). *Terrorists under the bridge: Applied theatre and empathy.* Unpublished manuscript.

Quijano, Anibal. (2000). Coloniality of Power, Eurocentrism, and Latin America. *Nepantla: Views from South* 1, no. 3: 533–80.

Ravitch, Diane. (2014). Public Education: Who Are the Corporate Reformers? March 28. As retrieved from: http://billmoyers.com/2014/03/28/public-education-who-are-the-corporate-reformers/

Rivage-Seul, D. (2006). *The emperor's god: Misunderstandings of Christianity.* Berea, KY: Berea College.

Santos, Boaventura de Sousa (2005, 2009). General Introduction: Reinventing Social Emancipation: Toward New Manifestos. In Boaventura de Sousa Santos (Ed.), *Democratizing Democracy. Beyond the Liberal Democratic Canon* (pp. xvii–xxxiii). London: Verso.

Santos, B. S. (2009). A Non-Occidentalist West? Learned Ignorance and Ecology of Knowledge. *Theory, Culture & Society,* Vol. 26 (7–8): 103–125.

Stetsenko, Anna. (2002). Vygotsky's cultural-historical activity theory: Collaborative practice and knowledge construction process. In D. Robbins and A. Stetsenko (Eds.), *Vygotsky's psychology: Voices from the past and present.* New York: Nova Science Press.

CHAPTER TWO

Paulo Freire and the Continuing Struggle to Decolonize Education[1]

ANTONIA DARDER

More than forty years after Paulo Freire's (1971) book *Pedagogy of the Oppressed* was first released in English, the inequalities and injustices that he was addressing then continue to persist in the United States and around the world. In many instances these conditions have worsened in the past two decades, with the infusion of neoliberal imperatives of privatization, deregulation, and the free market into practices of education. It is important then to begin our discussion about the legacy of Freire here, in that it has often been precisely Freire's revolutionary critique of capitalism and the link of schooling to class struggle that have been stripped away, resulting in watered-down, diluted versions of his ideas.

As a scholar of color who was born a colonized subject in Puerto Rico and reared in abject poverty in the United States, there is no way that anyone can convince me that the center of gravity of oppression for those of us deemed "other" is simply the psychological aberration of white people toward our so-called "race." Rather, I argue adamantly that the racialization processes experienced by the marginalized are intimately tied to the material domination and exploitation of our communities by the wealthy and powerful elite—and enacted, for the most part, by those who are not themselves affluent but answer the siren call of capital daily.

With this in mind, I want to argue that, although seldom spoken about or acknowledged in traditional discourses about Freire's work, there are particular ways in which radical black, Latino, Native American, and Asian American working-class communities of the '60s and '70s engaged the deep potential inherent in Paulo Freire's treatise. For many of us, Freire was one of a few educational theorists and philosophers of the time who spoke to our grounded understanding of racialized oppression as powerfully linked to the larger international imperialist project. In other words, if we were to counter the impact of the historical and contemporary wounds of slavery and colonialism on our lives, we had to begin by engaging the manner in which racism is inextricably tied to the imperatives of social class formation and material exclusion.

For activists of color, the struggle was not foremost about "celebrating diversity" or cultural identity or even the acknowledgement of our cultural legitimacy, but rather a struggle for our humanity and our survival, given that we had suffered, in the flesh, the violence of oppression at every level of our existence. With this in mind, the more radical arms of the civil rights era, such as the Black Panthers, the Young Lords, the American Indian Movement, the Chicano Movement, the Asian American Movement, the Third World Women's Alliance, and others, recognized that our local political struggles for self-determination had to also be anchored to the larger international class struggle against the ravages and advancement of capitalism. As formerly colonized populations, Chicano, Puerto Rican, American Indian, and Native Hawaiian groups also framed their struggle within the context and impact of a long history of colonization. Hence, important links were made between the economic imperatives that led to the colonization of our lands and the enslavement of our African American brothers and sisters. Moreover, the engagement of Paulo Freire's work was as much about the political decolonization of our communities, as it was a personal process of decolonizing of our hearts, bodies, and minds.

In this sense, Freire's recognition that the oppressor/oppressed dialectic was also housed within the oppressed, echoed concerns raised by W.E.B. Du Bois, Jose Marti, Pedro Albizu Campos, Frantz Fanon, and Albert Memmi to name a few—activists, educators, or writers of color of the 20th century who spoke to this phenomenon in their political articulations about the struggles of oppressed populations. Theorists of color wrote of our twin being, Black Skin/White Masks, double consciousness, biculturalism, and so on, which spoke to the collision of not simply two cultures, but where deep asymmetrical relations of power led to the subordination and systematic erasure of the histories of racialized populations located at the margins of U.S. hegemony.

Restoring the integrity of our voices and centering our cultural and historical knowledge of survival became an important political project, in an era when our voices and participation remained relatively absent or silent from the spheres of power and privilege. It was also a time during which the "other" was treated routinely as an object or thing to be manipulated, as a reserve army of workers or soldiers to defend the economic and military agendas of the wealthy and powerful. And traditional education, springing out of the one-dimensionality of capitalist logic, served as an institution of *thingification*, as articulated by Aime Cesaire

(2001), who expressed great concern for the destruction of communities, societies, and nations and for the "millions of men [and women] torn from their gods, their land, their habits, their life—from life, from the dance, from wisdom" (p. 178). In response, radical theorists of color fought to challenge the racialized culture of class formation, which systematically worked to erode a sense of belonging, identity, and language, from poor working-class communities of color, while stripping us of our history, cultural knowledge, and language.

As a young woman, reading *Pedagogy of the Oppressed* changed the course of my life as an educator and political activist. This was for many reasons but perhaps, in particular, because he looked and felt more like my own people—people exiled from our lands. At the time, he was exiled from Brazil for his emancipatory efforts with the impoverished people from the countryside, yet he attributed so much of his pedagogical formulation to what he learned in his relationship with those who were dispossessed. Paulo inspired in activists and educators of color a political clarity and commitment.

Freire challenged us to embody our commitment to social consciousness and political transformation, within the relationships we forged with those within and outside of our cultural communities. What we sensed then, almost instinctually, was that a pedagogy of the oppressed was not only for the classroom, but rather a living pedagogy that had to be infused into all aspects of our lives, including our politics. This is to say that teaching to transgress constituted for us a moral stance, often belittled and diminished in mainstream political discourses—so much so that it brought bell hooks (1994) to write, "It always astounds me when progressive people act as though it is somehow a naive moral position to believe that our lives must be a living example of our politics" (p. 48).

For those who were betrayed by our schooling, Freire offered the possibility of an educational project for our children, tied to a larger democratic vision—one that resonated with our anti-colonial struggles for self-determination and our desire to control our own destinies. Hence, Freire's pedagogy was also a pedagogy of transgression—transgression of oppressive ideas, attitudes, structures, and practices within education that debilitate our humanity.

THE BETRAYAL OF MULTICULTURALISM

In the early history of the civil rights educational struggles, educators and activists of color saw multicultural education a possible counter-hegemonic mechanism for decolonizing the curriculum and transforming classroom life. In the '70s notions of biculturalism (tied to the struggle for bilingualism) began to evolve and efforts were forged toward developing culturally relevant pedagogy. Many of these pedagogical efforts were founded on principles of dialogue, reflection, problem posing, critique, and conscientizaçao that Freire evoked in *Pedagogy of the Oppressed*. These principles challenged cultural invasion and the banking model of education, and called for a problem-posing pedagogy that would support the evolution of critical consciousness in disenfranchised communities. Freire's notion of cultural invasion was overwhelmingly salient to those of us with histories of genocide, slavery, and colonization.

However, as critical multicultural education efforts began to take hold in the late 1970s and early '80s, reactionary conservative backlash and liberal rewriting of multiculturalism began to steadily erode the transformative intent of the project. Many of the multicultural education efforts that took hold in schools in the late '80s and '90s not only conserved a racializing hierarchical structure of power, but also intensified the process of hegemonic class formation within communities of color (Darder & Torres, 2004).

As communities of color utilized a politics of identity to call for fundamental changes to gross inequalities at work in the social and economic arenas of the nation, the Reagan administration's 1983 report, *A Nation at Risk*,[2] served as an effective educational neoliberal strategy to thwart the social advancement for equality in the United States. With the veiled contention that schools should serve as economic engines to ensure the global superiority of the nation, the accountability movement began to gain traction. It is worth noting that the national policies brewing during this period were not only tied to education. The process of deregulation, privatization, and the erosion of the safety net resulted in an economic corporate boom in the decade that followed, while neoliberal policies countered the gains made by the civil rights movement (Darder, 2012a). One disastrous impact to communities of color was the unprecedented increase in the number of U.S. incarcerations from 1985 to 2010, which resulted in an overwhelming number of poor, working-class inmates of color—more than 70% of whom were considered to be functionally illiterate.[3]

Anchored in deficit notions, conservative "whitewashed" expectations of multicultural education became the vanguard, while discussions about the "race" problem or "race" as the determining factor in the academic underachievement of students of color prevailed in educational debates (Darder & Torres, 2004). True to the colonizing politics of the times, many radical educators, particularly those of color, who remained aligned with Freire's pedagogical and political concerns, were pushed out and marginalized as new mainstream multicultural education gurus descended on the stage offering more palatable approaches, which served to distort revolutionary pedagogical discourses that originated within the decolonizing struggles of oppressed communities.

Often well-meaning discourses of urgency, justified by "culture of poverty" interpretations that placed the blame for poverty on our children, families, and culture (Leacock, 1971), were used as handy rationale for curtailing efforts toward self-determination and opportunities to evolve and advance in the process of decision making, even within our own communities. As a consequence, many of us found our efforts warped into unrecognizable proportions, rationalizing once again the superiority of white multicultural educators. Token educators of color, who followed their lead, were effectively integrated into schools and teacher preparation programs to marginalize decolonizing discourses and practices of more radical educators of color—a phenomenon whose consequence is being dramatically felt across the entire educational landscape today, as scholarship tied to cultural and language subordination in schools has gone out of vogue and now is considered passé in the "flat world" of neoliberal multiculturalism (Darder, 2012b). In the process, the revolutionary potential of multicultural curriculum, text, and pedagogy has been all but stripped away, while a fractured curriculum of cultural songs, stories, holidays, and heroes prevails.

With the eclipse of the so-called "multicultural age" in education, persisting problems and concerns raised by educators of color for almost a century now fall on deaf ears, as the instrumental ideology of neoliberal education policies has created limited matrices of accountability, which deliberately discount historical and contemporary community concerns related to culture, language, poverty, pedagogy, and power. Instead, the numbers game of high-stakes testing, the standardization of knowledge, and teaching to the test are the order of the day, shrouded in the institutionalization of Common Core standards.

Consequently, we find ourselves more deeply mired in Western ethnocentric (universal) notions of humanity, in which individualism (object-based, future-focused), and materialism counter the legitimacy of subordinate cultural community values and traditions. Additionally, this leads to the negation of our worldviews—including the marginalization of communal life, ancestral knowledge, or spiritual traditions that might enhance the teaching and learning of all children. More often than not, well-meaning educators seeking to address the needs of working-class communities of color continue to be entrapped in a deficit paradigm of difference.

Even more disconcerting, when critical educators of color (at all levels of education) attempt to challenge deficit notions through our teaching and research, mainstream educators, many of whom pride themselves in being social justice advocates or anti-racist educators, greet us with resistance and unparalleled requests for legitimacy of claims, deeply anchored within our particular cultural paradigms and philosophical assumptions of humanity and community self-determination. These paradigms and assumptions often reside outside many well-intended but still colonizing social values and epistemological priorities or directives, which objectify and render students from poor and working-class communities of color passive agents of their own learning.

This, of course, echoes the historical project of colonization, anchored in a conceptual narrative and epistemological design that legitimizes and naturalizes the cultural, economic, and military domination, exploitation, and dispossession of the majority of the world's population—in the name of democracy, progress, and profit. There is no question that the dehumanizing currents of the contemporary neoliberal agenda—which show global trends of increasing inequalities—require us to grapple seriously with the struggle for our humanity, as Freire argued, in the face of oppressive forces that seek to colonize every aspect of our lives, from birth to death. This is precisely why the issue of the political economy must remain central to any decolonizing pedagogy or methodology of emancipatory leadership.

We need only consult history to confirm that the politics of colonization has been rooted in a violent project of economic exploitation and racialization, which has provided the hegemonic apparatus to justify imperialist expansionism, unmerciful genocide, and conquest of those deemed "less human." Here, Freire's notion of "capitalism as the root of domination" (Shor & Freire, 1986, p. 47) is useful in this analysis, in that it connects past and current colonizing forces to how the capacity for productivity of a population is perceived within a capitalist society. This is to say that the ultimate worth of an individual or a people has been literally tied to their capacity to contribute to capitalist accumulation. As such, rather than pedagogical concern for our humanity, sovereignty, or the evolution of critical consciousness in the interest of cultural democracy, educational objectives within the United States are directed toward the potential of students to become good consumers. In this context, democracy becomes conflated with unbridled consumption.

Moreover, schools, as economic engines, function effectively in the process of class formation and the production of a national workforce that is in sync with the requirements of the labor market and a reserve army that can meet the military demands of a culture of perpetual war. It is here, where the politics of meritocracy in the United States, in conjunction with high-stakes testing, is effectively normalized and utilized to sort, sift, reward, or exclude students, accordingly. As would be expected, the children of the affluent rise to the top, while the majority of poor and working-class students of color populate the rosters of the academically underachieving—where they, their families, their culture, their language, and even their intelligence are all deemed suspect and responsible for their academic failure (Darder, 2012a). All the while, the larger institutional structures, economic inequalities, and educational exclusions that negatively impact the lives of working-class students remain veiled in a victim-blaming discourse of accountability, personal choice, and the myth of equality for all.

THE CULTURAL CONTEXT

Central to Freire's pedagogical thesis is the significance of the cultural context in the process of knowledge production. This is as true to the larger context of class formation as it is to the question of bicultural formation, wherein students must daily navigate the tensions and injustices of the subordinate/dominant divide. Hence, Freire's work has been and continues to be significant to critical educators, educational leaders, and activists of color, in that it reinforces the political necessity of contextual knowledge linked to communal and ancestral knowledge, which does not transcend the individual subject nor the material conditions that shape the histories and everyday relationships of formerly colonized and enslaved populations, both in the United States and abroad.

From this vantage point, if we are to genuinely contend with the educational difficulties of students from working-class, racialized communities, we must look beyond simply the personal or individual. We must seek answers, as Freire argued, within the histories of economic, social, and political structures of oppression, so that we might better understand the forces that give rise to inequalities and social exclusion, as they currently exist within our lives as educators and those of our students. Moreover, this call for the *enfleshment of knowledge* moves us away from those colonizing abstractions and separations of the body (and the land) that have always worked in the colonizing interest of the powerful and wealthy. This is to say that the underlying purpose of hegemonic power is to legitimize and conceal imperial/colonial relations. As such, the political work of the oppressed has always required the unveiling, naming, and challenging of asymmetrical relations of power and their consequences within schools, communities, and the larger society.

It is from this political imperative that philosophical critiques related to objectivity, absolute knowledge, reductionism, ethnocentrism, and elitism, as well as structural critiques of class inequalities, cultural invasion, racism, sexism, heterosexism, and so on have been waged. For some, this may echo the mantra of intersectionality, so often heard in oppositional discourses. However, as Rodolfo Torres and I have argued in *After Race: Racism After Multiculturalism* (2004), many intersectionality arguments still fail to confront the totalizing impact of capitalism. That is, racism, sexism, heterosexism, disablism, and all forms of oppression are implicated in an interlocking set of relations that preserve and sustain the interests of capital.

Beyond the obvious material dispossession, Freire spoke repeatedly about the manner in which conditions of economic exploitation and domination dehumanize us, distorting our capacity to love one another, the world, and ourselves. In concert with Antonio Gramsci (1971) before him, Freire was well aware of how even well-meaning educators, through lack of critical moral leadership, participate in disabling the hearts, minds, and bodies of students—an act that stunts the development of social agency and the political understanding necessary to challenge and transform the social and material conditions that betray our freedom.

THE STRUGGLE FOR OUR HUMANITY

Freire's notions of *armed love* and his dialectics of revolutionary practice have provided many activists and educators from disenfranchised communities a critical political foundation for liberatory struggles and a pedagogy committed to the collective and ongoing struggle for our emancipation. Freire (1971) insisted that while both humanization and dehumanization are alternatives, only the first could serve as our vocation—a vocation that he believed could be "thwarted by injustice, exploitation, oppression, and the violence perpetrated by oppressors, but affirmed by the yearning of the oppressed for freedom and justice" (p. 13).

Starting from the realization that we live in an "unfree" and unequal world, Freire (1971) affirmed that our struggle for our humanization had to "involve our struggle for the emancipation of labor and for the overcoming of our alienation" (p. 28), so that we might affirm ourselves as full subjects of our own lives and of history. However, the pursuit of our full humanity, he argued, could not "be carried out in isolation or as individuals, but only in the fellowship and solidarity" (p. 28) of community and social movement. Thus, relationships of solidarity, built through collective labor, remain central to our politics and our pedagogy, given that it is "in the process of revolution…that human beings in communion liberate each other" (Freire & Freire, 1994, p. 114).

For Freire, our capacity to live free required a fundamental shift in how leaders, educators, and students define our lives and the conditions of our labor. This requires decolonizing of the mind, through ridding ourselves of colonizing ideologies of domination, the establishment of solidarity with others, the existence of meaningful choices in our lives, the recognition of ourselves as subjects of history, the courage to speak out when necessary, and a well-developed sense of empowerment, in order that we might name, critique, decolonize, and reinvent our world collectively, in the interest of social justice, human rights, and economic democracy.

In waging struggles for social change, it has always been imperative that those who have been oppressed recognize that domination does not exist within a closed world from which there is no exit. Instead, Freire (1971) reminded us that "this struggle is possible only because dehumanization, although a concrete historical fact, is not a given destiny but the result of an unjust order that engenders violence,…which in turn dehumanizes the oppressed" (p. 16). Significant here is Paulo's acknowledgment of the psychological, physical, and spiritual violence that communities of color have endured for centuries at the hands of colonizers.

Moreover, his political and intellectual courage in linking this question of violence to intentionality was particularly important to our history of struggle. That is to say, although Freire never condoned violence in any of his speeches or his writings, he clearly recognized that there was a very different phenomenon at work in violence that is engendered by those who seek to dominate and exploit and violence that is generated by the fight of the oppressed to counter their dehumanization. "And this fight, because of the purpose given it by the oppressed, will actually constitute an act of love opposing the lovelessness which lies at the heart of the oppressors' violence, lovelessness even when clothed in false generosity" (p. 44).

And as such, Freire supported, until his death, our possibility and potential to remake history through our commitment to struggle. For it is precisely because "oppression exists as an impermanent, incomplete, and changing historical phenomenon—constructed by human beings" (p. 36) that we as empowered and decolonized subjects of history possess the possibility of transforming its configuration. Our task then as critical educators committed to a just world is to embrace fully this dialectical understanding of our relationship with the world, so that together we might transform our teaching and learning into a revolutionary praxis—a critical praxis that encompasses reflection, dialogue, and action, wherein theory and practice are regenerating and in an ongoing alliance.

Paulo knew that this way of life requires great discipline and a critical commitment to move beyond piety, sentimentalism, and individualistic gestures, so that we might "risk an act of love" (p. 35) and enter into sustaining and nurturing political relationships of dialogue and solidarity—communal relationships grounded in our unwavering fidelity to break out of the domesticating and colonizing conditions that trick us into complicity with "an economy that is incapable of developing programs according to human needs and that coexists indifferently to the hunger of millions to whom everything is denied" (Freire, 1997, p. 36).

In *Pedagogy of the Heart*, Freire (1997) urged us to construct within schools and communities what he called "advanced forms of social organizations...capable of surpassing this articulated chaos of corporate interests" (p. 36). This, of course, points to corporate policies of an economic Darwinism that promote deregulation, the free market, nationalism, and militarism through an ethnocentric ethos of "survival of the fittest," which shamelessly justifies its brutal impact upon millions of people and on the destruction of the earth's ecosystem.

Freire acknowledged that radical struggle by those who dare to exercise their political will and capacity within schools could be severely curtailed by a tendency to become "hardened," in response to the bureaucracy's backlash toward those who critique the system and seek change. He recognized that, more often than not, this phenomenon is prevalent because educators (and in particular, educators of color) committed to a liberatory pedagogy within schools and communities are perceived by institutional gatekeepers as disruptive or dangerous. Meanwhile, critical leadership practices to cultivate greater freedom and autonomy are discouraged or punished, even by those who would call themselves our allies. Educational policies of control not only work to inanimate teachers and students of color, but also serve to "deter the drive to search, that restlessness and creativity that characterizes life" (Freire, 1971, p. 60). In response, Freire insisted that the aim of true learning must expose the contradictions and courageously challenge those practices that objectify and dispirit us, preventing our political expression as full cultural citizens of the world.

Paulo recognized and often spoke of the enormity and difficulty of the pedagogical vision that he proposed. Nevertheless, he could see no other alternative to the restoration of our humanity than to eradicate the debilitating fatalism and imposing myths that seek to alienate and render us passive, while underhandedly seeking our consensus and participation in our own oppression, through notions of morality that reinforce our disempowerment. With this in mind, former Black Panther Assata Shakur (1987), who has lived exiled in Cuba since 1979, writes, "Nobody in the world, nobody in history, has ever gotten their freedom by appealing to the moral sense of the people who were oppressing them" (p. 139). Hence, Freire and others of his time argued that no one can empower the oppressed, but rather it is the oppressed who must empower themselves, if true liberation is to prevail.

Indeed, Freire's vision entails the need for an ongoing political process of personal and community struggle, which demands our ongoing critical vigilance. Fundamental here is our sustained, collective labor—a labor born of love, but deeply anchored in an unceasing political commitment to know, through both theory and practice, the nature of the beast that preys upon our humanity; and with this knowledge, fight with unwavering hope and solidarity. For many of us from poor and working-class communities of color, the option of struggle was never a choice, but rather a political necessity if we were to forge our self-determination and ensure our right to exist, in sync, with the cultural wisdom forged from our lived histories of survival as tribes, nations, and peoples.

EDUCATION AS A POLITICAL ACT

Within Paulo Freire's (1993) revolutionary vision, education never is, has been, or will be a neutral enterprise. About this he wrote, "It does not matter where or when it has taken place, whether it is more or less complex, education has always been a political act" (p. 127). Paulo was adamant on this question, as were the educators of color during the last five decades who have followed his precepts. Moreover, Freire agreed that an activist and educator's political orientation had to be explicit. He wrote, "In the name of the respect I should have for my students, I do not see why I should omit or hide my political stance by proclaiming a neutral position that does not exist. On the contrary, my role as teacher is to assent the student's right to compare, to choose, to rupture, to decide"(Freire, 1998, p. 68).

Oftentimes this has been a significant point of contention for radical educators of color, given that within the classroom, whether conscious of it or not, teachers perpetuate dominant values, beliefs, myths, and meanings through the authority they exert over students. The rub here is that these dominant views are so normalized and naturalized that those enacting them are often oblivious of the colonizing imposition of their worldview on working-class students and parents from racialized communities. Hence, what is painfully clear again is that education can colonize or decolonize; it all depends on the assumptions, intent, and purpose of the pedagogical leadership we enact through our practice.

Unfortunately, more often than not, schooling conditions students to ascribe to the dominant norms and cultural assumptions of the prevailing social order. In addition, it socializes students to accept their prescribed role or place within the larger social order—a role or place that historically has been predicated by the political economy and its colonizing institutional structures. Schools, then, are both enmeshed in the political economy of a society and at its service. This is an aspect that receives little attention, for example, in the preparation of teachers. Yet, Freire in dialogue with Donaldo Macedo (1998) rightly asserted, "The more you deny the political dimension of education, the more you assume the moral potential to blame the victims" (p. 123) and to perpetuate deficit myths about those who are seen as "other." By so doing, one colludes with educational policies and practices that result in wholesale inequalities and social exclusions.

For this reason, our pedagogy with students from culturally marginalized communities must be shaped by a critical decolonizing epistemology, one that discards commonsensical acceptance of the racializing social order and unveils structures of capitalist exploitation that disable disenfranchised communities. Such a critical pedagogical approach embodies through curricula, activities, texts, and classroom relations the conditions for student empowerment as an ethical and moral imperative. Instead of educating students of color to become assimilated objects, reliable workers, complacent and obedient citizens, and out-of-control consumers, radical educators committed to a decolonizing education work to cultivate in their students a critical understanding of their everyday lives, while integrating, with respect and dignity, the wisdom of their lived cultural knowledge.

To accomplish this requires that educators understand how, as a consequence of cultural, linguistic, and economic subjugation, racialized populations everywhere have been systematically exploited and dispossessed. And, in the process, the impact of these histories creates particular challenges and struggles that are intimately addressed by the survival strategies of our communities. Hence, to divorce children of color from their cultural knowledge and histories is to set them up either to fail miserably or to live an imitation of life.

The debilitating impact of mainstream education in many communities poses a challenge, wherein critical educators must work to unveil the hidden curriculum that informs the current use of standardized curricula, materials, textbooks, testing and assessment tools, promotion criteria, and institutional relationships, in an effort to critically infuse our teaching with a decolonizing vision of schools and community life (Darder, 2012a). By so doing, the task at hand, then, is not to reproduce the traditional social arrangements that support and perpetuate inequality and suffering, but rather to actively work to transform them, in the interest of self-determination and culturally democratic life.

Furthermore, unwillingness to suspend belief in the superiority of Western culture and its mantra of modernity—attached to classed, racialized, patriarchal, and heterosexist codes of conduct and assumptions—has been one of the most difficult issues that activists and educators of color have confronted in trying to create alliances across dominant/subordinate divides. But what is clear for those of us who have remained in this protracted struggle is this: if there is to be a genuinely decolonizing approach to education, it demands the democratic participation of educators, parents, students, and members from historically marginalized communities.

Unfortunately, the unmerciful arrogance often still enacted by white educators who consider themselves more competent to tell our stories or to educate our children has been an area of major conflict for many black, Latino, and Native American educators over the years. It is like folks in a New Zealand context believing that because they have read books about Maori communities; perhaps have a Maori friend or two; and perhaps lived or hung out for awhile within a Maori community here and there, they are now equipped to proclaim and legitimize the needs of Maori communities, even without the participation of members from these communities.

It is this sort of mental border-crosser that frequently becomes tremendously problematic to the larger decolonizing project in education. Does this mean that whites cannot be part of this struggle? Of course they can and they must be! But they must enter carefully, aware of their privilege and their internalized hegemonic assumptions about the abilities and capacities of those who are racialized, which may inadvertently betray their well-meaning intentions if they are not self-vigilant. The only remedy here is the willingness to remain in ongoing dialogue as full peers and comrades, offering their privilege, knowledge and resources in the service of the larger struggle for emancipation. This is what Paulo often referred to as "class suicide."

THE STRUGGLE IN TUCSON

Although there are pompous educational and political theorists who seek to discredit or render Paulo Freire's work irrelevant to the struggles of today, I argue that for working-class communities of color who continue to wage decolonizing struggles for educational justice, Freire's writings persist as an important intellectual force, inspiring literacy programs, popular education programs, youth programs, labor education initiatives, and independent schools in poor and working-class communities of color. Black New Yorkers for Educational Excellence, the Institute for Cultural and Linguistic Democracy, La Escuelita, El Centro de La Raza, Pedro Albizu Campo High School, and the Raza Studies High School program, in Tucson, Arizona, were all established on Freire's pedagogical principles. I want to very briefly speak to the Tucson program, a highly effective ethnic studies program shut down earlier this year. The program was eliminated after a prolonged, brutal campaign to demonize students, teachers, and their community.

One of the rights gains in the hard-fought struggle of the '60s and '70s was the inclusion of ethnic studies into the educational curriculum—a right that is steadily being eroded in the current climate of neoliberal multiculturalism. At its best, ethnic studies courses offered a place for African American, Puerto Rican, Chicano, Native American, and Asian American students to learn their histories and to forge political consciousness with respect to the larger struggle for democratic life. In the sanctuary of these classrooms, the different cultural histories and the dynamics of their location within the U.S. landscape found a place to be openly engaged, as simply a commonplace process of knowledge production. In this way, the knowledge and wisdom inherent in students' cultural histories and the epistemological power of different ways of knowing could find room for critical engagement. Similarly, a pedagogical process of decolonization, with social justice as a central concern, sat at the heart of the curriculum, as it did in the Raza Studies high school program.

For more than a decade, the high school program achieved unprecedented success with working-class students, most of whom were Chicano, Mexicano, or Native American—student populations that have been subjected to almost two centuries of marginalization and dispossession in the Southwest. Beyond the typical college enrollment marker of success, these high school students demonstrated through their practices in the community that they had undergone an effective process of cultural and political formation—one that assisted them to begin disrupting the cultural invasion of generations.

The program resulted in a large number of these students electing over the years to participate collectively in school and public forums to speak on issues and concerns related to their educational and community needs. The students formed political study circles and strategized ways in which they might work together toward greater self-determination in their communities. In the program, students read textbooks that spoke of their own histories and the conditions that shaped their lives. They learned about technology in ways that nurtured their critical understanding of media literacy, and they became media producers of videos and CDs that spoke of their everyday lives and their educational struggles.

Students who had never before felt so engaged in their education were now actively present and involved in a pedagogical process that was meaningful and that culturally resonated with their histories and community life. In the process of their intellectual formation, one of the books that was required reading was *Pedagogy of the Oppressed*. In 2012, the book, along with six others, was banned by public school officials. Teachers were told to stay away from any book that made "race, ethnicity and oppression…central themes."[4]

Today the Raza Studies program remains at the center of a major political struggle, as Arizona passed measures to ban the program, thwart undocumented immigrant mobility in the state, and reinforce English-only practices in the classroom. State educational officials harassed teachers in the Raza Studies program, accusing them of separatism, reversed racism, inclusion of subversive texts in the curriculum, dissemination of anti-American views, and brainwashing of students.[5] Despite the inflammatory and reactionary tone of the accusations made against them in newspapers and during court proceedings, Tucson educators and activists continue to fight back, in an effort to provide a humanizing educational experience for their students—an educational experience that places texts about students' histories, cultural values, and traditions at the center of the pedagogical process, so these can be juxtaposed with the reading of required textbooks.

In place of the competitive and individualistic culture of mainstream education, the decolonizing pedagogy of the Raza Studies program focused on the communal learning of students. *En lak'ech: Tu eres mi otro yo* (You are my other I), for example, serves as one of their decolonizing principles for classroom life. The powerful principle of *En lak'ech*, derived from an indigenous reading of the world, pedagogically resonates with students' deep communal and interdependent relationships to one another, to the land, and to all living beings. And it is precisely the power of the collective political grace that such a decolonizing educational process has awakened in students that has caused the fear-based responses of modern-day white settlers of Arizona, many of whom came from big cities to stake their retirement claims on land that was systematically usurped from indigenous people.

For the Tucson activists and educators of color, Paulo Freire's pedagogical promise for the transformation of education remains a revolutionary inspiration today—just as it was for those who embraced his ideas in the '60s and '70s. Yes, there are many texts today that offer a new generation of educators an assortment of readings and varied interpretations regarding the experiences of racialized communities in the United States and abroad. Yet it was Paulo Freire's powerful and resounding message of revolutionary love and radical hope that ignited the minds and hearts of educators, students, and community members involved in the educational struggle in Tucson.

PAULO: AN EMISSARY OF HOPE

Despite the overwhelming nature of the political project that informed his dreams, Paulo Freire (1997) remains an emissary of hope for the oppressed. His ethical commitment to a radical hope is anchored in his lifelong revolutionary commitment to counter all forms of poverty and injustice, to contest the arbitrary power of the society's ruling class, to unveil the dehumanizing forces of violence within schools and society, and to confront the destructive consequences of capitalist dominion over the earth.

In *Politics of Education,* Freire (1985) spoke of revolutionary vision. "A revolutionary vision," he wrote, "tends to be dynamic rather than static; tends toward life rather than death; toward the future as a challenge to [our] creativity rather than as a repetition of the present; toward love as liberation of subjects rather than as possessiveness; toward the emotion of life rather than cold abstractions; toward men [and women] who organize themselves reflectively for actions rather than order; to creative and communicative language rather than prescriptive signals; to reflective challenges rather than domesticating slogans; and to values that are lived rather than myths that are imposed" (p. 82).

Whether the educators and students of Tucson are able to save the program or not is not the salient point here (although the hope is that the program will continue). Rather, what is extraordinary is that through their practice and experiences within a decolonizing pedagogical process, the students and their teachers accepted "the challenge to creativity," refusing to repeat the past. In similar ways, decolonizing struggles against racializing worldviews persists around the world today. Yet decolonizing struggles require of us a sincere thirst for freedom, tireless commitment, and a bountiful solidarity for others. Labor that is born of love and justice is what can make a new world possible; for only collectively, and in solidarity, can we reinvent the old histories of oppression and forge emancipatory futures.

Whether in Palestine, the streets of London or Greece, the Dine reservations of New Mexico, the Zapatistas in Chiapas, the indigenous struggle in Colombia, within Aboriginal or Maori communities of Australia and New Zealand, or the struggle for Raza Studies in Tucson, there are oppressed communities everywhere that persist in the fight for justice, and who still today embrace the man from Recife as a bright guiding light of liberation.

NOTES

1. This chapter is the text of a keynote address given at the International Conference on Paulo Freire at Waikato University, Hamilton, New Zealand, on November 28, 2012.
2. See: http://datacenter.spps.org/uploads/SOTW_A_Nation_at_Risk_1983.pdf
3. See: http://www.teachsafeschools.org/literacy-programs.html
4. De la Torre, M. (2012). "Arizona schools forced to ban ethnic-studies books" in Ethicsdaily. com. See: http://www.ethicsdaily.com/arizona-schools-forced-to-ban-ethnic-studies-books-cms-19217
5. Richardson, V. (2009). "School head fights 'ethnic Chauvinism' in Arizona" in *The Washington Times*. See: http://www.washingtontimes.com/news/2009/jul/28/school-head-fights-ethnic-chauvinism-in-arizona/?page=all

REFERENCES

Cesaire, A. (2001). *Discourse on colonialism*. New York, NY: Monthly Review Press.

Darder, A. (2012a). *Culture and power in the classroom*. Boulder, CO: Paradigm.

Darder, A. (2012b). Neoliberalism in the academic borderlands: A dialogue with Antonia Darder. In P. W. Orelus & C. S. Malott (Eds.), *Radical voices for democratic schooling: Exposing neoliberal Inequalities*. New York, NY: Palgrave Macmillan.

Darder, A., & Torres, R. D. (2004). *After race: Racism after multiculturalism*. Albany, NY: SUNY Press.

Freire, P. (1971). *Pedagogy of the oppressed*. New York, NY: Seabury Press.

Freire, P. (1985). *Politics of education*. Westport, CT: Bergin & Garvey.

Freire. P. (1997). *Pedagogy of the heart*. New York, NY: Continuum.

Freire, P. (1998). *Pedagogy of freedom* (p. 68). New York, NY: Continuum.

Freire, P., & Freire, A. M. A. (1994). *Pedagogy of hope: Reliving "Pedagogy of the oppressed."* New York, NY: Continuum.

Freire, P., & Macedo, D. (1998). *Literacy: Reading the word and the world*. Westport, CT: Bergin & Garvey.

Gramsci, A. (1971) *Selections from "The prison notebooks."* New York, NY: International.

hooks, b. (1994). *Teaching to transgress*. New York, NY: Routledge.

Leacock, E. (1971). *The culture of poverty: A critique*. New York, NY: Simon & Schuster.

Shakur, A. (1987). *Assata: An autobiography*. Brooklyn, NY: Lawrence Hill.

Shor, I., & Freire, P. (1986). *Pedagogy of liberation*. New York, NY: Praeger.

CHAPTER THREE

Equity as Critical Praxis: The Self-Development of Te Whare Wānanga o Awanuiārangi

GRAHAM HINGANGAROA SMITH

INTRODUCTION

Our struggle for equity in New Zealand (NZ) is both similar to and different from the struggle for equality by other indigenous peoples. Māori as a cultural minority have consistently argued for the recognition and validity of their own cultural frame of reference as well as increased economic and resource parity in their own right alongside the dominant Pakeha (non-Māori population) in NZ. Such arguments for cultural, social, and economic inclusion might simply be interpreted as potentially assimilating of different cultural groups into a homogenous form of capitalism and exploitation that in the end is a continuance of colonization. As Freire forewarned in his text *Pedagogy of the Oppressed* (1972) the danger here is that the oppressed may become the oppressors or in our sense the 'colonized become the colonizers' as they take on and replicate dominant hegemony.

In this sense education and schooling become important sites of struggle. An important task therefore is to redevelop schooling and education away from the inevitability of the reproduction of dominant cultural, social, and economic norms. This is the project that has been taken up by Te Whare Wānanga o Awanuiārangi, an indigenous higher education institution. While this project is enormous and ultimately reaches beyond education and into the realm of politics, the formation of a critical consciousness and a transforming politics that positively reposition education and schooling of Māori is important. This project is not developed against the notion of the national interest; rather, it engages the prevailing silence on important questions such as "Whose interests are represented in the notion of the national interest?" or indeed "Whose interests are served within the current definitions of what counts as the national interest?" On the contrary it is important to rescue the 'transforming possibilities' that reside within a notion of the "public good" responsibility of the state. Education and schooling need to encourage thinking that goes beyond narrow, captured manipulations of democratic practice that, in turn, enable the uncritical reproduction of social, cultural, and economic dominance.

For Māori the current accent on neoliberal, market-led education and schooling practice is detrimental to notions of collective responsibility embedded in words such as *society, social, public* and *community*. This is reinforced formally (government policy) and informally (public hegemony). In this latter example, dominant Pakeha consent to neoliberal hegemonies of the possessive individual, individual rights and freedoms, consumer sovereignty, consumption, and accumulation politics needs to be critically interrogated as these notions collide with Māori/indigenous cultural views and thereby have become a new formation of colonization formed at the intersection of cultural oppression and economic exploitation (see Apple, 1979, 1993, 2003).

This chapter describes the rise of a Whare Wānanga, a Māori institution of higher learning, and its struggle to grow within the neoliberal education context of NZ and to develop an educational site of resistance that simultaneously builds Māori citizens who have excellent skills in both Māori and Pakeha languages, knowledge, and culture and who also have the critical tools to resist and transform those aspects of the neoliberal economic thrust that continue to colonize and exploit our communities and their interests. In this sense this institution exemplifies the important concern not simply to describe our pathology but to do something about it as well.

PREAMBLE

Since the 1980s there have been three Wānanga (Māori cultural-based, tertiary institutions) that have developed within the provision of higher education in New Zealand. New Zealand has a total population of about 4 million people and a population of about 450,000 Māori who are resident in New Zealand and about 100,000 more residing in other countries, the majority in Australia. New Zealand was/is formally colonized by Britain, which signed a treaty (the Treaty of Waitangi, 1840) with Māori. This treaty ostensibly guaranteed rights and privileges to Māori including the protection of the British Crown in exchange for governance rights by the Crown over the lands and resources of New Zealand. Britain maintains a physical presence in the governance of New Zealand through the Office of the Governor General who is often referred to as the "Queen's Representative." Subsequent to the 1840 signing of the treaty, Māori experience of British colonization has been similar to that of other indigenous peoples within the outreach of the British Empire (now called the Commonwealth). While there have been benefits from this contact, the overall impact is that today Māori suffer widespread and highly disproportionate levels of social, cultural, and economic underdevelopment as compared with the dominant Pakeha (non-Māori) population. Education and schooling have been significant sites for colonization, through both the production and reproduction of educational underdevelopment that has been both intentionally and unintentionally perpetrated through multiple means and sites. There is an increasing body of research and literature from international and national sources that attempts to identify and analyse the causes of the underlying issues that impact Māori. Over the years various government interventions developed from within the educational system have been applied with limited success. In 1982 a significant self-development movement evolved out of Māori communities that initiated what I describe elsewhere as the "Māori Education Revolution" (Smith, G. H., 1997). At the seat of this revolution were some core ideas that have been generalized as Kaupapa Māori (Māori Philosophy and Principles). This revolution is marked by the following principles:

- *Conscientization*: Coming to understand the stark realities of the neoliberal economic changes in New Zealand and its overt and inequitable impact on Māori and therefore the subsequent conscientizing of Māori to the fact that our struggle was not just about our culture, but also over structural elements such as economics, power, and ideology, that is, a need to simultaneously struggle for structuralist and culturalist change.
- *Resistance*: Enactment of self-development.
- *Transforming*: Not just transformation as an outcome, but a continuous cycle of reflective and reflexive transforming.

In the 1980s an educational self-development revolution by Māori was begun. This was the genesis of the Māori language revitalization movement beginning with Te Kohanga Reo (Pre-School Language Nests) to Kura Kaupapa Māori (Immersion Elementary Schools) to Kura Tuarua (Immersion Secondary Schools) to Wānanga (Māori Higher Education Institutions). All of these initiatives were started as alternative, self-developing responses by Māori communities outside of (and often in reaction to) the system. Each of the three Wānanga has developed differently and has shaped their institutions to respond to different Māori educational needs. Te Whare Wānanga o Awanuiārangi has developed itself within a context of the indigenous-university and aims to provide opportunities for Māori and Iwi development from doctoral to certificate level. I should note that our position is that we do not position ourselves as a university as described within the New Zealand Education Act. We are clear that we are a Whare Wānanga and have specific responsibilities to perform under the Education Act, but that we offer similar programmes as those offered at existing universities at graduate-level teaching as well as in research.

HISTORICAL BACKGROUND

Te Whare Wānanga o Awanuiārangi is a relatively young institution within the overall context of tertiary education provision in New Zealand. It was begun by the Māori tribal nation of Ngāti Awa in 1989 as a self-development initiative. This development was not easy; in fact, it would be more accurate to say that its existence was very much the result of struggle against the dominant mono-cultural system on the part of key individuals who had the vision and the foresight to enact their dream. The key individual was Professor Hirini Moko Mead, who was also the Chairman of the tribal council of the Ngāti Awa tribe at that time. He announced his proposal that Ngāti Awa establish a Whare Wānanga some years ago at a specially convened Hui at Te Hokowhitu Marae of the Ngāti Pukeko Hapū of Ngāti Awa. I was also at this Hui and was asked to contribute, given my educational background, as a teacher and as the then Pro Vice Chancellor (Māori) at the University of Auckland. While the idea of the Whare Wānanga was positively received at the time, there was some scepticism expressed by those who worried about the resources that would be required to establish such an entity. It took a further two years for the ideas to become manifest. In the early stages of establishment, Professor Mead co-opted two local identities to assist: Mr. Hohepa (Joe) Mason and Mr. Peter McLay, both of whom had educational backgrounds. A further issue raised at this Hui was an appropriate name. It took some time before the name "Te Whare Wānanga o Awanuiārangi" emerged and Mr. Monte Ohia (an official with the New Zealand Qualifications Authority [NZQA] at that time) is credited with giving encouragement for this ancestoral name that embraced Mātaatua people as well as other tribes throughout New Zealand.

When I am asked today about how to establish a Whare Wānanga or an alternative institution, I usually respond by saying that you need a strong vision that is encapsulated in an inspiring name. If the vision is appropriately powerful it will provide the necessary impetus and direction to your struggle to establish your institution. All of the other important elements such as a strategic plan, funding, programmes and courses, staffing, and so on will flow from the vision and be enacted through the strategic plan.

An important part of the establishment of Te Whare Wānanga o Awanuiārangi has been the necessity to engage in a struggle to build it. *Struggle* might be seen as a positive element in this regard. In building the institution from the ground up, the supporters have not only had to get their hands dirty, they have also had to sort out in their heads what they are struggling for and what they are struggling against. This element is important as it strengthens the commitment to the kaupapa or the integrating philosophy, particularly when times become difficult.

Te Whare Wānanga o Awanuiārangi is an outcome of the embedded transforming philosophy within the Te Kohanga Reo (Language Nest—immersion pre-school) revolution. As such, this revolution should not be understood so much in terms of the physical manifestations of the institutional entities of Te Kohanga Reo, Kura Kaupapa Māori, or for that matter Wānanga. Indeed I would argue that the real Māori education revolution of the 1980s was much more profound; it "was a revolution in thinking; it was a shift by Māori from being 'reactive' to being 'proactive'—to taking more responsibility to make change for themselves and not wait for other people's permission." (G. H. Smith, 1999).

I will not go into detail concerning the historical struggle to establish Te Whare Wānanga o Awanuiārangi at this point, but there are some important elements that need to be understood. First, Te Whare Wānanga o Awanuiārangi (because it has also been established partially as a result of a Treaty Claim in 1999) is simultaneously a Crown and an Iwi tertiary partnership, which along with the other two Wānanga form part of a unique group, distinctive from other New Zealand tertiary institutions. Second, Te Whare Wānanga o Awanuiārangi has a foundational relationship with its founding Iwi of Ngāti Awa. Third, the Whare Wānanga itself and Ngāti Awa own its physical plant, buildings, and land, and this again is quite different from other New Zealand tertiary institutions and universities in which the government owns almost all their buildings and other capital assets. Thus, the government's fiscal investment in the Wānanga is limited to mostly operational support through EFT's funding. At one level this might be viewed as a structural inequity; on another, it could also be interpreted as being more independent of the system. Of course, all of the concerns related to the neoliberal strategies of devolution and privatization of responsibility of public education need to be countered. While these institutions use the Treaty of Waitangi to mediate these issues, there are still a large number of inequities that disproportionately accrue to the Wānanga Sector and Te Whare Wānanga o Awanuiārangi in particular as a result of not receiving (as the neoliberal level playing field of equity promises) the same treatment as other like institutions.

CONTEMPORARY SITUATION

Te Whare Wānanga o Awanuiārangi adjusted its branding in 2011 and added the international descriptor *indigenous-university* to its title. This adjustment has been carefully positioned. Te Whare Wānanga o Awanuiārangi does *not* wish to be a university as prescribed within the University Act *nor* does it aspire to be constrained by the existing functions of a university. However, Te Whare Wānanga o Awanuiārangi aspires to be *like* a university in terms of its graduate and research aims, and its Māori and indigenous emphasis also needs to be seen as a distinctive characteristic. There are a number of other distinguishing features that are best captured in the adjectival description of the compound word *indigenous-university*, particularly our international alignment with other like institutions, for example, the Sami University College of Norway, the First Nations University of Canada, the Indigenous University of Bolivia, and Haskell Indian University of the United States.

Te Whare Wānanga o Awanuiārangi is an institution that is simultaneously responsive to both generic Māori and specific Iwi aspirations both within and through the educational programmes of the institution. Notwithstanding this, the Wānanga is also shaped by the Education Act 1989, which provides the official description and parameters of the academic responsibilities. Wānanga are given statutory recognition under section 162 of the Education Act 1989. Wānanga are regarded as the peers of universities, polytechnics, and colleges of education. Section 162(4)(b)(IV) states

> A Wānanga is characterised by teaching and research that maintains, advances, and disseminates knowledge and develops intellectual independence, and assists the application of knowledge regarding āhuatanga Māori (Māori life) according to tikanga Māori (Māori custom).

Overall, there are two main underpinnings to the academic emphasis of the institution: Māori knowledge and cultural excellence and world knowledge excellence.

TE WHARE WĀNANGA O AWANUIĀRANGI

Te Whare Wānanga o Awanuiārangi in 2014 has approximately 3,200 EFTS (this translates to about 7,700 students including part-time students). It employs around 180 staff members, 90% of whom are of Māori descent. The institution has three major sites of delivery in Whakatāne, Auckland, and Northland; we also work with about 300 tribal marae (Māori Meeting House sites) over a three-year cycle.

We have three schools; the School of Iwi Development, the School of Undergraduate Studies and the School of Indigenous Graduate Studies. We also host five institutes; the National Institute of Māori and Indigenous Education; the Institute for Post-Treaty Settlement Futures; the Institute for Māori and Indigenous Science; the Institute for Technology, Design and Creativity; and the National Institute for Māori and Indigenous Performing Arts.

We have attracted a critical mass of Māori PhD-qualified staff and faculty including eleven Māori professors (this is a significant number compared with the university sector more generally). Our programmes extend from Adult Community Education (ACE) certificates and diplomas to degrees, graduate diplomas, and master's and doctoral degrees. All of our programmes are intentionally shaped to positively impact Māori social, economic, and cultural growth. More than 90% of students are Māori (approximately 51% of whom are engaged in degree programmes). Of our graduate student numbers, 190 are master's students and 90 are doctoral students. All of our degree students are expected to undertake "critical studies" as core components.

WHAT IS UNIQUE ABOUT US?

The word *Whare* distinguishes Te Whare Wānanga o Awanuiārangi from the other two Wānanga. We have always described ourselves as a *Whare Wānanga*[1] as opposed to just using the single term *Wānanga*.[2] Moreover, the term *Whare Wānanga* positions Awanuiārangi as a tertiary entity for higher learning including undergraduate and graduate studies. Thus, we teach a broad mandate of programmes from level one to doctoral level. Furthermore, we are able to deliver across the whole of New Zealand where and as appropriate to engage in transforming education.

The term *transforming education* is deliberately ambiguous and both meanings are intended. We need to focus on outcomes that are transforming given that for the most part the status quo way of educating is problematic in that Māori educational underdevelopment tends to be reproduced. In using the term *transforming education* we are calling attention to the need to enact change both in the process and the outcomes of Māori/indigenous education.

A further aspect of our institutional stance to transforming is a concern to move beyond a developmental emphasis of growing change from the bottom up. The problem here is the linear, instrumental, project-oriented approach derived from human development theory that sees change occurring through an incremental maturation process, beginning in childhood. We have attempted to problematize this approach. Our notion of transforming is premised on the assumption that the Māori struggle within and through education is not one struggle, but includes many struggles. We therefore accept the need to engage in a 360-degree approach to move beyond singular projects of change to engaging in multiple strategies, within multiple sites—sometimes these may need to be engaged with simultaneously. The point here is that colonization is not found in one place or is one shape; it is being perpetrated in many sites often in many guises; as a consequence there is a need to be critically literate and be able to respond appropriately to these new formations of colonizing.

Te Whare Wānanga o Awanuiārangi is also intentionally positioned to respond to its immediate social-geographic context of the Bay of Plenty and we therefore build our planning strategies and programmes accordingly. For example, the Māori population in the Bay of Plenty is growing faster than most other regions in New Zealand and it already contains more Māori than most provinces (see the BERL 2014 report). Furthermore, this region is significantly underdeveloped in respect of Māori access, participation, retention, and success in higher education.

We also have a focus on the emerging Māori economy and its associated workforce needs. The emerging Māori economy is estimated to be around $37 billion and growing. It is also significantly rural, located in tribal territories, and is therefore largely asset based (and not liquid). The challenge for the Wānanga is to assist building work opportunities and employment that derives from Māori organisations and tribal interests. This also connects with the post-Treaty settlement context and the need to help facilitate the post-Treaty environment given that a Treaty settlement is a beginning not an, ending. We should also be helping to fill the vacuum created by the settlement process as Māori and Pakeha contemplate new futures and new social and political arrangements in the new New Zealand going forward.

Te Whare Wānanga o Awanuiārangi is located in the rural resort town of Whakatāne. It attracts large numbers of tourists to attractive surf beaches and sunshine and brings in tourists chasing eco-tourism experiences. Whakatāne is also known as the sunshine capital of New Zealand. A key stance adopted by the Wānanga has been to position it within a context of rurality rather than rural. Rurality is a concept that puts rural experience and life at the centre of consideration rather than on the periphery. The notion of rurality acknowledges the reality of rural lifestyle as being at the forefront of consideration rather than being seen/ constructed as the reflection of urban experience. This shift in perspective is important as Te Whare Wānanga o Awanuiārangi attempts to respond to the special needs of the Eastern Bay of Plenty and to the large population of Māori who still live in tribal and marae contexts. This understanding also helps shape our institutional programmes to link more effectively to our local needs and expectations.

CRITICALLY UNPACKING NEW FORMATIONS OF COLONIZATION

The Māori education revolution is predicated on the development of a critical analysis that examines culturalist and structuralist issues. We need to understand the politics of struggle and the critical importance of deconstructing neoliberal hegemony that legitimates and reproduces the existing dominant cultural, social, political, and economic order. Particular hegemonies accrue around the following issues:

1. **Equity** (Narrowing an assertion of the level playing field ideology has the effect of simply maintaining the status quo and reproducing existing inequalities)
2. **Democracy** (Dominant interests are reproduced when minority populations have to depend on a system of one person, one vote and majority rule)
3. **Individualism** (Individual rights and freedoms uphold capitalist values of the possessive individual and often conflict with Māori values of collectivity, social responsibility, reciprocity, and extended family responsibilities [whanaungatanga])
4. **Devolution** (Illusion of Power Sharing: the devolution of responsibility, but the power and control over funding and resources remain at the centre of government)
5. **Choice** (Choices are offered within defined parameters; choice is supposedly a natural derivative of individual freedoms; it becomes a way to explain failures of the system—the responsibility for failure resides with individuals who made poor choices, e.g., unemployment, educational failure. In this sense the state (government) exports failure back to citizens.)
6. **Science Reification** (The accent on Western science, the rise of positivism and the techno-rationality are accompanied by a rise in the attack on the arts and on non-mainstream language, knowledge, and culture. This trend is also marked by STEM curriculum, more targeted funding to sciences and associated research, e.g., in science scholarships)
7. **Accountability** (The rise of neoliberal economics and the free market is accompanied by a commensurate rise in the notion of the surveillance society, coercive power, and moral authoritarianism, e.g., more police, more rules and regulations, rise of traditional family values and conservative religious views, "dob in your neighbor" campaigns underpinned by whistle-blower legislation)
8. **Privatization** (The abdication by the state of its "public good" responsibilities needs to be resisted by Māori; the creation of private wealth off the back of publicly owned assets reproduces structured inequalities by potentially widening the gap between those already socially and economically advantaged and those who are not)

This is the new terrain on which the colonization of Māori needs to be fought against. This is why critically informed studies are important for Māori—first to recognize these new formations of colonization and second to do something about them. A further concern is to critically understand that colonization has not magically disappeared; rather, it is coming at us in new shapes and in multiples sites, sometimes simultaneously. While the traditional sites of colonization have been schooling, the church, and government policies, the new forms of colonization are significantly economic. As such the neoliberal economic emphasis might be considered a series of new formations of colonization shaped at the intersection of cultural oppression and economic exploitation. This phenomenon has seen a sharp rise in the interest in intellectual and cultural property rights by indigenous peoples as the commodification of culture takes effect. This point about multiple sites of colonization and resistance connects with Antonio Gramsci's (1971) strategic notions of war of position and war of manoever.

ENACTING CRITICAL STRUGGLE

Staff and students interested in developing transforming education must develop understandings and practices that are founded on critical insights that enable Māori to respond appropriately to the societal context of unequal power relations. These power inequalities exist in multiple sites and are enabled in a complexity of ways. Things become more complicated when different shapes of inequality overlap and compound their impact. For example, the power differential that undermines Māori life chances are often multiplied in a convergence of 'dominant: Pakeha: economic' interests. This intersection of interests occurs because Māori exist within a societal context of unequal power, social, economic, and cultural relations. Subsequently there is a need to make more appropriate space for the existence of the validity and legitimacy of Māori ways of knowing, being, thinking, and acting. Most Māori still want to be Māori. For example, there is a need to protect Māori language, knowledge, and culture from the mono-cultural system that tends to reinforce and reproduce the dominant non-Māori cultural perspective, and perhaps even attack and undermine minority cultural forms. An important and distinctive feature of the programmes taught at Te Whare Wānanga o Awanuiārangi is that all students are exposed to critical studies and understandings. In this sense all students need to understand how these colonizing forces work and how they might be countered. This project involves a dual perspective, a critical view of one's own colonization as well as a critical view of how colonization is perpetrated over Māori by external interests.

EQUITY AND CRITICAL PRAXIS

One of the key struggles for Māori has been a long-standing contestation with the neoliberal state over the meaning and practice of equity. This struggle has been prominent since 1982 when New Zealand, under the David Lange–led government, formally moved away from a welfare-driven economy to the notion of the "free market" economy. This shift was announced on television during an interview with the prime minister of the time, David Lange. When pressed on the issue of equity, Lange proffered this definition—Equity is unequal input for equal outcome. The parameters of what was at stake were evident in a very awkward exchange that subsequently ensued between Lange and his minister of finance, the Hon. Roger Douglas, the architect of the neoliberal approach that was to be adopted (later referred to as Rogernomics). The very next night on television, Douglas publicly corrected Lange's statement by announcing that the prime minister had "got it wrong" and that equity was to be reframed going forward, stating that "equity means treating every New Zealander exactly the same."

The policy implications of these definition shifts are profound. In more colloquial speech we see a shift from compensatory forms of equity application and practice to the notion of the level playing field, an exporting of state/public responsibility to individual responsibility by means of a "user pays" hegemony. More recently we have seen other policy strategies as well, such as distributive equity—targeted applications of selected equity provision within groups of need. These different approaches need to be critically understood within the societal condition of unequal power relations. For example, the "level playing field" ideology may in the end simply reproduce and maintain existing inequalities and unequal relations of power.

Individualism (individual freedoms, rights, the possessive individual) undermines the capacity to enact social, public, and collective responsibilities. Even in the academy the privileging of individual academic achievement through the Performance-Based Research Fund (PBRF) and other competitive systems enables and rewards individual meritocracy to the detriment of building a more powerful and collaborative community of scholars. There are some important shifts that we should take up in order to become more effective in transforming our condition. We need to move from an emphasis on self-determination to being self-determining; from an emphasis on conscientization to enactment; from an emphasis on transformation (as goal) to transforming (as a process). Other concepts that should be engaged include the emphasis on the capitalistic notions of the possessive individual, techno-rationality and scientific reification.

We should understand the politics of distraction and to clearly know what we are struggling for and against. In this sense there is a need to move beyond simply describing what's gone wrong to enacting solutions and change. Put another way, this is a move beyond what counts to more precisely identifying what we want, how we get it, how we know when we have it, and whether or not it is effective and makes the appropriate difference.

We need to shift our transforming model from a linear conception to a circular praxis framework.

TRANSFORMATIVE PRAXIS

Underpinning the Māori intervention elements described above are important understandings about transformative praxis and, by extension, critical pedagogy. The intervention strategies applied by Māori in New Zealand are complex and respond simultaneously to multiple formations of oppression and exploitation. That is, multiple formed oppressions need to be responded to by multiple formed resistance strategies. This flexible response is necessary because the shape of the struggle with which Māori are engaged is neither singular, nor linear, nor instrumental.

The Kaupapa Māori educational interventions represent the evolution of a more sophisticated response by Māori to freeing themselves from multiple oppression(s) and exploitation. In particular, the very emergence of Kaupapa Māori as an intervention strategy critiques and reconstitutes the Western dominant notions of conscientization, resistance, and transformative praxis in different configurations. In particular, Māori reconfiguration rejects the notion that each of these concepts stands individually, or that they are necessarily to be interpreted as being an instrumental progression from conscientization, to resistance, to praxis. That is, one state is not necessarily a prerequisite or contingent on the other states. Thus the following popular representation of transformative action (based on a predominantly Western type of thinking) needs to be critically engaged.

Figure 3.1. Linear Change Configuration.

The position implicit within the new formations of Māori intervention (and that may have wider significance for other indigenous populations) is that *all* of the above components are important; *all* need to be held simultaneously; all stand in equal relation to each other. This representation might best be understood as a cycle. For example:

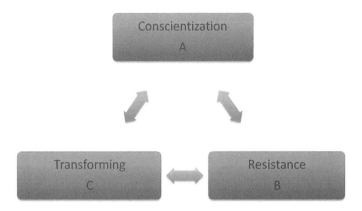

Figure 3.2. Circular Praxis Configuration.

A further point here is that individuals and groups enter the cycle from any position and do not necessarily (in reflecting on Māori experience within Kaupapa Māori interventions) have to start at the point of conscientization. In other words, individuals have been caught up in a transformative praxis unconsciously, and subsequently conscientization and transforming action have developed later. For example, some parents took their children to Kohanga Reo (because it was the only early childhood option in the town), and this later led to the parents becoming conscientized about the politics of language revitalisation and highly active participants in a resistance movement (G. H. Smith, 1999). This is a significant critique of much of the writing on these concepts that tend to portray a *linear,* instrumental progression through the stages of conscientization, resistance, and transformative action. Māori experience tends to suggest that these elements may occur in any order and indeed may all occur simultaneously. It is important to note as well that the arrows in Figure 2 go in both directions, which reinforces the idea of simultaneous engagement with more than one element. It is also an inclusive representation of struggle and moves beyond the hierarchical representation implied in the linear model. In the figure 2 all Māori can be plotted somewhere on the circle (some are standing still, some are going backwards, others are well advanced)—the point is that every Māori is in the struggle whether they like it or not, whether they know it or not.

One of the most exciting developments with respect to the organic resistance initiatives of Māori in the 1980s and 1990s has been the discernible shift and maturing in the way resistance activities are being understood and practiced.

Now a greater emphasis is placed on attempting to take into account structuralist concerns (economic, ideological, and power structures) as well as culturalist responses (related to agency). Some of the important factors that the Māori resistance initiatives attempt to engage with relate to economic, ideological, and power dimensions, which are derived from the nexus of state dominant Pakeha cultural interests (Smith, G. H., 1999).

Where indigenous people are in educational crises, indigenous educators and teachers must be trained to be "change agents" to develop transformation of the undesirable circumstances. They must develop a radical pedagogy (a teaching approach that will develop positive change). Such pedagogy must also be informed by their own cultural preferences and respond to their own critical circumstances. I believe there is much to inform other indigenous contexts from the lessons we have learned from the struggle established in Te Whare Wānanga o Awanuiārangi. In particular, the need to put a critical focus on the processes of transforming, and on positive transformative outcomes. What are they? How can they be achieved? Do indigenous people's needs and aspirations require different schooling approaches? Who benefits? Such critical questions, which relate to the task of teachers being change agents, must not only inform our teacher education approaches, they must also inform the work of all indigenous educators. Furthermore they must also ensure the buy-in from the communities they are purporting to serve.

TRANSFORMING EDUCATION

I now share some of the key intervention elements that have underpinned this period of positive and proactive change since the 1980s and that have helped shape the Te Whare Wānanga o Awanuiārangi strategic direction. These change elements are worth identifying and sharing as they may provide insight or stimulate similar ideas for catalyzing transformation in other education sites. Again, it is important to critically reflect on these strategies—some may fit and be immediately relevant and applicable, yet others might need to be recast to fit your specific context, others again may be totally irrelevant. The few points that are shared here are merely a selection of a much larger number of key elements that have made the indigenous education and schooling revolution a relative success in our situation and we would recognize that we still have limitations in some areas.

In order to lead change and to support education transformation of indigenous learners the following strategies are important:

A. THERE IS A NEED TO MAKE AND LEAD
CHANGE OURSELVES

A key learning that we have made within our Māori context is that no one else can make the changes for us—we have to make them ourselves. The commitment has to be ours—we have to lead it. Others can help, but ultimately it is indigenous people who have to act. We need to move beyond waiting for a "cargo plane to land" or for someone else to do it. We need to develop a transformative struggle that is inclusive and respectful of everyone. Doing it we should ensure greater buy-in from the people for whom the changes are intended. We need to draw on our cultural ways of collective work: of extended family obligation and our values of sharing and reciprocity. In New Zealand we have had to deliberately reteach much of this, as it had been lost to some of our culturally dislocated relatives and the generations who were raised in the urban settings.

Acting and doing sometimes require courage, or they require someone just to start something. This is how Te Wānanga Awanuiārangi began. Literally we started with our imaginations. As noted earlier, once we had decided what we wanted to do the next step was to get a board, four nails, and a pot of paint. An empty prefab was found, a name was chosen and written on the board, the board was nailed on the wall, and we had started a Māori tertiary institution. We knew we needed funding, a plan, a CEO, courses, faculty, and other facilities—but the critical thing was that we started; we nailed our name to the wall and began. Everything else has been methodically built over time, beginning with a strategic plan. Today, several years later, Te Whare Wānanga o Awanuiārangi teaches to the PhD level, has a wide range of programmes and is a multimillion-dollar entity, funded by the tribes with assistance from the government. Strategic planning was a very important factor here.

In summary, there is a need to see the distinction between self-determination (as an outcome) and being self-determining (as a process). That is, the focus of our struggle must be to be actively engaged (self-determining) rather than simply passively engaged with a utopian/rhetorical ideal (self-determination). Being self-determining in my view is to live out self-determination in everyday practice. In this sense, self-determination becomes the vision and the goal; to be self-determining describes the practice of enacting self-determination every moment. In many ways there is a profound question here for indigenous people who are already self-governing and/or who purport to have self-determination. That is, is the way in which we live our lives and engage with the structures of our society an enactment of self-determination? In other words, are we genuinely being self-determining? The implication of this question is that it is possible not only to have self-governance and self-determination politically, but also to live our everyday existence in culturally, socially, and economically oppressed ways. Many small states may understand these phenomena as development dependency or structural indebtedness. Both of these situations are good examples of what I view as new formations of colonization. For many small self-governing states, issues around education development become complicated when confronted with these issues and choices that may put into opposition cultural knowledge excellence on the one hand and the need to develop skills to enable access to labor markets in order to support economic goals on the other. Often and tragically, the international forces driving economic development seem to have little concern for the issue of localized cultural knowledge excellence (apart perhaps from a few individuals). It is apparent that many of the international funding and development agencies too often have narrow perspectives on these issues and often do not appreciate these ends, regarding them as impediments to economic outcomes. There is a large set of Pacific literature on this; see Sitiveni Halapua (1982), M. Meleisia and P. Meleisea (1987) and Thaman (2003). A subsequent tragedy is that often in these small nations, states, and tribes, the education and schooling opportunities that are offered may end up not delivering excellence in either the cultural or the economic development domain. There are important issues for Māori learning communities to reflect on here.

B. THERE IS A NEED TO CENTRALIZE THE ISSUE OF TRANSFORMING

Transforming needs to become our focus in education. Why? Because for the most part the status quo way of doing things has not delivered significant change in the existing circumstances of high and disproportionate levels of socioeconomic marginalization and/or of educational underachievement. We cannot simply go on reproducing the same poor outcomes.

The focus on transformation as outcomes of our transforming intent means that we need to know the answers to the following:

- How do we get transformation?
- What counts as real and meaningful transformation?
- How do we know that transformation is effective and sustainable?
- Whose interests are served by the transformation?

Furthermore, there is a need to understand the implicit rationale or theoretical basis to our preferred transformation strategies in order to make the intervention potential portable and therefore able to be transferred and applied in other sites where change is required such as health, economics, housing, and the like. We have learned from our experience that we need to move beyond linear, instrumental notions of transformation. These linear modes of transforming tend to create needs hierarchies and as a result develop competition for limited resources. Often these competitive strategies divide us against each other. Our new approach is to move away from an emphasis on linear models of transformation and reconceptualize our transforming strategies as a circular praxis (following G. H. Smith, 1997). This approach is predicated on the presumption that the necessary changes that need to occur are many; our needs are to be found in multiple sites; and our strategies also need to be multiple. This 360-degree approach to engage with multiple colonizing forces often requires multiple resistances that often need to be applied simultaneously. The important point here is that we must move beyond single policy initiatives of transformation (as implied in the linear framework) to asserting transformation needing to occur in multiple forms. In respect to policy, this may mean the need for government to focus on the "whole of government" strategies involving several ministries engaging with the same issue from different bases at the same time. For example, many of the education issues overlap with health, social development, economic development, and so on. We should also be able to relate our vision of what we are trying to achieve to the actual process of change and transformation, for example, around Claus Offe's legitimation-crisis' change cycle and Jurgen Habermas's incremental cycle of social change (Offe, 1984; Habermas, 1974). That is, a vision will usually be achieved incrementally and we need to understand the pace and nature of change and therefore identify and celebrate the incremental victories along the way to the realization of the ultimate or utopian vision.

More recently we have de-emphasized using the noun *transformation* to now emphasizing the verb *transforming*. We have moved to distinguish between transformation as an outcome and transforming as a process. That is, we have shifted from a focus on descriptive, long-term outcomes (utopian vision) to now recognizing the need to enact transforming in our everyday behaviours and to enact it as an ongoing dynamic process.

In shifting to a concentration on transforming we are able to celebrate the incremental victories along the way to the full realization of the transformation vision and goal. That is, we do not want to overly focus on realizing the end point of transformation—as some of these visions are more aspirational or utopian and may require a lot of time before they are realized. The collapse of overly generalized utopian visions such as civil rights and gender equity and so on lost a lot of support from the 1970s onwards, as people's interest waned in these movements because they lost faith waiting to realize the ultimate outcome. Having noted the prior importance of the notion of transforming as opposed to transformation, there is still a case for long-term, utopian visions. A utopian vision can give impetus and direction to our transforming struggles.

C. THERE IS A NEED TO BECOME MORE LITERATE ABOUT NEW FORMATIONS OF COLONIZATION

There is need to understand colonization more profoundly rather than simply within the traditional understandings of "the schools did it to us," "the missionaries and churches did it to us" or "the state and colonial governments did it to us." All of these traditional explanations have elements of truth and are part of the explanation. However, there are some who believe that because we understand these elements that colonization can be controlled or even that colonization has disappeared.

The term *post-colonial* is often confused as meaning this; it does not mean this—but I think a number of people misinterpret the preoccupation with post-colonial studies as being after the period of colonization. This is not the case—colonization has not gone away; in many instances it has just changed its form. This is the point—many are still looking through the old critical lenses and fail to see the new formations of colonization and subsequently how the new blockages are formed in the face of indigenous aspirations. We need to develop new critical literacies, which enable us to analyze the various scenarios correctly to enable the appropriate resistance or intervention to be developed. As long as we continue to misread this situation we will continue to produce ill-fitting and ineffective resistance measures.

Some of the old forms of colonization have been embedded in schooling and education and we know them by different labels. For example, we should still be aware of the contradictory and colonizing nature of curriculum that is driven by deficit theory and/or self-esteem theory; we also have critical theory understandings that illuminate the dangers for indigenous cultures contained in the notions of the selected curriculum and the social construction of knowledge. That is, any curriculum is a selection of knowledge by someone or by people with particular interests (cf. Bernstein, 1971, 1973, and Young, 1971). Once Māori understood this about the curriculum we could respond more effectively—hence the rise of alternative education and schooling where we could better influence what was to count as the curriculum. Examinations and testing are also socially and culturally constructed phenomena that need attention to ensure they are fairly and equitably applied.

There are other new formations of colonization that arise at the intersection of cultural oppression and economic exploitation. These occur around the commodification of knowledge—the buying and selling of knowledge through manipulating cultural and intellectual property regimes, enacting the regulatory effects of patents, copyrights, and trademarks. This is a major issue at present and is one of the key elements of the free trade agreements for example as regulated

in the General Agreement on Tariffs and Trade (GATT) and Trade-Related Aspects of Intellectual Property Rights (TRIPs) initiatives. The attendant values that
allow this kind of exploitation are contained in the neoliberal economic values of
individualism, privatization, competition, the free market, and so on. Having rendered this critique, I do not want to completely dismiss the potential of neoliberal
economics to also act in positive ways for indigenous interests.

D. THERE IS A NEED TO PUT OUR OWN INDIGENOUS LANGUAGES, KNOWLEDGES, AND CULTURES AT THE CENTER OF OUR EDUCATION REVITALIZATION

This is important in order to harness the emotional energy related to identity
and culture to enhance learning more generally. Dr. Lee Brown, a colleague at the
University of British Columbia, has written some powerful work on this aspect
using the medicine wheel (Brown, 2004). The point here is that identity is linked
to language, knowledge, and culture.

Place is also important: land, Mother Earth. I am reminded of a story about
one of our elders, Rima Edwards,[4] and his evidence that he presented in a land
claim hearing in the Waitangi tribunal hearing. It took him a day and a half
of giving the context of place before he actually reached the person whom he
wanted to talk about in his evidence—his total evidence took two and a half days
of traditional stories, chants, songs, and oral history. The point is that place, our
traditional context, is important—but it may be that we have to begin the work of
finding new concepts of place within our language and oral traditions as climate
change and rising oceans threaten many of our traditional homelands. The por-
tentous issue of climate change and its impact in the Pacific must be part of the
context in which Pacific Rim nations plan for the future.

Some other examples of indigenous Māori knowledge being important in its
own right are the work of the Elder Kino Hughes (over 400 traditional songs
memorized, sung, and recorded); the work of Emily Schuster, a Māori weaver who
worked on special knots for the NASA space programme; the Te Māori art exhi-
bition at the New York Metropolitan Museum of Art, which had been considered
artifacts in New Zealand and yet virtually overnight after being displayed in New
York were then considered objects of art (and subsequently imbued with status and
economic worth). The key point here is that knowledge is arbitrary.

In general it took a while to realize both as a people, as an education and schooling system and as a nation that fundamentally Māori still want to be Māori—that
Māori were not prepared to sacrifice their culture, language, knowledge, or identities and become brown-skinned Pakeha (non-Māori New Zealanders). Most

indigenous people I have encountered have the same sentiment—they still want to be indigenous.

CONCLUSION—OUR STRUGGLE IS TO BE TRANSFORMING

Finally I want to summarize some key points about Māori struggle for equity in New Zealand. Our struggle is not just for social and economic inclusion; it is also for our language, knowledge, and culture. For Māori, these issues are interdependent. While I am concerned about what happens in New Zealand, I do acknowledge the need and suffering of other peoples. An important point is that all of us need to struggle to transform our existing marginal conditions.

In this writing, I use *struggle* to encapsulate the contested, unequal power relationships between dominant Pakeha (non-Māori) and subordinate/d Māori social, cultural, and economic interests. Education and schooling are critical sites to be struggled over. Schools and education are implicated in the production and reproduction of these unequal relations of power and subsequent social, economic, and cultural inequities. My ultimate argument is to enable every citizen in our country to enjoy levels of social, economic, and cultural well-being that engender a positive national pride and sense of belonging.

I view the notion of struggle positively as it can also provide clarity of what we are for as much as what we stand against. We should be clear that our struggle for Māori educational liberation is also a struggle for the rescuing of the legitimacy of the educational and schooling system as a whole (e.g., for every 100 non-Māori children 75 will leave with a level 2 NCEA qualification as opposed to 48 Māori).[5] While I have concentrated on Māori struggle, I do fully acknowledge that many of these issues also draw in educators more generally. In this sense some of the issues identified in relation to Māori may also transcend the specificities of cultural context.

Our struggle is now—Tomorrow is too late—today is tomorrow—we can not afford to continue to wait; to continue deciding on how we might react; to continue waiting for someone else to come up with answers; to continue to rely on others to lead. In regard to our cultural survival everyone must become a leader. Urgency is of the utmost priority to the extent that our talking should not be about what we *might* do but rather about what we *have* done (accent on the past tense). We need to move beyond the description of our morbidity to enacting change.

Our struggle is both cultural and structural—It is not either/or; institutional, government, and societal structures (as well as people) need to be challenged and where necessary changed. In other words we need to develop new literacies to enable transforming, to enable identifying systemic and people blockages and to react to them as appropriate. Otherwise our transforming endeavours will not be long term; they will simply be short-term, one-off projects.

Our struggle is not one struggle—It is composed of multiple struggles that occur in many places, often simultaneously. Our resistance has to be the same—to multiple sites of incursion, often at the same time. We need to move beyond being the recipients of the single policy approach with respect to government intervention strategies. The fact that the majority of our people still remain socially and economically marginalized is evidence that selected policy applications have had limited effect. Singular policy interventions are and have been insufficient. There is no silver bullet; no magic pill; no single policy. There is need to invest in change on a broad range of fronts—a 360-degree approach. Some of these investments in change we need to take responsibility for ourselves, and others are situated in the public policy domain (note Gramsci's war of position, war of manoeuvre, 1971; WE need to be alert to the criticism of essentialism when arguing for collective struggle as Maori and it is useful to draw notions like Spivak's 'strategic essentialism' to support the idea of collective struggle).

Our struggle is also with ourselves—It rests not just on the competitive or possessive individual, but also on our families, on our communities, on our tribes, on our people as a whole. We must defend our cultural propensity toward collectivity and to revitalize and re-empower our abilities to collaborate and socialize. We need to reinstate, value, and practice the collective power that resides in the group. We must proactively rebuild the social, rebuild the concept of the public interest and public good responsibilities against the hegemony of the primacy of the individual. It is not just about what "I" can do, but, perhaps more so about what "we" can do responsibly and collectively.

Our struggle must be positive and proactive—We must move beyond being debilitated by negative and reactive politics. Our struggle must shift from over-emphasizing our pathology to accentuating our collective well-being. We cannot afford to remain trapped or debilitated by our historical discontent. While we must not forget our histories, they must become the levers for building and informing our futures. All minority interest groups must have a hand in naming our own world and futures; if we procrastinate others will do it for us.

Our struggle must be to become more self-determining—Indigenous communities who live in colonized situations of unequal power relations often need to break away from the disempowerment of social, economic, and intellectual dependency and to assume increased power and responsibility for their own well-being. We must move beyond the rhetoric of self-determination (an outcome) to being self-determining (a process). In other words, we must enact self-determination in our every day, every hour, every minute practice, not just hold it as a utopian ideal. We must recognize the incremental victories along the pathway to our transformative vision. This not a movement away or against dominant cultures—it is a positive assertion about the need to make space for minority cultures and to proactively protect languages and cultures that might be at risk. More often it is also about protecting the original cultures and languages that belong in the soil and landscapes of countries that have been colonized.

Our struggle is for our minds—There is a need to understand our own complicity in forming our own domination, exploitation, dependency, and oppression. We need to re-educate ourselves out of false consciousness and to free our minds from hegemony. Education has been a major factor in embedding indigenous inferiority. We must reclaim the power of education to act in our interests. An important decolonizing act therefore, is to struggle over the meaning and intention of education and schooling. It needs to serve all people and not simply be a means to reproduce dominant cultural expectations at the expense of indigenous interests. More positively, there is a need to reinstate a utopian vision in order to give direction and impetus to our transforming struggles.

Our struggle to become "more fully human" (Freire, 1971) is correlated to our ability to transform the education system. This task is urgent and critical. Failure to do so will give credence to the lament about the irrelevance of public education made by Janine Terbasket, an Okanagan graduate student from Kelowna, Canada: *"My only problem is that I went to school to get educated."*

NOTES

1. Traditional description for House of Higher Learning; note that all the existing universities use the phrase, "Te Whare Wānanga o…" when describing themselves.
2. A contemporary term that describes a site of Māori learning.
3. This story related by the Hon. Justice Joseph V. Williams, Te Whare Wānanga o Awanuiārangi Graduation Speech, April 19, 2013.
4. The National Certificate of Educational Achievement (NCEA) is the official secondary school qualification in New Zealand. Ministry of Education (2012).

REFERENCES

Apple, M. W. (1979). *Ideology and curriculum*. London, England: Routledge & Kegan Paul.

Apple, M. W. (1993). *Official knowledge*. New York, NY: Routledge.

Apple, M. W. (Ed.). (2003). *The state and the politics of knowledge*. New York, NY: RoutledgeFalmer.

BERL Report. (2014, April). *The economic contribution of the Wānanga sector*.

Bernstein, B. (1971). *Class, codes and control: Vol. 1. Theoretical studies towards a sociology of language*. London, England: Routledge & Kegan Paul.

Bernstein, B. (Ed.). (1973). *Class, codes and control: Vol. 2. Applied studies towards a sociology of language.* London, England: Routledge & Kegan Paul.

Brown, L. (2004). *Making the Classroom a Healthy Place: The Development of Affective Competency in Aboriginal Pedagogy.* Unpublished PhD Thesis; Faculty of Graduate Studies, Dept. of Ed. Studies, University of British Columbia, B.C., Canada.

Gramsci, A. (1971). *Selections from "The prison notebooks"* (Q. Hoare & G. Smith, Eds. & Trans.). London, England: Lawrence & Wishart.

Habermas, J. (1974). *Theory and practice* (J. Viertel, Trans.). London, England: Heinemann.

Hoskins, T. & Jones, A. (Eds.). (2012). *Interview Kaupapa Māori: The dangers of domestication. New Zealand Journal of Educational Studies, 47*(2).

Halapua, S. (1982). *Fisherman of Tonga: Their means of survival.* Institute of Pacific Studies in association with the Institute of Marine Resources, University of the South Pacific, Suva, Fiji.

McLean, M. & Orbell, M. (1975). *Traditional songs of the Māori.* Auckland, New Zealand: A.H. & A.W. Reed Ltd.

Meleisea, M., & Meleisea, P. (Eds.). (1987). *Lagaga: A short history of Western Samoa.* Suva, Fiji: Institute of Pacific Studies.

Ministry of Education. (2012). *Me Kōrero—let's talk! Ka Hikitia—accelerating success 2013–2017.* Wellington, New Zealand: Ministry of Education.

Offe, C. (1984). *Contradictions of the welfare state.* London, England: Hutchison.

Smith, G. H. (1990a). The politics of reforming Māori education. In H. Lauder & C. Wylie (Eds.), *Towards successful schooling* (pp. 73–88). London, England: Falmer.

Smith, G. H. (1990b). Taha Māori: Pakeha capture. In J. Codd, R. Harker, & R. Nash (Eds.), *Political issues in N.Z. education* (pp. 183–197). Palmerston North, New Zealand: Dunmore Press.

Smith, G. H. (1992) Education: Biculturalism or separatism? In D. Novitz & B. Willmott (Eds.), *New Zealand in crisis* (pp. 157–165). Wellington, New Zealand: G.P. Books.

Smith, G. H. (1997). *Kaupapa Māori: Theory and praxis* (Doctoral dissertation). Education Department, University of Auckland, New Zealand. International Research Institute for Māori and Indigenous Education.

Smith, G. H. (1999). Paulo Freire: Lessons in transformative praxis. In P. Roberts (Ed.), *Paulo Freire, politics and pedagogy: Reflections from Aotearoa-New Zealand* (pp. 35–43). Palmerston North, New Zealand: Dunmore Press.

Smith, G. H., & Smith, L. T. (1990). In J. Marshall et al. *Myths and Realities.* Palmerston North, New Zealand: Dunmore Press.

Smith, L. T. (1999). *Decolonizing methodologies: Research and indigenous peoples.* London, England: Zed Books.

Spivak, G. C. (1990). *The Post Colonial Critic: Interviews, Strategies, Dialogues.* London and New York: Routledge-Taylor Francis Group.

Stack, M., Coulter, D., Grosjean, G., Mazawi, A., & Smith, G. (Eds.). (2006). *Fostering tomorrow's educational leaders.* British Columbia, Canada: Gov. Print.

Thaman, K. (2003). Decolonizing Pacific studies: Indigenous perspectives, knowledge and wisdom in higher education. *The Contemporary Pacific, 15*(1), 7.

Young, M. (1971). *Knowledge and control.* London, England: Collier Macmillan.

CHAPTER FOUR

Paulo Freire and the Idea of Openness

PETER ROBERTS

There has been a flurry of pronouncements over recent years about new forms of openness in scholarly and pedagogical activity. Reference has been made to open education, open learning, open knowledge, open technology, open content, open source, open access, and open courseware (Iiyoshi & Kumar, 2008). In surveying some of this work, it sometimes appears as if such initiatives have come from nowhere, with a history no older than a decade or two and no discernible epistemological or ethical roots. Openness is often viewed merely as an unfolding reality: an outcome of new social practices and modes of cultural life in the digital age. Attention also needs to be paid, however, to the philosophical heritage of discourses on openness and to some of the conceptual contours of openness as an ideal.

This chapter considers what it might mean to talk of openness as an educational virtue. Drawing principally on the work of Paulo Freire but with prior reference to Aristotle and a range of other thinkers, I set out to show that openness has ontological, epistemological, and ethical dimensions. Openness has application in multiple areas of educational life and can serve as a principle for both lifelong learning and social organization. The optimal pursuit of openness in pedagogical settings, I shall argue, requires the presence of other virtues and can be contrasted with various forms of closure, including dogmatism, excessive certainty, and an unreflective rejection of either the old or the new. Openness, it will be noted, also has its limits and education has an important role to play in identifying these.

OPENNESS AS A VIRTUE

In what senses might openness be considered a virtue? To address this question, it is first necessary to ask what we mean by *virtue*. A concern with virtues and the virtuous person has a lengthy history in Western philosophy and is often traced back to the ancient Greeks. Among the early Greek thinkers, it is Aristotle, in his *Nichomachean Ethics*, who pays closest attention to the nature and significance of virtues. For Aristotle, virtues are neither feelings nor faculties but dispositions (Aristotle, 1976, p. 99). Aristotle defines a virtue as "a purposive disposition, lying in a mean that is relative to us and determined by rational principle, and by that which a prudent man would use to determine it" (pp. 102–103). The doctrine of the mean specifies, in the realm of human virtue, that which is neither excessive nor deficient. Thus, in relation to fear and confidence, we might see rashness as the excessive tendency, cowardice as the deficiency, and courage as the mean (p. 104). Deficiency and excess, Aristotle notes, are "*not* one and the same for all" (p. 100, emphasis in original).

Aristotle distinguishes between two types of virtue: intellectual and moral. Intellectual virtue, he says, "owes both its inception and its growth chiefly to instruction, and for this reason needs time and experience" (p. 91). Moral virtues "are engendered in us neither *by* nor *contrary to* nature; we are constituted by nature to receive them, but their full development in us is due to habit" (p. 91, emphasis in original). We acquire virtues by exercising them; we learn, Aristotle maintains, by doing (p. 91). For Aristotle, the supreme good is happiness (*eudaimonia*), and art of living a good life is to be found in practical wisdom (*phronesis*). The happy person, according to Aristotle, is "one who is active in accordance with complete virtue, and who is adequately furnished with external goods, and that not for some unspecified period but throughout a complete life" (p. 84).

Aristotle does not identify openness as one of the virtues. He does, however, discuss a number of dispositions that might be said to be compatible with openness, such as truthfulness, resourcefulness, understanding, and patience. If we were to adopt an Aristotelian perspective on the question of virtue, we would want to ask whether openness might reasonably be said to constitute the mean, and if so, what might be seen as corresponding dispositions of excess or deficiency. This presupposes, however, that openness is best understood as a disposition. There is certainly a strong case that can be made for seeing it in this light, by focusing on the notion of open-mindedness. Open-mindedness, as Riggs (2010) points out, is often among the most highly valued of epistemic or intellectual virtues (see also Steutel & Spiecker, 1997).

But equating openness with open-mindedness and locating it within the tradition of virtue epistemology, which can be distinguished from virtue ethics (Crisp, 2010), arguably fails to capture adequately the connotations of the term in contemporary discourses on open education, open source, open access, and the like. Thus, while we might from an Aristotelian viewpoint regard open-mindedness as a virtue, with, say, closed-mindedness as the deficiency, it is not clear exactly how we should characterize the excess. A term such as 'intellectual permeability', indicating an indiscriminate openness to everything, could be a candidate, but this has a certain clumsiness to it. There are, moreover, some traditions of thought in which this kind of disposition is regarded as desirable. In the *Tao Te Ching*, for instance, Lao Tzu says: "My mind is that of a fool—how blank! / Vulgar people are clear / I alone am drowsy. / Vulgar people are alert" (Lao Tzu, 1963, ch. 20). As George Miller (1996) points out, we "can infer from Lao Tzu's perspective that the mind etched with intractable distinctions is the closed mind; the open mind is 'blank and muddled'" (p. 64). For a follower of the *Tao Te Ching*, then, permeability in allowing thoughts to pass freely, without a deliberate attempt to order the contents of the intellect or make judgments about quality, is a worthwhile state of mind and precisely the kind of openness that should be cultivated.

Openness, I want to suggest, is inclusive of, but not limited to, open-mindedness. Openness is, or can be, not merely an individual disposition (cf. McMahon, 1990) but also a particular orientation to action and relationships, a property of systems, and an organizing principle for social organization. Openness has not one but several opposites. Most have something to do with closure. Closed-mindedness is one example, but we might also talk about closed systems and closed societies. Indeed, when attention is drawn to the need for openness, it is frequently in response to something less than open in the social world—e.g., the censoring of websites or e-mails, or the withholding of institutional information, or the stifling of open debate.

Discussions of this kind have theoretical antecedents in earlier defenses of openness in social and economic organization, among the best known of which are Karl Popper's (1974) *The Open Society and Its Enemies* and Friedrich Hayek's (1944) *The Road to Serfdom*. In policy and political arenas, closure is often considered in relation to trade and other forms of international exchange. Thus, we find a burgeoning policy rhetoric on the need for free trade, portrayed as the easing of barriers to the movement of goods and services from one country to another. At the same time, countries such as North Korea and Iran are, in U.S. political discourse particularly, often portrayed as quintessential examples of closed societies, where involvement with the outside world is minimal.

An Aristotelian framework, then, does not take us far enough when analyzing openness as a virtue. It is helpful nonetheless in prompting deeper investigation of the philosophical underpinnings to any discussion of virtue, and Aristotle's influence on contemporary ethics cannot be underestimated. Aristotle's more recent interpreters, such as Alasdair MacIntyre (2007), have accepted the importance for ethical theory of examining virtues but have sought to go beyond Aristotle's "metaphysical biology." Following the initial publication of his modern philosophical classic *After Virtue* in 1981, MacIntyre, influenced by Aquinas, has gone on to qualify his critique of Aristotle's position. "What I came to recognize," MacIntyre observes, "was that my conception of human beings as virtuous or vicious needed not only a metaphysical, but also a biological grounding, although not an especially Aristotelian one" (2007, p. xi). Richard Rorty (1980), too, while respecting Aristotle's attempt to break away from Plato's theory of forms, is critical of the lingering universalism in Aristotelian epistemology. Aristotle, it seems, retained a conception of the intellect as something special—something immaterial and separable from the body (1976, pp. 40–41).

Neither MacIntyre nor Rorty has made openness a key subject of philosophical inquiry, but both might be said to be implicitly committed to it. Indeed, Rorty has often been seen as one of the main proponents of a new openness in conceptualizing the task of philosophy. Rorty (1980, 1989) has argued against foundationalist thinking in philosophy and demonstrated the value of other forms of writing—particularly literature—in advancing liberal goals such as solidarity. Stanley Cavell (1999) and Martha Nussbaum (1990) are among the other philosophers in a growing list who have taken literature seriously as a source of potential insight in addressing ethical questions. Nussbaum is self-consciously Aristotelian in her approach but Cavell owes more to Wittgenstein, who, along with Nietzsche, paved the way for a subsequent radical reappraisal of the nature and purpose of philosophical work. Nietzsche's task, as he saw it, was to provide a revaluation of all values (cf. Nietzsche, 1901/1968, 1883–1892/1976, 1887 & 1908/1989, 1886/1990), while Wittgenstein, in his later writings at least (Wittgenstein, 1958), was concerned principally with questions of language, meaning, and logic. Both, however, can be regarded as prophetic in foreshadowing a new ethos of openness not only as a philosophical concept but also as a mode of being and living.

The influence of Nietzsche in particular can also be detected in the work of other thinkers whom we might call philosophers of openness, such as Karl Jaspers, Simone de Beauvoir, Hans Gadamer, Jacques Derrida, and Gilles Deleuze, among others. Jaspers, who wrote a book on Nietzsche (Jaspers, 1965) and referred to him often in his other published writings, has been described by one commentator as "the metaphysician of tolerance" (Durfee, 1970). Others (e.g., Salamun, 1988, 1990) have stressed the importance of openness in Jaspers's ethical and political theory. Simone de Beauvoir's (1948) emphasis on *ambiguity*, a notion some see as distinctively female in its epistemological orientation (Miller, 1996), places her in a tradition of thought that values the openness of imagination and is comfortable with uncertainty. Beauvoir, along with her compatriots Jean-Paul Sartre and Albert Camus, developed her ideas not just through works of philosophical non-fiction but also via novels and other forms of literary expression. Gadamer and Derrida, while differing from each other in many ways, were responsible, perhaps more than any other thinkers in the second half of the twentieth century, for fostering an opening of the text: Gadamer in the tradition of hermeneutics, as exemplified in his magnum opus *Truth and Method* (2004), and Derrida through deconstruction, beginning with his classic work *Of Grammatology* (1976). Deleuze, alone and in collaboration with Felix Guattari, addressed openness in systems, including systems of thought (see, e.g., Deleuze, 1997; Deleuze & Guattari, 1996).

For these thinkers, however, education is not a key concern. In developing a distinctively educational account of openness as a virtue, the work of Paulo Freire is especially helpful. Born in 1921 in Recife, Brazil, Freire first came into international prominence through his work with illiterate adults. Freire developed a unique approach to the teaching of reading and writing, linking "word" with "world" and basing literacy programs on the realities of everyday life for impoverished Brazilians. Rather than employing a language for literacy instruction that was dislocated from the lives of learners, Freire would begin with words such as *favela* (slum) and *tijolo* (brick). He encouraged dialogue rather than monologue in literacy learning, built upon (but did not rest with) the experiences of learners, and allowed participants to learn to problematize aspects of their social world. He was later to apply similar principles, but with appropriate modifications for different contexts, in programs in Chile and Guinea-Bissau, among other countries.

Freire gained worldwide educational attention with the publication of his classic work, *Pedagogy of the Oppressed* (Freire, 1972b) in English in 1970. Forced into exile with the military coup in Brazil in 1964, he was not able to return permanently to his home country until 1980, after which he became active in the Brazilian Workers Party. He held the demanding position of Secretary of Education for the municipality of São Paulo from 1989 to 1991, and in his last years he devoted himself mainly to his writing. He published prolifically in the last ten years of his life, co-authoring a number of dialogical "talking" books with Ira Shor (Freire & Shor, 1987), Donaldo Macedo (Freire & Macedo, 1987), Antonio Faundez (Freire & Faundez, 1989), and Myles Horton (Horton & Freire, 1990), among others. He also authored several volumes on his own during this period, some of which were published posthumously (Freire, 1993, 1994, 1996, 1997a, 1998a, 1998b, 1998c, 2004, 2007).

Freire was in heavy demand as a speaker in many parts of the world from the early 1970s until his death in 1997. Numerous books and articles have been published on his theory and practice over the years; to date, however, relatively little direct attention has been paid to the importance of openness as a theme in his work. The next section takes up this theme, and in my conclusion I consider some of the implications of this analysis for the new discourses on open education, open knowledge, and open access.

A PEDAGOGY OF OPENNESS: THE WORK OF PAULO FREIRE

The theme of openness provides an arc connecting Freire's earliest books with his last. Openness can be regarded as a pivotal feature of both Freire's educational theory and his pedagogical practice. Openness has a close connection with other epistemological and ethical virtues in Freire's philosophy but it is not reducible to them. Openness, from a Freirean perspective, is tied tightly to the very essence of being human: the ontological and historical vocation of humanization. Humanization, as Freire conceives of it, is a process of becoming more fully human through critical, dialogical praxis: reflection and action upon the world in order to transform it (Freire, 1972b). As humans, we are *unfinished* beings. The process of humanization is never complete: as the world (and we ourselves) are transformed, there will always be a need for further reflection and action. Often, we are impeded in this pursuit, and thus dehumanized, by oppressive social structures, practices, and attitudes.

Addressing oppression in its myriad forms is, for Freire, a *social* process: we never liberate ourselves alone. Knowing, too, from a Freirean viewpoint, is necessarily incomplete: we can never know *absolutely*; instead, we can only come closer to knowing the essence that explains an object of study. Freire's account of liberating education grew from his practical experience as a literacy educator working with impoverished adults in both urban settings and rural peasant communities. As such, there is a close link between liberation and the process of struggle against oppression. This does not, however, explain Freire's theory of liberation fully, for there is also a heavy reliance, particularly in his later works, on a virtue-based account of human formation and flourishing. This is especially significant when considering the concept of openness.

Education: The Practice of Freedom (Freire, 1976), while not published in English until after *Pedagogy of the Oppressed* (Freire, 1972b), was written prior to the latter text and conveyed in careful detail not only Freire's approach to adult literacy education but also his commitment to openness as an ideal. *Education: The Practice of Freedom* was also published under the title *Education for Critical Consciousness*. Together with *Pedagogy of the Oppressed* (Freire, 1972b) and *Cultural Action for Freedom* (Freire, 1972a), it is one of three key works in Freire's first important phase as an international educational writer (see further, Roberts, 2000). In *Education: The Practice of Freedom* Freire discusses the concept of openness in relation to the historical development of Brazilian society and as a feature of what he called "critical consciousness."

Citing Popper's (1974) *The Open Society and Its Enemies*, among other sources, Freire charts some of the key features of Brazil's movement from a closed society through a transitional period in the 1950s and early 1960s toward greater openness. In a closed state, Brazil lacked autonomous status, generating cultural alienation and a reliance (as a raw materials export-based economy) on external markets. In the earlier decades of the twentieth century the country remained fundamentally "backward" (Freire's use of this word has not endeared him to all readers), with very high rates of illiteracy and deep social inequalities. Dialogue was discouraged. As changes that had begun with the industrial revolution gradually exerted an influence over Brazilian society, the steady state of closure that had been maintained for decades "was split apart with the rupture of the forces which had kept it in equilibrium" (Freire, 1976, p. 9). Yet, while urban centers became progressively more open, rural areas remained closed. Landowners maintained tight control over production and profits in peasant communities, with many in the northeast of Brazil in particular suffering horrific rates of disease, malnutrition, and infant mortality. As Freire puts it, "Brazil was a society no longer totally closed but not yet truly open: a society in the *process* of opening" (p. 9, emphasis in original). With the military coup in 1964, the risk of a "catastrophic" return to even greater closure was heightened (p. 10).

The path to greater openness, Freire (1976) argued, was to be found not through the naïve consciousness that prevailed in urban areas during the period of transition but in the development of a more critical consciousness. Among the features of critical consciousness, as a concept specifically applicable to the Brazilian context at that time (and not necessarily directly transferable to other settings), Freire speaks of "depth in the interpretation of problems," "the testing of one's findings," an "openness to revision," a refusal to transfer responsibility, "the practice of dialogue rather than polemics," and "receptivity to the new for reasons beyond mere novelty" (p. 18). Critical consciousness, Freire makes clear, demands "the good sense not to reject the old just because it is old"; we should, he says, accept what is valid in both the old and the new (p. 18). Under military rule, Brazil had become authoritarian and rigid, with a culture of silence and inaction. Critical consciousness stands opposed to this. It is "characteristic of authentically democratic regimes and corresponds to highly permeable, interrogative, restless and dialogical forms of life" (pp. 18–19).

These early ideas on openness find further elaboration in multiple books across the rest of Freire's writing career. There is not space to comment in detail on all such references, but several key points can be made. As Freire's thought developed, he paid increasing attention to what we might call educational virtues. (For a fuller discussion of this dimension of Freire's work, see Roberts, 2010.) Freire had in mind, among other things, dispositions, qualities, or characteristics of being human that had particular value in teaching and learning situations. Some of the most commonly mentioned virtues of this kind include humility, the ability to listen, care of and respect for those with whom we work in educational settings, tolerance, an inquiring and investigative frame of mind, and a willingness to take risks (Freire, 1998a, 1998c).

This virtues-based approach was consistent with, rather than an alternative to, the persistent Freirean theme of liberation as a process of struggling against oppression (Roberts, 2008). For it is exactly qualities of the kind identified above that must be present if the process of struggle is to be a liberating one. Not all forms of struggle, Freire demonstrated, are liberating. Educational virtues spring from broader human ideals, the most important of which, for Freire, is *love* (Freire, 1997a). Freire had taken heed in his early writings of Che Guevara's portrayal of love as a revolutionary virtue, and in later works this becomes a dominant theme. Love for Freire applies to multiple dimensions of human existence. It is love of the physical environment, of the process of study, and of our fellow human beings. We are, Freire insisted, beings of communication, and love, as exemplified by the respect we show to others, our commitment to them, and our willingness to enter into dialogue with them is an integral part of bringing this feature of our ontology to life.

Educational virtues can be found in individual teachers and students, but they can also be present in groups and evident in systems, structures, policies, and practices. An attitude of openness is a permanent orientation: as unfinished beings, we should, Freire believed, always be open to new ways of understanding the world, new approaches to addressing old problems, new forms of learning, and new modes of communication. Technology should neither be embraced uncritically nor rejected in a reactionary manner (Freire, 2004). Openness can be contrasted with dogmatism, which Freire spoke against repeatedly and had observed among those on both the political left and the political right (see Escobar, Fernandez, & Guevara-Niebla, with Freire, 1994; Freire, 1997a). Openness is closely connected with our *creativity* as human beings: our ability to make history (though not always, as Marx would have reminded us, under circumstances of our own choosing) and form ourselves as cultural beings (Freire, 1972a, 1972b, 1976, 1994, 1998a). Openness from a Freirean standpoint also implies other principles of educational importance.

To be open in our orientation to education, and to human life more generally, is to accept that the world (including the inner world of thoughts and feelings) is undergoing constant change. Transformation thus becomes not merely possible but one of the defining features of our existence. A commitment to openness, for Freire, also implies a willingness not only to live with but also to actively embrace uncertainty (Freire, 1997a, 1998a, 2007). In his later works, Freire spoke often of the need to become less certain of some of our certainties, and he continued to admit to his own doubts and restlessness right up to the time of his death.

The virtue of openness, as understood by Freire, can be found in reading, in dialogue, in seeking to know, in our relation to the Other, in the way we respond to criticism, and in our attitude to life itself. In reading, we must, Freire insisted, be open to being challenged by the text and to the possibility of challenging it (Freire

& Shor, 1987). Dialogue cannot occur without an openness to the process of communication and a trust in the ability of others to engage likewise (Freire, 1972b, 1976). Without an openness to the Other, we remain locked in a self-centered or ethnocentric world (cf. Freire, 1996, 1998a, 2004, 2007). Openness to constructive criticism allows us to continue growing as learners, teachers, and researchers. While Freire did retain certain key pedagogical principles throughout his educational career (e.g., a commitment to dialogue and to the value of a critical orientation to the world), he also modified, deepened and extended his thinking in many areas—partly in response to criticism from feminist and postmodern scholars, among others (see Freire, 1997b; Freire & Macedo, 1993, 1995; Mayo, 1999; Roberts, 2000).

A passage from one of Freire's last books, *Pedagogy of Freedom* (Freire, 1998a), captures very effectively the position he had reached after a lifetime of reflection, writing, teaching, and social action, and is worth quoting in full:

> In essence, the correct posture of one who does not consider him- or herself to be the sole possessor of the truth or the passive object of ideology or gossip is the attitude of permanent openness. Openness to approaching and being approached, to questioning and being questioned, to agreeing and disagreeing. It is an openness to life itself and to its vicissitudes. An openness to those who call on us and to the many and varied signs that catch our interests, from the song of the bird, to the falling rain or the rain that is about to drop from the darkening sky, to the gentle smile of innocence and the sullen face of disapproval, to the arms open to receive and the body stiff with refusal and fear. It is in my permanent openness to life that I give myself entirely, my critical thought, my feeling, my curiosity, my desire, all that I am. (p. 119)

This statement, almost poetic in its lyricism and quite unlike most forms of educational writing, completes the arc that started with *Education: The Practice of Freedom* (Freire, 1976). Freire was aware of the importance of openness from his earliest work. From an initial focus on openness as the open society and the open (critical) mind, Freire broadened the scope of his inquiry to include other dimensions of an open orientation to ourselves, others, and the wider world. When Freire's work is examined holistically, openness can be seen as a mode of educational life incorporating reason, emotion, and willing (Roberts, 2010). It is exemplified by a well-rounded critical consciousness, and it is forged through our actions, our relationships, and our dialogue with other human beings.

CONCLUSION: LIMITS AND POSSIBILITIES

While Freire was largely celebratory in his attitude toward openness, this does not mean he was unaware of its limits. Those limits were of more than one kind. Freire recognized that we are all shaped by social and cultural norms—by the dominant structures and ideas and practices of our time—and that these can limit our ability to identify problems, take a different perspective on complex issues, or conceive of alternatives. He argued, however, that we are *conditioned* rather than *determined* by these influences. Education has a key role to play in allowing us to confront our prejudices, encounter others who see the world in a different way, and, where appropriate, change our views. Freire also demonstrated that some limits to openness are justified. He made it plain, for example, that he did not favor an "anything goes" approach to pedagogy. Teaching and learning should not be so open that discipline and structure disappear altogether. Freire stressed that educational dialogue, while not closing off opportunities for going down potentially fruitful unanticipated pathways, should also have a strong sense of purpose and rigor (see Freire & Shor, 1987; Horton & Freire, 1990).

We also need to acknowledge Freire's limits. This is not the place to consider in detail the various critiques of Freire's work. These have been discussed at length elsewhere (e.g., Freire, 1997b; Freire & Macedo, 1993, 1995; Mayo, 1999; Roberts, 2000, 2003, 2010). Briefly, however, it can be noted that a number of dimensions of Freire's thought remained underdeveloped at the time of his death. He was just beginning, for example, to explore in a more focused manner questions relating to the world environmental crisis. In his last works he spoke about the importance of respecting the environment—caring for it, as we should care for others—and he was supportive of efforts to enhance ecological awareness, but his ideas were still in their early stages. Freire's acquaintance with postmodern and poststructuralist currents in social theory was also somewhat limited. In the 1990s he started to refer to a postmodern orientation to the world, seeing this as compatible with the spirit of openness and contrary to the dogmatism he had observed among some of his colleagues on the political left. Again, however, he said little about specific theorists and anyone searching in Freire's publications for a lengthy engagement with influential postmodern and poststructuralist texts will be disappointed. Despite the importance of virtues in his later work, Freire did not find it necessary to comment at length on other areas of inquiry where virtue is a central theme—e.g., virtue ethics. He spoke directly and indirectly about the significance of care but did not refer to scholarship on the ethics of care. He stressed the need for emotional as well as rational development but did not ground his discussion in the literature on the philosophy of emotion. These limits are not fatal to the coherence or rigor of Freire's work but they point to deeper questions relating to the ethics of the Other in Freire's approach to openness (see further, Peters & Roberts, 2011).

What can we learn from Freire that is worth knowing in considering current discourses on openness? Freire was not an Aristotelian scholar but he would have accepted much of what Aristotle had to say about the nature of virtue. The spirit of openness toward new ways of philosophizing, new ways of addressing ethical questions, characteristic of thinkers such as Nietzsche, Wittgenstein, Jaspers, Rorty, Cavell, Nussbaum, Derrida, and others, was also shared by Freire, even though he differed from these thinkers on some important matters of philosophical substance and style. Openness from a Freirean perspective is not merely open-mindedness, though that is no small part of it; openness for Freire is also always within certain limits—some of which need to be challenged, others of which are desirable for educational purposes. From Freire, we can learn that there is no *one* virtue of openness but many *virtues* of openness. Or, to put this another way, we might say that the virtue of openness can and should be conceived, displayed, and experienced in different ways, depending on the context. In the educational realm, some virtues of openness are evident in intellectual or epistemological dispositions; others are exhibited in our ethical conduct. It is possible, however, to go beyond this and speak of virtues of openness being evident in the way systems operate, institutions are organized, or societies are structured.

These distinctions are worth keeping in mind when contemplating contemporary claims about the need for greater openness in education and scholarship. It is often *implied* that openness is a virtue, but the senses in which this might be so are not always considered carefully. From Freire, we learn the value of unpacking some of the ontological, epistemological, ethical, and political assumptions that underpin our thinking about openness. Freire teaches us to be context-specific in the forms of openness we seek to uphold or explain or limit. Within some educational contexts, there may be multiple virtues of openness evident at any given time, and there is merit in analyzing these for the respective contributions they make to teaching and learning in those contexts. Freire shows that openness is not merely a technical matter, where changes in procedures alone will suffice, or a set of rules to be followed, or a prescription of dispositions to be developed, or a checklist of methods to be employed by the teacher. Educational openness, from a Freirean perspective, is an orientation to life itself—to the way we live in the world, individually and collectively, within and outside institutions, in countries with different histories and problems and opportunities. Embracing openness, but not uncritically so, and within limits, is very much a holistic commitment but one that has arguably never been more needed than at the current time.

ACKNOWLEDGMENT

An earlier version of this chapter was published in M.A. Peters and P. Roberts (2011), *The Virtues of Openness: Education, Science, and Scholarship in the Digital Age,* Boulder, CO: Paradigm.

REFERENCES

Aristotle. (1976). *Ethics* (J.A.K. Thomson, Trans.). Harmondsworth, England: Penguin.
Beauvoir, de, S. (1948). *The ethics of ambiguity* (B. Frechtman, Trans.). New York, NY: Citadel Press.
Cavell, S. (1999). *The claim of reason.* New York, NY: Oxford University Press.
Crisp, R. (2010). Virtue ethics and virtue epistemology. *Metaphilosophy, 41*(1/2), 22–40.
Deleuze, G. (1997). *Negotiations* (M. Joughin, Trans.). New York, NY: Columbia University Press.
Deleuze, G., & Guattari, F. (1996). *What is philosophy?* (J. Tomlinson & G. Burchell, Trans.). New York, NY: Columbia University Press.
Derrida, J. (1976). *Of grammatology* (G. Spivak, Trans.). Baltimore, MD: Johns Hopkins University Press.
Durfee, H.A. (1970). Karl Jaspers as metaphysician of tolerance. *International Journal for Philosophy of Religion, 1*(4), 201–210.
Escobar, M., Fernandez, A.L., & Guevara-Niebla, G., with Freire, P. (1994). *Paulo Freire on higher education: A dialogue at the National University of Mexico.* Albany, NY: SUNY Press.
Freire, P. (1972a). *Cultural action for freedom.* Harmondsworth, England: Penguin.
Freire, P. (1972b). *Pedagogy of the oppressed.* Harmondsworth, England: Penguin.
Freire, P. (1976). *Education: The practice of freedom.* London, England: Writers and Readers.
Freire, P. (1985). *The politics of education.* London, England: Macmillan.
Freire, P. (1993). *Pedagogy of the city.* New York, NY: Continuum.
Freire, P. (1994). *Pedagogy of hope.* New York, NY: Continuum.
Freire, P. (1996). *Letters to Cristina: Reflections on my life and work.* London, England: Routledge.
Freire, P. (1997a). *Pedagogy of the heart.* New York, NY: Continuum.
Freire, P. (1997b). A response. In P. Freire, J.W. Fraser, D. Macedo, T. McKinnon, & W.T. Stokes (Eds.), *Mentoring the mentor: A critical dialogue with Paulo Freire* (pp. 303–329). New York, NY: Peter Lang.
Freire, P. (1998a). *Pedagogy of freedom: Ethics, democracy, and civic courage.* Lanham, MD: Rowman & Littlefield.
Freire, P. (1998b). *Politics and education.* Los Angeles, CA: UCLA Latin American Center Publications.
Freire, P. (1998c). *Teachers as cultural workers: Letters to those who dare teach.* Boulder, CO: Westview Press.
Freire, P. (2004). *Pedagogy of indignation.* Boulder, CO: Paradigm.
Freire, P. (2007). *Daring to dream.* Boulder, CO: Paradigm.
Freire, P., & Faundez, A. (1989). *Learning to question: A pedagogy of liberation.* Geneva, Switzerland: World Council of Churches.
Freire, P., & Macedo, D. (1987). *Literacy: Reading the word and the world.* London, England: Routledge.
Freire, P., & Macedo, D. (1993). A dialogue with Paulo Freire. In P. McLaren & P. Leonard (Eds.), *Paulo Freire: A critical encounter* (pp. 169–176). London, England: Routledge.
Freire, P., & Macedo, D. (1995). A dialogue: Culture, language, and race. *Harvard Educational Review, 65*(3), 377–402.
Freire, P., & Shor, I. (1987). *A pedagogy for liberation.* London, England: Macmillan.
Gadamer, H-G. (2004). *Truth and method* (J. Weinsheimer & D.G. Marshall, Trans.). London, England: Continuum.
Hayek, F. (1944). *The road to serfdom.* London, England: Routledge & Kegan Paul.
Heidegger, M. (1977). *The question concerning technology and other essays* (W. Lovitt, Trans.). New York, NY: Harper & Row.

Horton, M., & Freire, P. (1990). *We make the road by walking: Conversations on education and social change.* Philadelphia, PA: Temple University Press.

Iiyoshi, T., & Kumar, M. S. V. (Eds.). (2008). *Opening up education.* Cambridge, MA: MIT Press.

Jaspers, K. (1965). *Nietzsche: An introduction to the understanding of his philosophical activity* (C. F. Wallraff & F. J. Schmitz, Trans.). Tucson: University of Arizona Press.

Lao Tzu. (1963). *Tao te ching* (D. C. Lau, Trans.). London, England: Penguin.

MacIntyre, A. (2007). *After virtue* (3rd ed.). Notre Dame, IN: University of Notre Dame Press.

Mayo, P. (1999). *Gramsci, Freire and adult education: Possibilities for transformative action.* London, England: Zed Books.

McMahon, C. (1990). Openness. *Canadian Journal of Philosophy, 20*(1), 29–46.

Miller, G. D. (1996). Open-mindedness and muddled minds: Fusion in confusion. *The Journal of Value Inquiry, 30*, 63–80.

Nietzsche, F. (1968). *The will to power* (W. Kaufmann, Trans., W. Kaufman & R. J. Hollingdale, Eds.). New York, NY: Vintage Books. (Original work published 1901)

Nietzsche, F. (1976). *Thus spoke Zarathustra.* In W. Kaufmann (Ed.), *The portable Nietzsche* (pp. 103–439). Harmondsworth, England: Penguin. (Original work published 1883–1892)

Nietzsche, F. (1989). *On the genealogy of morals* and *Ecce homo* (W. Kaufmann, Trans.). New York: Vintage Books. (Original works published 1887 and 1908)

Nietzsche, F. (1990). *Beyond good and evil* (Rev. ed.) (R. J. Hollingdale, Trans.). Harmondsworth, England: Penguin. (Original work published 1886)

Nussbaum, M. (1990). *Love's knowledge: Essays on philosophy and literature.* New York, NY: Oxford University Press.

Peters, M.A., & Roberts, P. (2011). *The virtues of openness: Education, science, and scholarship in the digital age.* Boulder, CO: Paradigm.

Popper, K. (1974). *The open society and its enemies* (5th ed., Vols. 1 & 2) London, England: Routledge & Kegan Paul.

Riggs, W. (2010). Open-mindedness. *Metaphilosophy, 41*(1/2), 172–188.

Roberts, P. (2000). *Education, literacy, and humanization: Exploring the work of Paulo Freire.* Westport, CT: Bergin & Garvey.

Roberts, P. (2003). Epistemology, ethics and education: Addressing dilemmas of difference in the work of Paulo Freire. *Studies in Philosophy of Education, 22*(2), 157–173.

Roberts, P. (2008). Liberation, oppression and education: Extending Freirean ideas. *Journal of Educational Thought, 42*(1), 83–97.

Roberts, P. (2010). *Paulo Freire in the 21st century: Education, dialogue and transformation.* Boulder, CO: Paradigm.

Rorty, R. (1980). *Philosophy and the mirror of nature.* Princeton, NJ: Princeton University Press.

Rorty, R. (1989). *Contingency, irony, and solidarity.* Cambridge, England: Cambridge University Press.

Salamun, K. (1988). Moral implications of Karl Jaspers' existentialism. *Philosophy and Phenomenological Research, 49*(2), 317–323.

Salamun, K. (1990). The ethos of humanity in Karl Jaspers' political philosophy. *Man and World, 23*, 225–230.

Steutel, J., & Spiecker, B. (1997). Rational passions and intellectual virtues: A conceptual analysis. *Studies in Philosophy and Education, 16*, 59–71.

Wittgenstein, L. (1958). *Philosophical investigations* (2nd ed.) (G. E. M. Anscombe, Trans.). Oxford, England: Basil Blackwell.

CHAPTER FIVE

Freeing Ourselves: An Indigenous Response to Neo colonial Dominance in Research, Classrooms, Schools, and Education Systems

RUSSELL BISHOP

INTRODUCTION

This then is the great humanistic and historical task of the oppressed: to liberate themselves and their oppressors as well. The oppressors, who oppress, exploit and rape by virtue of their power, cannot find in this power the strength to liberate either the oppressed or themselves. Only power that springs from the weakness of the oppressed will be sufficiently strong to free both.

(FREIRE, 1972, P. 21)

This chapter draws from the book *Freeing Ourselves*, published in 2011 by Sense Publishers, which draws together many previously published articles and book chapters that I have produced during the past 20 years of work in the field of indigenous education. This journey over time has led me from researching the impact of colonisation on my mother's Māori family to an appreciation of just what research in Māori contexts involves. The lessons learnt here also appealed to me, as an ex–secondary school teacher, as being a means by which we could re-theorise the marginalisation of Māori students in mainstream classrooms. From this understanding we could develop a means whereby educators could reposition themselves discursively and create caring and learning relationships within mainstream classrooms that would see Māori students benefiting from their participation in education. From these theoretical beginnings grew a large-scale classroom-based project that eventually developed into a comprehensive principle-based education reform based on theory that is now being implemented, in two different forms, in 150 secondary schools in New Zealand.[1] I have included in the text the full references to the original works that this book draws together so that the interested reader can follow up on some of the topics raised here in more detail. However, what I have attempted to produce in this chapter is not just a compilation of a series of papers, but rather a record of the development of a theoretical positioning that has grown into a project that has now begun to make a difference to Māori students' life chances.

Fundamental to this theorising and practice were the understandings promoted by Paulo Freire forty years ago, that the answers to the conditions that oppressed peoples found themselves in were not to be found in the language or epistemologies of the oppressors, but rather in that of the oppressed. This realisation was confirmed when I understood that research in Māori contexts needed to be conducted dialogically within the worldview and understandings of the people with whom I was working. This realisation also led me to understand how dialogue in its widest sense is crucial for developing a means whereby Māori students would be able to participate successfully in education.

I wish to acknowledge many of the people who have been supportive in this work during the past twenty years. The early theorising of Graham Smith who, in following Freire's notions of the essential interaction of conscientisation, resistance and praxis, developed the first iterations of what has become known as Kaupapa Māori research. Linda Smith's early work with decolonising methodologies was inspirational to developing my own understanding of how Kaupapa Māori research and pedagogy might work. Ted Glynn and Keith Ballard took on the unenviable task of teaching me the craft of being an academic and worked with me for many years. Mere Berryman then took on the task of partnering much of the work during the past decade, which has included her co-authoring many papers and books. Now I am working with many schools, their leaders, teachers, students, and communities and I can look back and see the genesis of the ideas in this book and I wish to thank them all for the parts they have played in the development of the theory and practice described in these pages.

THE CURRENT CONTEXT

The major challenge facing education in New Zealand today is the continuing social, economic, and political disparities within our nation, primarily between the descendants of the European colonisers (Pākehā) and the indigenous Māori people. Māori have higher levels of unemployment; are more likely to be employed in low-paying jobs; have much higher levels of incarceration, illness, and poverty than do the rest of the population; and are generally under-represented in the positive social and economic indicators of society. These disparities are outcomes of a process of colonisation that removed Māori control and power over their resource base, language, and culture and promoted non-Māori ways of making sense of the world.

Given a different set of relationships, we could have seen Māori people being full participants in the emerging economy and society of the new nation, instead of being marginalised and minoritised, a process of colonisation that has resulted in Māori being over-represented in the negative indices of society, and under-represented in the positive (Bishop & Glynn, 1999; Walker, 1990). As Colin James (2008) wrote recently in a *New Zealand Herald* column titled "Nation's Duty to Protect Vulnerable":

> Iwi and hapū were protected in theory by the Treaty of Waitangi. Māori were made equal 'subjects' (citizens). In fact, they were largely dispossessed of their assets, their culture and their self-respect. It wasn't genocide but it crushed morale. Hapū and whānau were less able to ensure their members' welfare. In part the gang violence can be traced to that dispossession and demoralisation. In short, Governments here for 140 years failed the 'responsibility to protect' test for a large and distinguishable minority of our citizens. Only with the initiation of the Treaty of Waitangi process of truth and reconciliation and compensation a generation ago have governments recognised this past failure and attended to it…. Rebuilding assets and morale is a multi-generation task…[and indicates] the paramount necessity [for the state] to invest well in our children,…reversing the demoralisation of iwi is a demanding project, this responsibility to protect.

The necessity to invest well in our children was also the subject of a recent report to Parliament, *Inquiry Into Making the Schooling System Work for Every Child*, by the Education and Science Committee of the House of Representatives (2008). In their report, they point to the part education should play in addressing disparities in terms of the impact on Māori as a people, and as people expected to contribute to the nation. They pointed out that because Māori represent 28% of newborn New Zealanders, the increasing proportion of Māori in the population means that unless "the gap between the performance of Māori students and others is not addressed, the negative consequences for New Zealand will grow exponentially" (p. 10). Professor Mason Durie (1994) is quoted as saying that "until the disparity in Māori achievement is corrected, Māori will continue to feature disproportionately in indicators of poor outcomes, *and will be a wasted resource for New Zealand*" (p. 10, emphasis added). In other words, impact on society is seen as the result of a strong "connection between non-engagement with school and youth offending" (p. 11) and

> as employment becomes less labour-intensive, and more dependent on the use of technology, fewer jobs will be available for those who lack functional literacy and numeracy.

The larger the group, the more difficult will it be for New Zealand to create and sustain a high-performing, internationally competitive economy. (p. 11)

The Education Counts website[2] also identifies a substantial body of evidence demonstrating that students who are not well served by the education system are heavily disadvantaged later in life, in terms of their earning and employment potential and their health and wellbeing. For example, those with higher levels of education are more likely to participate in the labour market, face lower risks of unemployment, have greater access to further training and receive higher earnings on average. Conversely, people with no formal school qualifications have unemployment rates far exceeding those with qualifications, and have the lowest median incomes:

> In 2006, the unemployment rate for those with a bachelor's degree or higher was 2.1 percent; for those with another tertiary qualification 2.9 percent; with only a school qualification 4.1 percent; and with no qualification 5.2 percent.... The median weekly income for those with bachelors' and higher degrees was $785; for those with other tertiary qualifications it was $575; for those with school qualifications it was $335; and for those with no qualifications $310. (Education and Science Committee, 2008, pp. 10–11)

The Education Counts website also contends that young people leaving school without any qualifications may have difficulty performing in the workforce and may face difficulties in terms of lifelong learning or returning to formal study in later years. They suggest that a considerable number of research studies show a strong connection between those who leave school early and unemployment and/or lower incomes, which are in turn generally related to poverty and dependence on income support.

In his submission to the Education and Science Committee (cited above), Judge Andrew Becroft, the Principal Youth Court Judge, estimated that up to 80% of offenders in the Youth Court are not attending school, either because they are not enrolled or because they are suspended or excluded. He continued by suggesting that between 25% and 30% of youth offences takes place between 9:00 a.m. and 3:00 p.m. Judge Becroft proposed that "engaging all young people of compulsory school age in education would reduce the crime rate among this group significantly" (Education and Science Committee, p. 11).

In terms of offending, the report noted that young Māori offend at twice the rate of young Pasifika people and at four times the rate of young Pākehā, and in the experience of Judge Becroft, failure at school contributes to the establishment of a vicious circle that leads to recidivist offending. The Ministry of Social Development also presented evidence that gaining stable employment helps young offenders to desist from offending, particularly if their jobs offer learning opportunities. However, "students who fail at school clearly have less chance of obtaining such employment" (Education and Science Committee, pp. 10–11). The educational disparities that afflict Māori are stark. The overall academic achievement levels of Māori students are low; more leave school without any qualifications than do their non-Māori counterparts; their retention rate to age 17 is far less than that for non-Māori; their rate of suspension from school is three to five times higher, depending on gender; they are over-represented in special education programmes for behavioural issues; they enrol in preschool programmes in lower proportions than do other groups; they tend to be over-represented in low-stream education classes; they receive less academic feedback than do children of the majority culture; they are more likely than other students to be found in vocational curriculum streams; they leave school earlier, with fewer formal qualifications; and they enrol in tertiary education in lower proportions (Hood, 2008; Ministry of Education, 2005). Further, while these outcomes are most clearly exhibited in secondary schools, the foundations for these problems commence in the primary school years. Indeed there are indications (Crooks, Hamilton, & Caygill, 2000; Wylie, Thompson, & Lythe, 1999) that while there are achievement differentials evident on children entering primary school, it is by years 4 and 5 that these achievement differentials begin to stand out starkly.

Despite the choice provided by Māori-medium education in New Zealand,[3] the vast majority of Māori students attend public/mainstream schools and are taught by non-Māori teachers who have problems relating to and addressing the educational needs of Māori students (Bishop & Berryman, 2006). In addition, decades of educational reforms and policies such as integration, multiculturalism, and biculturalism have failed to provide adequate support for teachers to address systemic shortcomings and models of reform based on deficiencies of the home in terms of literacy resources (Nash, 1993). More recently, neuro-philosophy claims about the deficiencies of the brain (Clark, 2006) have done little to alleviate the situation. These reforms have made very little difference for the large proportion of Māori students who have attended mainstream schools since these educational disparities were first statistically identified more than forty years ago (Hunn, 1960).

Addressing these educational disparities is a difficult, yet necessary, task for educators at all levels within our system. Most countries that have diverse ethnic student populations will attest to this fact, for this is where educational disparities really show themselves: among the marginalised and minoritised peoples within mainstream educational settings.

KAUPAPA MĀORI RESPONSES

The book *Freeing Ourselves* looks at three examples of how an indigenous people have freed themselves from neo colonial oppression in a way that also suggests how other minoritised peoples can similarly liberate themselves. The book also highlights how such an approach has redirected the actions of the oppressors to discursively reposition themselves through an ongoing process of conscientisation in relation to the representations of Māori as a minoritised group.

Although the book primarily focuses on addressing educational disparities in mainstream/public school settings, the first example examines an indigenous initiative in research within Aotearoa/New Zealand termed Kaupapa (agenda/ philosophy) Māori research. I commenced this project in 1990 as part of a group of people led by Graham and Linda Smith who were developing a means of wresting control over what constituted research into Māori people's lives away from the dominance of the traditional academy. This work has been through many iterations but it is fundamental to the study of addressing educational disparities because if sense-making and knowledge-producing processes remain in the control of the dominant group, what Scheurich and Young (1997) term epistemological racism is maintained; this is where the social history of the dominant group in society is used to produce solutions for those dominated. Hence, freeing ourselves from neo colonial dominance becomes of primary importance in research so that models of reform for the oppressed groups can be developed from within the epistemological frameworks of those groups rather than from within the dominant epistemology. Recent studies conducted within Māori contexts serve to illustrate this process. This agenda for research is concerned with how research practice might realise Māori desires for self-determination while addressing ongoing research issues of Initiation, Benefits, Representation, Legitimacy and Accountability (IBRLA).

Research such as this suggests that it is the cultural aspirations, understandings, and practices of Māori people that implement and organise the research process and positions researchers in such a way as to operationalise self-determination (agentic positioning and behaviour) for research participants. The cultural context positions the participants by constructing the story lines, and with them the cultural metaphors and images, as well as the "thinking as usual," the talk/ language through which research participation and researcher/researched relationships are constituted. Kaupapa Māori research rejects outsider control over what constitutes the text's call for authority and truth. A Kaupapa Māori position therefore promotes what Lincoln and Denzin (1994) term an epistemological version of validity. Such an approach to validity locates the power within Māori cultural practices where what is acceptable and what is not acceptable research is determined and defined by the research community itself.

The second example in *Freeing Ourselves* addresses the situation in New Zealand where, despite decades of educational reform, there has been little if any shift in the educational disparities that afflict the large proportion of Māori students who attend mainstream/public schools. In contexts such as these, one must consider how theories and models of reform that draw from relational discourses, that are fundamental to indigenous people's epistemologies, may provide sufficient conditions for education reform. I commenced one such project in the late 1990s when considering education reform, from the theoretical position of Kaupapa Māori research, and making an examination of appropriate Māori cultural metaphors used in Māori medium schooling. I developed a model whereby educators could create learning contexts within their classrooms that would allow Māori students to bring their own sense-making processes into the classroom, where what they knew was legitimate and not marginalised. This model suggested that teachers needed to develop pedagogic relationships and interactions: where power is shared between self-determining individuals within non-dominating relations of interdependence; where culture counts; where learning is interactive, dialogic and spiraled; where participants are connected to one another through the establishment of a common vision for what constitutes excellence in educational outcomes. This pedagogy has since been developed further and termed a Culturally Responsive Pedagogy of Relations, which is in Freirean terms a "Pedagogy of Hope."

I was then fortunate enough to attract funding that provided me with the opportunity to examine what a culturally responsive pedagogy of relations might look like in practice. In 2001, we began a professional development project for teachers that eventually grew in to what is now called Te Kotahitanga, which is now a large-scale project that aims to improve the educational achievement of Māori students in mainstream/public schools (Bishop, Berryman, Powell, & Teddy, 2005; Bishop, Berryman, Tiakiwai, & Richardson, 2003).

The project commenced in 2001, seeking and sought to address the self-determination of Māori secondary school students by talking with them and others participating in their education about just what is involved in limiting and /or improving their educational achievement through an examination of the main influences on Māori students' educational achievement. The project sought to examine how a number of groups might address this issue and commenced with the gathering of a number of narratives of students' classroom experiences and meanings by the process of collaborative storying (Bishop, 1996) from a range of engaged and non-engaged Māori students (as defined by their schools), in five non-structurally modified mainstream secondary schools. These stories were also complemented by the gathering of stories of experience and meaning from those parenting these students, their principals, and their teachers. Since then the project has grown, and is now being implemented in fifty secondary schools in New Zealand where there is evidence of very acceptable changes in the schooling experiences and outcomes for Māori students (Bishop, Berryman, Cavanagh, & Teddy, 2007, 2009).

It is clear from working with teachers' attempts to address educational disparities in their own classrooms that what is effective for Māori is effective for other minoritised students. This understanding has major implications for what many educators are identifying as the most pressing problem facing us in education today. That problem is the interaction between increasingly diverse student populations and the associated persistent pattern of educational disparities affecting indigenous peoples and populations of colour, poverty, different abilities, and new migrants. This problem is exacerbated by the continuing lack of diversity among the teaching force who demonstrate discursive positionings and pedagogic practices more appropriate to monocultural populations.

The third example in *Freeing Ourselves* is about developing a model for freeing public schools and the education system that supports them from neo-colonial dominance by scaling up, that is, extending and sustaining effective, indigenous/minoritised-based education reform as opposed to education reform that is based on dominant group understandings. Scaling up such education reform has the potential to have a major impact on the disparities that exist in society, because deepening and expanding the benefits of effective education reform programmes will change the status quo of historical, ongoing, and seemingly immutable disparities. Nevertheless, I am not claiming that educational reform on its own can cure historical disparities; however, it is clear that educational reform can play a major part in a comprehensive approach to addressing social, economic, and political disparities.

Current approaches to scaling up educational reform have not worked for indigenous and other minoritised students. Most attempts are short term, poorly funded at the outset, and often abandoned before any real changes can be seen, soon to be replaced by some "bold new initiative." In contrast, the model identified in this chapter suggests that educational reforms need to have built into them, from the very outset, those elements that will see them sustained in the original sites and spread to others. These elements will allow educational reforms to be scaled up with the confidence that the reform will not only be able to be sustained in existing and new sites, but that, above all, will also work to reduce disparities and realise the potential of those students currently not well served by education. Put simply, educational reforms that can be sustained and extended can have an impact on educational and social disparities through increasing the educational opportunities for students previously denied these options, on a scale currently not available in most Western countries.

Again, I am fortunate that, with a group of colleagues, which this time includes those from another institution, Te Whare Wānanga o Awanuiārangi, a Māori tribal university, we have been able to attract sufficient funds to support one hundred secondary schools to implement this model as a means of moving their institutions toward being responsive to Māori students' learning needs.

So overall, *Freeing Ourselves* records the development of a means where, just as Paulo Freire predicted it should, educational reform has grown out of the power of the oppressed. It commenced by our initially wresting control over what constitutes research into Māori people's lives from the dominant groups. It then meant that we could use this control to establish professional development for teachers that makes sense to Māori students and not just to the teachers (although that happens as well), and then designing a model to expand this process to a large number of sites in New Zealand.

ACKNOWLEDGMENT

This chapter has been previously published as the Introduction to Russell Bishop's 2011 book, *Freeing Ourselves* (Rotterdam, The Netherlands: Sense Publishers) and has been edited by Mere Berryman. It formed the basis of Russell's keynote address at the Freire: The Global Legacy conference in Hamilton, New Zealand, November 2012, and here it appears with the kind permission of Peter de Liefde, Founder and Owner of Sense Publishers.

NOTES

1. There are approximately 320 secondary schools in New Zealand.
2. This is the Ministry of Education website: https://www.educationcounts.govt.nz/. Its aim is to increase the availability and accessibility of information about education statistics and research in New Zealand via this website.
3. Adrienne Alton-Lee (2007, 2008) provides us with evidence that students in Māori-medium classrooms are achieving at higher rates than their contemporaries in mainstream schools.

REFERENCES

Alton-Lee, A. (2007). The Iterative Best Evidence Synthesis Programme, New Zealand. In *Evidence in education: Linking research and policy*. Paris, France: Centre for Educational Research and Innovation (OECD).

Alton-Lee, A. (2008, November). *Te Kotahitanga using research and development (R & D) to make a much bigger difference for our children and our society*. Keynote address presented at the inaugural Te Kotahitanga Voices conference, University of Waikato, Hamilton, New Zealand.

Bishop, R. (1996). *Collaborative research stories: Whakawhanaungatanga*. Palmerston North, New Zealand: Dunmore Press.

Bishop, R. (2011). *Freeing ourselves*. Rotterdam, The Netherlands: Sense Publishers.

Bishop, R., & Berryman, M. (2006). *Culture speaks: Cultural relationships and classroom learning*. Wellington, New Zealand: Huia Publishers.

Bishop, R., Berryman, M., Cavanagh, T., & Teddy, L. (2007). *Te Kotahitanga Phase 3 whanaungatanga: Establishing a culturally responsive pedagogy of relations in mainstream secondary school classrooms*. Wellington, New Zealand: Ministry of Education.

Bishop, R., Berryman, M., Cavanagh, T., & Teddy, L. (2009). Te Kotahitanga: Addressing educational disparities facing Maori students in New Zealand. *Teaching and Teacher Education, 25,* 734–742.

Bishop, R., Berryman, M., Cavanagh, T., Teddy, L., & Clapham, S. (2005). *Te Kotahitanga: Phase III: Whanaungatanga. Improving the educational achievement of Maori students in mainstream schools.* Wellington, New Zealand: Ministry of Education.

Bishop, R., Berryman, M., Powell, A., & Teddy, L. (2005) *Te Kotahitanga: Improving the educational achievement of Māori students in mainstream education Phase 2: Towards a whole school approach.* Wellington, New Zealand: Ministry of Education.

Bishop, R., Berryman, M., Tiakiwai, S., & Richardson, C. (2003). *Te Kotahitanga: The experiences of year 9 and 10 Maori students in mainstream classrooms.* Wellington, New Zealand: Ministry of Education.

Bishop, R., & Glynn, T. (1999). *Culture counts: Changing power relations in education.* Palmerston North, New Zealand: Dunmore Press.

Clark, J. A. (2006). The gap between the highest and lowest school achievers: Philosophical arguments for downplaying teacher expectation theory. *New Zealand Journal of Educational Studies, 41*(2), 367–382.

Crooks, T., Hamilton, K., & Caygill, R. (2000). *New Zealand's national education monitoring project: Maori student achievement, 1995–2000* [Electronic version]. Retrieved May 9, 2007, from http://nemp.otago.ac.nz/i_probe.htm

Durie, M. (1994) *Whaiora: Maori health development.* Oxford, UK: Oxford University Press.

Education and Science Committee. (2008). *Inquiry into making the school system work for every child* (I.2A). Retrieved December 23, 2008, from http://www.parliament.nz/en-NZ/SC/Reports/7/f/3/48DBSCH_SCR3979_1-Inquiry-into-making-the-school-system-work-for.htm

Freire, P. (1972). *Pedagogy of the oppressed.* New York, NY: Herder & Herder.

Hood, D. (2008). *Statistical analysis of Maori students' participation and achievement data.* Unpublished paper.

Hunn, J. (1960). *Report on Department of Maori Affairs.* Wellington, New Zealand: Department of Maori Affairs.

James, C. (2008, July 1). Nation's duty to protect vulnerable. *New Zealand Herald.* Retrieved December 23, 2008, from http://www.nzherald.co.nz/colin-james/news/article.cfm?a_id=338&objected=10519201/

Lincoln, Y. S., & Denzin, N. K. (1994). The fifth moment. In N. K. Denzin & Y. S. Lincoln (Eds.), *Handbook of qualitative research* (pp. 575–586). Thousand Oaks, CA: Sage.

Ministry of Education. (2005). *Making a bigger difference for all students: Hangaia he huarahi hei whakarewa ake i ngā tauira katoa. Schooling Strategy 2005–2010.* Wellington, New Zealand: Ministry of Education.

Nash, R. (1993). *Succeeding generations: Family resources and access to education in New Zealand.* Auckland, New Zealand: Oxford University Press.

Scheurich, J. J., & Young, M. D. (1997). Coloring epistemologies: Are our research epistemologies racially biased? *Educational Researcher, 26*(4), 4–16.

Walker, R. (1990). *Ka whawhai tonu matou: Struggle without end.* Auckland, New Zealand: Penguin.

Wylie, C., Thompson, J., & Lythe, C. (1999). *Competent children at 8: Families, early education, and schools.* Wellington, New Zealand: New Zealand Council for Educational Research.

CHAPTER SIX

Humanization in Decolonizing Educational Research: A Tree of Life Metaphor

RENEE BAYNES

The Tree of Life is an ancient motif that appears in many cultures and religions. The Tree is symbolic of the interconnected nature of our world(s) and is often used as a reminder of the sacredness of life and its connection to the earth. This chapter uses the metaphor of the Tree of Life to explore the methodology of Participatory Action Research in a decolonizing educational project. A group of science teachers explored the possibilities of the mandated inclusion of Aboriginal and Torres Strait Islander Histories and Cultures in the new national Australian Curriculum. The chapter connects Freirean ideas of *conscientizção* and humanization through the processes explored by the teachers and the educational outcomes sought. The importance of nourishment, protection, and interconnectedness related to the Tree of Life is explored in this context.

INTRODUCTION

Through the process of my doctoral work I spent much time musing on the methodology of Participatory Action Research (PAR) and searching for a way of representing my work that could relate to both critical and indigenous[1] understandings. From the perspectives of both the critical tradition and indigenous methodologies, the theme of interconnectedness was one that recurred throughout my reading of theoretical underpinnings. More than this, interconnectedness was a theme through the work itself, manifesting in unexpected and serendipitous ways. In some Australian Aboriginal understandings, it was explained to me by a Kamilaroi woman that serendipity and intuition are intertwined (D. Moodie, personal communication, September 1, 2011). If a person is "on the right track," connected to country and listening to her or his intuition, serendipitous things would happen. This conversation led me to think of the fortunate and unexpected events that happened in the PAR journey as more than just mere coincidence. Trying to represent my newfound understanding of the methodology in a scholarly way became difficult. I was searching for a way of representing ideas quite separate from white Western epistemology. As a white researcher, this was a particular challenge.

It was at this juncture (serendipitously perhaps) that I picked up my volume of *Native Science* (Cajete, 2000) and re-read some chapters. In this book, I found a Native American description of the Tree of Life. In the cyclical development of the teachings of the Tree I found a parallel to the personal and professional development of myself as a researcher/participant and the teacher participants of my PAR project. The cycles within cycles, interconnectedness, and growth of the Tree of Life drew together the purpose and critical intent of the project. In this chapter I develop the Tree of Life metaphor for PAR and link the critical intent to a decolonizing educational research from a Freirean perspective.

THE TREE OF LIFE

The motif of the Tree of Life appears prominently in cultures around the world. The symbol is usually understood as a representation of the interconnectedness of life and the spiritual and physical worlds (Cook, 1974). The Tree is a metaphor for the cycles of renewal and dynamic creativity that has acquired a permanent significance and adaptability in changing worldviews, theological systems and ideologies (James, 1966). Tree metaphors are often also used in Western traditions of knowledge and truth. The Tree of Life metaphor seems to be in contrast to rationalist scientific thought. The eighteenth century saw Enlightenment thinking give credence to only two realms of experience, reason and sensory perception, giving no room for the recognition of imagination and non-physical realms (Cook, 1974). The scientific primacy placed on empirical, measurable cause and effect data marginalizes the idea of situated, interpretive, multiple realities as "soft" research (at best) (Semali & Kincheloe, 1999). Rather than a structural approach to a tree metaphor as might be found in the scientific tradition, the Tree of Life recognizes more than physical, measurable sensations as sources of information, also acknowledging intuition and inspiration.

Cajete (2000) describes the teachings of the Tree of Life as a "metaphor for life, healing, vision and transformation" (p. 285). Central to the teachings of the

Tree are four great human development stages, which bring forth the key meanings and teachings of the Tree:

> Through an understanding of "protection" (the shade of the Tree), we come to see how the Earth provides for human life and well-being. In understanding the nature of "nourishment" (the fruit of the Tree), we come to see what we need to grow, to live a good life. We come to understand how we are nourished through the relationships we have at all levels of our nature and from all other sources that share life with us. We also come to know that as we are nourished, so must we nourish others in return. As a tree grows through different stages—from seed to sapling, to mature tree, and to old tree—we see that growth and change are the key dynamics to life. We also learn that growth and change reflect self-determination, movement toward our true potential through the trials and tribulations, the "weather of our lives." "Wholeness" is the finding and reflection of the face, heart, and foundation through which our lives become a conscious part of a greater whole, of part of a life process rooted to a larger past, present and future ecology of the mind and spirit. (p. 286)

In linking the description by Cajete to my work with Aboriginal and Torres Strait Islander knowledges, I spoke with one of my cultural consultants about Aboriginal understandings of the Tree of Life. As a Ngarrindjeri man, he told me a story he'd recently adapted for a primary school student play:

> There was once an old Goanna Lady who was a healer. She moved from tribe to tribe using her medicine to help people. By making her way between nations she brought the people together and gave them a common connection. When she died a medicine tree grew in the place where she was buried. The Goanna lady's tree continued to bring together the nations and provided a place of healing. (D. Nikkelson, personal communication, March 30, 2011)

Again, the theme of interconnectedness comes to the fore. There are several parallels in this Indigenous Australian understanding to the Native American representation of the Tree above. Through her healing knowledge and status as a healer the Goanna Lady connected to country and to people in a way that promoted peace. The Goanna Lady's tree provided a place of nourishment and protection for future generations. Growth and stages of life are present through the representation of age and death. There is also renewal through the continuation of the Goanna Lady's healing provided by the tree that grew where she was buried. Interconnectedness is present through all of these metaphors in terms of healing, country, and people.

In recognizing the similarities between the narratives of the Tree, while acknowledging the differences and not essentializing indigenous knowledge, the adoption of a metaphor of life, healing, vision, and transformation fitted with my own understandings of my PAR methodology, the personal and professional growth of myself and the other project participants, as well as our critical intent in working within the study.

THE RESEARCH STUDY

The research project described in this chapter aimed to illuminate the intellectual, epistemological and pragmatic processes that teachers undertake when engaging with indigenous knowledges in science classrooms. The focus of the research was engagement of epistemologies and content outside of Western modern science traditions and the sense teachers made of these alternate ways of knowing in the context of science education. The methodology aimed to highlight the relationship between this (re)conceptualization of science education and teacher praxis. The implementation of the new Australian Curriculum provided an impetus for the inclusion of different cultural understandings (and specifically Indigenous Australian understandings), of science (Australian Curriculum Assessment and Reporting Authority, 2011).

I was the researcher/participant, and six mostly secondary school–based science teachers were part of the research group. All participants except one identified as white Australians, with the other participant identifying as a Murri person (Queensland Indigenous person). Although the research project began with six participants, owing to external factors such as teacher transfer and additional workloads gained during the project, not all participants were contributing by the project's conclusion. For the purposes of this chapter, data have been taken only from those who participated in the entire project.

In total four PAR cycles were completed. In the first cycle the group members considered what they wanted to achieve through the project and set some goals to work toward. The second cycle saw consideration of where the group saw indigenous knowledges fitting within the curriculum and discipline areas of science that they needed to teach. The third cycle saw the remaining participants implementing their teaching plans in the classroom, while the fourth cycle considered ways of moving forward with their pedagogical praxis. Data were collected in the form of recordings and resulting transcripts from group meetings and individual discussions with the participants, documentary evidence of lessons/units planned and classroom observation of teaching. This chapter draws on a small subset of the larger data pool of the research project, focusing on group meetings and individual discussions.

The choice of a PAR methodology allowed the teachers involved in the project to connect theory and practice to collectively (re)create knowledge (Kemmis, 1981; Kemmis & McTaggart, 2005; McIntyre, 2008). The cyclical process of PAR is one of continual reflection and action involving collaboration between participants in the research (Griffiths, 2009). The choice of PAR as a method and the strategies for data collection and analysis were reflective of a critical research perspective. The methodology showed a concern for locating the project within the social and political landscape, seeking emancipatory outcomes and reflected a concern with praxis. The underlying tenets of PAR as applied in the project can be described as a collective commitment to investigate an issue; a desire to engage in individual and collective action leading to a useful solution that benefits the people involved; and the building of alliances between the researcher and the participants in the planning, implementation, and dissemination of the research process (McIntyre, 2008). As knowledge is collectively generated, it was hoped that the practices that emerged from the PAR process would be aligned with teachers' pedagogies and promote a lasting opportunity for changes in practice.

The theoretical frameworks often identified as underpinning PAR were congruent with the critical concerns of the project. Critical theory has contributed to PAR through the examination of social, political, and economic structures that influence the social participation of individuals and their practice (Kemmis, 2008; McIntyre, 2008). The idea of *conscientização* (Freire, 1989), developing a critical consciousness, is inherent in the reflexive and social nature of the PAR process. Freire recognized the role of praxis as action in and reflection on the world in order to change it (Freire, 2009). The critical self-inquiry and reflection processes of PAR and the importance of these for effecting social change has been recognized by practitioners of PAR as drawing on Freire's work (Fals Borda & Rahman, 1991; Herr & Anderson, 2005; McIntyre, 2008).

PAR AND INDIGENOUS METHODOLOGIES

Because the research project was working with both Indigenous and non-Indigenous people and engaging with indigenous ways of knowing and being, I selected a method that could be deployed recognizing the cultural sensitivities inherent in the topic. I was conscious of the power differentials between indigenous knowledges and Western scientific knowledges as well as the potential for me as a white researcher to be seen as appropriating indigenous ways of knowing. As Semali and Kincheloe (1999) warn, it is important that Western people do not speak and act for indigenous people and that indigenous people form allies outside their local communities.

This project was formed with a focus on relationships and collaborative thought, action, and generation of knowledge. As Brydon-Miller, Kral, Maguire, Noffke, and Sabhlok (2013) highlight,

> PAR is in keeping with Indigenous cosmologies where relationships are at the center, a form of research that is "evaluated by participant-driven criteria" (Denzin and Lincoln, 2008, p. 11). It is a decolonizing of methods of academia, a political stance in the redistribution of power with a focus on sharing and mutual respect. (p. 395)

Indigenous methodologies can be described as research by and for Indigenous people. Writing from a Maori standpoint, Smith (2012) emphasizes the importance of building trust in relationships within indigenous methodologies. Important questions around the researcher's intent are highlighted: *Who owns the research? Who will benefit?* and *How will the results be disseminated?* Smith sees these questions as part of larger judgments that indigenous communities make surrounding the researcher, in which questions such as *Does he/she have a good heart? What baggage do they carry?* and *Can they actually do anything?* (p. 10) are equally important. As the researcher in this project, I was always conscious of these types of questions as critiques of my methodology from an indigenous standpoint.

There is an intersection between most critically based PAR projects and indigenous methodologies in that both seek to critique the notion of the unproblematic creation of scientific knowledge. The frameworks employed by PAR can complement indigenous methodologies through challenging the positivist scientific positions of objectivism and neutrality (Shiva, 1997). In the case of this project, indigenous methodological stances informed the PAR process, in particular through my critical theory/pedagogy lens and engagement with the importance of reciprocity in relationships.

Freirean ideas have been used in indigenous methodologies as well as with PAR. Freire's theory of conscientization (Freire, 2009), "his belief in critical reflection as essential for individual and social change, and his commitment to the democratic dialectical unification of theory and practice have contributed significantly to the field of participatory action research" (McIntyre, 2008, p. 3). Similarly, Freire's development of counter-hegemonic approaches to knowledge construction within oppressed communities has informed many of the strategies practitioners use in PAR projects (McIntyre, 2008). Conscientization is also part of some indigenous methodologies; for example, Smith (2012) draws on Freire's thoughts around "naming the world" and the power that this gives to hegemonic groups in knowledge claims to suggest the Indigenous project of *Naming* to (re)name the landscape with indigenous names. Here the possibilities of synergies between indigenous methodologies and PAR emerge: both are aiming for a critical consciousness in analyzing the legitimacy and power of knowledge.

A TREE OF LIFE METAPHOR FOR THIS PROJECT

Protection—The shade of the Tree

Freire described the banking model of education as the act of a teacher making deposits of information that the students receive passively; he articulated this as an exercise of domination, indoctrinating the oppressed into the world of oppression (Freire, 2009). In the project described here, the teachers attempted to free themselves of the indoctrinating ways of schooling, while still acting within the prescribed system, to provide a liberating experience for their classes and themselves as educators. In providing a pedagogical space for well-being and growth, they were acting in the shade of the Tree, recognizing the need for human life and well-being.

Through expressions of alienation and domination, dehumanization takes place (Freire, 1970). In working to reduce the alienation of the Other, as indigenous cultures in the colonized world are still seen, the work was very much a humanizing and decolonial project. The process of working toward a pedagogy that was humanizing and liberating had the effect of promoting conscientization in the teachers themselves. In actively opposing oppression in their own praxis, the teachers advanced in terms of human becoming as they more clearly began to see the oppressive ways of the curriculum and their peers around them and actively engaged in promoting change. As Freire observed, "Liberation can not exist within men's consciousness, isolated from the world; it exists in the praxis of men" (Freire, 1970, p. 3).

In challenging the status quo of marginalization of indigenous ways of knowing within the scientific frame, the teachers promoted an educative space in which indigenous knowledge was seen as synergistic with Western scientific ideas. Freire, speaking of the humanist revolutionary educator, said of the teacher that "from the outset, her efforts must coincide with those of the students to engage in critical thinking and the process of mutual humanisation" (Freire, 2009, p. 75)

One of the teacher participants in the project, Cristy, told us of her experience in approaching the resistance some students had to seeing how indigenous knowledge could be science and the impact of presenting indigenous knowledge in the science classroom.

> Aboriginal and indigenous knowledges and perspectives, "how is this science?," but that was the perfect way of promoting that this is science and that we can work together, irrespective of where we come from and what we bring to the table, to pass on knowledge and critical thinking.

Nourishment—the fruit of the Tree

In understanding what is needed for growth and promotion of a good life in terms of nourishment of the Tree, all participants, including me, thrived on the successes of the teachers in the classroom. For teacher participant Cristy, nourishment came through having one Aboriginal student actively involved in the teaching of a physics unit, incorporating didgeridoo playing and the sharing of his family's knowledge of traditional hunting and food gathering. She noted:

That was just so, so empowering for him but also for the other students as well because they were asking him questions. It was such an interactive lesson that—and the boys all responded so positively to it—I can't imagine why this whole concept is not a good idea.

In reflecting on Cristy's experience, another teacher participant, Alan, observed:

It could be the case that this is a lot more powerful than just making [connections]—I think the idea of recognition of value in other people's cultures is really important, recognition of Indigenous people [having] a long history in their countryside, in the land and what they have to offer is pretty big. The ability for our Indigenous students to say, well this is how this works and then use the science vocab to describe it, I think that was—I think for someone to do that, that's showing that they've thought about it.

For me as the researcher/participant in the process, one of the most nourishing moments in our group discussions came when one of the teachers articulated his thoughts on the power of indigenous knowledge in the classroom to promote *conscientizção* in students:

It opens up and it makes people think, oh there's value in that and there's value in you and value in [indigenous knowledge].

Through the PAR process, teaching experiences were shared, allowing for encouragement and critical reflection to build new ways of considering praxis in terms of pedagogy and challenging the status quo. Without this nourishment from successes and from one another, the potential of the project to stall was a real danger. Initially, the project had ten teacher participants. Perhaps those who did not find the nourishment they needed in the process found it more difficult to proceed through the PAR cycles. Several participants did not proceed past the first or second cycle. The implications of challenging their own praxis and the institutional status quo may have proved too difficult for them to proceed to actual implementation in the classroom. Fears of "stepping on cultural toes" and ensuring that their other reporting and curricular commitments were met became insurmountable obstacles to classroom implementation.

Growth and Change

The idea of the growth of the Tree through the cycles of life reflects well the progress of a PAR project. The cyclical nature of PAR fosters action and critical reflection at each stage of the research process. Participants are challenged to reflect on their actions to inform their future praxis. Through this constant reflection, critical consciousness grows and potential grows from the trials and tribulations of the process. At the beginning of the project, several participants had trouble envisioning how their science teaching practice could contain indigenous knowledge and epistemologically struggled with the different ways of knowing:

> I think parts of the Indigenous knowledge, I don't even know if that's the umbrella term of what it is, but I think parts of it are scientific and parts of it are mythology which to me in my definition, in my head, that's not science. So like, I don't see how I'm going to be able to…but then I can't really just cut it, can I? Cut it in bits?

However, by the end of the second cycle, the same teacher had better reconciled Western science and indigenous knowledge and saw the potential for incorporation quite differently:

> Something that's really good that's come out of, I think, what we've been doing, is that I think I've got a more positive outlook with what I can do…. Like at the moment I'm teaching a unit that I've never taught before, which is forces, and machines and things like that. And I'm kinda kicking myself for not having thought of taking an Indigenous perspective with one of the assignments…. I've been thinking about Indigenous tools, Indigenous weapons and that stuff just fits so perfectly into looking at levers, looking at incline planes, like it would be a really, really good unit.

Similarly, one of the participants who worked within the project until its completion moved from seeing indigenous knowledges being incorporated into units in specific areas such as astronomy and geology to seeing unlimited potential:

> I think you could almost write a science book using activities based around indigenous experience.

Wholeness

The project became an ongoing exercise in decolonization and humanization for the participants. Through the *conscientizção* achieved by the teachers, their commitment to a teaching praxis that is humanizing has been stimulated and they continue to challenge institutional barriers presented to them. While the inclusion of Indigenous ways of knowing has been mandated by the new Australian Curriculum, when considering the whole of the context within their own schools, teachers have found that this may not be valued or supported. Their efforts in the project work have often been little acknowledged and in some cases dismissed. This was evident when one of the teachers had heated discussions with peers around their perceived lack of importance of the Aboriginal and Torres Strait Islander Histories and Cultures Priority in science teaching.

Resistance to the inclusion of indigenous knowledges in the science classroom was presented both actively and passively. Only two of the original group of ten teachers completed the project. The teachers' most common reason for leaving the project was time constraints owing to the job expectations placed on them. Many cited the pressures of preparing and implementing assessment and reporting structures required by the current neoliberal educational system. Teachers felt they were unable to commit the time to gaining the necessary knowledge and skills to respectfully and non-tokenistically implement their ideas in the classroom.

In some cases, resistance also came from the teachers' peers within their schools. In one instance, a unit and assessment plan written by a participant was to be implemented across a Year 8 cohort. Even though the unit had been written and resourced for all teachers to work with, one teacher refused to use it in his classes. This meant that only half the cohort experienced lessons with indigenous content.

The limitations on teachers' practice and agency within the schooling system impacted their praxis and their ability to challenge the status quo. While individual teachers promoted humanizing curriculums, the dehumanizing influences of the system were not easy to overcome. Perception of these institutional limitations and conforming pressures proved to be an important point of consciousness for the sustained motivation of participants. As Freire observed,

> The educator who chooses a humanist option, that is, a liberating one, will not be capable of carrying out the obligation bound up in the theme of his option, unless he has been able through his own *praxis* accurately to perceive the dialectical relationships between consciousness and the world or between man and the world. (1970, p. 3). (Original emphasis)

While this quite negative representation of wholeness in terms of understanding the contextual aspects of the school system was a strong theme, a positive wholeness was also inherent in the project. Linking to the idea of nourishment through the successes of the teachers, the collective knowledge generation of the PAR process provided an interconnectedness of the participants and me as a researcher/participant. Through this critical analysis of the systemic influences and historical and social forces conscientization was achieved, ensuring that there was a "reflection of the face, heart, and foundation through which our lives become a conscious part of a greater whole" (Cajete, 2000, p. 286). Participants challenged themselves to maintain their integrity of purpose in the face of the oppositions they encountered. Through future planning of activities to carry on the work of the project, such as whole school staff professional development sessions run by the teachers themselves, participants reminded themselves "of part of a life process rooted to a larger past, present and future ecology of the mind and spirit" (Cajete, 2000, p. 286)

CONCLUSION

Many critical PAR projects share a desire to be liberating and humanizing. The choice of project research area often centers on situations in which dehumanization is oppressing individuals and groups. Participants experienced liberating and humanizing research processes through considering how science teachers incorporate indigenous knowledges and ways of knowing in their teaching practice. Through recognizing the dehumanization inherent in the school system, and the potential of indigenous knowledges to humanize the learning experience for their students, they developed their own critical consciousness.

The development of the PAR process in the project could be explained through a Tree of Life metaphor. The critical consciousness developed and the motivation within the participants to effect change through their praxis reflects the idea of protection of the Tree. The cyclical nature of PAR fits well with notions of growth and change of the Tree, especially given the critical perspective used (and gained). Nourishment became particularly important to the participants in terms of celebrating the successes of the project to be able to keep moving forward. Wholeness was reflected through the recognition of the contextual and historical forces that influenced both teachers' practice and praxis.

NOTE

1. In this chapter capitalization is used to differentiate indigenous peoples and Australian Aboriginal and Torres Strait Islander peoples (Indigenous).

REFERENCES

Australian Curriculum Assessment and Reporting Authority. (2011). The Australian curriculum. Retrieved October 13, 2011, from http://www.australiancurriculum.edu.au/Home

Baynes, R. (2013). The tree of life as a methodological metaphor. In W. Midgley, K. Trimmer, & A. Davies (Eds.), *Metaphors in, for and of educational research* (pp. 145–155). Newcastle Upon Tyne, England: Cambridge Scholars.

Brydon-Miller, M., Kral, M., Maguire, P., Noffke, S. E., & Sabhlok, A. (2013). Jazz and the Banyan tree: Roots and riffs on participatory aciton research. In N. K. Denzin & Y. S. Lincoln (Eds.), *The Sage handbook of qualitative research* (4th ed.). Los Angeles, CA: Sage.

Cajete, G. (2000). *Native science natural laws of interdependence*. Santa Fe, NM: Clear Light.

Cook, R. (1974). *The tree of life: Symbol of the center*. London: Thames and Judson.

Fals Borda, O., & Rahman, M. A. (1991). *Action and knowledge: Breaking the monopoly with participatory action research*. New York, NY: Apex Press.

Freire, P. (1970). Notes on humanisation and its educational implications. Retrieved October, 16, 2013, from http://acervo.paulofreire.org/xmlui/bitstream/handle/7891/1540/FPF_OPF_09_009.pdf

Freire, P. (1989). *Learning to question a pedagogy of liberation.* New York, NY: Continuum.

Freire, P. (2009). *Pedagogy of the oppressed.* New York, NY: Continuum.

Griffiths, M. (2009). Action research for/as/mindful of social justice. In S. E. Noffke & B. Somekh (Eds.), *The Sage handbook of educational action research* (pp. 85–98). Los Angeles, CA: Sage.

Herr, K., & Anderson, G. L. (2005). *The action research dissertation: A guide for students and faculty.* Thousand Oaks, CA: Sage.

James, B. O. (1966). *The tree of life.* Leiden, Netherlands: E. J. Brill.

Kemmis, S. (1981). Introduction. In Deakin University School of Education. Open Campus Program (Ed.), *The action research reader.* Warun Ponds, Victoria, Australia: Deakin University, Open Campus Program.

Kemmis, S. (2008). Critical theory and participatory action research. In P. Reason & R. Bradbury (Eds.), *The Sage handbook of action research participative inquiry and practice.* London, England: Sage.

Kemmis, S., & McTaggart, R. (2005). Participatory action research communicative action and the public sphere. In N. K. Denzin & Y. S. Lincoln (Eds.), *The Sage handbook of qualitative research* (3rd ed.). Thousand Oaks, CA: Sage.

McIntyre, A. (2008). *Participatory action research.* Los Angeles, CA: Sage.

Semali, L. M., & Kincheloe, J. L. (1999). Introduction: What is Indigenous knowledge and why should we study it? In L. M. Semali & J. L. Kincheloe (Eds.), *What is indigenous knowledge? Voices from the academy* (pp. 3–57). New York, NY: Falmer Press.

Shiva, V. (1997). *Biopiracy: The plunder of nature and knowledge.* Boston, MA: South End Press.

Smith, L. T. (2012). *Decolonizing methodologies* (2nd ed.). Dunedin, NZ: Otago University Press.

CHAPTER SEVEN

Warfare as Pedagogy: Shaping Curriculum From the Margins; A Freirean Counter-Narrative of War

ERIC D. TORRES

"AT PEACE NOW"

That was the sublime headline for the front page of *The Pilot*, my hometown local newspaper on Wednesday, July 2, 2008, followed by "Soldier Made Famous by Photo Dies in Pinehurst," a rather discrete subtitle that sounded like a whisper in a town that took pride in its dignified and highly manicured Old South celebrations. A noticeably downsized version of the *Army Times*–copyrighted picture of medic Joseph Patrick Dwyer carrying an injured Iraqi boy, taken by photographer Warren Zinn, was strategically placed on the upper right side to illustrate the story. Dwyer, originally from New York, had signed up "to fight for his country" immediately after the terrorist attacks of September 11, 2001, according to the source. "He felt like it was something he had to do," said Matina Dwyer, his wife, to senior writers Matthew Moriarty and John Chappell (2008). I immediately remembered the image from the time it was widely showcased by the national media in order to build up public support for the war in Iraq in 2003. It is a great picture indeed. One of those that make history: Dwyer, in full battle gear, runs as he holds a barefoot half-naked, darker skinned young boy, who looks at the camera while holding his stomach with his right hand, and his right knee with his left hand; revealing pain through a half open mouth, and horror through a tense facial expression and wide-open, dark eyes. Dwyer does not look at the camera. Breathing through his mouth, reveals his exhaustion. A slight inclination forward denotes hurried but careful movement and direction. He seems to be focused on the ground, ready for the next step. The 45-degree angle formed by the lines of his body and his eye line, though, reveals that he is only ready for the next step. The firmness of his right arm holding the boy reveals his resolution, and the delicate touch of his left hand on the boy's hurting leg shows his compassion. The fact that he is married is highlighted by the existence of a line suggested by his wedding ring finger, which intersects, right in the middle, the projection of another line suggested, in the opposite direction, by the automatic rifle that hangs heavily from his right shoulder, creating a visual balance for his paradoxical commitments. Dwyer stands tall. But that harsh vertical line is softened by a diagonal suggested by the way the frightened boy lies on his arms, with his head at a higher level than his feet. It conveys the idea of power and mercy.

Dwyer's image became an icon right at the beginning of the war and the picture, unsurprisingly, acquired a life of its own, separated from the life of the man. Four summers ago, though, the picture was not the focus of the news. Neither was the man. It was the soldier made famous by the picture. In a perverse way, the picture outlived the man. The picture was well, alive, and, ironically, still in the larger picture. How to report that a decorated hero has committed suicide? How to spell out the political investment on his image as a warrior? How to explain his disenfranchisement? How to decode what makes him different? What meaning does a story like this have and how does it become history? How is our collective memory constructed? Why was our town crier whispering?

Rationalizing the pain of the man, the press in general reported the fatal event as another case of post-traumatic stress disorder (PTSD) and, without further discussion, quietly justified it and moved on to cover the next crisis. Warren Zinn, the photographer, did something else. He immediately returned to the place of the original photo shooting but this time with a CNN crew. Zinn was looking for the kid "to make sure he was alive and to show what happens to the people after the U.S. comes to places like this." According to Christian Lowe (2003) from the *Marine Corps Times*, reporting for USAToday, Zinn said that image was very important to him because it was one of the first ones he had ever taken "that showed raw human emotion." When he found the boy, he gave him a copy of the famous picture. CNN, in its turn, as reported by the same source, confirmed that the boy was in fact alive, and through this made-for-the-media recollection not only reproduced the desired meaning of the original picture, but also reinforced it creating the picture of the boy holding the picture of the soldier holding the same boy, in a flagrantly vicious manipulation of hermeneutics.

Why flagrant? Why vicious? Because I am under the powerful impression that in front of us a very important element has been surreptitiously removed, limiting the scope of meaning of the picture, and reducing the possibilities to understand the larger situation from which it had been excised. Zygmunt Bauman, in his book *Life in Fragments* (1995), has very appealingly explained the ways and means through which one can separate deeds and morals in modern society, and suggested that the principal tool for that severance—as I argue is the case here—is what he calls *adiaphorization*:

> Making certain actions, or certain objects of action, morally neutral or irrelevant exempt from the category of phenomena suitable for moral evaluation. The effect of adiaphorization is achieved by excluding some categories of people from the realm of moral subjects, or through covering up the link between partial action and the ultimate effect of co-ordinated moves, or through enthroning procedural discipline and personal loyalty in the role of all-overriding criterion of moral performance. (p. 149)

Within this framework of understanding, bodily weakness, for example, or an insufficient ability to submit and to fit, as in the specific case of Joseph Patrick Dwyer, the man, is exclusively seen as a symptom of ill health, and as such medicalized or articulated as a case for psychiatric treatment. As a socially constructed description of a human condition, then, PTSD would only respond to the declared main general purpose of the war, the war in Iraq in this case: to free people and save lives. This paradox of "creative destruction" (p. 152), says Bauman, explains and justifies the suffering of a few as a low price to be paid for the happiness of the many.

Ali Sattar, the Iraqi boy, was alive indeed. According to the same *Army Times* report only one of the two holes on the walls of his home, produced by the indiscriminate U.S. bombing of his neighborhood, was visibly repaired. The repaired and un-repaired holes together with a big scar along his leg and a pronounced and still painful limp were most likely constant reminders of something that somehow had already been internalized but, obviously, insufficiently understood, because neither he nor his father, according to the same source, seemed to be able to comprehend Zinn's visit. Not even at face value. Their lives went on and continue to go on in a different frame, which CNN could not co-opt for its coverage.

Back in town, I have to say, I was saddened by the tragedy of a man who lived in my community. But as the story unfolded, I was sorry for his wife too. She was not at home when it happened. Reportedly, she had left the family home, taking their daughter, some time before the incident occurred. But I was appalled by the pressure put on her to explain what had happened, as if she had any explaining to do. "He was just never the same when he came back; because of all the things he saw," said Matina Dwyer to Michael Moriarty (2008). What he saw she did not specify. "He never regretted going over there, doing what he did," she said very clearly for the record. What he did she did not specify either. She expressed frustration for the insufficient avenues and resources to help returning soldiers, as well as hope that her husband's death would bring attention to this issue. And, finally, in the stern tone of those who hurt, heightened by the eloquence that only an awareness of both her husband's human ordeal and her own vulnerable condition as a military widow talking to an audience that included the military can afford, she passed along the following message: "He couldn't actually come home. He was still there in his mind" (p. 11). Is this the voice of her ego defending itself against an anxiety for the loss of love, and her symbolization—"he couldn't come home," ergo *it must have not happened*—a lighter way to carry the conflict with the world of others, the military world on which she depends, thus identifying with her aggressor? Or is there an implicit critique in her choice of words saying that since "he was still there in his mind," and something reproachable happened, then it must have happened over there—before his mind devoured and spiritually vacant body returned to her—and not here, where she was expected to deal with it all by herself; entering into the metaphorical and interpretative world of *plausible deniability*, as they call it in Washington?

I really do not know and I must admit that it still upsets me. But what upsets me is not being able to know whether it is "fear of loss" or "threat to lose" that informs her saying. That would just be a very selfish and intellectually vain pursuit. Maybe it is both, or, for that matter, perhaps none of the above, as often said in Washington, and I really missed the point! What upsets me is precisely that whatever it is, or however it may be described, I know it is wrong. And that knowledge, as any other knowledge, should never work as a substitute for transforming unjust situations in our midst. Awareness calls for a response: she lived in my community and I really did not know what to do.

That unintended summer awareness and the deep feeling of empathy it generated remind me now of Paulo Freire's idea of conscientization and his profoundly moral effort to humanize the oppressor as two simultaneous processes that necessarily inform each other. They also remind me of the unintended qualities of learning that Alice Balint so well describes and Deborah Britzman in *Novel Education* (2006) quotes:

> Learning and its symbolization…is composed of a radical and original uncertainty and a promise. Not knowing but still needing to respond can make one nervous…. Mistakes and misunderstandings are not the outside of education but rather are constitutive of its very possibility. (p. 43).

Britzman (2006) convincingly argues, from a psychoanalytical perspective, that understanding our own acts as beyond and even in contradiction to our consciousness is part of an educational process about us and about us in relation to others. Through it "we are entering the space of thinking about thinking, an exploration, however uncertain, of how one feels in the world of others and what this intimate knowledge may mean." That exploration, she suggests, is like a commentary on our ability to self-represent. If you agree with her, as I do, then you may want to look at it in the same way you look at democracy as a political process, because "it allows people to speak, give voice to their concerns, be as difficult as they can be, and be heard" (p. 59).

I situate curriculum as a process of social construction in an effort to theorize how the U.S. National Security doctrine informs education public policy, and discern how this scenario becomes a pedagogical warfare. Following Patrick Slattery's recommendations in *Curriculum Development in the Postmodern Era* (2006), I decided to embed my initial reflection in a real-life situation, one that could not only honor the tension between ideas and emotions that configure and sustain our condition as human beings in all its complexity, but one that could also allow the personal and more subjective—even the marginal—construction of meaning that welcomes but is certainly not limited to the autobiographical, in order to emphasize the belief that knowledge is created "in a context that necessarily reflects human interests, values, and actions" (p. 36). I am reading the world, as Freire would say. I propose to understand curriculum as a hermeneutical process and to differentiate it from a commodified version that can be passed along to others just like the famous photo of a soldier holding a boy, as a linear fact that pretends to be free of pretensions. In the hopeful spirit of social justice, I argue that curriculum can be understood as the attribute of unhinging questioning. This is the ability to make questions that include the perspective of the other, and a practical effort to respond to them as we understand the experience from the point of view of the self in contrast to the perception of the experience of self in relation to others. This is an effort to write a counternarrative of war that offers a perspective from the margins of the structures of power.

THE OFFICIAL STORY

In his book *Surprise, Security, and the American Experience* (2004), Yale history professor John Lewis Gaddis knowledgeably inscribes the U.S. grand strategy on national security within the larger context of American history. It is a fine attempt to understand the terrorist attacks of September 11, 2001, in the context of the process of American political and economical expansionism, and a worthwhile attempt to speculate about its consequences in terms of security and defense. Whether you agree with his conclusion or not is an entirely different story. I mention this book because it is in itself a very powerful example of curriculum as a social construction. At the beginning, Gaddis (2004) makes an interesting and honest disclosure of the limits of his endeavor: the events are too recent. For that reason, he admits, the accuracy of his historical writing is diminished by both its own shortness of perspective and access to rather fewer resources. It is, in his own words, "a premature effort to treat as history an event that remains inescapably part of our present" (p. 4). For the same reasons, though, Gaddis (2004) says that his writing acquires relevance: however imperfect the exercise may be, he argues, "an incomplete map is better than no map at all" (p. 5). Later on, in an autobiographical mood, he quotes Ewan Macdougall, one of his undergraduate students at Yale, probably the same age as Joseph Patrick Dwyer, saying one evening shortly after the terrorist attacks, and probably at about the same time that Dwyer decided that fighting the war was something *he had to do*:

> I love this country. I love this place. I love what we are doing here tonight. I love it so much that I'm prepared to defend our right to do it, which is why I'm joining the Marines. It's people like me who make it possible for people like you to be here doing what you're doing. (p. 116)

To which a consenting Gaddis (2004) interestingly added: "Our ability as a democracy to question all values depends upon our faith in and our determination to defend *certain* values" [the emphasis is his]; because, he argues, "they are the bedrock beliefs that make it possible for *us* to be here and for so many *others* to wish to be" [the emphasis is mine]. (p. 116). For Gaddis (2004), even if they are "social constructions," it is more important that "it's *our society that constructed them*" [again, the emphasis is his]; and "*that* [here, the emphasis is mine] is what makes them worth fighting for, as so many others have done before us" (p. 117). The language of his methodological disclosure, despite its glorious, scientific aim, cannot unveil what comes veiled by default, and cannot but continue to hide both the split into good and bad of his reasoning, and the gap between the self and the other that informs his writing. Split and gap are automatically transferred to all other dichotomies of analytical relations: you and I, us and them. And, even more, he claims that "Americans have the opportunity once again to do so much designing [in the world]" (p. 113). By deciding to reduce his self-proclaimed historical account to an immediate relation of cause and effect, its self-assessed sense of relevance, in fact, not only forecloses any possibility for empathy to generate any significant knowledge. Also, most important, his semantic structure indicates that it is not just a current conjuncture but, as a matter of fact, the confirmation of a historical pattern, wherein the confirmation of a historical pattern is not as relevant as the as-a-matter-of-fact tone with which it is assessed.

Gaddis (2004) concludes his account in the same autobiographical tone quoting Schuyler Schouten, another undergraduate student of his at Yale, when he asked "in the dark and fearful days that followed September 11th," whether it "would be OK now for us to be patriotic." To which Gaddis (2004) straightforwardly responded: "Yes, I think it would" (p. 118), assuming the whole situation as something that needed to be explained rather than interpreted. Semantics, here, is working like a dark room, it allows you to say and not to say; suggest and suggest not; explain, veil, and imply in such a convincing way that it is hard to imagine that what is being said, described, or redescribed could be otherwise. That is, precisely, the power of semantics, and, for that matter, of the semantics of power.

The understanding of curriculum as a social construction, then, should help us to systematically identify and interrogate the assumptions that form and inform our reflection, even subconsciously. In this sense, I could argue, for example, that Zinn—the photographer—and Gaddis—the historiographer—have something in common. While they connect logic and emotion to deliberately reduce the boundaries of imagination, in the larger picture, it is obvious that they secure themselves in an ideological lockdown to cope with the fears they happen to share, instead of making that same connection to stretch those boundaries and negotiate alternative meanings, allowing their perception to be openly affected, gain more understanding, and move on.

In order to counterbalance the tendency of simply building on top of unquestioned assumptions, a more comprehensive as well as challenging vision for curriculum and curriculum development is needed, one that transcends reading the word and helps to differentiate between functional literacy and critical literacy. The curricular question here, then, should not inquire about specific contents about what happened, but, as Kwame Anthony Appiah points out in *The Ethics of Identity* (2005): "The real debates…are about in what narratives we will embed them; they are about which of the many true stories we will tell" (p. 207). Patrick Slattery (2006) has articulated what he calls a kaleidoscopic vision in that respect: "Curriculum development in the postmodern era will challenge the traditional approach of modern logical positivism to the study of history as a linear timeline of events…. It will encourage autobiographical reflection, narrative inquiry, revisionist interpretation, and contextual understanding" (p. 36). It is precisely within this kaleidoscopic framework that I explore the possibility of reading the official documents that contain and explain the national security strategy of the United States of America as an authentic expression of modern logical positivism and as conveyors of a curriculum designed as a linear projection to the future of a *desired history*, expressed both through a grand vision, and a continually updated matching timeline of events that logs concrete accomplishments and challenges within a preconfigured grand strategy toward that vision.

THE ORIGINAL UNCERTAINTY

Like any other citizen, you and I are already expected to create a life, consciously or not, with the materials that history gives us as the American experience. According to Appiah (2005), to create a life is fundamentally a hermeneutical process that ends up configuring what he calls a person's ethical self:

Your character, your circumstances, your psychological constitution, including the beliefs and preferences generated by the interaction of your innate endowments and your experience: all these need to be taken into account in shaping a life. They are not constraints on that shaping; they are its materials. As we come to maturity, the identities we make, our individualities, are interpretive responses to our talents and disabilities, and the changing social, semantic, and material contexts we enter at birth; and we develop our identities dialectically with our capacities and circumstances, because the latter are in part the product of what our identities lead us to do. (p. 163)

But how are we supposed to create a life tied to the preconfiguration of a desired future? Notice that the subject has been surreptitiously changed: it would not be just like asking Joseph Patrick Dwyer to look at the picture, but instead to ask him to continue to look like the picture regardless of his circumstances. Signifier and signified have, let's say, switched roles. What kind of personal identities could this kind of blueprint generate? What kind of impact will this social engineering experiment have on our experience as autonomous individuals? Will there be any possibility of unhinging questioning or dialogical space? Is this the kind of uncertainty with which Matina Dwyer was struggling, and, thus, her powerfully sublime existential appeal to look at the context? I really don't know. But an awareness of this radical and original uncertainty looks like a new beginning and a promise to me. Deborah Britzman (2006) puts it this way: "The capacity to think well about injustice and justice belongs to beginnings and now to education, which, after all, is the ego's second chance" (p. 58). So, looking for a second chance, one could revisit the marketplace of ideas and once there, it could be reasonably argued that if the famous picture of the soldier holding a boy conveyed the idea of power and mercy, then Matina Dwyer's quotation conveys the idea of agency and grace, an argument that could potentially lead to a healthy, necessary, and insightful gender consideration, but the bottom line would remain the same: the unquestionable need to understand the power dynamic between autonomy and collective identities. I follow Appiah (2005) for this analysis:

Autonomy, we know, is conventionally described as an ideal of self-authorship. But the metaphor should remind us that we write in a language we did not ourselves make. If we are authors of ourselves, it is the state and society that provide us with the tools and the contexts of our authorship; we may shape our selves, but others shape our shaping. And so, if the state cannot but affect our souls, we can fairly ask both how it does and how it *should* do so [the emphasis is his]. (p. 157)

Figuring out how things work as opposed to how they should work is, in this case, an important digression that comes from what Appiah himself calls his rooted liberal cosmopolitanism. But it is also a Critical Pedagogy interest, which Slattery (2006), in the best Freirean spirit, synthesizes as rooted in the premises that oppression is based in the reproduction of privileged knowledge codes and practices; that facts and values are inseparable and inscribed by ideology; that language is a key element in the formation of subjectivities, and, thus, critical literacy—the ability to negotiate passages through social systems and structures—is more important than functional literacy—the ability to decode and compute (p. 193). Within this framework one could legitimately ask, for example, what kind of risks the U.S. national security doctrine could pose to critical pedagogy. Peter McLaren, in *Pedagogy and Praxis in the Age of Empire* (2007), responds in this way: "Proponents and practitioners of critical pedagogy have long feared being cast into the pit of academic hell for being perceived not only as dangerously irrelevant [*sic*] [irreverent] to United States democracy but also as politically treasonous" (p. 33), mainly because critical pedagogy earned an early reputation as a fierce critic of U.S. imperialism and capitalist exploitation. But according to McLaren (2007) himself, things have changed. Today critical educators have become "so absorbed by the cosmopolitanized liberalism of the post-modernized left" that critical pedagogy "no longer serves as a trenchant challenge to capital and U.S. economic and military hegemony" (p. 33). He insists, in a militant tone, that "what is needed as a major step towards social justice is a transformation of the social relations of production." (p. 34). While this is true, perhaps it is the militant lens he uses what prevents him from fully assaying the power of re-description. Perhaps it is that same militant tone what prevents others to listen to what he has to say. I believe that the pedagogical exposure of the contradictions of the free market ideology continues to be a valid alternative and a valid response that summons us to return to the radical Freirean *naming* and original uncertainty and promise that education offers and that, as Britzman (2006) reminds us, is constitutive of its very possibility.

Nevertheless, McLaren (2007) is absolutely right when he asserts that tolerance must become a liberating rather than a repressive force. As such, "pure tolerance of 'free' speech must be challenged when it impedes the chances of creating a context in which people can live free of fear and violence" (p. 52). This assertion is rooted in the deepest Freirean tradition because in rejecting manipulation, Freire never accepted thoughtless spontaneity. Therefore, it is not just a matter of being tolerant, but rather a matter of creating an alternative frame of counterhegemonic meaning. Persisting in a language that scorns the other does not advance this kind of creativity. We frequently forget that it is also important to humanize the oppressor. Consequently, understanding education as the ego's second chance, and trying to understand and expose the blueprint embedded in the U.S. National Security Strategy, it is only fair to ask to what extent the state should be allowed, as the state, to intervene in the process of interpretation through which each of us is supposed to build an identity. In this sense, one thing is clear for McLaren (2007): "Critical educators need to consider citizenship outside of a narrowly nationalist sense in a manner that situates them in a larger practice of global citizenship and solidarity" (p. 86). In a similar manner, Gaddis (2004) gives us an important lead, which is to acknowledge the moral ambiguity of our history: "We got to where we are by means that we cannot today, in their entirety, comfortably endorse" (p. 33). I argue that Appiah's (2005) rooted cosmopolitanism and Slattery's (2006) critical theory offer a useful framework to understand education as part of a very complex mechanism to secure a generational transfer of ideology. Here I join them to understand education as part of a complex mechanism to secure global ideological transfer and to redescribe warfare as its pedagogy.

PEDAGOGICAL WARFARE

As an educator, I have always been interested in understanding the effects of war on children who survive it. Because of its horrendous effects there is no greater human disaster. The physical, mental, moral, and spiritual marks that it produces have no comparison because they not only affect real individuals, they also affect generations. Consequently, the drama is not only each suffering child. That would be, in fact, just the tip of the iceberg, an atrocious starting point. The challenge comes with the need to understand the pedagogical process it triggers and especially with the efforts to comprehend its effects in its multiple levels of complexity. My interest in the effects of war on children who survive it is not limited, though, to those who are targeted in acts of war. It is about children in general, including those who suffer the effects of war from the *winner's* side, if there is such a thing as a winner's side. I believe everyone loses in a war. I am interested in knowing how warfare is used as pedagogy in the American experience.

Back in the seventies, in the midst of an ongoing ideological warfare—whose victorious end was claimed by former President George W. Bush in the presentation of his National Security Strategy—Ivan Illich (1970/2002), properly so, argued that in a schooled society, just like ours, war making always finds an educational rationale. I believe that his is still a valid assertion because, regardless of its content, an educational rationale has the potential to acquire a life in itself and soon, if not systematically challenged, may acquire a symbolic value that has the potential to profusely permeate the collective memory of any given historical community. The U.S. National Security Strategy's educational rationale was clearly stated by President Bush: "Today our enemies have seen the results of what civilized nations can, and will, do against regimes that harbor, support, and use terrorism to achieve their political goals." (2002, p. 8). I borrow Illich's expression *pedagogical warfare* to establish a connection between war and education.

War, as an annihilating phenomenon, is an expression of cultural and social disconnectedness. As educators we know that dissonance inevitably precedes the emergence of a new cognitive paradigm. But when we deal with war what emerges from that dissonance is not a new cognitive paradigm, but a commodified version of knowledge dressed up as a ritual. I use the word ritual in the same sense Peter McLaren (1999) defines it in *Schooling as a Ritual Performance*: "They form the warp on which the tapestry of culture is woven, thereby, '*creating*' the world for the social actor. They grow conjuncturally out of the cultural and political mediations that shape the contours of groups and institutions, serving as agencies of socialization" (p. 38). [The emphasis is mine.] Illich (1970/2002) reminds us that rituals can hide the discrepancies and conflicts between social principles and social organizations, and "as long as an individual is not explicitly conscious of the ritual character of the process through which he was initiated to the forces which shape his cosmos, he cannot break the spell and shape a new cosmos" (p. 51). I define pedagogical warfare as a scenario created through critical literacy aimed at producing systematic pedagogical dissonance.

Rituals frequently serve normative functions. Such is the case of, among many others, the notions of patriotism and national pride. They are governed by beliefs rooted in psychic structures established through a continuous process of socialization. As part of a strategically increasing military presence in all high school campuses, I found several years ago a very interesting example of recruitment propaganda contained in a brochure that is made available to all students: *"MARINES. THE FEW. THE PROUD." (2002)*. Its direct text and distinct imagery mutually reinforce each other in an unambiguous message: war can be embedded in education, and education can be embedded in war. Making use of powerful marketing techniques, it effectively conveys the core of a philosophy of life making it sound attractive:

> Time and time again, the Marines have been called into service to protect our nation's interests. We operate around the world as America's quick strike expeditionary force, ready at the moment's notice to effectively insert our warriors into any situation that calls for it. We are proud to be America's shining tip of the spear, and we are ready for the next victory. Maybe you can be one of us. (p.6)

But depending on how you look at it, the brochure could also be disconcerting and appalling. Its language unabashedly describes both the curriculum and the philosophy of education that supports it:

> No one simply joins the Marines, because the title must be earned. Marine Corps Recruit Training is where the separation begins: the weak from the strong, the child from the adult, the civilian from the Marine. The 13 weeks will break away all the things that bind you to the excesses of the past. And in the end, you will become a confident member of the finest warrior force in the world. You'll be a United States Marine. (p. 2)

I argue that this is not just a marketing product. At its core is a sample that represents a philosophy that abruptly assumes that we are all enmeshed in a sort of sacred commonality of interests and that those interests need to be protected from others excluded from the definition of *we*. It assumes that those interests admit no limits and that its protection does not recognize any sovereign barrier in the world. It assumes that warfare has its own logicality and that it can be imposed anywhere at the moment needed. It assumes war as a cultural trait and that only warriors express the fullness of its human condition. Finally, it assumes military supremacy as a lead and structuring value and, finally, that education is just a natural selection process.

H. E. Goemans in *War & Punishment* (2000) has developed an interesting theory about war and war termination that is widely accepted among and used by both public policy makers and political science academic circles. I find it extremely interesting because it is, coincidently, a very sophisticated version of the brochure. Goemans redescribes war and war termination as learning processes: "War makes agreement possible because war provides information" (p. 27). "Once a war starts, and the belligerents spend some time fighting each other, they acquire new information about their own as well as their adversaries' capabilities and the costs of war. They also begin to learn more about both sides' resolve. Specifically, continuous combat will tell both sides all sorts of things about the final outcome on the battlefield that they can never know before the war" (p. 28). As war progresses, he explains, at least one side must discover that its original estimate was wrong. The resolve to go to war expressed by former President Bush (2002), somehow shockingly renewed by presidential candidate Mitt Romney, may be better understood in the light of this strategic learning theory. But it also sheds light over its limitations and contradictions, since the United States is no longer dealing with traditional warfare but with something different. As former President Bush explained, "We will disrupt and destroy terrorist organizations by defending the United States, the American people, and our interests at home and abroad by identifying and destroying the threat before it reaches our borders.... We will not hesitate to act alone, if necessary, to exercise our right to self defense by acting preemptively against such terrorists" (p. 6). In this pedagogical warfare, what are the pedagogical practices that will enable us to unlearn bad lessons well learned in the past? What are the questions that will bring the discussion back to the educational field and reconnect it to democracy as a "site of struggle" in Henry Giroux's (2005, p xxxiii) words? From the field of education I argue that dissonance generates new knowledge. From the field of political science I argue that war is a negative sum game. From the intersection of both, hereon, following Freire, I argue that critical literacy constitutes a site for hermeneutical conflict that is essential to democratic citizenry.

A SITE FOR HERMENEUTICAL CONFLICT

I must explain here that the selection of Matina Dwyer's narrative is not a random event. The process of coming to see other human beings as "one of us" rather than as "them," asserts Richard Rorty (1989), and I agree, is basically a matter of detailed description of what "unfamiliar people" are like and of redescription of what we ourselves are like. Oddly enough, though, this is not a task for philosophy, political philosophy, or for any other theory, Rorty says, but for genres such as ethnography, the journalist's report, the comic book, the docudrama, the novel, the movie, and the TV program. "They have gradually, but steadily, replaced the sermon and the treatise as the principal vehicles of moral change and progress" (p. xvi). I explore this postmodern assertion here and explore its pedagogical implications. Consequently, I situate myself in a site that is temporary, contingent, ambiguous, and densely populated by binary oppositions. I call it a site for hermeneutical conflict. At the same time, I situate myself in front of Matina Dwyer, allow myself to listen to her voice, and let language flow with curiosity toward displacement, defenses, and affect, paying attention, as Deborah Britzman (2006) suggests, "to guarded statements, utterances that mislead, misrecognize and abject, and taking note of the little procedures of resistance to interpretation that service desire" (p. 6).

In a rather subliminal way, Matina Dwyer's narrative challenges not only the objectivity of Gaddis's research, for example, but objectivity in itself as she embodies what Zygmunt Bauman (1995) has poignantly described as "our modern ambivalence about might, force, and coercion" (p. 139). This is precisely the postmodern gist of her voice: one person's enabling and spawning process is another person's cogent hindrance. Clearly, a great deal of power is absolutely essential to crease and disjoint signifiers in Matina Dwyer's unscripted narrative so that what they mean may be perceived as expected or desired, or even as right or better, if you will. Matina Dwyer's voice, though, embeds the critique that is necessary to transcend modernity, the "frontier civilization" that Bauman describes as one that "re-creates itself and rejuvenates through a constant supply of lands to conquer and ever new invitations to, or pretexts for, transgression" (p. 140). I find Matina Dwyer's *plausible deniability* fascinating in an era of insecurity and unrestricted surveillance such as ours, where unrealistic images are blatantly used for ideological management.

Ushering in a time of fear, not too long ago, former President George W. Bush (2002) strongly argued in the aftermath of unprecedented terrorist attacks on North American soil, that "our enemies have openly declared that they are seeking weapons of mass destruction, and evidence indicates that they are doing so with determination" (p. 4). Up to this day, more than a decade later, even though that evidence has been proved wrong, and even fabricated, and as President Obama switched the American berserker focus of the previous administration back to Al Qaeda and Afghanistan in the Middle East, and despite a chronicle of an announced retreat from Afghanistan, the hawkish rationale seems to be well and alive in different scenarios. Notwithstanding the increasingly negative perception of war by the public, it continues to inform the debate and determine threat inflation, as it besets the continued failure of the marketplace of ideas through the power of redescription.

At the beginning of the twenty-first century, national security has acquired urgent and exceptional relevance. The U.S. National Security Strategy inscribes education within the frame of national security doctrine and has strategically situated its domestic effects under the umbrella of homeland security policy. Education, in no uncertain terms, became one of nine general foreign policy strategies designed to expand what former President George W. Bush (2002) so intriguingly called a "circle of development" process, which was, hole-and-corner, engrained within another one, more powerful, identified as War on Terror.

In a promising vision, delivered to the world almost one year after the terrorist attacks in New York and Washington, D.C. in 2001, President Bush considered literacy and learning as the "foundation of democracy" (p. 23). Obviously, no one could ever disagree with an assertion of the sort. But a careful reading and analysis of the official documentation that defined national security and regulated its policy making, nevertheless, reveals not only that literacy and learning had been obstreperously foreshortened to unpretentious functions played within an innocuous structure, but confirms that this notion of education was seamlessly articulated to a larger political agenda: "to open societies" (p. 21). The implications and challenges that this vision continues to carry have not been sufficiently discussed in pedagogical terms. What does it mean to open societies? What does it mean to open societies in a context of terror? I argue that the political project contained in the U.S. National Security Strategy, read as curriculum, models coercion in service of individual self-assertion.

Both political project and curriculum have ostensibly anchored their fundamental belief in a particular interpretation of history at the end of the cold war: "The militant visions of class, nation, and race which promised utopia and delivered misery have been defeated and discredited," said President Bush (2002) and he stoutly ascertained that there is only one "sustainable model for national success: freedom, democracy and free enterprise" (p. 1). I strongly believe in democracy and adhere to democratic principles, but precisely because of that, I think it is neither possible nor plausible to pretend to conflate those three concepts and make them work as if they were one. I follow Jeffrey Weeks as cited by Bauman (1995) to frame an alternative argument: "Humanity is not an essence to be realized, but a pragmatic construction, a perspective, to be developed through the articulation of a variety of individual projects, of differences, which constitute our humanity in the broadest sense" (p. 162).

As I continue to reflect on national security doctrine trying to discern the way in which the notions of democracy, freedom, and free market are described and inscribed in it, many complex questions have come to my mind constituting altogether a multidimensional imaginary puzzle. What constitutes a threat to democracy? What constitutes a threat to a democratic state? What is the repertoire of legal responses to a threat against a democratic state? Is there any difference between a legal and a legitimate response? Does the subjectivity involved in the perception of a threat play any role in the legitimacy and or the legality of the response of a democratic state? Do responses to perceived threats challenge, dispute, or contest the concepts and institutions of democracy and of a democratic state as we understand them now? I have even been wondering whether we actually share such an understanding. Beyond academic definitions, how is democracy experienced under real-life exceptional circumstances? Of course I do not pretend to have a conclusive answer to all or any of these questions at all. But after careful consideration, I must say, there is still one idea against which I have not yet been persuaded: a liberal democracy may and, in fact, will roll back during a period of perceived threat.

Such a unique phenomenon may not only be interesting because of its political implications, but it certainly acquires dramatic philosophical tones because it operates through a sequence of sublime mechanisms where language and images play a main role. Let's just look at the mainstream media or, better yet, a simple school textbook. The expressions *force*, *violence*, *extremism*, *terror*, and *terrorist violence* are used in a sort of exchangeable way to describe an undesirable situation, essentially in contrast to the notions of law enforcement and order, bolstering the modern conceit that they belong to two different categories. Bauman (1995) points out that what this verbal distinction hides is that, in fact, the former—used to counter violence condemned as illegitimate, gratuitous, and harmful—is also about certain ordering, "but not the one which the makers of the distinction had in mind" (p. 141). This means that the distinction is, in point of fact, being made between the desired order and all the rest. Consequently, aware of the power of language, it would be a significant pedagogical experience just to ask for the role that coercion plays in this language puzzle.

Jennifer Holmes, for example, in *Terrorism and Democratic Stability* (2001) affirms, correctly, I believe, that "to understand the consequences of violence on democratic stability, violence coming from terrorist groups and violence emanating from the state must be studied together" (p. 10). What she implies is that, instead of just asking what unleashes violence one should also ask for the consequences of violent responses. Within this more comprehensive perspective, she asserts, "Violence can be observed as cause of further instability, instead of merely a manifestation of a preexisting conflict."(p. 11) Her inclusive approach helps us to avoid a traditional assessment of the state in terms of law and order and encourages us to look at the larger, more complex, and dynamic picture drawn by its fundamental constitutional role.

Terror as a phenomenon of political violence and the way we understand it from a democratic perspective depends heavily on the historical, political, social, and economic context in which we inscribe it, as well as on how the groups and individuals who participate in or respond to the actions we call terror relate to the world in which they act. I grew up and lived my young adult life in the midst of a situation like that in Peru and—not without fear—survived the bloody crossfire. Seventy thousand people didn't, and I am still troubled by that. The violent scenario comes back to my mind but now in global scale.

An important lesson learned from the past about warfare as pedagogy is that the context for terrorism does not consist entirely of objective historical factors. Equally important to understanding terrorism is its symbolic context. Patricio Silva in *Collective Memories, Fears, and Consensus* (1999) warns us that "how it is perceived determines its subjective conditions" (p. 178). The power of using the term, he argues, resides in its symbolic appeal and, most important, in its capacity to outlast short-term strategic failures. If you agree with him, as I happen to do, it is easy to understand why it persists, almost ineluctably, despite negative outcomes: "Terrorism projects images, communicates messages, and creates myths that transcend historical circumstances and can motivate future generations" (p. 179). Another important lesson learned from the past is that the understanding of terror and its complexity is contingent upon our understanding of terrorism as a conflict of political nature. Obviously, there is always a self-presentation of those who use terror and a construction that governments and publics place on it. But, in fact, when people choose to call the actions of others terror or to label others as terrorists, then this choice often has a sort of prescriptive relevance and not only a moral connotation. Martha Crenshaw in "Thoughts on Relating Terrorism to Historical Contexts" (1995) explains that "political language affects the perceptions of audiences and their expectations about how the problem evoked in a particular way will be treated" (p. 17). The vocabulary used to define or identify a problem, consequently, may also indicate a preferred solution.

A CULTURE OF FEAR

The overarching official document that originally contained and explained the *National Security Strategy of the United States of America* after September 11 was published by the White House in September 2002, just a couple of months after the newly created Office of Homeland Security published *The National Strategy for Homeland Security* in July 2002. Since then, both documents guided both homeland and national security public policy making. These documents were followed by *The National Security Strategy of the United States of America* in March 2006, which is a more sophisticated version of the original document. It gives an official historical version of what was described as the successes and challenges of the context at that particular time, and most important, described the way ahead giving a sort of road map for a desired version of the future, which is also part of the document. Shortly thereafter, when the cost of the war and foreign policies in the Middle East started to be increasingly questioned, two other important documents were made public: *The National Strategy for Combating Terrorism*, Washington, September 2006; and *9/11 Five Years Later: Successes and Challenges*, Washington, September 2006. From a political and pedagogical point of view, these documents are of the utmost importance: they legitimized the War on Terror as a civilizing process:

> Today our enemies have seen the results of what civilized nations can, and will, do against regimes that harbor, support, and use terrorism to achieve their political goals. Afghanistan has been liberated; coalition forces continue to hunt down the Taliban and al-Qaeda. But it is not only this battlefield on which we will engage terrorists. Thousands of trained terrorists remain at large with cells in North America, South America, Europe, Africa, the Middle East, and across Asia. (The White House, 2002a, p. 5)

It is easy to be overwhelmed by the realization that war makers have enormous power. The narrative continues to go in the same direction but claims to be approaching a halt in a continued search of legitimacy. But like any other legitimation strategy, this one hides as much as it reveals. Concerned by the deterioration of democratic powers in America, Cornel West (2004) has talked and written extensively about what he considers a sort of sedimentation of democratic values, and has made the case for a strong differentiation between democratic commitment and flag-waving patriotism. "Democratic commitment," he strongly argues, "confronts American hypocrisy and mendacity in the name of public interest; flag-waving patriotism promotes American innocence and purity in the name of national glory" (p. 103). The problem West (2004) sees here is by all odds engrained in the cultural makeup of American society, which in his own words is "not knowing how to deal with our traditional fear of too many liberties, and our deep distrust of one another" (p. 6). This fear, in turn, he concludes, manifests itself in a politics that is about winning a political game and not about producing better lives for all. Robert Jay Lifton (2003) has an interesting take on this issue as well. As a psychiatrist interested in the human condition in extreme situations, he describes the American experience as a superpower syndrome: "We have long had a national self-image that involves an ability to call forth reservoirs of strength when we need it, and a sense of a protected existence peculiar to America in an otherwise precarious world" (p. 125). As a consequence, he argues, this sort of exceptional condition makes us feel as if it were almost un-American to be vulnerable. Notice here that one condition is immediately implicated by the other. They are presented as irremediably inseparable. But in all reality, for an ordinary flag-waving citizen, it is the equivalent to claiming a power that is unlimited just to compensate the intolerable idea of not being invulnerable, and to compensate the intolerable emotion of being vulnerable. So, "one solution," says Lifton (2003), "is to maintain the illusion of invulnerability," even when that means that the superpower "runs the danger of taking increasingly draconian actions to sustain that illusion" (p. 129).

Michael Lerner describes this illusionary state of consciousness as cynical realism in *The Left Hand of God* (2007). This state of consciousness is characterized by a heightened state of alert and a profound sense of fear. In this very human condition, he explains, there is a battle of all against all, where others will necessarily dominate you unless you dominate them first. For Lerner (2007), here, fear of the other is the most common of the senses, and as such the prism of our human diffraction and the cause of the fragmentation of our lives. Within this logic, "security for ourselves, our families, our communities, or our nation depends on our ability to get advantage over them before they get it over us" (p. 77). But Lerner (2007) gives a good dressing down and warns us that when fear dominates, what happens is that all our experiences are discerned through this lens, prevailing over other parts of our cultural heritage precisely because they validate those fears. Consequently "people seek to maximize their own advantage." Fear is not only, then, an alienating force, but also "the energy that summons us to the market" (p. 80). I argue that it is also the straining force that motivates the need to open other societies as foreign policy. There is an intrinsic weakness in governments, says Howard Zinn in *A Power Governments Cannot Suppress* (2007), "however massive their armies, however vast their wealth, however they control images and information, because their power depends on the obedience of citizens, of soldiers, of civil servants, of journalists and writers and teachers and artists" (p. 13). And any government's power, he concludes, may become futile when critically confronted by an educated citizenry.

L'ENFANT ET LES SORTILÈGES

In an effort to do away with the debris produced after so much official neatness during the Bush administration, a twice-sworn President Barack Obama turned his undivided attention to national security matters during his second day in office, and continued to untwine the arras of policies woven by his predecessor over the previous eight years. He signed executive orders designed to close Guantánamo Bay prison within a year, prohibit extreme interrogation practices, and revisit military tribunals for suspected terrorists. "Shuttering the detention facility is intended to show that U.S. foreign policy is in metamorphosis," President Obama said during a press conference. "The message that we are sending around the world is that the United States intends to prosecute the ongoing struggle against violence and terrorism" but will do so "in a manner consistent with our values and our ideals. We are not, as I said at our inauguration, going to continue with a false choice between our safety and our ideals" he concluded as highlighted by National Public Radio on January 22, 2009.

There is indeed an enthrallment in the narrative of national security documents and of national security issues. It pretends to be about dislodging violence, but in fact it just redescribes its redistribution. I argue that they are powerful artifacts that very efficiently perform what Bauman (1995) so interestingly describes as an ordering activity:

> Ordering makes protruding the difference previously unnoticed and creates a difference where there was none; it splits the set of objects within the field about to be ordered into such as fit the order and such as do not. The latter must be coerced to change themselves or to change their places. (p. 140)

The fact that the executive orders to close Guantánamo Bay prison within a year, prohibit extreme interrogation practices, and revisit military tribunals for suspected terrorists have certainly been hard to implement and have not been completed reveals not only that these are complicated issues but that, in fact, they are just the tip of underpinning structures that cannot be easily removed. With President Obama, I think that the choice is not between safety and ideals, as he has digressed, but rather a matter of consistency. The real choice will be where he decides to re-inscribe his digression. That was not very clear during his successful campaign for re-election and continues to remain the same during his second term.

The disruption created by such fit impetus reminds me of the powerful script written by Sidonie-Gabrielle Colette in 1917, *Divertissements pour ma fille*, for which Maurice Ravel (1925) composed the opera *L'Enfant et les Sortilèges*. In this story a boy conflicted by time and mathematical problems tears off the wallpaper of his room, knocks over his clock, and rips apart his favorite book, just to see that the characters that inhabited his little world—within which and with whom he had safely grown for years—are free, have a life of their own, and heatedly struggle and riot to continue to make the same sense even without their context. This is the story of a strange place in time where a boy comes face-to-face with the very objects from which he had just been distanced but has no other option than to negotiate with them a new space. This is also, coincidently, the story of our modern day so well captured by Colette (1936) herself, in *Mes Apprentissages*: "By means of an image we are often able to hold on to our lost belongings. But it is the desperateness of losing which picks the flowers of memory, binds the bouquet" (p. 67). The desperateness of losing, in this case, brings us back to Matina Dwyer's dilemma and her fragile human condition, to the picture of the boy holding the photo of a soldier holding that same boy, to the warps in which culture and memory are woven, to schooling rituals and their force to force.

Back in 1999, an FBI report on *Counterterrorism Threat Assessment* to the U.S. Department of Justice indicated way before the terrorist attacks in New York and Washington, D.C., that Osama Bin Laden's objectives—"driving U.S. and Western forces from the Arabian Peninsula, removing Saudi Arabia's ruling family from power, 'liberating' Palestine, and overthrowing 'Western-oriented' governments in predominantly Muslim countries"—had established him as a leading figure among extremists who shared a similar ideological orientation. But the most alarming assessment contained in this little-known document came in one of its conclusions: "While Bin Laden is one of the most recognized proponents and key financier of this broad movement, he does not control or direct all such extremism. Should either he or Al-Qaeda cease to exist, this international movement would, in all likelihood, continue" (U.S. Department of Justice, Federal Bureau of Investigation, 1999, p. 55).

The Al-Qaeda attacks of September 11, 2001, ushered in a time of fear that is now more than twelve years old. Some scholars are beginning to refer to it as the "perpetual war," since there seems to be no obvious conclusion on the horizon but rather a sort of metastasis. But most important, a disturbing pattern emerged just from a purely academic examination, a pattern of disrespect for the law. The response of the state to politically subversive violence has repeatedly weakened the fluidity of the constitutional order.

"We've been fighting the wrong battle," Frank Cillufo, a former White House Homeland Security official, has said unflinchingly, to *Time* magazine's Amanda Ripley (2008). "The real center of gravity of the enemy is their narrative. It is ideologically bankrupt" (p. 47). I think he is absolutely right. Howard Caygill (1993) has managed to articulate a clear image to illustrate the current world scenario:

> With the limits for territorial expansion themselves reaching the limit,…reasoned civility and sovereign violence threaten to collapse into each other…. The potential for violence displaced to the periphery returns to the center with increasing speed. The border between civility and violence is no longer to be found at the limit of a sovereign, territorial space, but now traverses that space. (p. 52)

For the same reason, I am afraid, shouldn't an ideology that cynically infuses fear and its narrative of creative destruction be included in the same theoretical category? President Barack Obama (2009a), in his inaugural speech, made an eloquent appeal to an uncompromising "recognition, on part of every American, that we have duties to ourselves, our nation, *and the world*." [The emphasis is mine.] Alluding to the promise of citizenship, he ceremoniously ushered in what he called a "new era of responsibility." A few days before, in spite of it all, he had already approved his first act of war, this time in Pakistani territory. "Last Friday [January 13, 2009], unmanned U.S. Predator drones fired missiles at houses in Pakistan's Federally Administered Tribal Areas, or FATA, killing as many as twenty-two people, including at least three children," reported Amy Goodman (2009b) on her radio show *Democracy Now* on January 30, 2009. The Pakistani Prime Minister Yousaf Raza Gilani told an audience at the World Economic Forum in Davos the day before of her report that "U.S. drone attacks were 'counterproductive' and ended up uniting local communities with militants." On the other end, Goodman (2009b) reported that U.S. Defense Secretary Robert M. Gates, then a remnant component of the former Bush administration in the Obama administration, indicated at a Senate Armed Services Committee hearing on Tuesday, January 28, that "such strikes will continue and that Pakistani officials are aware of U.S. policy on this matter."

How can one make sense of the sense of duty to which President Obama made reference in his inaugural speech if it is embedded in a renewed war scenario without undergoing derisive feelings? To provide a sense in advance of what that might be, a few weeks later, then U.S. Homeland Security Secretary Janet Napolitano (Spiegel Online, 2009) revealed to *Der Spiegel* some elements of what could be interestingly identified as a formal strategy of deradicalization. When asked for the specific reason she did not mention the word *terrorism* during her first testimony to the U.S. Congress, she said:

> In my speech, although I did not use the word "terrorism," I referred to "man-caused" disasters. That is perhaps only a nuance, but it demonstrates that we want to move away from the politics of fear toward a policy of being prepared for all risks that can occur.

The admitted sophistication of Secretary Napolitano suggests, though, that the appeal to a new era of responsibility is nothing more—and nothing less—than an appeal to procedural correctness, and that the sense of duty that it entails is no other but the ritualized belief that organizations are moved only by an impersonal logic of self-propelling principles, where individuals that act within the realm of bureaucratic action are actually divested of their moral autonomy and educated both to distrust their own moral judgment and not to exercise it. What does this contradiction mean in pedagogical terms? Does it mean that metacognition and critical thinking can or should go only so far?

DEPERSONALIZING WAR

The provision of security has long been recognized as one of the most important functions of a democratic government. It took centuries for the modern state to evolve and gain exclusive control of the means of violence. But history is evolving in a way Max Weber did not foresee. Peter Singer, in *Corporate Warriors: The Rise of the Privatized Military Industry* (2003), has identified and started to describe an overall global pattern, "one of growing reliance by individuals, corporations, states, and international organizations on military services supplied not just by public institutions but also by the non-sovereign private market." (p. 18). The privatized military industry, for him, may very well represent the new face of warfare. The birth and growth of this kind of industry, he asserts, and I agree, does not only mean that the monopoly of force from the state is broken, but that "the state's role in the security sphere has now become deprivileged" (p. 18). One can only wonder what kind of effect this change will produce in the process of shaping an identity. The unknown territory brings us back, once again, to the opposition between order keeping and violence; law enforcement and order; insurgency and counterinsurgency, narratives and counternarratives. I think this scenario is not as simple as former President George W. Bush assumed in his promising view of the world. The end of the cold war has allowed internal conflicts to implode states, and international conflicts have caused wars between neighboring states. Simultaneously, globalization has created immense areas where people starve and live under disparaging human conditions of insecurity, and has facilitated the emergence and re-emergence of conflict groups not bound to any one state. As Singer (2003) has very well pointed out, there was a vacuum in the market of security that was exacerbated, he believes, by a context where global threats and their authors too easily acquired notoriety, and traditional responses to insecurity came to the fore as weak and inappropriate, to say the least (p. 233). But if the privatized military industry represents the new face of warfare, the increased use of Unmanned Aircraft Systems (UAS) during the Obama administration over the Federally Administered Tribal Areas in Pakistan, for example, represents both a renewed attempt to depersonalize war and a sophisticated remake of the old deleterious voice of self-deception. It is not casual that such a territory gained narrow focus in the war against terror. The region is nominally controlled by the central and federal government of Pakistan. But the constitution of Pakistan governs FATA only through the same rules that were left by the British in 1901. The president of Pakistan has an authority weakened by the remains of colonial tradition. This has created, in Western terms, a political vacuum that serves, as in Colette's story of the boy and the spell, the interests of insurgents that have found refuge in an ungovernable territory and the interests of a superpower syndrome that seeks to improve its multibillion conventional war means over its much needed and less costly capabilities of counterinsurgency. Robert M. Gates (2009) made such an interesting digression in "A Balanced Strategy: Reprogramming the Pentagon for a New Age," an article written shortly before his confirmation as U.S. Secretary of Defense by newly elected President Barack Obama and that eventually cleared his reappointment in office. He said:

> We should be modest about what military force can accomplish and what technology can accomplish. The advances in precision, sensor, information, and satellite technologies have

led to extraordinary gains in what the U.S. military can do. The Taliban were dispatched within three months; Saddam's regime was toppled in three weeks. A button can be pushed in Nevada, and seconds later a pickup truck will explode in Mosul…. But no one should ever neglect the psychological, cultural, political, and human dimensions of warfare. War is inevitably tragic, inefficient, and uncertain, and it is important to be skeptical of systems analyses, computer models, game theories, or doctrines that suggest otherwise. (p. 39)

But such an expression of unconventional thinking unfortunately does not find its reflection in reality. According to peace organizations Voices for Creative Nonviolence (www.vcnv.org) and Nevada Desert Experience (www. nevadadesertexperience.org) U.S. drone bombings reportedly have killed at least 687 Pakistani civilians since 2006. During that time, U.S. Predator drones allegedly carried out at least sixty strikes inside Pakistan, but hit just ten of their actual targets. In early April 2009, a group of fourteen peace activists were arrested for protesting outside Creech Air Force Base in Nevada, where U.S. Air Force personnel pilot the unmanned drones used in Pakistan and which Gates (2009) mentions in his *Foreign Affairs* article. Peace activist Father Louis Vitale, Franciscan friar, explained it this way to Amy Goodman (2009c):

Well, you know, it works out rather nicely. They [the pilots and sensor operators] live with their families in Las Vegas. They drive out and drop the kids off at school, drive out in the morning, fly their missions, drop their bombs. They can go home and have dinner with their family in the evening.

Unsurprisingly, the corporate media does not report on these kinds of events. After all, how does one seriously report what some of the soldiers have described as an intriguing arcade experience? How does one explain the way they embody a sense of duty that has no sense of moral accountability? How does one illustrate a scenario where the act of carefully watching dramatically overlaps with the condition of being observed and, yet, the overlap does not enhance a sense of consciousness but creates a black hole of disenfranchisement that allows for sort of intermediary beings to roam and transgress the boundaries between the sacred and the profane? What stories are the intermediaries telling and how are they becoming history? Unfortunately, a mostly rural population estimated to be about 3,341,070 people in 2000, according to official Pakistani sources and Gregory Copley (2007) from the International Strategic Studies Association (http://128.121.186.47/ ISSA/reports/SouthAsia/index), for example, remains at large in a deadly crossfire, trying to find refuge in the midst of a situation that may very well exemplify what Secretary Janet Napolitano has redescribed as man-caused disasters.

In such a scenario, when the formal argument alludes to politics and we decode its discourse in modern Western political science categories, we are confronted with a basic dynamic that revolves around two opposing poles: the search for community and harmony and the pursuit of power. Benedetto Fontana explains in

"Gramsci on Politics and State" (2002) that politics is the activity that search-es the common ground or space within which the common good or public end may be pursued, but, concurrently, it is also a competitive struggle for interest and advantage. From a psychoanalytical perspective, though, as Britzman so inter-estingly explains in *Novel Education* (2006), contrary feelings and opposite poles such as the ones explained above are grouped under the experience of the sublime. This is a site, she observes, "where thought encounters its limits and becomes groundlessness, thereby alienating its perception." (p. 7). When thought becomes sublime, she continues, there is a sort of madness: "We are unable to turn away from our fascination of being, at least momentarily, without our own nature to comprehend ourselves" (p. 7).

MORAL PROGRESS

The traditional philosophical way of describing what we mean as "human solidar-ity," says Rorty (1989), is that there is "something within each of us that resonates to the presence of this same thing in other human beings" (p. 189). He argues, though, that we better "try not to want something which stands beyond history and institutions" (p. 189). His warning is rooted in the historical evidence that suggests that the force of "us" is, typically, in contrast with the force of a "they," which also happens to be made up of human beings, who in a contrastive logic, happen to be the "wrong" kind of human beings and, unfortunately, too often and too easily wiped out. Rorty considers, for example, the attitude of contemporary American liberals concerning the unending hopelessness and misery of the lives of the young blacks in American cities, just like those drowning on TV after Hurri-cane Katrina, as typical. "Do we say that these people must be helped because they are our fellow human beings?" he asks. "We may, but it is more persuasive, morally as well as politically, to describe them as our fellow Americans—to insist that it is outrageous that an American should live without hope." (p. 190). The important point he makes is that "our sense of solidarity is at its strongest when those with whom solidarity is expressed are thought of as 'one of us,' where 'us' means some-thing smaller and more local than the human race" (p. 191).

It is for that reason that Rorty (1989) argues for an understanding of solidar-ity as "the ability to see more and more traditional differences (of tribe, religion, race, customs, and the like) as unimportant when compared with similarities with respect to pain and humiliation" (p. 192). Human history, according to Howard Zinn (2007), is not only about competition and cruelty, it is also about "compas-sion, sacrifice, courage, and kindness" (p. 270). In this very same sense, explaining his understanding of education for political literacy, Freire (1985) says: "Although the educator in the domesticating model always remains the educator of learners, the educator for freedom has to die, so to speak, as the exclusive educator of the learners, that is, as the one educating them. Conversely, the educator must propose to the learners that they too die, so to speak, as the exclusive learners of the educators so that they can be reborn as real learners-educators of the self-educator and self-learner" (p. 105). Matina Dwyer's plausible deniability is precisely that, a note to self, a reminder to make the decision to listen to the voice of otherness, and not to conform to the expectations of others apparently more powerful, as a way to set a higher moral standard for our lives. Her statement is criticality and creativity symbolically used to prevent evil from winning. It is both an act of resistance and a site for redeeming prospective projection.

SOMETHING CULTURAL

In *A power governments cannot suppress* Howard Zinn (2007) reflects on how a person, in the midst of war and injustice, can manage "to stay socially engaged, committed to the struggle, and remain healthy without burning out or becoming resigned or cynical" (p. 267). His response is like anything simple: "if we do act, in however small a way, we don't have to wait for some grand utopian future;...to live now as we think human beings should live, in defiance of all that is bad around us, is itself a marvelous victory" (p. 270). This simplicity, though, encompasses a uniquely radical perspective, one that breeds a dynamic of passion that is not exhausted by rational calculation, but reflects and diffracts the very complex process of learning into its unerring meaning. This is why Paulo Freire continues to be so relevant in the transformative education processes around the world. Zinn was able to capture this particular interest in the underlying phenomenology of what is considered historically relevant, and continues the Freirean model by focusing on the person herself rather than on the events. In this way, Zinn—in the same way Freire was—was not only critical and keen to the ease with which historical explanations can easily be turned into self-serving justifications, but through his historiography, Zinn spoke to possibility in the same way Freire did through his whole production of popular pedagogy. Each issue they depict, each dilemma they unfold, each voice they echo, opens up and refers to a particular kind of being-in-the-world. And the most inspiring treat of their writing is that in each case, the person described is not a stranger, but someone we ourselves, at one time or another, could have been, or even better, could become.

Freire's greatest treat as an educator, I believe, is that he openly acknowledges that his writing is not neutral and that through it he wants to bring into the light those victories mentioned above because for him, at the end of the day, the standard scholarly practice minimizes our present freedom by privileging Truth at the expense of truthfulness. As a result, the historical material with which he deals as an intellectual is not just a matter of objectivity, balance, and methodological distance, but from a philosophical perspective, the only truth that may interest him, if any at all, is rather problematical, unfinished, unpretending, and, most of all, alive. As an activist, Paulo Freire walked the talk, seeking to inspire others as he highlighted the creative power of ordinary people struggling for a better world. And, as a socially engaged human being himself, he certainly believed that even though our future is unpredictable, he had hope and believed that change can certainly be induced; that speaking truthfully is a far more fitting ambition than speaking the Truth; and that transformation often starts as something cultural. I describe it as the pedagogical site where dissent is expressed and both consciousness and unconsciousness are shaped. In the end, education is a perspective to be developed at a crossroad, an unhinging critical point, and a juncture with a possible future.

REFERENCES

Acosta, S. (2007, September 20). *La influencia militar de EE.UU. en América Latina. serie: "De la seguridad nacional a la seguridad democrática."* Radio Netherlands.

Appiah, K. A. (2005). *The ethics of identity.* Princeton, NJ: Princeton University Press.

Ball, M. S. (1993). *The word and the law.* Chicago, IL: University of Chicago Press.

Bauman, Z. (1995). *Life in fragments: Essays in postmodern morality.* Malden, MA: Blackwell.

Britzman, D. P. (1998). Is there a queer pedagogy? Or, stop reading straight. In W. F. Pinar (Ed.), *Curriculum toward new identities.* New York, NY: Garland.

Britzman, D. P. (2006). *Novel education: Psychoanalytic studies of learning and not learning.* New York, NY: Peter Lang.

Bush, G. W. (2002). *The national security strategy of the United States.* Washington, DC: The White House.

Bush, G. W. (2006). *The national security strategy of the United States.* Washington, DC: The White House.

Caygill, H. (1993). Violence, Civility, and the Predicament of Philosophy. In D. Campbell & M. Dillon (Eds.), *The Political Subject of Violence.* Manchester, England: Manchester University Press.

Chomsky, N. (2001). *Media control: The spectacular achievements of propaganda.* New York, NY: Seven Stories Press.

Chomsky, N. (2003). *Hegemony or survival: America's quest for global dominance.* New York, NY: Owl Books.

Chomsky, N. (2006). *Failed states: the abuse of power and the assault on democracy.* New York, NY: Owl Books.

Colette, S. (1936). *Mes Apprentissages.* Paris, France: Hachette.

Copley, G. (2007). *Pakistan: the delicacy, and inevitability, of the political transition now underway.* GIS. ISSA.

Crenshaw, M. (1995). Thoughts on relating terrorism to historical contexts. In M. Crenshaw (Ed.), *Terrorism in context.* University Park: Pennsylvania State University Press.

Dantley, M. E. (2007). Re-radicalizing the consciousness in educational leadership: The critically spiritual imperative toward keeping the promise. In D. L. Carlson & C. P. Gause (Eds.), *Keeping the promise: Essays on leadership, democracy, and education*. New York, NY: Peter Lang.

Didion, J. (2006). *The year of magical thinking*. New York, NY: Knopf.

Fischer, M. (2000). *The liberal peace: Ethical, historical, and philosophical aspects* (BCSIA Discussion Paper 2000–2007). Cambridge, MA: Kennedy School of Government, Harvard University.

Fontana, B. (2002). Gramsci on politics and state. *Journal of Classical Sociology, 2*, 157–178.

Forsythe, D. P. (1992). Democracy, war, and covert action. *Journal of Peace Research, 29*, 385.

Freire P. (1985). *The politics of education: Culture, power, and liberation*. New York, NY: Bergin & Garvey.

Gaddis, J. L. (2004). *Surprise, security, and the American experience*. Cambridge, MA: Harvard University Press.

Gates, R. M. (2008). *National security: What new expertise is needed?* U.S. Department of Defense. Office of the Assistant Secretary of Defense (Public Affairs). Speech to the Association of American Universities (Washington, DC) as delivered on Monday, April 14, 2008.

Gates, R. M. (2009). A balanced strategy: Reprogramming the Pentagon for a new age. *Foreign Affairs, 88*(1), 28–40.

Giroux, H. A. (2005). *Schooling and the struggle for public life: Democracy's promise and education's challenge*. Boulder, CO: Paradigm.

Giroux, H. A. (2006). *America on the verge*. New York, NY: Palgrave Macmillan.

Giroux, H. A., & R. I. Simon. (1989). *Popular culture, schooling, and everyday life*. New York, NY: Bergin & Garvey.

Goemans, H. E. (2000). *War & punishment: The causes of war termination & the First World War*. Princeton, NJ: Princeton University Press.

Goodman, A. (2009a). Despite Gitmo closure and torture ban, Obama admin converges with several Bush policies in so-called "War on Terror." *Democracy Now*. Retrieved from www.democracynow.org./2009/2/20

Goodman, A. (2009b). Obama continues Bush policy of deadly air strikes in Pakistan. *Democracy Now*. Retrieved from www.democracynow.org.2009/1/30

Goodman, A. (2009c). Peace activists arrested after protesting U.S. drones in Nevada. *Democracy Now*. Retrieved from www.democracynow.org/2009/4/14

Gorman, S., Y. J. Dreazen, & A. Cole. (2009, December 17). Insurgents hack U.S. drones. *The Wall Street Journal*.

Gornick, V. (2001). *The situation and the story: The art of personal narrative*. New York, NY: Farrar, Straus & Giroux.

Guignon, C. (2004). *On being authentic*. New York, NY: Routledge.

Habermas, J. (2006). *The divided West*. Cambridge, MA: Polity Press.

Herzog, K. (1993). *Finding their voice: Peruvian women's testimonies of war*. Valley Forge, PA: Trinity Press International.

Holmes, J. (2001). *Terrorism and democratic stability*. Manchester, England: Manchester University Press.

hooks, b. (1994). *Teaching to transgress: Education as the practice of freedom*. New York, NY: Routledge.

hooks, b. (2001). *All about love: New visions*. New York, NY: Perennial.

Hosenball, M., Isikoff, M., & Thomas, E. (2010, January 11). The radicalization of Umar Farouk Abdulmutallab. *Newsweek*.

Illich, I. (2002). *Deschooling society*. London, England: Marion Boyars. (Original work published 1970).

Jakobsen, P. (2005). *PRTs in Afghanistan: Successful but not sufficient* (DIIS Report 2005:6). Copenhagen, Denmark: Danish Institute for International Studies.

Kamrath, C. (2009). Randolph Bourne's malcontents: Culture politics, democratic practice, and the domestication of war, 1917–1918. *Culture, Theory, and Critique, 50*(1), 959–975.

Kincheloe, J. L. (1993). *Toward a critical politics of teacher thinking: Mapping the postmodern.* Westport, CT: Bergin & Garvey.

Kincheloe, J. L. (2005). On to the next level: Continuing the conceptualization of the bricolage. *Qualitative Inquiry, 11*(3).

Krujit, D. (1999). Exercises in state terrorism: The counterinsurgency campaigns in Guatemala and Peru. In K. Koonings & D. Krujit (Eds.), *Societies of fear: The legacy of civil war, violence, and terror in Latin America.* London, England: Zed Books.

Krujit, D., & Koonings, K. (1999). Violence and fear in Latin America. In K. Koonings & D. Krujit (Eds.), *Societies of fear: The legacy of civil war, violence, and terror in Latin America.* London, England: Zed Books.

Lerner, M. (2007). *The left hand of God: Healing America's political and spiritual crisis.* San Francisco, CA: HarperCollins.

Lifton, R. J. (1993). *The protean self: Human resilience in an age of fragmentation.* Chicago, IL: University of Chicago Press.

Lifton, R. J. (2003). *Superpower syndrome: America's apocalyptic confrontation with the world.* New York, NY: Thunder's Mouth Press.

Lowe, C. (2003). *Photographer finds boy from famous picture.* USAToday. July 6, 2003.

Maaluf, A. (2000*). In the name of identity: Violence and the need to belong* (B. Bray, Trans.). New York, NY: Arcade.

McDonald, M. (2002). Human security and the construction of security. *Global Society, 16*(2).

McLaren, P. (1999). *Schooling as a ritual performance: Toward a political economy of educational symbols and gestures.* Lanham, MD: Rowman & Littlefield.

McLaren, P., & Jaramillo, N. (2007). *Pedagogy and praxis in the age of empire: Towards a new humanism.* Rotterdam, The Netherlands: Sense.

Moriarty, M., & Chappell, J. (2008, July 2). At peace now. soldier made famous by photo dies in Pinehurst. *The Pilot, 89*(79).

Obama, B. (2009a, January 22). Inaugural address of Barack Obama. Full text of speech. *Chicago Tribune.* Retrieved from www.chicagotribune.com/news/politics/obama

Obama, B. (2009b). President Obama's speech at the Nobel Peace Prize ceremony in Oslo on December 11, 2009; as released by the White House. *The New York Times.*

Obama, B. (2009c). *Speech on strategy in Afghanistan as delivered at the U.S. Military Academy at West Point on December 1, 2009.* Washington, DC: Office of the President.

Pareja, P., & Torres, E. (1989). *Municipios y terrorismo: Impacto de la violencia política en los gobiernos locales.* Lima, Peru: Centro de Estudios Peruanos.

Poole D., & Rénique G. (2003, Winter). Terror and the privatized state: A Peruvian parable. *Radical History Review, 85,* 150–163.

Purpel, D. E., & McLaurin, W. M., Jr. (2004). *Reflections on the moral & spiritual crisis in education.* New York, NY: Peter Lang.

Ravel, M. (1925). *L'Enfant et les sortilèges.* Monte Carlo.

Richey, W. (2009, October 29). Obama endorses military commissions for Guantánamo detainees. *The Christian Science Monitor.* Retrieved from www.csmonitor.com/layout/set

Ripley, A. (2008). *Reverse Radicalism.* Time Magazine. March.

Rochester, J. M. (2003, Fall). Critical demagogues: What happens when ideology and teaching mix. *Education Next*, 77–82.

Rogers, K. (2008, June 3). Drone warriors—British, U.S. Reaper operators fly joint Afghanistan mission. *Las Vegas Review Journal.*

Rorty, R. (1989). *Contingency, irony, and solidarity.* New York, NY: Cambridge University Press.

Rorty, R. (1999). *Philosophy and social hope.* New York, NY: Penguin.

Shapiro, S. (2006). *Losing heart: The moral and spiritual miseducation of America's children.* Hillsdale, NJ: Lawrence Erlbaum.

Sharansky, N. (2005). *The case for democracy: The power of freedom to overcome tyranny & terror.* New York, NY: PublicAffairs.

Silliman, S. (2001, November 28). *DOJ Oversight: Preserving our freedoms while defending against terrorism.* Testimony. United States Senate Committee on the Judiciary. November 28, 2001. Retrieved from www.judiciary.senate.gov

Silliman, S. (2003). International legal constraints on strategic deception. In *Conference on strategic deception in modern democracies: Ethical, legal, and policy challenges, Chapel Hill, NC. Proceedings.* The Triangle Institute for Security Studies, The United States Army War College, The United States Naval Academy, and Duke University Kenan Institute for Ethics.

Silva, P. (1999). Collective memories, fears and consensus: The political psychology of the civilian democratic transition. In K. Koonings & D. Krujit (Eds.), *Societies of fear: The legacy of civil war, violence, and terror in Latin America.* London, England: Zed Books.

Singer, P. W. (2003). *Corporate warriors: The rise of the privatized military industry.* Ithaca, NY: Cornell University Press.

Singer, P. W. (2009). *Wired for war: The robotics revolution and conflict in the 21st century.* New York, NY: Penguin.

Slattery, P. (2006). *Curriculum development in the postmodern era.* New York, NY: Garland.

Sloan, S. (1995). Terrorism: How vulnerable is the United States? In S. Pelletiere (Ed.), *Terrorism: National security policy and the home front.* Washington, DC: The Strategic Studies Institute of the U.S. Army War College.

Spiegel Online. (2009, March 26) Away from the politics of fear: Interview with Homeland Security Secretary Janet Napolitano. Retrieved from www.spiegel.de/international/world

Spring, J. (2001). *The American school, 1642–2004.* Boston, MA: McGraw-Hill.

The White House. (2002a). *The national security strategy of the United States of America.* Washington, DC.

The White House. (2002b) *National strategy for homeland security.* Office of Homeland Security. Washington, DC.

The White House. (2006a) *The national security strategy of the United States of America.* Washington, DC.

The White House. (2006b) *National strategy for combating terrorism.* Washington, DC.

The White House. (2006c) *9/11 Five years later: Successes and challenges.* Washington, DC.

Totenberg, N. (2009). *Judge: Bagram prisoners may challenge detention.* NPR. Retrieved from www.npr.org/templates/story

U.S. Department of Justice, Federal Bureau of Investigation. (1999). *Terrorism in the United States. 30 years of terrorism. A special retrospective edition.* Counterterrorism Threat Assessment and Warning Unit, Counterterrorism Division. Washington, DC.

U.S. Marine Corps. (2002) *MARINES. THE FEW. THE PROUD.* Washington, DC.

Weeks, L. (2009). On second day in office, Obama keeps rolling. NPR. Retrieved from www.npr.org/templates/story

West, C. (2004). *Democracy matters: Winning the fight against imperialism.* New York, NY: Penguin.

White, D. (2006). Sen. Obama reacts to U.S. bill approving torture. About.com US Liberal Politics. Retrieved from www.usliberals.about.com

Zakaria, F. (1997). The rise of illiberal democracy. *Foreign Affairs, 76,* 22–43.

Zinn, H. (2007). *A power governments cannot suppress.* San Francisco, CA: City Light Books.

Zinn, H. (Writer), & Ellis, D., & Mueller, D. (Directors). (2004). *You can't be neutral on a moving train: A personal history of our time* [DVD].

Zinn, W. (2008, July 13). Ricochet: My shot made Joseph Dwyer famous. Did it also lead to his death? *The Washington Post,* p. B1.

CHAPTER EIGHT

Paulo Freire's Prophetic Voice at the Intersection of Liberation Pedagogy and Liberation Theology

DÉBORA B. A. JUNKER

INTRODUCTION

This chapter proposes a brief review of the contributions of Freire's education-al philosophy within the religious field by showing how his faith-based vision was influential for the emergence of liberation thoughts, which included the em-bryonic liberation theology of the late 1960s and early 1970s in Latin America. More specifically, it analyzes how religious groups, informed by Freire's teachings, started to reject practices and religious discourses that legitimized the subjugation and exploitation of marginalized people in order to reclaim the prophetic role of education in those settings. In addition, this chapter indicates how men and women, inspired by his ideas, began to realize that their struggles were not sim-ply results of fate or divine will, but consequences of a patriarchal and colonialist mentality materialized in situations of oppression. It concludes that Freire was a fundamental agent in the transformative process that took place in the context of Latin American Christian churches. His inspiring presence influenced a whole generation and still influences present generations. The prophetic vision of Freire has guided the path of those who understand education as an act of love and be-lieve that a world "more just and less ugly" is possible.

Paulo Freire—A Man of His Culture

Known as one of the most important philosophers of education in the twentieth century, Paulo Freire inspired many educators around the globe with his passionate insights on education as an act of love and courage. His global legacy has extended beyond the field of education influencing different fields such as philosophy, linguistics, psychology, communication, drama, and theology, among others. Specifically in the theological field, his contribution can be seen in the genesis of what came to be known as theology of liberation, a theology born in the midst of the pain and oppression of Latin America countries, and later recreated in other contexts of struggle such as Africa and Asia. Freire's work has been remarkably influential to many generations of religious educators around the globe who see in his work an inspiring force to revive the hope for a world of justice and peace. Certainly the dialogic character of his pedagogy has inspired many scholars from different fields contributing to a more holistic understanding of the process of teaching and learning and the involvement of participants in the process of education.

In the next section, some key historical aspects that have stimulated the development of Freire's liberation perspective highlight how he was part of a group of intellectuals and religious leaders that contributed significantly to the emergent liberationist endeavor that took place in Latin America.

A HISTORICAL OVERVIEW

The 1950s, 1960s, and 1970s were decades marked by the fertile and dynamic social movements that mobilized countries around the world to fight against social and structural injustices present in various layers of society. The seeds germinated in these decades gave birth to movements that were concrete testimonies of society's longing for a more humane and transformed reality. Some of these exemplary initiatives were the civil rights movement and women's rights movement in the United States, and the anti-apartheid movement and anti-colonialist movements in Africa, among other initiatives in different parts of the world.

In Latin America, intense political discord and class conflicts marked these decades. Events such as the consolidation of the Cuban Revolution, the growth of working-class trade unions, and the rise of left-wing political parties stirred Latin America. Particularly in Brazil, the strengthening of student movements, such as Catholic Youth Association (JUC) and Young Catholic Workers (JOC), stimulated a younger generation to envision new ideals in response to these conflicts as Brazilian citizens sought to challenge the colonial mentality of the country through many demonstrations in favor of the so-called basic social reforms. The Catholic Church, concerned with social inequalities generated by the model of capitalism established in the country, began to raise her voice as well. In 1952, the National Conference of Bishops of Brazil (CNBB) was founded and later, in 1955, the Latin American Episcopal Council (CELAM) was created. By the interest and involvement of the Catholic bishops in the social and economic problems affecting the country, the Brazilian Catholic Church—and some more progressive segments of the Protestant Church—experienced a significant revitalization of the churches around the country. Several leaders who advocated for the social and structural reforms recognized how education was a pivotal force either to support the status quo or to confront the inequities they tried to overcome. During this effervescent time, a space was opened in which novel educational approaches were welcomed. Paulo Freire's work emerged precisely within such contexts of controversy and possibilities.

Earlier in his life, after his father's death, Freire experienced a lack of material goods and became sensitive to the suffering that poor people had to endure in their lives. Later, as an educator, he was deeply touched by the severe situation of material and intellectual deprivation found in northeastern Brazil. From his engagement with education at different levels, Freire was able to develop a different pedagogy to educate illiterate adults based on their life experiences, work, and cultural context. He considered literacy not a mechanic process of teaching people to read and write, but instead a process through which they would break the silence imposed on them. Freire believed that these people could develop a critical consciousness about their situation in order to transform their individual and communal realities. Thus, his pedagogical paradigm, grounded in the ethical commitment to the oppressed, sought to stimulate students to dialogue, not only to read the words by their sociocultural contexts.

In 1963, Freire coordinated a literacy project in Angicos, in the state of Rio Grande do Norte (northeastern region of Brazil). In this project, 300 workers learned to read and write in 45 days. This remarkable experience gave him national visibility and recognition as an educator and philosopher of education. As a result, President João Goulart and Minister of Education Paulo de Tarso Santos nominated him to lead a National Literacy Program early in 1964. The aim was to teach millions of students throughout the country to read and write in the same short period experienced in Angicos. Unfortunately, shortly after his appointment, a coup led by the Brazilian military on April 1, 1964, dismantled Freire's literacy endeavor because his activities were considered subversive. Military leaders forced Freire into 16 years of exile (1964–1980) along with many Brazilian intellectuals, politicians, and religious popular leaders (Horton & Freire, 1990). During his exile period, Freire continued to develop his thinking and educational philosophy, and in 1967 he published one of his most significant works, *Education as the Practice of Freedom*. A year later, a major event took place in Latin America that would change the directions of the Catholic Church on the continent. The Second

General Conference of Bishops of Latin American held in Medellin, Colombia, in 1968 made a clear and prophetic "preferential option for the poor." This also influenced the Protestant Church.

According to Carlos Alberto Torres (1993), there is significant resemblance between the *Final Documents of Medellin* produced by the Catholic bishops and Freire's philosophy of education as expounded in his early books (pp. 120–121). Freire's pedagogical insights offered a methodological path to the emergent Catholic and Protestant theological thinking. After the conference in Medellin, the Church became increasingly concerned with issues of social inequality and recognized the need for greater involvement in the political process in society. Many priests, nuns, and lay pastoral workers became political activists in defense of the poor and in opposition to authoritarianism.

In regard to the characteristics of education in Latin America and the need for a liberating education, the *Final Documents of Medellin* states: "The task of educating our brothers [*sic*] does not consist in placing them into the cultural structures that exist around them, which can also be oppressive, but something much deeper. It consists in enabling them, as authors of their own progress, to develop a creative and original cultural world according to their own wealth, as fruit of their own efforts" (Gómez-Martínez, 1968). This statement parallels Freire's philosophy of education and his pedagogical principles of educating for critical consciousness and agency as expounded in his book *Education For Critical Consciousness*. According to Freire (1973), a critical education stimulates the critical attitudes necessary to enhance one's ability to confront the challenges and intervene in one's social reality in order to transform it (pp. 32–34). This critical thinking, he adds, "requires a strong sense of social responsibility and engagement in the task of transforming society" (p. 13). Another paragraph of the *Final Documents of Medellin* states its aim to "propose a vision of education, more in line with the overall development we advocate for our continent, which we would call the 'liberating education.' That is, the education in which the learner becomes subject of his own development" (Gómez-Martínez, 1968). Furthermore, the document asserts, "Education is indeed the key means of freeing people from all bondage and to make them ascend 'from less human conditions to more human conditions,' given that they are the 'principal agents of their success or their failure.'" Indeed, this document validates the principles Freire advocated in his approach to education.

In the same year, 1968, Freire first published his book *Pedagogy of the Oppressed* in which he declares, "Authentic liberation—the process of humanization—is not another deposit to be made in men. Liberation is a praxis: the action and reflection of men and women upon their world in order to transform it" (1968/1997b, p. 60). Freire's account of human beings as subjects of their own development and the unfinished character of human existence as "beings in the process of becoming—as unfinished, uncompleted beings" (p. 65) is a vital part of his great contribution and legacy not only to an effervescent Latin America, but also to humanity in general.

The new political, economic, and cultural circumstances that had created a favorable environment to rethink education also began to impact theology and the theological education practiced in Latin America, thanks to Freire's liberation philosophy and educational approach. For the first time in the history of Latin American Christianity, an autochthonous theological thought began to take shape. Motivated by the circumstances and continuous struggles of the Latin American people since colonial times, the new ideas functioned as fertilizers nourishing the arid soil that had received the evil seeds of social injustices and political indifference. Little by little, those reflections achieved consistence and depth and became the innovative theology to announce a new time to a wounded continent. Interestingly, the seeds of this theology began to sprout in different Latin American countries through several theologians. Some of them and their respective works are: Miguez Bonino (1967, Argentina), *La Fe en Busca de Eficacia* [The Faith in Search of Effectiveness]; Rubem Alves (1968, Brazil), *Teologia da Esperança* [A Theology of Human Hope]; Leonardo Boff (1970, Brazil), *Jesus Cristo Libertador* [Jesus Christ Liberator]; Juan Luis Segundo (1970, Uruguay), *De la Sociedad a la Teología* [From Society to Theology]; Gustavo Gutiérrez (1971, Peru), *Teologia de la Liberación: Perspectivas* [A Theology of Liberation: History, Politics and Salvation]; and Hugo Assmann (1971, Bolivia), *Opresión-Liberación. Desafío a los Cristianos* [Oppression-Liberation: The Challenge of Christians].

According to Freire (1984), liberation theology is "a prophetic, utopian theology, full of hope" that emerges from the "hopeless situation" of occupied societies (p. 544). Moreover, Freire's *Pedagogy of the Oppressed* played an important role in the emerging liberation theology. For instance, Gustavo Gutiérrez's book, *A Theology of Liberation* (1971), one of the most influential texts in the development of the emergent theology, draws insights from Freire's philosophy and argues that Freire's book is "one of the most creative and fruitful efforts implemented in Latin America" (p. 57). Leonardo Boff corroborates, saying that Paulo Freire, from the beginning was, and continues to be, considered one of the forebears of liberation theology (A. M. A. Freire, 2005, p. 596). Freire sought to develop an authentic and coherent faith throughout his life, and on several occasions referred to his commitment to the principles of the Christian faith. The experiences developed in the early stages of his life were pivotal in the formation of his human character, which is precisely what I explore in the next section.

The Former Christian Influences—Under the Shade of a Mango Tree[1]

From the parallels seen between Freire's educational philosophy and the *Final Documents of Medellin*, one can see the tremendous impact he made on the emerging theological thoughts in Latin America. His view of education, his passion to build a different world, and his commitment to justice compelled him to fight against the manipulative and oppressive forces that prevented people from experiencing freedom. Authors such as John Elias, Daniel Schipani, and Carlos Alberto Torres, among others, have indicated how Freire's intellectual formation was influenced by religious thinkers such as Jacques Maritain, Tristan de Ataide, Emmanuel Mounier, and Martin Buber. Through his engagement with the work of these intellectuals, Freire was able to develop his own perspective informed by his Christian convictions and his commitment to people, society, politics, and culture. However, it is clear that the religious nature of Freire's writings and the influence of his Christian faith were engendered in a much earlier period of his life. It was in the convivial atmosphere of his family that Freire gained the first insights of his educational philosophy.

On several occasions when referring to his formative years, Freire declared that he learned how to appreciate and cultivate openness to different perspectives as a result of the religious tolerance he experienced at home. Freire's mother was a Roman Catholic believer and his father was a follower of French spiritualism. Growing up in an atmosphere of religious respect and tolerance, Freire experienced firsthand what he called "the harmony and contradictions of his parents," which coexisted in a warm and open environment (Horton & Freire, 1990, p. 242). The welcoming disposition of their discussions helped Freire understand, at a very early age, that people with different opinions can and must be open to dialogue. In his conversation with Myles Horton, one of the founders of the Highlander Folk School,[2] he remembered how his parents would discuss their different perspectives on faith without imposing their view on each other, and would encourage their children to develop consistency "between proclaiming faith and having consistent behavior vis-à-vis this faith" (p. 243).

Although Freire admits that he did not feel comfortable speaking openly about his faith, he recognized the fundamental importance of faith to sustain and challenge him to overcome an oppressive reality in order to build a more humane society. According to Freire, "Having faith is not a problem; the problem is claiming to have it and, at the same time, contradicting it in action." (1998, p. 104). Freire also illustrates how his faith motivated his actions and pedagogical approach when he declares, "When I went first to meet with workers and peasants in Recife's slums, to teach and to learn from them, I have to confess that I did it pushed by my Christian faith" (Horton & Freire, 1990, p. 245). Certainly, the values learned in an earlier age would significantly influence the way he demonstrated coherence between his discourse and his praxis. Freire understood the concept of praxis not as simply action based on reflection, but as a complex relationship between theory and practice, a dialectical exercise in which oppressive structures are challenged. In praxis—action/reflection—human beings seek to understand critically their reality, and as historical beings commit themselves in favor of the oppressed and to the transformation of the world. In this sense, praxis emerges in the context of dialogue and fosters conscientization and transformation.

Another aspect of his social and educational philosophy refers to his openness to embrace others' perspectives, which is embodied in his profound respect for the experience and universe of the learners. Consistent with his educational vision, Freire respected the worldview of his students, their vocabulary, and their social location as a starting point of the educational process. According to him, it was impossible to talk about respect for students without taking into consideration the conditions in which they live and the knowledge derived from their life experiences. However, he advised that the educational process cannot stay at that level, but it needs to expand on what students know in order to advance the construction of their knowledge. In addition, he stressed that teachers who use irony to put down students and who discriminate or inhibit students' curiosity transgress fundamental ethical principles of the human condition. In his view, teachers should understand the perspective of the learners in order to facilitate the learning process by inviting them to become subjects of their own learning. This would be possible by stimulating decision making and responsibility by enabling learners to discuss the problems of their contexts, and by encouraging them to intervene in that context from the perspective of their agency and creative potential. In this framework, dialogue is the key and necessary component of the learning process, which occurs between two historical subjects while they analyze a dehumanizing reality, denounce it, and announce its transformation (Freire, 1970, p. 20).

According to Freire, the role of liberation education is to educate for critical consciousness with the ultimate goal of humanization and the building of a just society. He regards the ontological vocation of human beings "to be more" as a central construct of his theory that explicitly opposes any action that is destructive and inhuman. This is already a prophetic sensitivity embedded in the life of a person whose passion is the well-being of everyone—Christian praxis at its full stretch. For him, Christian faith was not an excuse to accept passively oppression that takes place, but an invitation demanding a historical commitment, a transforming activity, and a praxis of liberation that encompasses prophecy and hope. Hence, a faith that anchors itself in passivity and accommodation is an alienating faith and serves to promote injustices and inequities. In essence, it is a faith that contradicts the Christian message to love God and neighbors. Love in this respect is not an abstraction, but it materializes in concrete actions of solidarity and justice in face of oppressive socioeconomic and cultural situations.

Freire's educational approach informed by Christian principles became even more explicit through his involvement with the World Council of Churches. While teaching in the United States as a visiting professor at Harvard University, in 1969, Freire was invited to join the newly established Office of Education of the World Council of Churches (WCC) in Geneva. As a Special Consultant on Education, he was able to devote his efforts to assisting educational programs of recently independent countries in Asia and Africa. During a decade serving the WCC (1970–1980), Freire influenced the development of ecumenical education and had the opportunity to examine more closely the Church as an institution. While serving as a consultant, he was able to articulate more explicitly his concerns and criticisms about the oppressive nature of the institutional church, challenging Christians to embrace a more coherent position between their words and actions. In a collection of articles from Freire's lectures published by LADOC during 1970–1972, there are explicit references to how he understands the role of Christians and the Church (Freire, 1972). Particularly in the texts "Conscientizing as a Way of Liberating," "The Third World and Theology," and "The Educational Role of the Churches in Latin America," Freire draws from the Jewish and Christian traditions to build on themes such as hope, love, justice, freedom, and prophecy—denouncement and announcement. He declares,

> The word of God is inviting me to re-create the world, not for my brothers' domination, but for their liberation.... Listening to the word of God does not mean acting like empty vessels waiting to be filled with that word.... That is why I insist that a utopian and prophetic theology leads naturally to a cultural action for liberation and hence to conscientization. (1972, p. 12)

Some of these articles are dedicated to the discussion of the role of the Church in its prophetic dimension, which shall be discussed subsequently. In what follows, I bring into conversation the practical aspect of Freire's contributions to the local community of faith: the Base Ecclesial Communities.

THE GENESIS OF A NEW CHURCH—BASE ECCLESIAL COMMUNITIES

As seen above, in the late 1950s and early 1960s members of Catholic and Protestant churches such as Catholic Action, Church and Society in Latin America (ISAL), and Lutheran Pastoral People (PPL) started to reflect on the social conditions of the poverty of many people in Latin America and to question the reasons for these circumstances. In the early 1970s, young people, intellectuals, and priests entered the world of the poor, embracing their culture and their claims. Inspired by the methodology *See-Judge-Act*, also known as the hermeneutical circle, they recognized the new historical subject: the poor, the woman, the peasant, the native, and the black. Together with them, they sought new ways of reading the Bible in which the experience of the marginalized was part of the historical and spiritual meaning of the Bible and God's revelation. They started to reject interpretations of the Bible that legitimized oppression and exploitation, which, in some cases, had the concealed support of the ecclesiastical authorities who were silent amid the atrocities practiced by the military dictatorships.

Gradually, these Base Ecclesial Communities, that is, small groups primarily composed of lower-class, grassroots people, lay leaders, and priests, started to meet regularly to read the Bible, pray, and reflect on it theologically. While studying the Bible, they began to articulate a reading of the word (Bible) and the reading of the world (their reality) as postulated by Paulo Freire. Therefore, the local community started to experience a new model of religious education, a new process of learning, a new paradigm of studying the Bible and practicing Christian faith. These new groups became known as Base Ecclesial Communities (BECs), or *Comunidades Eclesiais de Base*, as they are known in Brazil. The impact of Vatican II in Latin America, and more specifically in Brazil, was without a doubt a fundamental element to the consolidation of the BECs. The Medellin Conference (1968) inspired the Church with the theme of liberation, and Puebla in 1979 with the evangelical option for the poor brought energy and hope for structural changes in a context marked by injustices.[3] Thus, BECs became an instrument toward a more just and friendly society.

From their very beginning, BECs played a relevant role in influencing the lives of many marginalized people in Brazil. The churches, thus, became a space to articulate an engaged reading of the Bible—one that lives out an incarnate spirituality that openly contests the political repression imposed on poor people. These communities, based on an ecclesiology grounded in the needs of the poor, represented a new paradigm born within popular sectors as a non-authoritarian and non-hierarchical way of being a community. As Boff comments:

> Christian life in the basic communities is characterized by the absence of alienating structures, by direct relationships, by reciprocity, by deep communion, by mutual assistance, by community of gospel ideals, by equality among members. The specific characteristics of society are absent here: rigid rules; hierarchies; prescribed relationships in a framework of a distinction of functions, qualities, and titles. (1986, p. 4)

It was through personal and communal readings of the Bible, collective prayers, songs and celebrations, and sociopolitical participation that these groups started to discover new ways of being together in solidarity with one another as brothers and sisters living out their dream for a better society. *Ecclesiogenesis* is the word Boff uses to describe the birth of this new church, a new concept of practicing the faith, a church in constant search of transformation from within.

The primary purpose of base communities—as a space for ordinary people to grow—was to read and reflect on the Bible in the context of their own daily struggles. People worked together to find new ways to understand their reality inspired by the message of the Bible. This was indeed a new perspective of living together as a community of faith. Because people in the community shared a specific geographical territory, they were able to establish relationships and to see their common needs. Together, they discussed their problems and were able to claim small improvements in the neighborhoods. The word of God was brought to bear on the problems of the group as they faced a world of scarcity: lack of electricity, sewers, paved streets, clinics, schools, and so forth. At the same time, they began to become conscious of their social and political situation. Essentially this meant grounding the reading of the Bible within the sociopolitical context of the participants. Consistent with Freire's thoughts, the ordinary people took courage to move from awareness to action.

BECs applied a participatory methodology that included the collaboration of all to discuss the problems and to seek together the solutions to those problems. If, for example, the issue was unemployment, there was a communal and concrete commitment to provide food for the family; at the same time, through a process of consciousness, they began to take a political stance toward the conditions that generated that situation. Seeking to improve their lives, they began organizing themselves through neighborhood associations, labor unions, political parties, and the like (Boff, 1984, p. 127). Within the community, they organized festivities, group projects, neighborhood credit unions, and efforts to resist land takeovers. Many services included women and men in clubs and small organizations: community gardens, mothers' clubs, adult literacy, and often support groups of popular movements. Consequently, this spirit of cooperation triggered the emergence of lay ministries that were multiplying from the community's demands. These services included the commitment of the CEBs with the poorest and the consequent relationship between professed faith and concrete life experiences.

Accordingly, BECs represented a popular space of intense participation, witness, and creative celebration in which Bible readings are rooted in daily life and a commitment to transformation. The Bible readings included not only the intellectual contribution of the priest or theologian, but also the perspective of lay people who began to hear the Good News, to interpret the Gospel message, and to find the liberating presence of God in the midst of their struggles. As the BECs started to spread across the country, the socially and politically active laity, through their praxis and leadership style, challenged the structures of the traditional church, especially the Roman Catholic Church.

It can be argued that the experience of many of the participants in the BECs exemplifies what Freire describes as the experience of Easter, the experience of new birth through which a person (oppressor or oppressed) can no longer remain as they were. In regard to the BECs' participants, their experiences also convey a sense of re-birth as they emerge from a culture of silence to speak their own word. As re-born people, they realize that their life's struggles are not simply the results of fate or divine will, but consequences of a patriarchal and colonialist enterprise that sought to deny their sense of human dignity. As seen above, in the context of Brazilian culture, BECs challenged conventional patterns of community life to become a more democratic, participatory, and holistic model of living that encompassed all dimensions of life. They become sources of inspiration allowing participants to create voluntary associations and a network of support to seek social changes.

The theological interpretation proposed by Latin American liberation theology, as experienced within BECs, is consistent with Freire's pedagogy because it starts from the reality of the people, from its concreteness and limits, but also from its possibilities. As people who have been denied the right to speak, they found in this environment the opportunity to speak their word, which represented the first stage in taking control and shaping their own destiny. As they analyzed and problematized their situations—and sought to solve their problems—they became protagonists of their own history. Certainly the coherence that BECs advocate between faith and the life is what Freire also engaged in his own life through his prophetic vision. This is the subject of the next section.

THE PROPHETIC CHURCH—COMMITTED TO TRANSFORMATION

The importance and influence of Freire's thought within religious contexts cannot be overemphasized. The world that Freire confronted in his time was one marked by inequalities, discrimination, and oppression exposed through governmental indifference, political repression, structural poverty, and violation of basic human rights. His ideal of education as the practice of freedom found a receptive soil to germinate even amidst adversity and atrocities that were perpetrated by dictatorial governments. With outside interest growing, his books appeared in other languages, embraced by other countries in Latin America, Africa, and Asia. The strength of his thought broke boundaries of language, race, and cultures because many of his readers recognized themselves in Freire's writings. Many years have passed since the initial impact of his ideas, and yet his educational approach remains relevant in today's context of a globalized market and the victims it produces. His genuine concerns for the poor and marginalized without distinction of color, race, gender, religious affiliation, or any other kind of discriminatory mark are necessary for both educational and religious institutions. Regarding the role of the Church, he challenged the churches, specifically in Latin America, to recognize that they are institutions "inserted into history and conditioned by concrete historical reality" (1972, p. 15), and as a result they cannot dismiss or forget their prophetic role, especially in contemporary context where discriminatory structures, ecological abuse, and unequal relations are so prevalent.

Freire's understanding of education as freedom rejects the compartmentalization of knowledge, which hinders, weakens, and prevents the historical subjects from changing their inhuman situations. In his perspective, a dialogic pedagogy must not subscribe to any imposing, excluding, and fatalistic type of education that dictates what and how to think, depriving learners of their sense of agency. Rather, Freire chooses to advocate for a pedagogy of hope, inclusion, and construction of a more humane and compassionate society where there should be a space for all. In order for this particular pedagogy to be implemented, a pedagogy of indignation must first erupt—one that positions itself against the objectification, domestication, and sanitization of people, which perpetuates discrimination and oppression. Because he recognizes the potential for each person to become more human by opening oneself to be educated, he affirms that "along with the denial of experiences of freedom we discover the necessity and feasibility to fight for freedom and autonomy against oppression and arbitrariness" (2000, p. 121). For that reason, Christians need to be prophetic voices in today's context to deliver to "the least of these" the message that another world is possible and desirable. Indeed, a new world is possible, not beyond the grave but here and now. In light of the present-day challenges the Church cannot, indeed dare not, be silent. The Church cannot suffer from apathy, lacking social commitment to the transformation of society and the world. Today, as it was in the past, the participants of the Church need to break the culture of silence because the neglected and illiterate Freire devoted his attention to in the past are the excluded from the context of today's global economy. Thus, motivated by her faith the Church needs to create emancipatory movements that promote life with justice. Against a spirituality of individualism so prevalent in contemporary societies, the Church needs to reclaim a spirituality of solidarity that is the heart of liberation theology. When contexts of solidarity prevail, there is no space for imperialist ideologies or idolatries of the market, neither space for human sacrifices. Therefore, no matter which configuration, Churches today are called to foster movements to read today's reality with critical awareness, enlightened by pedagogies of indignation and hope. Certainly, the prophetic Church cannot accomplish its task if she is not concerned with the creation of a critical consciousness. Such consciousness can only be attained through a deep involvement with the 'flow of history' and the context of pressing struggles in order to denounce all that is inhuman.

As Paulo Freire reminds us, the prophetic Church must move forward constantly, forever dying and forever being reborn (1984, p. 544). Every time we confront injustices, we are called to take a stance and to envision new possibilities. The utopia that feeds us needs to be cultivated in the minds and hearts of young people, but this is not enough. The vision of different and transformed realities needs to reach the hands and feet of a people so that it can be actualized through actions of solidarity and transformation. Utopia, for Freire, is not a kind of idealism, but a radical process of transformation in which a person becomes more fully human. He contends that only utopians can be prophetic, reacting against a culture of silence, but without giving up hope. Freire declares that oppressors and reactionaries cannot be utopians because they cannot be prophetic and hopeful. According to him, the prophet is not a "bearded wise person," but instead one who lives by "what one sees, what one hears, what one realizes, based on one's epistemological curiosity, watching out for signs that one seeks to understand, reading the world and the words, old and new" (2000, p. 118). Echoing Gustavo Gutiérrez (2008) when he says that theology must always be a love letter to God, to the Church, and to the people we serve, a Freirean approach requires that theology speak to the narratives of the suffering of God's children. It must be a letter of love that the people, whom the Church serves, understand, assimilate, and appropriate as their own.

The seeds tenderly planted in Freire's childhood germinated later in his youth, and became a strong tree—perhaps a mango tree whose fruits we can savor. This is the legacy that Freire offers to us: the seeds of transformation that need to be planted in our homes, cultivated in our communities, so they can thrive in our societies. However, as he reminds us, a critical reading of the world, as so many claim to possess, does not mean an immediate commitment to the struggle for liberation. This incessant struggle needs to become part of our minds, hearts, and actions until we see justice and peace for all human beings independent of their gender, race, ethnicity, sexual orientation, or religious affiliation. Freire's prophetic message offers us a redemptive dimension, which echoes his faith and reaches both our individual and our communal subjectivities. Freire (2012, p. 138) reminds us that God is a presence in history that does not prohibit human beings from making history, but rather inspires them to work not in favor of the powerful who exploit and control the powerless, but toward the transformation of the world, which restores the humanity of both. Initially, this redemptive process has an inward nature, which invites us to engage in our own development of conscientization. Subsequently, this emancipatory practice invites us to ascend as historical subjects who can intervene in history in order to transform society through our agency. Finally, as children of God, this liberating revelation calls us to embrace transcendence in the encounter with the God of shalom who delights in those who join in the historical construction of a new project of humankind, a different world "less ugly," less unjust, and more ethical and democratic.

NOTES

1. *Under the Shadow of the Mango Tree* (À Sombra desta Mangueira) is a reference to the original title of one of his books that has been translated into English as *Pedagogy of the Heart* (1998). In this book, Freire plays with the tropical memory of his childhood, bringing to his words the

warmth of the days in the northeast region of Brazil as a form of refuge and connection to his cultural roots. See Ana Maria Araújo Freire, *Pedagogy of the Heart*, note 2, p. 111.

2. Myles Horton was one of the founders of the Highlander Research and Education Center, formerly known as the Highlander Folk School, in Monteagle, Tennessee. During the 1950s, this school trained young people in nonviolence and leadership, becoming a critically important incubator of the American Civil Rights movement. Among those who received training in this school were the famous Rosa Parks, prior to her historic role in the Montgomery Bus Boycott, as well as Martin Luther King, Jr. See http://highlandercenter.org/media/timeline

3. The Second General Conference of the Latin America Bishops realized in Medellín, Colombia, in 1968; the Third General Conference of the Latin America Bishops realized in Puebla, Mexico, in 1979.

REFERENCES

Boff, L. (1984). *Church, charisma, and power: Liberation theology and the institutional church.* New York, NY: Crossroad.

Boff, L. (1986). *Ecclesiogenesis: The base communities reinvent the church.* Maryknoll, NY: Orbis.

Collins, D. E. (1977). *Paulo Freire, his life, works, and thought.* New York, NY: Paulist Press.

Foubert, C. (1978). *The church at the crossroads: Christians in Latin America, from Medellín to Puebla, 1968–1978.* Rome, Italy: Idoc International.

Freire, A. M. A. (Ed.). (1999). *A pedagogia da libertação em Paulo Freire* [The pedagogy of liberation in Paulo Freire]. São Paulo, Brazil: UNESP.

Freire, A. M. A. (2005). *Paulo Freire: Uma história de vida* [Paulo Freire: A life history]. São Paulo, Brazil: Villa das Letras Editora.

Freire, P. (n.d.). LADOC. Keyhole Series, no. 1. Division for Latin America, Washington, DC: USCC.

Freire, P. (1970). *Cultural action for freedom.* Cambridge, MA: Harvard Educational Review.

Freire, P. (1972). The educational role of the churches in Latin America, *Pasos, 9*, ISAL. Santiago, Chile. (15-18).

Freire, P. (1973). *Education for critical consciousness.* New York, NY: Seabury Press.

Freire, P. (1978). *Pedagogy in process: The letters to Guinea-Bissau.* New York, NY: Seabury Press.

Freire, P. (1984). Education, liberation and the church. *Religious Education, 79*(4), 524–545.

Freire, P. (1997). *Pedagogy of the oppressed.* New York, NY: Seabury Press.

Freire, P. (1998). *Pedagogy of the heart.* New York, NY: Continuum.

Freire, P. (2000). *A pedagogia da indignação. Cartas pedagógicas e outros escritos* [The pedagogy of indignation. Pedagogical letters and other writings]. São Paulo, Brazil: UNESP.

Freire, P. (2001). *Pedagogy of freedom: Ethics, democracy, and civic courage.* Lanham, MD: Rowman and Littlefield.

Freire, P. (2007). *Pedagogy of hope: Reliving "Pedagogy of the oppressed."* New York, NY: Continuum.

Freire, P. (2012). *À sombra desta mangueira* [Under the shadow of the mango tree]. Rio de Janeiro, Brazil: Civilização Brasileira.

Gómez-Martínez, J. L. (1968, September). *Documentos finales de Medellín.* Medellín, Colombia: Segunda Conferencia General del Episcopado Latinoamericano. Retrieved August 26, 2012, from http://www.ensayistas.org/critica/liberacion/medellin/medellin6.htm

Gutiérrez, G. (1971). *A theology of liberation: History, politics, and salvation.* Maryknoll, NY: Orbis.

Gutiérrez, G. (2008). *A teologia como carta de amor*. Voice_Feb2014.docxhttp://www.cebi.org.br/noti cia.php?secaoId=13&noticiaId=770) Retrieved September 7, 2012

Horton, M., & Freire, P. (1990). *We make the road by walking: Conversation on education and social change*. Philadelphia, PA: Temple University Press.

Schipani, D. (2002). *Paulo Freire: Educador cristiano*. Grand Rapids, MI: Libros Desafío.

Second Vatican Council. (1965). Gaudium et Spes: Pastoral constitution on the Church in the modern world. Retrieved from http://www.vatican.va

Torres, C. A. (1993). From the *Pedagogy of the oppressed* to *A luta continua*. In P. McLaren & P. Leonard (Eds.), *Paulo Freire: A critical encounter*. London, England: Routledge.

CHAPTER NINE

Social Emancipation and Human Rights

MAURO TORRES SIQUEIRA

HUMAN RIGHTS AND SUBORDINATE COSMOPOLITISM

Throughout the course of history, capitalist society has been building a path of domination, exploration, discrimination, imposition, and overvaluation of the rational over the emotional. Such a state of affairs is part of a historical and cultural process passed on through generations, establishing the dominant paradigm on how we comprehend the world (Santos, 2002).

In that sense, Santos (2006) revisits the concept of globalization, dividing it into hegemonic and counter-hegemonic globalization, as well as emancipation and multiculturalism. These issues will be addressed in this chapter, along with the correlation between these concepts and social emancipation and popular education as access to human rights.

Let us start with a discussion on the concept of globalization. In the words of Santos, it is defined as "a set of social relations that translate into intensification of transnational interactions, be they interstate, global capitalist or socio-cultural transnational practices" (Santos, 2001, p. 90).

Thereby, we note that globalization has implications of economic, environmental, political, and cultural character. Globalization must be discussed as the sets of social relations that are modified in accordance with the changes within themselves. That is why, according to Santos (2006), this concept should be realized in the plural (globalizations) instead of in the singular. To make his thesis didactic, he classifies it in two ways: hegemonic globalization—constituted by two processes: globalized localism and localized globalism—and counter-hegemonic globalization, characterized by an insurgent and subordinate cosmopolitism, by the common heritage of humankind, that is, a globalization in accordance with the project of society that respects local cultures, multicultural and emancipated.

Regarding hegemonic globalization, the author brings into discussion the universalist aspect of human rights, which tends to operate as a globalized localism in that most of the countries that constituted the Declaration of Human Rights were in a particular universe and that other cultures did not intervene in its production. Globalized localism, for the author, would be the result of local production that presents itself to the world as global—a local standard that is eventually appropriated by different localities. Another example of this would be multinational corporations that spread throughout the planet.

In turn, local globalism, according to Santos (2006, p. 406) "consists in the specific impact on the local conditions of practices and transnational imperatives that emerge from globalized localism." In other words, it refers to the global effects that are generated in certain places caused by external sources. An example is the effects of pollution on a region due to problems from others such as acid rain caused by polluting industries situated in neighboring areas. Another example can be seen in the determination of economic models by multilateral agencies that coerce countries into following local policies in the interest of transnational models.

According to Santos, we see that the localized globalisms and the globalized localisms write the plot of worldwide systems (top-down). However, there are resistances caused by them. They are the ones that Santos (2006) calls counter-hegemonic globalization (bottom-up). In counter-hegemonic globalization, insurgent subordinate cosmopolitism consists in the transnationally organized resistance against globalized localisms and localized globalisms (Santos, 2006, p. 406).

The use of the term *cosmopolitism* is founded upon a strategy that aims to transcend locality and seeks to gather demands from distinct social groups. The expression *subordinate* brings groups that were previously included in inferior social layers to light. It opposes top-down configurations of society.

Subordinate cosmopolitism is, as such, universalist, counter-hegemonic, and horizontal. This, to Santos (2006, p. 406):

> relates itself to a vast and heterogeneous set of initiatives, movements and organizations that partake in the struggle against social exclusion and discrimination, along with the environmental destruction produced by neoliberal globalization, using transnational articulations made possible by the revolution in information and communication technology.

Another point reflected in relation to the concept of globalizations in their counter-hegemonic aspect is the idea of a common heritage of humankind. To Santos (2006, p. 408):

> It is about values or resources that are meaningful only in as much as they are reported in the globe in their totality: the sustainability of human life on earth, for example, or environmental themes such as the protection of the ozone layer, the preservation of Antarctica, biodiversity and marine life.

In this context, according to Santos a transnational and globalized struggle exists for values or resources that, by their essence, are as global as the planet emerges.

EMANCIPATION AND MULTICULTURALISM: APPROXIMATIONS BETWEEN PAULO FREIRE AND BOAVENTURA SANTOS

The debate over social emancipation and multiculturalism is nestled in the thoughts of Paulo Freire and Boaventura de Sousa Santos, thinkers whose theoretical constructions cross paths and possess a high level of proximity, which I will discuss further in this chapter.

Santos takes on a fresh view of emancipation. His thinking arises from delving more deeply into the democratic perspective that contemplates dialogue between subjectivity, citizenship, and emancipation. For the author, in current contexts, socialism finds itself freed from the grotesque caricature of a "real socialism" and returns as the utopic view of a just society and the provider of a better life for all.

Santos (2003) led an international research project titled *Reinventing Social Emancipation: Toward New Manifestos*. The central aspects of this project are the concepts that gave credibility to the modern ideals of social emancipation and allowed them to find themselves questioned by the globalization phenomenon which, despite not being new, has been gaining an amplitude that has redefined contexts, configurations, objectives, means, and subjectivities in political and social struggles in the past few decades. This project has revealed that hegemonic globalization has been progressively confronted by another form of globalization: "alternative," "counter-hegemonic," instituted by the collective of initiatives, movements, and organizations, which, through "local and global links, networks, and alliances, fight against neoliberal globalization, mobilized by the desire of a better, fairer, and more pacific world which they believe is possible and feel they are entitled to" (Santos, 2003, p. 14).

This perspective of emancipation emerged in the First World Social Forum in Porto Alegre and continues to strengthen. "It is in this alternative globalization and its shock against neoliberal globalization that new paths for social emancipation are being created." This alternative viewpoint of globalization has its roots in

Marxism, along with the international strife in the context of global capitalism (Santos, 2003, p. 35).

> The success of emancipatory struggle depends on the alliances that its protagonists are capable of forging. In the beginning of the 21st century, these alliances must course a multiplicity of local, national, and global scales and must also embrace movements and struggles against different types of oppression. (Santos & Nunes, 2003, p. 64)

According to Santos and Nunes (2003), these struggles have been waged in a historical context, in which the emergence of different struggles and distinct collective actors has been observed: women, environmentalists, anti-racist movements. According to these authors, in facing the new configurations of globalized capitalism, it is no longer possible to attribute to a single collective actor—*global proletariat*—the principal part in the struggle against different forms of oppression, exclusion, and domination. There is, then, the emergence of a diversity of struggles and collective subjects. Therefore, "it becomes necessary to recontextualize the spacial scale of these struggles, which are waged in the national, supranational, and subnational spaces in which capitalism operates" (Santos, 2003, p. 35).

At the same time hegemonic globalization generates new forms of racism, it also creates conditions for the emergence of multiculturalism. Santos (2003) writes about multiculturalism, multicultural justice, collective rights and plural citizenship and describes them as terms that permeate the debate over the tension between difference and equality, between the demand for recognizing difference and a distribution that will enable the substantiation of equality. These tensions occur in the midst of the struggle by social movements with emancipatory perspectives against the Eurocentric reductionism of certain terms, seeking to propose more inclusive conceptions and, at the same time, being respectful of the difference between alternative conceptions and practices that yearn for human dignity (Santos & Nunes, 2003, p. 25).

At this juncture, Santos and Nunes (2003, p. 28), debate multiculturalism as a term wrapped in controversy and tension. The expression *multiculturalism* originally designated the coexistence of cultural formats or groups characterized by different cultures in the realm of "modern" societies. Therefore, this term has been used to designate cultural differences in a global and transnational context. In this way, there are different notions of multiculturalism; however, not all have an emancipatory meaning. It may be conservative as well as emancipatory. According to these authors, this term presents the same difficulties and potentials as the concept of culture. One of the dominant concepts refers to the paths to institutionalized knowledge in the West. However, there are other conceptions that recognize the existence of a cultural plurality, "defining them as complex totalities which blend with societies, allowing the characterization of ways of life based on material and symbolic conditions" (Santos & Nunes, 2003, p. 27).

Thus, Santos (2003) defends emancipatory multiculturalism, which is based on the recognition of difference and on the right to difference and coexistence, or the construction of a common life beyond differences of any sort. However, equality or difference, by itself, isn't sufficient for an emancipatory policy. The debate over human rights and its reinvention as multicultural rights—as well as the struggles of women and indigenous peoples—shows that the affirmation of equality based on universalist presuppositions, as well as the ones that determine the Western and individualistic conceptions of human rights, often leads to decharacterization and negation of different historical identities, cultures, and experiences.

In the studies of Freire, we bring to the forefront the hope in his writings that, given the discontent in a socialist experience while living a capitalist experience, urges a fairer and more human world, something that is still possible. The current context, according to him, allows us to transcend the negative model of soviet socialism as well as the authoritarian paradigm of the so-called real socialism:

> I refuse to believe that the socialist dream is over because I note that the social and material conditions by which it can flourish are there. Misery, injustice and oppression are there. Capitalism does not solve that, except for a minority. I believe that never, never in our History the socialist dream has been so visible, so palpable and so necessary as it is today, although, perhaps, in a much more difficult way to achieve. (Freire & Shor, 1997, p. 209)

In these terms, social emancipation will not happen by accident or concession, but by conquest, by the struggle within the human praxis. "Liberation, thus, is not unlike childbirth…. The man that is born from that birth is a new man viable only in and through overcoming the oppressor-oppressed contradiction, which is the liberation of us all" (Freire, 1991, p. 35).

Human emancipation in this light considers the whole humanization process, oppressor and oppressed alike. Thus the struggle of the oppressed is the struggle of men and women in search of the reconstruction of humanity, not perceiving themselves as oppressors, neither converting themselves into the oppressors of the oppressors, but as restorers of the humanity in both. And therein lies the great humanistic and historical task of the oppressed—liberating themselves and the oppressors (Freire, 1991, p. 30). According to Freire:

> Debating about multiculturality demands a critical analysis of its constitution, for multi-culturality does not consist of the juxtaposition of cultures, much less of exacerbated power of one over the other, but in freedom conquered, in the secured right of each one to move across each other's respects. (1997, p. 156)

With that said, the idea in which, to Freire, multiculturalism expresses itself as the critical dialogue between cultures in order to establish equivalent strengthening between collectives and individuals that glimpses more human ways of coexistence becomes clear.

Paulo Freire (1997, p. 198) criticizes the "right-wing" model of post-modernity, which defends the idea that social classes have become extinct, as well as idealism, dreams, and utopias. To the author, there is an imperative to adopt the democratic reality in which one cannot only conform joyfully that, in a certain society, man and woman are free in such a way that they even have equal rights to death and hunger. Therefore, they have the right to live on the streets, the right not to have old age supported, the right to simply not be anything at all (Freire, 1997, p. 157).

Hence, multiculturalism does not exclusively establish the assertion of the right to be different if that difference is characterized by social inequality. The right to difference between multiplicities of cultures is insufficient to ascertain that one is in a multicultural society.

According to Souza (2001, p. 123), the Freirean multicultural perspective is expressed as the concreteness of a critical dialogue between cultures, at the same time boosting actions that envision human forms of coexistence and individual and collective growth of all human beings. In this way, much like Boaventura de Souza Santos, Freire verifies the existence of different cultures or cultural aspects in the same national culture, despite finding themselves juxtaposed or in situations of domination and subordination. The challenge lies in extrapolating this cultural diversity by means of a critical dialogue between cultures and cultures within a multiculturality.

Therefore, we can turn to Boaventura de Souza Santos, who reinvents the concept of emancipation. To Santos (2005, p. 277) emancipation is no more than a set of procedural struggles without a defined end. What distinguishes it from other sets of struggles is the political feeling of their procedurality.

The similarity between Freire and Santos, from a conceptual viewpoint, is noted on the elements centralized in the respect for differences, in addition to disseminating, through their ideas, that dialogues between cultures are interrelated as a process of human emancipation. Multiculturalism seeks to incite, in this thinking, a horizontal dialogue between people, culture, peoples, territories, nations, and states.

MULTICULTURALITY AND EDUCATION FOR EMANCIPATION

Education and school are focal points in the struggle for emancipation. Liberating education is contrary to domination, be it classist, racist, sexist, or of any other nature. The battle against this disposition is waged through the illumination of reality, by debating it in a way in which one can confront manipulation. This way, "to better comprehend the exploration of workers, it can be done rigorously in a classroom.... Only in the classroom level can a better comprehension of such a subject and a change in it as a reality be achieved" (Freire & Shor, 1997, p. 207).

Freire points out that only political action can lead to transformation and social emancipation, but he also notes that education is the instrument for this action. Education is a path of struggle against dehumanization, against the distortion of the vocation of being more by the part of oppressed and oppressor. If we were to accept that this path of dehumanization were the human vocation, then there would be nothing we could do. The struggle for humanization, for free labor, for dealienation, for the affirmation of men as people, as "beings for themselves," only has meaning because dehumanization is not a given fate, but the result of an unjust "order" that generates violence from oppressors and this violence, the being less human (Freire, 1991, p. 30).

Thus, emancipation, according to Freire, is to appropriate and experience the power to pronounce the world, the experience of the human condition of being the subject of their own history. Freire proposes a popular education that seeks human liberation, humanization, and emancipation. His pedagogy encompasses a social and historical ontology, an ontology that, accepting or postulating human nature as necessary and inevitable, does not understand it as historically a priori. Human nature is constituted socially and historically (Freire, 2000, p. 119). Emancipation is a quotidian and historical enterprise crossed by challenges, dreams, utopias, resistances, and possibilities. Aspiring to liberty, humankind seeks to create spaces of autonomy through the disposition of mining, without stopping, in search of a renewed compromise with the emancipatory cause, be it on the personal or collective plane. Freire fights for human emancipation. This task, however, cannot be proposed by the dominant class. It must be fulfilled by those who dream of the reinvention of society, the recreation or reconstruction of society (Freire, 2001, p. 49).

In a capitalist society, there are many barriers on the path to human emancipation. Emancipation is, then, always a project. Emancipation for Paulo Freire is a quotidian living, not an intention to be fulfilled only in a distant future, maybe to be made meaningful only by others. This way, emancipatory practices by humankind will be effective both in daily life and in history. It occurs at all times in family relations, in school, at work, no matter the degree of intimacy or distance. In this sense, popular education is a fundamental space for individual and collective human emancipatory experiences. Hence, in the Freirean perspective, emancipation includes the living experience of material and subjective necessities; it comprehends the celebration and joy of life:

> This education towards freedom, this education tied to human rights in this perspective must be embracing, totalizing; it must come with the critical knowledge of the real and with the joy of living, and not only with the rigorous analysis of how society moves and wades; it must come with the revel that is life itself. But it must be done critically, and not naively. (Freire, 2001, p. 102)

At this point, Freire counters the banking approach to education. This approach does not promote emancipation; on the contrary, it reduces the human being to the status of "automaton," which is a negation of its ontological vocation of being more. It is an idea of a human as an "empty" being that the world "fills" with content, forming a particularized and mechanistic conscience. "In the 'banking' approach which we are criticizing, to which education is the act of depositing, transfering, transmitting knowledge and values, this overcoming is neither verified nor possible to be verified" (Freire, 1991, p. 59). Such education only contributes to silencing and the upkeep of contradiction.

Education, as thought of by Freire, is engraved in the dialogical concept of an education rooted in a problematizing comprehension of the act of knowing and the intentionality of changing the world. It is an education that evokes transformation, emancipation, and human liberation (Freire, 1991). The elite of society imposes its dominant class culture, language, syntax, semantics, affections, dreams, and projects. According to Freire, this hinders bilingualism, as well as "multilingualism, outside of multiculturality, and it does not exist as a spontaneous phenomenon, but as a phenomenon created, politically produced, worked, through hardships, in history." It is necessary that each cultural group organizes itself as historical subjects and struggles for a voice in society. To reach such goals it is necessary, therefore, "to have an educational practice that is coherent with these goals; a practice that demands new ethics based on respect for differences" (Freire, 1997, p. 157).

The human emancipation project defended by Freire implicates the question of multiculturalism. In his last works, Freire takes on the right to have and the need to respect differences. To Freire (1997, p. 156), multiculturality must be thought of as a theme that requires a critical analysis of its content: "Multiculturality is not the juxtaposition of cultures, much less in exacerbated power of one over the other, but in freedom conquered, in the secured right of each one to move across each other's respects." Thus, in a society possessing possibilities of multicultural emancipation, the challenge lies in establishing a critical analysis of educational practices, with the intention of not confusing a cultural juxtaposition for multiculturalism.

The multicultural perspective of Paulo Freire is expressed as a concreteness of a critical dialogue between cultures, enabling actions toward individual and collective growth of all humans. It refers to the educational processes that contribute to the "construction of mankind and the human being, of all the human beings in all the corners of the globe" (Souza, 2001, p. 124).

Freire is emphatic when he states that it is not enough to guarantee the right to diversity in a democratic society. He criticizes the "right wing" model of post-modernity, which spreads the idea that social classes have been suppressed, as well as ideologies, dreams, and utopias (Freire, 1997, p. 198). The perspective that the social class category has been abolished is seen in educational and sociological discourse, that workers are spread throughout two fronts: work, immediate survival. However, we understand that the debates in vogue today do not totally stray from the class issue, as, for example, the debates on the defense of nature, the ethnic struggles, women's struggles, the right to difference—in other words, the unequal manner by which different groups have participated in the process of producing and enjoying cultural goods and materials produced by humankind:

> At first, the struggle for the unity in diversity, which is obviously a political fight, impli-
> cates a mobilization and organization of cultural forces in which the *class division cannot be*
> *understated*, in the sense of an enlargement and the deepening and overcoming of a purely
> liberal democracy. (Freire, 1997, p. 157). (emphasis mine)

Therefore, multiculturalism is not simply the affirmation of the right to be different when this difference is marked by social inequality. The mere right to difference between cultural multiplicities is insufficient to determine that we are in a multicultural society. Thus, Freirean pedagogy has increasingly been put radically "in favor of the transformation of the conditions and life situations and the existence of majorities deprived of any economic, social, and political power" (Souza, 2001, p. 119). Facing this debate, Freire makes a distinction between a progressive post-modernity and a conservative, neoliberal one. He criticizes the latter, reaffirming the option for the excluded.

Freire and Boaventura identify, accordingly, that there are different cultures or cultural traces of a single national culture, although these find themselves juxtaposed or in subordinate or dominant positions. The challenge is, then, to transcend this cultural diversity by means of a critical dialogue between cultures and from cultures (interculturality), in a multiculturality (Souza, 2001, p. 123).

Multiculturality and interculturality are not spontaneous situations; they are projects, "*still desires, utopias, the goals of a few social groups, especially of the new social movements.*" (Souza, 2001, p. 124) In this way, multiculturality will become effective as a consequence of a politically, culturally, and historically motivated construction. Accordingly, this utopia and its hope and the desire for it will be able to become a new configuration of human coexistence (in its economic, political, and gnoseological dimensions) in the new global scenarios (Souza, 2001, p. 126). The experience in the World Social Forum has created opportunities for this global movement of expression, partition, and solidarity between peoples and cultures.

Popular education has a decisive part to play in this political construction for it presents the conditions of promoting learning focused on these multicultural values, as well as its class character. Miguel Arroyo (2001) defines popular education as an organized movement, a concept, a way of making education: "one of the most inquiring movements in pedagogical thought that is created and moves through adult and young education projects tied to popular movements in the fields and in the cities, all over Latin America" (Arroyo, 2001, p. 10).

However, there is no homogeneity when speaking of popular education. Beisiegel (1992), in discussing popular education policies in Brazil, points to its different possibilities, highlighting the experience of Paulo Freire and popular education given by the State. Even that could contribute the quality of life of the people, being able also to be executed through a liberating discourse or directed to the dimensions of an economy that promotes solidarity. Normally, it is directed to the service of the interests of the State. However, an education that realizes the democratic experience between those that live through its work is sought.

Here we understand both initiatives tied to social movements and the education provided by the state as popular education, where the education of the oppressed has a place, where a possibility of liberation can be seen. Access to education by the people equips them with the ability to think about reality, to refuse political and scientifical neutrality and to affirm concepts and practices of humanity.

Popular education thus emerges as a possibility for the affirmation of the condition of being a historical subject, stimulating processes that promote freedom, emancipation and individual and collective autonomy. Paulo Freire, in many of his works, expresses his comprehension of popular education linked to actions with the oppressed. Freire states that one of the primordial tasks of a radical, liberating and critical education (popular) "is working on the legitimacy of the ethical-political dream of overcoming an unjust reality" (Freire, 2001, p. 101). Hence, popular education, as defended by Freire, seeks the dream of the construction of society. Freire highlights that, despite the fact that education is not the boost for social transformation, transformation itself is an educational event:

> I know that education is not the boost for social change or transformation, but I know that social transformation is achieved through several small, big, great and humble tasks! I have been set with such tasks. I am a humble agent of the global task of transformation. Very well, I discover this, proclaim it, verbalize my option. (Freire, 2001, p. 60)

From this ideal, Freire debates the urgency of a liberating, democratic, unveiling, challenging education, a critical act of knowledge, of reading reality, of comprehending how society, school, as well as educational processes within social movements and practices work. Freire presents much diverse knowledge that is essential to educational action. We've highlighted two pieces of that knowledge that are said to be fundamental in the constitution of a popular emancipatory education by Freire: "the knowledge of History as possibility, and not as determination. The world 'is' not, the world is 'being'" (Freire, 2000, p. 85). Another is that "as a decidedly human experience, education is a way of intervention in the world" (Freire, 2000, p. 110).

From this knowledge, one seeks unity in diversity, one struggles for the possible dream, for necessary utopia, taking a stand in the perspective of inter- and multiculturality, for overcoming ghettoization and assimilationism in the critical interaction between cultures or present cultural traces. In other words,

To guarantee the development and enrichment of different cultures or present cultural traces. At the limit, one will be able to reach the construction of a democratic society not only representative, but participative. Contributions, these, that educational processes must not omit from social dynamics if not wanting to lose strength and the educational denomination. (Souza, 2001, p. 145)

According to Souza (2001, p. 127), the globalization model that is present has incited many "transculturations," mainly in the course of the past fifty years. However, it has not yielded results in regard to unity in the diversity of cultures, having only made possible a cultural diversity, or pluriculturality, which predominantly swings toward cultural fragmentation. In this way, many social movements have permanently denounced this as problematic. As an example, there are the many social movement protests that have arisen during international encounters with "world leaders" (Seattle, Davos, Genoa). Conversely, there are also the propositive actions of the World Social Forum, whose motto is "Another world is possible."

Santos (2003) states that multiculturalism can be an alternative to resistance in the face of transculturations provoked by current processes of hegemonic globalization, inscribing into that process the dialogue, respect, the sharing of differences.

The similarity of Freire and Boaventura, when these propose respect for difference and intercultural dialogue as the human emancipation process, becomes clear. Thus, popular education and social movements constitute the privileged "locus" of permanent learning in this process. From this perspective, multiculturalism constructs a horizontal dialogue between people, cultures, peoples, territories, nations, and states. According to Santos (2001, p. 560), emancipatory, multiculturalist, alternative social justice actions oppose unequal differentiation of identity, or domination. In this sense, it is possible to observe the emancipatory potential of human rights, including the formation of networks based on human rights and local initiatives, as well as the importance of individual and collective rights. We have the right to be equal when difference makes us inferior; we have the right to be different when equality decharacterizes us (Santos, 2006).

REFERENCES

Arroyo, M. (2001) A educação de jovens e adultos em tempos de exclusão. *Alfabetização e cidadania* (pp. 9–20). São Paulo, Brazil: RAAB.

Beisiegel, C. de R. (1992). Política e educação popular (a teoria e a prática de Paulo Freire no Brasil) (3ª. ed.). São Paulo, Brazil: Editora Ática.

Freire, P. (1991). *Pedagogia do oprimido* (19 ed.). Rio de Janeiro, Brazil: Paz e Terra.

Freire, P. (1997). *Pedagogia da esperança*: Um reencontro com a pedagogia do oprimido. São Paulo, Brazil: Paz e Terra.

Freire, P. (2000). *Pedagogia da autonomia* (14ª ed.). São Paulo: Paz e Terra.

Freire, P., & Shor, I. (1997). *Medo e ousadia*: O cotidiano do professor (7. ed.). Rio de Janeiro, Brazil: Paz e Terra.

Santos, B. de S. (org.). (2001). *Globalização:* Fatalidade ou utopia? Porto: Afrontamento.

Santos, B. de S. (2002). *Um discurso sobre as Ciências* (13. ed.). Porto: Edições Afrontamento.

Santos, B. de S. (2003). *Pela mão de Alice*: O social e o político na pós-modernidade (9 ed.). São Paulo, Brazil: Cortez.

Santos, B. de S. (2006). *A gramática do tempo*: Para uma nova cultura política. Porto: Edições Afrontamento.

Santos, B. de S. & Nunes, J. A. (2003). Introdução: Para ampliar o cânone do reconhecimento, da diferença e da igualdade. In Santos, B. S. *Reconhecer para libertar:* Os caminhos do cosmopolitismo multicultural. Rio de Janeiro, Brazil: Civilização Brasileira.

Souza, J. F. de. (2001). A pós-modernidade/mundo e suas implicações educativas na visão de Paulo Freire. In M. N. dos Santos Lima & A. R. Rosas (Orgs.), *Paulo Freire*—quando as ideias e os Afetos se Cruzam. Recife, Ed. Universitária UFPE/Prefeitura da Cidade de Recife.

Section 2:
Reading the World

The Popular Education Network of Australia (PENA) and Twenty-First-Century Critical Education

TRACEY OLLIS, JO WILLIAMS, ROB TOWNSEND, ANNE HARRIS, JORGE JORQUERA, AND LEA CAMPBELL

INTRODUCTION

Drawing on the philosophies and writings of Paulo Freire regarding education as activism, this chapter explores the history and activities of the Popular Education Network of Australia (PENA). The network, founded in 2009, involves educators, academics, and community workers working together on issues relating to critical pedagogy and social change in schools, communities, and adult education contexts. Two symposia have been organised on critical education in Australia. In 2010, Teaching and Learning for Social Justice and Action was the inaugural gathering. In 2012, Freire Reloaded: Learning and Teaching to Change the World featured a diverse range of workshops and Professor Antonia Darder as keynote speaker and observer. Through the perspectives and experiences of six academics involved in PENA, this chapter will explore the group's activities and reflect on the inspiration drawn from the work of Freire, Darder, and others. Creating spaces for discussion of critical pedagogy affords opportunities for academics, educators, teachers, and activists to reflect on their practice and also leads to further spontaneous networking and planning of action. We argue that there is continuing importance, in fact urgency, in producing places and spaces for conscientisation to occur, and for examples of critical education to be shared amongst twenty-first-century educators.

HISTORY OF POPULAR EDUCATION NETWORK OF
AUSTRALIA (PENA)

In late 2007, some early conversations were held between Jorge Jorquera, Tracey Ollis and Jo Williams about the need to establish a network of popular educators. We were motivated by the need to find a group of "fellow travellers" who were working in education from a critical perspective. All three of us were influenced and inspired by Paulo Freire's (1970) life and writing, and more broadly the theory and practice of critical pedagogy (Darder, Baltodano, & Torres, 2009). As activists we were interested in the connection and linkages between critical education work and the revolutionary educational possibilities of learning in and with social movements, solidarity groups and activist communities.

Life in the "swamp"[1] (working critically as an educator) is not easy in Australia; the neoliberal model of education and its alienating potential has impacted on the many layers of educational spaces and places where education occurs, such as primary and secondary schools, adult education and further (TAFE[2]), and higher education. We knew, however, that as we went about our critical education work, there were other like-minded educators and teachers, working critically across the same systems, and often similarly isolated from one another. What we needed in the first instance was to connect. One of the most important issues for the founding members was to create a space for critical reflexivity for teachers and educators to draw on their own and others' teaching and learning experiences. PENA would be not only a space for networking to occur, but also a space to reflect on one's own and others' practice.

As Freire (1970) so eloquently reminds us:

> For apart from inquiry, apart from the praxis, individuals cannot be truly human. Knowledge emerges only through invention and re-invention, through the restless, impatient, continuing, hopeful inquiry human beings pursue in the world, with the world, and with each other. (p. 53)

In reality we know that teachers are isolated, are poorly resourced, and are frequently working in systems in which the hegemony of broader political, economic, and cultural discourses will inevitably influence many. It takes a great deal of resistance to teach outside of these discourses and to push back against them, especially when working on one's own within a team that doesn't know about or support critical pedagogy. This speaks to why we pursued a popular education network and not a critical pedagogy network.

We were inspired by Paulo Freire's work and its revolutionary capacity for social change. We believed as educators that our work was not only to teach critically, but also to link the possibilities for criticality to the struggles of social and popular education movements. Like Freire we also understood critical education as necessarily linked to social critique and movement. We have seen the revolutionary capacity of education to push for human rights and justice around the world. Perhaps the most public recent example is the protests of the global Occupy movement against corporate excess and their cries for fairness and equity for the 99%. Similar youth and student-led protests in Vienna, Hungary, London, Quebec, Mexico, Chile, Greece, and other places have occurred, with communities responding to cuts to social services, rising education fees and other attacks through resistance to the austerity measures imposed by governments. Many of these student movements have also re-imagined the educational space, countering human needs to corporate objectives in curriculum and school and university organisation, Chile being a pertinent and inspiring example.

We see the revolutionary capacity for social change with the recent uprisings in Egypt, Libya, Tunisia, and Syria, where millions of protesters have fought for a change from the rule of repressive regimes, demanding the right of citizenship and democracy. In essence, PENA was formed, it is hoped, to inspire ourselves and other educators not only to work in the classrooms and other teaching spaces, but also to support educators to push back against an education system, indeed a global social system, that is inherently unjust and unequal. PENA was imagined as a place for educators to broaden the focus of our pedagogy to include linking our local education work to national and global struggles. This was envisioned as a two-way process, both educating and inspiring ourselves about current political struggles to enrich and deepen our pedagogical practices, and also growing alliances and practical networks to actually participate in broader collective action.

As Shaull (2000) claims in his now famous foreword to Freire's (1970) classic text *Pedagogy of the Oppressed*, all education work needs to work alongside sites of resistance and struggle:

> Education either functions as an instrument which is used to facilitate integration of the younger generation into the logic of the present system and bring about conformity or it becomes the practice of freedom, the means by which men and women deal critically and creatively with reality and discover how to participate in the transformation of their world. (p. 34)

From the early days of the PENA experience, when three like-minded educators discussed over coffee the need for a critical educators' network, we have grown enormously. The last symposium had more than one hundred people in attendance during two days, with significant attendance and contact from attendees at subsequent organising meetings. PENA is currently leading discussions around a potential boycott of the NAPLAN[3] testing regime in schools and planning for a third symposium. It is obvious from PENA's growth in membership that the need for educators to find a place to engage critically with one another is crucial and this is explored further in the next section.

PLACES AND SPACES FOR SHARING CRITICAL PEDAGOGY

While the spaces and places where this work can and must be done have changed and continue to change over time, our commitment to the principles of learning and teaching for anti-capitalist and inclusive social change is always in evidence, and they evolve with the changing landscape of Australian and international public debate, education policy and practices, and activism. This section will offer a brief overview of our activities to date, primarily our two symposia, their themes, and highlights. Each year, our commitment to open and equal access for all has mandated that our events remain completely free, with a particular commitment to cross-sectoral, intercultural invitation and participation. Our first symposium, Teaching and Learning for Social Justice and Action, was held at Victoria University (Footscray, Melbourne, Australia) on Saturday, October 30, 2010, and focused on the ways in which popular education upholds a social justice agenda and functions within community development. In this first publicly advertised gathering, we sought to overcome the isolating effects of a growing neoliberal agenda in education contexts, and to share insights from our work in practice, research, and policy areas.

From this inaugural event, we established publicly and clearly that we wanted to gather and dialogue in ways that were flexible, purposeful, and diverse. While we advertised a "call for papers," this was no business-as-usual conference announcement; many of us on the original committee were working in universities with output imperatives impinging on our every move. We were—and are—activists who resist the neoliberal demands for commodification of our intellectual and professional activities. Therefore, we strove from this first symposium and since to offer a range of options for participating in PENA spaces and places of sharing community, and the first call for papers reflected that, from a refereed conference format to a more informal and creative/activist format.

Participants could choose to submit or share a paper for refereeing, if they wanted or needed to pursue publication or refereed conference presentation for their own or their employers' requirements. Alternatively, storytelling, filmmaking, performance, and other interactive formats were encouraged, as well as non-refereed papers. Nevertheless, the overwhelming majority of contributions remained formal papers, a trend that we sought to address in our 2012 symposium with our "fresh air dialogues" between each presentation session. The themes touched on dynamic topics such as radicalising assessment, neighbourhood as a classroom and site of struggle, and critical (or "thick") global citizenship and democratising schools.

The weekend events were opened by well-known Australian popular educator Dr Rick Flowers, speaking on a history of popular education in Australia. Despite being entirely volunteer run, and with next to no resources, the symposium was a dynamic success with upward of eighty participants, increased networks, and a further development of perspectives and future goals for the group.

The 2012 symposium, Freire Reloaded—Learning and Teaching to Change the World, was held on April 27 and 28, 2012. The weekend was opened with two PENA book launches (from recent doctoral graduates): *A Critical Pedagogy of Embodied Education: Learning to Become an Activist*, by Dr Tracey Ollis, launched by visiting scholar Professor Antonia Darder; and *Ethnocinema: Intercultural Arts Education*, by Dr Anne Harris, launched by Associate Professor Michele Grossman and Dr Enza Gandolfo. This pre-symposium informal evening at the Footscray Bowls Club (Melbourne, Australia) featured music for social change by the Melbourne-based activist band the Conch,[4] and the kind of interactive, informal, and inexpensive sharing of community and ideas for which PENA is becoming widely known.

The Saturday symposium at Victoria University (Footscray, Melbourne, Australia) was opened by Karen Jackson of the Moondani Balluk Indigenous Academic Unit of Victoria University, who inspired participants with a passionate and political sharing of her heritage and the real meaning of offering a "welcome to country" to those of us on Kulin lands. Karen reminded participants of the responsibility that comes with that permission to enter country. Karen's compelling talk was powerful and moving, and called on us to "make changes where we can…and to work towards giving the ability to all people across the world to walk on country, and to do so together in the true spirit of deep listening and shared understanding." Karen's words were taken seriously by PENA members, who share a deep commitment to working closely with Aboriginal Australian activists, educators, and communities; to learning from them; and to collaborating where possible for justice and change.

The keynote address by Professor Antonia Darder was entitled "Reinventing Paulo Freire: A Critical Pedagogy of Love." Antonia brought the legacy of Paulo Freire to Melbourne, Australia, with an engaging and thought-provoking presentation that encouraged every one of us to consider the urgent need for struggle with, and for, the world's most oppressed peoples, and to ground our personal, political, and educational practices in a deep, revolutionary love. This inspiring address was followed by approximately twenty presentations linked to the overall themes of schools, activism, creative education, adult education, and communities. The program included presentations from people working in a range of sectors, and a dynamic range of perspectives. PENA identifies[5] as a "network of educators, academics, unionists, and community workers," and our activities and outputs reflect this, including strongly at the 2012 symposium. The presentations ranged from Indigenous perspectives in higher education (Mat Jakobi, Moon-dani Balluk), to Augusto Boal and Theatre of the Oppressed (Xris Reardon); from "Early School Leavers in Regional Areas" (Tim Fish, Ballarat Uni) to "Using Sport and Games to Educate About Human Rights" (Tanja Kovac, ECLC), to name just a few.

In addition to our symposia and other initiatives for creating radical and more traditional spaces and places for sharing (including the internet and social media), PENA continues to decentralise the creation and dissemination of activist educator knowledge amongst our members and more widely. Since that first October 2010 symposium, we have published a special issue of the journal *New Community Quarterly*,[6] established a significant online presence, maintained a reading group, presented sessions at a number of professional teacher association conferences, held regular social events, participated in the 2012 Australian EduFactory conference for students at the Australian National University and continued our ongoing campaigning. All of these activities within new and evolving shared spaces and places are volunteer driven and pulsing with the commitment and enthusiasm of like-minded workers and activists from a truly cross-sectoral community of PENA enthusiasts.

Particularly significant is the number of new schoolteachers who have joined PENA since the last symposium and are now a driving force in considering how and why the group might engage more broadly with teachers in schools. This is positive and fundamentally important if PENA is to grow as the multi-sectoral collective it was originally envisioned to be. That the activist base and leadership of PENA now stems so strongly from schoolteachers and vocational educators who are participating in current action and policy devises within Australian education systems is significant. This was always a major intention of PENA, and reflects a consciousness amongst the academic members that existing power hierarchies in education must be challenged, and that only broad coalitions of members can be truly representative of all sectors in education.

CONTEXT: THE BACKDROP OF NEOLIBERAL EDUCATION SYSTEMS IN AUSTRALIA

Australian federal and state/territory governments have provided much impetus for activism against the neoliberal agenda in recent years. The previous Australian Federal Gillard Labour government promised (since its time under previous leader Kevin Rudd) to revolutionise funding for schools. However, the review into schools funding, known colloquially as the "Gonski review" (DEEWR, 2011), recommended a boost of $5 billion into the education sectors, 75% of which was to go to public schools, which remains controversial. As is the case elsewhere in developed countries, the Australian schooling system is riddled with inequity, and the review highlighted that funding must be allocated according to need with resources increased for lower socioeconomic regions, for Aboriginal and Torres Strait Islander (ATSI) students, and for students with a disability. The review also highlighted the need for greater national coherence and consistency in teaching standards, education performance, and public accountability. Meanwhile a more recent briefing paper from the Victorian Department of Education and Early Childhood Development (DEECD, 2012) failed to mention the Gonski review and instead focused on improving teacher quality as the key to improved learning outcomes, suggesting teacher performance pay and bonuses as the means to achieving that. PENA activists developed and distributed publicly a response[7] that pointed out several issues with the arguments being made, as a means to "talk back" to the neoliberal discourse that underpins all current policy decisions, and an attempt to generate discussion on the real issues. Our response focused on the dangerous narrowing of the curriculum that occurs in an environment driven by performative and standardising measures; the unwillingness to acknowledge very real material (social and economic) barriers faced by our most marginalised communities in accessing quality education; and the ongoing omission of teacher, student, and community knowledge about what works, what is needed, in terms of the kind of quality teaching and learning to which we are all aspiring.

Concurrently the vocational education and skills training sector in Australia continues to undergo restructuring from federal and state/territory governments but mostly in opposite directions. The starkest example is that of the Victorian conservative Baillieu government's stripping of $300 million from the local vocational education and skills training sector in favour of supporting cheaper and less publicly accountable privatised training organisations. It is estimated that up to 2,000 teaching staff have been made redundant in 2012–2013, several vocational campuses across two eastern suburb institutions have announced closure, and regional institutes are in talks about possible mergers or partnerships between regional campuses of vocational institutes so they can survive. Many have noted the dire consequences this will have for equity in further education, particularly amongst women and other disadvantaged groups in Australian society.

The vocationalisation of higher education, where learning equals work, seems to be the only purpose of Australian education and learning. In this context, PENA seeks to challenge such a notion and publicly ask, "What about the social purpose of education/learning in Australia?" Universities throughout Australia are continuing to restructure, dumping entire programs and courses, reviewing faculty and school structures, offering places on demand, and so on. Again we ask, "For what purpose?" The professionalisation of education systems has led to a "managerialist" framework of education in which managers, accountants, and marketers outside of the academic disciplines manage university teaching programs, timetabling, learning support, technology requirements, "knowledge transfer," copyright and publishing, administration and, in some universities, even academic workload management. This has led to a disconnection between the philosophies of learning, the evolution of learning pedagogies and practices and the types of programs/courses we all offer.

In the face of such chaos, with highly insecure and disempowered staff and student bodies, the higher education sector is either stagnant with continued use of lecture/tutorial type of frameworks, which reflects what Freire (1970) decried as banking or knowledge transfer, or universities are giddy with visions of Massive Open Online Courses (MOOCS), which seem, without sound evidence, to be now driving policy agendas. For PENA, searing questions remain: Where is the scholarship of learning, and where is the commitment to equity, inclusion, and creativity in education, let alone the valuing of the social purpose of education for transformation or liberation? These stories will ring true with activist educators resisting the neoliberal agenda globally. The question is how to fight back, both within and beyond our classrooms.

THE FUTURE: CRITICAL PEDAGOGY AND THE LEGACIES OF FREIRE AND DARDER

From the outset, the decision to form the organisation that eventually became PENA was informed by the theoretical traditions of critical pedagogy and in particular by the work of Paulo Freire and Antonia Darder. Although Paulo Freire's work is born of struggles in South America and Antonia Darder's writing focuses primarily on the United States, the messages and learning we take from both of these profoundly internationalist writers and activists are deeply relevant to our struggles here in Australia. Moreover, critical educationalists understand that education can only be understood through a critique of a world where education policies internationally are shaped and restructured by an increasingly integrated and crisis-riddled international economy (Apple, 2010). As Darder (2011) suggests:

> Although Freire's historical, regional and class experiences were different from many of ours, his political purpose was clear and consistent. To achieve a liberatory practice, we had to challenge those conditions that limit our social agency and our capacity to intervene and transform our world. (p. 185)

Freire's and Darder's perspectives on the possibilities for education and social change, and moreover their challenging provocations for radical activist educators, provide useful and in fact urgently necessary ideas for the development of the theoretical framework we need in talking back to the neoliberal onslaught in education. Just as important, their work is full of real-life practical signposts to guide and indeed inspire those seeking to reclaim an activist space amidst the horrors of deepening inequality and injustice locally and across the globe.

The idea of a network of popular educators arose out of our frustrations and alienation working in higher education, in an environment of competition, individualism, marketisation, and privatisation. We wondered where the meaning was in what we were doing. All of us were engaged in "good work" in terms of educating our students from a specific pedagogical framework. We all shared Freire's vision of a world free from oppression. We brought to the collective our practices as critical educators, our histories in a range of activist organisations, and our stories of ongoing attempts to carve out space to work against the tide. However, it had also become clear that academia could all too readily see our good work depoliticised, fragmented, isolated, and disconnected from actual communities, or as Apple (2011) states, academia

> with its own hierarchies and disciplinary (and disciplining) techniques, the pursuit of academic credentials, bureaucratic and institutional rankings, tenure files, indeed the entire panoply of normalizing pressures surrounding institutions and careers—all of this seeks to ensure that we all think and "act" correctly. (p. 242)

So we had questions around the difficulties of collaboration, how to reconcile the "rules of the game" with our aspirations and values as critical educators seeking meaningful change in the areas of our work be it adult education, teacher education, racism in schools, or other. Our aspirations for the new collective were twofold: first, to strengthen our intellectual capacity to develop sharp critique of a fundamentally flawed system and give voice to emerging alternative visions and ideals, and second to build solidarity through collaborative practice that saw us theorising and, most critically, acting together, in the most powerful way possible, to bring those alternative visions to reality. We saw PENA as a means to "establish, cultivate, and support humanizing relationships [as we collectively struggled for]…social and economic justice…[able to]…break down the debilitating alienation and isolation" (Darder, 2011, p. 157) we often experienced in education institutions. Darder (2011) evokes Freire's vision for democratic, participatory alliances where "progressive teachers can participate in counterhegemonic political projects that do not dichotomize their work as cultural workers and social activists" (pp. 155–156).

PENA was also based on a rejection of the traditional power hierarchies between universities, schools, and other educational settings, and sought to make the case for shared learning and struggle across the sectors. We were keen to respond to Darder's (2011, p. 156) call for "alliances where a solidarity of differences is cultivated, [where] teachers from diverse communities and class positions can work together to create unifying, albeit heterogeneous and multifaceted, anti-capitalist political strategies to counter conservative efforts to destroy public schooling." Fortunately, most of the institutions we were working in allowed some space for critical practice and engaged activity, and most sought to foster genuine and respectful relationships with schools.

The hegemony of neoliberal policy, however, sees much of that work constrained, falling short of the kind of deep political and economic analysis that both Freire and Darder argue is critical to understanding the material bases of the inequity and exclusion in education and social systems globally. Furthermore, the seemingly intractable borders between educational sectors meant that all too often, and despite our best intentions, our activity within the formal boundaries of institutions remained strained, with limited trust and understanding between us and colleagues in schools and communities. We recognised that teachers trying to enact a critical pedagogy in schools shared our sense of alienation, and that in an education system plagued with guilt and powerlessness, solidarity was the antidote. We wanted to align ourselves with teachers out there struggling under the same conditions as we are, and through activist-driven collaboration outside of the formal walls of academia and schools, we found a space for collective consciousness-raising and felt able to channel our rage and despair into bold courage to speak out against social and economic injustice (Darder, 2011, p. 156).

PENA provides us with an opportunity to model democracy and to model solidarity. The kind of collaboration we are undertaking has a micro-importance in terms of ongoing work to develop liberatory and empowering practices for diverse classrooms, but also points us to the types of social movements required to make meaningful change. Darder (2011) explains that deep in Freire's work is the understanding that the struggle for just and empowering education is intrinsically linked to the broader project for human liberation, and that, moreover, alliances that foster movements capable of growing political strategy are critical, given that strong and democratic social movements are ultimately the only thing capable of forcing significant institutional change.

CONCLUSIONS AND THE FUTURE OF PENA

Currently, PENA has regular organising meetings of about ten to fifteen people and maintains a presence online and through social media. Our priority is the aforementioned campaign to initiate a boycott against the NAPLAN tests that has involved collaborating with an activist grouping within the teachers' union, and a group of literacy educators who have prepared a significant body of research documenting the problems with the tests. These alliances are enabling us to reach a broad group of people concerned with the testing regime, and we are hopeful that further public meetings will generate sufficient support to plan action for

2014. While the campaign against the tests is in itself a significant attempt to challenge the common language of neoliberal education, the collaboration and networking are likely to have positive consequences beyond the months ahead.

To date, PENA has been an inspiring experience for us, successfully bringing together a diverse group of educators across sectors, and providing a vehicle for increased networking, solidarity, and collaborations. For activist educators, the present challenge is to fight the marketisation of education and learning. In this struggle, PENA has proved to be a useful framework for developing our critique of a view of knowledge and learning that is bound up with commerce and productivity. Instead, together we are collectively considering and reframing our ongoing work in education as emancipatory practice, based on a view of knowledge and learning that values justice, authentic democracy, and fundamental social change.

ACKNOWLEDGMENTS

The authors would like to acknowledge that PENA is a living, evolving, breathing informal network and is constantly being shaped and driven by all its members. This chapter reflects the views of specific members within the network. The authors would like to acknowledge and thank all the current participants of PENA for their inspiration and participation in a new movement around popular education. We also thank Professor Antonia Darder for attending our 2012 symposium and inspiring us to collectively cry, smile, and then act! http://www.populareducation.org.au/

NOTES

1. See Beckett and Hager (2002), *Life Work and Learning, Practice in Postmodernity*, London, England: Routledge.
2. In Australia, the TAFE (Technical and Further Education) sector is roughly equivalent to what is known elsewhere as the vocational sector, community college, and, in some countries, as polytechnic institutions.
3. NAPLAN is the National Assessment Program—Literacy and Numeracy. These are Australia-wide tests conducted in all schools, the most prominent Australian version of the global emphasis on high-stakes testing. See, for example, W. Au. (2009). *Unequal by Design: High-Stakes Testing and the Standardization of Inequality*, New York, NY: Routledge.
4. www.theconch.org
5. On our website at http://www.populareducation.org.au and elsewhere.
6. Vol 9, No 3, Summer 2011. Issue 35. http://www.newcq.org/
7. Our response to the DEECD briefing paper can be accessed here: http://www.populareducation.org.au/?p=361

REFERENCES

Apple, M. (2010). Global crises, social justice, and education. In M. Apple (Ed.), *Global crises, social justice, and education*. New York, NY: Routledge.

Apple, M. (2011, September–December). The tasks of the critical scholar/activist in education: The contribution of José Gimeno Sacristán. *Revista de Educación, 356*, 235–250.

Au, W. (2009). *Unequal by design: High-stakes testing and the standardization of inequality*. New York, NY: Routledge.

Darder, A. (2011). *A dissident voice: Essays on culture, pedagogy, and power*. New York, NY: Peter Lang.

Darder, A. M., Baltodano, P., & Torres, R. (Eds.). (2009). *The critical pedagogy reader*. New York, NY: Routledge.

DEECD. (2012). *New directions for school leadership and the teaching profession* (Discussion paper). Melbourne, Australia: DEECD.

DEEWR. (2011). *Review of funding for schooling—final report*. Canberra, Australia: A.C.T. Department of Education, Employment and Workplace Relations.

Freire, P. (1970). *Pedagogy of the oppressed*. London, England: Penguin.

Shaull, R. (2000). Foreword. In P. Freire, *Pedagogy of the oppressed: 30th anniversary edition*. New York, NY: Continuum.

CHAPTER ELEVEN

Freire's Legacy for Communities Seeking Change in Sub-Saharan Africa

TIM BUDGE

INTRODUCTION

The 1960s and '70s were a time of optimism for emerging nations across Africa. Independence had been successfully negotiated in the 1960s by such countries as Botswana, Zambia, Tanzania, and Senegal and armed struggle across Portuguese African colonies, combined with political changes back in Portugal, led to independence in Angola, Guinea-Bissau and Cape Verde, and Mozambique in the mid-1970s.

Paulo Freire was involved with some of these emerging nations, especially Guinea-Bissau, which he visited a number of times and which is the subject of *Pedagogy in Process: The Letters to Guinea-Bissau* (Freire, 1978). Freire's book outlines his guidance to and interaction with educators involved in establishing a new approach to literacy and post-literacy, as well as Freire's reflections on different aspects of his visits to the country.

The new regime in Guinea-Bissau envisaged a radical, revolutionary approach to education and Freire was enlisted "as a collaborator" to help them design a mass literacy programme. This approach intended a "radical transformation of the educational system inherited by the colonizers" (Freire, 1978, p. 14) in which Freire saw literacy education as a "political act, directly related to production, to health, to the regular system of instruction, to the overall plan for the society to be realised" (1978, p. 13).

Apart from his more extensive involvement in Guinea-Bissau, Freire was involved with the former Portuguese colonies of São Tomé and Príncipe, Angola, and Mozambique. He was also involved in Tanzania, which he visited a number of times.

However, this chapter's real interest is in the trajectory of progress during the past forty years in different Sub-Saharan Africa (SSA) countries and how current contexts relate to Freire's radical ideas of politics, education, and change, particularly change at a community level. Given Freire's critique of the banking model of education, why is this model so prevalent, even now, and what does that in itself say about change for African communities?

Clearly, Africa is not one homogeneous state and it is not helpful to generalise by taking statistics from one or two countries and transposing them across all fifty-four African nations. Likewise, any simplistic analysis that leads to either a blanket "African pessimism" or "African optimism" needs to be resisted. However, it is true that on a regional basis, there are still some disturbing development indicators. According to the Africa Progress Panel (2012), 1 in 36 African women has a lifetime risk of maternal death, in contrast with developed nations, such as Australia where the same ratio is 1 in 13,300 (UNICEF, 2009). According to this report, up to 25% of elections are marred by violence and all but five African countries are rated in the lower half of Transparency International's Corruption Perception Index (as cited in Africa Progress Panel, 2012). Across Africa, 30 million children are out of school (Africa Progress Panel, 2012).

This topic is something of a personal, professional, and academic interest, since I've worked in international development for twenty years, much of it focused on Africa, and I am currently living in Zambia, working for an NGO, Plan International. My experience of living in Zambia inspired me to start reading Paulo Freire and to extend my thinking about how change happens in countries such as Zambia, a country also visited by Paulo Freire (Freire & Macedo, 1987).

Zambia provides an interesting example of one African country. It achieved independence from the British in the early 1960s without the widespread, armed struggle experienced by Guinea-Bissau, Mozambique, or others. It is a country with significant mineral resources and great agricultural potential, and political power has passed from one leader to the next through relatively peaceful national elections.

At independence, Zambia was one of the continent's richest nations; however, although there was initial growth after independence, a programme of nationalisation coincided with a slump in commodity prices and increased credit and fuel prices (World Bank, 2005). As a consequence, foreign debt increased (African Development Bank, 2001) and Zambia had many years of negative economic growth (UN DATA, 2012). Fortunately, since 2003, GDP growth rates are now over 5%.

In other words, there has been a fifty-year pattern of initial promise, then stagnation and negative growth, followed by more positive indicators.

Yet in Zambia, 45% of children under five years old are stunted (UN DATA, 2012), 70% or more of the population lives on less than US$1.25 per day (World Bank, 2012) and across many indicators, Zambia is behind levels established at independence.

It is also a country where the "banking model" of education predominates. Last year, I visited a preschool in a remote village, a community establishment supported by Plan International. Within a thatched-roofed, mud-brick setting, and with a community-trained volunteer teacher, all thirty children were sitting in two neat rows, facing the front and dutifully repeating everything the teacher recited to them. I commented to local staff that I was surprised to see such a formal approach to early childhood education, which, ideally, should be characterised by play, social interaction, and activities appropriate to child development (Moscow Framework, 2010). They agreed and noted that although we had encouraged play-based learning and while Plan International had helped set up the centre to be more interactive, the community wanted a "real school" and had made the very active choice to have their children sitting in neat rows facing the teacher, no doubt a better position from which to receive deposits of knowledge.

Zambia is not alone in this. Many writers have identified the apparent contagion of banking education across Africa. Okigbo (1996, p. 47) describes it as a "handicap" to supporting sustainable development and outlines how African education systems need to be cured of their "narration sickness." Okigbo linked the banking model to Western (and hence colonial) influences and concluded that changing the model could lead to greater participation, democracy, and development.

Nyirenda (1996) has a similar view of education in Africa, but links it to contemporary, not just past, power structures: "The existing education systems are designed by the elite and attempt to adjust people to given societies. People are treated as objects into which superior beings, that is the elite, pour knowledge" (Nyirenda, 1996, p. 12). This allows societies to remain unjust, with "economically and socially ordered patterns of dominance and subordination which are constituted and reproduced through the existing educational practices of the elite" (Nyirenda, 1996, p. 12). Unequal power arrangements are perpetuated (intentionally and unintentionally) through educational practices.

All of which asks why this approach to education is first so prevalent and second so difficult to remove or change. Serpell, Mumba, and Chansa-kabali (2011) write about the imposition of institutionalised public basic schools in Zambia. The Western cultural origins of this model can be traced to a process of "hegemonic imposition by Christian missionaries from Europe in the nineteenth and early twentieth centuries in the name of evangelization, and further entrenched by a colonial administration that shared with the missions assumptions of European cultural superiority and a view of African cultures as devoid of ideas relevant to the design of education" (Serpell et al., 2011, p. 79).

Tanzania's first president, Julius Nyerere, critiqued colonial education for its "emphasis on subservient attitudes" and because it "induced attitudes of human inequality, and in practice, underpinned the domination of the weak by the strong" (Nyerere, 1968, p. 269). For him, "The primary purpose of the colonial education system.... was to bring the colonized into the capitalist social and economic structure in which the colonized are more effectively exploited and dehumanized by their colonial masters" (as quoted in Mulenga, 2001).

Freire was also clear on the direct link between colonisation and banking education, which served the needs of the oppressor and in which the teacher projects absolute ignorance onto others, "a characteristic of the ideology of oppression" (Freire, 1970, p. 53). Freire recognised that colonial education was elitist and sought to de-Africanise the national population, as well as prepare low-level administrators who could serve the needs of the colonial bureaucracy. In this setting, colonised people's "hope of salvation lay in becoming 'white' or 'black with white souls'" (Freire, 1978, p. 13).

However, banking education across Africa is not just a relic of colonialism. After the wave of independence in the 1960s and '70s, this approach to education seems to have become further entrenched. Harber (1997) draws the link between education systems and the process of democratisation. He notes that the brief amount of time between the end of colonialism and democratic elections in newly independent nations did not allow for democratic processes and values to become properly established. Furthermore, uncertain political commitments from leaders, ethnic divisions, limited managerial and technical capacity, as well as the pressure of popular expectations all increased the complexity and obstacles to establishing strong, democratic institutions. Without a foundation for democracy, many of the excesses and imbalances of the existing power structures, including education systems, remained unchecked and unchanged.

Jackson and Rosberg (1982, 1984) highlighted how leaders of newly independent African nations gravitated toward a model of "personal rule," "a distinctive type of political system in which the rivalries and struggles of powerful and wilful men, rather than impersonal institutions, ideologies, public policies, or class interests, are fundamental in shaping political life" (Jackson & Rosberg, 1984, p. 421). This is a political system "composed of the privileged and powerful few in which the many are usually unmobilized, unorganized and therefore relatively powerless to command the attention and action of government" (Jackson & Rosberg, 1984, p. 423). Such a political setting provides huge obstacles to meaningful participation, democracy, and critical praxis. By and large, in these settings, political leaders remain unchallenged and resistant to change.

Fortunately, more recently there have been significant, positive developments in national governance and in political leadership in many African countries so that much of what was written in the 1970s and '80s is no longer universally valid. Theron (2011) has analysed the profiles of 158 African heads of state covering 1960 to 2010 and profiled a significant change in the career profile, age of appointment, education level, and area of expertise of African presidents. She notes, "Today, more leaders respect presidential terms limits, spend less time in power and adhere to democratic practices." She also notes a reduction in the number of "personal rulers."

Nevertheless, there is still the important question of how to respond to the contagion of banking education and attack the passivity that it creates and reinforces. For Freire and Nyerere at the start of the post-colonial period, a return to a society that existed before colonisation was necessary. For Freire, re-Africanisation and a re-claiming of culture were required (linking with Amílcar Cabral's view of culture). However, this needed to be a revolutionary and even militant undertaking, in which the middle class undertook "class suicide" in order to establish equality and a common orientation toward national reconstruction (Freire, 1978). A campaign of literacy and post-literacy was needed, overseen by a national council of ministries (Freire & Faundez, 1989). Education must serve national production, and in *Pedagogy in Process*, Freire speaks of the link between local organising and literacy and national "priorities as established by the 'Party'" (Freire, 1978, p. 63), thus emphasising the pre-eminence of the Party in leading national programmes, including education and literacy. In re-Africanisation, this vision of society does not include a return to a naïve or magical consciousness, but one in which there is ongoing critical reflection and self-awareness.

Nyerere is more forthright about the need to return to traditional African values and an African identity, which included, in his view, a return to a classless society: "I doubt if the equivalent of the word 'class' exists in any indigenous African language; for language describes the ideas of those who speak; and the idea of 'class' or 'caste' was non-existent in African society" (as quoted in Mulenga, 2001, p. 453). For Nyerere, values of cooperation, self-esteem, traditional family life, and communalism as well as human equality were the domain of African culture and the antithesis of colonialism. For him, socialism linked with this approach since it enabled the state to "prevent exploitation of one person by another" (Nyerere, 1968, p. 232).

However, others have questioned this return to traditional values. For some, it implies a kind of nostalgia for a culture that never really existed but yet somehow could be recreated. Others question the notion that pre-colonial African societies were without class or stratification. Even if Nyerere's tribe was devoid of class, this does not mean all African tribes are without class or stratification (Mazrui, 1996, in Mulenga, 2001).

Furthermore, as Simuyu argues (quoted in Harber, 1997, p. 14), pre-colonial African societies were in reality a "mixture of the rudiments of democratic tendencies and practices on the one hand and aristocratic, autocratic and/or militaristic tendencies, with varying degrees of despotism on the other." Colonialism overlaid this pattern with violence, discrimination, and exploitation, with colonial authorities enjoying power with few restrictions, a trend that perhaps influenced emerging leaders once they were in power themselves.

The persistence of deeply entrenched practices that emphasise the power imbalance between women and men seems to highlight that there are still deep power divisions in many African tribal cultures, divisions that seem relatively unaffected by colonialism. The high prevalence of child marriages—for example, 46% of girls below the age of 18 years are married in SSA compared with 21% in Latin America and the Caribbean (The Elders, 2012)—and initiation ceremonies— such as the *Chinamwali* ceremony for girls in the Chewa tribe, in which young girls are trained in how to please their husbands and in which they are exposed to a number of very predatory practices—suggest very strong power imbalances and inequalities, particularly for women (Tembo & Matenga, 2008).

The pattern of history since the 1970s suggests that Freire in particular was too idealistic, both in his view of how to overturn colonial education and in his perception of the political situation in Guinea-Bissau. In reading *Pedagogy in Process*, with all the benefit of forty years of hindsight, it is apparent that Freire had an almost unquestioning enthusiasm for the new regime in Guinea-Bissau and he seems overconfident that the literacy and post-literacy work would lead to a new, sustainable African society. In reality, as is widely accepted now, the Guinea-Bissau literacy programme failed.

It seems that in Guinea-Bissau, Freire faced two problems. First, the literacy programme was not value free but rather predicated on a particular view of society, in this case, a one-party, socialist state, with a clear, predetermined view of liberation and oppression. All learning took place within these parameters. As Harber writes, "Unfortunately, Freire often appears to favour the indoctrination of a new orthodoxy as favoured by the Revolutionary Party" (Harber, 1997, p. 36). Second, the programme was based on the assumption that the new government was committed to a level of common participation and democratisation of all people within the new country. In essence, this commitment required leaders who, despite their new found power, would be prepared to give away power to the people. Although Freire refers to "class suicide" as a choice that must be taken up by the middle class, in essence, the introduction and fulfilment of this type of programme also requires a type of suicide from political and bureaucratic leaders. Unfortunately, most governments and their leaders, including those in Africa since colonialism, have found this choice difficult, if not impossible, to make.

The conundrum can be summarised as follows: Banking education, an approach that reinforces docile populations and an over-respectful view of authority, apparently can only be tackled through strong leadership and national programmes prepared to envision and work toward a different model of power and participation. However, the legacy of banking education means national leaders have themselves benefited from the acceptance of authority that is inherent in this approach, making it doubly difficult for them to contemplate any change, since they have potentially the most to lose in the process.

It is my view that the missing element is a perspective on change as demanded and driven from below. Perhaps it is too much to expect any government, let alone one that has only recently taken charge, to be committed to the radical sharing of power that is the logical conclusion of Freire's approach to literacy. Perhaps the way forward is not so much a national literacy programme, as it is a claiming of power by those prepared to mobilise for their (still) unfulfilled rights. Just as independence was not offered up by colonial powers but had to be demanded and fought for by activists, independence leaders, and communities, perhaps a similar approach is needed now, even in post-colonial African societies. At the heart of this approach is a claiming of the right to participation and a recognition of the power of community organising. There is a suggestion that Freire saw this in Guinea-Bissau, as in his description of community organising work taking place in the city of Sedengal) (Freire, 1978, p. 162), a case study whose lessons he was also keen to pass on to the Commissioner of Education (Freire & Faundez, 1989). Interestingly, the link among education, mobilising, and organising was also something Freire discussed with Myles Horton, where Freire notes that it is "impossible to organize without educating and *being* educated by the very process of organizing" (Horton & Freire, 1990, p. 121) (emphasis in the original).

These dimensions will be explored by new research, through examining the ideas, activities, and progress of two community-based, membership-driven social movements working in SSA. In broad terms, the research will examine the movements' experience of local, community-led organising, as well as seek to identify and understand the impact that they have had at the local or even national level. If banking education leads to docile populations, have any lessons been learned from communities that have refused this role of passivity and compliance, and instead organised for their own agenda, rights, and well-being? Where does this organising go beyond basic and local cooperation at a more material level to a greater claim against power and authority, as a refusal against submissiveness? Furthermore, in these contexts, what reading of the word and the world is going on?

In approaching this research, it will be important not to overlay the ideas of Freire on to the approaches of the organisations as an interpretative grid, but rather to examine their praxis and look for points of resonance. Clearly, Freire's ideas have had a huge impact on the mainstream of theory and practice in community-based development work during the past forty years, (e.g., Chambers, 1983, 1997) and ActionAid's *Reflect* methodology (ActionAid, 2009), so it is reasonable to expect that some of his ideas have been taken up and absorbed at a practical and theoretical level. They have become almost common knowledge or even part of the canon of development theory.

However, it should be possible to have some kind of "dialogical exchange," at least between the legacy of his ideas and experience and lessons from these contemporary social movements: What is the discourse between Freire's ideas and the praxis of these organisations? The starting point for this dialogue will be to learn about these groups, including their histories, involvement of members, leadership models, campaigning approaches, their culture, and their stated approaches to learning, as well as seeking to reflect, it is hoped with them, on their experience of contributing to change and the impact they have been able to have in their communities and beyond.

The other dimension of the dialogue goes beyond the exchange between the praxis of the two organisations to include a broader reflection on the legacy of Freire for a new generation of community leaders and activists. Again, this cannot happen in a didactic way, but might be more of a fresh consideration of the relevance of his ideas within the context of local community organisations. Despite the generation gap and the vastly different worlds of Freire and contemporary SSA, it is hoped that his insights may contribute to the skills, knowledge, and practice of a broader set of organisations seeking change in their communities. The endpoint here is a contribution to the knowledge base of how local voices can be strengthened, democracy can be made more active and inclusive, and power structures can be made more accountable to constituencies and communities.

The research focuses on organisations that have the following characteristics: first, a membership base, which allows for internal democratic and participatory representation and which also is the basis for designation as a social movement; second, a commitment to action at different levels, including "practical" community-level initiatives right through to national or macro-level advocacy and campaigning; third, an awareness of the inter-relatedness of different issues that underpin this broad spectrum of action. In other words, there is a need for organisations that do not just act at different levels, but are also able to draw the connection between the need for this broad action and the links between apparent distinct micro-issues (such as reforestation) and macro-issues (for example, the negative impact of colonialism on traditional reverence for land).

The first such organisation is the Green Belt Movement (GBM), an organisation started in post-colonial Kenya in the late 1970s by the late Nobel Peace Prize laureate Professor Wangari Maathai. It began as an organisation to assist rural women in planting seedlings as a means to reduce soil degradation, improve local groundwater, and provide firewood. Implicit in the approach was a recognition that colonial rule had contributed to the loss of indigenous knowledge and respect for the environment and had encouraged practices that reduced biodiversity and local soil quality. Professor Maathai has spoken of her own experience as a child in rural Kenya, and how the traditional view of local fig trees as "trees of god" had been usurped by missionaries, who were keen to cut down these trees because the missionaries wanted the Africans to relate to a new god, one who could be "worshipped in a house called a church" (Maathai & Tippett, 2011).

Over time, Professor Maathai recognised that issues of degradation and food insecurity were symptomatic of "disempowerment, disenfranchisement, and a loss of the traditional values that had previously enabled communities to protect their environment [and] work together for mutual benefit." In an approach that resonates with the notion of critical consciousness (making use of a Kikuyu word, *kwimenya*, meaning "self-awareness," in empowerment seminars), GBM used a process that encouraged individuals to examine why they lack agency to change their circumstances, which in turn helped participants to recognise a political and societal dimension, and particularly that their trust in political leaders had been misplaced (Green Belt Movement, 2012).

Professor Maathai and the GBM lobbied and organised at a national level and confronted land-grabbing and corruption. This was at some personal cost to Maathai, who was often publicly ridiculed, as well as being physically attacked and jailed. Nevertheless, GBM's and her reputation grew and after multiparty elections in 2002, she was elected to Parliament and served as Assistant Minister. She was awarded the Nobel Peace Prize in 2004, noting herself that the Norwegian Nobel Committee had made the connection "between peace, sustainable management of resources, and good governance" (Maathai, 2006, p. 294). Professor Maathai died in 2011. GBM has planted 51 million trees since its beginnings in 1977 and has almost 4,000 community nurseries across Kenya.

Professor Maathai has also written about the links among passivity, colonialism, and African leadership, noting how "deculturization" continued after independence in many African states and how the new leaders in these states continued to "cultivate the culture of disempowerment, learned from the colonizers, that kept the great mass of people ignorant, fearful, passive, and obedient" (Maathai, 2009, p. 44). In her writings and her actions, she refused to accept the words and self-proclaimed status of these leaders but, more important, she mobilised others to challenge them.

The second organisation is the South African chapter of the Slum Dwellers International (SDI) movement. SDI started in India in the mid-1980s, supporting a network of women's collectives in the pavement slums of Mumbai. This grew into a national and then an international network of people living in slums and shantytowns. It now exists in thirty-three countries in Africa, Asia, and Latin America. The South African chapter was started in 1991. The members of this organisation are people living in shacks and slums; in India, its membership is at least 550,000 people (Patel & Bartlett, 2009). In South Africa, the movement comprises 55,000 households across 750 communities (SDI South African Alliance, 2012a). The work of SDI can be summarised in the following three objectives: first, "to create solidarity and unity of the urban poor so that they are well organised and equipped with the skills, knowledge and scale needed to create meaningful change"; second, to build "a national urban network of the poor for learning and lobbying"; and third, "to change the way our cities are planned and developed and how public funds are used so that they are inclusive, and that ordinary people are involved" (SDI South African Alliance, 2012b).

These organisations exemplify the "demand-driven approach" noted above and have their own individual focus on learning, mobilisation, and practical action that stretches from local to national level initiatives.

Both organisations are interested in and supportive of the planned research and see the possibility of mutual learning, rather than their organisations and members being the object of an extractive research process. Nevertheless, the research will present some practical challenges. First, it needs to be a genuinely collaborative effort, one that involves GBM and SDI in the design, scope, implementation, and analysis with some clear, tangible benefit and learning for the organisations and their members. It is hoped that the research will contribute to their praxis and future development. Second, there is the difficulty of co-designing a process that will adequately enable open reflection, the telling of stories, and a sharing of learning and history on the one hand, but still allow broader conclusions to be drawn from these two interesting but disparate movements on the other hand. Techniques such as "Most Significant Change" (Dart & Davies, 2003) and "Process Tracing" (White & Phillips, 2012), as well as the techniques developed in Participatory Rural Appraisals (Chambers, 1994) may allow greater insight into the organisations and also generate understandings that might be useful for others, including other social movements, development workers, and policy makers.

Finally, it is important to note that this "demand-driven" approach is a not a panacea, or that its absence is the only contributing cause of the lack of citizen involvement or meaningful change in African societies. However, the research may provide some practical guidance on how to generate alternative approaches to change and a chance to move away from too strong a focus on centrally driven, bureaucratic, or national programmes. On a personal level, I hope that it may help to guide my praxis as a development worker. It also seems an appropriate way to re-examine and continue to share the legacy of Paulo Freire, particularly as it relates to communities themselves that are seeking change.

REFERENCES

ActionAid. (2009). *Reflect*. Retrieved August 31, 2012, from http://www.reflect-action.org/

Africa Progress Panel. (2012). *Africa progress report 2012* (p. 116). Retrieved from http://www.africaprogresspanel.org/publications/policy-papers/africa-progress-report-2012/#.Ul3bkBy4ZhE

African Development Bank. (2001). Zambia-HIPC decision point under the Enhanced Framework. Retrieved September 29, 2012, from http://www.afdb.org/fileadmin/uploads/afdb/Documents/Financial-Information/ADB-BD-WP-2001-07-EN-HIPC-ZAMBIA-BOARD-APPROVAL-DOC-REVISED-ECA-18-JAN.PDF

Chambers, R. (1983). *Rural development: Putting the last first* (p. 246). London, England: Longman Scientific and Technical.

Chambers, R. (1994). Participatory Rural Appraisal (PRA): Analysis of experience. *World Development, 22*(9), 1253–1268. doi:10.1016/0305-750X(94)90003-5

Chambers, R. (1997). *Whose reality counts? Putting the first last* (p. 297). London, England: Intermediate.

Dart, J., & Davies, R. (2003). A Dialogical, Story-Based Evaluation Tool: The Most Significant Change Technique. American Journal of Evaluation, 24(2), 137–155. doi:10.1177/109821400302400202

Freire, P. (1970). *Pedagogy of the oppressed*. London, England: Penguin,.

Freire, P. (1978). *Pedagogy in process: The letters to Guinea-Bissau* (p. 178, three leaves of plates). New York, NY: Seabury Press.

Freire, P., & Faundez, A. (1989). *Learning to question: A pedagogy of liberation* (p. 142). New York, NY: Continuum.

Freire, P., & Macedo, D. (1987). *Literacy: Reading the word and the world* (p. 184). London, England: Routledge & Kegan Paul.

Green Belt Movement. (2012). Green Belt Movement: Our history. http://www.greenbelt-movement.org/who-we-are/our-history. Retrieved September 9, 2012, from http://www.greenbeltmovement.org/who-we-are/our-history

Harber, C. (1997). *Education, democracy, and political development in Africa* (pp. vii, 168). Brighton, England: Sussex Academic Press.

Horton, M., & Freire, P. (1990). *We make the road by walking: Conversations on education and social change* (pp. xxxvii, 256). Philadelphia, PA: Temple University Press.

Jackson, R. H., & Rosberg, C. G. (1982). *Personal rule in Black Africa : prince, autocrat, prophet, tyrant* (pp. xi, 316). Berkeley: University of California Press.

Jackson, R. H., & Rosberg, C. G. (1984). Personal rule: Theory and practice in Africa. *Comparative Politics, 16*(4), 421–442. Retrieved from http://www.jstor.org/stable/10.2307/421948

Maathai, W. (2006). *Unbowed*. London, England: Random House.

Maathai, W. (2009). *The challenge for Africa*. London, England: Random House.

Maathai, W., & Tippett, K. (2011). Planting the future with Wangari Maathai. *On Being With Krista Tippett*. American Public Media. Retrieved from http://www.onbeing.org/program/planting-future/142

Moscow Framework. (2010). Moscow Framework for Action and Cooperation: Harnessing the wealth of nations. In *World Conference on Childhood Care and Education* (p. 9). Moscow, Russia: UNESCO. Retrieved from http://unesdoc.unesco.org/images/0018/001898/189882e.pdf

Mulenga, D. C. (2001). Mwalimu Julius Nyerere: A critical review of his contributions to adult education and postcolonialism. *International Journal of Lifelong Education, 20*(6), 446–470. doi:10.1080/02601370110088436

Nyerere, J. K. (1968). *Freedom and socialism: Uhuru na ujamaa; A selection from writings and speeches, 1965–1967* (pp. xvi, 422). Dar Es Salaam, Tanzania: Oxford University Press.

Nyirenda, J. (1996). The relevance of Paulo Freire's contributions to education and development in present-day Africa. *Africa Media Review, 10*(1), 1–20. Retrieved from http://archive.lib.msu.edu/DMC/AfricanJournals/pdfs/africa media review/vol10no1/jamr010001001.pdf

Okigbo, C. (1996). Contextualising Freire in African sustainable development. *Africa Media Review, 10*(1), 31–53. Retrieved from http://archive.lib.msu.edu/DMC/AfricanJournals/pdfs/africa me dia review/vol10no1/jamr010001001.pdf

Patel, S., & Bartlett, S. (2009). Reflections on innovation, assessment, and social change: A SPARC case study. *Development in Practice, 19*(1), 3–15. doi:10.1080/09614520802576336

SDI South African Alliance. (2012a). *Brief history of the alliance.* Retrieved October 7, 2012, from http://sasdialliance.org.za/history/

SDI South African Alliance. (2012b). *Informal settlement network.* Retrieved October 7, 2012, from http://sasdialliance.org.za/about/isn/

Serpell, R., Mumba, P., & Chansa-kabali, T. (2011). Early educational foundations for the development of civic responsibility: An African experience. *New Directions for Child and Adolescent Development, 2011*(134), 77–93. doi:10.1002/cd

Tembo, R., & Matenga, C. R. (2008). *Extent and impact of child marriage in four districts of Zambia* (pp. 1–79). Lusaka: University of Zambia, Department of Development Studies.

The Elders. (2012). *Child marriage: The facts.* Retrieved October 08, 2012, from http://www.theelders.org/docs/child-marriage-factsheet.pdf

Theron, M. (2011). *African trends and transformation: The profiles of sub-Saharan African executive heads of state since independence* (Research Paper 17). Canberra, Australia: DLP. Retrieved from http://www.dlprog.org/ftp/download/PublicFolder/Executive Summary—African Trends and Trans formation.pdf

UN DATA. (2012). Stunting in Zambia. Retrieved September 29, 2012, from http://data.un.org/Data.aspx?q=gdp+growth+zambia&d=WDI&f=Indicator_Code:NY.GDP.MKTP.KD.ZG;Country_Code:ZMB

UNICEF. (2009). *The state of the world's children 2009: Maternal and newborn health* (p. 168). New York, NY: UNICEF. doi:10.1016/j.vacuum.2004.05.005

White, H., & Phillips, D. (2012). Addressing attribution of cause and effect in small"n" –impact evaluations: Towards an integrated framework. Retrieved from http://www.mande.co.uk/blog/wp-content/uploads/2012/06/White-Phillips-Small-n-Impact-Evaluation-WP-version.docx

World Bank. (2005). *Zambia poverty and vulnerability assessment* (p. 258). Washington, DC: World Bank. Retrieved from http://sarpn.org/documents/d0001457/PVA_Zambia_June2005b.pdf

World Bank. (2012). Poverty headcount ratio. Retrieved September 29, 2012, from http://data.worldbank.org/indicator/SI.POV.DDAY?page=1

CHAPTER TWELVE

Autoethnography in a Kabyle Landscape

SI BELKACEM TAIEB

INTRODUCTION

In my father's time in the mid-1900s, the Algerian labor force was expatriated to France and stacked in dormitories to work in French factories. I remember my father telling me that he used to have only one day off work a week. It was the only day he would get to do his cleaning tasks. Today, our people are lodged in suburbs, also called Zones of Educational Priority (geographical area within a city where resources in education are invested to "help" the immigrant to integrate into the society) or Prioritized Zones for Urbanization (ZUP). A ZUP is focused on answering the shortage of accommodation. It is a policy that took place in France between 1959 and 1967. A ZEP (Educationary Priority Zone) refers to cities or regions that received, in 1981, extra funding for the building of supplementary schools where "education" was an emphasis. We can of course understand what "education" meant knowing that in reality these places are used to park all the "Others" from different cultural and low economic backgrounds into social projects. It is the place where we had to surrender our self-esteem and identities in order to possibly gain access to the developed and rich world that began on the other side of the boulevard.

The town where I grew up was divided into two main sectors. The first was the European part with the factory that provided some of its employees with decent accommodation. This area was also made up of new housing built by Italian and Portuguese employees. The second part was located on the outskirts of town, just on the border of Luxembourg and Belgium, and was separated from the rest of the city by a boulevard. The accommodations were made up of apartment buildings of up to twenty floors high with thin walls and broken elevators as well as town-houses and semi-detached houses with a little garden. My father bought a house in the first part of the town and fortunately we did not grow up in the ZUP. But after I turned 13, my father decided to go back to Algeria, which was when life changed drastically. The Algerian government decided to change the education system from French to Arabic. As Kabyle educated in French, we were excluded from the Arabic Algerian society. Even though we fought for the decolonization of Algeria, we lost our country. It is with great sadness that my father decided to go back to France. In France, even though we had funds and excellent references, every attempt to break free from social alienation was in vain and we ended up in the ZUP.

My youth felt like the writing of a partition in which my family was trying to find harmony. In reality, we, the kids from the first generation growing up in France, became the battlefield of postcolonization. In this chapter, I propose to present the theoretical framework that supported my inquiry of cultural recovery. I find inspiration in Freire's works (1970, 1975, 1985; Freire & Macedo, 1987), I reflect on Foucault's work (1980, 1994) to understand the discursive methods of colonization that took place in the fragmentation of my colonized mind (Fanon, 1963, 1986), I reflect on the politics of knowledge and I make sense of them in a project that strives to support the reclaiming of my Kabyle voice in the building of an independent postcolonial Kabyle Self. In that regard, I present a theoretical indigenous decolonizing alternative to discourses of power to conclude with a rationale for my narrative as a Kabyle/Berber man from the Atlas Mountains of Algeria.

OVERCOMING FRAGMENTATION

Foucault (1980, 1994) and Fanon (1963, 1986) take a critical stand against oppression and describe the dynamics of colonial power. Foucault objectively studies the discursive methods that shape power into a discourse and Fanon explains the fragmentation of identity. Both lead to an understanding of the mechanism of subjugation of cultures, knowledge, and people. It is where I start in order to leave the colonial framework.

I use Foucault's references to illustrate what indigenous and colonized people experience (Foucault, 1980, 1994). I explain how one's knowledge can be subjugated by institutional racism. Together with the work of Fanon (1963, 1986),

I understand my experience of fragmentation. I use an indigenous holistic decolonizing methodology for the recovery of my Kabyle indigenous self. Freire (1970) taught me, with a *Pedagogy of the Oppressed* in action, a *Cultural Work for Emancipatory Projects*.

> Not infrequently, training course participants call attention to "the danger of 'conscientization'" in a way which reveals their own fear of freedom. Critical consciousness, they say, is anarchic; others add that critical consciousness may lead to disorder. But some confess: Why deny it? I was afraid of freedom. I am no longer afraid! (Preface, no page number)

I am endorsing support of Foucault's analysis of knowledge construction and its exploiting process (Foucault, 1980). Foucault provides a great understanding of the discursive methods that create "subjugated knowledge." Indeed, knowledge is subjugated in the sense that populations are being silenced by systems of oppression, control, and exploitation. Knowledge is subjugated because it is enslaved to the system of knowledge management developed by the so-called developed societies. There is a hierarchy of knowledge in which indigenous epistemologies are silenced. It always intrigues me to see how one can talk about the need to fight fragmentation, cutting down stories and experiences into isolated units such as phonemes of knowledge. The reader must then have a translator to change the whole thing back into a life story. It is a reanimation of what Whitehead (1929, pp. 5) calls in *The Aims of Education* "inert knowledge," so much so that the writer makes a powerless participation, unable to bring that dead matter back to life. Controlled by a few, knowledge becomes an elitist tool that can be used to manipulate a story into a system of control, reproducing a situation of alienation and power. This leads to the creation of a vortex in which every meaningful experience is swallowed and classified for academic enzymes to break down.

QUESTIONS OF LEADERSHIP AND KNOWLEDGE

In the process of gathering information in indigenous locations, I avoid an outcome in which indigenous people's stories are displaced, vulgarized, and taken away by the "powerful" anthropologists to be put in Western museums and libraries. Said (2002) explains the relationship between knowledge and power in *Power, Politics and Culture*:

> In the West, for instance, in certain fields, such as anthropology, history, cultural studies, feminist studies, it [knowledge] has influenced people to think about problems of power relationships between cultures and people, where dominance includes the power to represent and create, to control and to manipulate. In other words, it makes the argument for the connection between the production of knowledge and power. And specifically, because it was a historical work, it really looks at all of this in the age of empire. (p. 372)

The crisis of representation in research raised the issue of whether research-ers should be involved with the population. Denzin, Lincoln, and Smith (2008) explain:

> In North America, qualitative research operates in a complex historical field that crosscuts at least eight historical moments.... These moments overlap and simultaneously operate in the present. We define them as the traditional (1900–1950); the modernist, or golden age (1950–1970); blurred genres (1970–1986); the crisis of representation (1986–1990)....The blurred genres phase produced the next stage, the crisis of representation. Here researchers struggled with how to locate themselves in reflexive texts. A kind of methodological dias-pora took place, a two-way exodus. Humanists migrated to the social sciences, searching for new social theory, new ways to study popular culture and its local ethnographic contexts. (pp. 3–4)

This crisis did not go to the extreme of questioning why we needed to gather so much knowledge and how we could have organized an equitable redistribution of the knowledge on a global scale. Anthropologists tend to uproot knowledge that is supposed to stay connected to the place of discovery in order to stay active. The relationship with the researched is not equitable. Research is motivated by issues of competition, dominance, and power among anthropologists. This system is designed as a pyramid that aims to condition everyone to want to climb upward. By doing so, the energy of the struggle for victory strengthens the people on top.

Knowledge is not totally subjugated for everybody but is rather shared in some very intimate circles and in laboratory-like environments. There is a reason old patterns of positivist norms for experimentation want knowledge to remain with an elite. Bourdieu and Sayad (1964), in *Paysans Déracinés* (Uprooted Peasants), de-scribed knowledge, once "decontaminated" in processes that we can call uprooting:

> Most frequently, the uprooting creates a field favourable to the cultural contagion, weak-ening the collective defences that the group was opposing to borrowing and to innovation. Uprooted from his land and his house, dispossessed from his birth world that he owned, the peasant dies as a peasant: It is the end of the old *thafellah'th*, the peasantry, the total and intangible art of life that falls apart in one shot in its totality. The last descendants of the servants of a revered land are now one's slaves chained to their heritage in a hateful condition. (p. 56)

However, I believe in human agency and I stay the leader of my education. I learn about fragmentation from Fanon (1986); displacement and fragmentation are experienced by many of us, indigenous people, who were socialized in specific frameworks with chosen people, whose minds have been framed as well. Access to higher education means having access to a lot of knowledge and possibly power, but to access a level at which power can be changed into decisions means following the rules in the marketing of knowledge. A hierarchy is present at every level of the educational processes to protect the rules. The knowledge is actually gathered in places and languages that are supporting it, building walls around it. Later, Said (2004) insists on the connection between power and knowledge referring to the United States of America's example:

> In the last chapter (of *Orientalism*, 1978) I look at the role of the United States after classical empires were dismantled in World War II, to see, since the extraordinary role that the United States played as the last remaining imperial power, and the influence of that role upon knowledge and the production of knowledge. (p. 373)

And Said (1978) introduces the idea of control in this quest for power: "Once again, knowledge of subject races or Orientals is what makes their management easy and profitable, knowledge gives power, more power requires more knowledge, and so on in an increasingly profitable dialectic of information and control" (p. 36). Having knowledge means gaining control. Having the knowledge is having the power to manage populations and use their foundations to build up a system that will sow the seeds of acculturation and domesticate the population, turning it into a usable crowd. The power to control also comes in the capacity to manage the distribution services.

"BANKING EDUCATION" (FREIRE, 1970)

Universities are now pushing for more and more productivity. The more one does, the more wealth one brings to the system. Wealth is often measured in research dollars. Said (2004) explains in *Power, Politics and Culture*:

> As a systematic discourse Orientalism is written knowledge, but because it is in the world and directly about the world it is more than knowledge: it is power since, so far as the Oriental is concerned, Orientalism is the operative and effective knowledge by which he was delivered textually to the West, occupied by the West, milked by the West for his resources, humanly quashed by the West. (p. 26)

This idea of capitalizing knowledge to gain power leads me to compare schools with banks. The new bank customer has to go to a bank with his money. The customer opens an account and people are very friendly, trying to see what type of person he is, to see whom to refer this new investor to. Then the customer meets a representative who will offer him a chair, or not, according to the amount this newcomer brings or could bring in. After that he is sold a package that "helps" manage his money, a package that includes a number of possible transactions (number of deposits are unlimited but withdrawals are limited to a certain amount per day, Internet banking, credit cards, etc.). Once one is in the bank, they try to secure the client's loyalty to assure that he will come back and ask for more products. That is when one becomes part of the system. In the future every transaction that he will make will have to be done via the bank. They will decide where one can live and how one will live. Now it is even more interesting because the employer is actually in partnership with banks and "helps the new customer" choose the bank in which he will have his salary desposited. It is also what Freire (1970) calls "banking education":

> Education thus becomes an act of depositing, in which the students are the depositories and the teacher is the depositor. Instead of communicating, the teacher issues communiqués and makes deposits, which the students patiently receive, memorize, and repeat. This is the banking concept of education, in which the scope of action allowed to the student extends as far as receiving, filing, and storing the deposits. (pp. 45–46)

After describing the student as a passive and a submissive receptor engaged in a non-equitable relationship, Freire (1970) continues his metaphor describing the exchange transaction of knowledge in such a banking system. In Freire's theory (1970), teachers spend their knowledge on the student (received and oppressive knowledge that the student is not supposed to interfere with and does not really own).

> In the banking concept of education, knowledge is a gift bestowed by those who consider themselves knowledgeable upon those whom they consider to know nothing. Projecting an absolute ignorance onto others, a characteristic of the ideology of oppression, negates education and knowledge as processes of inquiry. The teacher presents himself to his students as their necessary opposite; by considering their ignorance absolute, he justifies his own existence. (p. 46)

You are from any part of the world and you carry so much knowledge. That knowledge is bought packaged and achieves maturity in boxes that get traded in a market according to the dominant pressures of the day. Societal pressure shapes it to fit into defined boxes. This neoliberal perspective of education turns the world into a battlefield for intellectual survival. Turning more and more to a research-intensive orientation, universities have to answer to the law of a market whether or not it is fair to everyone. It is clear that only a very small part of the population of the earth profits from the benefits that the market generates. Placed in banks and exchanged on the market, indigenous cultures become a good for which indigenous people have to fight to get access. Indigenous people are trapped in a system from which we need to emancipate ourselves, replacing the colonialist system; we now have to deal with cultural imperialism. It is for that reason that I return to the book *The Wretched of the Earth*, written by Fanon (1963). He explains the path to independence, as he sees it, using the example of Algeria during the War of Independence. That war still has an influence on what Berber people are going through today.

FRANTZ FANON IN A KABYLE LIFE STORY TODAY

Sartre (1963), in the preface to Fanon's *The Wretched of the Earth*, describes the starting point of my journey. He describes colonial violence and puts my thoughts into words. He says:

> Colonial violence not only aims at keeping these enslaved men at a respectful distance, it also seeks to dehumanize them. No effort is spared to demolish their traditions, to substitute our language for theirs, and to destroy their culture without giving them ours. We exhaust them into a mindless state. Ill fed and sick, if they resist, fear will finish the job: guns are pointed at the peasants; civilians come and settle on their land and force them to work for them under the whip. (p. 53)

I experienced Sartre's powerful statement during my education in France (Fanon, 1963). "Destroy their culture without giving them ours" (p. 1). An education based on expropriation and instrumentation is what I see in these words. Raised in France, I received an education that never gave me room to develop my personal cultural identity. This education was aspiring to make my culture disappear. I was provided with industrial tools to work on a land that was not mine. My soul was removed from its source to be exploited on international markets. I was going to school with French people in France and I was serving in my colonial society without being conscious of it. I was learning through my education to whiten the world. In the book *The Wounded Storyteller: Body, Illness, and Ethics*, Frank (1995) explains the phenomenon of the reverse of leadership and expropriation with the example of medicine.

> Both the divide that was crossed from the pre-modern to the modern and that from modern to postmodern involves issues of voice. The woman reported by Bourdieu seems to perceive that medicine has taken away her voice: [medicine assails her with words, she does not want to know and let her not knowing more about her sickness]. (p. 7)

The voice here is the powerful expression of the true self, meaning the one of heritage from the position of personal consciousness.

RECLAIMING A KABYLE VOICE

The voice Frank (1995) refers to is the one threatened by an authoritarian system of knowledge, as explained previously, as well as in the Freire statement (1970) on banking education. Frank then makes reference to Bourdieu's work (Bourdieu, 1961, 1972, 1980) in Algeria and quotes a Berber woman: "In the old days folk didn't know what illness was. They went to bed and they died. It is only nowadays that we've learned words like liver, lung, stomach and I don't know what!" (p. 5).

We understand here that the colonized who went to Western schools use a language foreign to the colonized kind and learned social reproduction of situations of oppression. Deepened in theoretical contexts, dominated by colonial discourses, the colonized learned the methods from the colonizer. They encouraged the domestication of the Imazighen, the first people of North Africa also called Berbers, placing them into the cages of the colonizer's methods. Fanon (1963) said that "in order to assimilate the culture of the oppressor and venture into his fold, the colonized subject has had to pawn off his intellectual possessions. For instance, one of the things he has to assimilate is the way the colonialist bourgeoisie thinks" (p. 79).

The colonized wants to decolonize. Artist or intellectual, he goes back to the traditional tools to communicate. He tries to go back to a time when he was independent and could innovate and look to the future from an independent perspective. He does not understand that his nation has changed. If the colonized wants to emancipate himself from his colonizing jail he needs to be in the present and find the tools to address the present situation. The colonized has a vision that is blurred by the will to rediscover what he had lost or changed. Fanon (1963) described the return of the colonized:

> When he decided to return to the routine of daily life, after having been roused to fever pitch by rubbing shoulders with his people, whoever they were and whoever they may be, all he brings back from his adventures are terribly sterile clichés. He places emphasis on customs, traditions, and costumes, and his painful, forced search seems but a banal quest for the exotic. (p. 225)

As a colonized intellectual myself, having grown up in France, I felt touched by what Fanon says when he describes the three steps of the work of the colonized. When I obtained my bachelor's degree in France, I had successfully "assimilated the colonizer's culture" (Fanon, 1963, p. 227). I made a name for myself and I proved that I was capable. At the same time, I answered my social anxieties and accepted the game of socialization in the context of colonization. I accepted the pressure. But as time went on, experiences grew and inequalities multiplied, leaving me no other choice than the one of reflecting critically on my experience and committing to the journey of healing. I had to go back to my roots. I distinguished myself from this machine that tried to shape me since I had roots in a foreign civilization. I refused injustice or the schizophrenic split self as a solution to my situation.

SPEAKING KABYLE IN ACADEMIA

I refused to live this life of an "angel" (Fanon, 1963) and I had to inscribe myself on the earth, to leave my imprint on it. Fanon (1963) describes so well the situation of the colonized in these words: "This painful and harrowing wrench is, however a necessity. Otherwise we will be faced with extremely serious psycho affective mutilations" (p. 223).

I am a part of the nation of "individuals without an anchorage, without borders, colorless, stateless, rootless, a body of angels" (p. 223). But I chose not to let that be my destiny. I threw myself into a master's degree that looked a lot like what Fanon describes as "an outsider relationship" with "my" people because I had not lived, or only in a fragmented way, with them. Wanting to come back to my origins is a "task of memory" (Fanon, 1963, p. 227). At the start of my PhD work, I was delving into my memory for stories, connectors, receptors, and transmitters to my Kabyle culture. I was socially acceptable because, in some way, I was exotizing myself, looking for an identity in a tradition and of going back home to Algeria. It was for this reason that I did not threaten the system that raised me and I was, in fact, even an exotic experience. Fanon (1963) explained:

> No colonialism draws its justification from the fact that the territories it occupies are culturally nonexistent. Colonialism will never be put to shame by exhibiting unknown cultural treasures under its noses. The colonized intellectual, at the very moment when he undertakes a work of art, fails to realize he is using techniques and a language borrowed from the occupier. He is content to cloak the instruments in a style that is meant to be national but which is strangely reminiscent of exoticism. (pp. 227–228)

Even if I did wish to produce a work that would be undermined by the colonizer, it was necessary for me to become aware of my motivation for this inquiry, to understand my context and to emancipate myself. I could then finally arrive at what Fanon describes as a "combat stage" in which the colonized "after having tried to lose himself among the people, with the people, will rouse the people" (Fanon, 1963, p. 227). By adopting a critical and participative approach to the Berber condition, I shook the social structures, dusted up the cultural conceptions and pushed for an actualization of my culture. My work is an inquiry that I wish to leave to my close and extended family. It is possible, however, that through this work only a trace of me would remain after my definitive departure for the land of the forgotten. Often I thought that this inquiry would be my last attempt to bring my contribution to Algeria, a land that is mine, but about which I know so little. I saw my work as a way of accepting my reality, but paradoxically, my reality then became the cornerstone for a liberating creation. Fanon (1963) explained:

> This creator, who decides to portray national truth, turns, paradoxically enough, to the past, and so looks at what is irrelevant to the present. What he aims for in this inner intentionality is the detritus of social thought, external appearances, relics, and knowledge frozen in time. The colonial intellectual however, who strives for cultural authenticity, must

recognize that national truth is first and foremost the national reality. He must press until he reaches that place of bubbling trepidation from which knowledge will emerge. (p. 230)

The independent nation was born from what she accepts, as she is now embracing her history, pain, and happiness, with shame and pride to keep her going on the journey. The Amazigh nation is a nation representing humanity. This work of the colonized intellectual, described by Fanon as the unavoidable road, a road used many times, is in fact for me a personal experience of liberation. For Fanon, the colonized intellectual cannot be on the right trajectory unless he leaves his bourgeois cloth behind, to take back his place with the people. Fanon (1963) stated:

> We must first and foremost rid ourselves of the very Western, very bourgeois, and hence very disparaging, idea that the masses are incapable of governing themselves. Experience has proven in fact that the masses fully understand the most complex issues. One of the greatest services the Algerian revolution had rendered to Algerian intellectuals was to put them in touch with the masses, to allow them to see the extreme, unspeakable poverty of the people and at the same time witness the awakening of their intelligence and the development of their consciousness. (p. 198)

CONCLUSION

Frank (1995) explains that to come back is to take back possession of one's history. It is a phenomenon that, according to him, characterizes postcolonial society. He introduces the concept of voice in his story. To whom does this history belong? To whom does this voice belong?

With colonization, and decolonization, the colonized took a second place in his personal history and culture. The anthropological work that aimed to make him better known made him become an "Other" to himself. Dispossessed of his own image, he would see himself only in the words of his colonizer. He would lose control of his representation system and give up the power to move in time and space, to become the object that could be moved. In the anthropology of neo-colonization, the colonized could either move from the hands of the colonizer, or move himself as the colonizer would move him. He was changed into a subject. However, through Freire (1970) I get a sense of what it is to be empowered in education and what it is to engage in reflection. Freire (1985) said that "to study is not to consume ideas but to create and re-create them" (p. 4), while also reminding us that "the act of study assumes a dialectical relationship between reader and author, whose reflections are found within the themes he treats. This dialectic involves the author's historical-sociological and ideological conditioning, which is usually not the same as that of the reader" (p. 4).

Even if liberation has already been explained many times, liberation does not exist as long as it is not lived. It is this need to live liberation that is the source and the reason for this work. The nation that I wished to live in is not the one of decolonization but the one of my indigenous culture. It was not an identity that separated us from the rest of the world but, on the contrary, unified us. Even if I wish to support social justice with my work and the rights of people for self-determination, which I have in common with Fanon, I do not wish to create a society based on the idea of domination and class struggle. The sovereign nation is the one that lives in a world of brotherhood, conscious of its human dimension. I find my way not through fighting, but by the positive and pacific expression of my cultural resilience, as my culture embraces the future of this planet.

REFERENCES

Bourdieu, P. (1961). *Sociologie de l'Algérie* [Algerian sociology]. Paris, France: Quadrige/PUF Ed.

Bourdieu, P. (1972). *Esquisse d'une théorie de la pratique* [Outline of a theory of practice]. Paris, France: Seuil Ed.

Bourdieu, P. (1980). *Le sens pratique* [The practical sense]. Paris, France: Éditions de Minuit.

Bourdieu, P., & Sayad, A. (1964). Paysans déracinés, bouleversements morphologiques et changements culturels en Algérie [Uprooted peasants, morphological upheavals and cultural changes in Algeria]. *Études rurales, 12*, 56–94.

Denzin, N.K., Lincoln, Y., & Smith L.T. (2008). *Handbook of critical and indigneous methodologies* (pp. 1–20). Thousand Oaks, CA: Sage.

Fanon, F. (1963). *The wretched of the earth* (C. Farrington, Trans.). New York, NY: Grove Press.

Fanon, F. (1986). *Black skin, white masks* (C. L. Markmann, Trans.). London, England: Pluto Press.

Foucault, M. (1980). *Power/knowledge: Selected interviews and other writings, 1972–1977*. London, England: Harvester Press.

Foucault, M. (1994). Genealogy of social criticism. In S. Seidman (Ed.), *The postmodern turn: New perspective on social theory* (pp. 39–45). Cambridge, England: Cambridge University Press.

Frank, A.W. (1995). *The wounded storyteller: Body, illness, and ethics*. Chicago, IL: University of Chicago Press.

Freire, P. (1970). *Pedagogy of the oppressed*. New York, NY: Seabury Press.

Freire, P. (1975). *Cultural action for freedom*. Cambridge, MA: Harvard Educational Review.

Freire, P. (1985). *The politics of education: Culture, power, and liberation*. South Hadley, MA: Bergin & Garvey.

Freire, P., & Macedo, D. (1987). *Literacy: Regarding the word and the world*. South Hadley, MA: Bergin & Garvey.

Mohia-Navet, N. (2008). L'expérience de terrain, Pour une approche relationnelle dans les sciences sociales [Field experience, For a relational approach to social sciences]. In *Terrains anthropologiques*. Paris, France: La Découverte.

Said, E. W. (1978). *Orientalism*. Gurgaon, India: Penguin.

Said, E. W. (2002). *Out of place: A memoir*. New York, NY: Knopf.

Said, E. W. (2004). *Power, politics and culture: Interviews with Edward W. Said and Gauri Viswanathan*. London, England: Bloomsbury.

Sartre, J. P. (1963). Preface. In F. Fanon, *The wretched of the earth* (p. 53). New York, NY: Grove Press.

Sayad, A., & Bourdieu, P. (1964). *Le déracinement: La crise de l'agriculture en Algérie*, [The uprooting: The crisis of Algerian agriculture]. Paris, France: Éditions de Minuit.

Whitehead, A. N. (1929). *The aims of education*. New York, NY: Macmillan.

CHAPTER THIRTEEN

Travellers in Time: A Critical Dialogue With the Gypsy Travellers of Lancashire

ALETHEA MELLING AND YASMEEN ALI

Education is an act of love, and thus an act of courage.
(FREIRE, P., *EDUCATION FOR CRITICAL CONSCIOUSNESS*,
2007, P. 33).

INTRODUCTION

The Traveller Communities of Lancashire are predominantly Romany and Irish. Their culture and language are oral rather than written. This not only limits the communities' ability to access services, but also limits their ability to articulate their views and to understand their rights. This chapter seeks to explore how Freire's pedagogy and the rich and colourful Traveller tradition of storytelling can be used successfully to engage the Traveller community in the production of a creative yet critical monologue that will facilitate not just reading, but reading their own reality and the development of a hopeful praxis. Moreover, it explores how the act of dialogue is an act of sharing a gift, the gift of education. In this chapter, we discuss how a group of undergraduates formed a learning community with the Travellers and how this became a vehicle for a new knowledge, leading to understanding, trust, and respect.

The Traveller community in the UK is complex and made up of a number of different ethnic and social groups. The generic term is Gypsy Travellers. This group consists of, first, Romany Gypsies, who have been recorded in the UK since the fifteenth century. They were originally referred to as Egyptians because of their dark complexion. It has been suggested that this group originated in India and moved into Europe, although this assertion has been contested by Okely and others (Clark, 2006, pp. 24–26). This ethnic group has been persecuted since the Middle Ages through purges and, more recently, through the genocide inflicted by the Third Reich (Clark, 2006, pp. 24–26). For example, in the time of Henry VIII in England, it was a capital offence to fraternise with Gypsies. Indigenous Travellers in the UK are Irish (Minceir) and Scottish Travellers (Nachins) and Welsh Gypsies (Kale). There are records indicating there were nomadic communities in Ireland centuries ago (Clark, 2006, p. 15). Added to this group are travelling show people and New Age Travellers. The former work in the travelling entertainment industry, such as fairgrounds and circuses. The latter consist of people from the non-nomadic community who are seeking an alternative lifestyle, often an environmentally sustainable lifestyle. Both these groups are usually well educated, the show people because they have to manage complex businesses, and the New Age Travellers because they are often from highly educated backgrounds seeking an ethically sound lifestyle for themselves and their children. However, the community that forms the basis of this study is that of the Irish Travellers.

THE CULTURAL CONTEXT

Irish Travellers have a lot in common with Romany Gypsies in the sense that they both have an oral rather than a written culture. The Romany speak Roma, which is derived from the Indian Sanskrit, and the Irish Travellers speak Shelta, which is a vernacular based on old English and Gaelic. Both these communities are Christian, although there is a Muslim Roma group in Eastern Europe (Education of Roma Children in Europe, 2013). The Irish Travellers are predominantly Roman Catholic, but there is a growing Evangelical Christian influence within this community. The Irish Travellers have very strict unwritten codes of behaviour around family and gender roles. They live in extended families and tend to practice consanguineous marriage, although this practice is not as predominant as it once was. Nevertheless, it is still unusual for a Traveller to marry a gorjio, or outsider. Travellers marry young, usually in their teenage years, and have large families. Sex outside of marriage is forbidden and young women are expected to remain chaste. The women stay at home to look after the house and the children and the men usually are self-employed in the construction, landscaping, and recycling of metals industries. Their work often takes them around the country from place to place.

In order to preserve their culture, it is usual for the Irish Traveller community to remove their children from school at about twelve years old. The girls will then help their mother at home and the boys will start work with their father and other male relatives. The community fears that outside influences may lead their young people into unacceptable forms of behaviour such as drug use and promiscuity (Clark, 2006, p. 213). Recently in the UK, this community has been the subject of a reality television show, *Big Fat Gypsy Wedding* (McNally, 2011). Many Travellers, including those who are the subject of this chapter, regard the programme as a gross misrepresentation of their culture.

Traveller culture is very passionate, emotional, and often physically violent. Children are strictly disciplined and both young men and women are expected to stand up for themselves. This behaviour manifests itself in the popular Traveller sport of bare fist boxing. Young boys are encouraged to box from an early age and the Traveller community have been criticised for participating in and organising child fights. Bare fist boxing, originally associated with Victorian fairgrounds, is illegal based on the grounds of health and safety, but it still continues as an underground movement, serving a significant illicit gambling industry. The Channel Four programme *Gypsy Blood* documents this sporting culture, looking at boxing as an expression of honour and masculinity within the Traveller community (Maguire, 2012). When Traveller families, or clans, fall out, altercations are brutal and can lead to fatalities. When such a feud is taking place, Traveller sites are unsafe for outsiders to visit. These extreme aspects of the Traveller culture are recreated by the popular media as images of deviance.

Traveller communities fall outside of what Antonio Gramsci referred to as the "dominant culture" (Jones, 2010, pp. 27–40) and adopt a lifestyle that is in many ways a challenge to the hegemony: rejection of a formal education where young people are indoctrinated with the values of the dominant culture, and a nomadic lifestyle. In 1924 social philosopher Mary Parker Follett discussed the denigration of diversity in her comments on conflict: "What people often mean by getting rid of conflict is getting rid of diversity, and it is of the utmost importance that these not be considered the same. We may wish to abolish conflict, but we cannot get rid of diversity. We must face life as it is and understand that diversity is its most essential feature.... Fear of difference is fear of life itself" (Follett, 1924, p. 300). Follett's considerations on the question of conflict and diversity and Gramsci's view of the ongoing negotiation of power between the state and the citizen are both interesting here. The state as the dominant culture ensures the acquiescence of the dominated through the provision of services, such as health, welfare, protection, and so forth. In order to access these services, minority communities must at least assimilate the central values of the dominant culture through the state education system and acquire the tools, such as a permanent address, literacy, numeracy, and Internet Communication Technologies (ICT), to access the services. As Ryder also notes, policy and practice in these areas assume a level of assimilation and that is why they fail (Ryder, 2010, pp. 56–60). Those marginalised from the dominant culture through poverty, illness, and, in this case, through culture cannot access the services effectively as they do not have the necessary human capital (Keeley, 2007, p. 10). Travellers therefore have some of the worst records of health, neonatal survival, and adult life expectancy of any ethnic group (James, 2007, pp. 367–388). This is particularly pertinent for antenatal care, as many Traveller women do not get the health checkups that are available to the wider society (Clark, 2006, pp. 192–194).

THE PEDAGOGY

The pedagogy employed must be sympathetic to valuing diversity and addressing the fear of difference. The University of Central Lancashire was asked by the Traveller Education Service to help develop the literacy skills of the young people on the site through student mentoring. In his work *Education for Critical Consciousness*, Paulo Freire (2007) discusses the concept of extension and its linguistic connotations. This concept has significance for this process, where the university students had been asked to extend literacy skills to the Travellers. It is very important in any truly authentic pedagogic process to avoid the negative connotations of extension. Freire notes that words form a "linguistic field" within a "conceptual field," thereby "expressing a vision of the world they reconstruct." Freire suggests that linguistically and therefore conceptually, the term extension, regardless of the context, held negative connotations: "It appears that the act of extension, in whatever sector it takes place, means that those carrying it out need to go to another part of the world, to 'normalise it' according to their way of viewing reality: to make it resemble their world" (Freire, 2007, p. 89). This act of extension, whereby the students bring their technical knowledge to the Traveller community, "must involve a relationship between human beings and the world, so as to make human beings better equipped to change the world." Otherwise, "the concept of extension which is characterised by the transference of techniques and knowledge is in direct contradiction with a truly humanist outlook" (Freire, 2007, p. 88).

The project posed a significant challenge. First, the Traveller community is notoriously closed and secretive. Travellers do not trust outsiders, referred to as gorjio. Owing to centuries of discrimination, the Traveller community have developed what Ryder (2010) describes as a strong "bonding" form of social capital that allows the community to function exclusively, with little linking to the dominant culture. There were concerns as to whether or not barriers to engagement could be broken and an inclusive learning community established. Freire stated, "Education is an act of love, and thus an act of courage," and it was through acts of courage on both sides that this learning community of young Travellers and university students developed (Freire, 2007, p. 33). Interaction required a humanising approach that would allow participants (staff, Travellers, and students) to remove their outer armour of preconception, prejudice, mistrust, and otherness, and to enter the dialogue as fellow human beings, with love, openness, tolerance, and curiosity.

In her opening address to the 2012 conference "Paulo Freire: A Global Legacy," Nita Freire talked about a hopeful praxis: how individuals and communities, if they engage critically and authentically in ethical and political struggles, can "ultimately transform" where they live (Freire, 2012). By using a pedagogy sympathetic to Freire's philosophy,[1] we worked with the Traveller community and university students to develop a critical monologue that facilitates reading their own reality through what Colin Lankshear refers to as a "humanising model of functional literacy" (Lankshear, 1993, pp. 111–118). Lankshear's discussion of domesticating versus liberating literacy is important here and to acquire such requires a similar pedagogy. A domesticating pedagogy demands that the student assimilate the dominant culture, whereas a liberating pedagogy allows students to develop a functional literacy, allowing them to pursue a humanising and hopeful praxis. This moment of praxis was most poignant in the creative monologue of a young Traveller whom we will refer to as Mary:

> My name is Mary, I am 25 years old. I travel around places.
> I am protesting against the banning of Travellers.
> I dream that Man can be peaceful. I want Travellers to be more wanted in cities. I can hear people. I can smell nature and horses. I can touch fences and walls.
> I remember when things were different. I am afraid of fairs ending. The best day of my life was when I didn't have a care in the world. The worst day of my life was full of worry when the law started.
> I am brave, blonde, married and funny. The object I can't live without is my phone.
> It is the day of the fair. I am protesting because I feeling frustrated. I am worried that I will say the right thing to bring the Travellers to Freedom. Will I do the right thing?
> Will I be a role model? Will I be a voice for the Gypsies?
> I am trying to be a voice for the future Travellers.
> If it weren't for the King then fairs such as Appleby and Cain Bridge wouldn't exist. Racism often goes on throughout the Travellers' communities, such as being accused of shoplifting and stealing and are hated for their background and religion. (Mary, 2012)

Unlike other ethnic minorities, the Traveller community does not ambitiously seek to be represented within the power structures of society such as politics and the law. A lack of human capital, namely, education and political alliances, and a low level of social capital outside of the immediate community make it difficult for Travellers to access services that support equality. Therefore, Travellers are almost routinely discriminated against in ways that would not be tolerated by any other ethnic group. Mary recalled trying to enter a well-known department store with her children when the security guard stopped her and said, "We don't want Gypsies in here as you will be thieving everything."[2] If the security guard had said, "We don't want Blacks, Pakistanis, and Indians," he would have been dismissed from his job on grounds of racial discrimination. The young woman said she had never stolen anything in her life, but this was not an isolated incident, but just part of the ongoing struggle the community had to endure to be accepted (Traveller, 2012). Travellers are a socially excluded group, with little access to redress.[3]

Developing a critical monologue necessitated developing critical capacity within the learning community. To develop a critical capacity, it was also necessary to engender a democracy. Freire believed that a lack of opportunity for concrete participation in democratic processes, through social exclusion, oppression, and other forms of marginalisation brought about by the dominant culture, results in an ingenuous approach to dealing with social and political issues: "The less critical capacity a group possesses, the more ingenuously it treats problems and the more superficially it discusses objects" (Freire, 2007, pp. 88-89). An important aspect of this pedagogic process was to create a democracy within what had become an eclectic learning community of adults and children, university students and Travellers, Muslims and Christians, Indian, Somalian, Pakistani, Irish and white British. The first act of courage was to cut through differences and seek common values. This sense of common understanding within the learning community was epitomised when we asked: What can Travellers teach the world? The Travellers believed that they could teach the world valuable skills in respect, modesty, living as a community, family, and culture. Interestingly, they identified a strong affinity with Muslims in terms of values and behaviour. Moreover, they wished to teach the world that Travellers are not "bad people," and that "we are human beings" (Mary, 2012). The latter point reflects how the Traveller community often feel that they are treated as subhuman by the dominant culture.

The question what can Travellers teach the world? immediately reverses the process of anti-dialogue that the dominant society has used to "educate" the Travellers for centuries. In the words of Stanley Aronowitz, "The locus of the learning process is shifted from the teacher to the student" (Aronowitz, 1993, pp. 8-9). From this simple dialogue it is possible to identify a number of important areas where the Traveller community can inform the dominant society. Successive governments and policy makers have sought answers to the question of cohesive communities, the respect agenda, family, sustainability, and culture. Here is a community that prides itself on faith, family, respect, the environment, and heritage. Moreover, it is a factor that is distinctly lacking in the dominant culture: humanity rather than neoliberal pragmatism.

The university students underwent a transformational experience as part of this project. They were subjected to humanity at its most authentic. The interaction between the Travellers was emotional and passionate, and at a level of intensity that the university students had not experienced. In a pragmatic education system, emotionality in the classroom is discouraged, even though it is through emotional references rather than reading books that we learn (Freire, N. , 2012). The passion and the physicality of the Traveller community initially disturbed the university students, as the Traveller young men in particular did not respond to the students' idea of what is "normal" classroom interaction. The young Traveller men also had issues regarding the university students, as they had little interaction with groups outside of their community and were suspicious as a form of self-preservation. To begin with, both groups behaved with some hostility toward each other. Nevertheless, the learning community worked together on forging an initially fragile democracy, which formed the basis of developing critical capacity within the learning community as a whole. Over the period of the project, both the university students and the Travellers moved through a really humanising process from an ingenuous attitude toward each other to a collaborative capacity for critical thought.

CONCLUSION

In his dialogue with Ira Shor, Freire agrees that a teacher must be an artist. Shor is referring to a need to recreate the visual and verbal aspects of the classroom and to shift passive learning to active learning. Shor seeks a colourful, vibrant, and dynamic learning environment (Shor, 1987, p. 117). The process of education needs to be a work of art, created by the whole learning community. Never has this been as pertinent as when working with the Traveller community whose language, culture, and heritage are built upon expression and emotionality. In order to engender the reading of reality, we worked with the oral tradition of storytelling and engaged the group in expressing their reality through fiction. An example of this is a short monologue by a young man whom we shall refer to as John:

John the Slave Boy.

My name is John. I am ten years old, I am on a big smelly ship. I am on the way to the Caribbean to be a slave. I am frightened in case I get killed and never see my family again. I dream of dying because I would rather be dead than be here. I want to be able to see my family again though. When will I see them? Will I ever see them again? I can hear banging, shouting, crying, squealing, coughing and sneezing. I can smell Pirates, rats and sweat. I can taste the smell of mice and bodies. I remember getting hit with a sword. I can see guns, people bleeding and injured. I am afraid of getting killed; what if I get thrown into the rivers and drown?
The best day of my life was just being with my family.
The worst day was when I stepped on to the ship and my life changed, then I got hit with a sword. I am good looking, skinny with a six pack and scars on my body. Life as a Traveller is terrifying because we were slaves, we were tortured we were threatened; we got beat up. An old-fashioned gun once shot me.

John's narrative is rich and vibrant. An oral culture with a strong emphasis on storytelling encourages a colourful and highly sensual vocabulary within the Traveller community. He is using storytelling as a way of dealing with his sense of otherness and identification with an oppressed minority, in this case a slave boy. Through this process, a ten-year-old boy is able to push through an ingenuous mind-set to read his own reality. This is a child with apparently "low levels of literacy," but a deep love of words and the ability to create physical sensation through narrative. This is a child who underachieves at school and will probably drop out in a couple of years. Yet this is a child with a mature and sophisticated level of emotional intelligence. The most powerful aspect of this process is that it is not a technique "extended" to the Traveller community by the hand of the university; it is the Travellers' own process that they have been able to share with the university students in a moment of collaborative conscientisation. The next step is to develop the critical monologue into a radio play for a wider audience.

This project was in fact a product of a failed assimilation process within the dominant education culture. As Ryder points out, the mainstream system does not attempt to accommodate the learning needs and aspirations of this ethnic group (Ryder, 2010, p. 52). Although the Report of the Stephen Lawrence Inquiry (recommendation 67)[4] emphasises the need for a curriculum that values cultural diversity, and recent movements have been forged to ensure the inclusion of minority cultures within educational provision, these "improvements" have bypassed the Traveller community. According to Clark (2006), in contrast to other ethnic minorities, there has been little input by Traveller communities into the development of the curriculum. Clark believes the reason for this is the rigid and inflexible education system rather than cultural reasons (Clark, 2006, p. 225). Moreover, many Traveller young people are racially bullied at school in ways that would not be tolerated by any other minority group. In the foreword to the governmental paper *The Inclusion of Gypsy, Roma, and Traveller Children and Young People*, Lord Adonis, the Parliamentary Under-Secretary of State Schools, UK, commented that "for far too long society has shunned people from these communities. This has resulted in their growing mistrust of authority and many generations not having a good education," thus leading to social marginalisation (Department for Children, Schools, and Families, 2008, p. 1-3). In his article "The Gypsies and Social Exclusion," Andrew Ryder elaborates on Adonis's point discussing how Traveller communities are excluded from "the benefits" of mainstream society (Ryder, 2010, pp. 52–60). Despite the rhetoric on inclusion and human rights, Traveller communities continue to be excluded from education. During the project, the Traveller young people worked on their critical monologues, asking the question: What if I ruled the world? The most popular answer was to ban school.

ACKNOWLEDGMENTS

We would like to thank the Traveller community in Preston, Patty Linfoot of the Divano Charity and Seb Smith of the Traveller Education Service, Lancashire, without whose help this project would not have happened. We would also like to thank Sam Broxton, Gillian Lynes, Fatima Younas, and Tony Ingham, our wonderful students. A great debt is owed to poet and artist Louise Walwein for having the creativity to move Freire's pedagogy to practice; Dr. Mahmood Chandia for acting as a valuable critical friend; and to the University of Central Lancashire. Finally, to Paulo Freire's legacy and ongoing influence, which continue to nurture our work in challenging times.

NOTES

1. Nita Freire stated that Paulo Freire hoped that students would "not repeat, copy or recreate, but use as a reference" (Freire, N. , 2012).
2. In his work on integralist narratives and redemptive anti-Gypsy politics, Michael Stewart explores how the dominant culture establishes a cultural connection between Gypsy Travellers and criminality. Stewart discusses this in the context of the Hungarian Roma community, but his comments have a resonance for the manner in which the wider society perceives Gypsy Travellers: "The cultural arguments which establish an inherent connection and inviolability as to the nature of gypsies, and present certain traits as normalised are, needless to say, dangerous as they serve the process of social habituation among the majority" (Stewart, 2012, p. 58).
3. Andrew Ryder defines social exclusion in this context as a denial of access to a range of life chances and opportunities caused by structural inequalities. He goes on to say that exclusion can be reflected "not only in material inequality, but spatial, institutional and political exclusion. It is a consequence of a complete rupture with society" (Ryder, 2010, p. 56).
4. The Stephen Lawrence Inquiry was initiated as a response to accusations of institutional racism within the police force following the murder of young black student Stephen Lawrence in 1993.

REFERENCES

Aronowitz, S. (1993). Paulo Freire's radical democratic humanism. In P. L. McLaren (Ed.), *Paulo Freire: A critical encounter* (pp. 8–9). New York, NY: Routledge.

Bishop, R. (2012). Freeing ourselves: A reflection on Paulo Freire's theories of liberation. *Paulo Freire: The Global Legacy Conference 2012.* Hamilton, New Zealand: Waikato University.

Clark, C. (2006). *Here to stay: Gypsy Travellers of Britain.* Hertfordshire, England: Hertfordshire University Press.

Department for Children, Schools, and Families. (2008). *Lord Andrew Adonis: The inclusion of Gypsy, Roma, and Traveller children and young people, DFCSF, Nottingham.* Nottingham, England: DFCSF.

Divano Charity. (n.d.). *Gypsy Roma Traveller.* Retrieved January 21, 2013, from http://www.gypsy romatraveller.com

Education of Roma Children in Europe. (2013). *Roma Muslims in the Balkans.* Retrieved January 30, 2013, from http://romafacts.uni-graz.at/index.php/culture/introduction/roma-muslims-in-the-balkans

Follett, M. P. (1924). *Creative experience.* New York, NY: Longman.

Freire, N. (2012). The Philosophy of Education Society of Australasia opening address. *Paulo Freire: The Global Legacy Conference 2012.* Hamilton, New Zealand: Waikato University.

Freire, P. (2007). *Education for critical consciousness.* New York, NY: Continuum.

Greenfield, M., & Ryder, A. (2010). *Roads to success: Economic and social inclusion of Gypsies and Travellers.* Buckingham, England: An Irish Traveller Movement in Britain Report.

James, Z. (2007). Policing marginal spaces: Controlling Gypsies and Travellers. *Criminology and Criminal Justice,* 367–388.

Jones, S. (2010). *Antonio Gramsci.* Oxford, England: Routledge.

Keeley, B. (2007). *Human capital: How what you know shapes your life.* Paris, France: Organisation for Economic Cooperation and Development (OECD) Insights.

Lancashire NHS. (2003). Retrieved January 18, 2013, from http://www.lancashirecare.nhs.uk/media/Publications/Quality_Account/Quality%20Account%202013-14/Quality%20Account%202013-14.pdf

Lankshear, C. (1993). Functional literacy. In P. M. Leonard (Ed.), *Paulo Freire: A critical encounter* (pp. 111–118). New York, NY: Routledge.

Linfoot, P. (2013, October 17). Divano Charity. (A. Melling, Interviewer)

Maguire, L. (Director). (2012). *Gypsy blood* [Motion picture]. England: Clear Story.

Mary. (2012, April). Creative monologue. (Y. Ali, Interviewer) Preston, England.

McNally, J. (2011). *Big fat Gypsy weddings.* London, England: Hodder & Stoughton.

Ryder, A. (2010). The Gypsies and social exclusion. *Social Work in Europe, 9*(3), 52–60.

Shor, P. F. (1987). *A pedagogy for liberation.* South Hadley, MA: Bergin & Garvey.

Smith, J. (2005, April 26). *Gypsies are 'Europe's most hated'.* BBC News. Retrieved January 18, 2013, from http://news.bbc.co.uk/2/hi/uk/4486245.stm

Stewart, M. (2012). *The Gypsy menace: Populism and the new anti-Gypsy politics.* London, England: C. Hurst.

Traveller. (2012, April). Discussion on Traveller rights at Leighton Traveller site, Preston. (A. Melling & Seb Smith, Interviewers)

Traveller Community from Leighton Site, Preston. (2012). *Travellers in time.* Preston, England: UCLan.

CHAPTER FOURTEEN

How the MST's Educational Principles in Brazil Respond to Global Capitalism, Neoliberalism, and "Reactionary Postmodernity"

JÚLIO EMÍLIO DINIZ-PEREIRA

INTRODUCTION

This chapter discusses how the Landless Workers Movement (Movimento dos Trabalhadores Rurais Sem Terra, or simply, MST), one of the largest and most important social movements in contemporary Latin America, which has struggled for agrarian reform as well as social and economic justice in Brazil, responds to three very important issues under which we live: global capitalism, neoliberalism, and, in Paulo Freire's words, "reactionary postmodernity." One of the lessons that the MST has learned from its history in Brazil is that it is not enough to struggle only for land. Education is also a quite important dimension of the MST's struggles. The MST pedagogy is linked to collective work and the construction of humanist and socialist values. Therefore, this chapter discusses how the MST's educational principles respond to these three very intertwined, contemporary issues.

"GLOBALIZATIONS"

Many scholars from several academic areas all over the world have been discussing the various phenomena associated with increasing globalization and its impact on different sectors of society. Well-known intellectuals such as Anthony Giddens, Boaventura de Sousa Santos, Eric Hobsbawm, Manuel Castells, Paul Hirst, Stuart Hall, William Robinson, and many others, assuming distinct political positions in this debate, contribute to the analyses of these highly complex phenomena. Indeed, as stated by Stromquist and Monkman (2000), "Globalization has many faces" (p. 4). While it is traditionally discussed only through the lens of economics, some academics have also dealt with the social, political, and cultural dimensions of globalization.

Addressing not only the economic, but also the political and ideological facets of globalization, McLaren (2000) prefers to conceive of these phenomena as capitalist domination on a global scale. Drawing upon William Robinson's ideas, he states that, in political and ideological terms, "globalization" has been mainly understood as "global capitalism."[1] McLaren (2000) examines the logics behind such a powerful ideology. He criticizes "a culturalist logic" in this conceptualization of globalization that reduces its meaning to a "standardization of commodities"—"the same designer clothes appearing in shopping plazas throughout the world." (McLaren & Farahmandpur, 2001, p. 137) According to McLaren, globalization is "inextricably tied to the politics of neoliberalism." In sum, he asserts that "the concept of globalization needs to be reformulated so that historical subjects or actors are granted the potential to challenge the hegemony of international capital in the defense of justice, solidarity, and the working class" (2001, p. 137).

While McLaren's criticisms of capitalist globalization are crucial, I find that his position does not fully consider the complexity of potential "globalizations." In my view, it is crucial to discuss, through the critical lens of "globalizations," the characteristics and potentialities of counter-hegemonic movements while simultaneously implementing concrete critical local-global actions, rather than simply summoning teachers to fight *against* "globalization," as McLaren suggests.

Santos (1997), grounded in Gramsci's concept of "hegemony," states that "there is strictly no single entity called globalization; there are, rather, *globalizations*, and we should use the term only in the plural" (the author's emphasis) (p. 3). Since globalization is a complex set of phenomena, we need to specify what we mean by "globalization." According to Stromquist and Monkman's analysis, "Globalization forces seem to be introducing a mix of homogenizing tendencies, but they are also opening space for new identities and contestation of established values and norms, many detrimental to the achievement of true social justice" (2000, p. 21).

There is no globalization without localization. Nothing is global in the beginning or, in other words, nothing is originally global. Meanwhile, localization is not only local but also global.[2] Santos describes the complexity of the interplay between local and global: "Though apparently monolithic, this process does combine highly differentiated situations and conditions, and for that reason it cannot be analyzed independently of the power relations that account for the different forms of time and space mobility" (1997, p. 4).

Santos suggests different modes of production of globalization, which give rise to distinct forms of globalization. The first, *globalized localism*, "consists of the process by which a given local phenomenon is successfully globalized" (1997, p. 4). As an example of this form, we have the globalization of American fast food, or the transformation of English into a worldwide language. The second mode of production of globalization is *localized globalism*, which refers to the impact of transnational practices and imperatives on local conditions that are restructured to respond to global realities. Deforestation and massive depletion of natural resources to pay for foreign debt and the ethnicization of the workplace are considered by Santos as examples of "localized globalism." Third, we have *cosmopolitanism*, which could also be called globalization of subordinate nation-states, regions, classes, and social groups or globalization of poor and oppressed people. Cosmopolitan activities include, among others, the global justice work of transnational feminist, labor, and environmental groups.

It is important to note that the first and second modes are *hegemonic* forms of globalization while the third one is an example of a *counter-hegemonic* form of globalization. As indicated by Santos, "the conflicts, resistances, struggles and coalitions clustering around cosmopolitanism...show that what we call globalization is in fact a set of arenas of cross-border struggles" (1997, p. 5).

Hence, one of the most important issues in this discussion has been the distinction between *hegemonic* and *counter-hegemonic* globalization, or between "globalization from above" and "globalization from below." On the one hand, as Santos (1998) points out, "the hegemonic processes of globalization are bringing about the intensification of social exclusion and marginalization of large bodies of population all over the world" (p. 461). On the other hand, against these hegemonic processes of globalization we have had grassroots initiatives, community innovations, and popular movements that try to counteract social exclusion, thus opening up spaces for democratic participation, for community building, and for alternatives to dominant forms of development and knowledge.

According to Santos, counter-hegemonic models occur in rural as well as in urban settings, and involve common people. In general, it is little known because it does not speak the language of hegemonic globalization. It becomes more apparent after the collapse of the models of grand-scale social transformation.

Land rights, urban infrastructure, drinking water, labor rights, gender equality, self-determination, biodiversity, the environment, and community justice are some of the concerns of counter-hegemonic globalization. These movements have had a wide variety of relations with the state—from no relation at all to complementary or confrontational relations.

The Landless Workers Movement is a national social and cultural movement in Brazil that acts locally and at the same time participates in a counter-hegemonic global alliance of peasants and small farmers called *Via Campesina*. In education, activist educators around the world have also tried to fight against conservative forms of education, teaching, and teacher education.[3]

As will be shown in the next section, hegemonic globalization—also called "global capitalism"—is strongly interwoven with the neoliberal ideology of the free market, which has been imposed worldwide through powerful institutions such as the World Trade Organization (WTO), the International Monetary Fund (IMF), and the World Bank, all of which have increased the disparity between rich and poor—both between and within nations—throughout the globe (McLaren, 2000).

NEOLIBERALISM

Although the term "neoliberalism" has been widely used in Latin America since the "Washington Consensus" was first presented to the World Bank in 1989 as "the formula" to promote economic growth in the region,[4] the ideology itself is not new.[5] As Chomsky (2000) reminded us, "Neoliberalism is centuries old, and its effects should not be unfamiliar" (p. 155).[6]

Apple (2001)[7] seems to agree that neoliberalism is not a new ideology. He points out the differences between neoliberalism and classical liberalism. Apple writes, "While the defining characteristic of neoliberalism is largely based on the central tenets of classical liberalism, in particular classic economic liberalism, there are crucial differences between classical liberalism and neoliberalism" (p. 71). He quotes Mark Olssen, who details the main differences between neoliberalism and classical liberalism (see Apple, 2001, pp. 71–72).

What is neoliberalism, then? What are its main principles? In short, neoliberal ideology holds that in order for corporations to maximize their profit and be able to compete in the global marketplace, an economy must be regulated by the market. As Apple (2001) writes, "For neoliberals, the world in essence is a vast supermarket" (p. 39). Consequently, the rule of the market is characterized by a minimum intervention from the state[8] and "deregulation." Phrases like "free market ideology" and "minimal state" are often linked to neoliberalism.

Privatization of all public and state-owned enterprises is another principle of the neoliberal ideology. Consequently, in order to achieve its goal, neoliberalism tries to spread the idea that "what is private is necessarily good and what is public is necessarily bad" (Apple, 2001, p. 38). In short, as Apple (2001), quoting Robert McChesney, states "neoliberalism is in essence 'capitalism with the gloves off'" (p. 18).

Bourdieu (1998) argues that "the strength of the neoliberal ideology is that it is based on a kind of social neo-Darwinism" (p. 42), that is, neoliberalism highlights both the logic of competition[9] and "the ideology of competence"[10] in our societies. The author insists that the neoliberal program destroys "collective references and solidarity" (p. 98).

The neoliberal ideology also tries to impose some concepts such as "democracy" and "citizenship" and make its definitions the only ones possible and acceptable. For neoliberals, "democracy" is conceived of as what Chomsky (1997, 2000) calls the "market democracy," which is a "top-down form of democracy" that attends to the interests of market "with the public kept to a 'spectator' role, not participating in the arena of decision making" (2000, p. 142).

Martin Carnoy, in the foreword to one of Paulo Freire's books, raises the following question: "Is globalized capital so powerful that the state is limited to the neoliberal agenda?" According to him, Freire would say "No" (Carnoy, 1997, p. 13). In Freire's view, neoliberalism has produced a pragmatic discourse "which speaks of a new history without classes, without struggle, without ideologies, without left, and without right" (1996, p. 114). He calls this highly ideological discourse "reactionary postmodernity."

"REACTIONARY POSTMODERNITY"

Freire (1996) argues that "reactionary postmodernity" has succeeded "in proclaiming the disappearance of ideologies and the emergence of a new history without social classes, therefore without antagonistic interests, without class struggle. They preach that there is no need to continue to speak about dreams, utopia, or social justice" (p. 84). Thus, Freire criticizes the fatalistic and triumphalist view of "the end of history,"[11] which proclaims that there is no future beyond capitalism. Freire states, "What we need to do now, according to this astute ideology, is focus on production without any preoccupation about what we are producing, who it benefits, or who it hurts" (1996, p. 84).

Bourdieu (1998) seems to agree with Freire's criticisms and also questions what he calls "a supposedly postmodern...version of the ideology of the end of ideology" (p. 42). He states that the neoliberal view "has succeeded in presenting itself as self-evident, that there is no alternative" (p. 29).[12] Consequently, "neoliberalism comes to be seen as an *inevitability*" (the author's emphasis). Bourdieu explains his perspective:

A whole set of presuppositions is being imposed as self-evident: it is taken for granted that maximum growth, and therefore productivity and competitiveness, are the ultimate and sole goal of human actions; or the economic forces cannot be resisted. Or again—a presupposition which is the basis of all the presuppositions of economics—a radical separation is made between the economic and the social. (1998, pp. 30-31)

According to Bourdieu, another important assumption in the neoliberal ideology is the language. He suggests that "there is a whole game with the connotations and associations of words like flexibility, *souplesse*, deregulation, which tends to imply that the neoliberal message is a universalist message of liberation" (1998, p. 31).

Freire responds to the neoliberals who proclaim the death of ideologies as well as the death of social classes and class struggle, claiming that it is "only possible to destroy ideologies ideologically" (1996, p. 188). He argues that "the leftist and rightist ideologies are still alive, but it is necessary for the rightists to preach that ideologies no longer exist so as to invigorate the Right" (1996, p. 84). Freire also responds to the "neoliberal, pragmatic discourse," claiming there is no future beyond capitalism. He writes:

The proclaimed triumph of capitalism and death of socialism actually just underlines the perversity of capitalism on the one hand and the enduring socialist dream on the other, if it is purified, with sacrifice and pain, from authoritarian distortion. Thus, the necessary dependence between socialism and democracy has been affirmed, in light of the failure of authoritarian socialism and the intrinsic evil of capitalism, which is insensitive to the pain of the exploited majorities. (1996, pp. 136–137)

Freire also states that "the dream of the popular majorities today is socialism as the mark of popular democracy. The fundamental point is not to end democracy, but to perfect it and have not capitalism but socialism as its filling" (1996, p. 137). Finally, he insists that "forging the unity between democracy and socialism is the challenge that inspires us. (...) The future is a problem, a possibility, and not inexorable" (1996, p. 137).

Although global capitalism, neoliberal ideology, and "reactionary postmodernity" have attempted to destroy our utopias[13] and our capacity to dream, the experience of the MST in Brazil offers evidence that the dream that "another world is possible"[14] is still very much alive.

RESPONSES FROM THE MST'S EDUCATIONAL PRINCIPLES[15]

Although the neoliberal agenda in Brazil has increased the number of landless people, as well as decreased educational opportunities for the poor population, the Landless Workers Movement (MST), in its thirty years of existence,[16] has struggled for agrarian reform as well as for social and economic justice in Brazil, achieving quite impressive results.

The movement is made up of people from some of the poorest segments of Brazilian society.[17] It mobilizes what Bales (1999), in the context of the current global economy, calls "disposable people."[18] The landless people are peasants whose lands have been expropriated and who been excluded from other basic rights of citizenship. They are also rural workers and unemployed people who struggle to be reintegrated into the labor markets and social arenas from which they have been expelled as a result of the unequal process of capitalist development (Fernandes, 2000; Wright & Wolford, 2003).

The landless people in Brazil struggle not simply for land, but for all the basic conditions of human existence. The Landless Workers Movement has three main goals: (1) to redistribute land to those who work it; (2) to achieve agrarian reform—which the movement considers to be much broader and more complex than land redistribution, and which must entail the attainment of the full scope of social rights that define full citizenship; and (3) to build a democratic socialist society.

The landless people are excluded not only from their lands, but also from other basic rights of citizenship. In order to conquer these rights, they have understood that the struggle for land is linked to the struggle for living with dignity. Through their struggles, they seek to trample other fences beyond those of the latifundium. Knocking down the invisible yet powerful fence around knowledge through an ambitious educational project is another challenge facing the MST.

AN OVERVIEW OF THE MST'S EDUCATIONAL WORK

One of the principal lessons that the Landless Workers Movement has learned from its history in Brazil is that it is not enough to struggle only for land. Education is another central dimension of the MST's struggles. Because of the high rates of illiteracy and low rates of schooling in the acampamentos (encampments) and assentamentos (settlements), the landless families consider formal education and schooling crucial. However, for the MST, education is not restricted to school and classroom. One's involvement with the entire movement is already considered the greater "school."

The MST's pedagogy, closely linked to a collective work ethic and the construction of humanist and socialist values, has been developing since the 1980s when the MST's education committees began discussing educational issues with the landless communities. The movement has also established pre-service and in-service teacher education programs for those who teach at schools in its settlements and encampments.

The educational principles of the MST have emerged from its praxis (practice and theory combined).[19] They have been established collectively through what the movement calls "método de princípios" ("method of principles"). The main purpose of this method is "to transform the accumulated lessons of all prior experiences and discussions into pedagogical principles that could lead (without prescribing) the educational work in all encampments and settlements in the country" (Caldart, 2000, p. 166).

The MST does not follow a unique pedagogy or an educational theory developed by a specific thinker. It constitutes itself as a pedagogical subject that incorporates various pedagogies and elements from many educational currents, adapting and modifying them according to people's needs in each settlement and encampment (Caldart, 2000; Harnecker, 2002).

A crucial aspect of the MST education project is that landless people must become subjects of their own pedagogy. The process of transforming people into educators who reflect upon their own education takes place through a permanent relationship between theory and practice. It is also a direct consequence of the fact that people are part of a social movement. Thus, "the landless people of the MST are not only the subjects of an educational experience and human development, but also challenge themselves to become the subjects of theoretical reflection upon the pedagogy that they live" (Caldart, 2000, p. 54; Harnecker, 2002).

As mentioned above, although this pedagogy goes beyond the school, it also passes through the school. However, for the school to incorporate the MST's pedagogy, there has to be a process of what the movement calls "school occupation."

The MST uses the term "school occupation" because the strategy landless people employ to force the state or the municipality to provide schools for their children is very similar to the one they use in order to occupy land. By occupying the school, the movement means "establishing the school first, beginning the work and the formal enrollments that they know are mandatory, despite precarious material conditions, and thus initiating the negotiations with the government in order to legalize the school" (Caldart, 2000, p. 240). The movement knows that if it starts first negotiating with local governments, the process of establishing a school may take months or even years (Caldart, 2000; Harnecker, 2002).

Caldart (2000; 2003a) discusses three other meanings of "school occupation" in the movement. First, because, as mentioned above, the landless families have mobilized themselves in order to struggle for the right to attend school, "school occupation" means the process of ensuring the extension of the social right to attend school to landless people. Second, the movement has taken on the task of organizing and articulating this mobilization in an organic way, producing a specific pedagogical project in the schools that have been conquered and training educators in a way that they can work toward this perspective. Thus, "school occupation" also means a planned and systematic process of incorporating the school into the movement's dynamic. Third, because the school is also seen as a political matter, "school occupation" means that the school is part of the strategy of struggling for agrarian reform, linking the movement's general concerns to its participants' political development.

Caldart (2000) states that traditional schooling and the movement demonstrate logics that contradict one another. Their identities are usually conflicting identities. On the one hand, as mentioned above, the MST, as a progressive social and cultural movement, increasingly insists upon humanist and socialist values in education. On the other hand, traditional schools usually subordinate themselves to the immediacy of market demands. For instance, in her research, Ribeiro (2001) found that parents and teachers in some settlement schools seemed to agree that it is really difficult to introduce cooperative relationships in teaching, even in the MST's schools, because school tends to promote competition, individualism, and submission.

As also mentioned above, in the MST's educational work, the children and the teachers are conceived of as "pedagogical subjects." They are seen as privileged links in the dialogue between the movement and the school (Beltrame, 2000).

The active participation of the MST children, who are also called the Sem Terrinha (little landless ones),[20] is a crucial element in the movement's educational work. Although the movement wishes to avoid transforming the pupils into premature adults, the MST strongly supports its children's active participation in the movement and, more specifically, in their schools.

Caldart (2000) states that, since the very beginning, the children have been an important part of the movement's dynamic through their participation, with their parents, in important MST actions such as mobilizations, demonstrations, and even land occupations. Moreover, the author argues, children have also been able to create their own space in the movement. They have organized themselves in order to demand their rights and make negotiations in their own communities.

Harnecker (2002) states that in settlements where work is organized in a collective way, the children often feel motivated to create their own organization. The author cites one settlement where "the children got used to holding weekly assemblies to analyze their daily problems and distribute the tasks they could take on in the settlement" (p. 92). In her opinion, these experiences make it easy for the school to be a miniature organization of the committees and work teams in the encampments and settlements.

Children's active participation also takes place at their schools. For instance, they may put pressure on teachers to change the curriculum to connect it more closely to their lives and realities. In Caldart's opinion, the children "are ready to assume their condition as subjects and, who knows, lead themselves in the process of occupying the school" (2000, p. 173).

The MST also emphasizes the importance of teachers' participation in the movement and their active involvement in the community. Caldart (2000) states that the MST's history of schooling has had the transformative effect of giving these teachers a specific collective identity that goes beyond their profession without abandoning it. To be a Sem Terra teacher, as Caldart argues, means to have "an identity that has been constructed simultaneously with the MST's progressive 'occupation' of the school" (p. 187).

According to Caldart, "Sem Terra teacher" is the name that can be given to an MST character who within herself[21] combines three different identity components: "first, the condition of being a woman and the whole grid of meanings that this implies from a human, social, political, and historical point of view; second, her professional identity as an educator; and third, her participation in an organization that struggles for land and that, in turn, produces new meanings for her condition as both a woman and an educator" (p. 187).

Caldart argues that at the same time that the MST is able to shape the educator's new identity, the emergence of the Sem Terra teachers leads to new characteristics for the movement's identity as well. One of the results of the construction of this new collective identity for teachers has been a significant increase in women's participation in the MST (see also Diniz-Pereira, 2013).

The teachers—more specifically, the female teachers—who began to participate in the MST as the wives of landless rural workers, brought a serious concern about the teaching profession to the larger struggle over land. According to Caldart (2000), "In the same sense that, earlier, [they] were important actors pressuring the MST to struggle for schools, [they] continue on the stage today, pressuring the MST to create more space for education on its agenda" (p. 186).

McCowan (2003) states that although the MST's national education committee formulates the principal orientations of the movement's educative work, and coordinators at the state and regional levels play the chief role in enforcing them, "teachers do have influence on pedagogical and organizational decision-making in schools" (p. 8). He argues that teacher participation seems to have a dual function in the MST: "firstly the 'organizational' aspect, creating a cooperative and efficient body of workers, and secondly to increase their identification with and commitment to the community and the movement" (p. 8).

CONCLUSION

To conclude, the ideology of neoliberalism has dominated global discourse and action when it comes to economic and educational reform, with disastrous consequences. The MST in Brazil has presented a stark contrast to this ideology, delivering hope and real opportunities for landless Brazilians. As their struggle to build the movement continues, the issue of education for social transformation becomes crucial.

ACKNOWLEDGMENT

Although this chapter is itself an original work, parts of it have been already published in, for example, J. E. Diniz-Pereira (2005), "Teacher Education for Social Transformation and Its Links to Progressive Social Movements: The Case of the Landless Workers Movement in Brazil," *Journal for Critical Education Policy Studies, 3*(2), 1–18; J. E. Diniz-Pereira (2012), "Global Capitalism, Neoliberalism, and 'Reactionary Postmodernity'" Responses From the "MST's Teacher Education Program in Brazil," in Matthew Knoester (Ed.), *International Struggles for Critical Democratic Education* (pp. 227–250), New York, NY: Peter Lang; and J. E. Diniz-Pereira (2013), *"How the Dreamers Are Born." Struggles for Social Justice and the Identity Construction of Activist Educators in Brazil*, New York, NY: Peter Lang.

NOTES

1. This seems to corroborate what Karl Marx and Friedrich Engels predicted in 1848 when they wrote the first edition of *The Communist Manifesto*. They stated then, "The need of a constantly expanding market for its products chases the bourgeoisie over the whole surface of the globe. It must nestle everywhere, settle everywhere, establish connections everywhere" (Marx & Engels, 1964, p. 63).
2. Apple (2003) suggests—and I strongly agree with him—that we "examine the mechanisms that link the global to the local; yet at the same time, also think about the specific relations of power at each level, ones that may not always be reducible to the automatic working out of global power onto the local" (p. 221).
3. The *Fórum Mundial de Educação* (World Education Forum) has been held in Porto Alegre, Brazil, as an attempt to build a counter-hegemonic global movement among activist educators all over the world.
4. The main "propositions" presented in the original paper, "Washington Consensus," were: privatization of state enterprises; deregulation; openness to foreign direct investment; trade liberalization; tax reform; fiscal discipline; and property rights (see Williamson, 1990).
5. The theoretical framework of one of the most recent versions of the neoliberal ideology comes from a group of conservative economists who draw upon the ideas of Professor Milton Friedman, 1976 Nobel laureate in Economics, from the University of Chicago. This group is usually known as the "Chicago Boys." This ideology was put into practice during the authoritarian regime of Augusto Pinochet in Chile during the 1970s, and also inspired other conservative administrations such as Margaret Thatcher's in England and Ronald Reagan's in the United States during the 1980s.
6. Chomsky cites the economic historian Paul Bairoch, who points out that economic liberalism in the nineteenth century served as a major element that explains the delay in the so-called Third World's industrialization, or even its "deindustrialization." Moreover, referring to the more recent past, Chomsky also cites the harmful influence of the IMF in Latin America pursuing what he calls "the 1950s version of today's 'Washington Consensus'" (2000, p. 155).

7. Apple (2001) analyzes in his book *Educating the "Right" Way* the politics of conservative restoration in education in the United States. He suggests that four conservative groups, *neoliberals*, *neoconservatives, authoritarian populists*, and the *new middle class*, make up a complex and sometimes contradictory alliance in order to establish and develop a quite conservative educational agenda in the United States. According to the author, *neoliberals*, the most powerful element in this conservative alliance, are "deeply committed to markets and to freedom as 'individual choice'" and strongly support and promote "educational marketization and privatization" (p. 11).

8. Apple (2003) highlights that neoliberalism "represents a powerful approach to economic governance. It is remarkably statist in orientation, with the state 'steering at a distance' and employing policy instruments and legislation to create, secure, and control market structures and relations instead of simply 'freeing' them" (p. 11).

9. In terms of competition for work, for instance, Bourdieu (1998) states that it "tends to generate a struggle of all against all, which destroys all the values of solidarity and humanity, and sometimes produces direct violence" (p. 84).

10. Bourdieu cites "the individualization of salaries and careers on the basis of individual performance and the consequent atomization of workers" as an example of what he calls "ideology of competence" (1998, p. 96).

11. After the Berlin Wall fell in 1989, Francis Fukuyama, a professor at the Johns Hopkins University, prematurely and naïvely announced the "End of History." He wrote: "What we may be witnessing is not just the end of the Cold War, or the passing of a particular period of post-war history, but the end of history as such: that is, the end point of mankind's ideological evolution and the universalization of Western Liberal democracy as the final form of human government" (1989, p. 4). Chomsky (2000) strongly criticizes this idea, stating that this is "the same 'end of history' [that] has confidently been proclaimed many times in the past, always wrongly" (p. 166).

12. The former British Prime Minister Margaret Thatcher was well known for justifying her neoliberal program with the acronym TINA for the phrase "There Is No Alternative" (to capitalism). THEMBA is a counter-acronym that has been recently coined in South Africa for the phrase "There Must Be an Alternative." In Zulu, the word *themba* means "hope."

13. For Freire (1985), to be utopian "is not to be merely idealistic or impractical but rather to engage in denunciation and annunciation," that is, "a dialogical praxis in which [leaders and the oppressed] together, in the act of analyzing a dehumanizing reality, denounce it while announcing its transformation in the name of the liberation of man [*sic*]" (p. 57).

14. "*Another world is possible*" is the slogan of the *Fórum Social Mundial* (World Social Forum) that has been held since 2001 in cities of the so-called Third World, such as Porto Alegre (Brazil) and Mumbai (India). The WSF, while explicitly opposing neoliberalism and a world dominated by capitalism, tries to build a counter-hegemonic global alliance among progressive groups and movements of civil society all over the world.

15. Much of the information that I share in this chapter draws heavily upon the works of the MST educator Roseli Salete Caldart. In addition to Caldart's work, documents of various kinds—books, booklets, magazine articles, journal articles, dissertations—that I collected during my fieldwork in Brazil provided me guidance in writing this chapter. I also took field notes throughout my fieldwork in Brazil. Finally, I draw upon information that was provided by the interviewees of my research: eleven women activist educators who have participated in the MST from four different Brazilian states.

16. The MST was officially established on January 20, 1984.

17. The MST is basically made up of poor people (peasants) from Brazil's rural areas. In Brazil, poverty remains more acute in rural areas than in urban areas. However, since only 21% of Brazilians live in rural areas, the urban share in the composition of poverty is higher. Moreover, poverty varies markedly across regions, with the northeast and the north reporting higher poverty rates than the southeast or the south.

18. This expression is used as the title of Bales's book (1999) about new slavery in the global economy. In order to discuss new forms of slave labor in global capitalism, the author does comparative research across five different countries—Thailand, Mauritania, Brazil, Pakistan, and India. In his chapter about Brazil, although Bales does not mention the MST, he cites the *Comissão Pastoral da Terra* (the Pastoral Land Commission), the CPT, as an antislavery movement in the country.

19. Paulo Freire defines praxis as "the unity between action and reflection." He argues that "one cannot change consciousness outside of praxis. But it must be emphasized that the praxis by which consciousness is changed is not only action but action *and* reflection. Thus there is a unity between practice and theory in which both are constructed, shaped, and reshaped in constant movement from practice to theory, then back to new practice" (1985, p. 124). (the author's emphasis).

20. This nickname identifies the children as *Sem Terra* subjects and an effective part of the MST dynamic. *Sem Terrinha* has at least three identity components: their condition as children, their condition as students, and their participation in the movement which, in turn, changes the meanings of their childhood and school experience. As Caldart (2000) states, "For the children, to participate in the MST has represented the possibility to live the childhood in a different way" (p. 195).

21. Most of the teachers who teach at schools in the MST's settlements and encampments are women of different ages and multiple ethnic origins. At the beginning of the MST's history, the movement reproduced the tradition that education is something for women and female teachers. Education was not deemed important enough to become an issue that the leaders and the landless men should be interested in (Caldart, 2000, pp. 186–187).

REFERENCES

Apple, M. W. (2001). *Educating the "right" way*. New York, NY: RoutledgeFalmer.

Apple, M. W. (Ed.). (2003). *The state and the politics of knowledge*. New York, NY: RoutledgeFalmer.

Apple, M. W., & Bean, J. A. (Eds.). (1995). *Democratic schools*. Alexandria, VA: AS. D.

Bales, K. (1999). *Disposable people: New slavery in the global economy*. Berkeley: University of California Press.

Beltrame, S. A. B. (2000). *M. T. professores e professoras: Sujeitos em movimento*. Unpublished doctoral dissertation, Universidade de São Paulo, Brazil.

Bourdieu, P. (1998). *Acts of resistance: Against the tyranny of the market*. New York, NY: New Press.

Caldart, R. S. (1997). *Educação em movimento: Formação de educadoras e educadores no M. T*. Petrópolis, Brazil: Vozes.

Caldart, R. S. (2000). *Pedagogia do Movimento Sem Terra*. Petrópolis, Brazil: Vozes.

Caldart, R. S. (2003a). A escola do campo em movimento. *Currículo Sem Fronteiras, 3*(1), 60–81.

Caldart, R. S. (2003b). Movimento Sem Terra: Lições de Pedagogia. *Currículo Sem Fronteiras, 3*(1), 50–59.

Carnoy, M. (1997). Foreword. In Paulo Freire, *Pedagogy of the heart*. New York, NY: Continuum.

Chomsky, N. (1997, November). Market democracy in a neoliberal order: Doctrines and reality. *Z. M.gazine*. Retrieved March 29, 2004, from http://www.chomsky.info/articles/199711.htm

Chomsky, N. (2000). *Chomsky on miseducation*. Lanham, MD: Rowman & Littlefield.

Clarke, J., & Newman, J. (1997). *The managerial state: Power, politics and ideology in the remaking of social welfare*. London, England: Sage.

Diniz-Pereira, J. E. (2013). *"How the dreamers are born." Struggles for social justice and the identity construction of activist educators in Brazil*. New York, NY: Peter Lang.

Fernandes, B. M. (2000). *A formação do M. T.no Brasil*. Petrópolis, Brazil: Vozes.

Freire, P. (1985). *The politics of education: Culture, power and liberation*. Westport, CT: Bergin & Garvey.

Freire, P. (1996). *Letters to Cristina: Reflections on my life and work*. New York, NY: Routledge.

Freire, P. (1997). *Pedagogy of the heart*. New York, NY: Continuum.

Freire, P. (1998). *Pedagogy of freedom: Ethics, democracy, and civic courage* Lanham, MD: Rowman & Littlefield.

Freire, P. (2000). *Pedagogy of the oppressed, 20th anniversary edition*. New York, NY: Continuum.

Fukuyama, F. (1989, Summer). The end of history? *The National Interest*, 3–18.

Harnecker, M. (2002). *Landless people: Building a social movement*. Havana, Cuba: Research Center Latin-American People's Memory (MEP. A..

Liston, D. P., & Zeichner, K. M. (1991). *Teacher education and the social conditions of schooling*. New York, NY: Routledge.

Marx, K. (1963). *The 18th Brumaire of Louis Bonaparte*. New York, NY: International.

Marx, K., & Engels, F. (1964). *The communist manifesto*. New York, NY: Washington Square Press.

McCowan, T. (2003, March). Participation and education in the Landless People's Movement in Brazil. *Journal of Critical Education Policy Studies, 1*(1), Article 5. Retrieved April 2, 2003, from http://www.jceps.com

McLaren, P. (2000). *Che Guevara, Paulo Freire, and the pedagogy of revolution*. Lanham, MD: Rowman & Littlefield.

McLaren, P., & Farahmandpur, R. (2001). Teaching against globalization and the new imperialism: Toward a revolutionary pedagogy. *Journal of Teacher Education, 52*(2), 136–150.

Ribeiro, M. (2001). Trabalho cooperativo no M. T.e ensino fundamental rural: Desafios à educação básica. *Revista Brasileira de Educação, 17*(1), 20–39.

Rodgers, C. R. (1998). *Morris R. Mitchell and the Putney Graduate School of Teacher Education, 1950–1964*. Unpublished doctoral dissertation, Harvard University, Cambridge, MA.

Santos, B. S. (1997). Toward a multicultural conception of human rights. *Zeitschrift für Rechtssoziologie, 18*(1), 1–15.

Santos, B. S. (1998). Participatory budgeting in Porto Alegre: Toward a redistributive democracy. *Politics and Society, 26*(4), 461–510.

Schon, D. (1983). *The reflective practitioner*. New York, NY: Basic Books.

Stromquist, N. P., & Monkman, K. (2000). *Globalization and education: Integration and contestation across cultures*. Lanham, MD: Rowman & Littlefield.

Williamson, J. (1990). What Washington means by policy reform. In J. Williamson (Ed.), *Latin America adjustment: How much has happened?* Washington, DC: Institute for International Economics.

Wright, A., & Wolford, W. (2003). *To inherit the earth: The Landless Movement and the struggle for a new Brazil*. Oakland, CA: Food First Books.

Zeichner, K. M. (2004, July). *Educating teachers for social justice in an era of accountability*. Keynote address presented at the annual meeting of the Australian Teacher Education Association, Bathurst, Australia.

CHAPTER FIFTEEN

Enough Is Enough— (de) Constructing Measurement Through Exposing Aspects of the Australian Curriculum in Mathematics as a White-Centric Epistemic Location

GLEN PARKES

INTRODUCTION

This chapter seeks to begin a discussion regarding the Australian Curriculum in Mathematics. This discussion seeks a change in focus, theory, and proof as to what can be measured and quantified, viewed through a qualitative lens of diversity. The premise of this discussion resides alongside the concept of "enough." a conceptualised quantification that rails against both the construct of (white) truth and logicality that underpin constructions of Western curricula and social policy.

Framing this discussion are Paulo Freire's culture-nature dichotomy and Kincheloe's concept of "multi-logicality" (critically viewing white Western ways (www) replicated through a curricula of outcomes, experiences, and epistemologies). Constructing and conceptualising measurement and thus quantity as being both moveable and experiential (potentially) rejects the logicality currently assumed within documented white-centric curricula and institutions.

Multi-logicality (potentially) supports a new direction in both mathematical understanding and direction in curricula. Constructing measurement as a moveable quantification denies an ongoing (white) colonisation of both curricula and what is legitimised as knowledge.

Mathematics is something that I have always understood. As a (white Western male) primary school student, I was always considered a high-achieving student who would apply theories and concepts presented to me in an unthinking (im)practical way. The quintessential good (read: privileged) student, I found room to engage, accept, and apply a seemingly abstract group of facts in an unthinking, lineal way. With apologies to the late Professor Julius Sumner Miller, why is it so?

Mathematics as concept presented to me throughout my school years was taught as a universal set of truths, beyond interpretation with an outright rejection of the potential for a diversity of situational approaches and solutions. Mathematics was true, it was about achieving an answer, which once obtained became an overt destination, a success—welcome to the inside, and leave all interpretive capacities and possibilities at the door. At this point (and as I am not a mathematician), the potential exists for this discussion to go in multiple directions. One direction (with apologies to music aficionados) explores the modern Western constructs of formal mathematics, replicated throughout Western society through documented curricula and plans for learning, which deny a history of mathematical thought and existence that did not require a formalised sequence of gatekeeping regarding knowledge and mathematics. The replication of such mathematical concepts in formal national plans for learning will be a focal point of this discussion. Linguistic constructions of concepts such as quantity are very much that of the white Western world, from the trophy cabinet excesses of colonisation practices to the numeric representations of people, places, and resources as they exist in society. Before such colonisation, extermination, and imposition of the white Western model of existence, how did First Nations people engage with the quantification and how were such practices represented in traditional epistemologies? Does quantification that stresses universality deny the existence or potential to mathematically position a numeric quantity as being that which is required for an experience or situation—or enough? Thus, this chapter will seek to explore an idea and the concept of enough as a mathematical construction that denies white Western universality and epistemologies of excess. Framing this exploration will be Freire's concept of the culture-nature dichotomy and Kincheloe's construction of multi-logicality in positioning quantification outside that which is deemed beyond question—mathematical knowledge and abstract (hegemonic) representation in formal white Western curricula.

THE FREIREAN CULTURE-NATURE DICHOTOMY

Freire theorised that the experience of people will incorporate multiple aspects of reality. This will incorporate experiences of nature and culture. Freire positions nature as being experiences in reality and culture as experiences with reality (Freire, 1972). Such enactments and experiences will impact knowledges in how they are legitimised through experience and transference. The imposition of specific knowledges as being engagements with and representations of reality denies the cultural productions and thus situatedness of knowledges across numerous social systems. Freire (1972) thus calls into question the universality of such knowledges, seeing epistemic legitimacy unquestionably incorporated and impacted through experience.

A further aspect of this dichotomy theorised by Freire is an acknowledgement that a critical engagement with knowledge will involve reading the world from which the knowledge came and the multiple representations and documentations of such knowledge (Freire, 1972). Through this theorised dichotomy, explored for implications through engaging with mathematics as critical knowledge and abstract representation, Freire opens up possibilities for exploration of the potential or possibility for knowledges to exist within the realities of experience and not just abstract representations. Is there potential for an experiential component of measurement and quantification, as culturally mediated enactments of and with reality to be incorporated and documented within the epistemic locale of the Australian Curriculum in Mathematics? I believe there is.

VIEWS FROM THE FIELD—DEFINING NUMERACY AND QUANTIFICATION IN THE AUSTRALIAN CURRICULUM IN MATHEMATICS

The Australian Curriculum in Mathematics specifically defines mathematical reasoning as incorporating a specific logicality that is notionally Western and specifically lineal in noting: "The curriculum focuses on developing increasingly sophisticated and refined mathematical understanding, fluency, logical reasoning, analytical thought and problem-solving skills." (Australian Curriculum in Mathematics, n.d.).

Further aspects of the subject-discipline-course rationale specify measurement as continuing a specific logical method of quantification. For example, students will "make meaningful measurements of quantities, choosing appropriate metric units of measurement. They build an understanding of the connections between units and calculate derived measures such as area, speed and density" (Australian

Curriculum in Mathematics, n.d.). Exploring such points of framing requires definitions to be created with regard to logical reasoning, analytic thought, and meaningful measurements. The positioning of such logicality from a hegemonic cultural perspective is framed within the epistemic legitimacy of a formal plan for learning—white Western curricula.

EXPERIENCE, REALITY, AND CULTURAL CREATIONS

Mathematics is described as a language, a means by which communication can occur between participants familiar with the cultural queues of that language. Language remains an important marker of cultural identity, impacting both communication and cultural replication in society (Kincheloe, 1999; McAllan, 2011). Freire (1973) theorises that the experiences of people with knowledge, and reality in their broader societies will have impacts on nature and culture, with nature positioned as experiences in reality and culture with reality. Thus, language, being a production of culture and marker of cultural identity, will legitimise specific knowledges through engagement with and knowledge of rules relating to such processes. Freire (1973) will thus position mathematics and hence quantification as a method of communication with society, incorporating cultural replications and productions. Frankenstein and Powell (1994) assert that this cultural element of mathematics as a production of culture is (potentially) framed against the rational, universal fact-based theory from which mathematics is approached and pedagogically transferred.

Freire positions knowledge as being experiential and denies the existence of facts that are not impacted by the societies and cultures engaged with them (1972, 1973). With mathematics, specifically with the process of quantification and arithmetic, the process for students is primarily answer based and lineal in the progression from problem to answer. Such lineal progressions, being documented through an engagement with a culturally mediated (mathematical) language, deny students choice with regard to finalising their response. This assumes an experience that is the same for all students, denying perspective from both truth and essentialised logic. The logic of quantification requires some thought and an example might illustrate this.

EXAMPLE ONE (OH) ONE

There are three students in a room and there are two apples in the same room. All students are to quantify how many apples are in the room and how many people will eat an apple.

Student one: there are two apples and there are three of us; therefore, one of us will not be able to eat an apple—one will miss out as two is less than three. 3 − 2 = 1— mathematics logic represented in abstract form.

Student two: there are three students and only two apples. Who grew the apple? Who is hungry? How might apples benefit all of us?

Student three: there are three students and only two apples. If we cut each apple into three pieces, we can all share the apples evenly.

In viewing the above example, the lineal progressive model of mathematics rationality is clearly espoused by student one. The mathematics spoken of by student one is without question, as the mathematical construction of two is less than three. However, what this scenario does not recognise is that straight mathematical logic is not something that can be applied devoid of the situation and experience of the students. Students two and three look at the situation and engage with mathematics to solve a problem, and as such humanise the process of engaging mathematics and hence quantification. The human element in mathematical quantification is thus constructed to solve problems and provide an answer that possesses meaning, perhaps justice, and definitely an apple for morning tea. What quantity of apples exists in the room? Students two and three decided there was (potentially) enough. Both students arrived at very different answers in responding to this mathematical dilemma, with their answers moving beyond simple numeric retorts to cultural responses to experience. Student one might also revisit the response that there are "not enough" apples, which enables the question Why? to be asked. Thus, the concept of enough seeks to position mathematics as a source of cultural communication, dynamic and moveable in its experiential application of quantification (Frankestein & Powell, 2002). Such cultural enactments and communication will have different purposes, messages, and narratives, and thus mathematics and hence quantification are potentially emancipated from the white Western cloak of universality. Meaning beyond numbers, potentially, enough!

MULTI-LOGICALITY—DEFINED AND EPISTEMICALLY DECENTRED

Kincheloe theorises a pedagogy of multi-logicality as being a starting point in locating Western knowledges as oppressive, constructed social systems, founded in claims of scientific rationality and subjugation of alternative ways of knowing (Kincheloe, 2008). Multi-logicality as an epistemic rejection of and confrontation of the colonial centrality of knowledge and power structures at once seeking to dismiss knowledges forms the delineated margins. Connell (2007) positions the premise of uncontested dominance sort through Western hegemonic practices as being an overt act of oppression, with traditional knowledge systems often critiqued for their lack of existence in abstraction, separate from the experience contained in such knowledges. Thus, multi-logicality seeks to broaden the epistemic base from which knowledge is created and engaged with. Knowledges in the Western sense are often universalised through formal documented curricula, thus removing the experiential component of such documented knowledges. Multi-logicality and hence the multi-logical educator will seek to move between epistemologies and knowledge systems (Kincheloe, 2008). This (potential) shift will have implications for engaging with curricula as a universal plan for learning and constructing the legitimacy of mathematics as documented in an abstracted form. Can the multi-logical pedagogue attach an experiential component to a language documented in abstract form? Knowledge without experience will lack relevance to the social worlds inhabited by students and the meaning attached to such an experiential component.

NUMERACY AND INDIFFERENCE IN WHITE WESTERN CURRICULA

Curriculum, as an instrument of social engineering, (potentially) reinforcing hegemonic power when constructed along (un)documented racial and epistemic (explicit curriculum) lines, can impact the existence and lived experience of those outside a preconceived norm (Nakata, 2007).

The school has long been touted as one of the few social agencies crucial to the development of genuinely democratic, just, and sustainable communities, although such pro-social orientations are by no means assured. Giroux (2010) has outlined the potential for social change embedded in the school: "While schools have had a long history of simply attempting to reproduce the ideological contours of the existing society, they are capable of so much more, and therein lies their danger and possibilities" (2010, p. 6).

However, when one looks beyond the rhetoric of formal white Western curricula, there would appear to be little genuine embrace of difference. In fact, contrary to the stated aims and objectives of the curriculum, a continued unthinking embedding of hegemonic notions of culture—in effect, a whitewashing of the curriculum—is evident. This whitewashing (potentially) engages in a (continued) colonisation of knowledge and knowing, discarding epistemologies that are essentialised as being "south" of mirrored hegemonic norms and reflections, intentionally masked as roadmaps, perspectives, and (un)embedded curricula priorities (Connell, 2007). Apple (1996, p. 22) refers to this compromise as being the politicisation of knowledge, with these decisions resulting in the establishment of what he describes as "official knowledge," delineated to achieve political aims. The application and establishment of mathematics as a language, born out of Western rationality and formal national plans for learning, frame such knowledge as beyond the question. Thus, as a language, mathematics is construed as a sequence of cultural enactments and the potential for universality across multiple cultural institutions is limited when framed alongside social spaces and decisions formed therein.

The unthinking embedding of mathematical language as being beyond question and solution based is a consistent theme of learning and curricula from the Western perspective. The origins of formal documented curricula in the Western context can perhaps be traced to Aristotle in formally classifying knowledge into specific categories, being theoretical, practical, and process (Carr & Kemmis, 1986). Classifying and categorising knowledge is a key attribute of Western curricula. Thus, the categorisation of Western knowledge legitimised through curricula, reinterpreted and "reinforced during the scientific revolution of the 17th and 18th centuries, to depict its own superiority," has enforced such written knowledges in formal learning and education (Kincheloe & Steinberg, 2005). Thus, there is the potential to position and define (white Western) curriculum as a sequence of coded instructions that seek to legitimise knowledges and hence privilege specific epistemic locations, essentially an epistemic instructions manual (Parkes, under review, 2012) locating white-centric ways of knowing and quantification at the centre of a legitimised learning experience.

DECENTERING PEDAGOGY, (RE)DEFINING LITERACY AND THE CRITICALITY OF ENOUGH

The role of formal curricula in legitimising Western and written epistemologies is a further application of a specific method of rationality (Austin, 2012). As a plan for learning, curricula will document the learning and knowledges that are valued and hence deemed important to members of society with influence in creating a documented plan for learning. Legitimising mathematical language as a broad plan for learning a collection of indisputable facts again dichotomises the construction of mathematical knowledge alongside cultural interpretation and replication (Austin, 2012). Austin (2012) sees the replication of Western epistemologies in curricula as an example of whiteness in claiming universality of knowledge and knowing. Kincheloe (2008) positions both multi-logicality and the multi-logical pedagogue as key ways of conceptualising past the white-centric ways of knowing, elevated within white-centric curricula (Austin, 2012). Freire (1972) positions dialogue as an essential tool and component of the critical and emancipatory educator and learning environment. It is appropriate to explore how a pedagogy of multi-logicality, incorporating a dialogical engagement with such mathematical content, might deconstruct and (potentially) decolonise the (white Western) mathematics curriculum and hence national plan for learning.

The (white Western) rationality that seeps out of the mathematics curriculum upholds the uni-logicality that Western enlightenment has provided to privileged epistemologies since the seventeenth century (Frankenstein & Powell, 1994). Such rationality is founded on mathematical proofs that, once accepted in the enlightened white Western tradition, become untouchable elements of absolute truths. When addressing mathematical problems incorporating an analysis or calculation of quantity, its representation will be in the form of abstract mathematics language, thus framing a uni-logicality to quantification therein. Such a claim of universality regarding mathematical language and thus quantification is troubling. Mathematics as a language is framed, positioned, and defined as social practice and cultural communication; however, white Western rationality has framed the transmission of such knowledge as being foundational to legitimised epistemologies and endeavour. Austin (2012, p. 169) positions such rationality as a bounded colonisation of experience, in essence a "hegemonic aura of universality." The vast collection, storehouse, and specificity of knowledges mediated through experience deny such universality and perhaps there exists potential for a rejection of hegemonic universality of what quantification is. This poses the question of white epistemic creation and location: What knowledge is valuable? The term valuable, and hence the term value are troubling through their orientations of power. Giroux (1982, 2010) has theorised that such orientations incorporating an unthinking imbedding of abstract representation deny a discursive element to the learning, and the emancipatory possibilities of dialogue.

Freire (1973) sees the use of dialogue in multiple learning situations and thus documented curricula as being an essential element of education as a mechanism to liberate the process of learning and knowledge construction. Such pedagogic enactments will deny teacher universality regarding knowledge content and interpretations, instead seeking an engagement based on power sharing and collaboration. Thus, again the Freirean positioning of dialogue provides a framework for (seeking) liberation to be an essential aspect of a learning environment (Freire, 1973). The process of this will be twofold, with a dialectical engagement incorporating liberation through education while also emancipating the process of education through power sharing and the construction of knowledge. What evidence exists of the potential of such an engagement with the Australian Mathematics Curriculum and constructions of measurement?

HEGEMONICS TWO (OH) TWO—DIALOGUE, PRAXIS, AND THE QUANTIFICATION OF ENOUGH

In deconstructing what quantification is and how one might look like beyond a white cloak of hegemonic replication, a pertinent discussion might invoke how such knowledges might be included in a formal plan for learning and explored with a critical pedagogue. This discussion is succinctly dichotomised through acknowledging that a national plan for learning is a white Western construction, thus limiting the potential for knowledges contained therein to encourage a critical praxis through exploration, dialogue, and critique. The potential for dialogue and critique will be influenced by the pedagogic design and approach and thus critical enactments presented therein. McLaren and Ryoo (2012) position radical critical pedagogy as a potential pathway to removing dichotic extremes of knowledge and knowing. Freire (1972) sees such a "critical praxis" as being an "act of freedom" (McLaren, 2000; McLaren & Ryoo, 2012). Such a praxis incorporates knowing and knowledge as being part of the journey in education, while also engaging further aspects of the learning such as questioning, troubling, and the possibility of decentring that which is hegemonically unquestioned—abstract mathematical reasoning and quantification (McLaren, 2000). How might such a praxis be instructed when one looks at the Australian Mathematics Curriculum and the learning experiences defined therein?

HEGEMONIC UTILISATION, INDIGENOUS KNOWLEDGES, AND NUMERICAL EPISTEMIC LOCATIONS

One potential encounter and pedagogic design to problematise is the rationality presented through numeracy. Such problematisation might benefit from an engagement with traditional or Indigenous knowledges. Baynes (2012) has theorised the (potential) humanising impact Indigenous knowledges can have on the learning journey and formal Western curriculum. Kincheloe and Semali (1999) have defined Indigenous knowledges as the vast storehouse of experience and beliefs that are specific to individual nations of people and guide all aspects of life and existence. In such contexts numeracy will impact daily existence and practice of life with quantification specifically linked to the experiences of that day, while concurrently linking with knowledges of the past and possibilities for the future.

In defining traditional knowledges as such, the experiential component is paramount to engaging with such knowledges. The definition of traditional knowledge itself represents an act of white-centric neocolonial practice, as the classification and categorisation of knowledge is very much that of a white Western lineal progress narrative (McAllan, 2011). This potentially again raises the Freirean construction of the culture-nature dichotomy incorporating experiences with quantification and experiences of quantification (Freire, 1972). The realities of quantification in traditional communities are very much dichotomised with regard to the abstract numerical mathematics and the experience of everyday life and the inherent narrative in the representation of numbers. The narrative and experience (potentially) represented in the application of the concept of enough quantification is both rejected and framed outside the confines of numeric quantification as documented through curricula. Abstract numeric representation denies an engagement with the process of questioning the specific problem and the situatedness of the answer. Freire (1972) provides a mechanism to expand what quantification is through the application of the culture-nature dichotomy. The process of knowledge, incorporating numeracy and quantification, moves beyond fact to what Derrida theorises as being life spaces (Derrida, 1972). This importantly situates learning within the life spaces occupied by people and rejects the lineal spaces of documented curricula, hegemonic logicality, and abstract numerical representations. Numeric, abstract representations of life spaces, experiences, and solutions incorporating social spaces are indeterminate, removed from reality, and certainly not "enough."

URBANE ABSTRACTIONS AND THE STORIED SELF

Connell (2007) positions the white Western academe as being a hegemonic representation of the urban metropole and epistemic location. Positioning measurement and quantification, in their abstract numerical form, and lineal domains of meaning from within the metropolitan epistemic locale reinforces an unquestioning meritocracy within such abstractions. The Australian Curriculum in Mathematics, through engaging in a discipline-based plan for learning, reinforces the epistemic centrality theorised by Connell (2007) through denying a social engagement regarding quantification and the process of formulating an academic response. Freire (1972) opens up possibilities, through dialogue and educational engagements of and with knowledge as nature and culture, to question learning and engage knowledge from multiple paradigms of existence. Thus, the potential remains for quantification to possess multiple lenses projecting the storied self as incorporating numeric legitimacy. Such legitimacy will not seek or claim universality regarding quantification from a solution, proof, or experiential perspective.

There exists the possibility for such epistemic and ontological positioning to expose social structures as gatekeeping mechanisms for the legitimacy of knowledges and reshape society to resonate with the lived experiences of the life spaces contained therein. Incorporating such life spaces and experiences, or the storied self, in the process of numeracy and quantification rails against the subjugated segregation Foucault (1972) theorised as incorporating the I-other dialect. Utilising the storied self in multiple experiences within a formal curricula, and hence the national curricula in mathematics, will require cultural enactments incorporating quantification, to me the situational need of the students beyond demarcated abstract representation and numbers without meaning.

(DE) CONSTRUCTING NUMERACY—WHEN ENOUGH IS ENOUGH

Mathematics, numeracy, and quantification were things that I understood, through personal expectation and that of the education system formulated in my image. As a white Western male in a hegemonically privileged country, my epistemic location and was (and is) formally positioned at the centre of the learning journey—through language, documented white-centric practices, and legitimised epistemologies. The social systems of Western education and epistemic enlightenment deny an engagement from both a critical perspective and situatedness of mathematical reasoning. But further to this quantification as documented in the Australian Curriculum in Mathematics and practiced in abstract numerical form denies an engagement with knowledge as social practice with emancipatory possibilities through participation and application.(SENSE?) Freire, through exposing the dichotomised and hegemonically situatedness of such knowledges, has begun a conversation that seeks to delegitimise colonial outposts of knowledge and language represented through formal Western curricula. The Australian Curriculum in Mathematics, as such a colonial epistemic location, utilises abstract mathematical language to achieve absolute numeric solutions devoid of experience.

Continuing the legacy of Freire through reshaping quantification will assist in meeting the needs of students engaged in the learning journey and decentring hegemonic absolutism of abstract numerical representation. Quantification, incorporating numeracy, might one day be formulated as being more than an abstraction, and with this the possibility of being enough.

REFERENCES

Apple, M. (1996). *Cultural politics and education*. New York, NY: Teachers College Press.

Austin, J. (Ed.). (2005). *Culture and identity*. Frenchs Forrest, Australia: Pearson Education Australia.

Austin, J. (2012). Decentering the WWW (white western ways). In R. Brock, C. Malott, & L. Villaverde (Eds.), *Teaching Joe L. Kincheloe*. New York, NY: Peter Lang.

Austin, J., & Hickey, A. (2008). Critical pedagogical practice through cultural studies. *International Journal of Humanities, 6*(1), 133–140.

Australian Curriculum in Mathematics. (n.d.). Retrieved October 1, 2012, from http://www.australiancurriculum.edu.au/

Baynes, R. (2012). *Humanisation in de-colonising educational research: A tree of life metaphor.* Unpublished manuscript.

Carr, W., & Kemmis, S. (1986). *Becoming critical: Education knowledge and action research.* London, England: Falmer.

Connell, R. (2007). *Southern theory.* Crows Nest, Australia: Allen & Unwin.

Derrida, J. (1972). *Positions.* Chicago, IL: University of Chicago Press.

Foucault, M. (1972). *The archaeology of knowledge & the discourse on language.* New York, NY: Harper Colophon.

Frankenstein, M., & Powell, A. B. (1994). Toward liberatory mathematics: Paulo Freire's epistemology and ethnomathematics. In P. McLaren & C. Lankshear (Eds.), *The politics of liberation: Paths from Freire* (pp. 74–99). London, England: Routledge.

Freire, P. (1972). *Pedagogy of the oppressed.* New York, NY: Herder & Herder.

Freire, P. (1973). *Education for critical consciousness.* New York, NY: Continuum.

Giroux, H. A. (1982). *Theory and resistance in education: A pedagogy for the opposition.* Boston, MA: Bergin & Garvey.

Giroux, H. A. (2010). *In defence of public school teachers in a time of crisis.* Retrieved October 2, 2011, from http://fightbacktcnj.wordpress.com/2010/04/15/henry-giroux-in-defense-of-public-school-teachers-in-a-time-of-crisis/

Kincheloe, J. L. (1999). The struggle to define and reinvent whiteness: A pedagogical analysis. *College Literature, 26*(3), 162.

Kincheloe, J. L. (2008). *Knowledge and critical pedagogy.* Dordrecht, The Netherlands: Springer.

Kincheloe, J. L. & Semali, S. (1999). *What is Indigenous Knowledge? Voices from the academy.* New York, NY: Falmer.

Kincheloe, J. L., & Steinberg, S. (Eds) (2005). *Things you don't know about schools.* New York: Palgrave Press.

McAllan, F. (2011). Getting 'post racial' in the 'Australian' state: What remains overlooked in the premise 'getting beyond racism'? *Critical Race and Whiteness Studies, 7*(1), 1–21.

McLaren, P., & Ryoo, J. (2012). Revolutionary critical pedagogy against capitalist multicultural education. In H. Kashope, M. Singh, & R. Race (Eds.), *Precarious international multicultural education. Hegemony, dissent and rising alternatives.* Rotterdam, The Netherlands: Sense.

McLaren, P. (2000). Paulo Freire's pedagogy of possibility. In S. Steiner, H. Krank, P. McLaren, & R. Bahruth (Eds.), *Freirean pedagogy, praxis, and possibilities: Projects for the new millennium.* New York, NY: Taylor & Francis.

Nakata, M. (2007). *Disciplining the savages, savaging the disciplines.* Canberra, Australia: Aboriginal Studies Press.

Parkes, G. (2012). *The potential for the learning presented in the Australian Curriculum in English for the positive representation of difference.* Unpublished honors thesis, University of Southern Queensland, Australia.

CHAPTER SIXTEEN

Shattering Silence in Kinshasa—Reading the World With Freire Under the Mango Tree

HOLGER NORD

It could be said that Africa invented Man, that the Semites invented God and that Europe in-vented the world.

(MAZRUI, 1986, P. 23)

The more historically anesthetized [we are,]...the less future we have.

(FREIRE, 1997, P. 101)

INTRODUCTORY NOTES: SILENCE—READING—MANGO TREES

Shattering Silence

When writing his book *Cultural Action for Freedom*, Paulo Freire (1972a) noted that masses are educated within and through a culture of silence that not only prevents them from true, i.e., transformative, learning but also prohibits them from creatively taking part in the transformation of their own society and therefore pro-hibits them from being (p. 30). The following reflections and introspections seek to contextualise this process and to show aspects of certain mechanisms of silencing in some of the schools of Kinshasa, capital of the Democratic Republic of Congo (DRC), drawing also on aspects of post-colonial education and language policies and their domesticating impact. "Shattering Silence," in this context, refers to the notion that submissive silence is "shattering" and devastating, while at the same time alluding to the author's intention to also indicate possibilities and sketches of transformation or transformative praxis, in order to continue a discourse of hope, enriched by "knowledge…born out of a practice that must be illuminated by theory in a permanent and dialectic process: from practice to theory to practice" (A. M. Freire, 2008), and eventually to sustain Freire's project of freedom and humanity on a global stage. The following considerations are based on personal experiences during a brief project in Kinshasa (DRC) in January 2012, when I had the opportunity to visit schools and to organise a four-day workshop for English teachers under the patronage of the Christian education provider *Eglise du Christ Au Congo*.

Reading the World

"Reading the world" must be understood here as an ongoing intellectual investigation, in the Barthesian sense, into the process of signification, i.e. the construction of meaning in acts and interaction, etc., through the use of ambivalent signs. Consequently this process must be *semiologically* analysed—exposure of a variety of relationships between the signifier and signified—in order to expose the signs' ambiguities within themselves (Barthes, 1972, pp. 128–129). This demystification process, here *"shattering silence,"* seeks to provide tools to "break [the] submissive silence" (Freire, 1972a, p. 16) and to identify aspects of alienation.

The repression used to return the masses to their silence is preceded and accompanied by a myth-making effort to identify as diabolical all thought-language, which uses words as alienation, domination, oppression, liberation, humanization, and autonomy (Freire, 1972a, pp. 16–17).

Under the mango tree

With the image of the mango tree Paulo Freire describes his personal need to find refuge and seclusion from the world—*under the mango tree*—not to establish the educator's separation from the world but rather the educator's confirmation of being *with* the world. The world provides us with experiences, situations, and ongoing questions that require reflections, inner discussions, and the search for answers and responses. This kind of isolation presupposes and cultivates the inextricable attachment to the world: "I need the world as the world needs me" (Freire, 1997, p. 30). In this chapter, the imaginative mango tree provides me, the author, with a personal platform to present thoughts, emotions, and an intellectual space that allows me to ask questions, converse, and discuss not only with myself but also with Paulo Freire as my intellectual inspiration, my inner Socrates and professional friend, raising concerns of personal experience within the wider context of pedagogy and the world. This helps me to make sense of my actions in order to continue my search, my trials, and strengthen my hope.

THE RELEVANCE OF PAULO FREIRE TODAY

Recent commentaries on the Olympic Games of 2012 in London (Eden, 2012) featured Rodney Atkinson and his complaint about the opening ceremony with its "strong strands of the parochial Left" and the "assumption that the industrial revolution was oppressive." Rather, he continues, "[t]he Left never understands internationalism and the wealth which arises from free trade among free peoples and cultures." Consequentially, neoliberal viewpoints propagate globalisation as a "natural" and positive continuation of this process, "recasting the character of human life the world over" with "unprecedented vistas of promise." It almost follows as sheer common sense, to realise the "trends of the knowledge era furnish human beings and human societies with an unprecedented ability to create a free, prosperous, and empowering future" (Mazaar, 2005, pp. 1–9).

These visions of socioeconomic changes do not take into account the ongoing human suffering, exploitation, and commodification of humans and their needs and desires. On the contrary, the dark side of human cost is replaced by the myth of material growth together with the utopian ideal of a richer and therefore more humane and just society together with its socioethical progress. Inequality and injustice, exploitation and imperialism are delicately sugar-coated and presented as a temporary necessary evil, serving as justifiable means to a futuristic (materialistic) end, with education merely a "neutral" bystander. This worldview of neutrality is rejected and actively opposed by Paulo Freire's with a pedagogical framework that adheres to an educational radicality and totality that aim at transforming the lives of those who participate.

Under the mango tree with Paulo Freire (1)—subjectivity

We are approaching the mango tree, your mango tree, Paulo. Did you know that I have never seen a mango tree? Make me see it! Make me feel it, its shadow! This would be an opportune time to talk about my 'immediate objectivity' and my 'homeland', my location (Freire, 1997, p. 39). *I feel strong inhibitions because coming from Germany, Christian, middle class, there are many imperial traps and 'Irrwege'. Why are you smiling? Uh,…never to deny the importance of subjectivity and we never exist apart from each other but are in constant interaction?* (Freire, 1972a, p. 27) *Yes, no 'man' is an island.*

This tension and interaction reminds me of the dialectic between post- and neo-colonialism. While the process of colonialism could historically be regarded as a process of the past, its impact had such epic proportions that postcolonial debate has already integrated a neo-colonial perspective: looking at the territorial division, the state systems, the presentation and integration of culture, the dominance of European languages, the world of law and the discourse of globalisation (Mazrui, 1986, pp. 12–13). *With the colonial injustice being firmly embedded in post/neo-colonial practices, I strongly believe in the world's ongoing need to re-read and re-engage with your work, Paulo!*

An overview of some of Freire's seminal titles gives an indication of the scope and the direction of his educational framework. *Pedagogy of the Oppressed*, *Pedagogy of Hope*, and *Pedagogy of the Heart* point toward a pedagogical project that seeks to humanise the world by liberating the oppressed as well as the oppressors; embracing a universal objective and a positive stance against the disenchantment and dystopia of our times. These times include the supremacy of individual self-determination, the dominance of neoliberalism and the end of social dreams (see McLaren, 2011, p. 117), the replacement of equality and dignity through the propagation of global consumerism, and standardisations and/or privatisation of cultures and beliefs. The educational methodology and the overall pedagogical framework focus on people and their historical realities and the conditions that hinder them from becoming fully human when participating in this world. Rather than letting humans become means to a capitalist end, submitting to the laws of commodification and rules of the global market, his pedagogical project is based on love for the people and the world(s) they live in. He is driven by the never-ending possibilities of a new humanity, which renounces the fatalistic viewpoint that, "things are as they are because there is no other way" (Freire, 1997, p. 101).

Freire worked within the specific socioeconomic reality of the participants, following a methodological approach that included dialogue, *conscientization*, critical reflection, action, and praxis. He was especially concerned with the psychological damage of the dehumanisation of the world. Alienation, fatalism, marginalisation, uncritical reception, self-depreciation, and duality are aspects that reveal not only his affinity with Marxism but also his own endeavour to overcome the limiting and circular dichotomy between oppressors and the oppressed. Particularly in this context, Freire continues to remind us that there is no "neutral educational process," as it will always be generated from a specific ideological platform connected to a specific model of society that

> either functions as an instrument which is used to facilitate the integration of the younger generation into the logic of the present system and bring about conformity to it, or it becomes the 'practice of freedom', the means by which men and women deal critically and creatively with reality and discover to participate in the transformation of their world. (Shaull, as quoted in Freire, 1972b, pp. 13–14)

Under the mango tree with Paulo Freire (2)—humanistic stance

Paulo, when reading your work I notice a refreshing 'eclecticism', drawing on various disciplines and different and complementing viewpoints. It provides a "variety of sources, which, nevertheless, appear integrated in a peculiar fashion and at the serviced of [your] educational enterprise" (Schipani, 1984, p. 53). *But what is most important for me is your overarching organising and guiding principle, "an emphatic humanistic stance…it assumes a vision of life with man at the center"* (Schipani, 1984, p. 54). *This vision is the heart of faith, directed toward love for others, enabling us to humanise ourselves and begin to understand the purpose and the method of our educational practice. Before running into a monologue…better be silent at this point.*

COLONIAL SILENCE—"AFRICA" AND THE WHITE NOISE

Since the Second World War the chief vortex of disturbance has passed to Eastern Asia, where the same forces have liquidated or transformed the empires and traditional spheres of ascendancy of Britain, Holland, and France. Already it can be seen that these forces are gathering strength in Africa, which is the last remaining great colonial domain of European Powers. (Lewis, Scott, Wright, & Legum, 1951, p. 11)

The answer to the question "Who is African?" is more complex than it need be. It varies depending on individual. I seem to ask more questions than I answer. (Yoruba, 2012)

Africa is the world's second-largest and second-most-populous continent, covering about 30.2 million km² and 6% of the earth's total surface area; further, in encompasses various time zones and consists of 53 countries. It is surprising that despite its diversity people continue to refer to specific locations on the African continent with the single noun of "Africa." It appears that the Western discourse continues to propagate the colonial "consolidated vision" (Said, 1993, p. 122). The subsuming signifier "Africa" not only silences any local voices, contexts, and personal experiences but also perpetuates the colonial civilising (here: globalising) mission when constantly alluding to the big and slumbering "dark continent." The concept of Africa still serves a tacit racist framework wherein vast difference of voices, languages, cultures, and human lives fall into the criteria of skin-colour and all its sociocultural, intellectual, political, and economic imaginations are posited against the old colonial dichotomy of "us" versus "them," "a process of…depersonalization of Africans" (Mudimbe, 1988, p. 133). The sign of "Africa" continues to rest on the "metaphysics of difference, the quest for the civilizational and cultural ontology of blackness" (Zeleza, 2006, p. 15).

In his classic novella *Heart of Darkness*, Conrad establishes a persisting "image of Africa as 'the other world', the antithesis of Europe and therefore civilisation, an image of a place where man's vaunted intelligence and refinement are finally mocked by triumphant bestiality" (Achebe, 1977, p. 3). Accordingly, the voices of the Congolese form the dark and threatening background of the protagonist's journey. There is no volume to their banter because within the concept of bestiality the bearers of African voices only muster a collective "murmur," leading to a "violent babble of uncouth sounds" and finally to an "uproar of lamentable voices" (Conrad, 1999, p. 46). Only the civilised speech of the English has been recorded, is intelligible, and can be heard. It illustrates the silence that has been constructed and continues to guide our selective hearing, when we shout for help for Africa, establishing ourselves as helpers, redeemers, healers, doctors, and bearers of progress and at the same time ignoring, erasing, and obliterating the vast array of local voices, visions, and knowledge. "Africa is always imagined, represented and performed as a reality or a fiction in relation to master references—Europe, Whiteness, Christianity, Literacy, Development, Technology—…mirrors that reflect, indeed refract Africa in peculiar ways, reducing the continent to particular images, to a state of lack" (Zeleza, 2006, p. 16) and enlarges the perception of ourselves at the same time.

> We penetrated deeper and deeper into the heart of darkness. It was very quiet there. At night sometimes the roll of drums behind the curtain of tress would run up the river and remain sustained faintly, as if hovering in the air high over our heads, till the first break of day. Whether it meant war, peace, or prayer we could not tell…. We were wanderers on a prehistoric earth, on an earth that wore the aspect of an unknown planet. But suddenly…a burst of yells, a whirl of black limbs, a mass of hands clapping, of feet stamping, of bodies swaying…. The prehistoric man was cursing us, praying to us, welcoming us—who could tell? (Conrad, 1999, p. 63)

Western narratives "have radically silenced or converted African discourses" (Zeleza, 2006, p. 16). The misleading and reducing label of "dust and cave dwellers" deliberately seeks to keep the various voices silent or unintelligible. At the same time, the colonial discourses have prevailed and continue the discourse of colonisers and colonised, firmly embedded and disseminated by its established institutions, permanent structures of distribution of resources and permeated through the vortex created by globalised political, economic, and cultural power.

A BRIEF FORAY INTO CONGOLESE (COLONIAL) HISTORY

Aspects of silence in Congolese education

How entangled the roots of colonial conquest and mastery have become is particularly perplexing in the case of the constructions of national and international identities through education and its integrated language policies. There are currently about 17,500 secondary and primary schools in DRC with 10 tertiary universities, of which the majority are run by the Catholic Church, followed by the Protestant churches, the Muslim community, and a few state and international schools (Nyamuke, 2011). While this is at times applauded as a "remarkable openness to the religious formation of students" by the Congolese government (Faber, 2012), it is actually a direct result of the colonial period.

During that period missionaries, in their proselytising efforts, founded not only churches but also hospitals and schools in Leopold's Belgian Congo (Congo-initiative). Not by choice but rather through the common colonial centre-periphery structure and often by brute force, the colony adopted Belgian sociopolitical structures and approaches and thus began a "long history of encouraging faith based organisations…to be the primary provider of education" (Leinweber, 2012, p.1).

During Mobutu's reign, attempts to make Zaire (aka Belgian Congo) more independent—and as his personality became more messianic—led to the nationalisation of all educational institutes. However, owing to diplomatic and economic isolation and the Catholic Church resisting the cultural usurpation, the government could not financially sustain this project. As a result, Mobutu agreed on a hybrid system, the "convention system," which still underlies the structure of "post"-colonial DRCongo today. "This hybrid system allows the state to maintain control of the education system [curriculum, i.e., political] control, while religious organisations are responsible for the day-to-day operation of schools" (Leinweber, ibid.)

Lingala and its language policies

The official language of administration, law, parliament, i.e., power, is French, whereas Congolese engage in more than 200 languages. Lingala, acknowledged as a national language among Kikongo, Swahili, and Tshiluba, is only spoken around its capital. It has a very restricted status of lingua franca because of its very peculiar colonial history. In the nineteenth century *Ngala* was the lingua franca in the wider areas of Congo, while missionary linguists were searching for a unifying and practical language, serving the "civilizational authority" of Belgium and the European need for standardisation (Errington, 2008, p. 119). Formalising and regulating, they began to purify and prescribe the features of their new version of *Ngala*, which they changed into *Lingala*. At the same time, these processes not only solidified the status and prestige of the European languages but also helped in preserving the hierarchies among the indigenous themselves. Lingala became the language for the downstream people and Swahili for the other areas. "Lingala has been the undignified jargon of unproductive soldiers, government clerks, entertainers, and recently, of a power clique, all of them designated as *batoka chini*, people from down-river, i.e. from Kinshasa. Swahili as spoken in Katanga was a symbol of regionalism" (Fabian, as quoted in Appiah, 1993, p. 209).

The question of language policies remains highly contested, especially when former colonial languages, in particular English, continue to maintain or strengthen their position locally as well as globally. Due to the colonial design and limited access to intellectual resources among the colonial subjects, "the ordinary masses, proficient in their own languages that are not languages of the law, government and business, are [still] prevented from influencing reconceptualising of the dominant human rights discourses.…They are excluded from full participation in public affairs" (Zeleza, 2006, p. 21).

In the culture of silence the masses are "mute," that is, they are prohibited from creatively taking part in the transformations of their society and therefore prohibited from being (Freire, 1972a, p. 30).

In today's Congolese (here: Kinshasa) classroom it means that the children are not allowed to use Lingala in or outside class! When I interrupted an English class and asked whether the children were able to translate sentences into French, they obliged promptly. But when asked to translate the same phrases into Lingala, the kids reacted with shocked faces and silence. This was because it was prohibited by law to use Lingala in class, albeit, as I found out later, this applies "only" to social conversations but not to instructions. Clearly, teachers never use Lingala as a reference point in their teachings!

Under the mango tree with Paulo Freire (3)—dialogue

> *Paulo, it left me speechless and really troubled when students' and teachers' verbal interaction outside school is performed in Lingala! I am asking myself, and therefore you, how is dialogue possible? "Dialogue is the encounter between men, mediated by the world, in order to name the world…if it is in speaking in their word" (Freire, 1972b, p. 61). What is the role of colonial languages and the local, subordinate languages? In the end, there must not be restrictions on the naming process of the world and the medium we choose to do that, even if we draw on former colonial languages, right?*

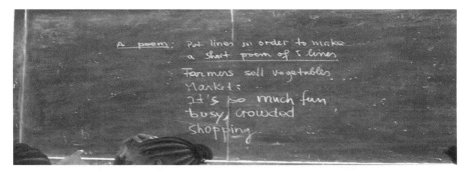

Figure 16.1. Poem instructions on the blackboard in a classroom in Kinshasa.

The binary of right and wrong

Another important observation was that a lot of the teaching appears to be generated from the governing principle of right or wrong, which, I suspect, helps to create the (see image no. 1) notion of education as "neutral." In this regard, classroom teaching keeps children silent because the content is separated from the learners as well as the teachers. Truth is being placed outside and above the realm of personal imagination, experience, and knowledge and belongs to external authorities such as scientific facts, grammar rules, or correct techniques. The concept of right/wrong enables the system to continue with its "paternalistic manipulation" (ibid, p. 64) and takes away the teacher's and student's creativity and independence.

This can be shown in the photo of the instructuions on the blackboard above: The teacher set the task of creating a poem about "At the Market." Normally, that could initiate open learning and allow the students to name their own worlds. Yet, my colleague wrote five "random" lines on the blackboard and instructed the class to order them—right/wrong principle—and then to write a short poem of five lines, integrating each phrase!

The class was not only confused but also very constricted in their work. In groups, they composed poems, only to turn to me at the end and asked me whether their poems were *correct*! The whole process could have led to a sense of greater authenticity and ownership without the restriction of selecting the teacher's phrases as well as limiting the experience to five sentences (and disallowing other languages to be presented).

A possible extension of silencing can also be seen in the sheer amount of bureaucratic demand, affecting teachers and students alike. Here in Kinshasa the teachers must submit three sets of documents for their classes, pertaining to

Figure 16.2. A staffroom in Kinshasa

curriculum, methodology, and an exact action plan (see the photo of the staffroom). These structures not only help sustain muteness, but also hinder change, human creativity, and individualisation. These burdens, organised by the anonymous authorities, contain regulations and prescriptions that drown the "modern man" in "levelling anonymity" and expel him "from the orbit of decisions" (Freire, 1974, p. 4).

Material conditions

The conditions for the ordinary Congolese population are very harsh with an erratic supply of electricity and water, and intermittent salary payment of low wages. To illustrate and personalise these circumstances: During my stay I visited a colleague's house. It consisted of two small rooms and a small kitchen area. This 25m² property was occupied by him, his wife, two children and his sister. The toilet, a hole in the ground, was shared by eight other families. Electricity was scarce and hygiene a daily issue. These material conditions do not provide the intellectual or physical space for rational discussions or dialogical conversations. There is no "mango tree" where they can feel or be fully human. These circumstances constantly re-introduce the "unseen grammar of commodity logic that serves as the regulatory lexicon of everyday life" (McLaren & Farahmand-pur, 2001, p. 144).

IN-CONCLUSION

As much as our personal hope is anchored in the ongoing fulfillment and completion of our "Dasein," so is the design of Freire's pedagogy of great and profound scale. The acceptance of the sense of inconclusion is also necessary in order to continue the search for improvement and in response to an ever-changing social reality and personal history. "One's inconclusion becomes critical, and they may never lack hope again...not so much the certainty of the *find*, but my movement in *search*" (Freire, 1997, p. 106).

My initiative in Kinshasa remains inconclusive, as my time was always marked by imminent departure and my role was never clear to myself: an "expert" on the one hand, an outsider on the other, and in between welcomed as a Christian brother. The activities in my workshop sought to initiate a soul-searching and critical reflection on educational practice with games such as "Tell a Lie," "Charade of Amazement," "Hollywood in Lingala," or the introduction of democratic classroom structures through peer assessment, "cheat" sheets or rubric negotiations, or concepts and training toward "true" dialogue. The Congolese teachers and students have been very curious, supportive and very eager, fully aware of the injustice, exploitation, and inhumane conditions. Many came voluntarily to the workshop and some started a network initiative for collaboration and professional exchange, defying material conditions but concentrating on the intellectual capacity!

In this context, the Christian discourse with concepts of kenosis (self-emtpying), the principle of agape (love of God), servitude, and hope have been very important and a constant source of encouragement. "My waiting (espera) makes sense only if I struggle and seek with hope (esperanza)" (Freire, as quoted in Schipani, 1984, p. 66). And it is faith that gives the strength for, the belief in, and the hope of a utopia of the liberation of man.

UNDER THE MANGO TREE WITH PAULO FREIRE (4)—PARTING

I came across the following poem by Ben Okri. I am sure you'll like it; it is my spiritual hug for you:

Harmony of Politics and Heart (I):
Mastery of material problems:
No spiritual way can reconcile.
Itself truthfully with the raw wound
Of starving multitudes.
We cannot use the word civilisation
As long as people die of starvation.
Those who do are cave-dwellers
Of the mind.

(OKRI, 1999)

REFERENCES

Achebe, C. (1977). *An image of Africa.* London, England: Penguin.

Appiah, K. A. (1993). *In my father's house: Africa in the philosophy of culture.* New York, NY: Oxford University Press.

Balogun, O. A. (2008). The idea of an "educated person" in contemporary African thought. *The Journal of Pan African Studies, 2*(3), 117–128.

Barthes, R. (1972). *Mythologies.* London, England: Vintage.

Blaut, J. M. (1992). *1492: The debate on colonialism, Eurocentrism and history.* Trenton, NJ: Butterworth-Heinemann.

Congoinitiative. *Church renewal and global mission.* Retrieved from http://www.congoinitiative.org/view.cfm?page_id=110

Conrad, J. (1999). *Heart of darkness & other stories.* Ware, England: Wordsworth Classics.

Eden, R. (2012, July 29). London 2012: Rowan Atkinson's brother criticises "Left-wing" opening ceremony. *The Telegraph*. Retrieved from http://www.telegraph.co.uk/sport/olympics/news/9434995/London-2012-Rowan-Atkinsons-brother-criticises-Left-wing-opening-ceremony.html

Errington, J. J. (2008). *Linguistics in a colonial world: A story of language, meaning and power.* Oxford, England: Blackwell.

Faber, C. (2012, July). Congolese educators, church leaders gather for ICOMB Consultation. Retrieved from http://www.mbconf.ca/home/products…/church_plants_welcomed/

Freire, A. M. (2008, March). *Nita—the Paulo Freire legacy.* Retrieved from http://www.google.com.au/#hl=en&sclient=psy-ab&q=nita+The+Paulo+and+Nita+Freire+International+Project+for+Critical+Pedagogy+the+legacy+powerpoint&oq=nita+The+Paulo+and+Nita+Freire+International+Project+for+Critical+Pedagogy+the+legacy+powerpoint&gs_l=hp.3

Freire, P. (1972a). *Cultural action for freedom.* Harmondsworth, England: Penguin.

Freire, P. (1972b). *Pedagogy of the oppressed.* Harmondsworth, England: Penguin.

Freire, P. (1974). *Education for critical consciousness.* New York, NY: Continuum.

Freire, P. (1997). *Pedagogy of the heart.* New York, NY: Continuum.

Giroux, H. A. (1997). *Pedagogy and the politics of hope: Theory, culture and schooling.* Boulder, CO: Westview Press.

Giroux, H. A. (2005, February). *Henry A. Giroux.* Retrieved from http://www.henryagiroux.com/online_articles/DarkTimes.htm

Lange, E. A. (2007). Transformative learning: The Trojan Horse of globalization? *Conference learning in community: Proceedings of the joint international conference of the Adult Education Research Conference (AERC).* Edited by Laura Servage and Tara Fenwick, Mount St. Vincent University, Halifax, Nova Scotia, Canada (pp. 355–360).

Leinweber, A. E. (2012). *Muslim public schools in post-conflict D.R. Congo.* London, England: Overseas Development Institute No. 22, 1–24.

Lewis, A. W., Scott, M., Wright, M., & Legum, C. (1951). *Attitude to Africa.* Harmondsworth, England: Penguin.

Mazaar, M. J. (2005). *Global trends 2005: An owner's manual for the next decade.* New York, NY: St. Martin's Press.

Mazrui, A. A. (1986). *The African heritage: A triple heritage.* London, England: BBC Publications.

McLaren, P. (1995). *Critical pedagogy and predatory culture. Oppositional politics in a postmodern era.* London, England: Routledge.

McLaren, P., & Farahmandpur, R. (2001). Teaching against globalisation and the new imperialism: Toward a revolutionary pedagogy. *Journal of Teacher Education, 52*(2), 136–150.

Mudimbe, V. Y. (1988). *The invention of Africa: Gnosis, philosophy, and the order of knowledge.* Bloomington: Indiana University Press.

Mulura, F. (2009, September). *Paulo Freire's development education methodology.* Retrieved from http://www.crvp.org/book/Series02/II-10/CH18.HTM

Naipaul, V. S. (2002). *The writer and the world.* London, England: Picador.

Nyamuke, A. I. (2011, July). Keynote address presented at the International Transforming Education conference, Darwin, Australia.

Okri, B. (1999). *Mental flight.* London, England: Phoenix House.

Said, E. W. (1993). *Culture and imperialism.* London, England: Vintage.

Schipani, D. S. (1984). *Conscientization and creativity: Paulo Freire and Christian education.* Lanham, MD: University Press of America.

Xpatulator.com. (2012, October). Congo Democratic Rep, Kinshasa. Retrieved from http://www.xpatulator.com/cost-of-living-review/Congo-Democratic-Rep-Kinshasa_56.cfm

Yoruba, C. (2012, May). *Who is African?* Retrieved from http://www.thisisafrica.me/opinion/detail/19481/Who-is-African%3F

Zeleza, P. T. (2006). The inventions of African identities and languages: The discursive and developmental implications. *Conference on African Linguistics* (pp. 14-26). Somervile, MA: Cascadilla Proceedings.

CHAPTER SEVENTEEN

Re-claiming Traditional Māori Ways of Knowing, Being, and Doing, to Re-frame Our Realities and Transform Our Worlds

LESLEY RAMEKA AND KURA PAUL-BURKE

Titiro whakamuri, whakarite ināianei, hei hāngai whakamua
(EMBRACE THE PAST, PREPARE NOW TO SHAPE THE FUTURE)

INTRODUCTION

The colonisation of New Zealand by the British was predicated upon the ranking of people into higher or lower forms of human existence and "assumptions of racial, religious, cultural and technological superiority" (Walker, 1990, p. 9). This was achieved, in part, by the economic growth and expansion of a Western imperialistic notion, which used colonisation as a vehicle for achieving power and control (L. Smith, 1999, 2008) perpetuating and enforcing the image of a successful, dominant Western elite over a perceived "lesser" inferior but conforming indigenous Māori culture (Johnston & Pratt, 2003). Māori were viewed as morally, socially, culturally, and intellectually inferior to Europeans. Hokowhitu (2004) stated the racial traits accorded to Māori included being depraved, sinful, idle, dirty, immoral, and unintelligent, the antithesis of those accorded to Europeans who were viewed as righteous, upright, intellectual, honourable, and liberal. With stereotypes such as these, the Māori child became schooled in the "psychology of colonialism."

This chapter briefly discusses the history of European schooling for Māori including early years education. It then explores the framings of the Māori learner, identity, and culture that resulted from the colonisation and European schooling for Māori. Finally, it investigates the need to reclaim and reframe Māori ways of knowing, being, and doing in order to make sense of the world and transform Māori realities.

THE HISTORY OF SCHOOLING FOR MĀORI

The history of European schooling for Māori in Aotearoa, New Zealand, is one of cultural dislocation, deprivation, and subjugation. Much has been researched and written on this by Barrington, Beaglehole, Belich, Binney, Bishop, Consedine and Consedine, King, Simon, Smith and Smith, and Walker. The early missionaries believed Māori lived in a state of "barbarism," with inferior intellect, language, and culture. Thus, in order to save their souls, Māori needed to be civilised and Europeanised (Belich, 2001; Harris, 2007; Hokowhitu, 2004; May, 2003, 2005). The aim of the early mission schools therefore was to interrupt the transmission of Māori culture, language, and worldviews and replace them with what was perceived to be the far superior and civilised European cultural norms, thus to transform Māori into "Brown Britons" (Belich, 2001).

Māori were schooled to provide a ready supply of workers but not to participate in higher education or access further employment opportunities. This limited curriculum was based upon the argument that Māori were "suited by nature to manual work" (Simon, 1998, p. 11). This two-tiered system of schooling was maintained over time and continued to be a source of cultural conflict and oppression for Māori children (Harris, 2007). Walker (1991, pp. 7–8) claimed that "this institutionalisation of racism within the Education Department and its schools explains the existence and entrenched nature of the education gap between Māori and Pākehā." These deficit perspectives of Māori have continued to inform and justify successive education policies. "State controlled education resulted in Māori being educated within a system that not only devalued them as a people but stressed the negative features of Māori knowledge and culture" (Berryman, 2008, p. 33).

The first infant school in New Zealand was reported in 1832 at Paihia. In 1833, Captain W. Jacobs visited the infant school, which taught around twenty-six young children, some European but mainly Māori. He was impressed with the moral culture of the school as much as with the school itself (May, Kaur, & Prochner, 2006). This is congruent with the aims and objectives of the British Infant School Society, established some eight years earlier, to save children from the deprivation of their home environments and to civilise them. May and colleagues (2006) highlighted the similarities in the rhetoric used to describe both young

British street children and Māori young children. "An infant school education, whether it was to remove young children from the British gutters, or their Māori 'kainga's' [homes], would save them from their uncivilised and disorderly worlds" (pp. 3–4). William Yates's (1835) account of early New Zealand also emphasised the need for such remedies. He stated:

> Formerly, a [Māori] parent would never correct a child for anything it might do; it was allowed to run riot in all that was vile, and have its own way in everything. The evil of this was palpable: in New Zealand, as in every other country, a spoiled child is a great plague; but if the pest was in any one place more severely felt than in another, it was here. Brought up in evil, and without restraint of law in their youth, it could be no great wonder if, as men, they indulged in every vice. (p. 241)

Urbanisation in the 1940s and 1950s resulted in up to 70% of the Māori population migrating from the rural tribal areas to urban environments and schools, where Māori educational disadvantage became increasingly visible in urban primary schools and raised issues for both primary and early childhood education (Hokowhitu, 2004). Urban teachers were unprepared for the influx of Māori children, and often identified them as failures, lacking the basic experiences of Pākehā children (May, 2005). This also coincided with intelligence and language research of the time and the ideas of cultural deficits, which positioned Māori children as both intellectually and linguistically deficient (Bishop & Glynn, 1999; Harris, 2007). The Māori child was therefore viewed as outside the norms of development and in need of remediation. In 1946, anthropologists Ernest and Pearl Beaglehole argued that there was a "need to bring to bear upon the Māori child a somewhat different technique of infant and child training" so that they would "fit more clearly into the patterns of Pākehā civilisations. By the time the child comes to Pākehā school it is already too late" (cited in May, 2005, p. 72).

In 1961, the Department of Māori Affairs, Hunn Report, for the first time provided statistical evidence of Māori disadvantage in the areas of health, housing, employment, and education. It identified the impact of the two-tiered schooling system and the subversion of Māori culture on Māori educational achievement, reporting a "statistical blackout" in higher education (Walker, 1991, p. 8). Blame for any "statistical blackout" was placed squarely with Māori parents and culture (Hokowhitu, 2004). The focus of successive education policies and practices was to rectify the "Māori problem" and overcome the perceived cultural inadequacies of Māori children (Fleras & Spoonley, 1999; Simon, 1986). The effects of these policies are still evident today, with Māori children disengaging from the education system, and consistently achieving disproportionately lower results on national averages (Smith & Smith, 1990). Hook (2007) added that this dissociation has resulted in a "dichotomy of existence for Māori, alienation of the minority, disengagement from the education system, loss of language, and loss of culture" (p. 2).

FRAMING MĀORI

With the devaluing of the Māori cultural base, Māori became conditioned to dominant Western perspectives, and began to accept European representations of Māori culture, identity, and knowledge. What it meant in effect was that being Māori was defined by the coloniser in a situation shaped by colonialism (Memmi (1957). Nandy (1983) likened this to "cognitive colonialism" or colonialism of the mind in that the perceived images of the dominant culture are a construct of colonialism, a false paradigm. These images further the cause of a colonising empire by creating a powerful intelligent all-knowing Western image in contrast to a weaker, unintelligent, un-knowing indigenous. The erosion of the Māori culture, Māori knowledge, and Māori identity served to protect and promote the interests of non-Māori (G. Smith, 1988, 1990; Walker, 1987, 1990). It provided space for non-Māori to dictate which aspects of Māori culture and knowledge were beneficial and relevant to them, and which weren't, disregarding the rest as subsidiary and/ or romantic (Bishop, 2008; G. Smith, 2009). Non-Māori were therefore able to justify their power positions and argue that it was better that they think for and act on behalf of Māori. Freire (1970, p. 112) framed this in the context of dominant elites, stating that the "dominant elites can and do think without the people— although they do not permit themselves the luxury of failing to think about the people in order to know them better and thus dominate them more efficiently." With this ideology, they were able to present the interests of the more dominant group "as the interests of all groups within society, thereby concealing and denying that subordinate groups interests are not being met, or even that they may have different interests (Coxon, Jenkins, Marshall, & Massey, 1994, p. 13).

FORCED IDENTITIES

Forced identities are those that are formed under conditions of deprivation and have been distorted by the realities of living within a marginal status. They are primarily defined by outsider groups and forced upon others who have little control over the process. The power to describe and define normality has remained with the coloniser, as has the ability to marginalise and pathologise others. With the power to define came control over the educational process, and the ability to dictate which aspects of Māori epistemologies were acceptable for application within the schooling arena. Māori students were therefore subjected to watered-down perspectives of their own culture as seen through the eyes of the oppressor. Māori were often portrayed as simple-minded, happy-go-lucky natives who were obedient and *grateful* to the oppressor, or dirty, sinful, irresponsible, unintelligent, lazy natives who were forever *blaming* the oppressor for the state that we have gotten ourselves into. Within these stereotypical frames, Māori began to accept and even joke about the assigned cultural dispositions. Memmi (1957, p. 81) described this when he stated that "he [sic] talks of it with amused affability, he jokes about it, he takes up all the usual expressions, perfects them and invents others." It becomes a survival mechanism, a happy-go-lucky, lazy, and unintelligent stance in life. The oppressed joke about their ignorance, their laziness, and their inability to compete with the oppressor, and after generations of exposure—their children believe it.

The inability of Western education curricula to place positive lenses on Māori children's identity, culture, and language perpetuates the concept that Māori culture and language are unintellectual, trivial, and strange. Māori knowledge is relegated to hobbies and extracurricular and after-school activities. The framing of Māori culture and identity as unworthy leads the Māori child to suffer an "identity problem because it binds them to minority group status with all its attendant disadvantages" (Walker, 1987, p. 176). Understanding and experiencing what it is to be Māori and accessing positive constructs of Māori success and achievement within educational and societal contexts are denied.

The loss of intellectual and cultural knowledges has been compounded by Māori being "constantly fed messages about their worthlessness, laziness, dependence and lack of 'higher' order human qualities" (L. Smith, 1999, p. 4). Berryman (2008) claimed that a "major contributor to this problem is that the years of colonisation have resulted in the coloniser, and not Māori, being largely responsible for defining what it is to be Māori" (p. 52). Within mainstream society, it is therefore no surprise to learn that Māori are failures at all levels of Western education paradigms.

RE-CLAIMING

It is only when the oppressed find the oppressor out and become involved in the organised struggle for their liberation that they begin to believe in themselves. This discovery cannot be purely intellectual but must involve action: nor can it be limited to mere activism, but must include serious reflection; only then will it be a praxis. (Freire, 1970, p. 47)

Reclaiming one's identity, or becoming the person one has always been, not only takes time but also is often a process of searching, learning, and unlearning (Parker, 2000). Reclaiming one's identity is a process of personal and cultural transformation that requires the unmasking of identities that are not one's own. Unmasking identities inherited as a legacy of domination and oppression such as slavery and colonisation are part of this process. These identities include negative attitudes to self that are oppressive and internalised. They also involve mostly unconscious beliefs about the superiority of the dominant culture and inferiority of one's own.

Unlearning what has been unconsciously internalised is an important part of the process of developing a positive cultural identity.

> Part of the process is learning their own history from the perspective of members of their own culture, reclaiming what has been lost or unknown to them, and reframing what has often been cast subconsciously as negative in a more positive way. (Tisdell, 2001, p. 147)

Berryman (2008, p. 28) suggested "that reconnection with one's own heritage enables greater opportunity and ability to reclaim the power to define oneself and, in so doing, defines solutions that will be more effective for Māori, now and in the future." Freire (1970) discussed the concept of "naming the world" whereby "those who have been denied their primordial right to speak their word must first reclaim this right and prevent the continuation of this dehumanizing aggression" (p. 61).

He asserted that the naming of the world is "an act of creation; it must not serve as a crafty instrument for the domination of one man by another…. The naming of the world, which is an act of creation and re-creation, is not possible if it is not infused by love" (p. 62). For Māori to identify and name ourselves as Māori means much more than to simply stand and declare: *I am Māori*. It means that we have learnt and are still learning from our educational past, that we are actively working to provide educational environments and curricula that permeate positive images of Māori as real and relevant for all children, of all races, toward the reclamation of Māori identities and, therefore, the transformation of our worlds.

Freire (1970) suggested that "reclaiming identity" is a living example of praxis of action and reflection and that true transformation and change can only be achieved if Māori learn to love or re-love ourselves first and not at the expense of the coloniser. To be able to forgive and then offer love and understanding of and for the aggressor is crucial in dismantling the violent acts of framing Māori and inflicting forced identities within Western educational constructs. The need to name comes not from the desire to oppress and dehumanise another, but to acknowledge, learn from, and move positively forward in the quest to become liberated and, in so doing, more human. As Freire (1970, p. 58) asserted, "the oppressed must unveil the world of oppression and through the praxis commit themselves to its transformation."

Learning to reclaim ourselves as Māori and learning what it means to us to be Māori are small steps in the act of naming ourselves. The courage to accept the past and learn from it requires the strength to grow as a person, as a Māori person, and become more "human" rather than "dehumanise" another through our own insecurities, confusion, and internal dilemma (Freire, 1970). This process often involves internal conflicts, internal questioning, and self-doubt as we search to free ourselves from the restraints of negative Western constructs of identities (Fanon, 1967; Memmi, 1957; Nandy, 1983). Walker (1990, p. 235) supports this when he wrote that "liberation from Pākehā (the dominant culture group in Aotearoa, New

Zealand) is not a gift conferred on the Māori by the oppressor. The Māori have to lead their own liberation struggle, a task Pākehā are free to join as auxiliaries."

REFRAMING

Memmi (1957) discussed the need to leave behind the "borrowed language of the coloniser," or in this context the borrowed educational philosophies and practices of non-Māori by establishing culturally appropriate educational pathways for Māori children, to benefit all children in Aotearoa, New Zealand. Reclaiming our ways of knowing, being, and doing is a theory of change. It attempts to empower communities by using the past as a learning tool in conceptualising what Māori need to do to ensure that our perspectives and knowledges are valued and represented appropriately. We need to "understand where the pain comes from and why…. All that mega-theory will not get us anywhere because without understanding, mega-theory does not mean anything, does not reflect reality, does not reflect people's experience" (Monture-Angus, 1995, p. 20). If Māori are to re-claim traditional Māori ways of knowing, being, and doing, to reframe our realities and transform our worlds, then it must be within an educational framework that identifies with and represents the "words, ideas, conditions and habits central to [our Māori] experience" (Shor, 1993, p. 31). Reframing Māori epistemologies in educational environments sets an agenda for change. It challenges the traditional modes of power and control between the oppressor and the oppressed. Reclaiming traditional Māori ways of knowing, being, and doing is critical to reimaging young Maori children, reframing their realities, and transforming their worlds.

KAUPAPA MAORI

Kaupapa can be translated as meaning strategy, principle, a way to proceed, a plan, or a philosophy. Embedded within the concept of kaupapa is a notion of acting strategically, of proceeding purposively (L. Smith, 1999). Kaupapa Māori is a movement of resistance and of revitalisation, incorporating theories that are embedded within te ao Māori (Berryman, 2008). "Kaupapa Māori speaks to the validity and legitimacy of being Māori and acting Māori: to be Māori is taken for granted. Māori language, culture, knowledge and values are accepted in their own right" (G. Smith, 1992, p. 15). Kaupapa Māori relates not only to Māori philosophies but also to actions and practices derived from such philosophies. Kaupapa Māori theory, therefore, is not new, nor is it a refurbished, refined, version of Western theories.

Kaupapa Māori is twofold: it provides a critique of existing structures, and seeks transformative strategies, thus creating space for other cultural perspectives to be recognised, and validated. This involves centralising the position of Māori knowledge, moving it from its marginal position of "abnormal" or "unofficial" knowledge to an equal status with Western knowledge. According to Barnes (2000), "Kaupapa Māori begins as a challenge to accepted norms and assumptions about knowledge and the way it is constructed and continues as a search for understanding within a Māori worldview" (p. 4).

Kaupapa Māori, according to G. Smith (1997), is both theory and transformative praxis. It has evolved from Māori communities and has succeeded in supporting fundamental structural changes in educational interventions. Kaupapa Māori theory has become an important and coherent philosophy and practice for raising Māori consciousness, supporting resistance and encouraging transformative action and reflection (praxis) in order to progress Māori cultural capital and learning outcomes within education. G. Smith (2003) referred to it as a revolution that involved a mindset shift of Māori people "away from waiting for things to be done to them, to doing things for themselves; a shift away from an emphasis on reactive politics to an emphasis on being more proactive; a shift from negative motivation to positive motivation" (G. Smith, 2003, p. 2).

Kaupapa Māori relates to learning and learners being seen as deeply located, embedded within Māori ways of knowing and being. Māori ways of knowing and being are fundamentally different from those of non-Māori, influenced and shaped by historical and contemporary interpretive systems or worlds. It is these interpretive systems that Māori learners inhabit, enact, and reflect in their learning. The systems consist of tools, patterns of reasoning, symbols, language, shared meanings, and customary practices that are required to competently participate within a particular social group, community, or culture (Weenie, 2008). Kaupapa Māori theory and practice provide a powerful vehicle to address the educational aspirations of Māori. As Mahuika and Bishop (2011) stated, "What has been identified as being essential is the realisation that at an abstract metaphorical level Māori cultural knowledge offers a framework for realistic and workable options for dealing with Māori educational underachievement" (p. 4). It is about affirming and legitimating Māori ways of knowing within wider New Zealand educational contexts.

CONCLUSION

In conclusion, reclaiming traditional Māori ways of knowing, being, and doing, to reframe our realities and transform our worlds, aims to locate positive constructs of identity for the Māori child, which are grounded in the material existence or experiential learnings of Māori (Freire, 1970). For as Marx pointed out, it is not the consciousness of men that determines their existence, but their social existence that determines their consciousness (Marx, 1958). It is about altering traditional constructs of education, of reclaiming and reframing Māori ways of knowing, being, and doing, in order to make sense of the world, to be an "active participant" and in so doing conceive faith in our epistemological frameworks, validating our sense of self and belonging within educational pursuits (Freire, 1970). A commitment to Māori epistemology is fundamental to reframing Māori realities. The relevance of the authentic "voice" of Māori and the experiential or lived experiences of that voice is the basis for positive, reflective, transformative action (Monture-Angus, 1995). As Freire (1970) wrote, "The oppressed must be their own example in the struggle for their own redemption" (p. 36).

Titirowhakamuri, whakarite ināianei, hei hāngai whakamua
(Embrace the past, prepare now to shape the future)

REFERENCES

Barnes, H. (2000). *Kaupapa Māori: Explaining the ordinary.* Auckland, New Zealand: Auckland University Press.

Belich, J. (2001). Foreword. In J. Simon & L. Tuhiwai Smith (Eds.), *A civilising mission? Perceptions and representations of the New Zealand native schools system.* Auckland, New Zealand: Auckland University Press.

Berryman, M. (2008). *Repositioning within indigenous discourses of transformation and self-determination.* Unpublished doctoral dissertation, University of Waikato, Hamilton, New Zealand. Retrieved from http://waikato.researchgateway.ac.nz/

Bishop, R. (1996). *Collaborative research stories: Whakawhanaungatanga.* Palmerston North, New Zealand: Dunmore Press.

Bishop, R. (1997). Maori people's concerns about research into their lives. *History of Education Review, 26*(1), 25–41.

Bishop, R. (1998). Freeing ourselves from neo-colonial domination in research: A Māori approach to creating knowledge. *International Journal of Qualitative Studies in Education, 11*(2), 199–219.

Bishop, R. (2008). Freeing ourselves from neo-colonial domination in research: A kaupapa Māori approach to creating knowledge. In N. Denzin & Y. Lincoln (Eds.), *The landscape of qualitative research* (pp. 145–184). Thousand Oaks, CA: Sage.

Bishop, R., & Glynn, T. (1999). *Culture counts: Changing power relations in education.* Palmerston North, New Zealand: Dunmore Press.

Coxon, E., Jenkins, K., Marshall, J., & Massey, J. (Eds.) (1994). *The politics of teaching and learning in Aoteaora, New Zealand.* Palmerston North, New Zealand: Dunmore Press.

Fanon, F. (1967). *Black skin, white masks.* New York, NY: Grove Press.

Fleras, A., & Spoonley, P. (1999). *Recalling Aotearoa: Indigenous politics and ethnic relations in New Zealand.* Auckland, New Zealand: Oxford University Press.

Freire, P. (1970). *Pedagogy of the oppressed.* London, England: Penguin.

Harris, F. (2007). *Re-constructing Māori children as achieving learners.* Unpublished doctoral dissertation, University of Canterbury, Christchurch, New Zealand.

Hokowhitu, B. (2004). Te taminga o te Matauranga: Colonisation in education. In T. M. Ka'ai, J. C. Moorfield, M. P. J. Reilly, & S. Mosley (Eds.), *Ki Te Whaiao—an introduction to Māori culture and society* (pp. 190–200). Auckland, New Zealand: Pearson Education New Zealand.

Hook, G. (2007). A future for Māori education Part II: The reintegration of culture and education. *MAI Review, 1,* Target Article. Retrieved from http://www.review.mai.ac.nz

Jackson, M. (1998). Research and the colonisation of Māori knowledge. In *Proceedings of Te OruRangahau Māori Research Conference* (pp. 70–78). Palmerston North, New Zealand: Massey University.

Johnston, P. M. (2001). *When indigenous knowledge destablises the border: Research in Aotearoa, New Zealand.* Paper presented at the Indigenous Knowledge Conference, Indigenous Peoples Program, Extension Division, University of Saskatchewan, Saskatoon, Canada.

Johnston, P. M., & Pratt, J. (2003).Culture, race and discourse. In J. Swann & J. Pratt (Eds.), *Educational research in practice continuum* (pp. 152–163). London, England: Continuum.

Mahuika, R., & Bishop, R. (2011). Review Paper 6: *Issues of culture and assessment in New Zealand education pertaining to Māori students.* University of Waikato. Retrieved from http://assessment. tki.org.nz/Media/Files/Mahuika-R.-and-Bishop-R.-Issues-of-culture-and-assessment-in-New-Zealand-education-pertaining-to-Maori-students-University-of-Waikato

Marx, K. (1958). *Selected works: Preface to a contribution to the critique of political economy.* Moscow, Russia: Foreign Languages.

May, H. (2003). School beginnings: A history of early years schooling. Case study one. Mission infant schools for Māori children, 1830–40s. *Research and Policy Series, No. 1.* Institute for Early Childhood Studies, Victoria University, Wellington, New Zealand.

May, H. (2005). *School beginnings. A 19th century colonial story.* Wellington, New Zealand: NZCER Press.

May, H., Kaur, B., & Prochner, L. (Eds.) (2006, November–December). *Reconceptualizing early childhood education: Research, theory and practice.* Paper presented at the Proceedings of 14th Conference. Rotorua, New Zealand, November 30–December 4.

Memmi, A. (1957). *The colonizer and the colonized.* New York, NY: Orion Press.

Monture-Angus, P. (1995). *Thunder in my soul: A Mohawk woman speaks.* Halifax, Nova Scotia, Canada: Fernwood.

Mutu, M. (2002). Barriers to tangatawhēnua participation in resource management. In M. Kawharu (Ed.), *Whēnua: Managing our resources.* Auckland, New Zealand: Reed Books.

Nandy, A. (1983). *The intimate enemy: Loss and recovery of self under colonialism.* Delhi, India: Oxford University Press.

O'Sullivan, D. (2007). Assimilation, biculturalism and rangatiratanga. In D. O'Sullivan (Ed.), *Beyond biculturalism and rangatiratanga.* Wellington, New Zealand: Huia.

Parker, M. (2000). *Organizational culture and identity. Unity and division at work.* London, England: Sage.

Pihama, L., Cram, F., & Walker, S. (2002). Creating methodological space: A literature review of kaupapa Māori research. *Canadian Journal of Native Education, 26*(1), 30–43.

Rao, J. (2003). *Selected works: Preface to a contribution to the critique of political economy.* Moscow, Russia: Foreign Languages.

Shor, I. (1993). Education is politics: Paulo Freire's critical pedagogy. In P. McLaren & P. Leonard (Eds.), *Paulo Freire: A critical encounter.* London, England: Routledge.

Simon, J. (1986). *Ideology in the schooling of Māori children*. Palmerston North, New Zealand: Department of Education, Massey University.

Simon, J. (Ed.) (1998). *Nga kura Māori: The native schools system, 1867–1969*. Auckland, New Zealand: Auckland University Press.

Smith, G. H. (1988). *Kura kaupapa Māori: Contesting and reclaiming education in Aotearoa*. Auckland, New Zealand: Education Department, University of Auckland.

Smith, G. H. (1990). *Research issues related to Māori education*. Paper presented at NZARE Special Interests Conference, Massey University, Palmerston North, New Zealand.

Smith, G. H. (1992). *Tane-nui-a-Rangi's legacy, propping up the sky: Kaupapa Māori resistance and intervention*. Paper presented at NZARE/AARE Joint Conference, Deakin University, Melbourne, Australia.

Smith, G. H. (2000). Māori education: Revolution and transformative action. *Canadian Journal of Native Education, 24*(1), 57–72.

Smith, G. H. (2003, December). *Kaupapa Māori theory: Theorizing indigenous transformation of education & schooling*. Paper presented at Kaupapa Māori Symposium NZARE/AARE Joint Conference, Auckland, New Zealand.

Smith, G. H. (2009). Protecting and respecting indigenous knowledge. In M. Battiste (Ed.), *Reclaiming indigenous voice and vision*. Vancouver, British Columbia, Canada: UBC Press.

Smith, L., & Smith, G. (1990). Ki te whai ao, ki te ao mārama: Crisis and change in Māori education. In A. Jones et al., *Myths and realities: Schooling in New Zealand* (pp. 123–155). Palmerston North, New Zealand: Dunmore Press.

Smith, L. T. (1992). Te Rapungaiteaomarama (The search for the world of light): Māori perspectives on research in education. In J. Morss & J. Linzey (Eds.), *Growing up: The politics of human learning*. Auckland, New Zealand: Longman Paul.

Smith, L. T. (1999). *Decolonizing methodologies: Research and indigenous peoples*. Dunedin, New Zealand: University of Otago Press.

Smith, L. T. (2008). On tricky ground: Researching the native in the age of uncertainty. In N. K. Denzin & Y. S. Lincoln (Eds.), *The landscape of qualitative research*. Thousand Oaks, CA: Sage.

Smith, L. T. (2009). Kaupapa Māori research. In M. Battiste (Ed.), *Reclaiming indigenous voice and vision*. Vancouver, British Columbia, Canada: UBC Press.

Tisdell, E. (2001). Spirituality and emancipatory adult education in women adult educators for social change. *Adult Education Quarterly, 50*(4), 308–333.

Walker, R. (1987). *Ngā Tautohetohe: Years of anger*. Auckland, New Zealand: Penguin.

Walker, R. (1990). *Kawhawhaitonumātou: Struggle without end*. Auckland, New Zealand: Penguin Books.

Walker, R. (1991). *Liberating Māori from educational subjection*. Auckland, New Zealand: Research Unit for Māori Education, University of Auckland.

Weenie, A. (2008). Curricular theorizing from the periphery. *Curriculum Inquiry, 38*(5), 545–557.

Yates, W. (1835). *An account of New Zealand*. London, England: Seeley & Burnside.

CHAPTER EIGHTEEN

Pakistan in Praxis: The Development of a Peer Education Programme as a Tool Kit in Developing Young People for Critical Consciousness

ALETHEA MELLING AND WAJID KHAN

INTRODUCTION

The purpose of this chapter is to discuss how the pedagogy of Paulo Freire has been successfully combined with transformational leadership training techniques in the development and delivery of a peer leadership programme for young people in Pakistan. It will explore how a group of University of Central Lancashire Community Leadership students from the Pakistani diaspora in Burnley, East Lancashire, UK, collaborated with students from the California Association of Student Councils, Stanford University, and students from the University of Gujrat,[1] Pakistan, to develop a peer-centred approach to developing leadership skills, with a strong focus on the concept of action/reflection praxis. Their objective was to develop, in the words of the late Michael Elliott, "a tool kit for change" (Elliott, 2011) that can be used by young people and communities. The outcome of the process was not only a "tool kit" for developing leadership skills, it also opened up the significant possibilities, and benefits from mobilising Pakistani undergraduates in Freire-influenced social action.

Pakistan is in a unique position in terms of a youth dividend. In 2004, the youth population ages 15 to 24 was estimated at 36 million (Faizunnisa, 2005, p. 1). Fifty-eight million are under the age of 15 (Zaidi, 2010). According to a British Council report, *Pakistan: The Next Generation,* the period of the dividend extends from the 1990s until 2045 (British Council, 2009). This gives approximately 50 years to capitalise on the benefits of a young population. However, against the demographics of promise, we also have a situation in which 50% of children do not have a formal secondary education and 36% have never been to school and therefore are assumed to be illiterate (Faizunnisa, 2005), and only 5% have access to higher education (British Council, 2009). Many of the young people lack the essential skills for a modern global labour market ("Perilous Journey," 2012, p. 13). Moreover, Faizunnisa, in a study of 8,074 young people, notes the gender discrepancy in education correlates with poverty, being wider at the most impoverished strata of society, with the gap narrowing substantially at the more affluent end wherein mothers themselves are more likely to be educated (Faizunnisa, 2005). According to recent surveys, young people are disillusioned with democracy. *The Economist* notes a generic cynicism toward politicians and the military ("Perilous Journey," 2012, p. 8). However, the British Council report also shows that young people love Pakistan and are keen to see strong economic and political development (British Council, 2009). Only 5% of Pakistan's young people manage to gain access to higher education. This chapter argues that the 5% can be effectively mobilised as peer educators to young people through a Freire-influenced model. Moreover, it concludes that this model can be extended to a programme of undergraduate-led social action.

In order to be effective in contemporary society within Pakistan and the world at large, young people need capacity building so that they can lead and make balanced and informed decisions about their lives, democracy, community, relationships, and work. Most important, young people need to be allowed to make an impact in the global economy and to contribute to the development of their communities. Faizunnisa notes the need to build up skills in young people and to raise their aspirations, and draws attention to an economically driven trend toward young people leaving education early in order to bring in an income. This is resulting in a generation of unskilled, low-wage manual labourers who do not have the knowledge or skill capacity to take on the challenges of a global economy or a fledgling democracy (Faizunnisa, 2005, p. 5). Today, there is a unique opportunity to develop a peer leadership and education programme to meet the growing needs of young people and the communities of Pakistan. Young people growing up in an increasing globalised existence face unprecedented pressures and often feel that their national, cultural, and personal identities are being swallowed up by a global system. Using the techniques of Freire in a peer educational context, it is possible to build young people's capacities in a way that respects and preserves their national, cultural, and personal identities, whilst building their skill levels for them to make an impact in a global context.

METHODOLOGY

At the University of Central Lancashire Centre for Volunteering and Community Leadership,[2] the process of peer-led community education and leadership is underpinned by the educational philosophy of the Brazilian educationalist, Paulo Freire. Freire was born in 1921 in Recife, Brazil. His main work was in adult literacy, but his main conceptual principles of problem-posing education are transferable to all learning contexts. In 1947, Freire began to work with adult illiterates from peasant communities in northeast Brazil. Until 1964, he was Professor of the History and Philosophy of Education at Recife University, and during the 1960s, he became well known for his involvement in an education movement to address widespread illiteracy. His empowering methods were originally supported by the federal government, and during 1963–1964, courses for programme coordinators were delivered in all states with a plan for 2,000 "cultural circles," or learning communities, to reach 200,000 illiterate peasants. This model, using a cascading effect, has influenced the peer leadership model presented at the University of Gujrat. However, following the 1964 coup in Brazil, Freire was imprisoned, as his methods were considered subversive (critical consciousness is dangerous because it empowers individuals to evaluate their situation). He was exiled to Chile, where he continued to develop his method, but he did not return to Brazil until 1979. During his exile, he was visiting Professor for the Study of Development and Social Change at Harvard University, as well as filling a position at the World Council of Churches in Geneva. After his return to Brazil, he was appointed Sao Paulo's Secretary of Education. He passed away in 1997 (Freire Institute, 2012).

Freire's concepts and pedagogy are deeply pertinent to the development of a youth-led peer leadership programme. The late Michael Cowen Elliott, BSG, the founder of the Freire Institute, conceptualised Freire's philosophy in his conviction that "uneducated," or illiterate people are not "empty vessels" that need filling up, but rather they need to be given a "tool kit" to critically examine their experience (Elliott, 2011). The process of the peer leadership training is therefore a tool kit to build up young people's capacity to be effective peer educators.

Michael Elliott's analogy of the "empty vessel" explains Freire's concept of "banking" education. Freire believed that the true purpose of education is the reconciliation of the "poles of contradiction" in the student/tutor relationship, so that both parties are simultaneously teachers and students (Freire, 1996, p. 53). This concept forms the basis of a strong peer education process. Friere uses the banking analogy to describe traditional forms of education:

> Education thus becomes an act of depositing, in which students are the depositories and the teacher is the depositor. Instead of Communicating, the teacher issues communiques and makes deposits, which the students patiently receive, memorise and repeat. This is the

banking concept of education in which the scope of action allowed to the students extends only as far as receiving, filing and storing the deposits. (Freire, 1996, p. 59)

In the banking analogy of education, "knowledge is a gift bestowed by those who consider themselves knowledgeable upon those whom they consider to know nothing" (Freire, 1996, p. 59). Within the banking analogy, Freire compares the student to the slave in the Hegelian dialectic—"their ignorance justifies the tutor's existence" (Freire, 1996). Freire believed in a mutual learning process, whereby the tutor and student share learning. The tutor cannot assume that he/she has the greater knowledge. The role of the tutor is to move the student from naïve, or magical (superstitious) consciousness, to "critical consciousness" (Freire, 2007, p. 39). Therefore, the action/reflection praxis is incredibly important in empowering individuals for positive change.

In his work *Education for Critical Consciousness*, Freire discusses the importance of making education meaningful. Unless it is meaningful, it is relatively useless to developing critical consciousness and an action/reflection praxis. Information without a situational context is simply information to be "banked" and it does not provide an authentic education. It does not promote critical thinking. This is why Freire advocated situational learning when working with rural, illiterate communities, and why we use this concept when working with young people as peer educators (Freire, 2007, p. 57).

The model of peer education developed by the students in Pakistan adheres closely to these concepts. The learning process is a situational problem-posing praxis, working in small groups with a peer educator. The process creates a dialogue. A "dialogue" from a Freirean perspective "presupposes equality among participants." There must be a mutual trust and respect for one another. Each participant must be open and aware that through the dialogue process, preconceived ideas and thoughts may well change and "new knowledge will be created" (Freire Institute, 2012). Freire believes that learning is a critical process of "conscientization," or developing a critical awareness of one's own reality (Freire Institute, 2012).

The banking process of educating young people is dangerous, particularly within the cultural context of certain parts of Pakistan. Young people who believe they are "empty vessels" to be filled up with the "gift of knowledge" by those who want to believe they have knowledge are vulnerable ("Perilous Journey," 2012, p. 9). The education system in Pakistan is sporadic, inconsistent, and fraught with corruption. There are frequent cases of teachers taking a salary but never turning up to teach, and the quality of teaching is very poor. Families, other than the most privileged, send their young people to Madrassas for an education. The teaching is free and the young people are usually fed, so this makes an attractive alternative to an unreliable and weak state system.[3] Importantly, Zaidi points out that the youth dividend in Pakistan is disproportionately male and this would transfer into the proportion of young people who are educated, particularly in poorer rural areas where young women would receive little or no education. Moreover, Zaidi emphasises the potential of young men from poorer backgrounds "to fall victim to radicalization, if left marginalized in the mainstream Pakistani society" (Zaidi, 2010).

Lipset (1960), quoted in Zaidi, identifies low levels of education as a factor "which tends to promote a simplified worldview of politics, and an uncompromising nature due to economic insecurity, which leads to a heightened state of stimulus to perceived disturbing events" (Zaidi, 2010). Young people from poor socioeconomic backgrounds have no opportunities to explore ideas, apply action/ reflection processes, or develop the skills necessary to take an active role in developing a modern democracy. To impose so-called knowledge (or usually misinformation, myths, and so forth) on young people without initiating an open process of dialogue, or without allowing an action/reflection praxis, is dictating, not teaching. Young people who do not have the tool kit for critical analysis are vulnerable to negative influence by people who fill them up with misinformation and hold control over them by denying them the process of conscientisation, or by keeping them in a state of naïve consciousness. "Education as the exercise of domination stimulates the credulity of students, with the ideological intent of indoctrinating them to adapt to the world of oppression" (Freire, 1996, p. 59).

DEVELOPING AN APPROPRIATE TOOL KIT

The first and most obvious question is, Why peer education? Why use young people to teach and develop other young people? In Pakistan, as in many other cultures, it is considered prudent to leave education and development of the young to parents and elders. Minhaj ul Haque states, "Parents are the unchallenged stakeholders in the lives of young people in Pakistan," "playing a critical role in socialising their children" (Haque, 2010, p. 1). Adults, parents and families, in particular, are intrinsic in shaping the values, morals, and beliefs of young people and it can be argued that no one is better placed to do that task. However, young people learn many of their skills and social norms from their peers. At the launch of the Laptop Project in the Punjab, Sharif expressed the hope that the youth will transform Pakistan in accordance with the ideals of Quaid-e-Azam[4] and Allama Iqbal,[5] and went on to state that "the youth will also evolve new ways of development and prosperity of the country and Pakistan" (Sharif, 2012).

Youth-led peer education is becoming internationally recognised as an important way forward. Organisations such as the British Red Cross (n.d.) and Save the Children (2004) are now investing heavily in the development of peer education and leadership training for young people as a means of addressing serious issues such as HIV and child exploitation. There is always a group leader whom young people look up to in the playground or street. That young person can be a positive or negative role model for their peers. In the model discussed here, student volunteers will work with young people and their parents[6] to train them as positive role models and educators within their respective communities so that they can then work to peer educate others; thus, the process will cascade. The overall aim is to create a regional and then provincial contingent of young peer educators who, supported by undergraduate volunteers, will then deliver training in leadership and key skills: ICT, literacy, numeracy, communication. By capacity building and empowering youth effectively, Pakistan can capitalise on its youth dividend.

The peer training for University of Gujrat students was delivered in May 2012 through the Global Youth Leaders Programme (hereafter GYL). This programme was developed in partnership with Dr. June Thompson, Director of the California Association of Student Councils (hereafter CASC), and Anton Lopukhin of the Association of Young Leaders (hereafter AYL) Russia. GYL is an unaffiliated body of like-minded individuals and organisations that share a common purpose in empowering young people for positive change through peer education and leadership. GYL has been delivering collaborative peer leadership programmes for a decade, with individual organisation histories going back to the 1950s (CASC, n.d.). The youth leadership conferences consist of up to two hundred participants, working in groups of eight to twelve people aged 13 to 24. Conferences last five days and are divided into two stages, and include staff development training for those who wish to become trainers themselves. Conferences consist of small groups, facilitated by peer leaders and educators who assist the young people in developing skills in communication, decision-making, interaction, strategic planning, and meeting facilitation. Practical training helps young people learn basic mediation skills and acquire oral presentation skills. There is a very supportive atmosphere and a positive attitude. The programme is run by an appropriate number of trainers, three gammas (who support the trainers) and a conference director (Gurjee, 2010; Melling & Khan, 2012).

The GYL programme is the result of combining the talents of young people with corporate training and staff development in a manner that is socially and culturally appropriate. The CASC and AYL have been influenced by the training methods of organisations such as Interaction Associates, Blanchard Training and Development, and Pfeiffer and Company to develop their programme (Association of Young Leaders, n.d.). The University of Central Lancashire Centre for Volunteering have incorporated the pedagogy of Freire and the transformational leadership theory of Yin Cheong: "A leader is one who not only adapts behaviour to the situation, but also transforms it" (Cheong in T. Bush & L. Bell (Eds.), 2002, pp. 59–65) This transformational model provides a workable structure on which to develop an appropriate leadership style. "Young leaders have a transformational role in developing their team to face challenges and to deal with testing projects effectively and efficiently" (Melling & Khan, 2012). The key task was to develop this model into a workable programme to be delivered by undergraduates within communities on a cascading basis.

There are significant challenges to the development of any project within Pakistan. The first and foremost is access and safety. Parts of Pakistan are considered dangerous for Western people to travel in and it is necessary to get the full support of the government before any joint work is carried out. The University of Central Lancashire worked with the Pakistan Consul General and the Pakistan Higher Education Commission in the planning of the programme. This project complements work currently undertaken by the Ministry of the Punjab in developing youth for positive change and overcoming negative cultures and practices that restrict young peoples' opportunities (Sharif, 2012). The second challenge is Pakistan's culture, and this is why Freire's pedagogy is so important, as it allows the programme to fully embrace the culture without losing any of its impact. The programme must be peer led or it simply becomes a vehicle for depositing knowledge. The programme had to be developed by and driven through the young people of Pakistan. Furthermore, the Freire approach allows the process to fully embrace cultural norms of behaviour and networking. For example, engagement with many Pakistani institutions or communities is dependent on the understanding of Baradarism, a cultural concept derived from the Persian meaning "brother" or "family." A person's influence within a community is therefore based upon his clan connections rather than his knowledge, ideology, or expertise. This challenge was mitigated, as the project leader was from the Pakistani Gujrat diaspora and had strong family connections within the necessary networks. Without this link, it would have been difficult to engage with any of the host institutions.[7]

The University of Gujrat engaged forty student volunteers to support the project (University of Gujrat, 2012). They came from a variety of academic disciplines, but the majority were studying social sciences. The students were put into "learning circles" or groups of ten for the duration of the training. Each group was led by two undergraduate peer educators from the UK and the United States. Of the two, at least one was from the Pakistani diaspora. The training utilised a blend of situational problem-posing techniques with formal leadership skill development. The methodology worked well as it allowed the students to understand the model within the context of their own culture. Moreover, there was a strong focus on the action/reflection praxis model and the development of dialogue. This concept was new to the Pakistani students as they had been taught in the banking style: "repeaters of texts, read but not known." As a result of an undemocratic approach to teaching, students are sometimes "incapable of taking up a cognitive position" (Freire, 1974, p. 133). However, if these young people were going to become peer educators in the transformational sense, they must understand the process of dialogue (a democratic exchange of views or a horizontal relationship) as opposed to anti-dialogue (a vertical relationship, or being told what to think) (Freire, 1970, p. 49). In *Education for Critical Consciousness*, Freire states: "The less critical capacity a group possesses, the more ingenuously it treats problems and the more superficially it discusses subjects" (Freire, 1970, p. 33). It was necessary to create a learning environment where "the class is not a class, but a meeting place where knowledge is sought and not transmitted" (Freire, 1970, p. 133).

The training was composed of five days of dialogue, or "a critical search for something" (Freire, 1970, p. 49). During this period, the students discussed what they would seek in an "ideal" peer educator. They also looked at themselves analytically through "time line" methodology, reflecting on particular incidents in their lives and how these had influenced decisions and actions. They worked on problem posing, applying theoretical concepts regarding such issues as conflict resolution within a situational context. The students engaged in dialogue on the dichotomy among consciensisation, culture, and tradition. This was particularly challenging, as any effective peer leadership/education process needs to fully respect and utilise the values and norms of the cultural group engaged.

One issue the peer education process at the University of Gujrat raised was that of emotionality. The training takes the student on an exploratory journey that opens up thinking and self-realisation in many ways, some of which are quite emotional. Moreover, the actual process of moving from a "naïve" way of thinking to consensisation is a challenging process for the student in itself. It is important therefore that the peer educators fully understand how to deal with emotionality in the learning group and to be able to provide a positive and supportive outlet, both for themselves and for the students (Gallagher & Harrington, 2012). This was done by creating "closure" sessions at the end of every day, in which the group could off-load and share their feelings openly with others. The end of the conference was incredibly emotional as it marked the end of one journey and the start of another. The process is transformational, and opens up new ways of thinking. It also raises the expectations of the students in terms of how they view themselves and the world around them. These expectations must be managed in an effective manner. Students cannot be pushed through a transformational process, ending up with no options to pursue the outcomes. Each student went away with personal learning goals and actions, and a new learning community was developed through online social networking sites. One collective goal is to keep the process alive by bringing the students from Pakistan to the UK to undertake stage two of their training and the staff development programme. With this in place, the students will be in a position to deliver the programme within the villages of Gujrat.

CONCLUSIONS

In his recent speech on education, Sharif spoke passionately about the need for Pakistan to develop its own destiny and how young people would be the key in this. He emphasized the need for Pakistan to make changes from within, rather than going outside with "a begging bowl" (Sharif, 2012). The objective of this programme is to support University of Gujrat students to develop a tool kit for change that will meet local and regional needs, with a wider long-term aim of introducing the concept to other regions. There is a significant issue with illiteracy in Pakistan, with one-third having literate fathers, and a much lower proportion, estimated at around 10% of the population, having literate mothers (Sultana, 2010, p. 1). A Freire-influenced programme that mobilizes undergraduates as peer educators in the delivery of a tool kit for change has the potential for a significant impact on communities.

Student or university engagement with local communities is not pervasive in Pakistan, other than for the purpose of social science research, although the recent Laptop Project in the Punjab is a step in the right direction (Sharif, 2012). Furthermore, there is no framework or infrastructure from which to deliver a student-led tool kit for change from the University of Gujrat. Nevertheless, the Pakistan Higher Education Commission has supported the development of this concept at the University of Gujrat and there is significant student interest. In May 2012, Khan and Melling conducted a consultative workshop to gauge the scope for developing such an infrastructure (Melling & Khan, 2012). This workshop opened up a much wider range of possibilities than youth leadership training alone.

For the purposes of the consultation, sixty participants were seated at nine round tables, each table representing a faculty: Botany, Mass Communication, English, Chemistry, Physics, Maths, Environmental Science, Psychology, Economics. Each table nominated a scribe and a presenter. The participants were briefed on the objectives of the exercise. Each table was asked to consider the following and write feedback in bullet-point format:

1. The benefit of such an infrastructure to the Gujrat community
2. The benefit to the individual student in taking part in such activity
3. The benefit to the university

The participants favoured focusing on the benefits that a specific faculty-related project could bring, rather than generic benefits.

This exercise was useful as it added further detailed insight into what the individual faculties could offer. However, there was no time to conduct a consultation into the barriers that faculties would face in the development and delivery of such programmes and how they might plan to overcome them. Even so, it presented a good starting point from which to develop a university-wide programme. The students and staff demonstrated a real understanding of peer-led social action and its benefits to community, students, and the university. Each representative group had the capacity to develop its own tool kit programme based on the subject area. Melling and Khan (2012) suggested that the university has a central infrastructure, which will have a supporting and coordinating role for satellite centres in each of the faculties. In partnership with University of Gujrat students, Melling and Khan produced a development framework. The students have the skills and enthusiasm to create a truly effective social action programme, influenced by the philosophy of Paulo Freire. They are ethically minded and wish to contribute to making a better society and would take up the challenge with enthusiasm should the infrastructure be in place.

ACKNOWLEDGMENTS

The authors would like to thank the Professor M. Nizamuddin, Vice Chancellor of the University of Gujrat, Pakistan, and all his staff and students for supporting this programme. Also, thanks to the Pakistan Higher Education Commission and the Pakistan Information Minister for their support. We would also like to extend our thanks to the Pakistan Consul General Mr Batthe for all his help in making this happen and promoting sustainability, Dr. June Thompson for all her support in directing the training in Pakistan, and all our GYL volunteers from the UK and United States. Finally, thank you to John Quirk, Director of the International Office, and Professor Keith Faulks at the University of Central Lancashire for giving us this opportunity.

NOTES

1. Gujrat in Pakistan is not to be confused with Gujrat in India.
2. The work of the Centre for Volunteering and Community Leadership has been named as an example of best practice in the recent Joseph Rowntree Foundation report in the ways that universities support communities in the UK (Robinson, Zass-Ogilvie, & Hudson, 2012).
3. Zaidi draws attention to the wider link between weak state infrastructures, of which education is only a part, and support for militancy: "Factoring in the support for militant religious groups and the rampant grievances against the US, it seems that the poor are more prepared to opt for militancy instead of an ineffective governance structure as a solution to their problems" (Zaidi, 2010).
4. Mohammed Ali Jinnah is referred to as Quaid e Azam, which is Urdu for "great leader."

5. Allama Iqbal, also referred to as Sir Muhammad Iqbal, was a philosopher and poet who was considered the founder of the Pakistan Movement.

6. Haque notes that as parents are important stakeholders in the lives of young people, their views must be included in any policy and practice (Haque, 2010).

7. The Ministry of the Punjab recognise that the practice of Baradarism has a negative impact on a young person's life chances and that if you do not know the right people you may be excluded from opportunities. During a recent programme of distributing laptops to young people, the Minister of the Punjab stated: "Laptops are being given to the talented students in recognition of their hard work and not on the basis of 'Baradarism' or any 'Safarish'" (Sharif, 2012).

REFERENCES

Association of Young Leaders. (n.d.). Retrieved from www.AYL.org.ru

British Council. (2009). *Pakistan: The next generation*. New York, NY: British Council.

British Red Cross. (n.d.). Peer education volunteering. Retrieved September 25, 2012, from http://www.redcross.org.uk/Get-involved/Volunteer/Volunteering-for-young-people/Peer-education-volunteering

California Association of Student Councils. (n.d.). Retrieved from www.casc.org.

Cheong, Y. (2002). Leadership and strategy. In T. Bush & L. Bell (Eds.), *Principles and practices of management* (pp. 59–65). London, England: Paul Chapman.

Commission on Integration and Cohesion. (2007). *Our shared future*. London, England: Cabinet Office.

Elliott, M. (2011). *Remembering Brother Michael: Gregorian Friar, Priest, Prophet, Activist, Missiologist, Educationalist and Friend*. Retrieved from http://michaelcelliott.wordpress.com/

Faizunnisa, A. (2005). *The poverty trap: Leveling the playing field for young people*. Islamabad, Pakistan: Population Council.

Freire Institute. (2012). Concepts used by Paulo Freire. Retrieved from www.freire.org/paulo-freire/concepts-used-by-paulo-freire/

Freire, P. (2007). *Education for critical consciousness*. New York, NY: Continuum.

Freire, P. (1996). *Pedagogy of the oppressed*. London, England: Penguin.

Freire, P. (1974). *Education for critical consciousness*. London: A&C Black.

Gallagher, A., & Harrington, F. (2012, July). *The impact on religious studies teachers of emotionality in the HE classroom; A research in progress*. Paper presented at the Foundations for the Future meeting, Greenwich, England.

Greenfield, M., & Ryder, A. (2010). *Roads to success: Economic and social inclusion of Gypsies and Travellers*. Buckingham, England: An Irish Traveller Movement in Britain Report.

Gurjee, A. M. (2010). *Empower to lead*. Preston, England: UCLan.

Haque, M. U. (2010). *Discrimination starts at home*. Islamabad, Pakistan: Population Council.

Melling, A., & Khan, W. (2012). *Development of a centre of volunteering and community leadership at the University of Gujrat*. Preston, England: UCLan.

Perilous journey. (2012, February 11). *The Economist*.

Robinson, F., Zass-Ogilvie, I., & Hudson, A. R. (2012, September). *How can universities support disadvantaged communities?* London, England: JRF.

Save the Children. (2004). *Effective peer education: Working with children and young people on sexual and reproductive health and HIV/AIDS*. London, England: Save the Children.

Sharif, M. S. (2012, February 18). Punjab government accomplishing development projects from its own resources. Retrieved from http://www.cm.punjab.gov.pk/index.php?q=node/1372

Sultana, M. (2010). *Two worlds under the same roof*. Islamabad, Pakistan: Population Council.

University of Gujrat. (2012, May). Closing ceremony of Global Youth Leadership conference at UOG. Retrieved from http://www.uog.edu.pk/index.php/news/events/561-closing-ceremony-of-global-youth-leadership-conference-at-uog

Zaidi, M. (2010). *A link between poverty & radicalization*. Islamabad, Pakistan: PAK Institute for Peace Studies.

CHAPTER NINETEEN

The Changing Life Patterns of the Veddhas of Sri Lanka: Translocation from a Forest Environment to an Agricultural Settlement

ASOKA JAYASENA AND SUSILA KUMARI EMBEKKE

INTRODUCTION

The accelerated Mahaweli Development Scheme was undertaken by the government of Sri Lanka in 1983. Under this scheme, several Veddha families were induced by the government of Sri Lanka to abandon their traditional forest homelands in the Dambana region and to move into newly created colonization scheme in Zone C of the Accelerated Mahaweli Development Scheme (AMDS). This chapter focuses on the life patterns of the Veddha families since their translocation from their forest environment to an agricultural settlement.

Veddhas and Theories About Their Origin

Veddhas refer to themselves as *wanniyalaiatto*, meaning "forest dwellers." They are an indigenous group of people living in Sri Lanka. They have lived in Sri Lanka for thousands of years as a group, preserving their ethnic identity. Seligmann (1911) has described the Veddhas as "one of the most primitive" racial groups. It is believed that the Veddhas have descended from the union of Prince Vijaya, considered as the founding father of the Sinhala nation, with Kuveni, the Yakka princess who befriended him and helped him to vanquish the Yakka clan, who are still considered to be the earliest inhabitants of Sri Lanka. The island's chronicle *Mahavansa*, written in the 6th century A.D., narrates the story of Vijaya, who arrived from India with five hundred of his retinue, took over the island with the help of Princess Kuveni. However, once he established his power in the island, he wanted to consecrate himself as the king of Sri Lanka. The members of his retinue were of opinion that this could only be properly done if there was a royal princess as his consort. Giving in to the wishes of his retinue, Vijaya repudiated Kuveni and got down a princess of royal birth from the Pandya country in south India. Hapless Kuveni, along with the two children she got from the union with Vijaya, was expelled from Vijaya's kingdom. During her journey and while on her way with the children, she met her death at the hands of some of her kinsmen, who were in hiding. The two children fled to the highlands located in the Ratnapura district and the union of the brother and the sister is supposed to have given rise to the Veddhas.

Because this is the accepted version of the story, it allows the Veddhas to claim that they are the autochthonous possessors of the land. The current scientific interpretation is that they are descended from the island's original Neolithic community dating from at least 14,000 B.C. However, it is accepted that the successive waves of immigration and colonization since Vijaya's arrival have repeatedly forced this indigenous community to choose between two survival strategies. One was either to be assimilated into other cultures or to retreat further and further into the forest, which was gradually shrinking with the opening of new settlements. It is an accepted fact that uncounted thousands of these original inhabitants have been absorbed into mainstream Sinhala society in the Northern Central regions and the Uva Provinces and those in the East Coast to the Tamil society in Sri Lanka.

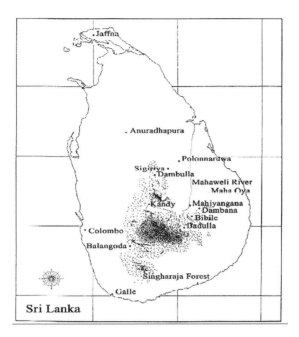

Figure 19.1. Map of Sri Lanka showing Veddha settlements.

Several authors have from time to time mentioned the Veddhas in their writings. Seligmann and Seligmann (1911) were some of the earliest authors. R. L. Spittel (1944) has pointed out that the Veddhas are a vanishing trail. Dharmadasa (1990) as well as Sugathapala (1972), who lived for sometime with the Veddhas studying their language, have acknowledged that Seligmann and Seligmann (1911) were unaware of the Vijaya – Kuveni legend. Senarath Paranavitana, the first Sinhalese archaeological commissioner, citing the word "milaka," identified in one of the early Brahmi inscriptions dated in the first century A.D., is of view that it refers to the autochthonous inhabitants of the island. He further adds that this term had no derogatory connotation and suggests that a section of this indigenous population apparently welcomed the new, prospering civilization established by the Aryans and that some became partners of the new civilization, while those who did not take that step were left to their traditional ways. This latter group is considered as the precursors of contemporary Veddhas.

Robert Knox (1861), who remained as a prisoner of the Kandyan king, and John Davy (1821) and Tennent (1860) all have mentioned Veddhas in their writings. The latter two in particular have mentioned that the Veddhas considered themselves to be belonging to a high caste. Seligmann and Seligmann (1911) too have endorsed this point when they stated that the Veddhas were ashamed to acknowledge any union with the Sinhalese. Nandadeva Wijesekara (1964) has put forward the notion that the Veddhas are an admixture of at least three racial types, namely, Negrito, Australoid, and Mediterranean. It is the view of some of the anthropologists that there is definitely a racial difference between the Veddhas and the other inhabitants of the island.

Original Way of Life

Preferring a nomadic way of life, the Veddhas resisted a settled lifestyle. They lived in huts built in areas close to rock caves and used them as shelters during the rainy season. In addition to hunting, which provided their main food, they supplemented their meal with fruits and bee honey. They also practiced *chena cultivation* (a burn and slash method). The grains they sowed were of a wide variety: *kurakkan*, maize, Indian corn, cow pea, and *mung* (green gram). Vegetables such as brinjals (eggplant), varieties of gourds, and fruits like plantains were popular among them. They did not take to dairy farming as they believed that the milk of the animals should be given to animals only. The children were fed with breast milk as long as they wanted it. The Veddhas' cooking habits were very primitive and the only ingredients they used were chillies and salt. Even though these food habits were considered primitive it is evident that their diet consisted of the basic requirements and was balanced and nutritious. They were averse to agriculture.

The original Veddha religion was a cult based on the worship of ancestral spirits such as *nayayaku* (a demon referred to as Naya). The Veddhas seek their blessings to keep their dead happy. However, recently there have been many conversions to Buddhism and Hinduism, depending on location. Their marriage customs were very simple. It involved the woman tying a bark rope, woven by herself, around the man who has been chosen by the elders to be her mate. This confirmed that the selected individual was her mate. The clothing of the Veddhas included a loincloth worn by the men below the waist; and the women normally wore a piece of cloth that covered their breasts and the knees. Their social structure was based on matrilineal rights.

Very little information is available about their population numbers. The 1881 Census gives a figure of 2,222 as the number of Veddhas in the island. However, the 1911 Census has recorded a figure of 5,342, while the 1921 census records a lower figure of 4,510. In the 1963 Census, the Veddhas had not been counted as a separate ethnic group, but it has been estimated that there were about 2,000 of them in 1985.

Three major groups of Veddhas have been identified. These are the Forest Veddhas, Village Veddhas, and Coast Veddhas. According to Seligmann and Seligmann (1911), the Coast Veddhas had intermarried a great deal with the Tamils and are Hindus, while the Village Veddhas, located in Bintenna and Tamankaduwa areas, had intermarried with the Sinhalese but yet remained primitive in nature.

The third group, the Jungle or Forest Veddhas are considered tamer. At present, the major group is located in Dambana and the person who is considered to be their chieftain resides there and normally, it is he who makes decisions pertaining to any aspect that affects them. But there are instances when his decisions were not heeded. This chapter actually focuses on a situation that arose when two sub-chieftains went against the chief's decision and decided to move out from their natural forest habitat and settle down in an agricultural settlement, in keeping with the wishes of the government of Sri Lanka.

Actually, the Veddhas are in a vulnerable position due to two reasons. One is that they never received secure land tenure deeds that recognized their custodianship over their traditional forest homelands. The second reason was that they had no say in any of the decisions made pertaining to them. Such decisions were made in far away Colombo, and they were never represented or consulted in such matters. The Veddhas do not understand the modern concepts of real estate belonging to individuals but they hold the view that they and their ancestors' spirits are part of the forest land which they are now living in, protecting them from all outside onslaughts. They do not understand the concept of acreage but know only the natural landmarks such as hills, rivers, and the like. This weakness, if one can calls it that, has resulted in them being repeatedly swindled out of their ancestral lands. What happened to them when the AMDS was undertaken by the government of Sri Lanka is the latest such episode that falls into this category.

In 1930s, 1940s, and 1950s, large irrigation and colonization schemes deprived the Veddhas of a major portion of their lands in Polonnaruwa, Mahiyangana, and Amparai. In 1977, the AMDS was launched. Under this scheme, traditional lands of the Veddhas were taken over for the benefits of other communities. No equitable compensation was offered to them. Instead, vast areas of forest land were logged and inundated or taken over. The lands lying between the western chain of reservoirs and the Maduru Oya irrigation dam were declared as the Maduru Oya National Park as a habitat for displaced wildlife and as a protected catchment area of the massive Maduru Oya reservoir. Entry to this national park as in the case of other national parks was by permit only. Thus, the forest lands where the Veddhas hunted for thousands of years were taken over and they were categorized as poachers and trespassers with barriers and outposts and guards stationed along the demarcated boundaries. Despite the Dambana chieftain's plea to "stop trying to convert us into cultivators," these hapless people were evacuated to villages in the Mahaweli Development Scheme Zones C and B by the government officials who had no clue about their ways of living nor understood their way of life. One such location was Hennanigala. About eight families who obstinately refused to be evacuated along with the Veddha chief were allowed to remain at Dambana, most likely with the idea that they would be forced to leave after the death of the chieftain, who at that time was quite old. This is confirmed in the 1987 Master

Plan for Maduru Oya National Park. However, Tisahamy, the Veddha chieftain, did not die until 1999, at the age of 96. The families that were evacuated were settled in Hennanigala under Kalu Appu, the sub-chief who agreed to the relocation. Thus, they started a new life at Hennanigala, the rockiest part of the land in the Mahaweli C Zone, as agriculturalists! (See Figure 2.). Hennanigala is bounded by Nawa–Medagama in the south, the irrigation channel Maduru Oya in the east, massive Hennanigala rock in the west, and in the north by the land area that came to be known as "North Hennanigala, the new abode of the Veddhas."

This chapter focuses on this group who were shifted against the wishes of their chieftain and what happened to them in the aftermath. Using Freire's cultural invasion theory this chapter intends to examine the lifestyle of this indigenous group of people and identify whether the change has been for their benefit or whether instead they jumped "from the frying pan into the fire."

Figure 19.2. Massive Hennanigala Rock.

Theory of Cultural Invasion

Freire's theory of cultural invasion emerged from his experiences in Brazil. The unequal relationship between the powerful landowners and the powerless peasants shaped and moulded Freire's views and ideas. According to Freire, a cultural invasion takes place when one group or a nation subjects another group to colonization. When this occurs, the group that was subjected to colonization loses their cultural identity as they begin to see reality through the eyes of their invaders. They begin to perceive that the culture of the invaders is far superior and that they cannot hold their own among this superior culture. They not only feel inferior but powerless as well. Thus, the oppressed inferiors absorb the culture of the oppressors and get alienated from their own culture. Moreover, the superior powers impose their values and norms upon the oppressed and this is purposefully achieved without taking into consideration their reality. According to Freire, cultural invasion simply implies the "superiority" of the invader and the "inferiority" of those who are invaded, as well as the imposition of the values by the former (Freire, 1993, p. 141). He further adds that "cultural invasion further signifies that the ultimate seat of decisions regarding the action of those who invaded lies not with them but with the invaders" (ibid.). Based on the above premise, this theory could be easily applied to examine the situation of the Veddhas after their relocation.

RESEARCH DESIGN

Using the above theoretical framework this chapter focuses on the life style of the Veddhas since their relocation from their traditional homelands to Hennanigala in 1983. The displaced group consisted of the Veddhas who were living in the villages of Kandeganvila, Kotabahiniya, Kotayayaya, Kurenvila, and Kotagasvila. All these areas were part of the acreage that was under the chieftain of Dambana.

The Purpose of the Study

The purpose of the study presented in this chapter was to identify whether there was any change in the lifestyle of the Veddhas since their translocation from a forest habitat to an agricultural settlement. In other words, to determine whether there was a cultural invasion by the dominant community that suppressed these helpless indigenous people.

Research Questions

What are the changes that have taken place in the lifestyle of the Veddhas after their translocation? The main research question was supported by a number of subsidiary questions that focused on:

- Living conditions—housing, toilet facilities, water supply, and other amenities including luxury items;
- Economic activities—occupations and the type of work engaged in by both men and women;

- Marriage, children, and family life—type of marriage, marriage partners, marital relationships;
- Children and the child-rearing practices—health care, punishments, and taboos;
- Socio-cultural practices—traditions and habits, religious practices, language, dress, food habits, health practices, status of women, social life;
- Changes in values and ethics.

Research Site

The research site selected for this study is Hennanigala, the new location where the evacuated members of the Veddha community was resettled. The boundaries, which demarcate Hennanigala, are described above. The research site is accessible by foot and vehicle both, and the two researchers were familiar with the area as they had undertaken previous research in the same location pertaining to the quality of life of the Veddha women. As such their prior knowledge of the area facilitated the study. Moreover, the principal of the school of Nawa Medagama, Maha Vidyalaya (who happened to be a student of the principal researcher), lived in the area, which was about two miles away from Hennanigala. In Sri Lanka, being the principal of a large, rural school like Nawa Medagama *Vidyalaya* (Nava Medagama school) carries a great deal of prestige and as such the principal is considered as a privileged, influential person. Since he had lived in the area for about thirty years, he is known to both the older and the younger generations. Also, there are some children from the Veddha community who have attended and are in attendance in this school. Therefore, he is known to almost everyone at Hennanigala. This made the researchers' task easier.

Research Sample

The research sample consisted of a number of first, second, and third generation families. Reaching out to the respondents was made easy, as all three generations lived in the same compound in most cases. Altogether, the sample consisted of 105 individuals—men, women, and children (see Table 1). When selecting the respondents an effort was made to get a purposive sample drawn from all three generations and some families that still had close ties with the kith and kin at Dambana.

Table 19.1. The Research Sample.

	Children	Men	Women
1st generation	–	05	12
2nd generation	13	06	18
3rd generation	22	09	20
Total	35	20	50

The last requirement was easily fulfilled as two daughters of the late chieftain readily volunteered as respondents. Out of the 650 families living in Hennanigala belonging to three generations, 105 members were interviewed while 25 family units were closely surveyed. Some of the respondents also came from some of the closely surveyed 25 families.

Research Methodology

The research was conducted using qualitative research methodology. Based on a single site case study, data was collected through interviews and observations. Eight research assistants who are post-graduate students trained in research methodology participated in the data collection. An open-ended brief questionnaire that focused on the aspects highlighted in the research questions was provided to the research assistants. They were given instructions to take down their observations and impressions, paying attention to the body language of the respondents as well. Apart from the interviews and observations, the researchers undertook a survey of a cross section of different categories of houses.

DISCUSSION

Living Conditions

Housing—When the Veddhas were moved from Dambana to Hennanigala, 53 families were given land for housing and cultivation (CENWOR, 1994). In addition, the Mahaweli Authority built houses for them. All of these houses adopted the same block plan. This type of house had a square area of about 120 square feet with a cooking area of about 40 square feet and a room with an area of another 40 square feet. It also had a small verandah of about 20 square feet. At the edge of the verandah there was a half wall on which people could sit. A block plan of this category of houses is shown in Figure 3. Some of these houses had tiled roofs, cement floors, and brick walls. Initially there were about 15 such houses at Hennanigala (see Figure 4). Those who did not get houses built a simple hut with mud that contained two or three rooms and a separate cooking area. There were instances where small boutiques were run in the front portion of the house, as can be seen in Figure 5. The last category of houses had only one room and the cooking area was separate. The main room was about 40 square feet. Various non-governmental organizations (NGOs) and outsiders helped the people to build the last two categories of houses by providing them with lavatory pans, tiles, and some other items necessary for building construction. Very often these houses had only one window.

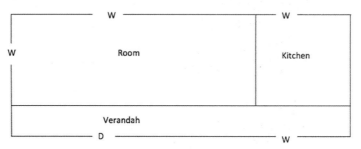

Figure 19.3. Ground Floor plan of a model house built by Mahaweli Authority.

The conditions now have changed immensely. Most of the first category of houses mentioned above have now been either demolished or extended. In place of the demolished buildings, new houses have been built that to a great extent resemble the houses of the Sinhalese people living in the nearby area. (See Figures 6 and 7.) These new houses have a large living area, a number of bedrooms, a verandah, and a large kitchen area (see Table 2). These houses were built with bricks and cement and then plastered. However, about 60% of the houses are without plaster even though people are living in them. Some of the floors are laid with cement. This resulted in the houses being dusty and unclean although the children were playing and eating in those surroundings. Their pets also lived with the people.

There were two houses among those that the researchers visited. These houses were painted with a cream colour and a touch of orange. At the extreme end of the compound was another house that is occupied by the daughter of the landowner. The daughter's house comes under the second category of the houses described above.

The most interesting feature that was noted in all these houses, both the new and old, was the tendency to keep the windows shut. The glass windowpanes in some of the new houses were covered with white or black polythene, either from the inside or on the outside. As a result the rooms and the living area in those houses were gloomy. However, about 40% of the houses were very clean. A majority of the houses indicated that little attention had been paid to cleanliness. In those houses, the clothes were strewn everywhere on chairs and beds. Some clothes were hung on a clothesline. The furniture used was made out of plastic.

Figure 19.4. The initial type of house built by Mahaweli Authority where an attempt has been made to expand and renovate.

Figure 19.5. Second category of houses built with mud.

Table 19.2. The number of rooms in the houses surveyed.

Number of rooms	Number of houses	Percentage
1 room	7	28%
2 rooms	4	16%
3 rooms	8	32%
4 rooms	5	20%
5 rooms	—	—
6 rooms	1	4%
Total		100%

Most of the houses had large gardens. Some had demarcated their boundaries by planting colourful hedges, which were trimmed in most cases. Some had used part of the garden to cultivate fruit trees and leafy vegetables. Some houses had potted Bougainvillea plants, which were kept in a row in the front of the house. In certain houses part of the space has been utilized to open a boutique, as could seen in Figure 5.

Figure 19.6. An incomplete modern house.

Figure 19.7. Completed new house.

Out of the houses that were surveyed, 40% had cement floors while 60% had mud and cowdung mixed floors. The doorframes in the one and two-roomed houses were very narrow and the number of doors was limited. The one and two-roomed houses had only the main door. Though the rooms were partitioned with walls, there were no doors to the rooms. The newly built houses had a separate fireplace with a chimney. Some houses had no chimney but the fireplace was built on an elevated platform. The houses built earlier had no special cooking area but the inhabitants had kept three stones or bricks and used that as the fireplace for cooking. This was the normal pattern in Dambana. Out of the 25 houses, 68% had separate kitchens. In 32% of the houses, cooking was done inside the house. It was quite amazing to see that none of the houses used clay pots and pans. All the houses had aluminum pots and pans and even their water was stored in aluminum pots. This is quite contrary to the habits of the educated Sinhalese people, the majority of whom still prefer to use clay pots and pans. In Dambana, the norm was the clay pots and pans.

Toilet Facilities— The Veddhas are not accustomed to using toilets. They roamed the jungle and made use of it whenever they wanted to relieve themselves. However, after they were relocated at Hennanigala, Mahaweli Authority was very particular that they get used to the habit of using toilets. Therefore, with help of several NGOs they provided the inhabitants with squatting pans and 750 rupees and instructed them to build their own water seal lavatories. When these researchers conducted their earlier study, only about 10% of the families had constructed what could be called a "lavatory" (CENWOR, 1994). They had constructed temporary structures that were covered with cadjans. They had dug a big hole and placed the squatting pan and were using it as a latrine. Those who did not even have this were using the Hennanigala rock or the bund of the tank for this purpose. As a result, when the rains set in the whole area got polluted and unhygienic. But the conditions have changed very much now. Practically every new house has a water seal lavatory that was constructed a few feet away from the house (see Figure 8).

Out of the 25 houses that were surveyed, 24 (96%) had toilets. This is a vast improvement from the situation in 1994. Out of these, 92% are water seal lavatories. There was no tap water available for use in the lavatories but the toilets were very clean. These were maintained very hygienically, and even cleaning brushes along with disinfectants were kept in the toilets. In the rest of the houses surveyed, 4% had pit latrines and the members of the first generation preferred to use these instead of the water seal toilets. At the same time, it was revealed that some members of the older generation, despite the availability of toilets, still prefer to use the tank bund as well as the open areas or the little bit of available jungle areas for this purpose. Some of them stated that the limited food consumption prevented them from the need to use toilets daily. However, the second and third generation members who had attended school at least for a few years indicated that their education prevented them from sticking to the habits of the older generation, as they are well aware it is unhygienic to do so. This is an indication that clearly shows that they have adopted the habits of the Sinhalese families living in the vicinity.

Figure 19.8. Showing the electricity lines that go through this locality and the newly built houses with a latrine built away from the house.

Figure 19.9. Hennanigala Tank —water source to many. Meets personal needs (bathing) and agricultural requirements.

Water Supply—When the Veddhas moved to Hennanigala, almost all of them got their water requirements from the adjoining massive tank. It was a common sight in 1994 to see the women carrying water from the tank to meet their household requirements. Actually they carry two pots of water, one on their head and one in the hand. The tank water was used for washing, bathing, and for agricultural purposes. However, even now, though 100% of the houses are not self-sufficient with the water requirements, about 80% of the houses have their own wells, in the compound which are nicely covered. Those who did not have their own well got water from a neighbour's well.

In addition, the researchers came across a few "community wells," which some people used as a group. Mahaweli Authority had dug a number of wells when the Veddhas were relocated but some of them had been closed down, as there were no underground springs. One community well had a surrounding wall, and the researchers noticed that on the day they visited the research site a group was cleaning the well by removing the water and adding purifying material such as charcoal bundles and various other medicinal herbs that they believe purify the water. In Dambana, of course, they were used to intricate water-purifying methods. Some others still use tank water or draw water from the irrigation channels. It is a common sight to see women and men enjoying their bath in the tank. This is not a rare sight in Sri Lanka, as most people enjoy their baths in the rivers and streams (see Figure 7). None of the houses had tap water. Electricity is a recent luxury in Hennanigala; at present a majority of the houses have electricity connections.

Other Amenities— Some of the new houses had very few storage facilities such as wooden cupboards or steel cupboards to store their belongings. In the smaller houses, the inhabitants' belongings were kept in cardboard boxes and stacked under beds or in the corner of a room. Most of the houses, almost 75%, have luxury items such as radios, television sets, and even laptop computers. However, those who lack "luxury items" very often visit a neighbour's house to watch television or listen to the radio.

Table 19.3. Luxury items (as defined by the Veddhas) available in the survey sample.

Item	Percentage
Radios	56%
Television sets	68%
Refrigerators	8%
Fans	16%
Electric Irons	20%
Mobile phones	04%
Tractors	08%
Bicycles	16%
Organ	04%
Sewing machines	12%
Three wheelers	08%

Apart from the above, people in a few houses had simply discarded radios and television sets that they said need to be repaired but, due to financial constraints, they could not afford to do so as this involved taking those items to a repair shop, which is not available close by. They indicated that since some of the houses do not have electricity they use car batteries to run the radios and the television sets. Old car batteries seem to be freely available for a nominal sum in garages and petrol sheds located in Medagama town. There are no telecommunication lines that run through the village and as a result no landline phones are available.

There is a strong sense of community feeling among them. They help one another and share what they have as a community. Lack of any specific facilities is not a great hindrance to them as such, as they are willing to share whatever they possess with the others in the community. This characteristic is hardly visible among the more civilized others living in the surrounding areas. Cultural invasion does not seem to have created an impact here!

The researchers noticed that in one house a young boy of about 19 years old was logging on to the Internet. When questioned, he said that they are trying to listen to music but his guilty face and that of his friend apparently created doubts in the minds of the researchers as to what they were searching for. However, there was no way to probe further. Since most of the parents are uneducated, even if the Internet and technology is used for erratic purposes, it is difficult to identify such activities or to implement precautionary measures. The other interesting feature that was denoted was that quite a large number of school children used bicycles to go to school. It is a common sight now but a few years back the school children used to walk long distances to reach their schools. We came across one boy in the study, about 16 years old, who, according to his mother, refused to go to school as he does not own a bicycle. The mother said that it is with difficulty that she feeds them at least a few meals and that she does not have the means to buy a bicycle for him. This particular boy who has refused to go to school as the mother failed to buy the bicycle apparently has gotten used to fishing in the tank with his friends as a leisure time activity. He eats the fish, with his friends, on the bund itself after cooking them over a fire. Cooking food over an open fire was one of the traditional ways of the Veddhas.

Another feature that was identified was the extensive use of plastic chairs, tables, buckets, and other utility items. This is a new trend that was not seen at Dambana. In areas closer to jungles, hardwood furniture is freely available and the use of plastic stuff is not the norm in Sri Lanka. However, these members of the relocated community of the Veddhas have got used to using cheaper furniture, which could mean two things. One is that they do not have the money to buy wooden furniture and the second is plastic chairs and tables are much easier to use, as these are not as heavy as wooden furniture. It is difficult to identify the exact reason even though one or two people indicated that plastic furniture is easier to maintain, more colourful, and easier to handle than wooden furniture. It was evident from their body language that they did not have sufficient funds to invest in wooden furniture even though they did not want to come out with this fact. Among 40% of the houses surveyed, many had electrical kitchen equipment such as food processors and electric grinders. A few water filters too were observed. The traditional grinding stone, which is a must in most of the houses belonging to Sinhalese and Tamils, was missing in these houses. The grinding stone is extensively used to grind pulses and various ingredients for cooking. It is not as expensive as blenders and other electrical equipment. Yet, it was a sad thing to denote that these traditional habits and ways of living are fast disappearing, even among the Veddhas.

During the research period, it was observed that many men were riding motorcycles and scooters but these men did not come from the surveyed 25 families. The roads in this locality are very narrow and it is difficult for two vehicles to cross each other. Even certain sections of the access roads are not motorable. The researchers were informed that a road development project is under way. The only evidence that could support this statement were heaps of stones and sand stacked in certain places by the road side. It is not possible to use cars as parts of the roads were washed away, but vans that had four-wheel drives were used by some who visited the locality. Researchers could not locate anyone from the area who owned a car or a van. Those who own scooters and motorcycles belonged to the second and third generation in Hennanigala.

Economic Activities

The traditional occupation of Veddhas was hunting and chena cultivation. At Dambana, they used to stay away from home and the family for long periods, hunting in the jungle and gathering food. Most of the food that was collected was preserved using traditional methods. Bee honey was used as a preservative. Dumping raw meat in honey and drying it in the sun was one method that they extensively adopted. However, since their relocation they lost this main food supply preservation method, as there was no jungle or a forest for them to continue their traditional way of life. In the surveyed sample, most of the men indicated that they have never touched a gun or a shotgun in their lives. A shotgun is what the Veddhas in Dambana still use and is quite different from modern firearms. When their forest land was acquired and preserved as the Maduru Oya National Park, they were strictly forbidden to enter the park for hunting. However, they were allowed to enter the park without any hunting equipment to collect medicinal herbs, which currently is a lucrative occupation. One woman said, "*Dan kavuruwath kaleta yanne naha. Wild life mahaththaruunta ahuvena neesa*" (Now no one goes to the forest because they will get caught to the wild life officers).

Overnight made farmers by the government, these people are unaware how to make a success of their agricultural occupations. To add insult to injury, these Veddhas got the most unsuitable area for paddy farming. They were given 2.5 acres of paddy land when they were relocated. But most of them have lost this land altogether, as they had leased it out to the Sinhalese people in the adjoining village. Those who still have it, up to now, despite a valiant effort to make a success of it, have failed miserably as could be seen from the paddy fields they owned. These fields are filled with weeds and the crop looked in need of water and manure very badly. It showed a contrasting picture when compared with the paddy fields owned by the Sinhalese people. Among the families surveyed in this research project, several women indicated that they leased out the land because their husbands had died and that they were heavily indebted to outsiders. At the same time, they also pointed out that the infertility of the land given to them made it impossible for them to make a profit. Complaining about this, one man said:

"...Teldeniyen aapu ayataa nam Honda idam dunna...aadivaasi apiwa ravattuwa......apaata labune nisaru idam...maasa dahaataka salaka dunna. Kumburu pennuwa. Athe mahansiyen nokanobi kumburu usvadduwa.... Eath ithin hariyata aswannak labune naha." (Those who came from Teldeniya got better land.... They deceived us—the indigenous people.... We got infertile land.... They gave us food coupons for 18 months.... They showed us the paddy fields....... We tried our best to cultivate this land without even proper food.... But we never got a rich harvest.)

Showing the foundation laid for a new house he further added: *"...Foundesama thiyena kella hadaganna vidiyalk naha..."* (I have no way to build this section where I have laid the foundation).

Chena cultivation was popular among the Veddhas when they were in Dambana. Here in Hennanigala, there was very little opportunity for them to indulge in chena cultivation due to lack of land. However, in certain sections of the land that they own some of them have undertaken chena cultivation. During the dry season, they set fire to the land and clean it up and fence it. After this initial task is over, both men and women work together and plant seasonal crops that they use for consumption and then sell the excess.

Occupations

Apart from engaging in agricultural activities, they also engage in animal rearing. But rearing cows is not very popular among the Veddhas in Dambana due to the late Veddha chief Tisahamy's, dictum that "Children should not be fed with animal milk," though it seems to be catching on. MILCO brand factory, which is one of the leading retailers in the milk trade in Sri Lanka, has entered the market and has persuaded some of these community members to rear cows and buffaloes. Those who engage in cattle rearing own about 5 to 6 cows. While some rear them for the milk, there were two families in the sample who breed cattle to sell for meat. A quota of the milk produced is consumed by the family and the rest is sold to tea kiosks in Medagama or to MILCO factory. Buffaloes are mostly reared for ploughing as well as to use the milk to make curd. Buffalo curd is in great demand among the villagers as a delicacy. However most of the work related to animal rearing, cutting grass and feeding the animals, milking, and moving them from place to place are undertaken by women (see Table 4).

Collecting medicinal herbs is another occupation in which men engage. They enter the forest reserve with permission and collect medicinal herbs that are used in the Ayurvedic system in Sri Lanka. This is the native medical practice that is widely prevalent and respected. Once upon a time it flourished in Sri Lanka and the Veddhas are accustomed to this system. They can identify these medicinal herbs in the forest and they do a lucrative business, as medicinal herbs are in great demand due to the high price in the market. Collecting bee honey is another task they used to engage in Dambana, however, collecting bee honey is quite a risky task as they have to enter thick jungle areas and the bees could attack them. Yet they still engage in it as it has a great demand for medicinal purposes.

The other types of occupations of the men in the surveyed sample are listed in Table 4.

Table 19.4. List of occupations of men in the research sample.

Type of occupation	Number	Percentage
Business (petty trade)	04	16%
Agriculture	10	40%
Labourers	06	24%
Fishing	01	04%
Collecting bee honey	01	04%
Police constable	01	04%
Cattle rearing	03	12%
Home gardening	04	16%
Driver	01	04%
Three wheeler driver	01	04%

In the home gardens, different types of vegetables are cultivated and the women take them to the Sunday fair. Casual labour jobs seem to be very popular among the men in the sample. It was indicated that contractors from Colombo come and recruit them for work sites in Colombo, the capital city. They indicated that they get paid well, about 18,000 rupees a month. Another man in the sample, Sudu Banda, said:

> "...*mata veda nathivunama mama kolomba hari gihin vedak soya gena karanawa...mata bus valayannapuluvan...bus eken bahina thena salakunak hithethiyagana bahalagihin aapa-suethanat aavith gamataenawa....*" (When I do not have work I go to Colombo in search of work.... I can travel by bus... I note the place where I get down from the bus by remembering a landmark and then come back to the same place and get in to a bus and come back to the village...)

It is mostly the young boys who engage in fishing in the reservoir and in the other irrigation channels. What they catch is not normally sold; rather, but they boil it there and eat it. Some men have taken fishing as an occupation. But the numbers are few, as it is against the Buddhist precepts. As shown in some of the pictures, running a small boutique in the home premises is catching up. It is not necessarily the men who engage in these minor business activities, but the women. What was freely available in these shops were mostly Disprin, Panadol, sweets, and what they referred to as *thuvala balm,* meaning plaster. There were two men in the selected sample who are earning money as vendors. They transported honey, fish, milk, and curd on their bicycles and go into interior villages to sell their wares. They get only a limited income. Another new occupation that the men have taken to is running a boutique in the town area. These men indicated that they earned about 800 to 1,500 rupees a day.

Occupations of women

In Dambana, women were considered as a "protected species." They were not allowed to come out of their houses and roam around on their own or talk and move with strangers. In Hennanigala, the situation has changed very much. Most women in Hennanigala, in addition to housework, cooking, and looking after children, also help their husbands in home garden cultivation. Two women who belonged to the surveyed sample had gone to the Middle East as domestics. In their absence, the husbands are doing housework and taking care of children. There were some women who are engaged in casual labour jobs such as replanting and harvesting. Some girls in the third generation, about five of them, had left the village to work in a garment factory in Malabe, a town closer to the capital city. Three of the women in the survey sample run the small shops that had been opened up in the home premises. Two other women in the survey sample are constantly away from home working on casual labour jobs. It was also revealed that girls from the third generation preferred to get jobs away from the village. Since they realized that they do not possess skills necessary to do any other jobs, they take whatever casual jobs that come their way. It was apparent that they no longer preferred the sheltered life they shared at Dambana. They are prepared for whatever challenges they have to face in their newly earned freedom.

Marriage, Children, and Family Life

In Dambana there was no legal marriage system. They had a traditional marriage system and they adhered to it. According the Veddha chief, any Veddha boy could marry any girl from their own community without legal formalities. However, in their system they made sure that the man had the capacity and certain assets with which he could support his mate. When these 53 main families were shifted to Hennanigala, they had a very low proportion of legal marriages (CENWOR, 1994, p. 54). However, due to lack of legal sanctions in the traditional system the women were vulnerable to insecurity. Few such cases were identified in the CENWOR study. They believed that once a man marries a woman, that man cannot bring another woman to the house as long as the first married woman lives. And men who violated this rule were punished. The CENWOR study (1994) clearly points out that no punishments were meted out to any of the men who violated the rule, including the sub-chieftain at Hennanigala at the time. At present, all marriages at Hennanigala are legally registered at the registration office at Medagama. However, this registration takes place after a man and a woman have lived together for a few weeks. Therefore, the woman was more secure as the man is legally bound to support the woman and any child by that marriage. This is a significant change in the marriage relationships. Another important change that had occurred is that the prevalent rule that the partners in the marriage should come from the same community is strictly not adhered to here. Both men and women have the freedom to marry anyone outside their community. Many such marriages are in existence today and it was revealed that such families are economically more stable and are doing better socially as well. The houses occupied by such couples were much cleaner and a distinct change in the lifestyle could be noticed. It was obvious such families were making a brave attempt to distance themselves from the main community and establish themselves as a distinct sub-cultural group.

One woman, Uuruwarige SuduKumi, who is a widow, categorically stated that women in this community never think of a second marriage during widowhood. Referring to herself, she stated that:

> *"Miniha keleta giyahama kavuda vedithiyala marala… eh venakota mage eka lamayek vivaha vela… anek haya denama punchipatto.…Monawath kanna thibunethnaha.… Mama thava deegekayannaona kale unath pita appek daruwanta hiriharakarananhinda mama bande naha…"* (Someone shot and killed my husband when he went to the forest.… By that time one of my children was already married.… The other six were very tiny.… We did not have any food even.… Even though I was young enough to marry again I did not want an outsider to ill treat my children…)

The second generation members in the survey group stated that the third generation young people insisted that marriages should be legally registered and that they always preferred to live away from the main family. Very often they put up a house in the compound of the parents' house but supported themselves. They did not have any elaborate marriage ceremonies as they cannot afford it but minor celebrations had taken place after registration.

Marital Relationships and Family Life

The women in the first and the second generation freely admitted that abuse and assault were common features in their marriages but the third generation women stated that they have very cordial relationships and that they are not abused by their husbands. They stated that their husbands helped them in household activities as well, which is a complete change from the first and second generation situation. Both second and third generation women in the sample admitted that they resorted to birth control practices and that they are guided and educated by the Public Health Nurse (PHN) and the Public Health Inspector (PHI). A larger age gap between the children was openly visible among the third generation members. Consequently, the numbers of children in such families were limited. Since most of them get married at the tender age of 16, they use birth control methods for about three years before they conceive a child. Also the lack of economic stability also prevented them from practicing birth control methods.

It was evident that their family life is very peaceful and happy despite the economic difficulties they faced. Most of all the faith they have about the fidelity to each other is very strong. It was revealed that sometimes the men stay away from the family at a stretch of about 15 to 20 days when they go out to work. Yet, these women believed that the men would never indulge in illicit affairs or other sexual relationships. They also indicated that they preferred to remain single even if they become widows at a very young age. Another feature that was identified was the support they give their children even if they are married. If the man who marries their daughter has no land the parents of the girl would give away about half an acre of their land to their daughter so that the new couple could put up a house and start their new life away from the parents. A majority of the third generation children have created new family units away from the parents' home. Yet, there were about 30% among the surveyed family units who still lived with the parents. Details of one such case was divulged by one UruVarige Sudu Banda, when he said:

> "*Mage duwge miniha valaha gahala athkadala as penne naha.... Eka ahak yanthamata penawa... Avurudu pahak vithara mahansi gattha...rupiyal 90000 vithara danata nayawela thiyenewa. Eh aya rakabalaganne api... digatama clinic ekkayanawa...*" (My daughter's husband was attacked by a bear.... His hands are broken.... His eyes too are damaged.... There is a slight vision in one eye....We have tried to cure him for the last five years....We have got into debt for about 90,000 rupees.... We only look after him.... We take him to the clinic regularly...)

The above is a strong case that indicates the family solidarity even though they do not have adequate means. When it is only one child, the parents prefer to keep the child with them even after marriage. H. M. Seelawthie and K. H. Ariyasena, who have acquired the more Sinhalized names, stated that their daughter stay with them even after her marriage. They still regret very much that they could not host a grand function to celebrate their daughter's wedding. It is the general opinion of the surveyed families that the caste and creed of the person whom their child marries is immaterial to them as long as the person is a caring and decent individual who will contribute to creating a happy family. The statement made by one mother pertaining to this aspect was:

"*Api kavuruth minissune… oyakula mala beda ape atharanaha…ape daruwa rakabalaganna-vanam eka thamai apataona…*" (We are all human beings…. We do not have this caste and creed differences…. If the person is looking after our child and is caring…that is what we want.)

This is clear evidence that discloses that they do not have any taboos pertaining to the selection of marriage partners. It apparently is a drastic attitudinal change from the "Dambana mentality," which indicated that they would expel anyone who marries outside their community. However, it must be mentioned here that the Sinhalese and the Tamils, especially the conservative generation, still consider caste and creed when selecting marriage partners for their children even though during the past few decades changes are gradually taking place. Therefore, it is evident that in Hennanigala there are no restrictions that prevent them from choosing a man or a woman from outside who belongs to a different community. Yet there were a few in the surveyed sample who did not approve of such mixing. They were of the opinion that the Veddha community will be soon extinct if such habits are encouraged. It was also learnt that eloping with the man or the woman of their choice has become a common occurrence at Hennanigala. According to some older women, they would not have dared to do it at Dambana. Here, "Who cares?" was the comment of this woman.

However, what was evident is that these third generation women are much luckier than the first and second generation women as they receive much tenderness, love, and cooperation from their wedded partners. Several young wives in the surveyed sample were vehement in their protests where they stated that "they will not live with them if they are authoritative or if they beat us up." One of them actually added that if such a situation arose that she will not hesitate to leave the husband. One further added, "*eheme unoth api medaperadi-gata yanawa*" (If such a situation arose we are going to the Middle East). This statement could be clearly attributed to the changes that have been taking place in the lives of women in Sri Lanka; where an exodus of them has migrated to the Middle East with the intention of making their lives as well as the lives of their offspring much better. In fact, according to government sources the income that they remit to Sri Lanka is the highest foreign exchange that comes into the country! It is evident that Veddha women at Hennanigala, too, would soon be a part of that category.

Children, Family Size and Child-Rearing Practices

Children are loved and cared for among most of the families in Sri Lanka irrespective of their wealth, status, or ethnicity. However, it cannot be denied that many reports that contradict this statement have emerged recently. Hennanigala was not much different from the norm as the parents loved and cherished their children and worked very hard to give a better life to their children. Some of them have succeeded in their effort as some have reached high standards in life especially through education. One such case is the "Siriwardena" girl who was admitted to the University of Peradeniya. After earning a degree she changed her surname to Siriwardena, giving up her clan surname, "UruVarige," which would have enabled any one to identify her as one from the Veddha clan. Researchers came across several girls in the sample who are studying at Nawa Medagama MahaVidyalaya and one of them, in fact, is the Head Girl of the school. According to the principal of the school, she is highly intelligent, very well behaved, and talented.

It was evident that limiting the number of children to a few, as shown from the data in Table 5, could be one reason that enabled the parents to bestow better care and pay more attention to their children. A majority of the women in the younger generation had nothing but praise for the Family Heath Nurse (FHN), Public Health Nurse (PHN), and the Public Health Inspector (PHI), who guided them meticulously to make a success of their family life. The information provided to them about birth control and health care, they said, was very informative. This is quite contradictory to the belief of the older generation who had a strong resistance to birth control, as they believed "It as a sin to prevent a birth." However, it is apparent that there is an attitudinal change pertaining to this. The other important factor is the age gap between the children.

Table 19.5. The number of children in the closely surveyed 25 family units.

Number of family units	Number of children
3	1
6	2
5	3
3	4
4	5
3	3
1	-
Total: 25	

Though the women of the older generation had a child practically every year, circumstances have changed and among the surveyed families the age gap between the children were wide ranging, from 3–5 years. Knowledge gained from mass media and the health clinics that are regularly held have contributed to this attitudinal change in limiting the number of children as well as maintaining a healthy gap between each child. The researchers were informed that some women have decided to get themselves sterilized after three children and that their husbands had no objection as such. They indicated that they could look after the children better when the numbers are limited.

Though the earlier tendency was to have the children delivered at home using the services of their clan midwife, the situation has changed as all the women who were interviewed disclosed that they gave birth to their children in the hospital. Inevitably, this was due to the influence of the PHN who had guided them through the ordeal quite competently. This has resulted in a reduction in the number of infantile deaths, which had been quite prevalent among the first generation women at Hennanigala. However, after they come home with the baby, they resort to some of the traditional practices such as bathing with boiled medicinal herbs and inhaling burnt garlic smoke, which they believe contributes to an increase in the breast milk. Whatever the advice they got from the health officials, they continue breast-feeding the child for a long time. This habit is sustained by the belief that they will not conceive again as long as they breast-feed the child. If the mother lacks breast milk, it is a common practice to put the child to the breast of another woman who has a sufficient quantity of milk. They also take care to inoculate and immunize the children during the relevant time periods as instructed by the heath officials. This is a positive change where the younger generation has benefitted immensely. Even though cow milk is available, they prefer to use powdered or tinned milk, such as Lakspray and Anchor, if they can afford it. But it was clear that almost 80% of the children got only breast milk. The children's diet is also supplemented with other local brews such as Kanji, which is a soup made out of rice and ground leaves; triposha; maize; and tinned milk. Though the earlier habit was to feed the child with *kurakkanpittu, kurakkanthalapa* (food made out of Kurakkan seeds) and yams, they have resorted to the easier way and these local foods made at home have been replaced by ready-made foods such as "5 minutes instant noodles" and the different varieties of biscuits. However, one anomaly that was identified was that they are not in the habit of purifying water before drinking.

As indicated earlier most of the houses (about 60%) are were well swept and clean and the children were dressed in clean clothes. Cleaning is a habit that the children have acquired in school and one that they insist that their mothers should practice. Earlier they used to wear clothes that were stitched in the village by someone who owned a sewing machine but the pattern has changed. The majority of them are now wearing ready-made skirts and T-shirts which have been purchased from the Nawa Medagama market. Yet, some children were minus undergarments. According to the women, they bathed the children daily and washed all the previous day's clothing in the morning. One woman said, "*Api veddounath pirisiduwa innawa*" (Though we are Veddhas we stay clean). This was supported by the fact that in almost all the houses the researchers visited clothes were hanging on outside lines. They also used soap, a new habit they have acquired, as the older practice was to use different kinds of herbs to wash the hair and to apply on the body. They had used charcoal to clean their teeth earlier, but they have now acquired the habit of using toothpaste and toothbrushes. The children normally sleep with one of the parents until they are about 5–6 years old. Then they are shifted to another room. Otherwise, the woman sleeps with the little ones while the father sleeps with the older male children. Beds are rare; sleeping on mats laid on the bare floor is the norm.

The children are punished by their parents and grandparents when they do something wrong. They still observe traditional customs when a girl comes of age. They build a hut away from the house, where the girl stays with an older woman till she is bathed and taken inside after seven days in accordance to the auspicious times observing all the rituals. All the clothes and the utensils the girl used within the seven days are completely destroyed. This is also an event they celebrate. Even among Sinhalese people, some of these traditions are still observed.

Socio-Cultural Practices

Some of the religious practices, food, health habits, and social life, as well as the status of women in Hennanigala have changed over the years. The people at Dambana worshipped different cults and Nayayaku, the spirits of their dead ancestors, which they believed protected them from any harm. However, these habits have changed over the years and almost every one of them has become a Buddhist. All the houses that the researchers visited had a picture of Lord Buddha. They light an oil lamp outside their house to venerate Lord Buddha and to seek divine help. They also make offerings to God Kataragama, as they believe that he is their guardian deity. They visit the Mahiyangana temple, which is supposed to have been visited by Lord Buddha himself in one of his three visits to the island. They take an active role in the annual pageant held in the temple. In addition they offer alms to the priests living in the close by Buddhist temple and some of them even observe *atasil*, the eight precepts, on the Full Moon Poya day. The children are enrolled in the Sunday school. All children below the age of 15 attend Sunday school clad in white. They participate in all Buddhist religious activities and believe in life after death; rebirth is a concept in Buddhism. Because of their belief, they said they do not want to do "wrong things." But this has not prevented them from practicing their earlier religious practices such as hunting if the opportunity presents itself. And still, when they fall ill, they resort to various other practices such as *yak natum* and *kohomba kankariya* (dancing ceremonies performed to cure the ill and bring peace of mind). They do not keep any statues inside their houses. In a few houses, they had erected two lamp posts.

Inside one of these they light a lamp to Lord Buddha and in the other to all the gods they believed in.

The Veddhas have a language of their own that the outsiders will find difficult to understand. However, now the people at Hennanigala do not speak the Vedi language at all, though the leaders have a tendency to switch on to that when they speak to outsiders. Researchers felt that this is to impress upon the outsiders the importance of their culture and that they are still adherents of their traditions and habits. Nothing is further from the truth than this. However, the rest of the community members speak very clear Sinhala without the slightest trace of Veddha influence. This also could be attributed to the fact that they receive their education at school in Sinhala, which they have to do willingly or unwillingly if they are to continue their education. Also, if they used the Veddha language they would have been subjected to much humiliation in the school, as there is no school exclusively for the Veddha children. They study with the others.

Figure 19.10. Clothes the boys and girls wear —the new trend.

The clothes and dress that the men and women wear reflect, to a great extent, the changes that have come over them. At Dambana, men had long beards and they used to wear a loin cloth and a sarong over it when they met strangers. They had long hair, which they tied in a knot. At Hennanigala, all men had cut their hair short and they wear sarongs and shirts or trousers and shirts. The children wear the school uniform when they go to school, which is comprised of blue trousers and a white shirt. The girls wore a white uniform when they went to school but at home they were clad in skirts and blouses or jackets to match. The women of the third generation all wore stylish skirts and blouses in matching colours. Both men and women wore ornaments. What the men wore resembled a talisman while the women and the girls wore bead chains, and plastic and glass bangles (see Figures 10 and 11). Some of the older women wore an ankle-length cloth and jacket while others wore a dress, which is referred to as a *lungi* (see Figure 11). The pregnant women were wearing maternity dresses.

Figure 19.11. Showing the clothes the women wear.

Most of the families are supposed to have three meals a day but from what the researchers gathered it was evident that they are satisfied if they could have two meals a day. Their staple food is rice and they make a valiant effort to have at least one meal of rice with a leafy vegetable and meat or fish. Meat is a rare delicacy now, as they cannot hunt, but fish is available as some members of the community indulge in fishing in the tank (See picture 9). They supplement the other meals with yams and bread. They have gotten used to bread since coming to Hennanigala. Tobacco is extensively used by the men. Both gender groups chew betel. It was revealed that there are some men who are addicted to liquor, a habit that they have acquired at Hennanigala due to the influence of the outsiders.

CHANGES IN VALUES AND ETHICS

Their values and ethics have changed much since their arrival here. They prefer to seek Western medical treatment when they fall ill. Still, they respect their elders.

They treat visitors with respect and courtesy and offer tea, fruits, or whatever they have to the visitor. As soon as someone walks into the house, they offer a chair and come and talk very respectfully to the visitor. They also have not lost their habit of sharing whatever they have with the others. Those who are short of food are often provided with some by the others. Sometimes they share the harvest with others in the community. Despite their poverty, the community feeling is very strong among them.

Education Levels and Aspirations

Education is greatly valued by the Hennanigala community. This is mostly because they see that a significant change has occurred in those who got some kind of education. As such, they make a great effort to educate their young even though they are aware that they cannot reach great heights due to their poverty. Though the CENWOR study (1994) reported that the attendance of the Veddha children at school was very poor, the principal of the Meda Mahagama Vidyalaya on the contrary informed the researchers that the few Veddha children in his school are very conscientious, well-behaved, and dedicated students. At the time of this study, two of the girls had registered for external degrees and they followed classes conducted at Mahiyangana, the closest city to Hennanigala. Most of the children in the second and third generation have completed junior secondary education and the number of girls in this category is much higher than the boys. A few mothers in the sample complained that it is difficult to keep the boys at school. They demand more facilities and privileges, like the boy who had given up schooling due to the inability of the parents to buy him a bicycle to commute to school. Almost all the little children of preschool age attend a preschool, which is located closer to Hennanigala, and the others who have transport facilities attend one, located closer to Nawa Medagama. As a result of the influence of schooling, these children are interested in different sports. Cricket is their favourite game but they also play other games. The young generation has lot of aspirations and so do the parents, who want their children to do well in studies and get better jobs. They believe that the younger generation has a future at Hennanigala and that it is too late to go back to their old ways of life. After getting used to a new way of life in which there is more freedom, the young generation does not want to be *bandapu vahallu* (tied bound slaves) anymore if they can prevent it.

Social Life

There is nothing much to describe as with regard to the social life of these people. They are working very hard to earn their living and therefore have very little time for recreation. But they have a culture of their own, featuring songs and dances with a special rhythm and sound. The women do not dance but they do sing their songs. They do not have many social functions but they celebrate weddings. However, their unstable economic conditions have limited these activities. A recent addition to their culture is the interest in cricket. Some boys even travel to other areas to play cricket. Recently, they played a cricket match with the ministers of the government!

CONCLUSIONS

What emerges from this study is that based on Freire's concepts, a cultural invasion has taken place to a great extent. Though the first generation of the Veddhas found it difficult to get adjusted to the new environment and remained socially isolated, the later generations have got over this difficulty and have managed to get assimilated into the neighbouring communities. The attempt of the government of Sri Lanka to make the Veddhas successful agriculturalists has failed to a large extent but invariably a change in the traditional lifestyle has occurred. This in turn has affected their housing, occupations, marital relationships, child rearing, food habits, health, education, transport, language, and ethics and values.

They have changed from food gatherers to food growers. Agriculture has become their main source of livelihood and is supplemented by other occupations such as fishing. They now live in a planned settlement even though planning is not 100% perfect. They have adapted to a changing lifestyle. Their housing and other facilities have improved. Some of them own larger houses with facilities. Considerable changes in the family life, too, were identified and the customary marriage habits have declined. The fact that they rely on a legal marriage has given a strong sense of security, especially to the women. Marital relationships, too, have changed, moving toward more gender equality. The decline in the family size is a significant change. The younger generation follows the advice of the PHN and PHI to create a more hygienic environment for their children to grow up in. They also have gotten used to immunization programs. These are healthy signs. The desire to inculcate better toilet habits even though full potential has not been reached yet are signs of better sanitary conditions. The role of women has changed considerably and a significant difference can be seen between the traditional Veddha women and those at Hennanigala, especially the members of the third generation. They have escaped from strict restrictions imposed on social relations, marriage, and even in their dress code and other habits at Dambana. The abuse that most of the first generation women experienced is no longer seen among the third generation. Now they participate more actively in all activities and keep home fires burning even in the absence of the husband. In addition, women are active in non-traditional occupations such as cultivation, trading, and even migrating to other countries as domestics. Obtaining a university education could be classified as a distinct step forward. The practice of birth control and the change in childbearing age are really great advances when considering the traditional nature of the society into which they were born. All these could be categorized as the result of their newly acquired freedom.

They have taken to Buddhism as their main religion but other cults are worshipped. The new generation's reluctance to speak the Veddha language and instead use the Sinhala language marks a deviation from their age-old traditions. It is evident that education has played a vital role in creating this change. There is no doubt that education has opened up new vistas for them and their parents, who are very hopeful that their children will reach great heights. This fact has motivated them to go through many hardships and difficulties to educate their children. This indicates a change in their aspirations.

Even though they still practice some of the traditional methods of healing that they are used to, they have more faith now in Western medicine. Now they dress more like Sinhala people and it is difficult to identify them in a group among the other Sinhala villagers.

All this indicates that cultural invasion has indeed taken place. Though earlier generations had regrets about coming to Hennanigala and their decision to relocate themselves from the forest habitat, the later generations seem to appreciate that they were able to get away from that strict secluded environment. They do not want to be called Veddhas anymore. It is evident that their lifestyle has changed to a great extent and that the process of integration has been rapid. The traditional lifestyle is fast disappearing and it seems as if a whole new world is opening up for them even though the challenges are many.

REFERENCES

Centre for Women's Research. (1994). *Veddhaah women: Impact of their translocation from a forest environment to agricultural settlements.* Colombo, Sri Lanka: CENWOR.

Davy, John J. (1821). *An account of the interior of Ceylon and of its inhabitants with travels in that island.* (Reprinted 1969). Dehiwala, Colombo, Sri Lanka: Thisara Prakshakayo.

Dharmadasa, K. N. O. (1990). *"Veddhas in the history of Sri Lanka: An introductory sketch."* ICES Series Ii. Sri Lanka: International Center for Ethnic Studies.

Freire, Paulo P. (1993) *Pedagogy of the oppressed.* London, England: Penguin Books.

Knox, Robert R. (1861). *An historical relation of Ceylon.* Colombo, Sri Lanka: M. D. Gunasena.

Seligmann, C. G., & Seligmann, B. Z. (1911). *The Veddhas.* Cambridge, England: Cambridge University Press.

Spittel, R. L. (1944). *Vanished trails.* Colombo, Sri Lanka: Lake House.

Sugathapala De Silva, M.W. (1972). *Vedda language of Ceylon.* München: R. Kitzinger.

Tennent, J. E. (1860). *An account of the island of Ceylon* Vol. 2 (4th ed.). London, England: Longman, Green, Longman, and Roberts.

Wijesekara, Nandadeva N. (1964). *The Veddhas in transition.* Colombo, Sri Lanka: M.D. Gunasena and Company.

CHAPTER TWENTY

On the Streets with Paulo Freire and Simone Weil, Talking With Gamilaraay Students About Hèlio Oiticica

CHARLOTTE SEXTON

Paulo Freire stated, "Hope is an ontological need. Hopelessness is but hope that has lost its bearings, and become a distortion of that ontological need" (2004, p. 2). Time in the world dries all tears and the unforgiven is forgotten. But it is not enough that tears be wiped away or death avenged. Emmanuel Levinas stated that "hope then is to hope for the reparation of the irreparable; it is to hope for the present" (2008, p. 93). Hope also requires a methodology and strategy expressed through multiple psychological, social, cultural, political, and economic possibilities. Becoming hopeful involves processes of transformation, self-determination, and independence; decolonising our minds from the web of jargon and ideas proliferating from official discourses of failure and brokenness; healing our minds, bodies, and spirits and connecting with a community and moving forward. The community seems willing to accept and expect pervasive hopelessness from particular individuals, groups, and places.

Hope offers the possibility of a new beginning and is intrinsic to Freire's concept of the Easter Experience, a radicalising encounter with the oppressed through education. The Easter Experience involves a "practice of freedom the means by which men and women deal critically and creatively with reality and discover how to participate in the transformation of their world" (Shaul in Freire, 2000, p. 34). One then invents new ways of living one's life and of living with others. Freire (2000, p. 61) states that one can experience a "profound rebirth." Those who undergo an Easter Experience "must take on a new form of existence, they can no longer remain as they were" (Freire, 2000, p. 61). These processes and experiences involve a break from the "circle of certainty" (Freire, 2000, p. 39) within which reality is imprisoned. One is able to enter into reality, so that, knowing it better, one can transform it. One is "rescued from narcissism or psychologism" (Goulet in Freire, 2005, p. ix) and comes into "dialogue with others whose historical 'vocation' is to become transforming agents of their social reality" (Goulet in Freire, 2005, p. ix). In a world of proliferating and disempowering discourses, apparatuses and institutions of violence and inequality, one becomes a subject rather than an object of his or her own history (Goulet in Freire, 2005, p. ix).

This transformation became of interest to me as someone who experienced educational disadvantage, became homeless, and experienced radicalisation within a commitment to holistic healing and justice. This statement indicates that my experience of tertiary education was that of marginalisation and vulnerability in relation to the traditions of education, knowledge, and history, which have the power to deliver the concepts, the vocabulary, and the axioms that are dehumanizing and offensive. A number of discourses within the arts and sciences deny the talents, skills, knowledge, and ideas of vulnerable groups and individuals. Their agency to create new ideas, their ways of being, and their right to self-determination in the world are undermined and compromised. The identity and experience of marginalised students are disavowed, masked, and hidden as a precondition for academic survival and success.

Academic research is determined by law and a philosophy of law based on the family, bourgeois or civil society, and the State. Universities now presuppose the possibility of a rigorous delimitation of thresholds or frontiers "between the familial and the non-familial, between the foreign and the non-foreign, the citizen and the non-citizen" and "between private and public, private and public law" (Dufourmantelle & Derrida, 2000, pp. 47–49). This is a global, political, economic, and legal environment where marginalized and vulnerable people "don't matter, are plain irritating, or are viewed as downright dangerous" (Smith, 2012, p. 221). Jacques Derrida writes of this oppressive deliminitation of space and human rights: "It is often techno-political-scientific mutation that obliges us to deconstruct...such mutation itself deconstructs what are claimed as these naturally obvious things or these untouchable axioms" (Dufourmantelle & Derrida, 2000, p. 45). Writing from an indigenous perspective, Linda Tuhiwai Smith observes that the task of many vulnerable and marginalized students or researchers is "to survive and do exceedingly well in an education system that denies the knowledge held by their own peoples. They are not necessarily successful in the system in terms of credentials, but are able to decode and demystify the system in order to learn and be educated without being damaged" (Smith, 2012, pp. 222–223). Flick Grey and Merinda Epstein are researchers who have introduced a perspective of people who have lived the experience of mental distress known as a mental health issue or mental illness: "Value is almost never ascribed to the learning that follows challenges to our mental health. It makes sense to value these experiences" (Our Consumer Place, 2010, p. 13).

The dispossession of becoming homeless or psychiatric incarceration is an event that evicts us from ourselves through which we are deprived of basic human rights. At no moment can a previous bereavement serve as a model for this violence and injustice.

I survived this temporary dispossession and destitution and found a warm, protected, and private apartment in Moree, a small agricultural town in northwest New South Wales. Having this secure and safe home was fundamental in engendering hope. French theologian, political activist, and philosopher, Simone Weil recognized the right to a home: "To be rooted is perhaps the most important and least recognized need of the human soul" (Weil, 2007, p. 43). To be fulfilled, one must feel a sense of belonging in society, that you are a part of the human family with a role to play and a responsibility for the well-being of others. Weil argued that humans have a need to experience and participate in the life of their community with heart and body—not just intellect:

> A human being has roots by virtue of his real, active and natural participation in the life of a community which preserves in living shape certain particular treasures of the past and certain particular expectations of the future. (Weil, 2007, p. 43)

The Easter Experience is not the sole domain and heroism of political radicals, revolutionaries, and anarchists but can be found amid ordinary lives and might also involve a decision to leave an abusive relationship; reading Weil and Freire in a Kings Cross women's refuge; recovery from drug and alcohol dependence and a decision to follow a twelve-step program for addicts; discharge from psychiatric care after twenty years; a decision to enrol in an art course or undertake adult literacy classes; refusal of a doctorate; the dishonour of exclusion from an educational institution; exclusion from a Buddhist monastery; an artist's decision to cease creating and exhibiting work after critical self-examination and reflection; living with an acquired brain injury after a serious accident; starting a new home after a period of homelessness; collecting retro ironstone crockery from opportunity shops after losing everything; surviving a suicide attempt; a religious conversion; diagnosis of a serious illness or disability; a decision to leave a church community.

The creative transformation of one's life and reality can come about through the liminal movement between states and statuses that alter mind, soul, health, and society. Liminality involves a period of separation or withdrawal from normal society and the enactment of rituals, rites of passage, and pilgrimages. The normal rules and social conventions associated with work, authority, and the law are overturned and reversed. There may be moments of scatological excess, confrontation, dissent, and even violence. One's identity and status are erased to be made anew.

Liminality also occurs when entire societies or large groups experience a sudden event, crisis, or collapse. These periods are both destructive and constructive with the emergence of new ideas and practices and significant cultural and social change. Rational and objective thought is undermined because of the disappearance of historical structures and institutions and because of the traumatic stress of liminal crisis.

This condition is also present in contemporary rural communities in Australia and the aboriginal communities that live in these towns who have experienced loss of traditional oral history and knowledge in the face of radical change in the new global market economy. Beyond the metropolitan centres of Australia, rural communities expose the fault lines of economic and cultural history. One is in the presence of an *other community* (Lingis, 1994, p. 10), which troubles, doubles, and shadows the cosmopolitan image of affluence, choice, mobility, elitism, and distraction offered by the metropolis.

The Easter Experience is also associated with the suffering of enforced exile, displacement, and forced migration. One's arrival is "marked by rage, fears, suffering, early longing, love, broken hope, and also by a certain shy hope, one that signals return. There is also the wish and the need to remake oneself, remake one's broken dream" (Freire, 2007, p. 66). Paulo Freire describes the domestic situation of exiles "who began to buy a piece of furniture or two for their homes only after four or five years in exile. Their half-empty homes seemed to speak, eloquently, of their loyalty to a distant land. In fact, their half-empty rooms not only seemed to wish to speak to them of their longing to return, but looked as if the movers had just paid a visit and they were actually moving back" (Freire, 2004, p. 24).

The memory and symbols of exile are turned over in the mind while they are watched and observed. In a prism they are never static, but saturated with new meanings that expand and shift in emphasis and nuance over time. These symbols can then generate cultural consciousness and empowerment that alters our relations with nature and social forces. Freire stated: "To the tumult of the soul belongs also the pain of the broken dream, utopia lost" (Freire, 2004, p. 24). *No one goes anywhere alone* (Freire, 2004, p. 23).

One must not succumb to nostalgia for one's origins, one's past, and one's family. A break from one's past involves grief, loss, even dishonour, but also transformation as oppression, affliction, and even loneliness give way to healing and hopefulness. We are then able to nurture life and develop greater efficacy and agency. We develop the unshakeable compassion necessary for cultural, historical, and spiritual affirmation and solidarity. *A free mind can achieve all things* (Eckhart, 1994, p. 5).

Moree is a small agricultural town which sits on the banks of the Mehi River in the country of the Kamilaroi or Gamilaraay people. The town takes its name from a traditional word meaning "long water hole." The Gamilaraay people carved trees or Dendroglyphs, which Etheridge observed were located near burial sites and initiation grounds (Etheridge, 1918, p. 2). The "scar trees" marked "places for sacred men's and women's business, ceremonial grounds and the scarred trees were just a warning for those particular places" (Border Rivers-Gwydir Catchment Management Authority, 2010, p. 9). Aboriginal lawyer, activist, and intellectual Noel Pearson argues that the fundamental ontological need for Aboriginal people is that the soul has a home. For many, Moree and the surrounding country is a "cultural hearth" (Pearson, 2011, p. 74) or "homeland of the soul" (Pearson, 2011, p. 171) where one must return.

Moree's population is below the threshold of the growth/decline required for a rural town to prosper in Australia. Many residents live with the effects of smoking, drug and alcohol abuse, diabetes, heart disease, cancer, obesity, suicide, lower levels of education and literacy, and lower life expectancy. They experience a reduced sense of efficacy, low self-esteem, and constrained agency. Moree has the third highest rate of domestic violence in NSW (Australian Broadcasting Commission, 2011, para. 1). The community also experiences visible child abuse including child sex abuse and animal cruelty.

Community members from low socio-economic groups do not have access to safe and nutritious food or lead active and healthy lives. The local agricultural industry does not have the capacity or the concern to contribute to overall welfare, nor does it contribute to goods and services in the town in ways that are socially responsible and environmentally sound. Discarded fast food packaging from the local McDonald's and Kentucky Fried Chicken outlets litters the roads.

Many residents lack the resources, skills, and self-esteem required to leave these destructive and invalidating situations and practices. This lack of financial and social capital includes structural barriers that create situations of dependence and reduced agency and efficacy. Moree is a community where community development seems to fail due to greed, nepotism, and ignorance. On a personal level, there is resistance to change and transformation as this would entail feeling, self-examination, and some measure of responsibility. A human response to suffering is to become cold and cruel.

In 1965, Aboriginal activist Charles Perkins and a group of students from the University of Sydney came to Moree to draw attention to racism in rural NSW towns. This was a significant event in Aboriginal self-determination and was known as the Freedom Ride. Aboriginal people were excluded from clubs, the local swimming pool, and cafes in Moree. The local public swimming pool became a scene of violence as the Freedom Riders attempted to assist Aboriginal children from Top Camp, the reserve outside the town, to enter while locals angrily stood outside defending the ban. This was one of the more public and significant events that led to the 1967 Referendum, which changed sections of the Australian Federal Constitution.

In 1987, Race Discrimination Commissioner Irene Moss found pronounced disadvantage in the living standards and socio-economic expectations of Aborigines living in the near-by border community, Toomelah, and concluded that the situation came about through racial discrimination (Human Rights and Equal Opportunity Commission, 1988, p. 1). The subsequent Human Rights and Equal Opportunity report stated that its purpose was to "ascertain facts, to identify problems and to look for solutions. It did not undertake a search for culprits or seek to attribute blame to individuals" (Human Rights and Equal Opportunity Commission, 1988, p. 2). Their aim was to "report on the present and look to the future. It is for historians to investigate and document the past" (Human Rights and Equal Opportunity Commission, 1988, p. 2).

In 2008 the Special Commission of Inquiry Into Child Protection Services in New South Wales heard evidence of abuse and neglect of children at Toomelah and Boggabilla. The Hon. James Wood (2008, p. 823) concluded "no intervention will be successful until many, and particularly leaders within the community, want their lives, and the lives of their children, to change and subsequently begin to participate actively in causing that change. It is not only the responsibility of government and nongovernment agencies." Wood (2008, p. 824) went on to identify "the need for the local community and the broader community, particularly those delivering services in the area, to acquire a better understanding of the history that led to these communities becoming dysfunctional, and of the differences in culture that might lead to a better understanding and partnership." In 2012 community health workers in Toomelah were reported to have experienced vicarious traumatisation after exposures to cases of child abuse (Australian Broadcasting Corporation, 2012).

This is a town where one can witness the effects of structural violence on opportunities to access employment, education, and health services. Paul Farmer pessimistically describes structural violence as an "insidious assault on dignity" (1996, p. 261). Professional workers in health, education, and community services lack competence to value and respect the lives of clients with diverse and complex needs. Stress, shame, humiliation, and denigration impact one's social status and self-esteem in a cycle of disability, death, and conflict. Structural violence attempts to measure and explain permanent disability and suffering from an "event assault" or "sustained and insidious suffering" (Farmer, 1996, p. 261) associated with poverty, discrimination, racism, institutional elitism, and sexism in healthcare, the legal system, and education. The effect is war-like conditions and devastating political systems. Structural violence includes physical violence, psychological violence, and the systematic frustration of aspirations. Robyn Williams writes:

> This means that the predominant social order denies one category of people's access to the prerequisites of effective participation in a system developed and controlled by powerful

interest groups. These prerequisites include organisational and communication skills, financial resources, and commitment of personnel and trained staff. (Williams, 2012, p. 13)

One-dimensional and deterministic welfare programs give power to specialist educational, medical, welfare, and community development workers, who are often professionally ambitious and intellectually narcissistic, in an industry that "has an entrenched interest in cultivating and maintaining behavioural dependency by many of its clients" (Pearson, 2009, p. 256). Anti-poverty programs and anti-violence campaigns too often produce what Aboriginal lawyer, activist, and intellectual Noel Pearson calls "opulent disasters" (Pearson, 2009, p. 165) because they deny the oppressed an active role in learning from their experiences and shaping the trajectory of change. He writes of the entrenched mentality and culture of victimhood in marginalised Aboriginal communities:

> Victimhood starts as an outlook or a mentality and becomes an identity....Victims do not take responsibility for what they eat or drink, for their health and mental wellbeing; their families become dysfunctional and their children are damaged even before they are born. (Pearson, 2009, pp. 240–241)

This situation is linked to epidemic levels of lateral violence in so many communities. Aboriginal and Torres Strait Justice Commissioner Mick Gooder states that the "harmful behaviour perpetrated within oppressed communities by members of that community" is "internalised colonialism" (Human Rights and Equal Opportunity Commission, 2008 para. 6). Bullying, gossip, jealousy, shaming, social exclusion, organisational conflict, and domestic violence often escalate into violent crime. Freire (2000, p. 62) calls this "horizontal violence." Men and women "treat others as mere objects; instead of nurturing life, they kill life; instead of searching for life, they flee from it. And these are oppressor characteristics" (Freire, 2000, p. 129).

Those who speak out against lateral violence in Aboriginal communities are calling for an end to victimhood, negativity, and judgment, and for accountable leadership. Marcia Langton (2008, para. 2) describes the "big bunga way" or "big man syndrome" of personal aggrandisement amid an astonishing variety of mental and physical forms of abuse that have become the norm in far too many communities and families. She argues that there is a "wide cultural, moral and increasingly political rift" (Langton, 2011, para. 1) between the "professional class" (Behrendt, Larkin, Griew, & Kelly, 2012, p. xi) of educated aboriginal intellectuals and rural and remote communities who witness "the horrors of life" (Langton, 2011, para. 1) amid the "fairy tale" (Price, 2009) versions of their culture promoted in some sectors of the media, tourism, the arts, and the entertainment industry.

Kristen Neff (2011, p. 21) describes the links between self-esteem and lateral violence, which is used to make a group or individual feel stronger, superior, and not to have to change. Cliques or groups are formed that ostracise and control outsiders, those marginal others who are despised, feared, and even hated in a cycle of guilt and humiliation for both the shamed and shamer. Those who become targets include people living with unmanageable addictions, homeless persons, those living with mental illnesses who are not well, persons living with disabilities who resist the metaphysical, psychological, and material violence of carers and support services, those who are charged with criminal offenses, or indigenous communities when they are experiencing despair and dysfunction. Other targets include those who dissent, speak out against the culture of silence that allows dysfunctional communities and self-interested, unaccountable government and community service delivery. The re-enactment of shaming creates trauma. When assaults on self-esteem in public institutions (including TAFE colleges and universities) and services are coupled with traumatic abuse in dysfunctional families or at the hands of others, individuals coming from these troubled backgrounds must work extremely hard to create healthy relationships and self-concepts.

A young middle class anarchist university student says of the beautiful girls lined up outside a nightclub that they are "trash" just because they dress differently to her. By putting others down, we actually harm ourselves. We create disconnection and isolation. Lateral violence includes a passive-aggressive tendency among women to manage their dominance of others (Cox, 1996, p. 185). This type of violence is present among both the clients of women's refuges and the welfare workers who support them, and in competitive intellectual and creative environments such as universities and arts industries. This behaviour is a response to being in a powerless position and a way of ensuring one's protective power. The powerful victims are those women who lock into an ongoing victim status. By identifying as victims they avoid being responsible and accountable for their abuse of others. They protect their territory by reinforcing images of powerlessness.

Harassment, bullying, and attacks may be symptomatic of the existential angst that can accompany disputes. This type of lateral violence occurs when there is a lack of competence in responding to the unpredictable, unknown, or uncontrollable needs of a group or individual. Short-term, cost-effective, and reactionary responses to crisis create a class of society who are disempowered, traumatised, angry, or just apathetic. The identity and well-being of an individual or group are diminished. Language, legislation, institutions, culture, public space, and public discourse are marked by social exclusion.

In contrast to adversarial conflict that is emotionally and intellectually disempowering are "culturally safe" practices in which there is "no assault, challenge or denial of a person's identity, of who they are and what they need" (Williams, 2012). Spiritual, social, cultural, emotional, and physical safety requires and generates shared respect, shared meaning, shared knowledge, and experience. Cultural safety promotes dialogues, growth, learning, collaboration, dignity and response in the context of our relationships and communities. We can understand how and why an individual or group has learned to make sense of and respond to their experiences, and then use these insights to create new ways of seeing, thinking, and doing.

Sharing shame, humiliation, dehumanisation, guilt, and inability to be assertive creates the conditions of transgenerational transmission of trauma, "biosocial degeneration" (Volkan, 2009, p. 11) and the promotion of hatred (Volkan & Fowler, 2009, para. 1). Biosocial degeneration is a consequence of massive trauma suffered by a population and is evident in high rates of violent crime and trauma suffered by children. If trauma is not dealt with and in the absence of appropriate mourning processes, the stage is set for a re-enactment of a violent past at some time in the future (Volkan, 2004b, p. 483). Volkan states:

> The victimized group suffers extreme losses, shame, and humiliation, as well as helplessness and an inability to assert itself. Members of a massively traumatized group cannot successfully go through a mourning process over their losses or reverse their shame, humiliation and helplessness. They cannot assert themselves in socially or politically adaptive ways and may end up internalizing a sense of helpless rage, idealizing masochism, or becoming prone to maladaptive sadistic outbursts—manifestations that are all shared by their community at large. In short, members of a massively traumatized group cannot successfully complete certain psychological tasks and they, then, transmit such tasks to the children of the next generation(s) along with the conscious and unconscious shared wish that the next generation(s) will resolve them. (2004a, para. 1)

One of the hallmarks of trauma is that it leads to incoherent personal, historical, and cultural narratives. Specific states of mind can be deeply engrained as a form of memory of trauma, a lasting effect of the traumatic experience. States of fear, anger, or shame can then re-emerge in an individual's responses. A traumatic event can start the emotional or interpersonal disregulation that spawns a vicious cycle of increased negative behaviour as the person or community continues to react to the cultural, political, social, and economic environment's invalidation and the environment increasingly devalues them. Besides caring for people with individual post-traumatic stress disorder (PTSD), and working through their own responses to trauma, indigenous mental health workers may be able to develop and enact strategies to interrupt the vicious cycle of transgenerational transmission of shared trauma.

Maria Tumarkin's (2005) description of a *traumascape*, a landscape marked by the need of people to build memorials where traumatic events occurred, is useful when contemplating the psychological geography around Moree. The past is always alive and playing out in the memory and grief of unresolved loss and trauma. In 2000, a memorial was unveiled outside Bingara near Moree to mark the Myall Creek Massacre of thirty unarmed Wirrayaraay members of the Gamilaraay nation. The memorial was vandalised in 2005. Another memorial plaque was erected in Moree to commemorate "Top Camp" when Aborigines were moved from the reserve at Terry Hie Hie in the early 1920s to live on the banks of the Mehi River. These memorial stones have a "change function" (Volkan, 2001) for the groups whose members have been affected by the trauma and their descendants. The monuments and the attached plaques are "like boxes in which the unfinished psychological processes of an affected group are kept locked up" (Volkan, 2001, p. 10). They can either postpone or become instruments for the work of mourning. The monuments in Moree have not sufficiently "cooled" to be appreciated aesthetically as art.

Myall Creek, Top Camp, the Mission, the local artesian pool complex, Stanley Village, Birrewey Place, Dingwell Place, Toomelah, Boggabilla, and Slaughterhouse Creek are daily reminders that the transgenerational transmission of trauma has created psychological injury for many residents. The missions and reserves around Moree were like refugee camps that required a passport or identity papers to leave. These places are psychologically "hot" (Volkan, 2001, p. 11), as they can induce immediate and intense feelings. The community experiences what Volkan describes as "chosen traumas" (2004a, para. 2). Imagery associated with these events causes a group to feel helpless, victimized, and humiliated by another group. The massacres, reserves, and missions around Moree are chosen to be mythologized in collective memory. Forgiveness, healing, responsibility, and accountability are prevented.

Volkan (2004a, para. 2) asserts that when a group or community adopts chosen traumas, it may develop an "exaggerated entitlement ideology" or "belief system that asserts that a group has a right to own what they wish to have." The pronounced welfare dependency of community members in Moree and the visibility of its welfare sector are symptomatic of this entitlement ideology. The abuse of the welfare system distracts the oppressed from the true causes of their problems and from the solutions.

This construction of history and identity risks creating cultural ghettoes from the entrenched self-hatred of victims who take for granted a life of violence, ignorance, dysfunction, and dependence in country towns, border communities, and town camps. The hostile encounter with the other, with the unknown, with the limits of one's understanding or knowledge produces a "defensive identity" (Castells, 2011, p. 61) or retrenchment of the known. Turkish novelist Elif Shafak warns of the dangers of identity politics in cultural and literary studies:

> It is not healthy for a human being to stare at his own image. Knowledge that takes us not beyond ourselves is worse than ignorance. We have no connection with the world beyond that which we take for granted. (Shafak, 2010)

Shafak advocates for universal and local culture that is from here and everywhere. The rise of identity politics among the academically educated "techno-meritocracy" (Castells, 2003, p. 39), a community of technologically and intellectually competent peers, has been accompanied by a rising tide of "particularisms, racisms and nationalisms" (Guattari, 1992, p. 16). This class does not lack knowledge but risks becoming elitist, distant, and disconnected through the pursuit of narcissistic intellectual knowledge rather than experience. *Learned wisdom brings arrogance* (Gyuto Monks of Tibet, 2003, p. 90). The professional education classes are not immune from lateral violence through loss of judgment, victimisation of complexity and loss of courage that constitute a culture of silence and complicity. For example when figures are charged with being representatives of culture and as victimised representatives rather than creative and independent individuals. Freedom, awareness, insight, healing, and justice are endangered by ignorance, acceptance of habits, addictions, reaction, repression, nepotism, and corruption.

Care for a community involves the ethical and compassionate care for self and others through *being* and *doing*. Freire (2005, p. 12) writes that the responsibility of this process "cannot be acquired intellectually, but only through experience." Such knowledge creates dialectics between those who belong to a group and the description of visitors that "brings us into touch with the lives of strangers" (Geertz, 1973, p. 16). Geertz calls this process *Thick Description* (Geertz, 1973, p. 3). How does a community or place become meaningful to outsiders such as the university-educated workers with specialist skills and knowledge who come to live and work in Moree, who must create affirmative and transformative opportunities for those they work with? Many experience privileges and mobility not available to their clients. A number fail to integrate into the community or connect with their clients. Some work with the community for professional advancement in law, medicine, the arts, and education. There is a risk of appropriating and objectifying the experience and culture of the other for narcissistic self-gratification and professional advancement.

Going deeply into a community or place does not have to be serious. Understanding community and place is a work of imagination rather than logic. It involves savouring what is at hand rather than analysing. It can be a gentle and playful practice. It requires patience and kindness: acceptance without looking for results, without achieving goals, without trying to create an ideal of how it should be. Self-reflective knowledge involves seizing what is understandable, nurturing it, and letting it develop its own subtleties. Life becomes a continuous process of discovering and finding things out.

Lives that appear to have been shattered and irreparably broken can in fact show little sense of despair and hopelessness but instead, beyond explanation, develop immense affirmation, freedom, and peace. We have the ability to thrive.

Resilience requires basic trust, a sense of being at home in the world where we are able to trust ourselves and other people. Meaningful changes in mental and physical health, longevity, happiness, resilience, and wisdom for individuals and communities are based on self-reflection and caring relationships. We will still experience setbacks and make mistakes. Offence and disputes will occur. When we trust our mind, we can feel wholesome, healthy, and sane. We make friends with ourselves. The worst war is the war in which we make enemies with ourselves. Self-hatred has created an acceptance of psychotropic-politics in the modern medical industrial military complex: ideological terror that uses "strange other-ness" to promote passive acceptance of the global prescription of psychotropics in the neuro-techno-pacification of resistant behaviour or critical voices and minds.

The experience of wisdom brings inner peace (Gyuto Monks of Tibet, 2003, p. 90). Building trust and peace could involve accepting the generous offer of a col-league to buy lunch and engaging in impassioned conversations where one's mind is accepted and one's thoughts and expressions are listened to, discerned, and val-ued; receiving two goldfish from a domestic violence worker; walking to visit the horses kept at the Moree Showground; picking the figs, lemons, or mulberries that hang over the back fences in Ballah Lane; stopping to watch a group of parrots feeding; cooking lamb and quince casserole for a visitor; caring for abused animals; riding a bicycle down a country road; holding a homemade cup-cake bought from a country school fete; buying honey and olives at a local market; op-shopping with Gamilaraay mothers; talking with Gamilaraay literacy students about Brazilian artist Hèlio Oiticica; feeling the warmth of the sun on oneself while sitting on a step on a winter day; taking in the starry night sky in a remote community; diving into the local swimming pool in the heat of summer; or pouring healing sands from a sacred mandala into the Mehi River. We can find in the uniqueness of our story, a unity that transcends and includes differences. Freire writes: "We carry with us the memory of many fabrics, self-soaked in our history, our culture; a memory, sometimes scattered, sometimes sharp and clear . . ." (Freire, 2004, p. 23).

In 1968, radical Brazilian artist Hèlio Oiticica declared on a parongole (a music genre) in tribute to murdered criminal and associate Cara de Cavalo, Seja marginal, seja herói. In 2009, not long after I moved to Moree, a fire destroyed a large body of Oiticica's work. Shortly after this, I destroyed my art and donated my belongings to charity. When living in Moree, I heard the news of British fashion designer Alexander McQueen's suicide and John Galliano's dependence on drugs and alcohol. I was aware that I had survived and of the abjection and shame of others—even the beautiful, the rich, and the famous fall from grace and shatter blind into fragments. Moment after moment of dying, letting go, and gratitude for everything and ev-eryone is a catalyst for making peace with ourselves, with our lives, and with oth-ers. This is a lifelong journey, purpose, work, and practice. On October 26, 2012, I attended a rally for Reclaim the Night in Moree. Amongst the marchers were relatives of Theresa Binge. She disappeared from Boggabilla in 2003. Her body was discovered on the side of the road near Boomi. Her murderer has not been found and charged. In November 2012, a local youth stabbed another teenager, who died.

Experiencing sadness, pain, and hardship is a part of life for all. We may try to repress and minimise our pain with drugs and alcohol, sex, anger, violence, food, sadness, distraction, sensation, busyness, gossip, fantasy, control or abuse of others, or amassing wealth and possessions. We cannot be cured of our suffering or medicated and psychoanalysed out of it. We can accept pain without being paralysed by it. We can use the experiences that cause us pain and suffering such as abuse or oppression for a purpose. We can create change through changing the expression on our face. When we reflect on and accept a feeling, a moment, an event, or our past, we can develop the skills to choose our reaction and explore new avenues of authentic living and authentic knowledge.

A mind motivated by compassion reaches out to know the world and others just as the heart reaches out through love and humility. Hope is for the transformation of lives and communities through feeling shame, observing, listening, and talking about justice and injustice—and then taking action. Wisdom arising from life's journey brings hope for the reunification and reconstruction of fractured lives and worlds. Entering that experience long enough to endure it, deliberately and consciously for transformation to occur, is a challenge that knows no end. The work of peace, justice, forgiveness, and acceptance are intrinsic to the ontology of hope.

REFERENCES

Australian Broadcasting Corporation. (2010). Bess Nungarrayi Price on the NT Intervention. Retrieved from http://www.abc.net.au/tv/bigideas/stories/2010/02/15/2819622.htm

Australian Broadcasting Corporation. (2011). Moree rates high in domestic violence stats. Retrieved from http://www.abc.net.au/news/2011-08-12/moree-rates-high-in-domestic-violence-stats/2836970

Australian Broadcasting Corporation. (2012). Abuse stories highlight concerns for towns like Toomelah. Retrieved from http://www.abc.net.au/7.30/content/2012/s3538245.htm

Australian Human Rights Commission. (2011). Indigenous communities must address lateral violence. Retrieved from http://humanrights.gov.au/about/media/news/2011/98_11.html

Behrendt, L., Larkin, S., Griew, R., & Kelly, P. (2012). Review of higher education access and outcomes for Aboriginal and Torres Strait Islander People: Final report. Canberra: Australia: Department of Industry, Innovation, Science, Research and Tertiary Education. Behrendt, Larkin, Griew & Kelly. Retrieved from http://www.innovation.gov.au/HigherEducation/IndigenousHigherEducation/ReviewOfIndigenousHigherEducation/FinalReport/index.html

Border Rivers-Gwydir Catchment Management Authority. (2010). Our home, our country: Ngalingu Walaaybaa. Inverell and Moree, Australia: NSW Government.

Brett, G., & Figueiredo, L. (Eds.). (2007). *Oiticica in London*. London, England: Tate Publishing.

Buoyancy Foundation of Victoria. (2003). *Nothing wrong: Self care for those who have been abused or who abuse substances*. Richmond, Victoria, Australia: Buoyancy Foundation of Victoria.

Castells, M. (2003). *The Internet galaxy: Reflections on the Internet, business and society*. Oxford, England: Oxford University Press.

Castells, M,. (2011). *The power of identity*. Volume 2 of *The information age: Economy, society, and culture*. Cambridge, MA: Blackwell.

Cox, E. (1996). *Leading women: Tactics for making the difference*. Milsons Point, Australia: Random House.

Dangalaba, M. (2012). Am I white enough for you? [Web log post]. *The Northern Myth*. Retrieved from http://blogs.crikey.com.au/northern/2012/08/20/am-i-white-enough-for-you/

Dufourmantelle, A., & Derrida, J. (2000). *Of hospitality*. Stanford, CA: Stanford University Press.

Eckhart, M. (1994). *Selected writings*. London, England: Penguin.

Etheridge, R., Jr. (1918). *The dendroglyphs or carved trees of New South Wales*. Sydney, Australia: William Applegate Gullick.

Farmer, P. (1996). On suffering and structural violence: A view from below. *Daedalus, 125* (1). Retrieved from http://www.jstor.org/discover/10.2307/20027362?uid=3737536&uid=2129&uid=2&uid=70&uid=4&sid=21101342982117

Freire, P. (2000). *Pedagogy of the oppressed*. London, England: Continuum.

Freire, P. (2004). *Pedagogy of hope: Reliving 'Pedagogy of the oppressed.'* London, England: Continuum.

Freire, P. (2005). *Education for critical consciousness*. London, England: Continuum.

Freire, P. (2007). *Pedagogy of the heart*. London, England: Continuum.

Geertz, C. (1973). *The interpretation of cultures*. New York, NY: Basic Books.

Guattari, F. (1992). Regimes, pathways, subjectivities. In J. Crary & S. Kwinter (Eds.), *Incorporations* (pp. 16–37). New York, NY: Zone.

Gyuto Monks of Tibet. (2003). *Heal your heart: Simple words of wisdom*. Sydney, Australia: ABC Enterprises.

Human Rights and Equal Opportunity Commission. (1988). *Toomelah report: Report on problems and needs of aborigines living on the NSW-Queensland border*. Sydney. Australia: Einfeld, Killer & Mundine.

Huxley, H. (2011, May 7). Life of a throwaway tweet. *The Sydney Morning Herald*. Retrieved from: http://www.smh.com.au/national/long-life-of-a-throwaway-tweet-20110506-1ebsc.html

Langton, M. (2008). The end of "big men" politics. *Griffith REVIEW, 22*. Retrieved from https://griffithreview.com/edition-22-moneysexpower/the-end-of-big-men-politics

Langton, M. (2011, April 15). Aboriginal sophisticates betray bush sisters. *The Australian*. Retrieved from http://www.theaustralian.com.au/national-affairs/opinion/aboriginal-sophisticates-betray-bush-sisters/story-e6frgd0x-1226039349353

Levinas, E. (2008). *Existence and existents*. Pittsburgh, PA: Duquesne University Press.

Lingis, A. (1994). *The community of those who have nothing in common*. Bloomington: Indiana University Press.

Neff, K. (2011). *Self-compassion: Stop beating yourself up and leave insecurity behind*. London, England: Hodder & Stoughton.

New South Wales Department of Premier and Cabinet. (2008). *Report of the Special Commission of Inquiry Into Child Protection Services in NSW* (Vol. 2). Sydney, Australia: Wood. Retrieved from http://www.dpc.nsw.gov.au/__data/assets/pdf_file/0011/33797/Volume_2_-_Special_Commission_of_Inquiry_into_Child_Protection_Services_in_New_South_Wales.pdf

Our Consumer Place. (2010). *So you have a "mental illness"…what now?* North Melbourne, Australia: Victorian Department of Health & Our Consumer Place.

Pearson, N. (2009). *Up from the mission.* Collingwood, Australia: Black Inc.

Pearson, N. (2011). *Radical hope: Education and equality in Australia.* Collingwood, Australia: Black Inc.

Price, B. (2009). Against change for the wrong reasons. Retrieved from http://www.theaustralian.com.au/opinion/against-change-for-the-wrong-reasons/story-e6frg6zo-1225766571739?nk=d071ea12ce9006d386396d6fb3337cde

Ramírez, M. (2007). *Hélio Oiticica: The body of colour.* London, England: Tate Publishing, with the Museum of Fine Arts, Houston, TX.

SBS. (2012). *Aboriginal or not.* Retrieved from http://www.sbs.com.au/insight/episode/transcript/490/Aboriginal-or-not

Shafak, E. (2010). *The politics of fiction.* Retrieved from www.ted.com/talks/elif_shafak_the_politics_of_fiction.html

Smith, L. (2012). *Decolonizing methodologies: Research and indigenous peoples.* London, England: Zed Books.

Tumarkin, M. (2005). *Traumascapes: The power and fate of places transformed by tragedy.* Carlton, Australia: Melbourne University Press.

Volkan, V. (2001). *Massive shared trauma and hot places.* Retrieved from http://www.austenriggs.org/images/uploads/Trauma%20and%20HOT%20PLACES.pdf

Volkan, V. (2004a). *Chosen trauma: The political ideology of entitlement and violence.* Retrieved from http://www.vamikvolkan.com/Chosen-Trauma,-the-Political-Ideology-of-Entitlement-and-Violence.php

Volkan, V. (2004b). Traumatized societies and psychological care: Expanding the concept of preventative medicine. In D. Knaffo (Ed.), *Living with terror, working with trauma: A clinician's handbook* (pp. 480–484). Lanham, MD: Rowman & Littlefield.

Volkan, V. (2009). The next chapter: Consequences of societal trauma. In P. Gobodo-Madikizela & C. Van de Merve (Eds.), *Memory, narrative and forgiveness: Perspectives on the unfinished journeys of the past* (pp. 1–26). Newcastle, England: Cambridge Scholars Publishing.

Volkan, V., & Fowler, C. (2009). Large group narcissism and political leadership. *Psychiatric Annals, 39*(4). Retrieved from http://www.vamikvolkan.com/Large-group-Narcissism-and-Political-Leaders.php

Weil, S. (2007). *The need for roots.* London, England: Routledge.

Williams, R. (2012). *Cultural safety: What does it mean for our work practice?* Retrieved from http://diplomaofcasemanagement2012.neitwiki.wikispaces.net/file/view/RevisedCulturalSafetyPaper-pha.pdf

Wood, J. (2008) *Report of the special commission of inquiry into child protection services in NSW* (Vol. 2). Sydney, Australia: New South Wales Department of Premier and Cabinet. Retrieved from http://www.dpc.nsw.gov.au/__data/assets/pdf_file/0011/33797/Volume_2_-_Special_Commission_of_Inquiry_into_Child_Protection_Services_in_New_South_Wales.pdf

Teaching English for Academic Purposes in a Japanese Setting: Problematizing and Dialogizing Essentialist Constructions of Language Pedagogy, Culture, and Identity

GLENN TOH

INTRODUCTION

This chapter is about opening up space for critical pedagogical practices in a Japanese EAP (English for Academic Purposes) setting. In recent years, universities in Japan have been actively seeking to have a steadily increasing number of their academic content courses delivered in English instead of Japanese. This is in response to the pressing need for Japanese universities to globalize amid calls for reform and reinvention, given a moribund curriculum (Goodman & Phillips, 2003), not least because many universities are also facing the pressure of falling enrollments due to a low birth rate and gradually imploding population (Burgess, 2010). Along with this new development has come an increased demand for courses in EAP.

In this chapter, I will argue that prevalent beliefs and practices relating to English language teaching (ELT) in Japan, while seen in many quarters as being instrumental, pragmatic (Kubota, 2011b), and ideologically "neutral," are intrinsically and epistemologically repressive. The late (and practically sudden) introduction of academic courses in English (Burgess, 2010) will further accentuate this problem, while exhibiting the ingredients of an external superimposition on both

English teachers and students, with serious implications for teacher and student subjectivities. This is apart from opening up entirely different sites of contention. I will argue that inherent in various curricular and pedagogical practices relating to having academic courses in English as well as in the teaching of EAP is the potential for the emergence of inequalities and repression, in turn realized in ideologized practices and commodified icons such as the standardized English test (TOEIC in Japan), the English entrance examination, and a predominantly skills-based deficit curriculum.

My discussion will draw on current literature providing theoretical and professional articulations on (a) the appropriation of English in Japan; (b) the role and positioning of ELT in academia in Japan and the subject positioning of English teachers and EFL students; (c) prevailing discourses bearing on curriculum planning and delivery, vis-à-vis the emancipatory ideals to be found in critical approaches to pedagogy; as well as (d) my own lived experience as a language teacher. Attention will be given to how repressive and reductionist controls are dissimulated beneath the veneer of conventionality, orthodoxy, and regularity of English teaching in the country. Finally, I will discuss strategies that can be adopted to counter powerfully essentialist constructions of language, culture, and identity vis-à-vis the EAP curriculum.

WHY ACADEMIC COURSES IN ENGLISH AT THIS TIME?

In this section, I would like to examine the way the English language and its global spread (Phillipson, 2008) has been perceived and appropriated in Japan, beginning with the observation that Japan has had to work through serious challenges relating to the English language (Aspinall, 2003). In the throes of the Pacific War, English was viewed as the language of the enemy (Oda, 2007). In the years of economic prosperity that began in the 1960s extending all the way to the late 1980s, the spread of English was viewed cautiously—as a threat to Japanese national identity and was therefore regarded as a culturally imperialistic (Hashimoto, 2007) force that needed to be countered by a rhetoric of resistance.

Furthermore, Japan as a nation has contended with matters to do with language, culture, and identity, epitomized not least in a proliferation of publications discussing the nature of Japaneseness and what it means to be Japanese. Such writings often and unfortunately play to a monolithic conceptualization of Japaneseness as being bound to an ethno-primordial form of Japanese ethnicity, language, and culture, articulated in a genre of literature known as *nihonjinron* writings that reify the uniqueness of the Japanese people (Befu, 1984, 2001). In *nihonjinron* writings, the Japanese language is treated as both a symbol and corollary of such uniqueness. Given this, the current push toward having academic courses taught and assessed in English becomes somewhat a curious if not surprising development. It might be noted here that even the University of Tokyo, an old and venerated institution, took the unusual step of conducting one of its entrance ceremonies in English in the fall of 2011 (University of Tokyo, 2011).

To better appreciate what is happening, it should be noted that Japan has, in recent years, been facing the problem of a low birth rate and imploding population (Burgess, 2010), to the point that universities have been experiencing falling enrollments. As part of trying to contain this trend, the government has embarked on an initiative to attract more foreign students into Japanese universities, launching an important project called the Internationalization Hub Consolidation Project (Global 30 Project, for short), which is an important milestone in terms of its expressed aims to internationalize Japanese universities. The official language of courses conducted under the auspices of this project at the thirteen designated universities in the country is none other than English (Rivers, 2010). An important point to note here is that Global 30 is primarily a project for attracting more overseas enrollments and is not inherently or conceptually thought of as one that will have any great or stimulating impact on existing classes run in Japanese. Indeed, we are told that Japanese students will not be studying alongside foreign enrollees in the Global 30 English medium courses (Rivers, 2010).

Nevertheless, outside of the thirteen designated Global 30 universities, other institutions, notably those in the densely populated Kanto and Kansai regions but also stretching to northern reaches in Tohoku and west in Kyushu, have tapped into the same rhetoric of internationalization and have also begun to conduct content courses in English. An outcome of this has been the increased demand for EAP courses, the reason being that Japanese students, even up to the time of entrance to university, have only had content subjects taught to them in Japanese. Content courses in English in university would consequently be extremely new and challenging. EAP is therefore crucial for content courses conducted in English to be realistic or viable.

REASONS FOR INTEREST IN ENGLISH

Despite the nationalistic view that English works as a culturally imperialistic force that competes against Japanese culture in zero-sum fashion (Aspinall, 2003), English teaching continues in schools and universities as well as the ubiquitous conversation schools very commonly found around train or bus stations. As of late, universities even want to have their content courses delivered in English. Why would this be the case?

The teaching and learning of English in Japan is sustained by ideologies and practices that nurture discursively constructed myths and iconic entities. To explain this "draw" toward English, it can be noted that the teaching and learning of English is part of a powerful narrative that romanticizes and commodifies the English language alongside its association with whiteness (Kubota, 2011a). The model of English held in high esteem is American English, with British English coming in a distant second. White teachers with American accents are keenly sought after, whereas black teachers or those with other accents (e.g., Australian or African American) are not (Honna, 2008; Kubota, 2002). English and the imagined freedoms of a western lifestyle are objects of desire for the Japanese people and Japanese women in particular are especially vulnerable to an English language that is discursively linked to an exotic world of English speakers as well as cultural fantasies associated with commodifications of whiteness (Kubota, 2011a).

In addition, English is closely tied in with the rhetoric of instrumentalism (Kubota, 2011b), how a mastery of English is seen as a way to wider career opportunities while opening up hypothetical global spaces (Kubota, 2011a). It is believed that a mastery of English will open up work opportunities, especially with regard to getting coveted overseas posts or appointments. Parents of university-age children likewise believe that an increased exposure to English beyond merely sending their offspring to conversation schools will increase their chances of landing better-paid and more glamorous jobs upon graduation. Such parents find their justification in the fact that large companies such as Rakuten and Uniqlo have begun to use English as their workplace language. Decision makers, on their part, latch onto rhetoric that naturalizes English as "the default language of international communication," rhetoric that links "global" English to strongly corporate interests (Phillipson, 2008, p. 4).

Such "mythicizing" (Freire, 2000, p. 168) enacts a brave new world of far-reaching possibilities for willing colluders (or consumers). Universities are able to harness this rhetoric not unlike the way dominant elites in Roman times spoke of the need to give "bread and circus" to the masses (Freire, 2000, p. 141), where English concocts a "bread and circus" formula to impress parents and students, not forgetting the very decision makers themselves. The flipside is that such collusion legitimates the workings of an oppression that bears down on parents, students, and decision makers alike, willing colluders notwithstanding. This in turn illustrates what Freire (2000, p. 127) notes to be an "existential duality," "embodying an ambiguity imposed on [such colluders] by the [very] situation of oppression," a fairly exemplary case of how "such persons retain the oppressor within themselves" (p. 155).

POWERFUL IDEOLOGIES AND NARRATIVES LINKED TO ENGLISH AND ELT

Bearing the above discussion in mind, I turn now to examine how entrenched practices that reflect particularized understandings of teaching and learning can present (or constitute) seriously limiting situations for the work of teachers. To do this, I draw on my own lived experience as a language teacher while following the work of educators who have founded their praxis on the realities of lived professional encounters (Freire, 2000). The work of these educators addresses (a) issues of ideology and power as they bear on language, culture, and education (Apple, 2000, 2002; Lee, 2002; Murphey, 2004; Spack, 1998); (b) the realities, challenges, and exigencies of teaching and learning in unique contextual situations (Hayes, 2010; Rivers, 2013; Tsui, 2007); and (c) the importance of teacher-generated narratives enacting teacher agency and action and how they can ameliorate the polarizing forces of institutional politics (Alderson, 2009; Apple, 2000; Rivers, 2013; Tsui, 2007).

Concerning Curriculum and Assessment

The workings of ideology in approaches to curriculum design and assessment can be seen in the way they exercise controls on how institutions and decision makers can or cannot act, with strong ramifications for teacher and student subjectivities. From my own experience in Japan, examples of this include the practice of using the TOEIC test as a measurement of proficiency, the English entrance examination as a bastion (and vestige) of unchanging practice (Aspinall, 2003; Murphey, 2004; Stanlaw, 2004), a curriculum that is strongly bound within a skills-based deficit model of planning and delivery (Lea & Street, 2000), and a 4-skills syllabus that reifies a narrow TESOL/TEFL curricular framework (Holliday, 2005). For enlightened decision makers, maneuvering decisions around these monolithic "givens" can prove very difficult. Teachers who are concerned with humanizing the curriculum, critical praxis, and teacher and student subjectivities also face challenges when seeking out the space for dialogical and emancipatory practices that promote openness, fairness, and equity.

The Panoptics of TOEIC. The TOEIC test maintains a panoptic presence in Japanese ELT. Epitomizing a circumscription of practice, it is panoptic in the way it becomes the preoccupation of parents, teachers, employers, administrators, and policy makers alike. Test scores, curves, and other graphical statistics command their own mythical presence, with many institutions keeping detailed graphs of individual students' progress. It would not be too unreasonable to say that

TOEIC is the make-or-break in a student's success or failure when it comes to his or her English. Institutions use TOEIC statistics as a way of advertising. Programs in academic English do not escape the panoptic presence of the TOEIC. In my own experience, the success of EAP programs I have taught or even the evaluation my own teaching has been measured via its auspices. The "effectiveness" of a teacher's teaching can be called into question with regard to students' TOEIC scores, while English program coordinators can be summoned to account if TOEIC statistics skew toward being unfavorable. As TOEIC is a bit item multiple-choice test of truncated listening to passages and largely decontextualized reading of extracts, such a form of testing becomes a serious challenge to teachers who believe that language is about engaging students realistically with socio-historical and socio-dialogical contexts of meaning production (Bakhtin, 1986).

While the influence of TOEIC can ultimately be better understood experientially by teachers and students in situations in which it exerts a heavy hand on classroom practices, for example, when teachers are obliged to rehearse students in question-answering techniques, an understanding of TOEIC's ideological dimensions must come through a probe into the origins of the test itself. TOEIC finds its roots in big business, and discussions of TOEIC seldom ever escape its close connections to the business world. This is despite protestations and remonstrations of its nonprofitability (Kubota, 2011b). The test itself is administered by the Institute for International Business Communication (IIBC) and was developed in 1979 "in response to the initiative of a Japanese entrepreneur who mobilized business leaders and retired government officials" to develop a test for Japanese learners (Kubota, 2011b, p. 250). It is not surprising that IIBC has, of late, aroused suspicions about its "interest in profit making" in the way it creates "testing needs by means of research and publicity that are subsidized by the money generated by test fees" (Kubota, 2011b, p. 250). If there is truth in these suspicions, then the close links between TOEIC and higher education institutions in Japan would add a dimension of commercialism to measurements of students' English proficiency. This is beside the fact that its reliance on a multiple-choice format for test reading, listening, and grammar (Kubota, 2011b) is fundamentally at odds with the work of engaging students with the discursive, dialogical, and socio-constructivist aspects of language, typifying its use in the making of meaning (Bakhtin, 1986).

Teachers are caught in a bind. It is valuable and necessary for teachers like me to spend time engaging students in discursive and dialogical aspects of thought and meaning-making. The dilemma, however, is that in some universities, students' TOEIC scores can contribute up to 50% of their final EAP grade. How teachers have to straddle the demands of engendering academic literacy on one hand while having to work on atomistic language drills as part of test preparation on the other hand becomes a veritable fight against oppression.

The Entrance Examination. Murphey (2004) describes how the Japanese university English entrance examination is a construct of human politics and powerful agendas. Much like the TOEIC, the examinations rely on discrete test items testing atomized components of language such as phrasal verbs, sentence connectors, or word order. Aspinall (2003) highlights how the entrance examination is much more than a language test per se, in that it represents closely protected professional turf of Japanese teachers of English, one which is guarded vigilantly and not to be ceded to forces of change from the outside. Hence, when Murphey (2004) relates how, as part of his duties on the examination committee at his university, he tried to introduce index of facility (IF) and index of discrimination (ID) research into test item construction, the responses he met with from both colleagues and administration were decidedly negative. Here again, the implications for EAP are serious in that the very examinations administered to potential students, apart from not being founded on the ways language is used in academia, have also been problematized for their (lack of) validity.

My own experience of this is striking. I was asked to be part of an entrance examination committee at my then place of work in a small private university in the Kanto region that taught a significant proportion of its undergraduate courses in English. The chairperson of the committee was, not insignificantly, also in charge of TOEIC preparation courses. The committee members were made up of the chairperson, one other TOEIC preparation teacher and three academic English teachers (one each from the United States and the United Kingdom, and me). Both TOEIC teachers were Japanese.

At the first meeting, the chairperson handed out printed sheets with outlines of the types of test items to be set and the person to be in charge of coming up with the items. There were to be items requiring reordering of scrambled clauses and phrases, translation of short (decontextualized) sentences from Japanese to English, responses to conversation routines such as common enquiries made at bus stops or train stations, and multiple-choice items testing grammar, denotative, and idiomatic meanings. I had to come up with two reading passages of about three hundred words each. The first passage had to be accompanied by true-false questions on factual information that students had to draw from the passage and the second by multiple-choice questions covering denotative meanings and factual content.

Given the fact that university courses required both exposition and argumentation of ideas, I quickly suggested that questions inviting original responses on thematic or topical issues should follow at least one of the reading passages. This suggestion was not accepted. Two reasons were offered.

The first was that exposition and argumentation were "not tested" at Japanese university examinations, nor were students required to offer spontaneous or original responses. There was simply no precedence for this. Moreover, the university, being a Japanese university, should not be seen to deviate from what other universities were doing. To substantiate this, a collection of past-year papers from different universities was duly produced.

The second was that my task was to design items that tested "reading comprehension." Since it was "reading comprehension" (and not writing or thinking skills) that was being tested, students could not possibly be required to do any of these in their responses. This was beside the fact that entrance examination scores had to be numerically quantifiable in absolute terms. Items that sought one-word answers or items requiring answers that were either "absolutely right" or "absolutely wrong" were the only ones that lent themselves to this type of scoring. Answers requiring spontaneous or critical responses were difficult and time consuming to mark since they could not be scored or quantified in numerical terms. Numerical scores were considered the most "objective" and "accurate" way of assessing language ability.

Of course, the irony was that students taking this entrance examination that the committee was in charge of preparing would ultimately be admitted into courses that required them to engage with topical and thematic issues in written mode. One is reminded of how inflexibility or a reluctance to change suggests the workings of an oppressor consciousness seeking to inanimate or immobilize new ideas (Freire, 2000).

I finally came up with two passages, one on Tiger Woods and the other on ballet performances, complete with the true-false and multiple-choice items—as instructed.

The Skills-Based Deficit Model and the 4-Skills Syllabus. If TOEIC and the entrance examination represent anomalies in the way language ability is measured and in the way students are assessed for admission, the skills-based deficit model of curriculum planning and the 4-skills syllabus represent circumscribed conceptualizations of language teaching (Holliday, 2005; Lea & Street, 2000), which are, once again, not in keeping with the facilitation of knowledge and meaning-making that language for academia demands. My own reasoning is that this is due to what Goodwin (1994) describes as discursively constructed controls or limitations that bear on both cognitive and perceptual parameters of professional practice or simply because dominant practices in TESOL/TEFL teacher certification tend to legitimate the centrality of essentialized methods and lesson planning and delivery practices rather than substantive issues to do with student empowerment and teacher agency. I return to this matter in a later section.

TEACHING ENGLISH FOR ACADEMIC PURPOSES IN A JAPANESE SETTING | 343

Concerning Narrow Conceptualizations of English and English Speakers

In Japan, language, culture, and ethnicity are viewed monolithically (de Mente, 2005). English is associated with "English-speaking peoples," taken stereotypically to mean white people from America and Britain, and to a lesser extent from Australia and other native-English-speaking countries (Kubota, 2002). This can be seen in materials written and produced for both ELT and English studies, which target the Japanese market. Takahashi's (1996) *British and American Cultural Readers*, for example, has reading material that typifies the English as being "bold and brave, yet inflexible and stubborn, as proud and haughty, yet correct and courteous" (p. 1), that British humor is to be prominently found in puns to which listeners respond with groans, and that displeasure is expressed through taboo words such as "blimey" or "bollocks" (p. 28). Americans, on their part, are typified as people who like to shop and that they do most of the shopping in department stores, supermarkets, shopping malls, and hypermarkets (Takahashi, 1996). Dennis, Saito, and Hayagoshi (1996) have passages explaining the Proms and Rule Britannia, the design of English gardens and traditions such as the Oxford and Cambridge boat race. Both books come complete with Japanese annotations.

Concerning Particularized Conceptualizations of Internationalization and Globalization

It has been mentioned that having more English in the university curriculum comes as part of Japan's effort at internationalizing its university courses and campuses (Burgess, 2010; Rivers, 2010). However, in the case of Japan, prevailing discourses to do with internationalization and globalization should be examined for their subtleties and nuances, particularly because they are, paradoxically, founded on an ideological substratum of nationalism.

Japan exhibits characteristics of the closed societies captured in Freire (1985): "rigid hierarchical social structure" and certainly a "precarious and selective education system whose schools are an instrument of maintaining the status quo" (Freire, 1985, p. 75). In Japan, the notion of a closed society also means that discussions of internationalization and globalization cannot be separated from nationalistic sentiments. Hashimoto (2007) describes an internationalization founded on motivations of strengthening nationalism. Describing a six-chapter report, the "Prime Minister's Commission on Japan's Goals in the 21st Century," an important document released by an advisory commission set up by the then Prime Minister, Keizo Obuchi, she notes that globalization is viewed negatively in the document (Hashimoto, 2007) and that Japan's remonstrations of looking outward are at best equivocal. This can be seen in both the subtitle of the report, translated to mean "Japan's frontier lies within Japan" (Hashimoto, 2007, p. 30), and the following extract from the commission's report that circumlocutiously points to an inward-looking agenda:

> Should we not face the future of the world and engage with it body and soul? By doing so, even if sometimes we wrestle with contradictions, surely the good qualities of the Japanese...will be honed into qualities possessing universality. If we live with such an attitude, we will come to see that Japan's frontier lies within. (Prime Minister's Commission, 2000, Preface, as cited in Hashimoto, 2007, p. 30)

Aspinall (2003) similarly describes the nationalistic belief that internationalism is only possible if Japanese people are strongly rooted in their own history, culture, and traditions. Describing Prime Minister Yasuhiro Nakasone's concept of "healthy nationalism," Aspinall (2003, p. 111) argues that "healthy nationalism" is merely a "more internationally acceptable face" of what in reality is *nihonjinron* ideology emerging in discussions about "mutual respect" across borders. Indeed, de Mente (2005, p. 192) notes that the "image that Japan gives of being 'international' is mostly mirage" and that "intellectually and emotionally, the average Japanese is far from being 'international'". He captures how internationalism for Japan is circumscribed and indexed with particular reference to the Japanese self rather than to the larger world beyond:

> Many Japanese believe that internationalism is little more than being able to communicate with the rest of the world well enough that they can explain themselves and the Japanese system to foreigners—following which foreigners will finally understand Japan and will accept Japan's system. (de Mente, 2005, p. 192)

No doubt, such particularized understandings of internationalization and internationalism cast a shadow of suspicion over Japan's late but ardent interest in having more English, much as such an initiative is linked palpably to internationalizing its university campuses. Internationalization of campuses through having more English seems incompatible with an inward-looking agenda.

IN THE WAKE OF INVASIVE, TOP-DOWN IMPOSITIONS

It is amid such a confluence of conflicting ideologies that EAP and content courses in English are now being brought into the university curriculum. Administrators who are keen to have more English, in the main, view English as a financial lifeline as well as something novel in a bid to "reinvigorate" both campus and curriculum (Burgess, 2010). In reality, however, the late and sudden introduction of content courses in English and EAP is not without various degrees of trauma for and invasiveness in the system and certainly does not happen as seamlessly as may be assumed.

Concerning Academic Faculty

One important question is with regard to the academic faculty who will be teaching these content courses in English—whether they will be existing Japanese faculty who would have all along been teaching their areas of expertise in Japanese, or whether they will be academics from overseas. Concerning the latter, further questions will arise over recruitment and work conditions. Rivers (2010) relates candidly the problems that typically surface in this area include less than ideal contractual conditions for overseas hires (limited-terms contracts, unpromising prospects for career advancement), the lack of inter-cultural competence among Japanese incumbents as well as a general unwillingness among local staff to adapt to campus internationalization initiatives (Rivers, 2010)—all symptomatic of the possibility that the new changes represent forms of top-down imposition not supported further down the hierarchy.

Concerning Teachers and Students

EAP teachers, given a prevalence of extremely generalist-universalist views of the work of language teaching, will all too commonly (or all too-conveniently) be assimilated from the ranks of teachers of general English who may or may not be familiar with the practices (let alone some of the dialogical and emancipatory practices) of EAP. Lea and Street (2000) describe three approaches to teaching language for the purposes of higher education. The first is based on a deficit model of teaching and learning wherein grammar and structure are "banked" or drilled into students (Friere, 2000). The second model focuses on (powerful) academic genres and sees teaching and learning as being about having students acculturated into these genres. The third approach views language socio-historically and socio-constructively as a means toward meaning-making and knowledge production, wherein students are encouraged to critique existing formulations of knowledge and meaning in and through language.

From experience, English teachers co-opted into teaching EAP are often given a very simple brief—which is for them to get students up to speed with their English so that they can listen to lectures, takes notes, answer tutorial questions, and write term papers. EAP is conceptualized as a necessary stepping-stone toward "effective" English and is often conceived of in deficit or remedial terms—the crude belief that students' English needs to be "fixed" (Lea & Street, 2000). The dilemma here is a fairly stark one: if students are unable to understand lectures and comprehend reading material from course texts and websites, would it not mean that EAP teaching is unsuccessful? One should remain mindful of the fact that students are admitted to university through entrance exams that, for the longest time, have been constructed out of bit items testing discrete language structures. Writing, thinking, and research skills are not tested. This is to be coupled with the fact that students are required to take TOEIC, yet another bit item test, at regular intervals with their numerical scores indicating "progress." Little or no consideration is given to more emancipatory roles that language can play in students' education—how language can be used for critique and dialogization of powerful formulations of ideas as they influence and are in turn influenced by different socio-histories (Bakhtin, 1986). One is reminded of the controls and limitations that come alongside cognitive and perceptual parameters of professional practice that Goodwin (1994) describes.

Concerning Equivocal Tropes of Internationalization and Traumatizing Pushes and Pulls

The current push for English begs the question of whether it represents a genuine initiative toward internationalization, or whether the changes are merely cosmetic, creating, as it were, an "English for Cosmetic Purposes." The answer to this question has implications for the overall tenability and sustainability of corresponding campus internationalization efforts. However, while the matter is being debated, various high-handed pushes and pulls of manipulation (Friere, 2000) will continue. Every "push" outward toward some form or semblance of internationalization will only be followed by a "pull" backward (Burgess, 2010). Similarly, teachers work hard to get students ready for the rigors of academic discussion only to be hamstrung by conservative elements within institutional portals that place their stakes on preserving the status quo (Rivers, 2010), for example, picayune atomized test items representing old testing practices (Aspinall, 2003; Stanlaw, 2004). There are calculated machinations toward Othering overseas faculty (often called "foreign" teachers) and micro-political moves among staff members against the opening up of campuses (Rivers, 2010). Contradicting, confusing, traumatizing, and oppressive, such is the nature of the challenges confronting teachers opting for more conscionable approaches toward educating students.

RESISTANCE AND CRITICAL REPONSES

Teachers like me may, of course, keep silent. This would mean proceeding unquestioningly with the ubiquitous exercises found in the set texts, continuing with extensive reading programs using the ubiquitous graded readers, doing the necessary legwork for making logistical arrangements to run those ubiquitous self-access or E-learning centers. Such an approach to "teaching" is not difficult to sustain—it involves "simply passing on...prescriptions formulated in the teacher's office" (Freire, 2005, p. 37); but it does not encourage "act[s] of creation" or "releasing other creative acts" on the part of learners (p. 39).

An alternative to this sort of existence is for a teacher to consider what the humanizing and emancipatory discourses of critical pedagogy have to offer. "Not to act is to let the powerful win" becomes an apt reminder, in this connection (Apple, 2000, p. 175). Behind the introduction of new initiatives (in this case, English into an incumbently Japanese system) are ideologies and agendas that precipitate new hegemonies, new contestations, and power struggles. Critical pedagogy also allows teachers to account for inconsistencies, incongruities, contradictions, perplexities, power inequalities, and oppressions arising from late or sudden changes to a system. In the present case, these are to be found in (a) the brief to teach academic English while students and English language levels are inadequately and incongruously assessed through TOEIC; (b) the brief to teach academic English in oppressive circumstances in which the success or failure of content courses in English hinge on whether or not students' "improve" in their English; (c) the pressure of linking content courses in English to increased enrollments and institutional solvency; (d) subaltern teacher subjectivities (Apple, 2002) resulting from being cast in the role of remediators; (e) student subjectivities resulting from being Othered as *foreign* language learners alongside the slur of their being "deficient" in English; (f) the teaching and learning of English predicated on obtuse and exaggerated constructions of whiteness; (g) historically unsettled prejudices toward things and matters foreign, including English. These would surely be conundrums that suggest the inner workings of manipulation and oppression (Freire, 2000), to be exposed through an uncovering of ideologies that feed into the cultural politics of inequality and exploitation (Apple, 2000).

CLASSROOM STRATEGIES

To engender greater critical awareness, I use movies and other materials that scramble and destabilize stereotyped representations of people, places, and cultures, be they renditions of Japaneseness, foreignness, or whiteness. This is consistent with the role of teachers "to propose problems about...codified existential situations in order to help...learners arrive at a more and more critical view of... reality" (Freire, 1985, p. 55). Hence, I introduce movies that bring in Japanese characters born and bred not in Japan, but in Manchuria, for example, and who speak Mandarin (and not Japanese) as a first language. I tell students that the famous Japanese conductor, Seiji Ozawa, was not born in Japan, but in Manchuria. I use video clips widely available on YouTube that feature Japanese Americans who fought for their country in the Pacific War and were decorated for their bravery; or white people who are speakers of perfect Cantonese or Mandarin. Students get to see in language class that meaning and knowledge are located in socio-historically bound (and borne) realities rather than in stereotypes that straitjacket people, race, identity, culture, and language. I introduce and sometimes read aloud short stories in English written not by native speakers of the language, but by people from diverse regions as the Philippines, Sri Lanka, or my native Singapore. Such stories illustrate how a diversity of cultural specificities and lived experiences can be communicated through language. I also make it a point to refer to different ethnic communities living in Japan (Brazilian, Filipino, Korean, Chinese, Iranian) and to their languages and cultures, which, it is hoped, in the not too distant future will be recognized as being an integral part of a Japan that thrives outside the bigoted constrictions (and constructs) of *nihonjinron* stereotyping.

In doing the above, I seek to engender a climate of having students enter into a "dialectical relationship with their social reality" (Freire, 2005, p. 30), thinking beyond stock or prescribed conceptualizations of knowledge, content, and meaning and to foster a classroom culture that appreciates the value of diversity, variety, and enriched conversations. This is in keeping with a generative (and generous) spirit of openness to diversity and difference, which should rightly be very much a part of academic inquiry.

CONCLUSION

The introduction of content courses in English and EAP into Japanese higher education is neither simple and innocent nor straightforward and unencumbered. At best, it represents a way of keeping up with developments that legitimate and cheerlead English as the language of globalization (Phillipson, 2008). At worst, it is an untidy and oppressive way of keeping up with appearances to show how institutions are doing their part to look progressive in their bid to survive the current population and monetary crunch. Both scenarios reveal a lack of foresight and insight on the part of institutions and their decision makers—the former because of Japan's seriously ambivalent attitudes regarding the English language itself and its lack of acumen with regard to critical approaches to teaching the language; and the latter because matters relating to language, ideology, and power require deep insight into how human feelings and subjectivities are impacted.

For courses in English and EAP to work in (and for) Japan, insights into critical approaches to understanding prevailing discourses and current developments as well as into critical approaches to pedagogy must surely prove crucial.

REFERENCES

Alderson, J. C. (2009). The micropolitics of research and publication. In J. C. Alderson (Ed.), *The politics of language education: Individuals and institutions* (pp. 222–236). Bristol, England: Multilingual Matters.

Apple, M. (2000). *Official knowledge: Democratic education in a conservative age.* New York, NY: Routledge.

Apple, M. (2002). *Power, meaning and identity: Essays in critical education studies.* New York, NY: Peter Lang.

Aspinall, R. (2003). Japanese nationalism and the reform of English language teaching. In R. Goodman & D. Phillips (Eds.), *Can the Japanese change their education system?* (pp. 103–118). Wallingford, England: Symposium.

Bakhtin, M. M. (1986). The problem of speech genres. In C. Emerson & M. Holquist (Eds.), *M. M. Bakhtin: Speech genres and other late essays* (pp. 60–102). Austin: University of Texas Press.

Befu, H. (1984). Civilization and culture: Japan in search of identity. *Senri Ethnological Studies, 16*, 59–75.

Befu, H. (2001). *Hegemony of homogeneity.* Melbourne, Australia: Transpacific Press.

Burgess, C. (2010, March 23). Higher education: Opening up or closing in? Contradictory reform goals could scotch chances of success. *The Japan Times* [Electronic version]. Retrieved June 1, 2011, from http://search.japantimes.co.jp/cgi-bin/fl20100323zg.html

de Mente, B. L. (2005). *Japan unmasked: the character and culture of the Japanese.* Tokyo, Japan: Tuttle Publishing.

Dennis, I., Saito, K., & Hayagoshi, H. (1996). *The isle of Britain.* Tokyo, Japan: Asahi Press.

Freire, P. (1985). *The politics of education: Culture, power and liberation.* Westport, CT: Bergin & Garvey.

Freire, P. (2000). *Pedagogy of the oppressed, 30th anniversary edition* (M. B. Ramos, Trans.). New York, NY: Continuum.

Freire, P. (2005). *Education for critical consciousness.* New York, NY: Continuum.

Goodman, R., & Phillips, D. (Eds.). (2003). *Can the Japanese change their education system?* Wallingford, England: Symposium.

Goodwin, C. (1994). Professional vision. *American Anthropologist, 96*(3), 606–633.

Hashimoto, K. (2007). Japan's language policy and the "Lost Decade." In A. Tsui & J. Tollefson (Eds.), *Language policy, culture, and identity in Asian contexts* (pp. 25–36). Mahwah, NJ: Lawrence Erlbaum.

Hayes, D. (2010). Duty and service: Life and career of a Tamil teacher of English in Sri Lanka. *TESOL Quarterly, 44*(1), 58–83

Holliday, A. (2005). *The struggle to teach English as an international language.* Oxford, England: Oxford University Press.

Honna, N. (2008). *English as a multicultural language in Asian contexts: Issues and ideas.* Tokyo, Japan: Kuroshio.

Kubota, R. (2002). The impact of globalization on language teaching in Japan. In D. Block & D. Cameron (Eds.), *Globalization and language teaching* (pp. 13–28). London, England: Routledge.

Kubota, R. (2011a). Learning a foreign language as leisure and consumption: Enjoyment, desire, and the business of *eikaiwa*. *International Journal of Bilingual Education and Bilingualism, 14*(4), 473–488.

Kubota, R. (2011b). Questioning linguistic instrumentalism: English, neoliberalism, and language tests in Japan. *Linguistics and Education, 22*, 248–260.

Lea, M., & Street, B. (2000). Student writing and staff feedback in higher education: An academic literacies approach. In M. Lea & B. Stierer (Eds.), *Student writing in higher education: New contexts* (pp. 32–46). Buckingham, England: SRHE and Open University Press.

Lee, S. (2002). Koreans—a mistreated minority in Japan: Hope and challenges for Japan's true internalization. In R. Donahue (Ed.), *Exploring Japaneseness: On Japanese enactments of culture and consciousness* (pp. 183–195). Westport, CT: Ablex.

Murphey, T. (2004). Participation, (dis-)identification, and Japanese university entrance exams. *TESOL Quarterly, 38*(4), 700–710.

Oda, M. (2007). Globalization or the world in English: Is Japan ready to face the waves? *International Multilingual Research Journal, 1*(2), 119–126.

Phillipson, R. (2008). The linguistic imperialism of neoliberal empire. *Critical Inquiry in Language Studies, 5*(1), 1–43.

Rivers, D. J. (2010). Ideologies of internationalization and the treatment of diversity within Japanese higher education. *Journal of Higher Education Policy and Management, 32*(5), 442–454.

Rivers, D. J. (2013). Institutionalized native-speakerism: Voices of dissent and acts of resistance. In S. A. Houghton & D. J. Rivers (Eds.), *Native-speakerism in foreign language education: Intergroup dynamics in Japan* (pp. 75–91). Clevedon, England: Multilingual Matters.

Spack, R. (1998). The (in)visibility of the personal in academe. In V. Zamel & R. Spack (Eds.), *Negotiating academic literacies: Teaching and learning across languages and cultures* (pp. 293–316). Mahwah, NJ: Lawrence Erlbaum.

Stanlaw, J. (2004). *Japanese English: Language and culture contact.* Hong Kong: Hong Kong University Press.

Takahashi, K. (1996). *British and American cultural readers.* Tokyo, Japan: Ikubundo.

Tsui, A. (2007). Complexities of identity formation: A narrative inquiry of an EFL teacher. *TESOL Quarterly, 41*(4), 657–671.

University of Tokyo. (2011). The University of Tokyo Entrance Ceremony, October 4, 2011. Retrieved September 15, 2012, from www.a.u-tokyo.ac.jp/english/oicehp-e/.../20110901-1e.pdf

The Customer Knows Best: The Opposite of the Banking Concept in the Case of the United Arab Emirates

LIZ JACKSON

Freire's *Pedagogy of the Oppressed* (1989) has inspired a generation of educators to teach with the transformation of co-creative student learners in mind. To engage in *dialogue* rather than deposit information is at the heart of the critique of banking education, encouraging educators to be mindful of students' best interests, as understood by the students themselves. This pedagogy is seen as inherently political and revolutionary, as it seeks not the maintenance of the status quo in society, but rather the consciousness-raising and revolutionary transformation of the oppressed class(es), as the teacher partners with students to learn and teach collaboratively using a problem-based approach.

As Freire has acknowledged, this perspective is not readily transportable, however. There are contexts in which applying pedagogy of the oppressed, presumably in contrast with the banking model, poses interesting challenges. In this chapter, postcolonial higher education in the United Arab Emirates (UAE) will be explored to consider unique implications of Freire's educational perspective of pedagogy of the oppressed versus banking education in a radically different setting from that which Freire and many Freirean educators work within today. In the UAE, teaching faculty is recruited from Western, traditional centers of power, to teach according to students' interests and needs. An inversion of the banking conception power dynamic is normalized, as these Western expat "laborer-bankers" are charged with teaching to the interests and perspectives of postcolonial national students. Thus, the nature and mode of deposits are controlled and dictated by the customer, not the banker. In opposition to banking education, but not quite in line with pedagogy of the oppressed either, what it means to be an educator lacking power and authority will be explored here, with an eye also to generalities and similar circumstances, drawing out some unique implications of applying a Freirean view in one particular postcolonial context.

IS PEDAGOGY OF THE OPPRESSED UNIVERSALLY APPLICABLE?

I want to elaborate on some key points of pedagogy of the oppressed and banking education before discussing education in the UAE. Fundamental to appreciating pedagogy of the oppressed is to understand Freire's *a priori* or *de facto* model of oppressive colonial education, banking education. Banking education as seen by Freire holds the traditional relationship between student and teacher as dichotomous with regard to power. The banker-teacher has currency while the student has none. Thus, the teacher deposits knowledge in the student's account of the world, which the student must accept. As Freire writes with regard to banking education, "(a) the teacher teaches and the students are taught; (b) the teacher knows everything and the students know nothing," and so on (1989, p. 59). As the exclusive source of power, the teacher "regulates" the perception of reality of the students, facilitating their active re-viewing of the world from the perspective of the elite population of society. This education supports conservative social aims, reflecting social change as unnecessary and not worthwhile. Additionally, it enables a contradictory, schizophrenic perception of reality among the oppressed, who suffer from the detachment of their experience of the world from school knowledge.

From this interpersonal conception of *teacher versus student*, Freire urges "reconciling the poles": balancing the scale of power in educational practice. An educator must reject traditional banking education by seeing herself as equal with students, regarding student knowledge as equally valuable. As Freire understands, a liberatory educator "must abandon the educational goal of deposit-making and replace it with the posing of the problems of men [*sic*] in their relation with the world.... Problem-posing education entails at the outset that the teacher-student contradiction be resolved" (1989, pp. 66–67). Problem-posing education cannot be based on the teacher's presumption of the major problem(s) to be explored, however, but must be founded in the collaborative, dialogic exploration of the world of both students and teacher; again, in this educational context, the teacher and student must be equal and similarly powerful, knowledgeable, and creative. As Freire writes,

Through dialogue, the teacher-of-the-students and the students-of-the-teacher cease to exist and a new term emerges: teacher-student with students-teachers. The teacher is no longer merely the-one-who-teaches, but one who is himself taught in dialogue with the students, who in turn while being taught also teach. (1989, p. 67)

In contrasting these models of banking education and pedagogy of the oppressed, one can see power shift from the teacher to the student, as we move from the former practice to the latter. As Freire writes from a concrete context of rural farmers in Brazil, elaboration of other characteristics of the oppressed and oppressors are also readily at hand. There are material differences between the two groups. On the one hand, the oppressed are recognized as the "masses," "natives," or "savages" (1989, p. 41). The oppressors, on the other hand, can "dress, wear shoes, be educated, travel, and hear Beethoven" (1989, p. 43). Yet while the oppressors are materially and politically wealthy in contrast with the oppressed, they are not freer. They are trapped in a material world. Freire describes the self-destructive market fetishism of the oppressor class, observing that, "in the egoistic pursuit of *having* as a possessing class, they suffocate in their own possessions and no longer *are*; they merely *have*" (Freire, 1989, p. 45, emphasis in original). Paradoxically, in this condition the oppressors depend on those they oppress for their own liberation, as the oppressed naturally rebel in their quest for humanization, while the oppressors do not. Thus, the power dynamic between the two is not as clear as it initially seems, for both ultimately depend on the oppressed, not the oppressors, for the humanization and freedom of both:

As the oppressors dehumanize others and violate their rights, they themselves also become dehumanized. As the oppressed, fighting to be human, take away the oppressors' power to dominate and suppress, they restore to the oppressors the humanity they had lost in the exercise of oppression. (Freire, 1989, p. 42)

This complex picture of power, the oppressor, and the oppressed is additionally complicated by the phenomenon of the middle class, to which teachers typically belong. In this context, teachers are not oppressors but partly oppressed themselves, as they operate within a broader framework in which they are also relatively powerless. In *Teachers as Cultural Workers*, Freire describes this (2005) with reference to the ideology of conflating teaching with parenting, which delegitimizes teaching as a profession and disables teachers from protesting "in favor of their students by demanding better working conditions" (p. 9). In this emerging context of educator disempowerment, also marked by the production of teaching packages by "experts," teachers become fearful of administrators who are more representative of the oppressor class. Thus, teachers can be seen in some instances as more similar to oppressed students than to oppressors. Further, they may even be oppressed in relation to students. As Freire writes,

One of the challenges to progressive educators…is not to feel or to proceed as if they were inferior to dominant class learners…who arrogantly mistreat and belittle middle-class teachers. But on the other hand, nor should they feel superior…to the learners from the slums…. In the first case, educators must take neither a position of revenge nor of submission but the position of one who assumes responsible authority as an educator; nor, in the second case, may educators take a paternalistic or scornful attitude toward the lower-class children;…the educator is a politician. (2005, p. 129)

Here Freire testifies to the less than dichotomous political reality of teaching. Essentially, the teacher is not simply an oppressor; the label applies better to the educational administrator, who works to facilitate education that is not always in the interest of all students but rather alienates some from their own interests and needs. But this does not mean that the teacher necessarily represents the oppressed, either. Like a politician, the teacher is an actor within a political world, which has its opportunities and limitations. Within the pedagogy of the oppressed, the teacher works on behalf of the oppressed, while in banking education, the teacher works more in support of the oppressors.

Freire has cautioned against both the rash application and the simplified exportation of his pedagogy. In *Pedagogy of the Oppressed*, he warns first of the revolutionary educator, who wants to identify the problems of the oppressed for them, framing the debate for the oppressed, rather than collaborating in genuine dialogue. Macedo and Ana Maria Araújo Freire (2005) similarly relate how the well-intentioned middle-class educator can reproduce inequality while striving for student empowerment, when not truly cognizant of the effects of class privilege. They offer a story of a teacher who becomes angry when excluded from a community project, and accuses others of being insufficiently democratic. Macedo and Freire observe here that "in her mind, one can be empowered so long as the empowerment does not encroach on the 'expert's' privileged, powerful position" (2005, p. xix). These examples articulate a challenge for those who may be well intentioned but not honestly grappling with the difference their unequal class and political positions make to their practice. The teacher thinks she sees the oppressed as her partner, but she does not truly see them that way. She thinks she is diminishing oppressive power, yet she works unwittingly to entrench it.

Pedagogy of the oppressed has also been taken up as a method by a wide variety of international teachers. By neoliberal educators, it has been "assimilated to the prevailing obsession of North American education" of "transmitting knowledge to otherwise unprepared students" (Aronowitz, as quoted in Macedo & Freire, 2005, p. x). Against this backdrop Freire has stated, "I don't want to be imported or exported. It is impossible to export pedagogical practices without reinventing them. Please tell your fellow American educators not to import me. Ask them to re-create and rewrite my ideas" (Macedo & Freire, 2005, p. x). As Problem-Based Learning has become a global trend related to learning outcomes and international standardization, it has likewise become detached from Freirean goals of revolutionary consciousness-raising, instead morphing into a way to objectify educational practice, reducing the pedagogy to a method.

Conversely, much has been written about the overzealous demand for the student's voice in exaggerated versions of Freire-inspired dialogical pedagogy, which aim for social justice, but seem idealistic and simplistic to those focusing on the historical legacy of structural inequality in society (Jackson, 2008). Lugonés and Spelman (1983) articulate how for a former colonial subject or oppressed individual, skepticism about collaboration and engagement with former oppressors can be reasonable and well informed; they ask in this case for social justice educators to freely give autonomy and independence to others, not to force them to relate to and benefit the oppressor through dialogue initiated by the oppressor.

> Why should we want you to come into our world out of self-interest?…The task as described could be entered into with the intention of finding out as much as possible about us so as to better dominate us. The person engaged in this task would act as a spy. The motivation is not unfamiliar to us. We have heard it said that now that the Third World countries are more powerful as a bloc, westerners need to learn more about them, that it is in their self-interest to do so. Obviously there is no reason why people of color should welcome white/Anglo women into their world for the carrying out of this intention. (1983, p. 580)

Understanding power as multileveled, as Freire sees it, seems a slightly limited viewpoint; maybe the white teacher is at a material disadvantage in comparison with the students of color, for example. Power is not a single, one-way experience. At the same time, Lugonés and Spelman remind us that students should not be required to testify to their experiences and share with their educators just because their educators desire them to do so; maybe there is good reason for them to be cautious, or not see such a partnership as being in their own interests.

In the next section, I want to further consider the case mentioned previously, in which the educator is oppressed in comparison with the students. This is not the situation Freire invokes in elaborating pedagogy of the oppressed, though in re-creating his views in new situations Freire did observe and note that teachers themselves are not always oppressors but can belong more to the category of the oppressed. Yet even in this instance, Freire did not elaborate on the situation in which a teacher was oppressed in contrast to all of his or her students. Such a possibility is not obvious or evident in traditional educational settings, but it may be an emerging trend in the future, requiring the rethinking of revolutionary pedagogy in radically different situations from postcolonial Brazil, or the contemporary United States.

PEDAGOGY OF THE CUSTOMER? BANKING EDUCATION
IN THE UNITED ARAB EMIRATES

The United Arab Emirates (UAE) is new to schooling. Though its capital (Abu Dhabi) is now the most literate city in the Arab world (with a literacy rate of 94%), in 1971 upon gaining independence from the British, 75% of the population was illiterate ("Abu Dhabi Boasts," 2012). The first formal school there, a Kuwaiti mission school, opened in 1953 (Daleure, 2011, p. 53). Though today access to education is universal, owing to a historical lack of formal schooling and a related lack of Emirati educators, the school system is staffed primarily by expatriate workers. Originally most came from parts of the Arab world with histories of schooling, such as Egypt, Lebanon, and Jordan. Today, many also come from Canada, Australia, Ireland, the United States, and Britain. Expatriate educators work in schools, the Ministry of Education, in teacher training, and in higher education. "Emiratization" is now being emphasized, which means the training of locals to work in the field, to take over their educational system.

Of course, to be without schools is not to be without education. In the UAE, people traditionally facilitated education as religious study, in small groups and one-on-one. Many view this traditional Islamic education as more social constructivist in nature than the educational system of the UAE today (Hourani, Diallo, & Said, 2011, pp. 340–341), as it focused on the view that "All children have the capacity to learn…. The purpose of education is not viewed as one of 'correcting' or 'remediating' a sinful nature but rather one of guidance" (Reagan, 2000, pp. 191–192). As Freire might urge, it was community based and problem based, and encouraged students to interpret values and principles for themselves dialogically.

However, with the development of national postcolonial identities came an Emirati self-understanding framed in opposition to the West, wherein "attitudes, opinions, and values are societal rather than individually constructed" (Hourani et al., 2011, p. 344). Emiratis (like others in the Gulf) have come to see Islamic education and Western education as dichotomous models in this context. They recall that the former (Islamic education) was conducted in a homogeneous cultural context, where hierarchies and values were (during protectorate times) well entrenched. This differs from the more globalized, Western-influenced Emirati classroom today, which in a men's college might be taught by a Western woman in a skirt and sleeveless blouse, and in a women's college might be taught by a white man in a tie and blazer. In this diverse educational context, a sense of separate identities has emerged and developed, of traditional Islamic alongside and versus Western. This separation is not total, as the parties come together in UAE professional life. However, it does put Western educators there in an interesting place professionally, as one observer notes: "Western trained academics working in the

Gulf region have to censor their academic thrust of knowledge in order for it to fit adequately to the sensitive social, cultural and religious contexts within which they are operating" (Hourani et al., 2011, p. 352).

In this setting, banking education as understood in other colonial and post-colonial contexts is precluded by a reverse power disparity, in which students are empowered from a material, sociopolitical viewpoint over educators. Today in the Emirates, pay for newly licensed teachers is among the highest in the world. Teachers are recruited from traditional Western centers of power, and provided better pay and benefits in almost every case than they would receive in their home countries. Yet their pay is incomparable to the wealth of Emirati students. In Abu Dhabi, "citizens each have an average net worth of $17 million" (ABC News, 2007). The average student's disposable income there is likely to be at least twice that of his or her teachers. In the UAE, no Emirati need go without land, health care, or education (including higher education), which are increasingly seen elsewhere in the world as commodities, or things that people have to in some way earn through employment.

This disparity of wealth discourages Emiratization of education—Emiratis taking greater control over their educational system—as "Emiratis typically demand higher pay and shorter working hours in comparison with expatriates employed in the same job" (Raven, 2010, p. 16). Thus, in education, hiring quotas are applied. One can see in a university setting, for example, a young Emirati (no more than thirty-five-years old) with a local master's degree working as an Associate Provost, while middle-aged Westerners with doctoral degrees remain Assistant Provosts. This economic context negatively impacts Emiratis' motivation to pursue education and academic study in various fields and at different levels, as in the UAE, "nationals perceive that good jobs can be had with only a high-school diploma or less" (Daleure, 2011, p. 62).

The idea that Emiratis need to become competitive internationally also fails to motivate strong participation in rigorous educational opportunities, because there is no sense of a need to compete internationally. Research on student motivation to learn English has found, "No participant responded positively to the idea of going abroad to live for work or study, and the anecdotes that they told about their travels abroad generally tended to be negative" (Fields, 2011, p. 38). Emiratis do well without advanced education, and do not see greater opportunities globally than within Emirati society. Thus, the power dynamic of banking education, in which the teacher holds power over the student, does not apply here as a *de facto* or *a priori* tradition, as the teacher does not hold the key or any power over students.

Can there be pedagogy of the oppressed in such a situation? It has been acknowledged as Western teachers have been brought in as replacements for Arab (expatriate) teachers in the past few decades that the most modern pedagogical methods were not always implemented in early Emirati schools. In this context

Western teachers have been hired to engage in student-centered and problem-based learning that is more interactive and engaging. Freire would caution against such a simplistic reduction of his philosophy to method as implied here, however; one cannot just "export" pedagogy of the oppressed. At the same time, this global movement seems to have some Freirean characteristics, particularly as the aims of education in the discourses are conceived as encouraging critical thinking for social empowerment and greater indigenous autonomy (as in Emiratization), and enabling more effective, intentional, and/or thoughtful, community-shaped social change.

In any case, introduction of such a discourse in the UAE provides an interesting puzzle, as student-centered learning is challenged there by a "lack of willingness to learn interactively" among Emiratis (Raven, 2010, p. 18). Now, such an attitude of indifference toward active learning might make sense at the K–12 level, where students around the globe do not necessarily want to go to school and learn, and might not go to school if not compelled externally. Sidorkin writes of the unpaid labor of education as resembling slave labor in this context, as students are required to develop human capital through piles of homework, without any immediate or obvious personal reward for their nine-to-five labor (2007). Lack of willingness to actively engage has also been observed in places where student-centered approaches have recently emerged: where it is not traditional for students to speak in class critically and ask questions, and hence where it then becomes difficult for teachers to implement student-centered learning as a new practice.

At the tertiary level, indifference toward student-centered learning has a different character in the UAE, however. Emiratis apply to and attend colleges and universities to learn things, socialize, and gain training. Yet they do not necessarily see active processes, involved for instance with homework and projects, or participating fully in classroom discussions, as crucial components. Students express finding active learning inconvenient, distracting from other activities they could engage in. They view educators as responsible for depositing certain knowledge in them, in line with marketing and related discourses framing them as consumers of a product of knowledge in education. Their instructors cannot easily interrupt this situation, for how can you make someone engage?

The fairly unique power dynamic of UAE education, which opposes or rather reverses banking education, both supports and in turn is bolstered by a hybrid pedagogy of the oppressors that here I refer to as "Never Fail a Nahayan." The minister of education, Sheikh Nahayan, is known for supporting open, collaborative learning spaces and he will listen to any student's concerns, despite being quite busy as the minister as well as the chancellor of the three public universities in the UAE. Nahayan is not known for firing instructors whom students dislike. However, this does not stop educational professionals in the hierarchical, dual-track Emirati/expat society from fearing repercussions related to students not liking them, from the sheikh down to low-level managers. As a professor there, your supervisor may like you, but she may fear for her own job if you get a bad review from students while under her watch; thus, at all levels of education it is encouraged to not fail or otherwise offend students.

This feature of education in the UAE should not be attributed to the sheikh, for this power dynamic is not unique to Emirati education, but rather is an effect of an overall two-track system within the society, of the majority expatriates, and the minority who are citizens. In all spheres of Emirati life, expatriate workers, who go there specifically for work opportunities held as greater than those in their home countries, carry in them a sense of oppression, of not feeling free, as they fear repercussions for upsetting the wrong member of the oppressor class, Emiratis. It is illegal in the UAE to publish, even on a blog, critical things about the UAE or Emiratis. One hears tales of people being "sent home" for making crude gestures at the wrong Emirati in traffic, or for being accused of doing so. In this undemocratic postcolonial society, traditional power relations of East and West have been reversed. Implicit in this reversal is that the Emirati dictates to the Westerner how to educate. The Westerner is recruited as a type of consultant or laborer skilled in providing educational services, rather than as an expert or authority.

Student evaluations are part of faculty review in the UAE to a much greater extent than one would see in a Western society (Aubrey & Coombe, 2011). There is no tenure system, and though employment is given in three-year contracts for expatriates, one can be let go at any time, which means for most being sent back to their home country within a month. In this context, teachers are encouraged to provide for student learning outcomes and give students high grades without making class "too hard." Institutional research committees spend time determining how instructors cook their books to avoid failing students. And should a student have a last name such as "Nahayan," educators are likely to be extra careful around them. As one educator reported recently on an institution in Dubai, "The worst thing about the place is that the students know that they can complain to the head of the department and swiftly get the faculty member into trouble. The students will outrageously lie doing this, and get away with it easily" (Oasis, 2012). The teachers fear the students in this context, precluding pedagogy of the oppressed, which focuses on problems both parties observe, and demands a power balance, rather than the inversion of banking education.

To a limited extent, efforts toward problem-based learning for critical thinking have been found productive in the UAE, to promote social awareness and deeper social analysis (King, 2011; Raddawi, 2011). Yet fundamental to the Freirean approach is that the teacher does not presume to know what problems or "generative themes" to base consciousness-raising around. To demand students to identify problems in this context, if the students do not want to do so, could potentially resemble ethnocentric pestering, or the naïveté of structural difference discussed as being off-putting by Lugonés and Spelman (1983). Who would be served by the educator badgering students to critique their lives—whose framework would be privileged, and whose would be ignored here?

Additionally, as Emirati identity is constructed alongside a skeptical view of the West, such experiments are too adventurous for educators who are one or two paychecks away from financial struggling. The UAE may wish to import student-centered practices, but that does not mean it wants Westerners critiquing their students' way of life. "Never Fail a Nahayan" precludes then both banking education and pedagogy of the oppressed, as a reverse banking, or pedagogy of the oppressors, that must not challenge the status quo, precluding the educator's suggestion that something might be wrong with, or worth structurally changing in, students' lives and society.

CONCLUSION

Last year the Higher Colleges of Technology sent a Scottish instructor home for writing "I hate the UAE" on a balloon during the celebration of the fortieth anniversary of the country. The teacher protested that he merely hated the colors of the flag, according to a news report; he was fired when a student filed a complaint of his insult to the nation ("Teacher Sacked," 2011). Such stories are common within the UAE. Foreign workers must see themselves as guests in the world in which they live and work; they are not equal or free as they might see themselves to be in their home countries. In many cases, they do not fully understand the rules of society, yet are required to support them. This political disempowerment combined with wealth disparities in the society make education an act of service to the students and to the society, which the educator is reimbursed for providing, but of which the educator is not at liberty to conduct as an authority, a professional, or a political actor. The teacher is not entirely oppressed here, and it is hard to see a student usefully as an oppressor. Yet this context gives evidence to Freire's desire for an education conducted within equal relations, by equally empowered educators and students. It also reflects his caution against the deprofessionalization of education, and demonstrates both that education is always a political act, and that we cannot import methods in new contexts simply.

Though the UAE is unique, it is not the only place where teachers are beginning to fear their students in this new era of accountability. The well-known *Freakanomics* (Levitt & Dubner, 2005) follows U.S. teachers who cheat on tests "on behalf of the student…to help themselves not look like they're bad performers" (Dubner, 2011). In these emerging contexts, power is not as closely tied to knowledge as many educators and philosophers traditionally assume; if knowledge is power, students in the Emirates are definitely lacking it, though they are quite powerful in the context of their instructors' professional lives. The UAE context illustrates that pedagogy of the oppressed is not the reversal of the power dynamic of banking education. Pedagogy of the oppressed is a political act among concrete actors living in a material world whose roles and relationships to levels of power cannot be presumed *a priori*, but are unique to context.

REFERENCES

ABC News. (2007, October 22). World's richest city wants to be cultural capital of Arab world. *Good Morning America*. Retrieved from http://abcnews.go.com/GMA/story?id=3759878#.UIDAX rIgfng

Abu Dhabi boasts 94 per cent literacy rate. (2012). *The National*.

Aubrey, J., & Coombe, C. (2011). An investigation of occupational stressors and coping strategies among EFL teachers in the United Arab Emirates. In C. Gitsaki (Ed.), *Teaching and learning in the Arab world*. New York, NY: Peter Lang.

Daleure, G. (2011). Factors affecting performance in post-secondary education: A case study of Emirati males. In C. Gitsaki (Ed.), *Teaching and learning in the Arab world*. New York, NY: Peter Lang.

Dubner, S. (2011). Freakanomics: Tackling the problem of cheating teachers. *American Public Media*.

Fields, M. (2011). Learner motivation and strategy use among university students in the United Arab Emirates. In C. Gitsaki (Ed.), *Teaching and learning in the Arab world*. New York, NY: Peter Lang.

Freire, P. (1972/1989). *Pedagogy of the oppressed* (M. Bergman Ramos, Trans.). Melbourne, Victoria, Australia: Penguin.

Freire, P. (2005). *Teachers as cultural workers: Letters to those who dare teach*. Cambridge, England: Westview Press.

Gitsaki, C. (Ed.). (2007). *Teaching and learning in the Arab world*. New York, NY: Peter Lang.

Hourani, R. B., Diallo, I., & Said, A. (2011). Teaching in the Arabian Gulf: Arguments for the deconstruction of the current educational model. In C. Gitsaki (Ed.), *Teaching and learning in the Arab world*. New York, NY: Peter Lang.

Jackson, L. (2008). Dialogic pedagogy for social justice? A critical examination. *Studies in Philosophy and Education, 27*(2).

King, M. (2011). Implementing problem-based learning in the Gulf: A case study of Arab students. In C. Gitsaki (Ed.), *Teaching and learning in the Arab world*. New York, NY: Peter Lang.

Levitt, S. D., & Dubner, S. J. (2005). *Freakanomics*. New York, NY: HarperCollins.

Lugonés, M. C., & Spelman, E. V. (1983). Have we got a theory for you! Feminist theory, cultural imperialism, and the demand for 'the woman's voice.' *Women's International Forum*, 6.

Macedo, D., & Freire, A. M. A. (2005). Foreword. In P. Freire, *Teachers as cultural workers: Letters to those who dare teach*. Cambridge, England: Westview Press.

Oasis, S. (2012). A gallant addition to these pages [Web log post]. *HCT Sucks!* Retrieved from http://hctsucks.blogspot.hk/

Raddawi, R. (2011). Teaching critical thinking skills to Arab university students. In C. Gitsaki (Ed.), *Teaching and learning in the Arab world*. New York, NY: Peter Lang.

Raven, J. (2010). Emiratizing the education sector in the UAE: Contextualization and challenges. In N. Reynolds & M. Banfa (Eds.), *Developing a nation through educational Emiratization: Reflections on the development and implementation of a transformational teacher education program in the UAE*. Abu Dhabi, United Arab Emirates: Higher Colleges of Technology Press.

Reagan, T. (2000). *Non-western educational traditions: Alterative approaches to educational thought and practice*. Mahwah, NJ: Lawrence Erlbaum.

Sidorkin, A. (2007). Human capital and the labor of learning: A case of mistaken identity. *Educational Theory, 57*(2), 159–170.

Teacher sacked for offending UAE sentiments. (2011, November 29). *Emirates 24/7*.

CHAPTER TWENTY-THREE

Freire, Sublative Hope, and Early Childhood Education in Aotearoa New Zealand

BRADLEY HANNIGAN

There are many ways to read Freire. Some authors read Freire through a psycho-analytic lens, and so they see his writing as psychoanalytically inspired (e.g., Bingham, 2002). Other authors view Freire with a utopian gaze, and read his pedagogy of liberation as a utopian project (e.g., Giroux & McLaren, 1997). Still others read Freire within an anti-bias frame, and see his work as a theoretical resource for their own projects (e.g., Gunn, 2003). Freire (1994) himself commented on the variety of messages ascribed to him, pointing out that while some were his own intention, others have been ascribed to him without his agreement. What is clear is that there are as many interpretations of Freire's writing as there are interpreters. This is hardly surprising given Gadamer's (1975, p. 357) assertion that "what is fixed in writing has detached itself from the contingency of its origin and its author and made itself free for new relationships." Freire (1994, p. 47) himself also identified the virtues of rereading as a source of both creativity and possibility. The possibility of rereading Freire, both in terms of his message and into a highly localised context, is the starting point of this chapter.

I read Freire's work as a pragmatic philosopher and as someone embedded in early childhood education in Aotearoa New Zealand. As a pragmatic philosopher, I share Rorty's (1999) assumption that essences do not exist outside of human needs. This means that there is no essential Freire that can be comprehended, nor is there any need to attempt to do so. Rather, there is the possibility of fruitful rereading in the hope that something useful may emerge from the process—something that may stir humanity to action. Again, similar to Rorty (1989), I cannot claim to know in advance what that action might entail; that is up to others to decide. Instead, my task in this chapter is to frame Freire's writing as an example of sublative hope (my own term, which means a hope that both negates and preserves that which is hoped-against), and to apply that understanding to early childhood education in Aotearoa New Zealand. The first part of this chapter rereads Freire's philosophy of liberation using G. W. Hegel's (2001) concept of sublation. The second part of this chapter recounts one educator's experience of introducing Freire's writing to a group of registered early childhood teachers and the example of sublative hope that emerged from that interaction.

Given that readers might not be familiar with early childhood education in Aotearoa New Zealand, a brief introduction might be useful. The early childhood sector in Aotearoa New Zealand is non-compulsory, but it is also seen as a key sector in the strategic focus of the current government that have set their target at 98% of children having experienced early childhood education upon starting school by 2016. According to the most recent data, there were 4,439 licensed early childhood services in Aotearoa New Zealand in 2011 (Ministry of Education, 2011). Those services ranged from full-day, teacher-led childcare services and kindergartens, to parent-led playcentres and kohanga reo (Māori language nests). Participation in 2011 was at 94.7% and the average number of hours children spent in licensed early childhood services was 20.4 hours per week. The education and care sector and kindergartens employed 19,956 full-time equivalent teachers as of July 1, 2011, with the sector attracting $1.3 billion in funding in the 2012 budget.

Early childhood education in Aotearoa New Zealand is premised on the "aspiration for children to grow up as competent and confident learners and communicators, healthy in mind, body, and spirit, secure in their sense of belonging and in the knowledge that they make a valued contribution to society" (Ministry of Education, 1996, p. 9). This statement of hope reflects the value that early childhood teachers place in their role as advocates for children (Te One, 2010) and the socio-cultural underpinnings of the New Zealand Early Childhood Curriculum/ Te Whāriki (Dalli, 2003). Early childhood education in Aotearoa New Zealand is commonly seen as an important foundation for lifelong learning (New Zealand ECE Taskforce, 2011).

PART ONE: SUBLATION AND HOPE

Sublation

Several writers have linked Hegel and Freire, for example, Torres (1994), Schutte (1990), and Duarte (1999). Gadotti (1994), Freire's biographer, even wrote that "the dialectic between the Master and the Slave, developed by Hegel, can be considered the principal theoretical framework of *Pedagogy of the Oppressed.*" Freire (2005, p. 72) himself made open reference to Hegel in *Pedagogy of the Oppressed*; it is therefore not fresh news to read Freire with a Hegelian lens. In this part of the chapter, the argument is advanced that Hegel's (2001) notion of *aufheben* or *sublation* plays a central role in the logic of Freire's philosophical writing. Discussion of Hegel's idealism, his teleology, and his essentialism is not the focus here. In fact, these three concepts make little sense to my own pragmatist agenda (c.f. Rorty, 1979, 1989, 1999), and so are left aside. This practice of rereading is appropriate to both Gadamer's and Rorty's philosophies as a practice for both reinterpretation and the reinvigoration of language. It is appropriate insofar as neither author believes that there is such a thing as an essential understanding of a text, and because both authors, in a similar vein to Freire, believe that the work of interpretation and reinterpretation is unfinishable. I too agree with that perspective.

Hegel's philosophy is premised on a world and ideas of the world that are in a process of becoming (similar to Freire's [2005, p. 64] idea of humanity's "incompleteness, from which they move out in constant search"). For Hegel, *sublation* is the primary means of becoming, moving in and with the spirit of the world (Hegel, 2001), or by means of negation—moving beyond that which had once become, in the formulation, a differentiated being. In my reading of Hegel, the world of matter, and more specifically of ideas, is both in the process of becoming other as well as in the process of gathering its sediments—histories upon which the forward movement of the world and ideas of the world depend in order to flourish.

According to Hegel, becoming is a twofold process of negating and preserving. Hegel (2001, p. 36) defined sublation in the following way:

> "To sublate" has a twofold meaning in the language: on the one hand it means to preserve, to maintain, and equally it also means to cause to cease, to put an end to. Even "to preserve" includes negative elements, namely, that something is removed from its influences, in order to preserve it. Thus what is sublated is at the same time preserved; it has only lost its immediacy but is not on that account annihilated.

What this means is that where change occurs, the new state of affairs contains within it something of the old, so that the new is not the absolutely new, but rather emerges out of a dialectical *moving-beyond*, a becoming, and as such contains as a necessary element—that which came before.

One example of sublation at work can be seen in the historical development of early childhood education in Aotearoa New Zealand. In general terms, the socio-cultural project is an attempt to move beyond developmentalist understandings of children and learning (e.g., Bredekamp, 1987) to an approach which identifies learning as a socially and culturally mediated activity (e.g., Fleer, 1995). Early childhood education provision in New Zealand is guided at the curriculum level by documents that are premised on socio-cultural notions of learning in context (Nuttall, 2003). The reality, however, is not as simple as the one approach replacing the other. Socio-cultural writers have hoped for an early childhood education that supersedes developmentalism and have ended up with an approach in which developmentalism has been sublated: an approach in which developmentalism is both negated but, more particularly, simultaneously preserved: in curriculum elements such as age-appropriate learning outcomes, the importance of exploration to learning (i.e., personal constructivism), and the assumption that biological development influences both need and quality provision (Ministry of Education, 1996).

This notion of sublation is central to my rereading of Freire's philosophy of liberation. For example, Freire (2005) is enacting sublation when he writes that "it is only the oppressed who, by freeing themselves, can free their oppressors" (p. 56). He is saying that the preservation of one's humanity negates those whose aim and goal it is to dehumanise in the name of their own self-preservation. More subtly, it means that the reality of oppression, and later the memory of it, is retained as a catalyst for *moving-beyond*. There is a double sublation here: on the one side, oppression is the *ground* against which the hope for liberation launches itself—the material experience of oppression that gives rise to the need. On the other side, the oppressed through the process of their own liberation negate the oppressor but preserve oppression as a ground toward which there should be no return, but simultaneously the possibility of return: "the moment the new regimen hardens into a dominating 'bureaucracy' the humanist dimension of the struggle is lost and it is no longer possible to speak of liberation" (Freire, 2005, p. 57).

The resolution of the oppressor-oppressed contradiction, which Freire places at the heart of his humanist project, is a call to action. This process of resolution and subsequent transformation of society is another example of sublation in action. According to Hegel (2001, p. 37), "Something is sublated only in so far as it has entered into unity with its opposite." That process works itself out in a number of ways in *Pedagogy of the Oppressed*: as the resolution of the humanisation-dehumanisation contradiction, as the resolution of the oppressed-oppressor relationship, as the resolution of the theory and practice binary, and as the resolution of consciousness and ignorance in the form of conscientisation (*conscientizacion*).

Freire's departure from Hegel is similar to the parting of ways between developmentalists and socio-culturalists in early childhood education, at least as far as the content of sublation is concerned (but not the principle). Where Hegel (2001, p. 43) wrote about "being-for-self, which sublates the being-for-other," Freire (2005, p. 44) wrote about "the great humanistic and historical task of the oppressed: to liberate themselves and their oppressors as well." On the one side the individual, on the other side the social—but both examples of a sublative process. To see oneself in the other, the negation of a separate self and the simultaneous preservation of one's humanity, is the mark of a critical consciousness that may serve both idealism and a material dialectic of liberation. So too might it fund the notion of critical hope, as will be argued in the following section.

Sublative Hope

Freire's metaphysics of hope is no otherworldly thing. It is as much to do with being as it is to do with becoming. In *Pedagogy of the Heart* Freire (2007) writes of hope as a metaphysical foundation that gives human life a greater sense of meaning: a sense of searching; a possibility of fulfilment. The root of that possibility is in the incompleteness of being (Freire, 1998), which is felt as an "ontological need" (Freire, 1994, p. 2): a need to become other; to become freer, more equal as human beings. For Freire, the hope that humans create is constructed in social contexts that have dehumanisation as their mark; it is articulated by the shared language of ideas that promise a better life that is possible; it is afforded by human action that seeks to transform the world. This is therefore a mediated hope whose fullness comes from the *not* (Bloch, 1986) of human experience. Freire's metaphysics is one of both presence and absence; of unfinishedness and unfinishability; of hope and of the oppression that might one day be overcome.

For Freire, to hope is to be human, so much as to say, "It is impossible to exist without it" (Freire, 1998). His reframing of his classic *Pedagogy of the Oppressed* into a *Pedagogy of Hope* is ample justification for the claim that hope is a central motif of his writing. Writers like Giroux and McLaren (1997), Webb (2010), and Van Heertum (2006) have also amplified Freire's work on this topic. My own perspective is that rather than being thought of as an *essential* component of what it means to be human, hope is a tool that we humans use to make the world a better place. To think in this way does little to detract from Freire's message, but rather realigns his writing with my own neo-pragmatic assumptions (cf. Hannigan, 2011). Like all tools, hope can be more or less fit for purpose. To account for this, Freire wrote about "false hope" (1978, p. 70) and that "hope needs practice in order to become historical concreteness. That is why there is no hope in sheer hopefulness" (Freire, 1994, p. 2). This section argues that what is needed is a critical hope, one that is aware of sublation in its own structure and that offers itself as a praxis of critical reflection for early childhood educators.

The notion of sublative hope that I have in mind, in writing this chapter, is one that digs back into itself, in search of sublated elements of that which has been negated and yet simultaneously preserved. Sublative hope recognises the possibility that the point of departure—that state of affairs that is best left behind—may exist also in the goal ahead. The recognition of this possibility promotes wariness in the hopeful, wariness that one's aspiration for liberation might also contain the seeds of future injustice. It is a self-aware hope, one that sees the possibility of otherness, of unintended consequences, even in the articulation of a most cherished vision. It is a form of hope that is critical of its own complacency in the *goodness* of its vision, and that is suspicious of hope that does not recognise the possibility of the presence of that which is *hoped-against* (both as origin and destination).

A similar perspective of critical hope has been put forward by scholars in the Robust Hope Project developed at the University of West Sydney. This project aims to express utopian possibilities in education and education policy in the face of neoliberal marketisation (Singh & Sawyer, 2008). It is a project with synergy to Freire's (1994) own effort to get out from under pragmatic neoliberalism. The difference between robust hope and the idea of sublative hope is that the former establishes a framework of hope by which policy documents (and educational programmes: Arthur and Sawyer, 2009) may be critiqued and reinterpreted. The latter focus specifically on the sublated elements within the hope itself—those elements that appear as the possibility of the preservation of that which is hoped-against.

Sublative hope can be observed in two events from Freire's own life story. The first event occured in the story of a man of about forty, worn out by work, who stood up at one of his meetings held on the topic of family violence early in Freire's career. At this meeting, Freire was challenged on the elitism and privilege of his own position as researcher and disseminator. Freire (1994, p. 17) wrote about this experience as "searing his soul for good and all" and becoming a turning point in his own thinking: a turning point that Freire described as a key inspiration for *Pedagogy of the Oppressed*. Of that experience he also wrote that "though this talk was given thirty-two years ago, I have never forgotten it" (Freire, 1994, p. 19). Freire's hope for the liberation of the oppressed has, on this account, sublated within it his own history—a state of privilege that he hoped against not only as a point of departure, but also in the recognition of the possibility of return highlighted in his liberation philosophy (e.g., Freire, 2005, pp. 56, 86).

The second event or set of events highlighted by Freire (1994, p. 22) was the experience of depression that revisited him often as a young man, sparked off by "the relationship between rain, green, and mud or sticky clay." Freire recounted the debilitating nature of his illness, but he also recounted its cure: a cure that was found in his revisiting of the past, in the act of return to the places of his childhood. This time, in a much more personal sense, Freire (1994, p. 22) used sublation (the act of preserving that which is simultaneously negated) as a method for realising a better life and a better world: "at bottom, in the deepest 'why' of my pain, I was educating my hope." Freire's own experience of a better, less emotively debilitating life, depended on both a return to his point of origin and the recognition that without his own process of conscientisation there was every possibility that such debilitation could be a possibility of his future. This sublative thematic can also be recognised in *Pedagogy of the Oppressed*, where he wrote:

"A deepened consciousness of their situation leads people to apprehend that situation as an historical reality susceptible of transformation" (Freire, 2005, p. 85).

The aspiration statement of the New Zealand early childhood curriculum is one such hope that is often expressed in non-problematic, even dogmatic terms. It is a good aspiration, and one that for all intents and purposes captures the mood of the early childhood community in Aotearoa New Zealand. The notion of sublative hope that I am suggesting aims to make the possibility of the presence of that which is hoped-against conscious as a form of critical reflection. Sublative hope is therefore a form of conscientisation in which the themes of the articulated hope are understood to simultaneously contain the possibility of their negative correlate as origin and as a material possibility in the destination. Thus, the aspiration "for children to grow up as competent and confident learners and communicators, healthy in mind, body, and spirit, secure in their sense of belonging and in the knowledge that they make a valued contribution to society" (Ministry of Education, 1996, p. 9) preserves the historical epoch where young children did not grow as competent and confident learners, as well as a frontal element preserving that state that is negated as a possibility of return, that the origin might appear as an unintended consequence in the destination. For example, that a valued contribution to society might be cast in purely economic terms, or that children might be seen as one more form of human capital.

By recognising that one's hopeful action, however well intentioned, might also bring about the opposite result is the work of critical engagement: it is the recognition of the sublative elements in hope. Research carried out with teachers in one kindergarten association points out a lack of knowledge of Freire's writing, let alone a recognition of his key ideas. The following part of this chapter is an example of one educator introducing the concept of conscientisation to that group of teachers. That introduction is presented as an example of sublative hope, in support of the argument that sublative hope is useful as a tool for critical reflection.

PART TWO: FREIRE, SUBLATIVE HOPE, AND EARLY CHILDHOOD EDUCATION IN AOTEAROA NEW ZEALAND

There are several texts within early childhood studies that link Freire's writing with early childhood education; for example, Moss (2009) uses Freire's writing to highlight that dialogue and broad participation are key elements of democratic agency in the face of an increasingly marketised early childhood sector. From another perspective, Urban (2008) uses Freire's notion of dialogue to describe a folding synthesis wherein agents (in educational settings) use dialogue to codetermine a shared identity. Urban (2008) concludes his work by arguing that professional early childhood education systems require a good dose of hope, using Freire to state that not just any hope will do, but hope that is well considered, a hope that authors like Halpin (2007) and Johnston (2006) would call *robust*, and that I am calling sublative.

Early childhood writers in Aotearoa New Zealand have made good use of the critical edge in Freire's work. For example, writers like Ritchie (2003) use Freire's approach of decentring the teacher as the expert. Jenkin (2010) used Friere's writing to reflect on the *banking model of education*, while Morehu (2009) and Pau'ulvale (2011) have used Freire to focus on cultural transformation and the revitalisation of language as a praxis of liberation. Mitchell (2007) has used Freire to articulate children as citizens, whereas other authors like Te One (2008) and Williams, Broadley, and Te-Aho (2012) use Freire's notion of conscientisation to fuel their critique. These writers mention Freire as a theoretical collaborator among several rather than presenting a sustained use of his writing, with only Stephenson (2009) offering a more sustained use of his work.

Sublation at Te Awhina Marae

We sat together on a crisp winter's afternoon at Te Awhina Marae in Motueka. Thirty kindergarten teachers, the kaitohutohu Māori (Māori facilitator), and I had been welcomed on to the marae (in a process of powhiri), we had eaten together (kai whakanoa), and we had sat and shared our family histories (mihimihi). Such was the *kawa* or protocol of this particular marae; we came in as visitors and we were now custodians of the marae and its traditions. The meeting hall (wharenui) in which we sat was called Turangaapeke, after the ancestors of the people of that place. To begin the talk, I asked for a show of hands to tell us who had heard of the writer Paulo Freire; three people raised their hands. I then asked who had heard of *Pedagogy of the Oppressed*; not a hand remained up. In this room full of professional teachers, teachers who had trained at various times during the past three decades (and some before), some of whom were recent graduates from university teacher education programmes, not a single person had read, let alone heard of, *Pedagogy of the Oppressed*.

At the beginning of the presentation, teachers were asked: *What does it mean to be human* and *What situations dehumanise you?* For the first question, about half the teachers responded by identifying reasons premised on social or collectivist language (for example, "living together, having compassion for others, being part of society"), and the other half identified reasons premised on individualism (for example, "to have choices about how I live my life, being an individual, thinking and reasoning"). There were no responses that took a critical or questioning perspective on being human or responses that referred to institutions or their rules.

Teachers also commented on this being an unusual question and one that made them begin to think more deeply about their own humanity. This question also opened onto the possibility of dehumanisation.

On the question of situations that dehumanise them, participants highlighted socio-contextual pressures (e.g., "being put down by others, others taking away your [sic] power, to have choice removed") more than they did the individual effects of their dehumanisation (e.g., "life without emotion/spirit, feeling as though I have no control, self-doubt"). Three respondents out of the group mentioned institutional pressures such as laws, policies, and being "reduced to a number" as sources of dehumanisation. After that exercise, teachers made comments about not having thought of their experiences in this way before and one teacher told me that thinking in this way made her feel uneasy. When I asked why, she said that "it makes me think of the world differently." Where conversations about humanisation were difficult, conversations of dehumanisation were arduous; however, the recognition of dehumanisation opened the door to some of the sublated aspects of teachers' worldviews.

Once the buzz had died down, I continued with my presentation and showed the teachers how Freire had used the dialectic of humanisation and dehumanisation to argue for the creation of a more socially just society. This was a line of reasoning that resonated with teachers, as social justice and advocacy have a rich tradition in the history of early childhood education in Aotearoa New Zealand (e.g., May, 1997, 2009). However, when introduced to the idea that only those who are dehumanised can act as the architects of their own liberation, teachers did not register. The teachers took a nurturing and rescuing approach to liberation, one that hoped to empower, but that preserved the possibility of disempowerment as a consequence of their well-meaning action. In one conversation, a teacher talked about the need to educate parents about the value of the educational perspective used in kindergartens; this was met with wide agreement. When it was suggested that these parents must take an active role in liberating their own ideas, the old rescuing mentality appeared to give way to a more critically reflective approach, one that challenged and indeed overtook several of their former assumptions. Through this process of reflection, teachers were confronted with the possibility that their own hopes for education might also mean the dehumanisation of others.

The teachers were then asked: *What aspects of your kindergarten programme may dehumanise children?* Responses to this final question were revealing for three reasons: the first is that over half of the responses contained a critically reflective perspective: teachers began to ask questions like: "Do we make it feel too upper class? Do we cater to the beautiful people? Do we impose our beliefs about what is good for children? Do we truly listen and connect with children or do we see and hear what we want to?" All were critical and challenging questions of the teacher's own role in the potential dehumanisation of children. They were uncomfortable questions and each pointed to a sense of injustice that had previously, and quite unproblematically, gone under the radar as teachers went about their usual business of improving learning outcomes for children. Teachers had begun to ask questions of their aspirations for children and had begun to comprehend the sublative character of their hopes.

The second reason that responses were revealing is that nearly 75% of all responses identified institutional reasons for dehumanisation. Teachers had begun to see that the rules and regulations of the system they themselves worked within (and reproduced) contained not only the potential for education, but also the potential for dehumanising the lives of children. Teachers highlighted things such as "not giving children enough time to be themselves, the rules we put in place without having children's input, the expectation that children will do the same thing at the same time" as examples of their own role in the perpetuation of institutional norms. In Freirean terms, teachers had begun to think of their own role in the dehumanisation and oppression of children in their care. One teacher wrote about the common practice of "making assumptions about children's behaviour, taken from our perspective, without talking or listening." It was clear that this line of inquiry into the role of the teacher was making several teachers uncomfortable.

The third reason that the responses were revealing is that teachers had begun to consider the world of children in a wholly different way, and they had begun to see their role in that world as one that was not as simple as they had earlier thought—as one that is itself rich in the possibility of dehumanisation (alongside the more traditional early childhood aspiration toward humanisation). At the end of the workshop, one teacher pointed out that this way of thinking leads to "perpetual revolution" because it is human nature that some people will have and some people will not have—"there will always be someone who is dehumanised." I found that a fascinating statement and could only agree that it is entirely possible. Given my own philosophical perspective, I did not find the notion of there being no final or absolute state of liberation at the end of the process as alarming as her colleagues did. Another teacher spoke up, and in a quiet voice said what I think that many of us were thinking—"Maybe so, but that shouldn't stop us from doing what we can."

For a couple of hours, at least, the settled idea of the early childhood educator as heroine, rescuer, and vanguard of the educational species had been sublated by highlighting the possibility of that which is hoped-against being preserved, unwittingly, in praxis. For this group of teachers, the praxis of recognising the sublative elements of their hopes for children opened on to a vista of deeper critical engagement with their aspirations. Of course, a single intervention is not enough to shift thinking, but it is enough to plant a seed. In this regard, the praxis of sublating hope provided some degree of success in disturbing the status quo for these teachers. My hope is that with time and practice sublative hope might add another tool to the reflective toolbox, and become a useful rereading of Freire as a means of critical reflection.

Concluding statement

Freire's writing continues to act as a wellspring of knowledge for the praxis of critical reflection in early childhood education. This chapter has reread Friere by using Hegel's notion of sublation and by dropping the metaphysical elements of both authors' work in favour of neopragmatic assumptions around language and its uses. The language of both authors has been used to develop the notion of sublative hope, which I have put forward as a perspective of critical hope. The story of how Freire's writing was introduced to a group of experienced teachers was shared as a material correlate for the idea of sublative hope as a form of critical praxis. Further work using sublative hope as a theoretical platform for critical reflection with early childhood teachers may offer new insight into both reflective education and the praxis of critical hope. It is my own hope that others might make use of this work, build upon it, critique it, extend it, and reread it, though the possibility of it never finding utility can never fully be negated: but that, in a nutshell, is also the point.

REFERENCES

Arthur, L., & Sawyer, W. (2009). Robust hope, democracy and early childhood education. *Early Years, 29*(2), 163–175.

Bingham, C. (2002). On Paulo Freire's debt to psychoanalysis: Authority on the side of freedom. *Studies in Philosophy and Education, 24*(6), 447–464.

Bloch, E. (1986). *The principle of hope* (Vols. 1, 2, & 3) (N. Plaice, S. Plaice, & P. Knight, Trans.). Cambridge, MA: MIT Press.

Bredekamp, S. (Ed.). (1987). *Developmentally appropriate practice in early childhood programs servicing children from birth through age 8*. Washington, DC: NAEYC.

Dalli, C. (2003). *Professionalism in early childhood practice: Thinking through the debates*. Paper presented at the 13th annual conference of the European Early Childhood Education Research Association (EECERA), Glasgow, Scotland.

Duarte, E. M. (1999). Conscientizacion y Comunidad: A dialectical description of education as the struggle for freedom. *Studies in Philosophy and Education, 18*(6), 389–403.

Fleer, M. (Ed.). (1995). *DAP centrism: Challenging developmentally appropriate practice*. Watson, Australia: Australian Early Childhood Association.

Freire, P. (1994). *Pedagogy of hope: Reliving "Pedagogy of the oppressed"* (R. R. Barr, Trans.). New York, NY: Continuum.

Freire, P. (1998). *Pedagogy of freedom*. Lanham, MD: Rowman & Littlefield.

Freire, P. (2005). *Pedagogy of the oppressed* (M. Bergman Ramos, Trans.). New York, NY: Continuum.

Freire, P. (2007). *Pedagogy of the heart*. New York, NY: Continuum.

Gadamer, H. (1975). *Truth and method*. New York, NY: Continuum.

Gadotti, M. (1994). *Reading Paulo Freire* (J. Milton, Trans.). Albany, NY: SUNY Press.

Giroux, H., & McLaren, P. (1997). Paulo Freire, postmodernism, and the utopian imagination: A Blochian reading. In J. O. Daniel & T. Moylan (Eds.), *Not yet: Reconsidering Ernst Bloch* (pp. 138–162). London, England: Verso.

Gunn, A. (2003). A philosophical anchor for creating inclusive communities in early childhood education: Anti-bias philosophy and Te Whāriki: Early childhood curriculum. *Waikato Journal of Education, 9*, 129–141.

Halpin, D. (2007). Utopian spaces of "robust hope": The architecture and nature of progressive learning environments. *Asia-Pacific Journal of Teacher Education, 35*(3), 243–255.

Hannigan, B. (2011). Without ground: Suggesting an antifoundational approach to educational research in early childhood studies. *Proceedings of the New Zealand Association for Research in Education Conference and Annual Meeting 2010* (pp. 28–33). Wellington, New Zealand: NZARE.

Hegel, G. W. (2001). *Science of logic.* Retrieved from http://www.revalvaatio.org/wp/wp-content/uploads/hegel-science-of-logic.pdf

Jenkin, C. J. (2010). Supporting Tiriti-based curriculum delivery in mainstream early childhood education (Unpublished doctoral dissertation). Auckland University of Technology, Auckland, New Zealand.

Johnston, C. (2006, August 18). *Robust hope: Finding a home for early childhood intervention in the new early years landscape.* Paper presented at the annual conference of Early Childhood Intervention Australia, Victoria chapter, Melbourne, Australia.

May, H. (1997). *Discovery of early childhood: Mid eighteenth century Europe to twentieth century New Zealand.* Wellington, New Zealand: Bridget Williams Books.

May, H. (2009). *Politics in the playground: The world of early childhood in New Zealand* (2nd ed.). Dunedin, New Zealand: Otago University Press.

Ministry of Education. (1996). *Te Whāriki: He whāriki mātauranga mō ngā mokopuna o Aotearoa. Early childhood curriculum.* Wellington, New Zealand: Learning Media.

Ministry of Education. (2011). *Annual ECE census summary 2011.* Retrieved from http://www.educationcounts.govt.nz/__data/assets/word_doc/0016/103390/Annual-ECE-Summary-Report-2011_final.doc

Mitchell, L. M. (2007). *A new debate about children and childhood. Could it make a difference to early childhood pedagogy and policy?* (Unpublished doctoral dissertation). Victoria University of Wellington, Wellington, New Zealand.

Morehu, C. (2009). Language re-vitalisation and cultural transformation. *MAI Review, 1*, article 8. Retrieved from http://www.review.mai.ac.nz

Moss, P. (2009). *There are alternatives! Markets and democratic experimentalism in early childhood education and care.* The Hague, The Netherlands: Bernard van Leer Foundation.

New Zealand ECE Taskforce. (2011). *An agenda for amazing children.* Wellington, New Zealand: New Zealand ECE Taskforce.

Nuttall, J. (Ed.). (2003). *Weaving Te Whāriki: Aotearoa New Zealand's curriculum document in theory and practice.* Wellington, New Zealand: NZCER.

Pau'ulvale, D. L. (2011). *Laulōtaha: Tongan perspectives of "quality" in early childhood education* (Unpublished master's thesis). Auckland University of Technology, Auckland, New Zealand.

Ritchie, J. (2003). Bicultural development within an early childhood teacher education programme. *International Journal of Early Years Education, 11*(1), 43–56.

Rorty, R. (1979). *Philosophy and the mirror of nature.* Princeton, NJ: Princeton University Press.

Rorty, R. (1989). *Contingency, irony and solidarity.* Cambridge, England: Cambridge University Press.

Rorty, R. (1999). *Philosophy and social hope*. London, England: Penguin.

Schutte, O. M. (1990). The master-slave dialectic in Latin America: The social criticism of Zea, Friere and Roig. *The Owl of Minerva, 22*(1), 5–18.

Singh, M., & Sawyer, W. (2008). Democracy and robust hope: Queensland's education and training reforms for the future. *Education, Citizenship and Social Justice, 3*, 223–237.

Stephenson, A. (2009). *Skirmishes on the border: How children experienced, influenced and enacted the boundaries of curriculum in an early childhood education centre setting* (Unpublished doctoral dissertation). Victoria University of Wellington, Wellington, New Zealand.

Te One, S. (2008). *Perceptions of children's rights in three early childhood settings* (Unpublished doctoral dissertation). Victoria University of Wellington, Wellington, New Zealand.

Te One, S. (2010). Advocating for infants' rights in early childhood education. *Early Childhood Folio, 14*(1), 13–17.

Torres, C. A. (1994). Education and the archaeology of consciousness: Hegel and Freire. *Education Theory, 44*(4), 429–445.

Urban, M. (2008). Dealing with uncertainty: Challenges and possibilities for the early childhood profession. *European Early Childhood Education Research Journal, 16*(2), 135–152.

Van Heertum, R. (2006). Marcuse, Bloch and Freire: Reinvigorating a pedagogy of hope. *Policy Futures in Education, 4*(1), 45–51.

Webb, D. (2010). Paulo Freire and "the need for a kind of education in hope." *Cambridge Journal of Education, 40*(4), 327–339.

Williams, N. M., Broadley, M., & Te-Aho, K. L. (2012). *Ngā taonga whakaako: Bicultural competence in early childhood education*. Wellington, New Zealand: Ako Aotearoa National Centre for Tertiary Teaching Excellence.

Section 3:
Education as the Practice
of Freedom

A Freirean Approach to Internationalization in Higher Education Within the Context of Globalization

ROSETTA KHALIDEEN

INTRODUCTION

Internationalization in higher education is a phenomenon with which universities have been grappling for more than two and a half decades. Much has been written from varying perspectives about what constitutes the internationalization of a university and how "internationalized" activities can be facilitated. However, many writers have expressed concerns that universities still do not understand the true meaning of internationalization, and confusion exists between the concepts of internationalization and globalization (Bartlett, 2005; Bond, 2003; Hanson, 2010; Knight, 1997; Mestenhauser, 1998). The question often asked is: Are there differences between these two phenomena, or are they one and the same? Altbach and Knight (2007) are of the view that universities often see internationalization as synonymous with globalization, but suggest that although these two concepts are closely linked, they are different. These writers see globalization as the *context* in which internationalization takes place. Allen and Ogilvie (2004), differentiating between globalization and internationalization, note that "although linked, internationalization and globalization are different phenomena rather than interchangeable terms" (p. 73). Knight (2004) describes the connectedness between internationalization and globalization as the significant changes they each bring about in the way education is conceived and delivered. She says that "internationalization is changing the world of higher education and globalization is changing the world of internationalization" (p. 5).

Hanson (2010) notes that "globalization is a multifaceted phenomena and one of its major components is the internationalization of education" (p. 72). Khoo (2011), in her comparative study of internationalization in Canadian and Irish universities, found that internationalization and globalization are linked in that internationalization is used by these institutions as a response to globalization. Brunold-Conesa (2010) underscores that it is difficult to define internationalization because of the diverse purposes and learning outcomes associated with its practice. Similarly, it is also challenging to determine what constitutes globalization with all its complicated social, economic, cultural, and political facets. Brandenburg and De Wit (2011) posit that some view globalization and internationalization as opposed positions. Globalization is seen as creating wider gaps in our social and economic structures, while internationalization is perceived as building relationships and fostering engagement in collaborative activities. They believe that there is an existing tension that positions the two as opposing forces—a tension that ignores the fact that activities connected to globalization are conducted through internationalization, and hence there is a strong link between the two rather than a polarization. As can be seen, there are many contradictions and sometimes confusion with the understanding of globalization and internationalization, but no matter how the two are conceptualized, there is no doubt that globalization is having an impact on the internationalization of universities.

INTERNATIONALIZATION'S RESPONSE TO GLOBALIZATION

Globalization has changed and is still changing the way universities operate and how they prepare students to live and work in a new social and economic order. At the forefront of globalization are economic competitiveness, rapid technological advancements, a stronger realization of the interdependence of nations, and new and evolving trade relations. There is a new and growing world market that defines people as producers and consumers of goods and services. One of the many products with a place of prominence in global consumerism is information, and the "sale" of this information is intensifying competition among educational institutions in the international marketplace. Post-secondary institutions are catching on to the business model of globalization, which is based on increased profits from the flow of financial capital. Within this economic globalized context, many universities are choosing to market their "products" and services in the name of internationalization. Education is viewed as a commodity to be sold and universities are striving to attain the competitive advantage in the global marketplace. Ng (2012), expressing concern for the increased export of higher education in the

Asia Pacific region, notes that the sale of higher education services is becoming "a global, market-oriented and private industry" (p. 441).

Allen and Ogilvie (2004) allude to the new trend of universities becoming earnestly engaged in strategies to increase international student recruitment, whether on their home campus or on international campuses. These writers note that "universities are competitive in searching for students and marketing their courses/programs worldwide" (p. 76). The goal of these institutions is to build a reputation as "world class" universities so that they can position themselves to capitalize on the economic resources generated by an increased number of international students. Some smaller and less recognized universities are also joining the international marketing fray, and one wonders whether the purpose of an internationalized education is ever a consideration in the building up of an international student base. Altbach (2011) subscribes to the view that universities are using internationalization for financial gains and not paying sufficient attention to the educational experience. He points out that there has even been a rising trend wherein universities are using third party agents to assist with recruiting international students, and notes that "this trend is growing in size, scope and notoriety as international enrollments have become a compelling part of some universities' bottom lines" (p. 11). There has been a significant increase in academic entrepreneurialism during the past two decades, and universities are becoming big businesses for revenue generation through internationalization. Edmonds (2012) concurs that internationalization in higher education is premised on financial profits rather than on a long-term vision. She concludes that fees from international students are a critical source of revenue to help the bottom line of both universities and governments.

Here in the province of British Columbia, Canada, the government is pushing for an increase of 47,000 international students in post-secondary institutions over the next four years. Despite the surge in enrollment that these international students will bring, the government has not indicated any intent to increase funding to its public post-secondary institutions. Instead, attention is centered on the boost to the economy from international students spending millions of dollars on tuition, accommodation, and other living expenses. Also, while there is currently a cap on fees for domestic students in British Columbia, there is no such regulation on fees for international students, and colleges and universities are free to set their own international tuition rates.

The continuous cutbacks to education funding, in what is being described as an ongoing global economic crisis, are resulting in higher education shifting its goal from education for critical citizenship, public service, and civic leadership to education for revenue generation. Berkowitz (2012), referencing the recent report of the Advisory Panel on Canada's International Education Strategy, says that the report confirms international education as Canada's eleventh largest *export* and its single largest export to China. There are substantial economic benefits to international students studying in Canada's post-secondary institutions.

Within a context of revenue generation and education exportation, international students are brought (sometimes lured through false marketing), to university campuses in an attempt to achieve targeted enrollments and balanced budgets. Some universities set annual quotas for international students to compensate for a shortfall of domestic student registrations. Upon arriving at the educational institutions, international students find that their learning is not guided by a clear set of principles that would enable them to successfully engage in a comprehensive international education experience. International students are taught courses with North American content, which takes little account of their experiences, social, cultural, political, or ideological backgrounds. Their education is one that re-cultures them to fit into the climate of the country in which they find themselves. Internationalization in this sense is viewed as something that needs to be done for, or done *to*, these students, since they come to the developed world to be enlightened. The situation is no different in student exchanges for students who come from developing countries. International students who come to universities on these exchange programs thinking that they would be involved in a "learning exchange" find out very quickly that their learning takes them down a one-way street. Conversely, North American students who leave for the shores of the developing world to gain an international experience return with patronizing stories of how they had to take charge and lead educational activities for people too poor and undereducated to be in control of their own learning. Too often, the stories do not take into account the rich experiential learning students have gained from their study abroad time. The attitude is that *others* can learn from us, but we cannot learn from them.

To illustrate the sense of superiority of students from North America and other parts of the developed world, I would like to share my experience with a group of Canadian students who went on a work-study attachment to an elementary school in my native country, Guyana. The school was located in a rural area of the country and lacked adequate resources. On their return to Canada, the students shared with me their many concerns about the level of poverty that exists for "those poor Guyanese kids" who did not have access even to a TV at school. It was unfortunate that they were unable to watch *Sesame Street* and Big Bird as part of their classes. The school also lacked basic teaching equipment and there was no overhead projector for these visiting students to show some of the beautiful pictures of butterflies they had taken to Guyana for their science lessons. In speaking with the teacher of the class in rural Guyana, she confessed how saddened she was for these Canadian students who had spent an enormous amount of time comparing her school with schools in Canada. They could not see that despite the many economic challenges, students were still learning, and this in itself was a very positive outcome of their schooling. She said that the Canadian student group failed to see the bright-eyed enthusiasm of the kids who sat in circles and shared their "Anancy stories," told to them by their grandmothers. They did not need to watch a foreign TV show to which they would be unable to relate. They were having as much fun and learning new ideas as other kids in a Grade 2 classroom in an elementary school in Canada. This teacher also mentioned that the Canadian students had missed the boat by not allowing the kids to go outdoors during their science classes to actually find a collection of butterflies for their project, instead of using the pictures they had brought with them. The close-minded attitude of the Canadian students was that there is not much to learn from people who are facing economic hardships. Internationalization needs to challenge this notion, since such people survive because they are strong, resilient, creative, and inventive. There is much to learn from them.

INTERNATIONALIZATION AND SOCIAL TRANSFORMATION

The attitude the students displayed in their field placement in Guyana is a good example of what Stier (2002) describes as internationalization being premised on the interests and values of ethnocentrism and on a belief in self-superiority. If not thoughtfully designed, study abroad programs and student exchanges reinforce stereotypes instead of providing opportunities for students to meaningfully engage with new cultural and socio-economic communities. The purpose of the exchange becomes a superficial contact with different ways of being and seeing the world, and students are not challenged to cross cultural, ethnic, religious, or ideological boundaries. Within the university's classrooms, if internationalization does not allow for curriculum and activities to include differences, then both international and domestic students will lose out on the opportunity to develop shared global perspectives, values, and attitudes. Since universities claim that one of their goals is fostering global citizenship and civic responsibility, they should see one of the key roles of internationalization as bringing about social transformation. This means shifting attitudes of ethnocentrism to an increased ability to respect all people and to function in an interdependent world. Universities have to enable students to understand international and intercultural issues related to justice, equity, and fairness. This stance of internationalization is becoming lost to the now common goal of revenue generation.

With attention on social transformation, the pursuit of activities related to internationalization should be guided by principles of reciprocity, and should lead to increased knowledge and awareness of inequities both within groups and among different peoples. Universities are about instilling values and beliefs, and as such they are positioned to facilitate a transformed social order through the development of appropriate policies and practices. Internationalization has to develop caring, responsive global citizens through the transforming stances of teaching and learning (Hanson, 2010). Universities also articulate one of their primary roles as the generation of knowledge and such knowledge, if transformative, can lead to social change. Those who attend universities are supposed to be engaged in activities that foster critical thinking and the continual development of values, beliefs, attitudes, and ideologies. A critical function of the university would be to allow for spaces where people can individually and collectively think outside of the box, push the limits of paradigms, and question societal interests and pressures (Brenman, King, & Lebeau, 2004). Fundamental to a university education should be the building of a collective critical intellect to lead and shape social transformation. An enriching university education means having a broad-based education that goes beyond technical and rational knowledge production, and that includes the promotion of an engaged global citizenry for social change.

Universities ought to pay attention to their responsibility through internationalization to develop within their students, faculty, and the wider community the ability to solve international problems, while respecting other cultures, demonstrating concern for human rights, understanding the interdependence of humanity, and valuing acceptance and cooperation. What is "taught" or not "taught" in universities has profound implications for the creation of social change or the strengthening of the status quo. As was previously suggested, globalization is creating new political, social, and economic realities that cannot be ignored, and it will be the role of education to promote intercultural understanding, values, and beliefs that would question the legitimacy of these realities. The work of Paulo Freire, the famous influential Brazilian educator, provides a roadmap for educators to foster the values, skills, and dispositions that can influence education for global citizenship and social transformation.

FREIRE'S PEDAGOGY OF SOCIAL TRANSFORMATION

Freire began his work as a literacy educator in his native Brazil, where he worked with the peasant communities who were exploited by their masters, the rich landowners. He taught the poor and illiterate to read and write though the use of *generative* words to trigger dialogue that allowed them to critically reflect on their lives of poverty. These dialogic discussions led them to understand the reasons for their exploitation and the possibilities to make changes. Freire's pedagogical approach was enlightening, providing learners the opportunity to see their ongoing helplessness and their perceived inability to change the course of their lives as their development of a *false consciousness*. Through dialogue and critical reflection, people were brought to the realization (*new consciousness*) that they could act upon and change their situations (*conscientization*). They could take liberating action that would free them from the bondage of social, political, and economic inequities, not only for themselves as individuals, but also for their communities. This process of reflection and action Freire termed *praxis*.

At the heart of Freire's pedagogy is an ideology of education that views learning as more than traditional teaching in which the teacher is seen as the producer and transmitter of knowledge to students (Freire, 1992). Students are not blank slates on which the teacher has to write. Freire strongly felt that education is way beyond an encounter with the production of knowledge. Instead, he saw teaching and learning as a process of raising critical consciousness. Freire believed that it is as important to teach people to read the word as it is to read the "world." He saw conventional texts as more than neutral print on paper, and emphasized that *who* determines what should be printed is as important as *what* is printed. Freire underscored the importance of understanding how the textual world is controlled by those who have power and thus are those who would influence the context of the lives of the less powerful. He reminded educators that reading is not a passive act, and for one to become truly literate, he/she must have the ability to understand textual meaning in the context of societal power relations.

Freire was convinced that teachers have to understand the social situations of learners so that whatever is being "taught" will impact the world in which learners live. Changing the world to be a place where people are valued and treated fairly and where democracy exists is core to the beliefs of a Freirean pedagogy. As Dos Santos (2008) notes, "For Freire, education is more than the mere act of teaching how to read and write; it goes beyond teaching content" (p. 364). Freire strongly believed that educators must challenge learners to critically engage with their world so that they can understand and act upon it. He promoted a problem-posing education with the aim of social transformation. He encouraged educators to question curriculum and classroom activities, and to analyze the institutional and societal constraints that dominate educational practices.

As was noted, Freire's pedagogy for social transformation is rooted in the context of the oppression of the poor and illiterate in Brazil. Oppression takes many forms. "Internationalized universities" can be "oppressive spaces" for students who are marginalized and have no voice in their education. They are seen more or less as the "silent" financial contributors to the coffers of higher education. International students often arrive from countries where globalization has imposed restrictions on their social lives, skills, occupations, political systems, and economic consumerism. Globalization might have, in some nations, made a few people wealthier, but it has also worsened the situations of many and continues to increase rather than to narrow the gap between rich and poor countries. Many international students come from this context of inequity, which adds to the challenges they face when they arrive on the campuses of our universities. If international students are to be successful, then these are challenges that should be addressed through the educational experience in which they participate. Within the internationalized classroom, there should be discourse that recognizes and understands the differences of the political, social, and economic contexts that characterize globalized communities.

Khalideen (2008), in the study she conducted in collaboration with Blachford, O'Leary, and Ross at a Canadian university, notes that in exploring the participation of international students in their education process, she found that these students felt discriminated against by their professors. Students spoke of being ignored and left out of classroom discussions and having their perspectives on issues disregarded. They also felt ostracized by Canadian students and were unable to fully participate in group work and projects. These students were of the view that as international students, they had a responsibility to be contributors to an enriching educational experience for all university students. They could not understand why they were not more fully integrated into the institution and were treated as "outsiders." Knight (2011), in debunking some of the myths associated with internationalization, identifies a misunderstanding that more international students on a university campus can be equated with successful internationalization. She claims that the reality in many institutions is that international students are marginalized and excluded. These students lose the opportunity to have a broad and enriching educational experience that would impact their own culture and the culture of the host country. My experience has been that international students want to feel that they do count and that they have much to contribute to their educational endeavours. The educational opportunities for *all* students lie in engaging in critical discourse and building alliances between international and domestic students. These alliances are crucial, since global issues will require the participation and action from all people in today's interconnected world. One group of students remaining isolated in the classroom will find themselves robbed of the experience of a "complete" education. Faculty have to find creative ways to bring both international and local students together to collaboratively discover their realities. This implies changing the teaching process in the classroom to ensure freedom for *all* students to be involved in helping to shape the structure and content of their education. As Freire has so often pointed out, the teacher is not the great master and orator who has to fill the empty minds of students with predetermined knowledge. Education is a symbiotic relationship between teacher and students, allowing for an engaged pedagogy in which students can make suggestions, ask questions, and find answers.

Freire often reminded educators that there is no such thing as a neutral education. Whose knowledge counts, whose values are promoted, and whose are excluded are important in the design of the content and education process. Education can perpetuate the status quo, or it can facilitate changes to liberate and generate new ways of acting in the world (Macedo, 1994). What should drive the educational process is the relationship of respect and reciprocity that is cultivated between educator and students and among students themselves. Bartlett (2005) says that "for Freire, all learning is relational and knowledge is produced in interaction" (p. 346). Mayo (2004) coins this relationship as one of love. He says that "it is love that drives the progressive Freire-inspired educator forward in teaching and working for the dismantling of dehumanizing structures" (p. 3). An internationalized classroom characterized by student autonomy, respect, and caring relationships would allow learners to develop the ability to critically analyze, question, and take action on the societal issues that affect and shape their lives. Through dialogue and problem posing, learners will develop consciousness of structures of their society that contribute to inequality and oppression. Consciousness-raising around issues such as powerlessness, marginalization, disenfranchisement, and intolerance, among others, is important to a liberating education. Such transformative and engaged methods of teaching and learning need to be the norm in education, so that the dominant ways of being are deconstructed.

Preparing both international and domestic students who can positively contribute to a multinational, multi-ethnic, and multi-lingual world in an interconnected global economy is a challenge facing universities. Freire's focus on a transformative education that develops democratic citizens is undoubtedly key to the values people will need to cultivate to live in a globalized society. His definition of democracy suggests participation in a culture of equality. He recognizes that learners are not homogeneous but are complex and diverse, and implores that we need to cross boundaries if we are educating for empowerment. Faculty and students crossing the lines of difference and building inclusivity is indeed central to transformative learning. We live in one world, and national borders should not be viewed as classifications of people's power or powerlessness. We need to question how the world functions in creating freedom for some and disempowerment for others. Freire's call for transformation would suggest that we all need to become architects of social change breaking down the walls that keep us in prescribed spaces. Khalideen (2008), referencing the study she conducted with Blachford, O'Leary, and Ross, suggests that international students might not have been deliberately ignored and marginalized by their professors, but could have been treated this way as a result of the exclusion of *others* that is so ingrained within the ideologies of our social and political systems. As Harper, Patton, and Wooden (2009) note, colleges and universities are an integral part of a nation's political system, and as such their policies and practices, while privileging some groups, disadvantage others.

CONCLUSION

Even though internationalization seems to be one of the measures of success of post-secondary educational institutions, there is still a lack of clarity about its role.

More than a decade ago, Hinchcliff (2000) saw the role of internationalization as tied to universities educating their students for global citizenship, to keep pace with their peers across the world, to better serve the national and international communities, and to remain great universities. Internationalization means enabling students to become globally conscious and to have a critical understanding of how national and international issues intersect. For those who have been paying attention to the changing landscape of internationalization, there might be some consensus that we have veered away from the real intent and purposes of the "internationalized" university. The comments of Tsiligiris (2012) in discussing the highlights of the Going Global 2012 Conference confirm that many scholars in higher education admit that universities have lost touch with the initial intent of internationalization. There is a call to re-think internationalization with the hope of determining what its purpose, real aim, and mission ought to be.

The work of Paulo Freire can provide a framework for education to interrogate current practices of internationalization and to bring about reform. Rather than accept the rhetoric of internationalization, the reality of internationalization would see educators encouraged to transcend boundaries and to define their roles as supporting equity, fairness, and democracy within a global community. Freire would claim that we cannot advocate that people should be free while we remain complacent about education leading to freedom and liberation (Johnston & Goodman, 2006). Educators have an ethical responsibility to help students critically engage their world so that students can be enabled to determine the interventions that are necessary to bring about societal change within the context of globalization. Ongoing reflections and questioning can lead to the development of a critical consciousness of broader societal issues.

It is unfortunate that Freire's writings have not seriously entered into the discourse of internationalization even though many scholars have drawn on his works (Johnston & Goodman, 2006). There is some consensus among scholars that his pedagogical approach to social transformation is complex and sometimes unrealistic, and thus educators who try to follow his approach are often challenged. Lange (2012), in her critique of Chet Bowers' article characterizing Freire's transformative education as a Trojan horse of Western globalization, agrees that there has been an ongoing criticism of his dialogic pedagogy, with some criticisms being fair and others misplaced. She suggests that for a Freirean approach to education to be effective, the context within which such education will take place needs to be analyzed and understood prior to an approach being determined. However, within the literature on education for social transformation, there seems to be agreement that following narrowly prescribed education agendas will lead to the continuous powerlessness of people. Educators have to reflect on the social, cultural, and geo-political locations of themselves and their students, and how these shape the meaning of teaching and learning. Creating spaces for multi-perspective pedagogical encounters within our post-secondary institutions would help us to re-examine assumptions, attitudes, and behaviours with a view to questioning internationalization practices. Internationalization should support a vision of higher education that will develop transformative citizens with the dispositions of social justice, democracy, and equity to live in a context of global interdependence.

REFERENCES

Allen, M., & Ogilvie, L. (2004). Internationalization of higher education: Potentials and pitfalls for nursing education. *International Nursing Review, 51*(2), 73–80.

Altbach, P. G. (2011). Agents and third party recruiters in international higher education. *International Higher Education, 62*, 11–14.

Altbach, P. G., & Knight, J. (2007). The internationalization of higher education: Motivation and realities. *Journal of Studies in International Education, 11*(3), 290–305.

Bartlett, L. (2005). Dialogue, knowledge and teacher-student relations: Freirean pedagogy in theory and practice. *Comparative Education Review, 49*(3), 344–364.

Berkowitz, P. (2012). Internationalization helps Canada's economy and trade, says advisory panel. *University Affairs, 14.* Retrieved from http://universityaffairs.ca

Bond, S. L. (2003). *Untapped resources: Internationalizing the curriculum and classroom experience: A selected literature review.* Ottawa, Canada: Canadian Bureau for International Education.

Brandenburg, E., & De Wit, H. (2011). The end of internationalization. *International Higher Education, 62*, 15–17.

Brenman, J., King, R., & Lebeau, Y. (2004). *Report on the role of universities in the transformation of societies.* London, England: Association of Commonwealth Universities.

Brunold-Conesa, C. (2010). International education: The international baccalaureate, Montessori and global citizenship. *Journal of International Education, 9*(3), 250–272.

De Wit, H. (2011). The end of internationalization. *International Higher Education, 62*, 15–17.

Dos Santos, W. L. P. (2008). Scientific literacy: A Freirean perspective as radical view of humanistic science education. In J. W. Bloom & D. Trumbull (Eds.), *Issues and trends in science education.* New York, NY: Wiley Periodicals.

Edmonds, J. (2012, July 11). What internationalization should really be about. *University Affairs.*

Freire, P. (1992). *Pedagogy of hope.* London, England: Continuum.

Hanson, L. (2010). Global citizenship, global health and the internationalization of curriculum. *Journal of Studies in International Education, 14*(1), 70–88.

Harper, S. R., Patton, D., & Wooden, O. S. (2009). Access and equity for African American students in higher education: A critical race historical analysis of policy efforts. *Journal of Higher Education, 80*(4), 389–414.

Hinchcliff, J. (2000). *The globalization of education.* Paper presented at the TEND conference, Crossroads of the New Millennium, Abu Dhabi, United Arab Emirates.

Johnston, J., & Goodman, J. (2006). Hope and activism in the ivory tower: Freirean lessons for critical globalization research. *Globalization, 3*(1), 9–30.

Khalideen, R. (2008). Voiceless in the internationalized classroom: Diversity and the dynamics of difference. *The International Journal of Diversity in Organizations, Communities and Nations, 7*(6), 267–273.

Khoo, S. (2011). Ethical globalization or privileged internationalization? Exploring global citizenship and internationalization in Irish and Canadian universities. *Globalization, Societies and Education, 9*(3), 337–353.

Knight, J. (1997). Internationalization of higher education: A conceptual framework. In J. Knight & H. De Wit (Eds.), *Internationalization of higher education in the Asia Pacific countries.* Amsterdam, The Netherlands: European Association of International Education (EAIE).

Knight, J. (2004). Internationalization remodelled: Definition, approach and rationales. *Journal of Studies in International Education, 8*(1), 5–31.

Knight, J. (2011). Five myths about internationalization. *International Higher Education, 62*, 14–15.

Lange, E. A. (2012). Is Freirean transformative learning the Trojan horse of globalization and enemy of sustainability education? A response to C. A. Bowers. *Journal of Transformative Education, 10*(1), 3–21.

Macedo, D. (1994). *Literacies of power.* San Francisco, CA: Westview Press.

Mayo, P. (2004). *Liberating praxis: Paulo Freire's legacy for radical education and politics.* Rotterdam, The Netherlands: Sense.

Mestenhauser, J. A. (1998). Portraits of an international curriculum: An uncommon multidimensional perspective. In J. A. Mestenhauser & B. J. Ellingboe (Eds.), *Reforming the higher education curriculum: Internationalizing the campus.* Phoenix, AZ: Oryx Press.

Ng, S. W. (2012). Rethinking the mission of internationalization of higher education in the Asia-Pacific region. *Compare: A Journal of Comparative Education, 42*(3), 439–459.

Stier, J. (2002). *Internationalization in higher education: Unexplored possibilities and unavoidable challenges.* Paper presented at the European Conference on Educational Research, Lisbon, Portugal.

Tsiligiris, V. (2012). What's wrong with internationalization of higher education? It's the language, stupid! *Anglo Higher Education—Lifelong Learning and Professional Training*, 1–4. Retrieved from http://www.anglohigher.com/casestudies/casestudy-detail/57/39

A Dialogue About Dialogue: Freire and Bakhtin Talk Pedagogy in Response to Percy's "Problem"

LEON BENADE AND E. JAYNE WHITE

PERCY'S "PROBLEM"

In the paper "The Problem With Percy" (Bailin, 1999), a teacher laments the fate of her graduate student, Percy, who is having difficulty in a graduate class that requires him to engage in critical writing. Percy's problem, according to Bailin, is that he is unable to engage in critical thinking. Her claim is based on his inability to consistently conceptualise, argue, and theorise ideas in his writing. Bailin asserts that this problem goes beyond the acquisition and practice of skills or the demonstration of a disposition to critical thinking. Thus, the problem is not about Percy's ability to conceptualise ideas or his disposition to inquire (although she suggests that Percy may lack a "critical spirit" [p. 164]). His problem, she suggests, is epistemological—"he does not understand the enterprise of knowledge creation and evaluation" (p. 164). She argues that there are moral reasons educators should encourage students to develop the ability and disposition to evaluate reasons, justify claims, and make judgments. This justification resides in a preference for these activities over those acting out of "image, intuition or authority" (p. 168), and is particularly important in the context of "a flight from reason,…spread of religious fundamentalism,…proliferation of new age philosophy" and postmodernist rejection of rationality (p. 169). For Bailin, the solution for Percy lies in an initiation into the practice of critical thinking that will, in her view, lead to an "appreciation of the nature of the enterprise" (p. 169).

Percy's problem is frequently echoed by many lecturers throughout academic institutions and often forms the basis for academic decisions that are made in the years leading up to and following postgraduate study. As such, it forms the basis of an educational position of what constitutes valued knowledge and its correlates. In this chapter, we want to challenge the construction of knowledge that forms the basis for this problem from the perspectives of Freire (1921–1997) and Bakhtin (1895–1975)—two "dialogist" thinkers who variously argue for an attention to dialogue as central to meaning-making. From their perspectives we ask, "What are the roots of the problem?" and "How it might be understood?" Based on these interpretations, we propose that the "problem" itself is at the centre of the problem when viewed dialogically. For Bakhtin, this is because the construction of knowledge is not viewed as a social act; and for Freire, that it is not geared toward liberation and humanisation. The perspectives of both thinkers are therefore illuminated throughout this chapter and thus represent a comparative analysis of the pedagogical imperatives of each, and their pedagogical alternatives.

FREIRE AND BAKHTIN ON DIALOGISM

While Freire and Bakhtin are often summoned as protagonists in the field of educational dialogism, they do not necessarily share the same approaches to dialogue and its relationship to pedagogy. In the section that follows, we introduce some of the key ideas of both and their interface. We do this as a means of exploring alternative pedagogical approaches that might assist Bailin in her response to Percy. We begin by examining the philosophical origins of Bakhtin and Freire, and introduce some key ideas that might support or challenge a consideration of Percy's problem as a misunderstanding of "knowledge creation." In essence, we draw out the ontological and epistemological orientations of Freire and Bakhtin as divergent thinkers who share a dialogic premise but provide a very different pedagogical imperative. In making this claim, we suggest that any view of the two as similarly oriented is naïve, and fails to emphasise key philosophical differences and their associated outcry in the classroom.

Any consideration of Freire and Bakhtin would be negligent if it avoided at least a mention of their very different philosophical orientations. While neither would have claimed to represent a philosophical "tradition," both were heavily influenced by the work of philosophers they had access to during the diverse epochs in which they lived. Bakhtin's lifetime spent in Russia in the Stalin and post-Stalinistic era of suppression, coupled with his lifelong encounters with art and literature that formed the basis of his aesthetic imperative (White & Peters, 2012) seem a far cry from Freire's middle-class family life in Brazil that was forced to the brink of poverty by global economic depression. Both men's experience clearly influenced their orientations—leading Freire to focus on developing literacy among the poorest of Brazil; whereas, for Bakhtin, his Aesopian attention to literature created a means of exploring human experience through dialogue. Bakhtin's ultimate objective was attuned to dimensions of self and other that were at the forefront of philosophical thought throughout his lifetime—emanating, in particular, from his early engagement with German philosophy (Morson & Emerson, 1990). As such, his application in education is largely left to the interpretation of those who ponder his legacy[1] based on the chronotopes he himself occupied over his lifetime (White, 2012). As Brandist (2011) explains:

> It is only through such experimental meetings that the value and the limitations of the ideas themselves can be established, and that the experiences on which the ideas were based can be, in a sense, redeemed. Similarly, such engagements cast a new light on contemporary problems and on the established ways of approaching them. (p. xii)

Clear areas of ontological, epistemological, and ethical focus are evident in the work of both men. They reflect, however, significant differences in their thinking and ideological approaches to their work due to their unique backgrounds. Several recognisable currents influence each of them. The Catholicism of Freire's childhood echoes, for example, throughout his 1998 work, *Pedagogy of Freedom* (Benade, 2010) and the Russian Orthodox residue from Bakhtin's early experience cannot be ignored. This is particularly prevalent in his earliest works that emphasise morality and his life-long interest in Dostoevsky (Bakhtin, 1984). For Bakhtin, the anticipated presence of the "authorial other" who always understands might be interpreted as some sort of supreme being who knows and, most important, sees all; while for Freire the dialectical relationship between people and the world they live in expresses his commitment to social justice underpinned by a human desire for hope. It is from these origins that Freire rejects fatalism; while Bakhtin suggests there is always a loophole for individuals to be "other" than the way they have been positioned within the social milieu (Bakhtin, 1984). Being "seen" (and maintaining the agentic orientation), as well as *not* being fully discovered (that is, consummated) are key to Bakhtin's aesthetic and are of equal significance. In the final analysis, however, Bakhtin suggests that every individual is answerable for his/her acts and cannot hide behind systems as some sort of alibi. Thus, the dialogic act represents a "special form of free volition of one person in relation to others" (Bakhtin, 1993, in Nielsen, 1998, p. 219). It, too, is hopeful but oriented toward individual agency in concert with authorial discourse, rather than overcoming the oppressive systems in which individuals are located, as Freire required.

According to Roberts (2005), Freire's imperative may be partially attributed to his engagement with Christian Gospels that he perceived as a call to action. His life experiences gave him deep understanding of the plight of those marginalised socially, politically, and economically. It also led him to distrust capitalism, and he was particularly appalled by the "scourge of neoliberalism" (1998, p. 22). Bakhtin, on the other hand, was less focused on solving the "problem" than he was on examining the social experience of dialogue as a route to creative engagement with the problem. Though an associate of Matvei Kagan (and the Marburg School) and a student of Kantian philosophy, Bakhtin rejected any ultimate discourse that might consume thought. His attention to the discursive is highly evident in his strategic use of genre and heteroglossia that were developed out of his later writing (Bakhtin, 1984). As such, Bakhtin's ultimate "problem" occurs when there is no problem to be discussed, debated, or considered because it has already been resolved. In doing so, Bakhtin might say that monologism has been achieved—here there is no dialogue and, by association, no opportunity for creative thought. The dialogue ceases to exist and, by association, so does learning.

Informed by Hegelian thinking, Freire's dialogic approach was underpinned by his understanding of the dialectic. He regarded all relationships within the world as dialectical (Roberts, 2000). From this understanding arise several key concepts in Freire's thinking, especially notions of praxis and humanisation. These concepts enabled Freire to speak of knowledge creation and the central ethical focus of human life. It is here, we suggest, it will be found that, apart from some superficial similarities, Bakhtin and Freire most poignantly part company. Bakhtin rejected dialectics because he saw it was a key means of finalising language and thus a kind of consummation process resulting in the elimination of dialogue. Instead, his route to creativity was through the aesthetic process of evaluation and appreciation—*vzhivanie*, or "actively entering into him" as other (Bakhtin, 1986, p. 93). Underpinning Freire's idea of the dialectic was the view that it was not ever possible for either the world or people to be considered as finished or complete. Clearly, Bakhtin shared an unfinalised position but did so through Goethe's *Bildungsroman* notion of "becoming" in which characters are presented as complex, nuanced, accountable, and full of potential. This image provides a very different starting place to Freire, who argued that both oppressor and oppressed had to be liberated. Where Freire's (1985) interest was in the way people live *with* the world (rather than *in* the world as animals do) as a means of transforming the world (unlike animals who merely survive), Bakhtin was concerned with the form-shaping potential of subject-subject relations as "event"—as a means of both intersubjectivity and alterity. Where for Freire a transformable world is never complete, but is possible, for Bakhtin, dialogic encounters are always acts of becoming because they are never fully known by one or another (at least not until the point of death when dialogue is no longer possible).

There are various positions that might be taken in relation to Freire's dialectical prerogative when juxtaposed with Bakhtin's dialogics. Facundo (1984), for example, suggests Freire defaulted to the term dialectic when he had no way of addressing the "problem." Like Matusov (2009), Facundo argues that Freire's position is therefore irreconcilable because he promotes notions of love while invoking violence through his admiration of communist liberation. For Matusov, the tension between dialogue and social justice is incommensurably aligned in Freire's thesis. In contrast, Bakhtin rejected this dialectic outright, because he believed it shut down dialogue (a concept he lived with in Stalinist Russia). For him, dialogue is a process of uncertainty and chronotopic encounter, rather than a product of learning—an opening or threshold for discovery and awe (White, 2012). Freire, however, would never accept dialogue for its own sake. For him, dialogue must serve a purpose (Roberts, 2000). Herein lies the conundrum—Freire believed that some ideas were superior to others (Roberts, 2000), while for Bakhtin all voices were entitled to joust for their position within the dialogic event or act. For one, some ideologies are better than others; while for the other, they are all entitled to contribute to the dialogue on their own merit. This latter point has received criticism from those who suggest Bakhtin's avoidance of conflict and power, and associated reluctance to accept any non-negotiated "whole" is unsatisfying (Holquist & Liapunov, cited in Bakhtin, 1990), yet it might also be argued that his ideas have become increasingly relevant in contemporary "open" societies that reject totalitarianism (White, 2012).

The differences between these two thinkers may be partly attributed to their very different response to associated Marxist ideas—which they were both exposed to in their lifetimes. While Bakhtin was undoubtedly influenced by Marxist thought (as a result of the epoch in which he lived), his work is inter-animated by Marxist ideas of language (for a fuller discussion, see Brandist & Tihanov, 2000; Morson & Emerson, 1990). Bakhtin's rejection of "the language of revolution" (Roberts, 2005, p. 128) is keenly evident throughout his work—resulting in a distant rejection of any exclusive alignment to systems of thought. In contrast, Freire's treatment of Marx is evident in his notion of oppressor and oppressed. For Freire (1970/1996) it is the "injustice, exploitation, oppression, and the violence of the oppressors" (p. 26) that negates the human desire for freedom and therefore underpins his imperative. Yet, despite his use of these dualisms, Freire should also not be read as projecting an image of raw power and a world of simple binary opposites, in which there is no hope. Even so, Freire's treatment of Marx might be seen, from a Bakhtinian standpoint, as anti-dialogic. Indeed, in his critique of these two thinkers Matusov (2009) purports that Freire's work illuminates the tension between dialogue and social justice as incommensurable concepts. When forced into combination, these concepts, Matusov suggests, jeopardise the potential of dialogic thinking. Yet, for Freire, dialogue is the *pathway* to social justice (Mayo, 2004; see also Darder, 2002, cited in Mayo, 2004, p. 33). If achieved, this process enriches further dialogue. On the basis of these varying interpretations, and our own reading, we suggest that these two approaches to dialogue are irreconcilable and, as such, highlight some important issues when considered in relation to classroom practice.

PEDAGOGICAL ORIENTATIONS OF BAKHTIN AND FREIRE

Given their attention to dialogue as a primary route to transformation (Freire) and meaning-making (Bakhtin), it is hardly surprising that both men are frequently summoned as pedagogical informants under the broad term "dialogic pedagogy" (Bowers, 2005; Rule, 2011; van der Linden & Renshaw, 2004). Arising from their respective backgrounds, priorities, and philosophical inspirations, however, their interpretation of this concept and its manifestation in practice are vastly different. A frequent question posed to Freire was how his work, shaped around illiterate rural poor in a developing national context, could be transferred to a developed national and international context. He would usually answer by emphasising that his ideas did not reduce to a "method" that could be transposed; rather, it was important that educators, regardless of their context, consider what human ideals are important to pursue, and then to do so critically and dialogically (Roberts, 2000). Even so, Freirean pedagogical practices sought to alter learner perspectives on "culture." This positioning is psychological and, while devoted to freedom, it is a freedom that speaks to the learner through "problem posing" (Bingham & Biesta, 2010). As Macedo has pointed out, the methods fetish leads some "pseudocritical educators" to domesticate Freire (1997, p. 2).

Bakhtin, on the other hand, provides a very clear method in his later work *Speech Genres and Other Late Essays* (1986). Yet it was not a model that was overtly oriented to education *per se,* nor did it lend itself to universal application (as is evident by the increasingly diverse treatment of his ideas across disciplines in contemporary society). Bakhtin examines key concepts from his earlier thinking from a literary standpoint, and applies them to the social experience of language. As Holquist and Liapunov (in Bakhtin, 1990) explain, his method is concerned with not only the "relatively stable types" (p. xxi) of utterances, but also their *use* within the discourse. His position is thus philosophical—learning draws from dialogic interplay. It is here that genres play out at their keenest as an indication of the strategic orientation of the language in dialogue with other. While his life work is less overtly oriented toward pedagogy,[2] his overarching emphasis on dialogic relations (symbolised through art and literature) cannot be separated from this imperative. Only one of Bakhtin's works focuses explicitly on pedagogy. Here—as a secondary teacher of grammar at Oblast secondary school—Bakhtin (2004) explains teaching as a "return to life" whereby the students' right to their own language(s) are interlocuted with those that the teacher interprets as "art" through metaphoric analysis of the text:

Creative, original, exploratory thought that is in contact with the richness and complexity of life cannot develop on a substrate consisting of the forms of depersonalized, clichéd, abstract, bookish language. The further fate of a student's creative potential, to a great extent, depends on the language he takes with him out of high school. And this is the instructor's responsibility. (p. 24)

Freire's attention to the notion of *praxis* as a pedagogical imperative cannot be understated in any consideration of his ideas concerning education. Described as the reflection on the world followed up by new action, praxis is at the heart of the development of knowledge through what has been labelled as "conscientisation."[3] In Freirean terms, the popular consciousness is profoundly influenced by the ideology of the oppressor (Mayo, 2004), bringing about a false consciousness that will lead the oppressed to merely replicate and accept this ruling ideology as given. Conscientisation is the ascendance of critical consciousness over false consciousness, which Freire labeled as "semi-intransitive" and "naïve transitive consciousness" (1985). The process of conscientisation requires that the unjust structures of repression and domination be denounced and an alternative view be announced. Freire has been roundly criticised for this position, both for the imperial arrogance implied by his Platonism, and for the notion of a rigid, linear developmentally staged process. Giroux (1985), however, regards this shift away from mythical or magical understanding as a critical awakening to the sedimented nature of the historical context in which people find themselves.

Praxis, the "authentic union of action and reflection" (Freire, 1985, p. 87), can only exist where objective-subjective dialectic is maintained, namely, an appreciation that people make their own history and they are fundamentally influenced by the material realities of life in society with others—humans are conditioned, but not determined (Mayo, 2004). Equally fundamental is the notion that people can have a critical consciousness of this influence or conditioning on their lives (Freire, 1985). It is this consciousness that enables people to rise above the stark realities of survival and plan, predict, and dream: "Whereas animals adapt themselves to the world to survive, men modify the world in order *to be more*" (1985, p. 70; emphasis in original).

Bakhtin emphasises the "chronotopic threshold" as an opportunity to generate new ideas, new ways of thinking, and where "culture" is ultimately realised *in* dialogue (White, 2012). Reconciling cognition as one of many educative functions within a broader dialogic world means that Bakhtin's prerogative is for people to deeply engage at an *ontological* level in education. Emphasising "Being-as-event," Bakhtin suggests there is little time (or need) for reflection when one is in this moment—its aftermath is irrelevant beyond this immediate time-space dimension (inter-animated by the past and future). His attention to the creative energy of dialogue as lived experience suggests that "reality" is arrived at only through dialogic encounters in which ideas are tested, debated, and examined *in that moment*.

The associated notion of *Lebensphilosophie* (a philosophy of life) emphasises the point that learning *is* meaning. It is not an outcome, as such, but embedded in that process. The interrelationship of individuals through dialogue, therefore, does not require consensus but rather "a plurality of consciousnesses, with equal rights and each with its own world" (Bakhtin, 1984, p. 6). Thus, Bakhtin's characters are free to tell their own story amid others—even if it is (or is not) aligned to authorial imperatives—*provided that it has been creatively considered in dialogue*. An example of Bakhtin's "dialogic pedagogy" is offered by Roberts (2005), citing Dostoevsky's (1987) novel *The Brothers Karamazov*, in which characters debate, but do not "win" or "rise above"; instead, tensions are maintained throughout. Bakhtin called this treatment of the characters an act of polyphony—a concept that signaled two of his most important (and sustained) ideas—namely, the notion of answerability (*otvetstvennost*) and the architectronic of the aesthetic act:

> An aesthetic event must involve two non-coincident consciousnesses. In an ethical event, hero and author co-incide: I stand for my act. In a cognitive event, which deals with abstract truths, the hero is altogether absent. And finally in a religious event, there are two consciousnesses, but they are not even potentially equal; the other is supreme and all-embracing. (Morson & Emerson, 1990, p. 74)

Emphasis is drawn to accountability to and by other. Yet emphasis is simultaneously given to the axiologic (that is, value-oriented) engagement that takes place in the pedagogical meeting of one consciousness in the life of another and the presence of two (or more) consciousnesses in the act. Thus, for Bakhtin, attention is given to the social experience of meaning as a *praxis of praxis* (Matusov, 2012)—a philosophical tenet that underpins dialogic pedagogy. Any interpretation of this dialogic exchange and its creative potential is framed with the delicate process of intimacy and distance sought through "visual surplus" that is offered to subjects through social acts—both characterise the pedagogical relationship. The praxical relationship of people to the ever-changing nature of their material lives that they may pursue also lies at the heart of Freire's ethical position, but his orientation is toward humanisation. He announced this imperative at the very outset in his *Pedagogy of the Oppressed,* in which he declared that humanisation is the historical vocation of all people that is negated by oppression, but must be reasserted in a way that restores the humanity of both oppressors and oppressed (1970/1996, p. 26). It is clear that Freire did not see this ethical ideal as belonging to the individual human subject alone—rather, it was a collective, social effort that is not built on the "ethics of the marketplace with its crass insensitivity to the voice of genuine humanity but [on] the ethics of human aspiration. The ethics of human solidarity" (1998, p. 116). It is also evident that Freire did not see this struggle as one with a defined end. For him, as for Bakhtin, we are all incomplete and unfinished. In this respect, Freire reveals his Sartrean and phenomenological influences.

This is no cause for despair, however, but a commitment by virtue of our very humanity that compels us to be free according to Kirylo (2011).

Bakhtin's ethics are also oriented toward freedom, but it is freedom of a different kind. Bakhtin's imperative is toward the author of the experience in dialogic communication, rather than the individual alone. Bakhtin's rejection of Kant's fourth postulate,[4] however, heralds an approach that provides an opportunity for social encounters to act as counterpoints for any shared ethical ideal, and for individuals to express themselves beyond the collective. In this sense, solidarity is not Bakhtin's goal for learners. Far from it! Viewing the "event" as a co-experiencing of the world (Rule, 2011), Bakhtin offers scope for a consideration of interpretation as central to learning, and for learning to become an expression of reality based on dialogic encounter, not "truth." Bakhtin takes this further in his detailed description of the marketplace where carnivalesque genres operate as a counter to the authorial world, but never subsume them. Rather, the two sit alongside each other in a dialogic interplay composed of satire, irony, and ridicule. Here, consciousness is "free" but only for that moment, because there are other worlds in which one must live, and answer to, once the carnival is over. Such is the nature of Bakhtin's heteroglossia as a route to meaning in which encounters between different ideological positions are at the centre of his pedagogical expression. Both he and Freire, therefore, take a very different path to Percy's problem.

RETURNING TO PERCY

Responding to Bailin's (1999) rationale that Percy cannot engage in critical thinking because he "does not understand the enterprise of knowledge creation and evaluation, an enterprise which is constituted by the offering and assessing of reasons" (p. 164), Freire and Bakhtin offer much provocation. Yet, as Matusov (2009) explains, while Freire's approach might be part of Bakhtin's dialogism, not all of Bakhtin's ideas are embraced within Freire's kind of pedagogy. A Freirean approach must necessarily raise questions around ontology (What is Percy's relationship to the world? What is his teacher's relationship to the world?), epistemology (How might dialogue develop critical thinking, and with it, greater self-knowledge and knowledge of the world?) and ethics (What is the nature of the dialogic and pedagogic relationship between Percy and his teacher? What is the human value to Percy and his teacher of this relationship?). A Bakhtinian approach is fundamentally attuned to creative growth that exceeds an exclusive attention to purely cognitive acts that are characterised by processes of reasoning and logic. An epistemological question might, of necessity, arise from the observation that Percy's internally persuasive discourses (IPD) and their location within the classroom (and beyond) appear to be absent. A question Bakhtin might then ask of Bailin is:

To what extent does this classroom provide opportunities for IPD? And: To what extent do teachers grapple with their own IPD? (Matusov, 2009). Bakhtin might also be interested in Percy's interpretation and articulation of "the" problem or his interest in engaging with it at all, rather than his ability to grapple with a pre-established "topic" (Bailin, p. 161)—a concept Bibler (2009) calls "points of wonder." Percy's experience in the event of discussion would be the focus of Bakhtin's interrogation rather than the written assessment that came about in its aftermath.

Such ontological engagement *with* Percy, based on his own experiences and their polyphonic relationship with others, contrasts starkly with the instrumental drive of Bailin. Here the student has no need to be *granted* agency, but instead *claims* agency for himself in educational processes. Drawing from Bakhtin's dialogism, "teacher[s] cannot guarantee good teaching" (Matusov, 2011, p. 41) for themselves, or anyone else for that matter, because learning is ultimately determined by the student. Thus, the teacher's dilemma is how to maintain the freshness, uniqueness and local responsiveness of dialogues while simultaneously providing students with increasingly sophisticated tools for analysis and decision-making (techne); without abstracting ideas such that they do not allow meaningful encounter (Bazerman, Farmer, Halasek, & Williams, 2005).

Freire would equally reject such an approach to education, likening it to his notion of banking education, wherein the teacher "delivers communiqués" to students who are, in this model, merely passive recipients of pre-packaged, frozen information (1970/1996). For Freire, the first step in resolving this problem will be to reconcile the antagonistic relationship between teacher and student, who must now be conceived as co-learners on a shared journey. This reconceptualisation requires crossing the boundary that typically exists between teachers and students, leading to a "horizontal relationship" (Rule, 2011) that admits to a different perspective on knowledge. It does not seek to differentiate between what is known and the process of recreating and re-knowing (Connolly, 1980). The vehicle that mediates this process, for Freire, is dialogue as an event of critical consciousness between two partners, albeit at different stages of development, who seek to know. Freire wanted teachers to develop "problem-posing education" which used student daily life and context as a valid text for a dialogic education. Such an education removes the emphasis from the teacher as expert who has private ownership of knowledge to be transferred to passive consumers. Instead, it shifts the emphasis to teacher and student problematising the task or topic at hand in a way that not only invites different points of view but that is also focused on students reconstituting their world through their critical reflection. One of Freire's key contributions to education has, therefore, been his recognition of the non-neutrality of pedagogy, and this is particularly evident in his notion of conscientisation, which may be regarded as an outcome of problem-posing education. This, and other politically oriented concepts, argues Smith (1997/ 2002), might be also interpreted as non-dialogic from a Bakhtinian point of view. Indeed Wegerif (2013), in his interpretation of dialogic pedagogy, goes so far as to suggest that "Freire's practice was not really as dialogic as his rhetoric" (p. 26).

Dialogic pedagogy, from a Bakhtinian standpoint, is never fully defined by individual moves of the teacher (or, for that matter, the students); nor is it oriented to consensus or even, necessarily, intersubjectivity (although indeed this might occur nevertheless). A highly interactive and conversational class, a dialogic genre, might have less dialogicity in it than a lecture delivered in a monologue because the degree of dialogism is determined by the living nature of internally persuasive discourses in relation with authorial ones. As such, the form and content of classroom discourse cannot, in itself, claim dialogicity because "dialogue *is* the discourse of education" (Matusov, 2009, p. 76), not the conditions that surround it. For Bakhtin, there is no resolution at the end of class, or in "critical writing" projects such as those facing Percy. Rather, Bakhtin's attention is drawn toward the form shaping consciousness of other—where one maintains his own unity, but in dialogue with another there is mutual expansion. Seen in this light, *curriculum is the learner* rather than the subject (Miyazaki, 2007) and no distinction is thus made between pedagogical learning and pedagogy itself.

For Bakhtin, then, dialogic pedagogy is an invitation into a curriculum space. It starts from the *boundaries* that exist *between teacher and learner* as a means of recognising, and being informed by, differences that can be recognised therein. This is a complex process that is less eschatological than Freire might purport. As such, there is a dialogic origin *and* a dialogic existence of knowledge (Matusov, 2009). Questioning and answering are not isolated events within an individual but take shape in the act itself and its chronotope(s). A dialogic "attitude" means that learners expect to be surprised by this experience. While the teacher possesses certain epistemological knowledge that the student may not share (but there is a vice versa here), the teacher has to suspend epistemological certainty here. The student also brings his internally persuasive discourses that may alter truth: "Dialogue is always pregnant by new never-ending dialogic contributions" (Matusov 2009, pp. 85–86); thus, the student is invited into a curriculum space where a series of provocations may be offered for discussion but there is no pre-set endpoint or outcome beyond what Bakhtin loosely describes as "becoming" (in a Bildungsroman sense). What has prevented Percy from claiming his agency in this regard might also be sourced in classrooms and other pedagogical experiences well beyond Bailin's immediate influence. Bakhtin might even suggest that the best approach for Percy may be to release him from the didactic chronotope in which he (and his teacher) are lodged. From this perspective, both may be locked into pedagogical regimes that dismiss an attention to creative alternatives drawn from multiple orientations and ideologies of "image, intuition or authority" (Bailin, 1999, p. 168) as legitimate aspects of the dialogue at their peril.

Ironically, Freire's notion of dialogue begins where the traditional boundary between student and teacher is breached. In making space for student voice, however, the teacher does not uncritically celebrate that voice, for it may contain elements of oppressor consciousness that must be challenged by the teacher. Simultaneously, the dialogic process must also open the teacher to critique by the student, in a way, however, that it is not regarded as a personal attack (Mayo, 2004). Freire was clear that dialogue between teacher and student is not at first equal: "At the moment the teacher begins the dialogue, he or she knows a great deal, first in terms of knowledge and second in terms of the horizon that he or she wants to get to" (Shor & Freire, 1987, p. 103, as cited by Mayo, 2004, p. 52). Freire therefore expected teachers to have "a plan, a program, [and] a goal for the study" (Freire & Shor, 1987, p. 172, as cited by Roberts, 2000, p. 59). These ideas are consistent with Freire's view that a democratic education has an overt intention—"[t]here is no education without objectives, without ends" (1993, p. 116, cited by Mayo, 2004, p. 82). While this may seem that Freire would be in accord with what appears to be Bailin's directive approach with Percy, a wider appreciation of Freire is required. Benade (2010) suggests that Freire rejected authoritarianism, which he associated with discriminatory practices, such as racism, sexism, and cultural imperialism (he also associated authoritarianism with banking education). At the same time, however, Freire rejected the idea that a progressive educator is a laissez-faire "facilitator," a concept more appropriate to pseudocritical educators who misappropriate his notion of dialogue and engage instead in "group therapy" (Macedo, 1997, p. 4). Indeed, Freire saw both "manipulative authoritarianism [and] lawless permissiveness" as being opposed to "democratic radicalism" (2005, p. 115).

The likelihood Freire envisaged was that authoritarian approaches would be anti-dialogic, while laissez-faire approaches would deny rigour, leading to a dehumanising outcome in both cases (Roberts, 2000). As for Bakhtin, the key to learning is the dialogic relationship that develops in and through joint inquiry and evaluation. Yet Bakhtin's emphasis on the importance of not consuming another by making them think the same requires an evaluative stance that is also characterised by intimacy and answerability and cannot be located in end-point strategies such as those that Freire promotes. Because, as Bakhtin reminds us, learning is located in the dialogic act, the direction of the learning cannot be fixed and remains as uncertain for Bailin as it is for Percy. Seen from this viewpoint, Bailin might be less inclined to condemn Percy for lacking a "critical spirit" (1999, p. 164) than to examine her own practice and the extent to which she contributes to his lack of agency (as opposed to "skill"). Does Bailin, for instance, recognise that Percy is presenting a genre he orients toward what he thinks his teacher wants (evidenced by his comment, "So in THIS class YOU want us to base our conclusions on reason and evidence" [p. 168])? Does she care that in other classes Percy attends, a postmodern teacher has challenged reason and evidence? Perhaps Percy brings with him a different kind of logic, based on his experience as "other," to Bailin's cultural priorities? Maybe Percy simply wants to obtain his grade and get out of that classroom? Without Percy's voice, we are left to wonder. Surely it is dialogue that takes precedence over liberation—a central point of difference that both Bakhtin and Freire clearly grappled with, in varying ways, as a pedagogical imperative.

TAKING STOCK

Not withstanding their considerable differences, we can assert that the "problem" with Percy, when taken from both a Freirean and a Bakhtinian stance, might now be seen to belong in no small part to Bailin (and the systems that underpin her agenda), because as laudable as it is that critical thinkers offer and assess reasons, these represent mere engagement in theoretical reflection. For Bailin, knowledge comes from the reflection (*without the event*) on the action (*that the teacher has determined*) that the critical thinker (*seen as a lone player*) engages in after initially reflecting on reasons (and motives, acts, facts, knowledge, and opinion determined by the "curriculum") *that are exclusively framed as cognitive*. Percy, in his turn, is merely being coached to play a scholarly game, not to reflect on ways that he may implicitly or explicitly be acting to perpetuate oppression in whatever guise it may appear (as Freire might suggest); or to bring his own voice(s) to the dialogue as a source of provocation (as Bakhtin might invite him to do).

Given that this chapter reflects a view that analysing and addressing an educational or pedagogical problem from the perspective of historical thinkers require that more is known about the antecedents of those thinkers, it is consistent to consider whether that background has any implications for the consideration of Bailin's problem with Percy. Freire and Bakhtin see epistemology as relational; however, for Bakhtin, truth is created through plurality and unmerged consciousness, while for Freire, it is entirely possible to know the world (as praxes through reflection). It can therefore be argued that Freire emphasises the dialectic-dialogic that sees "the relation between oppositions as the crucial site of learning and transformation" (Rule, 2011, p. 931), while Bakhtin emphasises the dialogic-dialogic (here we take issue with Rule, 2011, who says both share in the former), rejecting dialectics as a quest toward one-ness. Instead, Bakhtin talks of a struggle between "two consciousnesses, their counterposition and their interrelations" (Bakhtin, 1986, p. 142). Both thinkers prioritised uncertainty (Roberts, 2005) and, for both men, this became clearer as their careers and their writing progressed. Yet, Bakhtin does not seek to liberate the learner from some disempowered place. His lack of direct attention to the political nature of learning has been criticised (see, for example, Bakhtin, 1993), but this seems less of an oversight than simply outside

Bakhtin's orientation. By contrast, Freire wanted to resolve a fundamental opposition, that being the oppressor-oppressed relationship.

At the heart of this distinction are the different epistemological and ontological approaches of the two thinkers. Matusov suggests that Freire's epistemology lies in reflective knowledge in dialogue and his ontology in humanity in dialogue that will lead to liberation. In this place, there was to be a better outcome. For Bakhtin, however, there was no outcome per se—the outcome was the dialogue itself, as a mutual and equal relationship. "The teacher can affect it but cannot determine it" (Matusov, 2009, p. 80). In contrast, Freire regarded the teacher as instrumental in creating the conditions for dialogue. Once the conditions are created, the relationship is one that recognises teacher and student as co-learners and that is characterised by the teacher's respect for the autonomy of the student. Bakhtin's emphasis was on the nature of that dialogue—such as the relation between characters (see Dostoevsky). Bakhtin's argument was that no other can have access to someone's consciousness—though they may speak to it they cannot predict the outcome of their dialogue. This is otherwise, for Bakhtin, a form of manipulation.

Bailin's problem with Percy has its basis in the epistemological experience of critical thinking. To "get" Percy to think critically, therefore, he has to engage with perspectives through a process of evaluation and judgment. Bakhtin's imperative is not to "get" Percy anywhere that he does not want to go, but instead to involve Percy in inquiries that are brought alive through dialogue—not as an end-point, but as the point itself. This approach is likely to be unpalatable for Bailin, whose resistance to alternative discourses is evidenced in her response to intuition or image as legitimate scholastic provocations. As such, we conclude by suggesting that Bailin has failed to recognise what Freire and Bakhtin knew all along—that Percy is a member of a community of learners, each with his or her own priorities and agendas. Within the community exist multiple perspectives and approaches to evaluation that may differ from the teacher's and, in doing so, advance both Percy *and the teacher's* ability to engage in this experience of living theorisation that may exist beyond dominant cognitive domains. For both Bakhtin and Freire, this is not merely an epistemological agenda. It is also ontological, ethical, and deeply dialogic—as Matusov (2009) suggests, "[w]e *know* only in a community, in which the knowledge is dialogically circulated" (p. 91). Dialogue and collaboration between teacher and student deepen the idea that the path to humanisation is taken up in solidarity with others: "The pursuit of full humanity…cannot be carried out in isolation or individualism, but only in fellowship and solidarity" (Freire, 1970/1996, p. 66). Such principles are, indeed, laudable.

If we are honest, we might confess we have all walked in Bailin's shoes as teachers. The notion of dialogic pedagogy seems a welcome antidote. Yet the extent to which either Bakhtin's or Freire's imperatives could thrive in classrooms is deeply contested when such claims are brought to the fore of examination. Taken together, they highlight the complex issues at play within monologic classrooms that are outcome driven and test oriented. The associated tendency to blame the student for a lack of critical thinking is merely a symptom of the cause. The provocations of both Bakhtin and Freire suggest, however, these practices are not only pedagogically unsound, but also deeply unethical. The alternatives offered by both men, and their diverse origins as well as approaches, give some support to the idea that dialogic pedagogy is often aspirational but not lived in classrooms across the world. The differences between Freire and Bakhtin—one who spent a lifetime working with adult students and writing about his strategies; and the other who spent a lifetime writing from a literary standpoint (albeit with clear pedagogical imperatives based on his teaching of grammar and lecturing experiences)—offer some insight into the reality of dialogic pedagogy. Perhaps Freire's tensions are not felt by Bakhtin because the latter did not set out to emancipate his subjects as the principal outcome. His faith in the agentic potential of subjects to gain what they need—given conditions of authentic dialogue—is profoundly optimistic, yet from a Freirean standpoint, possibly naïve in a classroom such as this. Just as Bailin may not be in a position to claim (or even to see) her ontological responsibilities, so Freire was constrained by his political imperatives. Yet this chapter concludes by asking, How possible, and indeed relevant, is it to conceptualise learning that has no end-point in contemporary society? And how might teachers suspend certainty in regimes of accountability? Surely this, as for Bakhtin, Freire, and even Bailin (as for any other teacher), must come down to a moral imperative as well as a practice. To what extent are we able to become participants in this dialogic process, suspending the stronghold of "knowledge" that is contained in narrow objectives and agendas? For Freire, this was not the agenda he upheld, yet he recognised the value of dialogue as a source of knowledge. Bakhtin rejected this agenda altogether, emphasising a much broader focus. In both cases, dialogue remains the imperative, yet how this might play out in the classroom is deeply linked to the ontologies that can be entertained in this domain. For Percy, as for Bailin, these are very limited in their current locale, especially when considered in the diverse framework we now call "dialogic pedagogy."

NOTES

1. The notion of "dialogic pedagogy" in relation to Bakhtinian philosophy has been internationally ignited in the recent development of a *Journal of Dialogic Pedagogy* (see http://dpj.pitt.edu/ojs/index.php/dpj2).
2. Bakhtin did spend a lot of his life in various teaching roles nevertheless. His brother was also a teacher.
3. Though not a label Freire necessarily approved of (Mayo, 2004).

4. Kant's fourth postulate is described as "a belief in the existence of other egos, as a morally established faith" (Lossky, 1951, as cited in Bell & Gardiner, 1998, p. 217).

REFERENCES

Aronowitz, S. (1998). Introduction. In P. Freire, *Pedagogy of freedom: Ethics, democracy and civic courage.* Lanham, MD: Rowman & Littlefield.

Bailin, S. (1999). The problem with Percy: Epistemology, understanding and critical thinking. *Informal Logic, 19*(2&3), 161–170.

Bakhtin, M. M. (1968). *Rabelais and his world* (H. Iswolsky, Trans.). Cambridge, MA: MIT Press.

Bakhtin, M. M. (1981). *The dialogic imagination: Four essays* (M. Holquist Ed., C. Emerson & M. Holquist, Trans.). Austin: University of Texas.

Bakhtin, M. M. (1984). *Problems of Dostoyevsky's poetic* (Vol. 8). Minneapolis: University of Minnesota Press.

Bakhtin, M. M. (1986). *Speech genres and other late essays* (V. W. McGee, Trans). Austin: University of Texas.

Bakhtin, M. M. (1990). *Art and answerability* (K. Brostrom, Trans.). Austin: University of Texas.

Bakhtin, M. M. (1993). *Toward a philosophy of the act.* M. Holquist & V. Liapunov, (Eds.); V. Liapunov (Trans. & Notes). Austin: University of Texas Press.

Bakhtin, M. M. (2004). Dialogic origin and dialogic pedagogy of grammar: Stylistics in teaching Russian language in secondary school. *Journal of Russian and East European Psychology, 42*(6), 12–49.

Bazerman, C., Farmer, F., Halasek, K., & Williams, J. M. (2005). Responses to Bakhtin's "Dialogic origins and dialogic pedagogy of grammar: Stylistics as part of Russian language instruction in secondary schools": Further responses and a tentative conclusion. *Written Communication, 22,* 363–374.

Bell, M., & Gardiner, M. E. (1998). *Bakhtin and the human sciences: No last words.* London, England: Sage Publications.

Benade, L. (2010). Freire's *Pedagogy of Freedom*: Its contribution to the development of ethical teacher professionality through the implementation of the New Zealand Curriculum. *Paideusis: Journal of the Canadian Philosophy of Education Society, 12*(1), 5–15.

Bibler, V. S. (2009). The foundation of the school of the dialogue of cultures. *Journal of Russian and East European Psychology, 47*(1), 34–60.

Bingham, C., & Biesta, G. J. (2010). *Jacques Ranciere: Education, truth, and emancipation.* New York, NY: Continuum.

Bowers, R. (2005). Freire (with Bakhtin) and the dialogic classroom seminar. *Alberta Journal of Educational Research, 51*(4), 368–378.

Brandist, C. (2011). Bakhtin and pedagogy. In E. J. White & M. Peters (Eds.), *Bakhtinian pedagogy: Opportunities and challenges for research, policy and practice in education across the globe* (pp. x–xii). New York, NY: Peter Lang.

Brandist, C., & Tihanov, G. (Eds.). (2000). *Materializing Bakhtin: The Bakhtin Circle and social theory.* London, England: Macmillan.

Connolly, R. (1980). Freire, praxis and education. In R. Mackie (Ed.), *Literacy and revolution: The pedagogy of Paulo Freire* (pp. 70–81). London, England: Pluto Press.

Darder, A. (2002). *Reinventing Paulo Freire: A pedagogy of love.* Boulder, CO: Westview.

Dosteovsky, F. (1990). *The Brothers Karamazov*, (R. Pevear & L. Volokhonsky, Trans.). London: David Campbell.

Facundo, B. (1984). *Freire-inspired programs in the United States and Puerto Rico: A critical evaluation.* Retrieved from http://www.uow.edu.au/arts/sts/bmartin/dissent/documents/Facundo/Facundo. html

Freire, P. (1970/1996). *Pedagogy of the oppressed* (M. Ramos, Trans.). London, England: Penguin Books.

Freire, P. (1972). *Cultural action for freedom.* Harmondsworth, England: Penguin.

Freire, P. (1974). *Freire: Education for critical consciousness.* New York, NY: Continuum.

Freire, P. (1978). *Pedagogy in process: The letters to Guinea-Bissau.* New York, NY: Seabury Press.

Freire, P. (1985). *The politics of education: Culture, power and liberation* (D. Macedo, Trans.). London, England: Macmillan.

Freire, P. (1993). *Pedagogy of the city.* New York, NY: Continuum.

Freire, P. (1998). *Pedagogy of freedom: Ethics, democracy and civic courage.* Lanham, MD: Rowman & Littlefield.

Freire, P. (2005). *Teachers as cultural workers: Letters to those who dare teach* (D. Macedo, D. Koike, & A. Oliveira, Trans.). Boulder, CO: Westview Press.

Freire, P., & Shor, I. (1987). *A pedagogy for liberation.* London, England: Macmillan.

Giroux, H. (1985). Introduction. In P. Freire, *The politics of education: Culture, power and liberation* (D. Macedo, Trans.). London, England: Macmillan.

Kirylo, J. D. (2011). *Paulo Freire: The man from Recife.* New York, NY: Peter Lang.

Macedo, D. (1997). An anti-method pedagogy: A Freirean perspective. In P. Freire (Ed.) with J. W. Fraser, D. Macedo, T. McKinnon, & W. T. Stokes, *Mentoring the mentor: A critical dialogue with Paulo Freire* (pp. 1–9). New York, NY: Peter Lang.

Mackie, R. (Ed.). (1980). *Literacy and revolution: The pedagogy of Paulo Freire.* London, England: Pluto Press.

Marjanovic-Shane, A. (2012). *Developing dialogic teacher orientation: Drowning and swimming at the same time.* Paper presented to the mini-Bakhtinian Conference on Dialogic Pedagogy, University of Delaware, Newark, Delaware.

Matusov, E. (2009). *Journey into dialogic pedagogy.* New York, NY: Nova Science.

Matusov, E. (2012). *Dialogic education for agency.* Paper presented to the mini-Bakhtinian Conference on Dialogic Pedagogy, University of Delaware, Newark, Delaware.

Matusov, E., & Marjanovic-Shane, A. (2012) *The state's educational neutrality: General theory of dialogic pedagogy.* Paper presented to the mini-Bakhtinian Conference on Dialogic Pedagogy, University of Delaware, Newark, Delaware.

Mayo, P. (2004). *Liberating praxis: Paulo Freire's legacy for radical education and politics.* Westport, CT: Praeger.

Miyazaki, K. (2007). *Teacher as imaginative learner: Egan, Saitou and Bakhtin.* Paper presented at the second annual Research Symposium on Imagination and Education, Vancouver, British Columbia, Canada.

Morson, G. S., & Emerson, C. (1990). *Mikhail Bakhtin: Creation of a prosaics.* Stanford, CA: Stanford University Press.

Nielsen, G. (1998). The norms of answerability: Bakhtin and the fourth postulate. In M. M. Bell & M. Gardiner (Eds.), *Bakhtin and the human sciences: No last words* (pp. 214–231). London, England: Sage.

Roberts, P. (2000). *Education, literacy, and humanization: An introduction to the work of Paulo Freire.* Westport, CT: Greenwood Press.

Roberts, P. (2005). Freire and Dostoevsky: Uncertainty, dialogue and transformation. *Journal of Transformative Education, 2.* Retrieved from http://jtd.sagepub.com/content/3/2/126.full.pdf

Rule, P. (2011). Bakhtin and Freire: Dialogue, dialectic and boundary learning. *Educational Philosophy and Theory, 43*(9), 924–942.

Shor, I. (1987). Monday morning fever: Critical literacy and the generative theme of "work." In I. Shor (Ed.), *Freire for the classroom: A sourcebook for liberatory teaching* (pp. 104–128. Portsmouth, NH: Boynton.

Shor, I., & Freire, P. (1987a). *Pedagogy for liberation dialogues on transforming education.* Westport, CT: Bergin & Harvey.

Shor, I., & Freire, P. (1987b). What is the "dialogical method" of teaching? *Journal of Education, 169*(3), 11–31.

Smith, M. K. (1997/2002). Paulo Freire and informal education. *The encyclopedia of informal education.* Retrieved from www.infed.org/thinkers/et-freire.htm

van der Linden, J., & Renshaw, P. (Eds). (2004). *Dialogic learning: Shifting perspectives to learning, instruction, and teaching.* Dordrecht, The Netherlands: Kluwer Academic.

Wegerif, R. (2013). *Dialogic: Education for the Internet age.* London, England: Routledge.

White, E. J. (2011). Bakhtinian dialogic and Vygotskian dialectic: Compatibilities and contradictions in the classroom. *Educational Philosophy and Theory.* Retrieved from http://onlinelibrary.wiley.com/doi/10.1111/j.1469-5812.2011.00814.x/full

White, E. J. (2012, December). *Circles, borders and chronotopes: Education at the boundary?* Paper presented at the Philosophy of Education Society of Australasia conference: Crossing the Boundaries in Education, Taiwan.

White, E. J., & Peters, M. (2012, August). *Creativity and the university: The collective creation of Vitebsk.* Paper presented at the Creative University conference, University of Waikato, Hamilton, New Zealand.

CHAPTER TWENTY-SIX

Voices of Resistance: Positioning Steiner Education as a Living Expression of Freire's Pedagogy of Freedom

ALTHEA LAMBERT

The world becomes empty and barren, unless something can arise anew again and again from the essence of human nature—something that permeates outer perception with soul and spirit. Therefore, when we educate this way, we give the human being full freedom and vitality for the rest of life.
—RUDOLF STEINER, 1927/1997, P. 76

INTRODUCTION

Voices of resistance are voices raised or expressed in resistance to unquestioningly accepting a loss of personal voice in favour of adopting the common or socially sanctioned voice. The socially sanctioned voice speaks *for* you, whereas the voice of resistance speaks *from* you. In this chapter, the voices of resistance come from young women[1] who, at the time of speaking (2009), were students at a Rudolf Steiner high school in Aotearoa-New Zealand. Their voices emerge from a year of intense, regular, critical conversations, which were the substance of a phenomenological study exploring the lived (or living) experience of Steiner education. This study culminated in my doctoral thesis (Lambert, 2011) and has unfolded for the first time in the literature the experience of Steiner education through the voices of the young women students. What our study showed overwhelmingly was that these young women experienced a deep sense of belonging with school and their school community, and with(in) themselves. They described their educational experience as "having the space to become."

This chapter centralises the voices of the young women to show that they see themselves as the authentic authorities of their own lives, and thus, they resist the social prescriptions of whether and how a woman's, or young woman's, voice can be heard. Theirs are voices of resistance because they resist simply in the act of speaking *from* themselves (Gilligan, 2011). They resist because they offer a different construction of "adolescent" and of "young woman." They resist because they have spoken out with passion and conviction. They resist because they challenge the social and cultural deference to adult authority. What strikes me is that in their resistance, I hear the living expression of Paulo Freire's pedagogy of freedom. Thus, Steiner and Freire meet.

Steiner Education, Rudolf Steiner's pedagogical approach (Steiner, 1996, 1997), is frequently referred to as "education toward freedom," though it preceded Freire's pedagogy by some fifty years. Through his educational approach, Rudolf Steiner sought to eliminate factory-like schooling, which has led humankind to become "more or less isolated in soul" (Steiner, 1997, p. 79). While it is rarely referred to as such, Steiner's is clearly a critical pedagogy in that it centralises social action; freedom of voice and personal authority as key forces and aims within education; and emphasises the importance of "the people" and the community over and above the oppressive capitalist focus on materialism and mechanisation.

Through the voices of the young women in this chapter, we are immediately connected to a global network of half of humanity who have, in myriad ways, resisted the "vestiges of patriarchy" (Gilligan, 2011, p. 32). In order for these narratives to have context, there is a need to divulge some detail—albeit relatively brief, considering the body of knowledge I am drawing upon—about the background of my work; the educational ideas of Freire and Steiner; and the importance of listening to young women. Bear with me as I unfold these details before I finally get to the key voices of this paper—the young women's.

This chapter opens a dialogue between two great critical educationists, Rudolf Steiner (1861–1925) and Paulo Freire (1921–1997), by directing attention toward some intersections of their respective pedagogies as anchored in the concrete experience of young women students. To my knowledge here is the first such space in which this dialogue has been opened. By illustrating these intersections through the voices of young women Steiner students, I also open a dialogue between academics (and educators) and young women, and between young women and society. As a social group that one of my colleagues referred to as "in the margin of the margins," the young women's voices narrate as the living educational experience of a pedagogical theory and thus also open a further dialogue between theory and living experience. Here are voices of resistance that speak above the mindless hum of what we have come to accept as education in many countries.

BACKGROUND

I come to this not as a long-time Freirean scholar, but as a passionate teacher and social researcher who, having encountered Freire's writings, cannot ignore their resonance with the voices in my own research studies. My research work in the human sciences has specifically focused on unfolding the personal narratives of young women students in Steiner education and on exploring the psychological, emotional, and spiritual journey of young women during adolescence. More broadly, my research aims to restore the balance of voice in education, in science, and in society.

The narratives presented here are taken from a larger set of individual exploratory conversations between twelve young women Steiner students (14 to 18 years old) and me. Over the 2009 school year our conversations generated 148 hours of recordings. The idea was to explore the living experience of their Steiner education by creating a space for the young women to talk and engage, as they wished, in critical questioning. The young women were under no obligation to "show up" to a conversation or to continue with the study should they wish not to, yet they all stayed with it. This understanding between us supported, according to the young women, a space where they could just talk without the need to feel they had to achieve anything in particular or meet any particular obligation. What they did find they achieved though, was a meeting with themselves.

So here in the forum of this chapter, I have attempted to present the essence of what I "heard without trying to listen," as well as "what I listened for in an effort to understand." I don't want to speak for these young women and to this end I include a significant amount of raw text (unedited conversational segments) and hope to impart the sense of authentic voice. Ultimately I still must ask a Freirean-type question: *Who speaks for whom* (Weiler, 2001)? Perhaps in what is spoken we might recognise aspects of our own experiences and ourselves, the sense of another's voice expressing what we may think or feel.[2] The narratives selected are all vetted and approved by the young women concerned, but they were specifically chosen by me to illustrate the voice of resistance, which links Steiner with Friere.

EDUCATION FOR FREEDOM: STEINER MEETS FREIRE

True education recognizes that human beings are co-workers in building humankind.
(Steiner, 1997, p. 81)

Rudolf Steiner, like Freire, situated his educational ideas and initiatives as "education toward freedom" and believed that education was inseparable from social action. In a universal sense, Steiner and Freire have been educational co-workers. Like Freire, Steiner also worked tirelessly to disseminate and apply his ideas toward social renewal. Both Freire and Steiner remind us that to be present in this world, to be alive, is to be already the "ethically responsible activist" (Freire, 1998). What Donaldo Macedo says of Freire could be said of Steiner:

> [he] courageously challenges us to break with the rigidity of a technicist training approach to education in order to embrace those fundamental knowledges that will prevent us from deceiving our conscience...and transform the ugliness of human misery, social injustices, and inequalities. (Macedo, 1998, p. xxxii)

Interestingly, the first Steiner school was established in conjunction with a factory. In 1919, Emil Molt, the owner of the Waldorf Astoria cigarette factory in Stuttgart, invited Rudolf Steiner to apply his educational approach in establishing a school for the children of the factory staff. Since then, more than 1,000 Steiner or "Waldorf" schools have been providing an alternative to orthodox schooling in more than 55 countries (Gidley, 2010a; Simpson, 2004). Steiner's educational initiatives were a direct and passionate response to the devastation of social order caused by a world war and his vision for social reform was to elevate education above a "factory-like" institution (Finser, 1997; Gidley, 2010b). He spoke out against human oppression, particularly during the rise of Nazism, and positioned himself and his educational philosophy as non-sectarian and non-denominational (Wilson, 1894/1964). Steiner died at the age of 64 when Freire was 4 years old, but like Freire, he also left a remarkable legacy of work. Gidley (2010a) calls Steiner a "futurist and grand theorist [who] had a macrocosmic perspective on time in relation to what he called the evolution of human consciousness." Between 1883 and 1925 he gave more than 5,000 lectures and published 33 books (Rudolf Steiner Archive, http://www.rsarchive.org). In 1924, less than a year before he died, Steiner gave a series of five lectures, which brought together the essence of his educational approach. In the introduction to the published volume of these lectures, *The Essentials of Education* (Steiner, 1997), Torin Finser writes:

> [Steiner] education [should] not be thought of as just a 'method' of teaching or a way of getting through the challenges of the present, but...a transformative, social impulse with far-reaching implications. (Finser, 1997, p. viii)

Similarly, Freire's work is not simply a "brilliant methodology" (Aronowitz, 1998) it is a living social impulse and imperative for "the adventurous struggle to remake the world each and every day" (Clarke, 1997, p. xxxii). Steiner also addresses this, speaking in Oxford in 1922:

> ...today's social issue is primarily one of education. Today we may ask ourselves, justifiably, what we can do that will make our society and social institutions less tragic and menacing. We have only one answer: those who have been educated through the creative activity of spirit must be given positions in the practical life of the community. (Steiner, 2004, p. 4)

Steiner saw an increasing social and political focus on "materialism." For him, this signified that "in a civilisation bound by matter [where] the genuine, living method of teaching, the real life of education [becomes] frozen" (Steiner, 1997, p. 79). Thus, he positioned his educational approach as a means of transforming society. He wrote of this in many verses such as the following, which have become foundational mantras for many Steiner teachers:

> To spend oneself in matter is to grind down souls.
> To find oneself in the spirit is to unite human beings.
> To see oneself in all humanity is to construct worlds. (Steiner, 1997, p. 82)

The spiritual impulse in Steiner education serves to awaken and reconnect both the learner and the teacher to their own spiritual wisdom. A Steiner school seeks to prepare children to become a social voice for the cultivation of harmony and freedom that they themselves have experienced through their education and thus Steiner education becomes a critical social and pedagogical impulse.

CRITICAL PEDAGOGY, THE PEDAGOGY OF FREEDOM AND LOVE IN THE TIME OF NEOLIBERALISM

Critical pedagogy demands that people repeatedly question their roles in society as either agents of social and economic transformation, or as those who participate in the asymmetrical relations of power and privilege and the reproduction of neoliberal ideology. (Smith & McLaren, 2010, p. 332)

The educational and pedagogical ideologies and practices of Paulo Freire are frequently, but not exclusively, linked with the term *critical pedagogy*. Like the identities of the young women whose narratives grace this chapter, the identity of critical pedagogy is really "a becoming thing" (Kincheloe, 2007; Smith & McLaren, 2010). Along its continuum, we find pedagogies of oppression shifting to pedagogies of hope, freedom, and love (McLaren, 2007). Critical pedagogy defies being defined—which might risk "limiting its constant evolution and reinvention" (Smith and McLaren, 2010, p. 332)—but it does have certain recognisable characteristics. One of these is resistance. In its heat, this resistance may emerge as McLaren's "revolutionary critical pedagogy" (McLaren, 2010) or it may simply appear as a student's courage to engage in critical dialogue. At the heart of resistance is the sense of being free enough in mind and soul, to speak or act in ways that are contra to the norm. The act of resistance embraces personal and political freedom. From the Freirean perspective, this is not the freedom to "merely choose between two or more options on a grid preapproved by legislative fiat" (the socially sanctioned choices), "it is the freedom to change the very grid in which the choices are lodged" (McLaren, 2007, p. 303). A pedagogy of freedom then must cultivate an inner freedom that empowers the human being to enact resistance.

> The most important thing for which we can prepare a child is the experience of freedom, at the right moment in life, through the understanding of one's own being. True freedom is an inward experience and is developed only when the human being is viewed in this way. As a teacher, I must say that I cannot pass on freedom to another human being—each must experience it individually. (Steiner, 1997, p. 66)

A Philosophy of Freedom (Steiner, 1894/1964) was Rudolf Steiner's first major published work and it became a foundational text for his pedagogical epistemology. Steiner describes this freedom in education as emerging from the teacher's genuine love and respect of the child's own creative process, and then teaching out of this love. Similarly for Freire, a pedagogy of freedom is "powered by love" (McLaren, 2007, p. 304). This is "…lovingness not only towards students but also the very process of teaching"—and in that love Freire reminds us of the voice of resistance: "It is indeed necessary that this love be an 'armed love' (Freire, 1998, pp. 40–41, as cited by McLaren, 2007, p. 304).

Freire and Steiner are not alone in placing love at the heart of teaching and learning. In his recent book co-authored with Parker Palmer, *The Heart of Higher Education* (Palmer & Zajonc, 2010), Arthur Zajonc asks this very question: "What should be at the center of our teaching and…learning…. What is our greatest hope for the young people we teach?" And he answers with a quote from the poet Rilke:

> To take love seriously and to bear and to learn it like a task, this is what [young] people need…. For one human being to love another, that is perhaps the most difficult of all our tasks, the ultimate…the work for which all other work is but a preparation. For this reason young people, who are beginners in everything, cannot yet know love; they have to learn it. (Rilke, quoted in Zajonc, 2010, pp. x–xi)

What room is there for love in the time of neoliberalism? Here in Aotearoa-New Zealand the grip of neoliberalism and its persistent and destructive intervention in education is painfully strong (Small, 2009). As standardised testing begins to take hold in New Zealand public schools, we seem to have fallen into draconian times, forgetting the beauty and power of love in, and for, teaching and learning. New Zealand's public education, at all levels, is becoming increasingly prescription driven and outcomes based (Phillips, 2012; Small, 2009) and is being shaped by the policies and documents of non-teachers who seek to produce "human resources" rather than socially responsible, creative human beings. As Freire tells it, prescriptions are not the answer:

> The tasks of the time…are interpreted by an "elite" and presented in the form of recipes, of prescriptions. And when men [*sic*] try to save themselves by following the prescriptions,

they drown in levelling anonymity, without hope, without faith, adjusted and domesticated. (Freire, 1974, p. 5)

In such an educational climate, the inspirational capacity of teachers is significantly compromised and "the (student's) creative power has been strangled" (Phillips, 2012, p. iv). Associate Professor Peter O'Connor, at Auckland University, tells us that "our schools remain in desperate need of transformation" and that there is "a vision of education far richer than our tired repetition of testing, national standards and a narrow focus on literacy and numeracy" (O'Connor, 2011, p. B5). This is the vision of Freire and Steiner —and it is mine—to cultivate and foster education and schooling that enriches and nurtures the human spirit and is founded in love. It is a vision that positions education as lifelong learning and learning for life:

> …every school should prepare children for the great school of adulthood, which is life itself. We must not learn at school for the sake of performance; rather, we must learn at school so that we can learn further from life…. What we foster in children often lives imperceptibly in the depths of their souls, and in later life it emerges. (Steiner, 2004, p. 12)

It is through the narratives of the young women in this chapter that we catch a glimpse of what lives in the depths of the souls of those receiving an education toward freedom.

YOUNG WOMEN AS A FORCE OF CHANGE

Listening to young women's voices can awaken and alert us to what we have silenced; our human desire for connection and for healthy balanced relationships in a society where all voices are heard. (Lambert, 2011, p. 67)

As young women reach adolescence they "struggle against losing voice" (Gilligan, 1982/1993, p. xxiii). As they resist conforming to a social norm of disconnection, which accompanies the initiation into adulthood in a patriarchal culture, they may experience a fall into silence (Brown & Gilligan, 1992). The theme of silence and "silencing" is one thread in Freire's writing that is deeply relevant to women's and young women's social and cultural experiences around the globe (Fagan, 2009). The culture of "silencing," secrecy, and hidden agendas is powerfully debilitating for young women (Gilligan, 2011; Martini, 2004; Oliver, 1999, 2001). Relational psychologist Carol Gilligan (1995, p. 124) tells us that adolescent girls are "pressed from within and without to take in and take on the interpretive framework of patriarchy." Gilligan's research (Brown & Gilligan, 1992; Gilligan, 1982/1993, 1995, 1997, 2004, 2011) exposed a paradox voiced by young women, which ironically was about voicelessness. What Gilligan and colleagues found was that, in their closer relationships, young women said they recognised a point at which they stayed silent because if they spoke they would lose relationship, but if they didn't speak they also felt they would lose relationship. This created a "relational impasse" (Brown & Gilligan 1992, p. 216), manifesting as "a paradoxical or dizzying sense of having to give up relationship for the sake of *relationships* (author's emphasis)" (Brown & Gilligan, 1992, p. 216).

The psychological cost of navigating between their own voices and culturally prescribed ones "forces an inner division...and creates a profound psychological shift" in young women (Brown & Gilligan, 1992, p. 216). The result is dissociation from their inner knowing. The struggle with "knowing and not knowing" raises a voice of resistance. By creating the space for young women to be heard, we can open "the silenced dialogue" (Oliver, 1999, p. 221) and provide the opportunity for young women to discover the intellectual and social competence that empowers women beyond the conventional stereotypes and male power structures (Gilligan, 1997, 2011; Oliver, 2001; Vadeboncoeur, 2005). What is occurring for young women reflects a cultural and social chasm or split in the psyche—a damaging disconnection from one's own voice that both men and women experience, particularly in Western cultures (Gilligan, 2002, 2011). Young women's experiences therefore, can potentially provide a map for both men and women, reminding us of where we exchanged our own voice for that which has been culturally prescribed (Gilligan, 2002; Pipher, 1994).

By inviting young women to contribute to the evolution of educational theory and practice, we can contribute a "different voice" (Gilligan, 1982/1993) to the pedagogy of freedom. It was the voices of the young women in my research that brought me to realise that Freire's educational ideals were linked to the experience of Steiner. In the Freirean context of critical pedagogy, inviting students to dialogue in their own learning is crucial (Smith & McLaren, 2010). The young women who speak in this chapter are not just participants in a research study, they are "the active knower(s)" (Aronowitz, 1998, p. 14). As the voice of resistance, their authority effectively shifts the seat of knowledge-power from the hegemonic voice, toward the voices of those frequently less heard thus redressing the balance of social voice.

THE VOICE OF RESISTANCE

The young women in this study (pseudonyms are used throughout this text) speak about their own awakenings to who they are becoming and describe their life-worlds in terms of their belonging—"in relationship with themselves and with others." They demonstrate self-awareness and their right to exercise their voices, though they don't always say they claim that right in every situation. They do say they are aware of such a right and that they are exploring it. They seem to move between their own awareness of belonging to themselves and their own becoming-in-the-world, they voice the experience of a fluid interactive freedom, which to me is like the sound of a free soul. They challenge the idea of a static benchmark identity, saying "how boring would that be"; and they re/author(ise) the text of adolescence. Their narratives are colourful, varied, and impermanent, but the experience of our conversations is indelible. Speaking from the space of "belonging to who they are becoming," these young women discover their lives through their relationships (Gilligan, 1997, 2011), which for them are creative endeavours. The young women in this study contribute to the re-creation of the social construction of young women and adolescence, which is already underway (Artz, 1996; Bloustien, 2003; Brown & Gilligan, 1992; Gilligan, 1997, 2011; Martini, 2004; Oliver, 2001; Vadeboncoeur & Patel Stevens, 2005) and seem to have the courage to dialogue with themselves and with the world. Rather than conform to a prescribed hegemonic discourse,[3] they see themselves as "always becoming" anchored in their sense of belonging with themselves in and of the world (Patel Stevens, 2005; Pipher, 1994; Vadeboncoeur, 2005).

In the process of exploring these young women's personal narratives, our methodology emerged. Our togetherness in relationship generated our methodology rather than us having followed a particular methodology devised by someone else. I called the methodology "love, connectedness, and wholeness" (and later "natural human science"), and following our year of conversations, I was able to describe this primarily using the work and philosophies of Carol Gilligan (2011) and Johann Wolfgang von Goethe (1749–1832) (Bortoft, 1998; Steiner, 2000). Other influences on the methodology were Goethean conversation (Kaplan, 2005), inner participation (Barnes, 2000), feminist methodologies and critical theory (Gilligan, 1995, 2011; Hawthorne, 2002; Oliver, 1999, 2001), and the "Listening Guide" (Gilligan, Spencer, Weinberg, & Bertsch, 2003). For further details on method and methodology, I refer the reader to Lambert (2011).

Our methodology came together in the common space of conversation. This type of conversation is where personal truth is discovered in process through creative and intuitive speaking and listening, and silence is revered as much as sound. In such conversation, truth "becomes" in the belongingness of the conversation (Lambert, 2011). Goethe describes the results of such intense connection as a living experience, which opens in us "a new organ of perception" (Goethe, as quoted in Robbins, 2005, p. 113) so that our senses are refreshed and we are able to see and hear differently. Unfolding the narrative in this study became a threading and re-threading process that relied on a way of seeing and hearing that has been described as "inner participation" (Barnes, 2000). It was a weaving back and forth through the layers of our conversations like the "breathing process" (depicted as a lemniscates or figure-eight) that Steiner describes in the teaching-learning dynamic (Lambert, 2011). This breathing quality arose through our relationships and characterised the whole study. It was how the young women described their experience of identity creation—like breathing into and out from the world.

The personal narratives that follow are derived from our individual conversations. The sections chosen are illustrative of some of the key intersections between Rudolf Steiner's pedagogical approach and Friere's pedagogy of freedom. My intention here is not to talk over these narratives with a deeply analytical voice, but rather to present them as they are because I believe they speak for themselves. I weave in my comments to draw these narratives together and highlight the resonance of the phenomenon of the Steiner education experience. Each narrative includes raw text from conversations as well as comments from me, which unfold the voices of the young women. The different themes of resistance emerged naturally from our conversations. We begin with Crystal describing her sense of *interconnectedness*, her *instinct* and something she calls her *in-born consciousness*. We move to Hera, Isis, and Zen describing a resistance to anonymity (resistance to adopting the socially and culturally sanctioned prescriptions for living). Ruby, Sally, Laura, and Gabriel voice narratives of love and belonging, which resist fear and displacement. Finally, the narrative from 'Natalie' is a natural drawing together of our conversational threads. Natalie raises a voice of resistance to "loss of voice" or resignation to silence. She speaks directly and clearly to say that her resistance is grounded in her spaces of 'belonging and becoming', from which she draws her sense of "who she is." This phrase—"belonging and becoming"—is the keynote of the living experience of Steiner education for these young women and exemplifies a pedagogy of freedom. In the following narratives, the text in italics is the raw voice of the young woman as transcribed from our conversations.

RESISTANCE TO THE MYTH OF SEPARATION AND THE MYTH OF "NOT KNOWING"

> *Well everything's connected. Everything's, you know—they say that a butterfly's wings flapping here can alter something over there…everything's connected…If you put a positive thought out there then something positive…sometimes actually happen(s)…and if you put a negative thought out…lots of times something like that will happen.* (Crystal, 14 years)

Crystal has been talking about an experience of a *mystic, outlandish, otherworldly beauty* she felt while hiking on Mount Ruapehu and we are discussing connection to nature and being part of the natural world. *Well everything's connected,* she concludes. When I ask whether "the butterfly effect" has been a direct experience of hers, Crystal says very definitely: *Yes.* She talks about getting back *what you put out there* and she is adamant that one person can affect the *larger picture* and even *change the course of history* if you *follow your dream*. Crystal frequently speaks out about "being herself" in a way that claims her "space" in life.

> *All I say to people is just to be yourself but I guess you have to have the space to be yourself and I guess it's other people allowing you to be yourself…the education I'm going through…we get the space to be ourselves…we get freedom of expression not having a uniform and…heaps of kinds of creative things I guess which is expressing yourself. Maybe if I was, you know, in a another school where it's so kind of regimented you wouldn't have that space…then you'd have to make the space yourself…to make that space you have to step out there and be different and not worry so much about what people think…if they have a problem with how I am then it's their problem, not my problem…if someone wants to hate you, then they're wasting all that energy…everyone's on a different path of learning about their awareness of how they're acting.* (Crystal, 14 years)

Crystal says this awareness is partly about making decisions: *The decisions you make affect lots of things…you can do things but also not [do] things as well.* She sees some of her peers *fake doing things because that's what they think teenagers do [for example] they have a boyfriend because that's what you're meant to do…people should be less worried about what others think of them.* Even though I have received the message loud and clear by now, Crystal reiterates her resistance:

> *(I) won't ever be the stereotypical teenager. I can see what it's like and I have no desire to do that. I really don't like it when people have this idea of popular—like this whole idea that people are better than them and that they're worse than someone else. How can you think that?…What makes you better than someone? People sometimes say to me 'oh you think you're better than me' and I don't even answer. It's not even like that. I just don't want to be doing what you're doing… Instead of looking at [it as] if someone's better or worse, I feel it's just different levels of awareness.* (Crystal, 14 years)

Crystal is not interested in the media images of young women. I ask her where, then, does she get her idea of how she wants to be, and Crystal tells me with a laugh: *Instinct!* In our next conversation, Crystal alludes to her instinct: *It's like you have some inborn sense of consciousness.*

RESISTANCE TO ANONYMITY AND PRESCRIPTIVE LIVING

Hera echoes Crystal's *space to be yourself*:

> *I think one of the things that Steiner tries to bring through is…just being yourself…doing the things you like to do instead of trying to portray something else, trying to be more superior. I guess Steiner people just accept who they are…they're pretty secure really. We're just individuals connecting with other individuals.* (Hera, 17 years)

Isis talks about creativity and the feeling of being "free" at Steiner school where, she says, it is unpressurised.

At state school I would have already had to choose what classes to take for the future and you can feel that pressure building already in your life. The state school is like a factory—you go in at one end and come out the other with some qualifications…[You have to] come up to teachers expectations because you'd be classed on your abilities.… By Year 9 they have careers day.… It really kind of weighs you down when you feel that responsibility that you're growing up. I really enjoy it here—we're all in one class people of different abilities, we're all really good at different things instead of just one thing…There's room to move within the topic.… Like you have main lesson time and it's focussing on one topic for nearly two hours and you can learn quite a bit but it really gives you room to do something creative about what you've learned.… It's a lot more free in a way. (Isis, 15 years)

Does that mean, then, that you're not just memorising information here (at school)?

Mmm. I think they give it to you in such an unpressurised way that you enjoy learning information and if you enjoy it, you remember it and you feel good at it and you kind of grow as a person and you know all this information instead of just one set. A lot more knowledgeable about what goes on around you instead of just little things. (Isis, 15 years)

Zen remembers her sense of freedom in kindergarten and early primary school where she felt she was *being at one with the earth…so much more imaginative and creative than other children.* Then, she says, she stopped caring about her schoolwork and *just dribbled into the high school* and she said she labeled herself *dumb—* until she changed her mind. She has had the freedom not to suffer under a label, she says. She tells how she actively chose "not to be dumb" and make her own path, which led her to "*succeed and achieve* academically as well as personally."

I was actually really bad—and then one year I decided I'd try and I did really well.… Compared to other schools they think we are dumb [but] I reckon here there's more of a chance to get better. Well it's your choice and if someone tells you that you're dumb all your life you kind of feel like you're labeled and that's what you are and you have to accept it. [Here] they teach us to think for ourselves so that's what we do. (Zen, 17 years)

RESISTANCE TO DISPLACEMENT AND FEAR

Ruby speaks protectively of her school and describes a space where she feels safe:

People say when I say I go to Steiner, 'Oh that crazy school with all those crazy people' and I say—'Nup'.… I used to go to a state school and I absolutely hated it. I used to get bullied and stuff, but I really like it here. (Ruby, 14 years)

For Sally, making her own path is looking attractive, but scary, as she says she wants to leave school and fly off. As she talks about going, she discovers her deep connection to her Steiner education. In her first comment here, she is telling how the idea of going into the big ocean (leaving school for the wider world) scares her.

In listening through the layers, I notice two things in particular. She is using a story to illustrate her point—a common medium in Steiner teaching—and (secondly) in telling the story, she leads herself to unfold her love of school (nothing compares to Steiner). At first, she talks about being ready to experience the wider world.

> Now that I've got to 16 I just want to spread my wings and fly off and do something else.... It kind of scares me though;...one of our teachers...talked about [the journey through school as] coming from the little family circle into the lake and how the class students are going from being in the lake to the ocean with the wider world, kind of thing. I guess that kind of sits really big in a way for me 'cause it seems really truthful the idea of going into the big ocean. (Sally, 16 years)

Sally then relates a story of how her last main lesson at school inspired her to *broaden her horizons,* and as she considers leaving school she reflects on her education.

> Ah, something I like about the Steiner school—nothing compares to Steiner...the way they teach it is different not lecturing and stuff, but letting your imagination work with the different ideas of what their world would look like. I think with state schools it's probably like you get the idea and you don't really broaden your horizon with it. You get the image and it just kind of sits there. (Sally, 16 years)

Here we have it: the sense of what Hera calls being *pretty secure*; of being individuals accepting who they are; of expressing yourself'; of feeling safe; of being allowed to be imaginative and creative; of not being labeled; and of being connected in what Laura called more of a family idea; all of this reveals the deep sense of belonging that is woven throughout our conversations. The following narratives for Laura and Gabriel show how, in our final conversations, we are beginning to unfold the sense of belonging.

> I think that in some ways our school has got more of say a family idea incorporated into it—per se—being with the same class all the time—so that you connect quite strongly with them.
> **What if you don't?**
> If you don't then maybe Steiner doesn't work.
> **Are there times (at school then)...when you [might have] felt 'where do I belong', 'what am I doing'?**
> I think in a peer group...there are times when it really matters who you hang out with and you're more concerned with who's cool rather than who we really belong with. It doesn't matter if you're a person who doesn't hang out with everyone. You don't need to do that. It's up to you who you connect with. There's going to be people who you do and you don't. It's all right! How you feel is how you feel about it. I feel it's important though that you're not going to feel diminished in relationship. (Laura, 15 years)

For Gabriel, the sense of freedom and individuality that others talked about emerges when she talks about her Steiner experience.

I think we're freer to create our own identity 'cause there's not so many people so there's not that kind of clique where you know you dress the same way as a whole bunch of people…whereas everyone's fairly individual at our school 'cause there's not many people so there's not really groups to be in…. I think people are freer to do what they want, to not really be judged by what they wear;… there's that sense of belonging with the class and the community. (Gabriel, 17 years)

As our year of conversations draws to a close, the phenomenon of belonging that has been living in the background of our conversations finally makes a cameo appearance in Natalie's clear articulation in our second last conversation.

RESISTANCE TO DISSOCIATION, LOSS OF VOICE, AND LACK OF FREEDOM: BELONGING AND BECOMING

I don't know if I particularly like that word 'belong'…. Do I have to belong?…for me that is one of the hardest questions: 'Why am I here?'…your purpose and what am I meant to do and all this kind of thing…. I don't like the word 'belonging' 'cause it's kind of like a tie—you're tied to something. I think you should always have that freedom. (Natalie, 18 years)

It is as if Natalie had somehow picked up the threads of all 148 hours of conversations and had drawn them together into what became the synthesis of our conversational tapestry—belonging and becoming. Natalie begins by critically engaging with the idea of belonging, then with stunning similarity to Simone de Beauvoir's well-known phrase—"One is not born, but rather becomes, a woman"—Natalie says: *You're not born particularly to belong somewhere, but you become who you are.* The following narratives from Natalie come (progressively) from the one conversation.

I think belonging is kind of the key thing when people (are) a little bit lost in life and they're like 'where do I belong' and I think it's that discovery of a love or who you are…and that's when you discover where you belong—it might even be a place. I think your whole teenage life you're kind of like 'where do I belong' where's my niche—that and 'who am I'.

Maybe you need somewhere to belong to find out who you are. I think you really need the sense of belonging to something to…be grounded and it might even just be your family 'cause I'm sure if you feel out of place in your family that you're going to feel really lost. There needs to be somewhere that you know is yours that keeps you grounded and that you can always go back to and find yourself again—you know, a safe place, I guess.

I can see it working in different aspect for—one of my friends—who had her mother die when I think she was 13 or 14 and her family is, you know, they're always there for each other and they share everything…but I don't think she gets the warmth she needs and I think coming to the school she's found somewhere she belongs and that's kind of helped her find out who she is and become a person…really strong about who she is and what she wants to do…an individual.

If I think about belonging I think there's two things I think. One of them is this whole creative side and creative world...bringing up new ideas and new ways of looking at things.... I think I'll always belong to a group of people with a creative mind—they can do anything, but they think about it differently. I belong to that type. The strongest one for me is my family in the kind of, the spirit...there's this understanding...that's my home that's where I'm meant to be...it's kind of like grounding—where I belong...to a group of people. It's where I started and everything I am is because of that basis. The older siblings and where I lived and then it gets bigger—the school and friends and stuff and because all of that makes you who you are, that's why you belong to it...but not so much you can't belong anywhere else. (Natalie, 18 years)

Natalie's articulation of the belonging-becoming dynamic shows the sense of how through belonging we become and through becoming we belong. I hear her tell me that belonging is connected to being a part of something bigger than yourself—a bigger whole. Natalie relates belonging, as a grounding experience, to the discovery of what you love (or of love itself) and of self-belonging. There is the sense of "fitting in somewhere" or "with someone," and a strong aspect of choice and thus freedom—we can choose what we belong to and what we acknowledge as contributing to our belonging and this can change throughout our lives.

Our belonging gives us an anchor, a place from which to go out and experience the world. Yet Natalie also tells of belonging in relation to being tied down and not being free. She steps back from belonging at first and says it seems to be a key thing in life when you are a little bit lost, though I don't sense she is talking about herself here. Perhaps it is because she doesn't feel lost that she may have sensed belonging as initially remote from her—that is, until she starts to talk about it. It is almost as if Natalie is able to stand back and really look at belonging, because she feels secure enough in her own belonging to do so. She says very clearly that she knows who she is and suggests that is because of her belonging: *Everything I am is because of that basis...all of that makes you who you are, that's why you belong to it.* And as if in summary, Natalie's empowered voice tells who she is through her friend's words.

My friend said that there's something about my smile when I come into a room that's welcoming and I quite like that—I do go out of my way to [connect]—I don't want to shut off someone. [Also] I'm not going to let what they think dictate how I'm going to act. I'm just going to choose what I'm going to do. (Natalie, 18 years)

CONCLUDING COMMENTS

Women in all cultures have constructed resistances and identities in response to the historical and social circumstances in which they have found themselves. (Weiler, 2001, p. 67)

Young women are, without doubt, socially and culturally marginalised and media manipulated (Oliver, 1999, 2001; Vadeboncoeur & Patel Stevens, 2005). What is different about my research is that it centralises a marginalised voice that is rarely heard. Women and girls around the globe across all cultures experience oppression (Weiler, 2001) and non-freedom and if, and when, we make spaces for their (our) voices to be heard, then indeed these are voices of resistance by the very fact they become visible in an otherwise continuing cloud of silencing and secrecy.

Through the narratives presented here, the young women have challenged the stereotypes and prescriptions created for adolescents, for women and for education. Instead of the fragmented experience of displacement, lost-ness and hopelessness experienced as symptoms of our "modern" education system (Gidley, 2005; Vadeboncoeur, 2005), we hear "belonging" and empowered voices, which are foundational to lifting oppression and educating for freedom (Freire, 1998; Steiner, 1997) as well as for successful learning and academic achievement (Faircloth, 2009). We are left imagining the world in which education, fed by love and not fear, truly cultivates the courage to speak, honours the wisdom of silence and restores the balance in social voice in an ethical and just forum. *If*, says William Ayres:

> schools [were]…places of curiosity, imagination and reflectiveness embodying a passion for the possible [instead of] little assembly lines and mini-prison workshops…[then]… we might encourage the search for meaning by helping young people develop a capacity to look through a wider range of perspectives—the various disciplines, the array of arts and expressions, a diversity of people as well as one's own experiences, or we might insist on obedience and conformity above all. (Ayres, 2005, p. x)

I believe the Steiner culture and the voices of the young women from it, are exemplary of this kind of education.

In this chapter, I have highlighted the importance of education for freedom with a particular focus on freedom of voice and the importance of resisting the loss of personal voice in favour of a socially sanctioned discourse. I speak about young women (and women) because that is my direct and authentic experience—through my research and through my life and because by including marginalised voices we begin to restore the balance. Listening to young women's voices reminds us of our connectedness, and can awaken and alert us to what we have silenced, such as our human desire for belonging. Through their voices we hear the living expression of a pedagogy of freedom as resistance to "compelled conformity" (Martini, 2004). Theirs is a voice of resistance—to adolescent stereotypes and to Freire's (1974, p. 5), "levelling anonymity." These young women resist the image of "discomfited, disinterested adolescent" (Vadeboncoeur, 2005) and refuse to be labeled—academically or socially—or cajoled into silence (Oliver, 1999, 2001). They name their belonging in the world that they recognise in the process of its becoming—the "unfinishedness" that Freire frequently refers to (Freire, 1974, 1998). These young women are courageous in voice and deed and tell us clearly and consistently of the importance of connectedness in the natural and social worlds and thus they resist the dominant cultural discourse of "separation" endorsed by the patriarchy (Freire, 1998; Gilligan, 2011; Weiler, 2001).

The narratives shared in this chapter contribute to the feminist critiques and readings of Freire that have raised the pivotal importance of recognising women's voices and feminist perspectives as expansive of, instructive to, and potentially different from Friere (and from other pedagogies of difference that intentionally or unintentionally perpetuate the perspectives of men and the [dominant] patriarchal voice) (Jackson, 2010; Weiler, 1991, 2001). In this chapter, the voices of young women elucidate key characteristics of Freire's pedagogy that focus on the connections and similarities, rather than on the separations and differences, between feminist pedagogies and Freire's (and Steiner's) pedagogical approaches. The key connections are that education should be a space of belonging where we are free to become (for example) socially involved, politically active, and culturally informed human beings.

Just as Freire requested of his pedagogy, saying, "Give yourself to it critically and with ever-expanding curiosity" (Freire, 1998, p. 27), the legacy of Freire's work in education clearly lives on as his ideas are critiqued, expanded, and evolved around the globe (Giroux, 2010; McLaren, 2007, 2010; McLaren & Kincheloe, 2007; Weiler, 2001). I hope that this chapter contributes to that expansion. Rudolf Steiner also encouraged the expansion and evolution of his pedagogical ideas and practices to match the social, political, and cultural environment in which they served (Steiner, 1995, 1997) and I believe my research contributes significantly to that end. Joining Steiner and Freire adds strength to what Gidley (2007) calls "the evolution of consciousness as a planetary imperative." For me, this means a "questioning" consciousness grounded in an ethic of connected collective care; valuing innate knowing and continued (actual and verbal) acts of reflection; and reviewing the balance of voice in all of our social, political, and cultural relationships. Perhaps this reflects Freire's idea of a "critical consciousness" (Freire, 1974) or McLaren's (2010, p. 10) "pedagogy of critique grounded in revolutionary love." Perhaps it is what Steiner calls "harmonious development" or what Crystal calls *some inborn sense of consciousness*.

The voices of resistance from the young women in this chapter make education a personal narrative, which by its temporal location or "historicity" is in critical dialogue with the world: the personal becomes political. Drawing on Freire's pedagogy of freedom, Aronowitz extrapolates on this relationship:

> ...the learner's capacity to situate herself in her own historicity...and to understand the complexity of the relations that have produced this situation...entails a critical examination

of received wisdom, not as a storehouse of eternal truths but as itself situated in its own historicity…. Thus, the active knower, not the mind as a repository of "information," is the goal of education. (Aronowitz, 1998, p. 14)

My writing about young women is an inclusive act, which draws our collective voices out into the social arena. I consider it my privilege and my social responsibility—answering Freire's call to ethical activism as "a conscious presence in the world" (Freire, 1998, p. 26), armed with love.

It is fitting that the last word comes from Laura (who "spoke" earlier in this chapter). Laura's spontaneous spoken reflection, given one evening over the phone, came after she had reviewed my final written "interpretations" of some of our key conversational threads. At the time of our conversations, she was 15. This reflection was given two years after our conversations, when she was 17. In this narrative, Laura is describing her thoughts on the process of our methodology as *"a stripping back to the core."* Laura describes her sense of emerging from the core of belonging in her own voice, to belonging with the world. Having taken herself inward, she is the one who has discovered her "core" (her own voice) and she is the one who takes herself on her outward journey to connect to the world of human experience. Laura shows how she takes the notion of "the freedom to belong and become" into her own life and then expresses it as a more universal human experience.

> *A stripping away of everything to the total core of you—exploring all the qualities that are you, your negative qualities as well, and the other side of you. Once you see it in you, you see it in others around you. You're being confronted with them and you may not deal with it for a while…until you look and say 'there are these qualities' [and] I'm seeing them in me then seeing them outside of me. [And] I'm seeing the other qualities as well like joy and beauty. I'm able to recognise joy and beauty in the world! And able to see that there will always be joy and beauty and taking that and bringing it in. It's an 'in—out—in—thing'. Becoming 'at one' with some of the qualities you don't like about yourself. Own who you are instead of letting these qualities own you [and] know that you are going to have an impact and it's going to change the world. (Laura, 17 years)*

For me, this is a young woman's wisdom, a mindful and timely voice of love. Here is also "the joy and the beauty that comes in the search of itself"—without which Freire tells us, "teaching and learning are not possible" (Freire, 1998, p. 125).

NOTES

1. Here, a note on language is pertinent: While I do use individual (pseudo)nyms in this chapter, I also frequently use the term "young women" as a collective noun, which was suggested for use by the twelve young women whose voices are included in this chapter. This is not to objectify; rather, it is for textual fluency in academic writing, and is a term that the twelve young women concerned suggested as the best collective term we could use (preferring it to "girls").

2. Of course, I speak for me, but I also speak for them. We are inextricably connected through having shared such prolonged, intense personal space and every day I hear them speak in me. They speak for themselves, but also for me. And in the complex web of our conversations, there are the spaces where we meet with one voice.

3. Pipher (1994) and Oliver (1999, 2001) refer to this as girls trying to navigate between their own sense of self (their own perception, their own voice) and what is culturally and socially prescribed as "right and acceptable" for women.

REFERENCES

Aronowitz, S. (1998). Introduction. In P. Freire, *Pedagogy of freedom: Ethics, democracy, and civic courage* (pp. xxxii, 1–19). Lanham, MD: Rowman & Littlefield.

Artz, S. (1996). *The life-worlds and practices of violent school-girls* (Doctoral dissertation abstract, University of Victoria, British Columbia, Canada). Retrieved from http://proquest.umi.com.ezproxy.aut.ac.nz/pqdlink?did=740044361&Fmt=7&clientId=7961&RQT=309&VName=PQD

Ayres, W. (2005). Introduction. In J. A. Vadeboncoeur & L. Patel Stevens (Eds.), *Re/constructing "the adolescent": Sign, symbol, and body* (pp. ix–xi). New York, NY: Peter Lang.

Barnes, J. (2000). Essay: Participatory science as a basis for a healing culture. In Rudolf Steiner, *Nature's open secret: Introductions to Goethe's scientific writings* (pp. 219–301). Spring Valley, NY: Anthroposophic Press.

Bloustien, G. (2003). *Girl making. A cross-cultural ethnography on the processes of growing up female.* New York, NY: Berghahn Books.

Bortoft, H. (1996). *The wholeness of nature. Goethe's way towards a science of conscious participation in nature.* New York, NY: Lindisfarne Books.

Brown, L. M., & Gilligan, C. (1992). *Meeting at the crossroads: Women's psychology and girls' development.* New York, NY: Ballantine Books.

Clarke, P. (1997). Translator's notes. In P. Freire, *Pedagogy of freedom: Ethics, democracy, and civic courage* (p. xxxii). Lanham, MD: Rowman & Littlefield.

Fagan, A. (2009). *The atlas of human rights: Mapping violations of freedom around the globe.* Berkeley: University of California Press.

Faircloth, B. (2009). Making the most of adolescence: Harnessing the search for identity to understand classroom belonging. *Journal of Adolescent Research, 24*(3), 321–348.

Finser, T. (1997). Introduction. In R. Steiner, *The essentials of education* (GA 308) (T. Finser, Trans., pp. vii–xiv). (First published in English 1926; Original translator unknown.) [Five lectures April 1924, Stuttgart.] Spring Valley, New York: Anthroposophic Press.

Freire, P. (1974). *Education for critical consciousness.* New York, NY: Continuum.

Freire, P. (1998). *Pedagogy of freedom: Ethics, democracy, and civic courage.* Lanham, MD: Rowman & Littlefield.

Gidley, J. (2005). Giving hope back to our young people: Creating a new spiritual mythology for western culture. *Journal of Futures Studies: Epistemology, Methods, Applied and Alternative Futures, 9*(3), 17–30.

Gidley, J. (2007). The evolution of consciousness as a planetary imperative: An integration of integral views. *Integral Review: A Transdisciplinary and Transcultural Journal for New Thought, Research and Praxis, 5*, 4–226.

Gidley, J. (2010a). Holistic education and visions of rehumanized futures. *Research on Steiner Education, 1*(2), 139–147. Retrieved from http://www.rosejourn.com/index.php/rose/article/viewFile/37/70

Gidley, J. (2010b). Turning tides: Creating dialogue between Rudolf Steiner and 21st century academic discourses. A brief report on Steiner-based academic research in Australia in context commissioned by the Rudolf Steiner Schools of Australia: An association (RSSA). *Research on Steiner Education, 1*(1), 101–107. Retrieved from http://www.rosejourn.com/index.php/rose/article/viewFile/17/58

Gilligan, C. (1982/1993). *In a different voice: Psychological theory and women's development.* Cambridge, MA: Harvard University Press.

Gilligan, C. (1995). Hearing the difference: Theorizing connection. *Hypatia, 10*(2), 120.

Gilligan, C. (1997). Getting civilized. In A. Oakley & J. Mitchell (Eds.), *Who's afraid of feminism? Seeing through the backlash* (pp. 13–28). New York, NY: New Press.

Gilligan, C. (2002). *The birth of pleasure.* New York, NY: Knopf.

Gilligan, C. (2004). Recovering Psyche. *Annual of Psychoanalysis, 32,* 131–147.

Gilligan, C. (2011). *Joining the resistance.* Cambridge, England: Polity Press.

Gilligan, C., Spencer, R., Weinberg, M. K., & Bertsch, T. (2003). On the Listening Guide: A voice-centered relational model. In P. M. Camic, J. E. Rhodes, & L. Yardley (Eds.), *Qualitative research in psychology: Expanding perspectives in methodology and design* (pp. 157–172). Washington, DC: American Psychological Association.

Giroux, H. (2010). Rethinking education as the practice of freedom: Paulo Freire and the promise of critical pedagogy. Retrieved from http://archive.truthout.org/10309_Giroux_Freire

Hawthorne, S. (2002). *Wild politics.* Melbourne, Australia: Spinfex.

Jackson, S. (2010). Crossing borders and changing pedagogies: From Giroux and Freire to feminist theories of education. *Gender and Education, 9*(4), 457–468.

Kaplan, A. (2005). Emerging out of Goethe: Conversation as a form of social inquiry. *Janus Head, 8*(1), 311–334. Retrieved from http://www.janushead.org/8-1/Kaplan.pdf

Kincheloe, J. (2007). Critical pedagogy in the twenty-first century: Evolution for survival. In P. McLaren & J. Kincheloe (Eds.), *Critical pedagogy: Where are we now?* (pp. 9–42). New York, NY: Peter Lang.

Lambert, A. (2011). *Belonging and becoming: Voices of harmonious being; Young women Steiner students explore their lifeworlds through Goethean conversation.* Unpublished doctoral dissertation, AUT University, Auckland, New Zealand. Retrieved from http://hdl.handle.net/10292/355

MacDonald, M. (2012). Afterword. In E. S. Richardson, *In the early world* (3rd ed., p. 231). Wellington, New Zealand: NZCER Press. (Original work published 1964)

Macedo, D. (1998). Foreword. In Paulo Freire, *Pedagogy of freedom: Ethics, democracy, and civic courage* (p. xxxii). Lanham, MD: Rowman & Littlefield.

Martini, M. (2004). *Students at risk: The lived meaning of compelled conformity* (Doctoral dissertation, Boise State University, Idaho). Retrieved from ProQuest Information and Learning Company, New York, database.

McLaren, P. (2007). The future of the past. In P. McLaren & J. Kincheloe (Eds.), *Critical pedagogy: Where are we now?* (pp. 289–314). New York, NY: Peter Lang.

McLaren, P. (2010). Revolutionary critical pedagogy. *InterActions: UCLA Journal of Education and Information Studies, 6*(2), 1–11.

Metcalfe, A., & Game, A. (2007). Becoming who you are: The time of education. *Time & Society, 16*(1), 43–59.

O'Connor, P. (2011, July 27). Narrow focus road to education failure. *The Dominion Post*, p. B5.

Oliver, K. (1999). Adolescent girls' body-narratives: Learning to desire and create a "fashionable" image. *Teachers College Record, 101*(2), 220–246.

Oliver, K. (2001). Images of the body from popular culture: Engaging adolescent girls in critical inquiry. *Sport, Education and Society, 6*(2), 143–164.

Palmer, P., & Zajonc, A. (Eds.). (2010). *The heart of higher education: A call to renewal*. San Francisco, CA: Jossey-Bass.

Patel Stevens, L. (2005). ReNaming "adolescence": Subjectivities in complex settings. In J. A. Vadeboncoeur & L. Patel Stevens (Eds.), *Re/constructing "the adolescent": Sign, symbol, and body* (pp. 271–282). New York, NY: Peter Lang.

Phillips, G. (2012). Foreword. In E. S. Richardson, *In the early world* (3rd ed.). Wellington, NZ: NZCER Press.

Pipher, M. (1994). *Reviving Ophelia: Saving the selves of adolescent girls*. New York, NY: Ballantine Books.

Robbins, B. D. (2005). New organs of perception: Goethean science as a cultural therapeutics. *Janus Head, 8*(1), 113–126. Retrieved from http://www.janushead.org/8-1/Robbins.pdf

Simpson, R. (2004, April). Demystifying Rudolf Steiner education: A personal journey. *Taruna College Newsletter*, 1–4.

Small, D. (2009, November). *Neoliberalism's fate. Implications for education*. Paper presented at the 37th annual conference of ANZCIES, University of New England, Armidale, Australia. Retrieved from http://ir.canterbury.ac.nz/bitstream/10092/4719/1/12623584_Neoliberalism's%20 Fate%20ANZCIES%20Paper.pdf

Smith, M., & McLaren, P. (2010). Critical Pedagogy: An Overview. *Childhood Education, 86*(5), 332–334.

Steiner, R. (1964). *The philosophy of freedom: The basis for a modern world conception* (GA 4) (M. Wilson, Trans.). Spring Valley, New York: Anthroposophic Press. (Original work published 1894)

Steiner, R. (1995). *The kingdom of childhood* (GA 311) (H. Fox, Original Trans. 1982; Anthroposophic Press Trans. 1995). [Seven lectures given in Torquay, August 12–20, 1924.] Spring Valley, New York: Anthroposophic Press.

Steiner, R. (1996). *The education of the child and early lectures on education* (2nd ed.) G. & M. Adams, Trans. For 'The education of the child' (GA 34) (Original German work published 1907); Various translations for 5 lectures given 1906-1911, Berlin & Nuremberg), Spring Valley, New York: Anthroposophic Press.

Steiner, R. (1997). *The essentials of education* (GA 308) (T. Finser, Trans.). (First published in English 1926; Original translator unknown.) [Five lectures April 1924, Stuttgart.] Spring Valley, New York: Anthroposophic Press.

Steiner, R. (2000). *Nature's open secret: Introductions to Goethe's scientific writings* (pp. 219–301). Spring Valley, New York: Anthroposophic Press.

Steiner, R. (2004). *The spiritual ground of education* (GA 305) (Anthroposophic Press, Trans.). [Nine Lectures, August 1922, Oxford.) Spring Valley, New York: Anthroposophic Press.

Vadeboncoeur, J. A. (2005). Naturalised, restricted, packaged and sold: Reifying the fictions of "adolescent" and "adolescence." In J. A. Vadeboncoeur & L. Patel Stevens (Eds.), *Re/constructing "the adolescent": Sign, symbol, and body* (pp. 1–24). New York, NY: Peter Lang.

Vadeboncoeur, J. A., & Patel Stevens, L. (Eds.). (2005). *Re/constructing "the adolescent": Sign, symbol, and body*. New York, NY: Peter Lang.

Weiler, K. (1991). Freire and a feminist pedagogy of difference. *Harvard Educational Review, 61*(4), 449–474.

Weiler, K. (2001). Rereading Paulo Freire. In K. Weiler (Ed.), *Feminist engagements: Reading, resisting, and revisioning male theorists in education and cultural studies* (pp. 67–87). New York, NY: Routledge.

Wilson, M. (1964). Introduction. In R. Steiner, *The philosophy of freedom: The basis for a modern world conception* (M. Wilson, Trans., pp. vii–xxii). Spring Valley, NY: Anthroposophic Press. (Original work published 1894)

Zajonc, A. (2010). Introduction. In P. Palmer & A. Zajonc (Eds.), *The heart of higher education: A call to renewal* (pp. x–xi). San Francisco, CA: Jossey-Bass.

CHAPTER TWENTY-SEVEN

Bilingual Education, Culture, and the Challenge of Developing Freirean Dispositions in Teacher Education

JACOB W. NEUMANN

Calls for developing Freirean dispositions among teacher candidates frequently appear in the critical teacher education literature (e.g., Bartolomé, 2004; Darder, Torres, & Baltodano, 2002; Major & Brock, 2003). Within the area of bilingual education, these calls are beginning to be specifically directed toward teacher candidates' dispositions about culture (e.g., Dantas-Whitney, Mize, & Waldschmidt, 2009). Such calls make sense, because as the bilingual education literature clearly shows, bilingual education fits a Freirean disposition toward culture well. Yet, developing Freirean dispositions toward culture among teacher education students presents significant challenges that have not yet been adequately addressed in the critical literature. In this chapter, I examine these challenges through the context of a social studies methods course that I teach at a university in the United States and through field research I conduct at a local middle school near my university. I find that even though bilingual education suits Freirean dispositions toward culture well, several factors collude to make this a complicated and difficult endeavor: uncertainty about the meaning of the term "culture," the challenge in changing teacher candidates' beliefs about education, and, perhaps most importantly, practical and conceptual obstacles to developing Freirean dispositions within teacher education.

THE SETTING

The University of Texas - Pan American is located in south Texas, approximately 20 miles from the U.S. border with Mexico, in a region known as the Rio Grande Valley. This is a region of daily border crossing—literally, economically, emotionally, and cognitively—as a constant flow of students, families, and commerce crisscrosses the border every day. Hidalgo County, where the university lies, is 90.7% "Hispanic or Latino"; 34.4% of county residents live below the poverty level; and 84.4% of county residents speak Spanish at home (U.S. Census, 2011). One of the courses that I teach here is an elementary social studies methods course to bilingual education majors. Like the county population, every semester my students are practically all Latina, many of whom speak Spanish as their first language. Indeed, Spanish fills my classroom. English is used for "official" purposes, such as whole-class discussions, presentations, and teaching demonstrations. But students often immediately switch back to Spanish for small-group discussions and one-on-one conversations.

The Murillo (2010) study of the students in this program, calls these students *mestiza*, meaning "women of mixed Mexican and indigenous heritage" (p. 277). Murillo claims that many of these students "have been raised in a system of silence and obedience" (p. 277). Latinos in "the Valley," despite being the majority ethnicity, have historically suffered social, economic, and educational discrimination from a much smaller percentage of whites (Guajardo & Guajardo, 2004). Murillo describes the educational discrimination many of these students have faced throughout their educational experience in Valley public schools. She quotes one student who explains that

> because my first language is Spanish, the elementary school decided to drop me down two grade levels and I was placed in kinder[garten].... From then on, I knew I had to overcome the obstacle of language. I learned English quick and now I think I've forgotten much of my Spanish. (p. 283)

It is in this setting that I work to lead my students toward Freirean dispositions about culture. This context would seem ripe for such an endeavor. My students, unlike the teacher candidates Bartolomé (2004) describes who "tend to see the social order as a fair and just one" (p. 100), need no convincing as to the power discrepancies, social injustice, and economic unfairness about which criticalists routinely try to convince educators. Yet, my students struggle with these dispositions, not because they do not understand them, but because they don't know what to do about them. Let me not suggest a clear division, however, because the understanding and the doing make up two parts of one whole. Here lies the problem, for my students and for the critical education literature. Most of the literature advocating the development of Freirean dispositions in teacher education focuses on the understanding side of the whole. But teachers and teacher candidates also need to know how to implement Freirean dispositions inside the congested and contested context of local schools. As Schussler, Stooksberry, and Bercaw (2010) put it, "Teachers must not only be inclined to achieve particular purposes but also be sensitive to the context of any teaching situation to know what knowledge and skills to put to use at any given time to achieve those purposes" (p. 351).

BILINGUAL EDUCATION, CULTURE, AND FREIREAN DISPOSITIONS

The term "disposition" holds a variety of meanings. According to Dottin (2009), "Dispositions…concern not only what professional educators can do (ability), but also what they are actually likely to do (actions)" (p. 85). Schussler and colleagues (2010) state that dispositions "involve an inclination to put one's ability to use and the sensitivity to know when a situation calls for specific skills" (p. 351). And Villegas (2007) claims that dispositions are "tendencies for individuals to act in a particular manner under particular circumstances" (p. 373). A Freirean disposition would include problem-posing, generating critical inquiry, dialoguing, being humble, seeking social justice, and loving people. When applied to culture, a Freirean disposition examines culture through problem-posing; it values people's culture as rich with significance, not unreflectively, but as a product of how people create worlds. Cultural analysis, then, emphasizes questions of value, purpose, and meaning.

Bilingual education clearly aligns with these dispositions toward culture. According to Freire (1985), "Language is one of culture's most immediate, authentic, and concrete expressions" (p. 183). Indeed, "culture" might be the watchword of bilingual education. "Learning in a diverse class incorporates the rich linguistic and cultural life experiences that each student brings to the classroom" (Ovando & Combs, 2006, p. 100). Incorporating students' culture is often claimed to be an essential component of teaching and learning within bilingual classrooms and with language minority students (Banks, 2006; Garcia, 1991; Moll, 1988; Ovando & Combs, 2006; Pérez & Torres-Guzmán, 2002; Trueba, 1989). It is commonly argued that because many second language learning students do not come to school with the same cultural and social experiences as native language speakers, instructional connections to students' home culture help them to more meaningfully grasp and relate to academic content.

Bilingual education scholars also argue for similar perspectives about culture as does Freire. At a foundational level, both bilingual education and Freirean praxis emphasize drawing from the lived experiences of students. Where Freire calls for faithfulness to historical and material circumstances (Freire, 2004), Trueba (1989) contends that "instruction [for language minority students] should be tailored to children's cultural knowledge and experiences" (p. 70). Where Freire invokes generative themes that "exist in people in their relations with the world" (Freire, 1993, p. 87), bilingual scholars often encourage teachers working with language minority students to utilize what Moll (1992) calls funds of knowledge, "cultural practices and bodies of knowledge and information that households use to survive, to get ahead or to thrive" (p. 21). Where Freire articulates problem-posing that "is constituted and organized by the students' view of the world, where their own generative themes are found" (Freire, 1993, p. 90), Baker (2006) describes classroom activities that help to develop students' awareness of cultural heritage.

Yet, even a glance at the literature on bilingual and multicultural education reveals a wide range of perspectives on how and why to integrate students' culture into teaching. These perspectives range from a traditional emphasis on academic success to a reconstructionist emphasis on critical social change. For example, Olmedo (2009) describes a school in a Mexican American community in Chicago that takes a traditional approach to learning, one focused on academic and social success and participating in American society (p. 35). On the other end of this spectrum, Pérez and Torres-Guzmán (2002) advocate for using students' culture in promoting what they call "cultural repertoire"—understanding and competence in different linguistic and cultural systems—that "enable[s] individuals to critically assess their world and to entertain the possibility of a different future" (p. 19).

Similarly, scholars have taken a range of approaches to incorporating Freire's work into their arguments for bilingual and multicultural education. I find this connection tacitly evident, for example, in Garcia's (1991) description of "exemplar" teachers of minority language students who utilize student-generated instructional themes. While some of the themes Garcia reports involve relatively innocuous topics such as dinosaurs, other themes take a decisively critical turn, as when a primary teacher addresses cultural experiences of Latino students or when one third grade teacher has a class investigate the dangers of pesticides after one student suggested that the class study "the stuff in the field that made my little brother sick" (p. 136). Many scholars, however, make explicit connections. Some scholars, such as Banks (2006) and Harmon and Jones (2005), offer oblique references to Freire when describing a multicultural curriculum that helps students "to use knowledge to guide action that will create a humane and just world" (Banks, 2006, p. 24). Other scholars incorporate elements of Freire's ideas, but drain them of their political and ontological imperative. For example, Arreguin-Anderson (2012) uses Freire's notion of generative themes as merely another instructional method for increasing students' academic achievement. A few scholars include Freire's work as an aside, as one of a list of approaches for bilingual literacy (e.g., Baker, 2006). Many scholars, however, do draw directly from Freire in advocating for a reconstructionist perspective within bilingual and multicultural education. For example, Freire holds that within problem-posing, "the teacher is no longer merely the-one-who-teaches, but one who is himself taught in dialogue with the students, who in turn while being taught also teach" (Freire, 1993, p. 61). In a similar manner, Ovando and Combs (2006), speaking to both problem-posing and generative themes, claim that:

> in this process, the teacher is no longer the "expert," but is discovering new ways of exploring knowledge along with the students. This might mean that sometimes students lead the class in new curricular directions, depending upon how a unit develops. The teacher might initiate the theme, but as it unfolds, students contribute considerably to gathering the knowledge base that the class develops. (p. 165)

Here we can infer into the educator's disposition. Many factors influence how teachers teach. Accountability exams, local administrative policies, and teachers' beliefs about content and students are just a few of the factors that help shape their classroom practices. The past several years have seen a surge in interest, especially in teacher education journals, in dispositions as another important factor that shapes teachers' practices. In the current analysis, a difference in dispositions is a logical inference as to one cause for the diversity of approaches to culture and to Freire within bilingual education. Dispositions are key, especially in teacher education programs, when thinking about the possibilities for critical teaching, because as Borko, Liston, and Whitcomb (2007) and Dottin (2009) both note, just because educators have the knowledge and skill to act in a particular way does not mean that they will be *inclined* to act that way.

Some scholars contend that dispositional development should be teacher educators' top priority (Diez, 2007; Eberly, Rand, & O'Connor, 2007; Schussler et al., 2010; Sockett, 2008). This presents a challenge on several levels. A genuine shift in students' thinking should be the goal and not a pretended shift to satiate instructor expectations. Critical education does not advance if teacher candidates view Freirean perspectives merely as "little more than a series of meaningless routines, tasks undertaken to please someone else's conception of what is important" (Eisner, 1985, p. 69). Teacher candidates' beliefs about education are also resistant to change (Richardson, 2003). These beliefs stem, in part, from a number of societal myths about teaching. According to Britzman (1986), these myths are that (1) everything depends on the teacher; (2) the teacher is the expert; and (3) teachers are self-made (p. 448). Acquired from societal discourse about education and from their own biographies, students bring these beliefs with them into teacher education. And they do not easily change. Britzman "argue[s] that the underlying values which coalesce in one's institutional biography, if unexamined, propel the cultural reproduction of authoritarian teaching practices and naturalize the contexts which generate such a cycle" (p. 443). Put simply, teacher education "tends…to reinforce the ideas and images of education that prospective teachers bring to their training" (p. 446).

CONCEPTUAL AND PRACTICAL OBSTACLES TO DEVELOPING FREIREAN DISPOSITIONS

In addition, as if the above obstacles do not present teacher educators with enough challenges, there are other practical and conceptual obstacles to helping teacher candidates acquire Freirean dispositions toward culture that have not received enough attention in the critical literature. One conceptual obstacle specifically relates to culture. My bilingual education students often want to incorporate their future students' culture into their teaching, but they have difficulty articulating just what they mean by "culture." The difficulty in determining what culture means is apparent in the literature. For example, on one hand, McDonough (2008) maps out a multicultural landscape that spans from "liberal multiculturalism" to "difference multiculturalism" to "transfigurative multiculturalism." Hidalgo (1993), on the other hand, situates culture at three overlapping levels: concrete, behavioral, and symbolic. "The concrete level reflects behavioral patterns, and the behavioral patterns reflect values (symbolic level), but those elements are interconnected and sometimes explain and interpret each other" (Schwartz, Mor-Sommerfeld, & Leikin, 2010, p. 193).

A problem for teacher educators who encourage the incorporation of culture into teaching, and one that I consistently encounter with my students, is that teachers and teacher candidates often think of the most visible characteristics (food, holidays, clothes, etc.), that is, the concrete level, as a group's "culture" (Hidalgo, 1993). Thus, an integration of culture often remains superficial, becoming a celebration of holidays or food, or a feel-good, "I'm okay, you're okay" look at living patterns and traditions. This is especially troublesome for critical educators working in bilingual education settings where culture is held as crucially important, because "foods, clothes, holidays and artifacts actually reveal very little about how ethnic groups experience and make meaning of the world" (Schwartz, et al., 2010, p. 190).

A focus on concrete levels of culture also impedes the wording implicit within Paulo Freire's writing. Freire (1973) writes about culture "as a systematic acquisition of human experience" (p. 48). This notion of culture incorporates the concrete, but reaches deep into the symbolic. It also speaks to the symbolism of language, in that "in reading the word, we also read the world," because in reading the word, "we read the world in which these words exist" (Freire, 1997, p. 304). But in reading the word-world, we are presented with the problem of renaming the world with new words, thus building new worlds. We change the world through the conscious, practical work of writing and rewriting the word-world (Freire & Macedo, 1987, as cited in Neumann, 2011, p. 613).

What I try to get my students to understand as a ripe source for inquiry is that "culture" itself is a contested idea. Bilingual educators hold culture to be an essential component of educating English language learners. Yet Menand (2001) claims that "there is also the problem that 'culture' names a rather amorphous entity. Human beings produce culture in the same sense that they produce carbon dioxide: they can't help it, but the stuff has absolutely no value in itself. It's just there" (p. 407).

While bilingual educators usually value the concept of culture as an effective educational tool, Menand (2001) seems to question the notion of valuing culture at all. If, as Menand holds, "culture is only a response to the conditions of life; when those conditions change—and in modern societies they change continuously—cultures change as well" (p. 407), just what is being used or compared in the effort to make meaning with students? Questions such as these are full of possibilities for helping teacher candidates to deepen their conceptions of culture.

There is another conceptual obstacle to implementing Freirean dispositions in classrooms, one that presents perhaps the largest challenge for my teacher education students. Critical scholars spend considerable time trying to convince educators of the value and verity of their arguments. While these efforts may be necessary with some audiences, my students need no convincing. Instead, they struggle with something much more fundamental within teaching: the shift in thinking from teaching as telling to teaching as inquiry. This is more than a simple methods problem. Critical pedagogy is often criticized for a perceived lack of suggestions for practical implementation (Crocco, 2006; Eisner, 2002; Evans, 2008; Knight & Pearl, 2000; Seltzer-Kelly, 2009; Wardekker & Miedema, 1997). But the obstacle I speak to here is less about blueprints for doing critical education and instead about the deeper problem of helping students learn to think of the teacher's role as generating inquiry for students. Fragnoli (2005) captures some of this difficulty in moving teacher candidates toward inquiry. Discomfort with content, lack of experience in creating inquiry activities, as well as practical time considerations can all impede teacher candidates' dispositions toward inquiry. Fragnoli cites three of her students' reflections on inquiry that reflect these insecurities.

- Even though I know deep down [that] this is an effective strategy…I am questioning my ability as a teacher to put all of this together. (p. 249)
- It is great but as a new teacher, will I have the resources to put this together? (p. 249)
- I think this is great. I enjoyed it, but will I use this in my classroom? I do not think I could. (p. 250)

Resources and time for planning are important issues within inquiry. I find, however, that the problem can also lie deeper. The saying goes that we teach the way we were taught. As Britzman (1986) puts it, "Years of classroom experience allow students to have very specific expectations of how teachers should act in the classroom" (p. 445). This, of course, applies to thinking about teaching. Because my teacher education students have experienced teaching as telling in social studies for most of their schooling history—teaching wherein the teacher provides students with facts, with answers, rather than creates experiences for them to explore and to engage with—my students have tremendous difficulty conceptualizing teaching as anything *other* than telling.

Let me offer an illustration. In my social studies methods course, I spend most of the semester trying to move my students' thinking about teaching social studies away from telling and toward inquiry, as well as help students to understand strategies for incorporating that inquiry into the daily demands of schooling. To start our journey toward inquiry, students examine their past experiences with social studies and create a sort of "to do" and "not to do" list of teacher behaviors by specifically focusing on things they remember *their* teachers doing that they both liked and disliked. We read articles on inquiry, such as Wolk's (2008) "School as Inquiry." We also spend considerable time creating activities that are inquiry based. For one class exercise, I have students create an activity in which kindergarten students will examine the concept of "needs and wants." Here I refer students to the Texas state curriculum, the "Texas Essential Knowledge and Skills," that mandates that kindergarten students study "needs and wants" under economics (Texas Education Agency, 2011). I give students no further directions because I want them to develop their own metacognition of how they think about teaching social studies. Without fail, my students bring to class activities that have kids simply sort items according to given definitions of needs and wants. That is, they *tell* kids what the answer is. But when I ask my students by which criteria do we determine a need or a want, lots of discussion ensues. It is only *after* this discussion that students see that the real thinking lies in wrestling with and not simply applying the concept. By the end of the semester, some students grasp the concept of creating inquiry, but many still create lessons that emphasize telling. Mine, then, is a work in progress. Helping my students to understand and embrace inquiry presents such a huge challenge in this course that I feel my students and I still barely scratch the surface of the notion of critical inquiry that addresses concepts such as fairness and justice.

These conceptual obstacles are practical problems as well. To effectively implement a Freirean disposition in the classroom, teachers and teacher candidates must understand and embrace inquiry—and be able to integrate it into their teaching. This change to inquiry is also not easy because "inquiry-based teaching is a profound change from business as usual" (Wolk, 2008, p. 116). Schools are crowded places, and teachers and teacher candidates can easily be overwhelmed by school realities (Bekerman & Zembylas, 2010). Teachers must negotiate a range of pressures on their time. In one local middle school where I have been conducting longitudinal qualitative research for the past three years, these pressures come in the forms of accountability mandates, homework initiatives, instructional rounds, the introduction of iPads, special populations, TELPAS, paperwork, the International Baccalaureate program, and more. Teachers here have so many other things to worry about that thinking about teaching is at number seven or eight on their to do lists (Neumann, 2012). All of these time constraints—both inside the classroom and on teachers' planning time—present real obstacles to integrating critical teaching.

Teacher education students quickly pick up on these pressures. The students in my social studies methods class, for example, are bombarded with images—from their own experience as students, from teachers they know, from their field experiences in schools—of hierarchical mandates and institutional structures that appear to them as constricting exoskeletons on their professional freedom in their future classrooms. One student's reflection is worth citing at length, for it illustrates the difficulty that students sense even in integrating constructivist, let alone critical structures in the classroom:

> I know that the majority of us in blocks are planning on being constructivist, but as I have been learning in field [experiences in local schools], this is a whole different story. This story [that we recently read in class] made me think of what other teachers in the field have told me. Even though most of them would love to be constructivist, they say that the curriculum their school follows does not allow for it. Others say that even if you try to be constructivist you have a chance of getting in trouble because the administration wants to see you drilling the students with direct instruction and assessments for the test to make the school exemplary. (Neumann & Meadows, 2011, p. 103)

Even experienced teachers can struggle to shift their teaching toward inquiry. The experience of one eighth grade social studies teacher at the middle school where I research offers a telling illustration of both the conceptual and practical challenges presented by teaching for inquiry. This teacher, Bill Trammell, has been teaching for more than ten years and two years ago was named his school's Teacher of the Year. Three years ago, Trammell told me that he felt his teaching was constricted because "I have to do the mile wide and inch deep type approach, because I'm given all these criteria and all these objectives, and it's such a sprint from the first day of school all the way to the [state accountability] test." (Neumann & Meadows, 2011, p. 104).

Last year, Trammell completely changed his teaching. He doesn't necessarily hold a Freirean disposition toward teaching, but he did try to structure his teaching around inquiry and move away from lecture. This change has proved to be extremely difficult. In addition to the time constraints discussed above and having to learn how to create inquiry units, Trammell is also faced with restructuring and resequencing his teaching to allow for inquiry while also fulfilling school district pacing and benchmark requirements. Now into the second year of this change process, he tells me that he still feels like he is a brand new teacher learning everything all over again.

CONCLUSION

Bilingual education is a natural context for Freirean dispositions toward culture. A Freirean disposition takes the academic relationship between bilingual education and culture and deepens it to help students develop the "capacity to apprehend reality" (Freire, 1998, p. 66). Teacher educators can play a crucial role in helping to develop these dispositions among teachers and teacher candidates. However, serious conceptual and practical obstacles exist to implementing Freirean dispositions, and teachers and teacher candidates need help learning how to negotiate them. These obstacles have not yet received the necessary attention within the critical literature. Many critical scholars argue for supplying teacher candidates with experiences to help them learn to recognize their own ideologies, biases, and preconceptions. Actions such as these are essential to stimulating critical teaching through teacher education programs. But changing beliefs is not enough to develop a Freirean disposition. Even if a critical orientation to the world is a choice (Wink & Almanzo, 1995), teachers and teacher candidates also need help learning how to implement those dispositions inside the classroom. Unless they have the skill to do so, critical teaching about culture can easily be just another thing teachers wish they could do inside their classrooms.

REFERENCES

Arreguin-Anderson, M. G. (2012). Mobile learning and teaching in culturally diverse environments. In C. G. Garcia, M. E. Reyes, & V. Lopez-Estrada, (Eds.), *Classroom connections to teaching: A resource for teachers of Latino students*. Dubuque, Iowa: Kendall/Hunt.

Baker, C. (2006). *Foundations of bilingual education and bilingualism* (4th ed.). Bristol, England: Multilingual Matters.

Banks, J. A. (2006). *Cultural diversity and education: Foundations, curriculum, and teaching* (5th ed.). Boston, MA: Pearson.

Bartolomé, L. I. (2004). Critical pedagogy and teacher education: Radicalizing prospective teachers. *Teacher Education Quarterly, 31*(1), 97–122.

Bekerman, Z., & Zembylas, M. (2010). Fearful symmetry: Palestinian and Jewish teachers confront contested narratives in integrated bilingual education. *Teaching and Teacher Education, 26*, 507–515.

Borko, H., Liston, D., & Whitcomb, J. A. (2007). Apples and fishes: The debate over dispositions in teacher education. *Journal of Teacher Education, 58*(5), 359–364.

Britzman, D. P. (1986). Cultural myths in the making of a teacher: Biography and social structure in teacher education. *Harvard Educational Review, 56*(4), 442–456.

Crocco, M. S. (2006). The invisible hand of theory in social studies education. In C. H. Cherryholmes, A. Segall, & E. E. Heilman (Eds.), *Social studies—the next generation* (pp. 231–236). New York, NY: Peter Lang.

Dantas-Whitney, M., Mize, K., & Waldschmidt, E. D. (2009). Integrating macro- and micro-level issues in ESOL/bilingual teacher education. In S. L. Groenke & J. A. Hatch (Eds.), *Critical pedagogy and teacher education in the neoliberal era: Small openings* (pp. 113–125). Dordrecht, Germany: Springer.

Darder, A., Torres, R., & Baltodano, M. (2002). Introduction. In A. Darder, R. Torres, & M. Baltodano (Eds.), *The critical pedagogy reader* (pp. 1–21). New York, NY: RoutledgeFalmer.

Diez, M. E. (2007). The role of coaching in working with dispositions. In M. E. Diez & J. Raths (Eds.), *Dispositions in teacher education* (pp. 203–218). Charlotte, NC: Information Age.

Dottin, E. S. (2009). Professional judgment and dispositions in teacher education. *Teaching and Teacher Education, 25*, 83–88.

Eberly, J. L., Rand, M. K., & O'Connor, T. (2007). Analyzing teachers' dispositions towards diversity: Using adult development theory. *Multicultural Education, 14*(4), 31–36.

Eisner, E. W. (1985). *The educational imagination: On the design and evaluation of school programs* (2nd ed.). New York, NY: Macmillan.

Eisner, E. W. (2002). *The educational imagination: On the design and evaluation of school programs* (3rd ed.). Upper Saddle River, NJ: Prentice Hall.

Evans, R. W. (2008). The (unfulfilled) promise of critical pedagogy. *Journal of Social Studies Research, 32*(2), 16–25.

Fragnoli, K. (2005). Historical inquiry in a methods classroom: Examining our beliefs and shedding our old ways. *The Social Studies, 96*(6), 247–251.

Freire, P. (1973). *Education for critical consciousness.* New York, NY: Seabury.

Freire, P. (1985). *The politics of education: Culture, power, and liberation.* New York, NY: Bergin & Garvey.

Freire, P. (1993). *Pedagogy of the oppressed.* New York, NY: Continuum.

Freire, P. (Ed.). (1997). *Mentoring the mentor: A critical dialogue with Paulo Freire.* New York, NY: Peter Lang.

Freire, P. (1998). *Pedagogy of freedom: Ethics, democracy, and civic courage.* Lanham, MD: Rowman & Littlefield.

Freire, P. (2004). *Pedagogy of indignation.* Boulder, CO: Paradigm.

Freire, P., & Macedo, D. (1987). *Literacy: Reading the word and the world.* South Hadley, MA: Bergin & Garvey.

Garcia, E. E. (1991). Effective instruction for language minority students: The teacher. *Journal of Education, 173*(2), 130–141.

Guajardo, M. A., & Guajardo, F. J. (2004). The impact of *Brown* on the Brown of south Texas: A micropolitical perspective on the education of Mexican Americans in a south Texas community. *American Educational Research Journal, 41*(3), 501–526.

Harmon, D. A., & Jones, T. S. (2005). *Elementary education: A reference handbook.* Santa Barbara, CA: ABC-CLIO.

Hidalgo, N. (1993). Multicultural teacher introspection. In T. Perry & J. Fraser (Eds.). *Freedom's plow: Teaching in the multicultural classroom* (pp. 99–106). New York: Routledge.

Knight, T., & Pearl, A. (2000). Democratic education and critical pedagogy. *The Urban Review, 32*(3), 197–226.

Major, E. M., & Brock, C. H. (2003). Fostering positive dispositions toward diversity: Dialogical explorations of a moral dilemma. *Teacher Education Quarterly, 30*(4), 7–26.

McDonough, T. (2008). The course of "culture" in multiculturalism. *Educational Theory, 58*(3), 321–342.

Menand, L. (2001). *The metaphysical club: A story of ideas in America.* New York, NY: Farrar, Straus & Giroux.

Moll, L. C. (1988). Some key issues in teaching Latino students. *Language Arts, 65*(5), 465–472.

Moll, L. C. (1992). Bilingual classroom studies and community analysis. *Educational Researcher, 21*(2), 20–24.

Murillo, L. A. (2010). Local literacies as counter-hegemonic practices: Deconstructing anti-Spanish ideologies in the Rio Grande Valley. In R. T. Jimenez, V. J. Risko, M. K. Hundley, & D. W. Rowe (Eds.), *59th Yearbook of the National Reading Conference* (pp. 276–287). Oak Creek, WI: National Reading Conference, Inc.

Murray, F. B. (2007). Disposition: A superfluous construct in teacher education. *Journal of Teacher Education, 58*(5), 381–387.

Neumann, J. W. (2011). Critical pedagogy and faith. *Educational Theory, 61*(5), 601–619.

Neumann, J. W. (2012, October). *Middle school social studies teachers' experiences with a new state-mandated accountability exam.* Paper presented at the meeting of the American Association for Teaching & Curriculum, San Antonio, TX.

Neumann, J. W., & Meadows, B. (2011). Problematizing notions of decontextualized "best practice." *Curriculum and Teaching Dialogue, 13*(1&2), 93–107.

Olmedo, I. M. (2009). Blending borders of language and culture: Schooling in La Villita. *Journal of Latinos and Education, 8*(1), 22–37.

Ovando, C. J., & Combs, M. C. (2006). *Bilingual and ESL classrooms: Teaching in multilingual contexts* (5th ed.). New York, NY: McGraw-Hill.

Pérez, B., & Torres-Guzmán, M. E. (2002). *Learning in two worlds: An integrated Spanish/English biliteracy approach* (3rd ed.). Boston, MA: Allyn & Bacon.

Richardson, V. (2003). Preservice teachers' beliefs. In J. Raths & A. C. McAninch (Eds.), *Teacher beliefs and classroom performance: The impact of teacher education* (pp. 1–22). Greenwich, CT: Information Age.

Schussler, D. L., Stooksberry, L. M., & Bercaw, L. A. (2010). Understanding teacher candidate dispositions: Reflecting to build self-awareness. *Journal of Teacher Education, 61*(4), 350–363.

Schwartz, M., Mor-Sommerfeld, A., & Leikin, M. (2010). Facing bilingual education: Kindergarten teachers' attitudes, strategies and challenges. *Language Awareness, 19*(3), 187–203.

Seltzer-Kelly, D. (2009). Adventures in critical pedagogy: A lesson in U.S. history. *Teacher Education Quarterly, 36*(1), 149–162.

Sockett, H. (2008). The moral and epistemic purposes of teacher education. In M. Cochran-Smith, S. Feiman-Nemser, D. J. McIntyre, & K. E. Demers (Eds.), *Handbook of research on teacher education* (3rd ed., pp. 45–65). New York, NY: Routledge.

Texas Education Agency. (2011). Chapter 113, Texas Essential Knowledge and Skills for social studies, subchapter A, elementary. Retrieved October 28, 2012, from http://ritter.tea.state.tx.us/rules/tac/chapter113/ch113a.html

Trueba, H. T. (1989). *Raising silent voices: Educating the linguistic minorities for the 21st century.* Boston, MA: Heinle & Heinle.

U.S. Census. (2011). State & county quickfacts—Hidalgo County, TX. Retrieved on October 24, 2012, from http://quickfacts.census.gov/qfd/states/48/48215.html

Villegas, A. M. (2007). Dispositions in teacher education: A look at social justice. *Journal of Teacher Education, 58*(5), 370–380.

Wardekker, W. L., & Miedema, S. (1997). Critical pedagogy: An evaluation and a direction for reformulation. *Curriculum Inquiry, 27*(1), 45–61.

Wink, J., & Almanzo, M. (1995). Critical pedagogy: A lens through which we see. In J. Frederickson (Ed.), *Reclaiming our voices: Bilingual education, critical pedagogy, & praxis* (pp. 210–223). Los Angeles, CA: California Association for Bilingual Education.

Wolk, S. (2008). School as inquiry. *Phi Delta Kappan, 90*(2), 115–122.

CHAPTER TWENTY-EIGHT

A Contribution to Perspectives on Educational Partnerships for Social Justice

JO WILLIAMS

This chapter explores the possibilities for educational partnerships for social justice and change. It attempts to develop a critique of the dominant conception of "partnerships" and "engagement" as an extension of neoliberal policy. Some initial thoughts toward the development of a Freirean perspective for partnerships are then offered, posing solidarity, struggle, and hope as the key alternative bases upon which collaboration in education might occur, and suggesting that public good rather than the market should provide the compass for educational objectives and strategies. In problematising educational partnerships, the chapter attempts to raise a number of questions and challenges for those wishing to consider how collaboration through education might contribute to breaking this neoliberal consensus and elaborating subversive alternatives in and through education.

INTRODUCTION

What excellence is this, that manages to "coexist with more than a billion inhabitants of the developing world who live in poverty," not to say misery? Not to mention the all but indifference with which it coexists with "pockets of poverty" and misery in its own, developed body. What excellence is this, that sleeps in peace while numberless men and women make their home in the street, and says it is their own fault that they are on the street? What excellence is this, that struggles so little, if it struggles at all, with discrimination for reason of sex, class, or race, as if to reject someone different, humiliate her, offend him, hold her in contempt, exploit her.... What excellence is this, that tepidly registers the millions of children who come into the world and do not remain, or not for long, or if they are more resistant, manage to stay a while, then take their leave of the world? (Freire, 1994, p. 94, as cited in McLaren, 2000, p. 191)

As a teacher, now teacher-educator, and of course as a human being, I am fundamentally concerned with the question of what we might do, in and through education, to advance the struggle for a more socially just world. The everyday horrors of "living normal," poor and marginalised, as more than 5 billion people across the globe do, might not always register in our teaching but it should. This is particularly so when in many cases those suffering the brunt of these social crimes are children. As noted by the Uruguayan poet Eduardo Galeano, very few of them are immune.

Day after day, children are denied the right to be children. The world treats rich kids as if they were money, teaching them to act the way money acts. The world treats poor kids as if they were garbage, to turn them into garbage. And those in the middle, neither rich nor poor, are chained to televisions and trained to live the life of prisoners. The few children who manage to be children must have a lot of magic and a lot of luck (Galeano, 2000, p. 11).

Talking about education for the 3 billion people who currently subsist on less than $3 a day, in a world where prices and expectations are increasingly internationalised, seems like an exercise in cruelty or cynicism. Indeed, it is naïve to consider educational innovation as a socially reforming tool in the context of a global socioeconomic order where the wealthiest few thousand do better than the billions of poor. But this is not just a problem for those in the misnamed "developing world." The limited possibilities of social mobility are not just restricted to Third World economies. According to Hertz, in the United States "children from low-income families have only a 1 per cent chance of reaching the top 5 per cent of the income distribution, versus children of the rich who have about a 22 per cent chance" (2006, p. i). Despite some persistent and optimistic notions that it is otherwise, Australia is not immune to what is a global trend of increasing wealth for the rich at the expense of the poor. One of a handful of privileged, wealthy nations globally, the "lucky country" has high levels of inequality in terms of all major social and economic indicators compared with other OECD countries (Australian Social Inclusion Board, 2012; Wilkinson & Pickett, 2010). Another report documents the disproportionate burden of increasing inequality and hardship on young people (Commonwealth Bank of Australia, 2010). Reports on national and international tests aimed at benchmarking both quality and equity in education continue to suggest that although fairing comparatively well in terms of "quality," Australia performs poorly in terms of equity, with patterns of disadvantage connecting low socioeconomic status, geography, indigeneity, and refugee status to poorer outcomes continuing and in some cases worsening over recent years (Nous Group & Melbourne Graduate School of Education, 2011; Thomson, Bortoli, Nicholas, Hillman, & Buckley, 2011).

Liberal society has, by and large, considered education a fundamental lever for progress, justice, and social change. Liberal policy in the 1930s, as well as post-war, exemplified this approach, with capitalist expansion and growth providing the basis for liberal policy couched in terms of welfare, equity, and opportunity, most famously espoused in Franklin D. Roosevelt's "Four Freedoms" address.

> There is nothing mysterious about the foundations of a healthy and strong democracy. The basic things expected by our people of their political and economic systems are simple. They are: Equality of opportunity for youth and for others; Jobs for those who can work; Security for those who need it; The ending of special privilege for the few; The preservation of civil liberties for all.[1]

However, the era of progressive or social liberalism (social-democracy) is certainly a relic of the past (Harvey, 2007; Wallerstein, 1995). In terms of substantive policy, neoliberalism has no room for any considerations that do not square with the bottom line. Education is now treated just like home equity, a commodity for sale on a market that benefits some much more than others, inevitably involving winners and losers (Down, 2009).

Giving lip service to equity and justice in education, the "New Paternalism" (MacGregor, 1999) has in fact substituted "aspiration" for "achievement," highlighting the fact that neoliberalism has failed to provide enrichment or even betterment for most. Instead, the emphasis has been shifted to the responsibility of individuals, where "the main stress is on getting the poor and those receiving public services to change their behavior and act more responsibly. The basically liberal idea that the better-off might have obligations to the poor, that the healthy might have obligations to the sick, and that the lucky should aid the unlucky" (p. 108) has been abandoned.

Since the Global Financial Crisis of 2008, there has been an opening for a renewed critique of neoliberal policy. To date, the policy vacuum has been mainly filled by the re-invention of social-democracy, where the exponents of Third Way politics use the language of liberal left discourse not to revive welfarism, but to take the opportunity to extend the reach of neoliberal individualism to every last corner of social organisation, even where previously "public good" may have prevailed (Cammack, 2007). It is through the use of this language of cooperation, reciprocity, and mutual benefit that neoliberalism has driven the development of educational partnerships and informed the concept of *engagement* in education. In this respect, the concepts of partnership and engagement in education policy tend to become code for marketisation and commercialisation in one of the last remaining (partial) "public utilities" of global capitalism.

It is argued here that the partnerships agenda is best considered part of the web of the "New Paternalism," a means by which to expand educational marketisation and commercialisation and to promote an aspirational culture; utilitarianism pretending to stamp its mark on "the end of history." Developing this analysis is especially pertinent at a time of neoliberal crisis, seeking to counter the false alternatives promoted by besieged neoliberal policy makers and given the urgent need for subversive frameworks. In addition, a critique of the hegemonic partnerships discourse may contribute to theorising social change education on the basis of a collective (community-partnership) practice that includes the classroom but is not limited to it. The general question underpinning the development of such a strategic commitment is, *What are the possibilities and challenges for educational collaboration for radical social justice in this climate of neoliberal hegemony in education policy?* Here Michael Apple's arguments are pertinent, when he states that

> in engaging in such critical analyses, it also must point to contradictions and to spaces of possible action. Thus, its aim is to critically examine current realities with a conceptual/political framework that emphasizes the spaces in which more progressive and counter-hegemonic actions can, or do, go on. This is an absolutely crucial step, since otherwise our research can simply lead to cynicism or despair. (Apple, 2010, p. 15)

The aim is to go beyond an academic critique of education partnerships and explore the possibilities of actual counter-hegemonic practices in the framework of engagement and partnership.

No alternative approach to engagement and partnerships could avoid a foundational discussion of the meanings and purpose of education and its place in the system of schooling under capitalism. The formal education system is fundamentally a hegemonic practice of capitalism aimed at the reproduction of labour and schooling in the dominant ideology (Freire, 1970/1996; Greaves, Hill, & Maisuria, 2007; Hill, 2001; Ponce, 1993). However, as with all capitalist structures, schooling engenders dialectically opposed forces from within itself. The very processes of learning and the relationships it presupposes, however restricted, give rise to counter-hegemonic forces, actions, and possibilities. Foreshadowing the following discussion is an ongoing question for all radical educators: *How might these contradictions form the basis for alternative perspectives and practices for education partnerships?*

This chapter attempts to contribute to the development of a theoretical understanding of the partnerships agenda in education as shaped by neoliberalism and as challenged by the growing crisis of the same. Moreover, as part of a larger PhD study, this chapter presents an initial attempt at drawing on a Freirean understanding of learning and education as a liberatory praxis to consider alternative possibilities in educational partnerships and engagement for social justice. With the intention of stimulating further discussion, an argument is made for the need to develop open but coherent frameworks based on solidarity, struggle, and hope, where public good rather than the market provides the compass for educational objectives and strategies, including partnerships.

PARTNERSHIPS AS A THIRD WAY NEOLIBERAL AGENDA

Internationally, the restructuring of schools and universities has been driven by the imperatives of neoliberalism, to ensure students are prepared "as enterprising workers and citizens with the prerequisite skills, knowledge and values to survive in a volatile and competitive global labour market" (Down, 2007, p. 51). For education, neoliberalism has involved increased privatisation and load shifting, mandated standards and outcomes, individualism and merciless competitiveness leading to winners and losers in the knowledge marketplace. The impacts of neoliberalism on equity and justice have been well documented, with Connell (2002) describing the effect in the Australian context as being one of a steady decline of interest in "equity" issues in education, accompanied by an erosion of the "idea of education as a common good" (p. 324).

Neoliberalism propagated the view of the minimalist state but in fact rested on policies aimed at strengthening the state, in terms of its role in the business of the market, while eroding the state's role in supporting the "public" (Harvey, 2007). The crisis of neoliberalism has brought to the attention of governing elites the importance of renewing the state's intervention in "the public" for the sake of political stability. This is not (except on occasion rhetorically) a return to Keynesianism, but rather about extending the strong arm of the state. Enter Third Way politics.

As profit rates diminished following the post-war boom, capital launched a three-decade attack on wages and living conditions, in the process hollowing out education as a ladder for social advancement (Harvey, 2007). At present, in the context of the growing economic and even political crisis of neoliberalism, with its increasing inability to provide wealth creation for the "middle classes" (Duménil & Lévy, 2011), centre and centre-left governments have responded by attempting to humanise the face of neoliberalism (replacing "trickle-down" with "hand-up") without altering any of the fundamentals of free market policy.

Before neoliberalism came along, education policy was driven by the welfare approach of post-war-boom capitalism. This was premised on the possibility and desirability of full employment in an exceptional period of global growth in production, where expanding the number of skilled workers was a necessity (Mandel, 1978). Welfarism, as a policy approach, was also based on a different balance of power between market, state, and civil society. The labour movements that grew through and out of the Depression and sustained a social democratic ascendency in the industrialised countries, provided a counter-balance to the power of the corporate sector and the basis for universalism and redistributive policies. As Coolsaet describes,

> The social democratic project offered more than just the defense of the weakest, however. By offering the outcasts of the time the prospect of an equal place in bourgeois society, and an improvement of their lot for present and future generations, it lent its own interpretation to the nineteenth-century idea of progress, inspired by its basic values of equality and solidarity. To realize such a project, power was required. The strategy for acquiring power came down to mobilization of the majority against the prosperous minority and subsequently the deployment of the state. That succeeded in many European countries. (Coolsaet, 2009, p. 108)

Neoliberalism not only reversed all these policies in practice but also promoted an ideological case for it—especially on the back of the so-called end of history, aimed at discrediting any alternatives. Much of what now transpires under the rubric of Third Way politics represents not a return to welfarism, but rather a new language for couching neoliberal policies, a language of "inclusion" necessary now that "history has kicked back in." The actual content of Third Way politics is firmly at odds with redistributive politics, preferring instead a new paternalism (MacGregor, 1999).

Over the past few decades, under a generalised call to reassert the "civic mission" of higher education institutions in developed countries (e.g., Benson, Harkavy, & Puckett, 2000; Brown & Muirhead, 2001; Fernández, Delpiano, & De Ferari, 2006; World Conference on Higher Education, 2009), a plethora of *partnerships* and *engagement activity* purportedly aimed at ameliorating the worst effects of the inequities of an increasingly marketised education system has been rolled out. Decades of activity concerning *educational access and success*, with both schools and universities being urged to *partner* and *engage* to make a difference to young people's lives and to strengthen communities (Australian Universities Community Engagement Alliance, 2008; Department of Early Childhood and Early Development, n.d.), has involved no shortage of energy and passion from well-meaning and progressive educators, invested in the name of education for social progress.

As elsewhere, in Australia, the partnership discourse in education has largely become a form for extending neoliberal ideology, targeting "losers" through so-called social inclusion initiatives, where they get a second chance to step up to the same competition, maybe having changed their "problematic attitudes" or "lack of aspirations." The policy rhetoric is about inclusion but the focus on the individual betrays the gutting of any substantive discourse of equity and progress. Instead, as Hursh (2007) notes, "For neoliberals, those who do not succeed are held to have made bad choices. Personal responsibility means nothing is society's fault. People have only themselves to blame" (p. 497). Moreover, in education, "neoliberal discourses often reduce notions of social justice to access to markets, ignoring differences in access to monetary, legal and social resources. Such an approach also eliminates the need to discuss different conceptions of social justice or the purpose of society, asserting that economic and technical responses to political questions are sufficient" (Hursh & Henderson, 2011, pp. 176–177).

This can be seen as consistent with the language of the university-community engagement agenda in Australia, as Holland notes:

> The need to direct the intellectual assets of all tertiary institutions toward the amelioration of major public challenges and opportunities offers a way to renew the role of higher education as a force for nation building and improving quality of life. Perhaps of even greater significance is the powerful role of intellectual capital in the development and success of all sectors of the world economy. Innovation is now the key to controlling world markets. *Engagement represents an adaptive response of universities to these new realities.* (Holland, 2005, p. 16, my emphasis)

Winter, Wiseman, and Muirhead (2006) note that neoliberal policy results in an emphasis on increasing private revenue and input into local issues and problem-solving in an increasingly corporatised university context and in the face of decreased public spending. They argue that "...the deepening Commonwealth Government focus on competitiveness, commercialization and funding cutbacks as the key drivers of higher education policy" (Winter, Wiseman, & Muirhead, 2005, p. 3) constitute a significant risk to achieving meaningful community outcomes through partnerships.

Fisher, Fabricant, and Simmons (2004, p. 31) argue that decreased public spending and pressure to find alternative sources of revenue leave universities with little choice but to raise fees income (one example is community engagement as a narrowly perceived recruiting exercise), or increase privatisation and corporate sponsorship. In discussing a definition of community engagement for universities, Sunderland, Muirhead, Parsons, and Holtom suggest that

> ...as both method and methodology, community engagement can be seen to be heavily consistent with certain social and economic policy trajectories such as increasing focus on community-government-industry "partnerships"; economic rationalism or neo-liberal economics; the downsizing of public institutions and funding in favour of increasing industry and community funding sources; the move toward community based (as opposed to state based) "grass roots" service delivery and community renewal; and the assumption that knowledge and learning must always be "applied" or "commercialised" if they are to be of "value." (2004, p. 5)

Using a critical discourse analysis, Peacock (2012, p. 311) considers the language of an Australian Universities Community Engagement Alliance (2008) discussion paper, and suggests an "uneasy synthesis of neoliberal, social inclusion and civic engagement discourses into a hybrid [university community engagement] discourse [which] semantically privileges neoliberal forms of engagement."

HEGEMONY OF IDEOLOGY

In an article discussing the rise and legitimation of "post-welfare learning policy" and New Labor in the UK, Mulderrig (2003) suggests that this process

> partly involves changing people's behaviour and values in order to create a new self-reliant, risk-prepared, enterprise culture. Government discourse becomes a central tool in legitimising and enacting this transition; in a supply-side economic system, where the government no longer makes guarantees of financial support, 'welfare' must be cast in a negative evaluative frame, where receiving it becomes 'dependency' and removing the need for it becomes 'empowerment'. Social services themselves moreover, are reorganised (or 'modernised') according to market models, in which internal competition is used to improve standards of delivery for users of that service who are recast as its 'consumers'. (para. 5)

This is all brought together as both compass and marketing strategy for Third Way politics, replacing any old social-democratic and liberal philosophical notions of justice and equity. Third Way policies in education have retained the key policy handle of neoliberalism in education, privatisation, and marketisation, and have added a complex of *regulatory* policies aimed at "including" those majorities who will not succeed. Such policies include an array of programs and initiatives that punish non-compliants—by way of social security benefits, managerialism in schools and general social *intrusion* (Agostinone-Wilson, 2006).

In his critique of Giddens's Third Way, Cammack (2007) notes how the very concept of social justice is redefined on the basis of capitalist logic, rather than being seen as fundamentally antagonistic to it. And as a result, Giddens is

> committed to the transformation not only of ideas of social justice but of all our ideas of society and of ourselves. The uncompromising logic at the core is that everything should be bent to the goal of making capitalism work. For this to happen, a commitment to competitiveness has to be part of the general disposition of every citizen. (Cammack, 2007, p. 20)

While the discourse surrounding university-school-community engagement has emerged out of and is immersed in a neoliberal reform paradigm, as elaborated above, this occurs in a contested environment. Not everyone is a "committed competitive being," and many educators resist this logic intuitively. Nor has neoliberalisation entirely done away with the liberal attitudes and ideas left over from past experiences. The influences of more communitarian ideas and experiences dating back to the radical critiques and practices that characterised educational experimentation in the late 1960s and early 1970s are also present. Such ideas and practices, however, are marginalised and are often co-opted by the neoliberal ideas that posit notions of social capital as substitutes for public funding, and glorify a culture of entrepreneurship disguised as initiative as opposed to a culture of resistance and community rebellion against the status quo.

In the current context, the proclaimed objectives of inclusion, that entice educators to take on partnership activity, can easily become a trap, creating frustration and building disillusion. As Freire (1970/1996) himself explains, words that cannot realise constructive, meaningful action—where educational actors are "deprived of their dimension of action" (p. 68)—are reduced to a benign *verbalism*.

> Human existence cannot be silent, nor can it be nourished by false words, but only by true words, with which men and women transform the world. To exist, humanly, is to name the world, to change it. Once named, the world in its turn reappears to the namers as a problem and requires of them a new naming. Human beings are not built in silence, but in word, in work, in action-reflection. (1970/1996, p. 69)

Instead of proving a way out, the dominant partnerships discourse offers, as Louw (2001, p. 97) argues, a "'false' reconciliation of social contradictions, that is, reconciliations serving the interests of the hegemonically dominant." This is counter-posed to an educational process understood not as a mechanism by which people are coerced into adapting to the existing learning environment, but as a total process of self-empowerment and education as advocated by Freire. A Freirean perspective explains how authentic social inclusion is only possible as and through a struggle against those sociopolitical structures that restrict participation in the whole human enterprise and atomise society, in a word, capitalism.

In this respect, it is important to recapture the fundamentally political content of Freire's pedagogy as foundation for avoiding "false solutions" in engagement and partnerships. It is this revolutionary aspect of Freire's work that has long been under-emphasised or removed altogether by many progressive educational theorists who claim to be influenced by his work. On this, McLaren is explicit when discussing the removal of the political content and analysis inherent in Freire's writings.

> The figure of Paulo Freire has been domesticated by liberals, progressives, and pseudo-Freireans who have tried incessantly to claim his legacy and teachings.... Hence it is necessary to re-possess Freire from those contemporary revisionists who would reduce him to the grand seigneur of classroom dialogue and would antiseptically excise the corporeal force of history from his pedagogical practices, (McLaren, 2000, p. xxii)

Such revisionists wish to

> limit [Freire's] legacy to its contribution to consciousness-raising...[and are] often victims of a subjectivism that occurs when people verbally denounce social injustice but leave intact the existing structures of society.... [Freire was] unwavering in [his] view that education and cultural processes aimed at liberation do not succeed by freeing people from their chains, but by preparing them collectively to free themselves. (McLaren, 2000, pp. 192–193)

Such a distorted use of Freire's work has the opposite effect, as it is used to "... camouflage existing capitalist social relations under a plethora of eirenic proclamations and classroom strategies. Real socialist alternatives are nowhere to be found ..." (McLaren, 2000, p. xxv).

Giroux also reflects on this:

> What has been lost in this analysis is Freire's legacy of revolutionary politics. For Freire, *problem solving education* suggests not a methodology but a social theory whose aim is the liberation of individuals and groups as historical subjects through a critical educational process that involves making the pedagogical more political and the political more pedagogical. (2000, p. 148, original emphasis)

Neoliberalism turns partnership and engagement policies into a dead end, and worse still a trap for well-meaning, liberal-minded educators. Goals in educational policy have to be set *apart from and against* market priorities; established *above* these market priorities to subvert them. Any authentic community engagement in education needs to break from the market-centered approach and provide other visions and concepts that could subvert the neoliberal intentions and objectives and produce a counter-hegemonic practice. Here Freire's (1970/1996) insistence on education as a partnership for fundamental social change can form the basis for an alternative and essentially anti-capitalist approach.

FREIREAN "PARTNERSHIPS"—SOLIDARITY, STRUGGLE— AS ALTERNATIVE

Freire, in problematising educational activity, argues for a process fundamentally rooted in the existential realisation of oppression (conscientisation) as the starting point for humanistic social practice. Any "engagement" not based on this is "false" and misleading.

In its desire to create an ideal model of the "good man," a naïvely conceived humanism often overlooks the concrete, existential, present situation of real people. Authentic humanism, in Pierre Furter's words, "consists in permitting the emergence of the awareness of our full humanity, as a condition and as an obligation, as a situation and as a project" (Furter, 1966, as cited in Freire, 1970/1996, pp. 74–75).

Without naming and subverting oppression and exploitation, and making this the guiding content, community engagement becomes deception.

In considering Freire's contribution to critical pedagogy, McLaren (2000) states that

> Freire believed that the challenge of transforming schools should be directed at overcoming socioeconomic injustice linked to the political and economic structures of society. Thus, any attempt at school reform that claims to be inspired by Freire but that is only concerned with social patterns of representation, interpretation, or communication, and that does not connect these patterns to redistributive measures and structures that reinforce such patterns, exempts itself from the most important insights of Freire's work. (p. 163)

Fiercely critical of neoliberalism, in particular its ideological hegemony, Mc-Laren (2000) stresses that "Freire perceived a major ideological tension to be situated in the ability of people to retain a concept of the political beyond a reified consumer identity constructed from the panoply of market logics and their demotic discourses" (p. 152).

The New Paternalism seeks to saturate engagement initiatives with the ideology of individualistic "aspiration" but cannot successfully drown all learning and community partnering in such, fundamentally because the aspirations mostly have nowhere to go. This creates the critical space for intervention and a counter-ideology based on the Freirean idea of identifying oppression and encouraging a critical consciousness. This "constitutes a shift in the form of agency" (McLaren, 2000, p. 157) and

> faced with the internalisation of hegemonic rules and regulations that cleaves the individual subject, Freire's method involves the ejection of the introjected subject positions of dominant groups. Such a move reactivates an examination of the dominant society and constitutes a shift in the form of agency, a movement from the social to the political. (p. 157)

This first stage—the radicalisation of the individual subject—engenders the opportunity and need for collective action: the moment of engagement. The actuality of engagement then turns to the possible, what each community can bring—large or small—into the struggle for social change. Subversion of the capitalist hegemony becomes the compass for engagement and collective solidarity, and hope the spirit that fuels every action and conversation.

Freire argued that

> the starting point for organizing the program content of education or political action must be the present, existential, concrete situation, reflecting the aspirations of the people. Utilizing certain basic contradictions, we must pose this existential, concrete, present situation

to the people as a problem which challenges them and requires a response—not just at the intellectual level, but at the level of action. (1970/1996, p. 77)

For Freire, educational engagement is fundamentally about, or marked by, the notion of solidarity. In *Pedagogy of the Oppressed*, he emphasised dialogue and solidarity as the basis for cooperation for change (1970/1996, chap. 4). Antonia Darder (2011) discusses Freire's vision for democratic, participatory alliances, where "... progressive teachers can participate in counterhegemonic political projects that do not dichotomize their work as cultural workers and social activists" (pp. 155–156) and "where a solidarity of differences is cultivated, [where] teachers from diverse communities and class positions can work together to create unifying, albeit heterogeneous and multifaceted, anti-capitalist political strategies to counter conservative efforts to destroy public schooling" (p. 156).

Of course this is not to deny the difficulties of such Freirean practice, especially in the context of relative mass political passivity—the most radical educators often forced back into the classroom as a haven for discussion, further separating them from community. At a time when governments are attempting to harness community support against educators and push through further neoliberal reforms, often couched in terms of "engagement" and on the basis of making schools more transparent to "the community," precisely the opposite is required.

FINAL THOUGHTS

With neoliberalism still dominant, success will continue to follow the rich kids and failure the poor ones. For those in between, the idea of learning to understand is increasingly replaced with the language of performance. Teachers too will be increasingly divided between those who hit targets and those who fail to. The idea of teachers who inspire inquiry and constructive rebellion will be left to another era.

A Freirean social praxis offers an alternative vision, but also strategic and tactical signposts to guide counter-hegemonic activity in such a context. Fundamentally, such an approach is rooted in a profound humility and commitment to the liberation of not just a few mismatched kids who improve their test scores or up their attendance rates, but the masses of young people and their families who are every day relegated to a world void of agency and increasingly void of hope. As McLaren so beautifully puts it,

> Freirean educators do not conceive of their work as an antidote to today's sociocultural ills and the declining level of ambition with respect to contemporary society's commitment to democracy. Rather, their efforts are patiently directed at creating counterhegemonic sites of political struggle, radically alternative epistemological frameworks, and adversarial

interpretations and cultural practices, as well as advocacy domains for disenfranchised groups. (2000, pp. 174–175)

This needs to become a much more concerted area of work for educators. A "joined-up emancipatory education-activism" is surely possible and certainly necessary.

NOTE

1. Roosevelt's speech can be found here: http://www.ourdocuments.gov/doc.php?flash= true&doc=70.

REFERENCES

Agostinone-Wilson, F. (2006). Downsized discourse: Classroom management, neoliberalism, and the shaping of correct workplace attitude. *Journal for Critical Education Policy Studies, 4*(2).

Apple, M. (2010). Global crises, social justice, and education. In M. Apple (Ed.), *Global crises, social justice, and education*. New York, NY: Routledge.

Australian Social Inclusion Board. (2012). *Social inclusion in Australia. How Australia is faring* (2nd ed.). Canberra, Australia: Commonwealth of Australia.

Australian Universities Community Engagement Alliance. (2008). *Position paper 2008–2010. Universities and community engagement*. Retrieved from http://aucea.com.au/wp-content/uploads/2010/06/universities_CE_2008_2010.pdf

Benson, L., Harkavy, I., & Puckett, J. (2000). An implementation revolution as a strategy for fulfilling the democratic promise of university-community partnerships: Penn-West Philadelphia as an experiment in progress. *Nonprofit and Voluntary Sector Quarterly, 29*(1), 24–45.

Brown, L., & Muirhead, B. (2001). The civic mission of Australian universities. Retrieved from http://espace.library.uq.edu.au/eserv/UQ:10360/csrc_munis01.pdf

Cammack, P. (2007). Competitiveness, social justice, and the third way. *Papers in the Politics of Global Competitiveness, Institute for Global Studies, Manchester Metropolitan University, 6*. Retrieved from e-space.openrepository.com/e-space/bitstream/2173/.../giddens.pdf

Commonwealth Bank of Australia. (2010). *Viewpoint. Economic vitality report March 2010*. Retrieved from http://www.commbank.com.au/viewpoint

Connell, R. W. (2002). Making the difference, then and now. *Discourse: Studies in the Cultural Politics of Education, 23*(3), 319–327.

Coolsaet, R. (2009). The social democratic malaise and world politics. *International Politics and Society, 2009*(1), 107–125. Retrieved from http://www.fes.de/ipg/sets_e/arc_e.htm

Darder, A. (2011). *A dissident voice. Essays on culture, pedagogy, and power*. New York, NY: Peter Lang.

Department of Early Childhood and Early Development. (n.d.). Education partnership resource. Evidence of the need for education partnerships. Retrieved from http://www.eduweb.vic.gov.au/edulibrary/public/partnerships/eduprtnrshpresource/evidenceandbenefits.pdf

Down, B. (2007). *Beyond the corporate university: Towards democracy, public spaces and a transformative pedagogy.* Paper presented at the Australian Association for Research in Education (AARE) annual conference, Fremantle, Australia.

Down, B. (2009). Schooling, productivity and the enterprising self: Beyond market values. *Critical Studies in Education, 50*(1), 51–64.

Duménil, G., & Lévy, D. (2011). *The crisis of neoliberalism.* Cambridge, MA: Harvard University Press.

Fernández, C., Delpiano, C., & De Ferari, J. M. (Eds.). (2006). *Responsabilidad social universitaria. Una manera de ser universidad: Teoría y práctica en la experiencia chilena.* Santiago de Chile: Proyecto Universidad: Construye País.

Fisher, R., Fabricant, M., & Simmons, L. (2004). Understanding contemporary university-community connections: Context, practice, and challenges. *Journal of Community Practice, 12*(3/4), 13–34.

Freire, P. (1970/1996). *Pedagogy of the oppressed.* London, England: Penguin.

Galeano, E. (2000). *Upside down: A primer for a looking-glass world.* New York, NY: Metropolitan Books.

Giroux, H. (2000). *Stealing innocence. Corporate culture's war on children.* New York, NY: Palgrave.

Greaves, N. M., Hill, D., & Maisuria, A. (2007). Embourgeoisment, immiseration, commodification—Marxism revisited: A critique of education in capitalist systems. *Journal for Critical Education Policy Studies, 5*(1).

Harvey, D. (2007). *A brief history of neoliberalism.* New York, NY: Oxford University Press.

Hertz, T. (2006). Understanding mobility in America. Retrieved from http://www.americanprogress. org/wp-content/uploads/issues/2006/04/Hertz_MobilityAnalysis.pdf

Hill, D. (2001). Global capital, neo-liberalism, and privatisation: The growth of educational inequality. In D. Hill & M. Cole (Eds.), *Schooling and equality: Fact, concept and policy.* London, England: Kogan Page.

Holland, B. (2005). *Scholarship and mission in the 21st century university: The role of engagement.* Paper presented at the Australian Universities Quality Forum 2005: Engaging Communities, Sydney, Australia.

Hursh, D. (2007). Assessing No Child Left Behind and the rise of neoliberal education policies. *American Educational Research Journal, 44*(3), 493–518.

Hursh, D. W., & Henderson, J. A. (2011). Contesting global neoliberalism and creating alternative futures. *Discourse: Studies in the Cultural Politics of Education, 32*(2), 171–185.

Louw, E. (2001). *The media and cultural production.* London, England: Sage.

MacGregor, S. (1999). Welfare, neo-liberalism and new paternalism: Three ways for social policy in late capitalist societies. *Capital and Class, 23*(1), 91–118.

Mandel, E. (1978). *Late capitalism.* London, England: Verso.

McLaren, P. (2000). *Che Guevara, Paulo Freire, and the pedagogy of revolution.* Lanham, MD: Rowman & Littlefield.

Mulderrig, J. (2003). Consuming education: A critical discourse analysis of social actors in New Labour's education policy. *Journal for Critical Education Policy Studies, 1*(1).

Nous Group & Melbourne Graduate School of Education. (2011). Schooling challenges and opportunities. A report for the Review of Funding for Schooling Panel. Retrieved from http://www.deewr. gov.au/Schooling/ReviewofFunding/Documents/Nous-SchoolingChallengesandOpportunities. doc

Peacock, D. (2012). Neoliberal social inclusion? The agenda of the Australian Universities Community Engagement Alliance. *Critical Studies in Education, 53*(3), 311–325.

Ponce, A. (1993). *Educación y lucha de clases* [Education and class struggle]. N.p.:Mexico: Editores Unidos.

Sunderland, N., Muirhead, B., Parsons, R., & Holtom, D. (2004). *Foundation paper*. Brisbane, Australia: Australian Consortium on Higher Education, Community Engagement, and Social Responsibility.

Thomson, S., Bortoli, L. D., Nicholas, M., Hillman, K., & Buckley, S. (2011). *Challenges for Australian education: Results from PISA 2009*. Camberwell, Australia: ACER Press, Australian Council for Educational Research Ltd.

Wallerstein, I. (1995). *After liberalism*. New York, NY: New Press.

Wilkinson, R., & Pickett, K. (2010). *The spirit level: Why equality is better for everyone*. London, England: Penguin.

Winter, A., Wiseman, J., & Muirhead, B. (2005). *Beyond rhetoric: University-community engagement in Victoria*. Brisbane, Australia: Eidos.

Winter, A., Wiseman, J., & Muirhead, B. (2006). University-community engagement in Australia: Practice, policy and public good. *Education, Citizenship and Social Justice, 1*(3), 211–230.

World Conference on Higher Education. (2009, July). *Communique*. Paper presented at the World Conference on Higher Education: The New Dynamics of Higher Education and Research for Societal Change and Development, Paris, France.

CHAPTER TWENTY-NINE

Working for the World

M. J. STUART

WORKING FOR THE WORLD

Using Bauman's (1998, p. 92) notion of two types of international travellers, tourist or indigent, I examine the issue of work for all. Politicians use terms for policies such as "Free to Grow," utilising the assumption that freedom is unproblematic. Freedom includes "the form of opportunities for participation in trade and production [which] can help to generate personal abundance as well as public resources for social facilities" (Sen, 1999, p. 11, cited in New Zealand Treasury, 2001, p. 20). As Zygmunt Bauman says, they are freed from the fetters of capital, in an uncertain world like guests in a caravan site (2000, pp. 23–24). For states, such policies have bio-political purposes, such as decreasing educational disadvantage, getting women of childbearing age into the workforce, and ensuring children receive good foundational education prior to school. The usefulness of such policies has been advocated (as cost-effective ways of managing demographic and economic risks) by a number of national and international publications (Minstrom 2011; NZ Treasury, 2001; Organisation for Economic Co-operation and Development [OECD], 2012, p. 33). They are indeed, a part of a global discourse about work, its value and as sites for actuarial investments.

Work has been framed as one security in an unsecure world, where the tourists, offered freedom, can migrate to gain financial benefits for themselves and their families. Parents are free to choose their preferred ECE centre; they are free to take on part- or full-time work. A neoliberal economic world offers "choice" and "freedom" to self-maximising entrepreneurs. The indigents, however, are unwelcomed, deemed risky, stopped at the border (e.g., International Monetary Fund [IMF], 2004, p. 21). It is the vagabonds that the state wishes to tame, to domesticate through their young children. They are set "free" to find their way in a global village. I argue Paulo Freire's concept that "It is not possible to have authority without freedom or vice versa" (1998, p. 99) may open itself to challenge, in a world with too much freedom.

Freire himself abhorred the mechanistic "practice of education...[as] a complex of techniques, naïvely considered to be neutral" (1972, p. 1), seeing it rather as a human act of knowing, of being located in the historical and cultural reality. Any ideas coming from another part of the world cannot be transplanted, he argued, but submitted to cultural scrutiny. However, in a global world, where people are mobile, workers relocate-able and relationships short-term, such scrutiny is increasingly difficult. The children of such workers are being provided with care, while their parents seek fulfillment through work as consumers. Such care is increasingly defined as a "good" supporting the wealth of society, the parents, and the child.

The good is traded in the marketplace, a "private good" that allows the mobile worker to tour the globe, seeking employment wherever her skills can be of service. As care for her preschool child is provided by credentialed carers, international agencies offer policy advice on the best, most efficient ECE practice across the Western world. Best practice advice on child development and curricula is increasingly allied to economic advice. In *Starting Strong 111*, curricula are viewed as ensuring national consistency across services and countries.

> It is important that all stakeholders agree on the contents of the pre-primary curriculum. Governments and parents may share common objectives, such as preparing children for school.... In multicultural societies, governments may want to create a skilled and knowledgeable workforce and prioritise shared values for building a sense of community. (OECD, 2012, p. 84)

Starting Strong111 utilises data demonstrating the cost-benefit value of ECE as an early intervention (e.g., Heckman & Masterov, 2007; Schweinhart, 2006, as cited in OECD, 2012, p. 33). In early educational discourse underpinned by Human Capital Theory (HCT), children are framed as requiring appropriate dispositions (Cunha et al., 2005, as cited in OECD, 2012, p. 33). Investment in ECE, the authors argue, has good outcomes for children (p. 36) as well as long-term benefits for the state (pp. 143–149)

A number of supra-national publications (e.g., OECD, the World Bank, and the International Monetary Fund) see HCT as offering a solution to "changing demographics, globalisation and the rise of the knowledge economy" (Keeley, 2007, p. 11). It is changing demographics presented as the "key" to economic success, and growth in a changing world where jobs move from country to country (Keeley, 2007). There is an assumption that, as education is a private good, "individuals consciously invest in themselves to improve their own, personal economic returns" (Keeley, 2007, p. 28), which, when aggregated, grow national competitive wealth (pp. 30–32). The HCT model assumes that free markets are central to economic growth and returns. Free markets require free trade, freely negotiated employment conditions, freedom from government intervention or tariffs, with freedom to maximise profits. Individuals have been granted "freedom" to succeed or fail on their own efforts; to become consumers where all things are "goods in the market."

Such freedom creates winners and losers, a dichotomy of the successful and the less successful. Many aspire to be winners, but as Bauman said, the world has become a "synoptican-style" society (2000, p. 85), where the many watch the few, while aspiring to be like them. Such aspirations, Bauman continued, are presented as the exercise of free will, where any failure is the responsibility of the individual. He cited Jeremy Seabrook's (2000, p. 88) insight that "the poor do not inhabit a separate culture from the rich. They must live in the same world," a world presented as a "warehouse" where the desire to choose is presented as "bliss." Bauman concluded that such constructs are less about emancipation than they are about a "redistribution of freedoms" (p. 90), which divides rather than unifies humanity. The idea of "progress" that underpins the concept of the modern state concerns the self-confident individual being in control of time, with a trust in the future.

Bauman (2000) cautioned about the cracks in a vision where progress has become de-regulated and privatized: an "individual enterprise" (p. 135). The modern world has assigned a prime value to work, which implied free choice. For those unsuccessful in gaining work, there was blame for "poverty and misery" (p. 137). However, work has undergone a change in the liquid society. It has been stripped of its "eschatological trappings" (p. 139), no longer promising security. There are now people who are free to move, who are constantly on the move, but such mobility has value for only one segment of society, the tourist. Such people thrive on change and uncertainty, seeing both as "opportunities," shorn of their bonds to any community save that of the global village with its short-term rewards. It is the vagabonds that now remain, as locals, who require state discipline and management: in need of a "community," which Bauman posits is the new "gospel" (p. 173), a defence against insecurity.

THE LOSS OF FREIRE'S CONCEPT: FREEDOM AS TECHNOLOGY

Nikolas Rose (1999) offered a critique of the modern concept of freedom, which arose from the specific character of economic relations under capitalism, not as unintended consequences, but as invention. One of these inventors was Friedrich von Hayek, who argued that freedom was supported by the evolution of human institutions. It is, however, Rose concluded, an object of government, a technology of governmentality, allied to and supporting political economy. It was the value of the individual to the governmental discourse that supported the argument of government as antithesis to freedom, the responsibility of each worker to his family, himself, and his work. It involved, Rose, continued, means of "self-education" (p. 73). Rose noted, like Freire and Bauman, that there were different paths for wealthy and poor families. The role of experts (who can specify roles and responsibilities and dictate societal norms, penetrating into the domain of the private) emerged in the eighteenth century. Experts offered counsel and guidance to the families of the poor, advising them on hygiene and prudent living.

It was the counsel of economic advisers, suggesting that education could both aid the individual, her family, and her country's wealth, that is of interest to the discourse of HCT in ECE. Economists from the Chicago School of Economics, Ted Schultz, Gary Becker, and Jacob Mincer, devised new technologies of governmentality. Education of individuals was defined as a private good. Skills that the individual accrued over a lifetime could ensure security of home, income, and financial stability.

Like Freire, these economists were interested in improving the lives of the poor such as the migrant farm worker (e.g., Schultz, 1959, 1961). However, they approached the problem from a perspective based on improvement through paid work alone. By privately investing in their own education and health care, individuals could, over their life span, improve their human capital. A migrant worker who took a factory job earned more than a farm worker. Many white workers earned more than blacks, these economists argued, because they invested in education or on-the-job training. It was because of such investment in training that the U.S. national income rose between 1929 and 1956 (Schultz, 1961, p. 13). A young student, choosing to invest in the future rather than spend in the present, could build up capital, which would, in later life, ensure the comfort of his family. "Free men are first and foremost the end to be served by economic endeavour.... By investing in themselves, people can enlarge the choice available to them. It is one way free men can enhance their welfare" (Schultz, 1961, p. 2). Schultz's colleagues, Gary Becker (e.g., 1994, p. 15) and Jacob Mincer, suggested that freeing the woman from the private care of her home to work in the public sphere would enhance her family's capital. This was a way of raising the less fortunate to a middle-class lifestyle. The "labor market cannot do much for school dropouts who can hardly read and never developed good work habits" (Becker, 1994, p. 21). To this, a second-generation HC theorist James Heckman offered a solution: preschooling for the disadvantaged could imbue traits needed in the workforce of the twenty-first century.

FREE TO CHOOSE? EDUCATION AS PALLIATIVE

Heckman was awarded a Nobel Prize in Economics in 2000 for his work on heterogeneity. As people are diverse, so economics needs a broader measure for its models, he posited. Here the data from the American early intervention programmes for poor, disadvantaged preschoolers offered a mine of information on longitudinal outcomes for education. Heckman and colleagues have published over the past decades, drawing on information from the Highscope-Perry, Headstart, and Abcederian findings on improved economic outcomes for "high-risk" children. Citing nineteenth-century economist Alfred Marshall's idea (1890, paragraph VI.IV.11, cited in Cunha & Heckman 2010, p. 1) that the "most valuable of all capital is that invested in human beings; and of that capital the most precious part is the result of the care and influence of the mother," they argued for home visits, preschooling for disadvantaged children, and enriched ECE environments. However, because some mothers have fewer advantages, the state may need to help some individuals. Investing in education for the disadvantaged was not only equitable, it was cost-effective for states (Cunha & Heckman, 2010; Heckman & Masterov, 2007). Both cognitive and noncognitive abilities are important and explain schooling and socioeconomic success: "Measured cognitive ability is susceptible to environmental influences, including in utero experiences" (Cunha & Heckman, 2010, p. 3). Early childhood is a "critical period" (p. 5) for skill formation. Experiences in ECE environments can support children to develop dispositions such as "patience, self control, temperament, time preference" (p. 4).

As a greater proportion of children are exposed to adverse social conditions than in the past, many young children are deprived of a wider family and community sphere, some economists think. Here ECE can compensate. This is especially important, as skills that are formed at one stage in the child's life cycle lay the foundation for consolidation at the next—acquiring skills is a dynamic process,

> A society that seeks to eliminate ethnic and income differentials in schooling and skill attainment must start with young children, and cannot rely on later tuition policy or job training to compensate for neglect in the early years. An important corollary is that public dollars will be more efficiently spent if more human capital investment is directed toward the young. (Blakeslee, 2005, p. 7)

This economic argument is supported by recent neurological research. Heckman and Jack Shonkoff have joined forces in an argument for enriched early childhood environments for young children (Knudsen, Heckman, Cameron, & Shonkoff, 2006). Combinations of "risk factors" have been found to demonstrate the "probability of adverse outcomes in the domains of cognitive, emotional, and social development, leading to diminished economic success and decreased quality of life in adulthood" (p. 1). Studies have used data from attachment theory, language and child development theory, together with neuroscience to suggest that states should consider ECE for young disadvantaged children.

> Experience is essential to the unfolding of brain development, the more adaptable the species, the more experience plays a role.... The implications of this...for human capital formation are striking. The workplace of the 21st century will favor individuals with intellectual flexibility, strong problem-solving skills, emotional resilience, and the capacity to work well with others in a continuously changing and highly competitive economic environment. (Knudsen et al., 2006, p. 10155)

Both Heckman's and Shonkoff's scientific findings have had influence on national and international policy (see, e.g., Alderman, 2011; Irwin, Siddiqi, & Hertzman, 2007; Vegas & Santibanez, 2010). The World Bank, for example, argues for the "good" of ECE, and with overtones of Bauman's tourists, notes that "educated migrants seek places where many other workers have similar skills" (Alderman, p. 21). The risk of the indigent is not made explicit. It is not so much the individual, but what they represent to the economy and their uses as labour, that is discussed (e.g., McCollum, 2008; World Bank, 2007, 2008). In a market for labour, it is those with skills who benefit the most. Many of the itinerants are children; child labour remains an international issue (Irwin et al., 2007, p. 37). The care of children is often invisible to policy makers in developing countries, who, based on inadequate evidence, assume that care is provided by the wider family (e.g., Irwin et al., 2007, p. 61). In fact, many solo parents have to leave their children home alone; with increasing urbanisation and mobility, many are isolated, or if they are close by, relatives are also in the workforce (Irwin et al., 2007, pp. 63–64). In developing countries, one in four mothers takes her children to work with her or leaves them in the care of siblings (pp. 64–65). Many report accidents and that children's health deteriorates (p. 67). This dichotomy of tourist/vagabond is the downside of freedom: of free choice, free markets, and free economic policies.

A PROBLEM OF FREEDOM

In New Zealand's context, it is the theory of the Chicago School of Economics rather than Freire that dominates in the twenty-first century. HCT has been evident in ECE both in the Labour Coalition and in the National Coalition Governments. National Minister of Education Anne Tolley appointed an Early Childhood Taskforce that reported to her on their findings in 2011 (Minstrom, 2011). If government invests in ECE, the authors suggest, this will be a prudent investment as "participation in high-quality early childhood education can make the difference between having a life of poverty and dependence or a life characterised by on-going self-development and positive social engagement" (Minstrom, 2011, p. 13). HCT theory, especially Heckman's view of ECE as an investment (e.g., Minstrom, pp. 22–41), has a central place in this policy document. Investments in disadvantaged children pay the greatest dividends (p. 24). Effective use of state monies, they suggest, will be targeting funding to increase participation of risky populations (pp. 14–32), including migrants (e.g., p. 189) and those whose parents wish to work. This is a change from the long-standing policy of funding ECE on a universal basis. The authors call for public-private partnerships in which employers do not see ECE care as a purely private family or government matter, but as an investment in their employees (pp. 15–16). While the term *freedom* is missing from the ECTR text, the term *choice* (p. 29, pp. 122–138) occurs frequently, as does the concept of enhanced personal and community responsibility for education. The role of the state is to invest prudently with actuarial intent to ensure the human capital of the future is not put at risk. Early Childhood has become a site of governmentality, where both parent and child are viewed as economic units, ordering their presences, exerting rational choice in an education marketplace—free to succeed or fail in a world that offers only dichotomies.

Nikolas Rose (1999, p. 94) suggested that a genealogy of freedom will make explicit the technical sets of practices, relations, and governmental devices. We need to discard the idea that freedom is a principle of "progressive" thought. Rather, it is infused with relations of power, which constructs us as subject in the dominant discourse. The discourse of HCT requires individuals to be freely responsible for their education, their employment, their life trajectory and that of their children. Without freedom, there is no self-mastery, no correct dispositions able to support our values and transform our life chances. Human freedom, Rose argues, using a governmentality discourse, is "essentially mechanistic"—the name "we give today to the kind of power one brings to bear on oneself and mode of bringing power to bear on others" (p. 96). We can ask the price that freedom "exacts from those who lack the resources to practice it" (p. 97). Freedom is, he concluded, problematic.

For the tourists and the vagabonds—what price freedom? Whether training and education will, in the Freirean concept, result in "concientisation" or merely the acquisition of marketable skills is a question yet to be decided. In the global village, the "oppressors" are no longer visible; education becomes reduced to methods and techniques. The responsibilisation of the parent, the worker, the child is a governmental technique that lays a heavy burden on each individual. The tourist has replaced the pilgrim, the economist, the prophet, the church as a firm (Ekelund et al., 1997). Risk is a concept removed from its sociocultural contexts to be presented as a consumer's opportunity. Rewards are short-term for the tourist, difficult to locate for the indigent; salvation is dependent on one's trading skills in the here and now. For children, they will be dependant of the right dispositions, once they have joined the workforce, in growing the country's competitive advantage, obeying no masters but themselves. With the "end of history" (Fukuyama, 1992), as argued by the economists of the Right, there is no "becoming"—only the development of the entrepreneurial self, seeking improvement in one's life trajectory. We need a reinvention of language to redefine education in noneconomic terms, lest we are cast adrift in our freedom.

REFERENCES

Alderman, H. (2011). *No small matter : The impact of poverty, shocks, and human capital investments in early childhood development.* World Bank. © World Bank. Retrieved from https://openknowledge. worldbank.com/handle/10986/2266 License: CC BY 3.0 IGO.

Bauman, Z. (1998). *Globalization: The human consequences.* New York, NY: Columbia University Press.

Bauman, Z. (2000). *Liquid modernity* (Vol. 9). Cambridge, England: Polity Press.

Becker, G. S., Murphy, K. M., & Tamura, R. (1994). Human capital, fertility, and economic growth. In G. S. Becker, *Human capital: A theoretical and empirical analysis with special reference to education* (3rd ed., pp. 323–350). Chicago, IL: University of Chicago Press.

Blakeslee, J. (Ed.). (2005). Inequality in America: What role for human capital policies? *Focus, 23*(5), 1–11. Retrieved from http://www.irp.wisc.edu/publications/focus/pdfs/foc233a.pdf

Cunha, F., Heckman, J. J., Lochner, L., & Masterov, D. V. (2005). *Interpreting the evidence on life cycle skill formation* (No. w11331). Cambridge MA: National Bureau of Economic Research.

Cunha, F., & Heckman, J. J. (2010). *Investing in our young people* (No. w16201). Cambridge MA: National Bureau of Economic Research.

Ekelund, R. B., Hébert, R. F., Tollison, R. D., Anderson, G. M., & Davidson, A. B. (1997). *Sacred trust: The medieval church as an economic firm.* New York, NY: Oxford University Press.

Freire, P. (1972). *Cultural action for freedom* (pp. 37–51). Harmondsworth, England: Penguin. Retrieved from www.thinkingtogether.org/rcream/archive/110/CulturalAction.pdf

Freire, P. (1973). Education, liberation and the church. *Study Encounter, 9*(1). Retrieved from http://www.acervo.paulofreire.org/xmlui/bitstream/handle/7891/1138/FPF_OPF_01_0002.pdf

Freire, P. (1998). *Pedagogy of freedom: Ethics, democracy, and civic courage.* Lanham, MD: Rowman & Littlefield.

Fukuyama, F. (1992). *The end of history and the last man.* New York, NY: Free Press. Retrieved from http://www.revalvaatio.org/wp/wp-content/uploads/fukuyama-the_end_of_history.pdf

Heckman, J. J., & Masterov, D. V. (2007). *The productivity argument for investing in young children* (Working Paper 5). Cambridge MA: National Bureau of Economic Research. Retrieved from http://jenni.uchicago.edu/Invest/FILES/dugger_2004-12-02_dvm.pdf.

International Monetary Fund. (2004). *United States: Selected issues* (IMF Country Report No. 04/228). Washington, DC: International Monetary Fund. Retrieved from www.imf.org/external/pubs/ft/scr/2004/cr04228.pdf

Irwin, L. G., Siddiqi, A., & Hertzman, C. (2007). *Early child development: A powerful equalizer.* Report prepared for the World Health Organization's Social Determinants of Health.

Keeley, B. (2007). *Human capital: How what you know shapes your life.* Paris, France: OECD. Retrieved from http://www.oecd.org/insights/humancapitalhowwhatyouknowshapesyourlife.htm

Knudsen, E. I., Heckman, J. J., Cameron, J. L., & Shonkoff, J. P. (2006). Economic, neurobiological, and behavioral perspectives on building America's future workforce. *Proceedings of the National Academy of Sciences, 103*(27), 10155–10162. Retrieved from http://www.pnas.org/content/103/27/10155.full?sid=5960ad3e-c5ea-43a7-b8df-95ad46dea66f

McCollum, K. (2008). *Long-distance learning makes the world a classroom.* Washington, DC: International Monetary Fund. Retrieved from http://www.imf.org/external/pubs/ft/survey/so/2008/RES082108A.htm

Minstrom, M. (2011). *An agenda for amazing children: ECE Taskforce report—early childhood.* Retrieved from *www.taskforce.ece.govt.nz/* Wellington: Early Childhood Taskforce Report

New Zealand Treasury. (2001). *Towards an inclusive economy* (Treasury Working Paper 01/15). Wellington: New Zealand Treasury. Retrieved from http://www.treasury.govt.nz/publications/research-policy/wp/2001/01-15

Organisation for Economic Co-operation and Development. (2012). *Starting Strong 111 : A quality toolbox for early education and care.* Paris, France: Organisation for Economic Co-operation and Development.

Rose, N. (1999). *Powers of freedom: Reframing political thought.* Cambridge, England: Cambridge University Press.

Schultz, T. (1959). Investment in man: An economist's view. *The Social Service Review, 33*(2), 109–117. Retrieved from www.sdstate.edu/sdsuarchives/collections/.../investment-in-man.pdf

Schultz, T. (1961). Investment in human capital. *The American Economic Review, 51*(1), 1–17. Retrieved from https://webspace.utexas.edu/hcleaver/www/330T/350kPEESchultzInvestmentHumanCapital.pdf

Vegas, E., & Santibanez, L. (2010). *The promise of early childhood development in Latin America and the Caribbean.* Washington, DC: World Bank. Retrieved from http://siteresources.worldbank.org/EDUCATION/Resources/278200-1099079877269/547664-1099079922573/ECD_LAC.pdf

Walker, S. (2011). Promoting equity through early child development interventions for children from birth through three years of age. In H. Alderman (Ed.), *No small matter: The impact of poverty, shocks, and human capital investment in early childhood development* (pp. 115–154). Washington DC: World Bank. Retrieved from http://siteresources.worldbank.org/EDUCATION/Resources/278200-1298568319076/nosmallmatter.pdf

World Bank. (2007). *Globalization of labor.* Retrieved from http://www.imf.org/external/pubs/ft/weo/2007/01/pdf/c5.pdf

World Bank. (2008). *Globalization: A brief overview.* Retrieved http://www.imf.org/external/np/exr/ib/2008/053008.htm

CHAPTER THIRTY

Education as an Aesthetic Exercise in Everyday School Performances

MURIEL YUEN-FUN LAW

INTRODUCTION

The discourse of constructivist learning has gained currency in Hong Kong schools, particularly when project learning has become one of the four curriculum tasks of the local educational reforms since the late 1990s. Official goals of project learning are to strengthen students' social and cognitive skills, and to enable them to construct knowledge about the contemporary world through learning experiences. Local research studies, however, indicate that social-inquiry through project learning reinforces existing social education that masks realities in ways the banking approach does in the Freirean sense. Yet, through seeming acts of inquiry, students re-enact prescribed curricular discourses and sustain established social order, more than merely receiving realities passively from the teacher-depositors.

Freire (Shor & Freire, 1987) considers education as "naturally an aesthetic exercise," that engages educators and learners in "a permanent process of formation" (p. 118). As an aesthetic project, education has to do with acts of knowing, unveiling, and giving life to our object of study (Shor & Freire, 1987). One way of implementing such a liberatory education with learners having little power to change the system of oppression—in my case, students—is to organize them through developing and carrying out educational projects "with" them (Freire, 2000, p. 54).

Between the two years 2010 and 2011, I experimented with one such "educational project" in a Hong Kong secondary school in the process of engaging the student participants with their individual social inquiry projects, referred to as Independent Enquiry Study (IES),[1] a school-based-assessment[2] component of the senior secondary school subject, Liberal Studies.[3] This "educational project" was an action research study on the use of drama in project learning in a Hong Kong senior secondary school classroom. It was also an experiment on the role and the potentials of drama in transforming a positivistic and cynical mode of social inquiry in the local context. During those two years, I visited three Hong Kong secondary schools, and had in-depth interviews with five subject teachers and thirty students who were to do the first-time-ever Hong Kong Diploma of Secondary Education (HKDSE) in March 2012. I conducted pedagogical action research with thirteen students at School A, one of the three schools, using drama as both a method and an analytical framework. This chapter draws on some of the action-research findings at School A. It discusses the use of drama as a method for meaningful social-inquiry learning and educational experiences in relation to Freire's dialogic pedagogy and the aesthetic nature of education. The chapter concerns the possibilities of reorienting education toward an aesthetic practice in a schooling context influenced by positivism and cynicism.

A GLIMPSE OF THE EVERYDAY SCHOOL EXPERIENCES IN A HONG KONG SCHOOL

To offer a glimpse of the everyday school experiences in the contemporary Hong Kong context, I'll begin with a page from my action-research reflective journal at School A, the research site.

My watch showed 2:20 p.m., and the school bell went off. Students in the classroom said good-bye to their teacher and shuffled outside into the corridor with their stationery and books. I flipped through my organizer and the school timetable to check whether I was in the right place at the right time. Which direction would the girls come from? The whole corridor was swarming with buzzing students who had just exited their classrooms on either side of the corridor, and were heading toward the staircases for the next block of classes. They and their teachers looked at me with curiosity. It was 2:30 p.m. Mr. Daniel[*] arrived, holding the key to the classroom door. He needed it in case the previous teacher who had occupied the room had locked it. Now, it was 2:40 p.m., 20 minutes after the school bell had rung, and the traffic along the corridor had died down. Oh, there they were! The girls appeared at the floor landing. They had had hall assembly the previous hour, and it often ends late, forcing the girls to move hastily from classroom to classroom, Mr. Daniel explained to me in this first action-research session.
(Extracted and revised from my reflective journal, September 21, 2010)

The above journal entry recorded the first action-research session in September 2010. The eighty-minute session turned out to be a sixty-minute session, twenty minutes short because of the hustle and bustle of moving between classrooms, and the scene described above from my journal wound up being a recurring scene in the remaining nine sessions, except that Mr. Daniel did not explain the girls' late arrival anymore. The pace of the school was relaxed. Unlike other Hong Kong schools, during the fifteen or so minutes I would wait outside the designated classroom, the few teachers along the corridor didn't yell at students to discipline them nor did they made a scene in smoothing out the traffic. Teachers were mostly gentle in manner, but tired in appearance. Students' relations with teachers at this school seemed to be more casual than those at many other Hong Kong schools. Rather than follow the usual pattern of addressing teachers as "Mr. X" and "Ms. Y," students greeted all teachers by their nicknames or first names.

In this first action-research session, the students and I warmed up by introducing one another in pairs with reference to a shape and a sound, a warm-up that enabled everybody to think metaphorically and bodily. Students were very quick to appreciate dramatic conventions such as Still-Image (or Tableaux) and Thought-Tracking (Neelands & Goode, 2000; O'Neill, 1995). Students used their own bodies to devise images of themselves, of people around them, and of the potential target informants of their IES projects. Presenting still-images of themselves and of the others as such crystallized students' perception of those people and enabled the students to further interpret and discuss their representation of themselves and others in relation to IES (Boal, 1995; Neelands & Goode, 2000). We had fun and laughed at ourselves and at the images we displayed while learning through a language of observation and representation tailored to the Liberal Studies students.

CONSTRUCTIVIST LEARNING AND EVERYDAY SCHOOL PERFORMANCES

For Hong Kong, the current education reforms began in the late 1990s. Critical analysis has shown that existing educational practices and reforms in Hong Kong are characterized by market-oriented managerialism (Ho, 2005a; Ngan & Lee, 2010; Tse, 2005). Education has functioned to reproduce and legitimate capitalistic and neoliberal ideologies, emphasizing vocational training and reinforcing students' behavioral and institutional values while at the same time distrusting frontline educators (Ho, 2005a, 2005b; Tse, 2005). The typical Hong Kong school is often thought of as "a social unit in itself, with its own rules, power structures and values system" (Morris & Adamson, 2010, p. 109), and as an instructional site where teachers and students are receivers of the school culture who are expected to work to strengthen the culture (Ngan & Lee, 2010).

The discourse of constructivist learning has gained currency in the Hong Kong educational scene, particularly when project learning became one of the four curriculum tasks[5] of the education reforms (Curriculum Development Committee, 2002; Curriculum Development Council [CDC],[6] 2001, 2007; Curriculum Development Institute [CDI], n.d.). Official goals of project learning are to strengthen students' social and cognitive skills, and to enable them to construct knowledge about the contemporary world through learning experiences (CDI, n.d.).

Liberal Studies (LS) and its integral component IES that has been in place since September 2009 in the Hong Kong school curriculum apparently stand a good chance of becoming a critical pedagogy, nurturing students' critical thinking and literacy (CDC, 2007; Hong Kong Examinations and Assessment Authority [HKEAA], 2009a, 2009b, 2010). Yet research on the earlier junior versions of the subject has shown that LS suffers from "narrative sickness," where lived realities are treated as "motionless, static, compartmentalized and predictable," using Freire's words (2000, p. 71). Discussions of social issues are organized mainly around a conflict-of-interest model and effect a reproduction of simple binary oppositional self-other relations (Law, 2006). The two-year study at School A, the case that I am discussing in this chapter, indicated that social inquiry carries a positivistic orientation, and the method of IES in understanding the social is inherently positivist and ahistorical (Law, 2012, pp. 51–56). Pedagogy and pedagogical practices concern the transmission of knowledge instrumental to the existing society. They share features similar to those characterizing the positivist discourse of traditional educational theory, which gave rise to the new sociology of education in the United States in the early 1970s (Giroux, 1981, 1985).

My action-research findings at School A further revealed that the participating students' process of social inquiry learning was one of dependence, and that they took part in repetitive acts of presenting and re-presenting a priori understanding of the social (Law, 2012, pp. 51–56). These students depended on authority figures—oftentimes the subject teacher—to assess their progress and to issue clear instructions for the IES work. They also depended on frameworks such as presentation templates to guide the practical work of planning and charting the research process. Most of the participating students stated that they could discern whether the teacher approved of their IES work by piecing together the teacher's various snippets of feedback. Even so, the students would have preferred clear and direct assessments from the subject teacher. Apart from these sources of help, the students depended on their own collective efforts in locating possible IES topics, as was the case with Emily, who found her own topic uninteresting because it represented the "leftovers" from her group-brainstorming ideas. Apparently, the task of identifying a truly interesting topic required far too much work on her part, and she would rather stay with the "leftover" topic. Another source of help was the presence of bounds, or limits, within which students might devise their projects' inquiry design. That was why Maggie chose a topic that featured many other projects similar in nature on the Web, as it made it far less difficult for her to search for information pertaining to her school assignments.

The dependent nature of students' IES processes should neither be subjected to simple criticism, nor be considered simply negative. It reflects how feeding students with procedural forms of knowledge, in fact, shapes the students' mode of learning over time. Subject teachers would feed students with templates of work that geared toward small tasks and such templates organized general school-based learning, including IES projects, into a series of disconnected acts performed in a repetitive way (see Appendix 1, Excerpt 1.1). In the small-group discussions, I asked students whether they really wanted to pursue an inquiry about the topic at hand, and all of them offered very similar responses, expressing ideas summed up by the comment "I treat it as an assignment only." The students went further, stating, "When it's submitted, it is submitted." Completing the learning tasks becomes meaningless labor, especially when experiences from the present work process are neither contiguous nor consistent with past and future work processes. Such a mode of learning arrests rather than contributes to students' independent inquiry. What is more, as technical forms, the types of templates mentioned above encourage students to perceive information in compartmentalized ways. Learning through these technical templates structures students' modes of thinking and working around the needs of the immediate present. Oftentimes, such needs are reduced mainly to the needs of teacher-assessors.

Research results showed that all of the student participants performed seeming acts of IES inquiry; and the majority of these student informants clearly knew what they did was mere repetitive performative acts that reproduced information that teachers would like them to present (Law, 2012, pp. 66–69). More than merely receiving realities passively from the teacher-depositors, students re-enact prescribed curricular discourses and sustain established social order through such performative acts. These students ended up refuting the examination authority's claim that the school-based assessment of their social inquiry project work can "reduce dependence on the result of public examinations…[and may] provide the most reliable indication of the actual abilities of candidates" (HKEAA, 2010). What is worse is that the students made dismissive remarks regarding their own inquiry work (Appendix 1, Excerpts 1.2 & 1.3). Nonetheless, students felt that they had to abide by this falsehood because it had real consequences for their subject grades. These frustrated students became cynical performers who were perceiving school-based assessment to be a falsehood. Borrowing from Peter Sloterdijk, Slavoj Žižek (1989), defines cynicism as "enlightened false consciousness" (p. 26), which applies to people who are aware that they are "following an illusion," but who nevertheless continue to follow it (p. 30). The students who participated in this study performed as good and diligent students would, and their objective was to strengthen their teacher-assessor's view of them as apt pupils capable of meeting assignment due dates, even though the students themselves had little or no faith in their IES-related activities.

DRAMA AS METHOD FOR CRITICAL DISCOVERY

Students' cynical IES practices in the Hong Kong context have posited a specific problem for a transformative pedagogy. Informed by Althusser and Foucault, Doyle McCarthy (1996) contends that, in contemporary culture, ideologies are not false consciousness in the Marxist sense but "lived practices" as they "provide the most fundamental frameworks through which people interpret, experience, and 'live' the conditions available to them" (p. 42). These students' IES cynical practices in Hong Kong come in the form of "lived practices," in the form of everyday performances of seeming acts of constructivist learning.

Freire (1970/2000) has called for educators and the oppressed to perceive the reality of oppression "not as a closed world from which there is no exit, but as a limiting situation which they can transform" (p. 49). For him, "It is *the perception* towards the limit-situations rather than the limit-situations in and of themselves that *creates a climate of hopelessness*" (emphasis added, p. 99). In the case of IES learning, however, it is the "lived practices" of the everyday performances in the forms of seeming acts of constructivist learning that has nurturing forms of cynical practices and cynical reasoning. Cynicism, in the form of "enlightened false consciousness," forms a limit-situation for the IES students. A limit situation as such would require not only a change of perception but a transformation of the pedagogical structure and the everyday performative practices at school. Such transformation would involve efforts in developing a different pedagogical structure for students to experience and experiment with social inquiry learning, and in developing a tool for the educators to illuminate where the limit-situations—here, cynicism—lie and what possible work could be done to transform the limit-situations.

Raymond Williams' discussion about the relationships between drama and society can shed light on this topic as it stands in Hong Kong. In his professorial inaugural lecture entitled "Drama in a Dramatized Society," Williams (1983) delineates how drama in society once comprised festive theatrical events that offered a break from accepted signs, thus helping forge "a more complex, more active, and more questioning world" (p. 16). What is more, he sees drama—with its dramatic presentations, attention-grabbing images, and role typifications—as a constructed component of everyday life. Williams states that his analysis of drama and society has revealed to him "not only as a way of seeing certain aspects of society but as a way of getting through to some of the fundamental conventions which we group as society itself" (p. 20). Williams's conception of drama in this latter sense is about conventions and the structuring of the conventions to frame and reframe social realities.

In this regard, drama serves as a method of critique, a lens for critical educators. If we consider schools in the Hong Kong context from this light of Williams's analysis, we can see that schools prescribe roles for teachers and students that are typified and ahistorical, and that the scripts of schools are pre-determined, organizing realities that reproduce themselves and sustain established social order.

In the section below, by drawing some findings from my action-research study on the use of drama in IES learning in a Hong Kong senior secondary school classroom, I argue that drama could be a potential instrument for students' critical discovery. It has the potential for transforming the limit-situations the constraint students' IES practices.

SUSPENDING TYPIFIED ROLES IN THE DRAMATIC ELSEWHERE

The action research at School A took place between April 2010 and December 2011. It explored how drama could be an analytical tool for social-inquiry learning and teaching. The research exploration aimed to find out how drama would enable the student participants to see and hear "the other," who had been rendered invisible and inaudible to the students by media and curricular discourses, and how drama would integrate into the students' social-inquiry learning their past and present experiences that have often been dismissed in their learning processes in general. The action research ran in two research cycles, involving thirteen students. I was the researcher-facilitator and Mr. Daniel, the subject teacher, was the non-participant observer.

Throughout the action-research process, individual students expressed their wish not to conduct any IES assignments. Emily and Cindy were two such students, and in fact, they quickly grew frustrated with the excessively monolithic and difficult set of IES tasks. Devising questionnaire items was a particularly difficult task. We spent one session refining the questionnaire design using functional role play. Here are my observations of this session, which I recorded in my reflective journal after the session.

> *Emily stared straight at the returned assignment: the questionnaire she had designed to collect data from the teenagers regarding how they see their own mental wellbeing. She was delighted with the grade received: "I've never received a passing grade in any other IES assignment before. I got one for this questionnaire design." "You did a good job," I said. Wincey and Yvonne were chitchatting about the grade I gave them. Cindy was slumped in a chair idling the time away, while she and the other girls in the room were supposed to be looking at the comments I had written on their draft questionnaires and getting ready for the Focus Group role play, in the quest for more ideas on how to revise the questionnaire items. That was the major purpose of the lesson.*

"Emily, why don't you begin first?" I asked. "Try to treat the classmates as your informants. Introduce your topic and interview them with your questionnaire, for real."

Emily picked a few items and asked the group for their answers. To her amazement, some of the ideas that popped into her head had never before come to mind when devising options for the questionnaire items. Her face glowed, and she was happy with the activities. Cindy was next and was unsure whether the role-play activity would be useful, but she was trying to finish the assigned task. It didn't take long, and she exclaimed, "Oh yes, why didn't I get that point down in my questionnaire?" Afterward, Cindy enthusiastically played the role of informant for the other classmates. Yvonne was very much into the role-play mode and asked her peers to put themselves in her informants' situation: teens who inflict physical harm on themselves. (Extracted and revised from my reflective journal, March 8, 2011)

Toward the end of the activity, the students began to say that the focus-group activity was useful. Cindy even asked why the activities had not been scheduled for earlier. Obviously, the functional role-play had animated these girls' experiences. The functional role play mediated the nature of questionnaire design, shifting the task from a solitary form to a group form. The social nature of drama oriented the girls, as a group, toward direct participation in and ownership of the processes of production.

What is more, role play in the dramatic elsewhere—in liminal space—temporarily suspended classroom realities that had inflexibly placed these students in the role of IES inquirers. In their everyday school performances, these students typified their inquirer roles through repetitive acts, most notably the act of completing templates. While performing these acts, the students were joining in the process of representing and relating themselves to the other in ways predetermined by the templates and the curricular and media discourses. In the liminal space of drama, these students could play diverse roles: individuals who draw on their own experiences to help shape wider understandings of a given issue; individuals who observe their own actions across dramatic acts; and individuals who, as learners, reflect on their experiences and raise questions about their IES inquiry to further develop it. By occupying the liminal space of drama, students in general can activate different roles and relate to themselves and others in ways different from those characteristic of everyday classroom realities.

RE-"IMAGING" AND REPOSITIONING THE SELF AND THE OTHER THROUGH DRAMA

"Does the post-80s include the post-90s?" Pearl asked.

Pearl's question came in the action-research session (September 28, 2010) during which we were exploring the notions of "teenager" and "the post-80s." The term "the post-80s" was coming into vogue in Hong Kong media and was ascribed to young Hong Kong activists born in the 1980s. The term itself gained widespread media circulation during protests against the Express Rail Link construction in January 2010 in Hong Kong. Though the post-80s youth-activist phenomenon was emerging as a promising social movement at the end of year 2009, mainstream-media discourses about those post-80s youths have generally been far less diverse and contested than they could have been. As usual, the restless-dangerous-youth discourse gained currency, dominating the media's treatment of related events and themes.

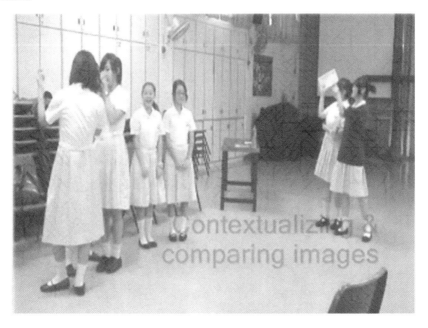

The phenomenon attracted the attention of Pearl and her friend Kim, as it had many other people in Hong Kong, chiefly because of media coverage. The two girls chose to look into the phenomenon's relationship with the local cultural and political scenes. To address these events and themes, I devised a session where the students in this action research would explore the notions of "teenager" and "the post-80s" using various dramatic conventions that specifically work with roles and role relationships. Students, in pairs or trios, took on the roles of the post-80s youth, identifying situations where these young people would have been active. Then, in still-images, these students showed what these post-80s were doing and with whom. When it came time to perform, the students presented still-images of youths at a protest site, thrusting their fists up toward the sky, or youths in front of computers, composing protest literature. After the nine students briefly embodied the post-80s youths with those still-images, I made use of the Thought-Tracking convention to help the students tap into the private thoughts of their roles

(Neelands & Goode, 2000, p. 91). Through the Thought-Tracking convention, these students-in-role gave a voice to post-80s youths that they embodied with the images. For about ten minutes, the students portrayed youths yelling in protest against Express Rail Link construction, youths planning the dissemination of protest materials, and youths wondering why so many of their peers had taken to the streets. The students then got out of the role of the post-80s youths and reflected upon the whole dramatic in-role experiences in relation to their understanding of the post-80s youth. Some of the students talked about their in-role experiences in class. One of the ideas brought up during these conversations was that these youths were not restless and dangerous but serious about a cause, an understanding that differed substantively from reductive mainstream-media representations.

To further make audible and visible the figures of post-80s youth, I used the Space Between convention (Neelands & Goode, 2000, p. 86) to invite these students to position themselves physically in relation to an empty chair that signified the protesting youths whom the students had previously embodied. This time, the students took on a different role, the youth figures' "significant other," as it were. The Space Between convention invited the students-in-role to locate themselves physically in proximity to a protesting youth (i.e., to the empty chair). The physical space between each individual student (now embodying the significant other) and the empty chair would symbolize how close or distant that particular significant other would be relative to the youth. In identifying both a place where the significant other would stand and a distance between that significant other and the youth (the empty chair), the students had to consider which significant other they would try to embody and also had to analyze the relationships between that particular significant other and the youth. Pearl and Kim, who chose the post-80s as their IES topics, situated themselves closest to the chair as they embodied the role of the youth's family members offering him encouraging remarks and unconditional love. Other students who took on the role of family members but who positioned themselves a greater distance from the empty chair did so to indicate their disapproval of the youth's social acts.

TOWARD A DIALOGIC PEDAGOGY

After those drama activities, I invited the students to return to their own IES topics and consider the materials they had chosen to read thus far (at the end of September 2010). In light of the Space Between convention that works on roles and the analysis of role relationships, students were to compile two lists: one list showing the views they had collected so far about their IES topics, and another list indicating views they would like to further collect to develop their IES inquiry. On almost all these students' first lists, *the subjects of inquiry* of these students' IES topics were talked about as if they were *the objects of inquiry* (see Appendix 2 for the lists that students compiled after the session of drama work, in the original written Chinese). Take, for instance, Hannah's topic on how teenagers view love and sexual intercourse; the materials she had collected featured university academics and media professionals commenting on teenagers' immature attitudes toward love and loving relationships. Take, for another instance, Emily, who had planned to investigate the causes of teenagers' health deteriorations, had collected reports from health experts, nutritionists, and medical professionals' reports. On their second lists, seven of the nine students taken part in the session stated that they would like to collect their subject's personal views of the matter. Their show of interest in understanding their IES subject was a promising sign that these student inquirers had witnessed—through drama—the importance of understanding *views of their subject of inquiry* rather than resting with simple univocal representation of their subject of inquiry.

In the dialogic pedagogy, Shor (Shor & Freire, 1987) sees the need to "include a global, critical dimension" which enables students to understand the familiar socially and historically (p. 104). Tyson Lewis (2009) contends that Freire's practice of dialogue functions to reconstruct and reconfigure the "narrative understanding of the world," which has been ideologically mystified by the banking education offered for the oppressed (p. 292). Lewis maintains that "critical pedagogy has to be supported by an aesthetic rupture of the visible/audible, transforming the detached, omniscient, authoritarian gaze of banking education into the interactive gesture of the glance" (p. 293). In the action-research session mentioned above students explored notions and images of post-80s youths. Students crystalized images of post-80s youths using their own bodies. In presenting those still-images as fragments of realities, students engaged in dramatic acts of *contextualizing* the "depersonalizing" media and curricular youth discourses, giving voice to post-80s youths. It exemplifies how drama works as a method that ruptures the "authoritarian gaze of banking education" of the restless-dangerous post-80s youth typeset by mainstream media discourses. At the same time, the dramatic conventions and the structuring of those conventions as a whole works as a method for assisting students to see the *need* of identifying points of view other than those circulated in the mainstream media, and points of view unheard, particularly those of their IES inquiry subject.

CONCLUDING REMARKS

Education as an aesthetic event is life-giving and creative, countering the oppressor consciousness that tends "to 'in-animate' everything and everyone it encounters" and "to deter the drive to search, the restlessness, and the creative power which characterize life," (Freire, 2000, pp. 59–60). In the case of IES learning in HK, positivism and cynicism kills life through a seeming social constructivist approach to social inquiry learning. Positivism dismisses learners' experiences and histories while cynicism calls upon students to reproduce the pre-established relationship, lifestyle, and meaning inherent within a closed system of known signs. Together, positivism and cynicism nurture a similar kind of oppressor consciousness.

Social inquiry in the *dramatic elsewhere*, as my action-research findings show, has potential for *reopening* the closed system of signs that frame cynical reasoning and acts. The liminal dramatic space and exploration through dramatic roles and real-life images activate students' experiences and feelings as tools for their own social inquiry, and offer them opportunities to perceive the reality of their social world through different lights. Drama as a method could further motivate and organize these students for their own transformative educational experiences.

Drama also functions as a lens, a conceptual tool for critical educators as it reveals how school conventions frame the realities of everyday school performances, typify students' roles as inquirers, and sustain their dependence on templates of work and on the teachers' assessment guides through the repetitive act of completing those templates. The challenge for critical educators would be to further discern and exercise their own political power and that of their students' to implement a liberatory and transformative education.

APPENDIX **1**

Excerpt 1.1

Muriel:	What do you expect students to do in IES? What would you like them to experience from the process?
Daniel:	We don't really expect this first cohort [of senior secondary students] to experience much out of IES, because we can't just compare them to students doing Liberal Studies at AS level [for HKALE].[7]…Well, we don't really have much expectation…. I don't have much expectation. I just expect that they follow our approach to finish an IES. That's all. So, as I told you last time, we do it in a very rigid mode. They follow the procedure we laid out, take it step by step and at the end put everything together. That's what I expect from them because they don't really have the ability to organize an IES.

(Translated from oral Chinese, Mr. Daniel Interview, December 16, 2011).

Excerpt 1.2

Muriel:	Now, it's been more than a year since you began the IES work; what would you say about the experiences of IES?
Cindy:	It's meaningless, a waste of energy and time. You've done something you've already known, doing things repetitively as if it is very analytical.
Maggie:	You've anticipated the answers already.
Cindy:	No, you have already got the answers, but you still need to find and prove what you've already known.
Maggie:	It's simply pointless.
Muriel:	I've glanced through your projects; some of you wrote in the conclusion and the reflections that you've discovered something….
Cindy:	Well, we bragged about it.
Bonnie:	You've got to write in that way.
Muriel:	Bragging? Really no discovery at all? It's all there as expected and known beforehand?
Cindy:	It's really like that. Like what I did was about making online friends, what they [the respondents] said about the cause and effects is known to everyone. Why bother to inquire about it?

(Translated from oral Chinese, SFGI, December 9, 2011).

Excerpt 1.3

Bonnie: English school-based assessment (SBA) is the most troublesome, it's troublesome all the time.

Hannah: It's troublesome all the time, there has been so many of them [*sic*: assessment tasks].

Bonnie: You've got so nervous. For example, they gave you [the topic] today to prepare something and you've got to present it the next day.... With IES, you go about doing something, but for English, you've got only one day to finish writing the one whole piece [*sic*: a presentation script], recite it the night before and speak in front of the video camera.... It makes you all tense up.

      (Translated from oral Chinese, SFGI, Dec 09, 2011).

Liam: [With SBA in Visual Arts], you've got to finish 6 artworks within 2 years. With one Visual Arts topic, there are three subtopics. For each subtopic, you've got to submit one artwork plus a portfolio that contains the content, things about [related] artists, the art media and the techniques learnt. It is so troublesome.... The assessment criteria have not been set out. They [HKEAA] kept revising the assessment criteria and we kept changing what we did when the assessment criteria changed.

      (Translated from oral Chinese, SFGI, December 16, 2011).

Appendix 2: Excerpts of Students, In-Class Written Work (in Original Written Chinese)

After the Space Between convention, students returned to their own IES topic and reviewed the materials they had read about their subject of inquiry. Students then compiled two lists of views:

1. they identified from the materials collected
2. they would like to collect to further develop their IES inquiry

NOTES

1. Under the Education Bureau's curriculum reform, a new senior secondary academic structure and a new school curriculum were established in September 2009. Liberal Studies was introduced in addition to Mathematics, Chinese language, and English language, forming the four core subjects of the new senior secondary curriculum. IES (Independent Enquiry Study) is an integral part of the Liberal Studies curriculum. The purpose of IES is for students "to integrate knowledge acquired from the Areas of Study [in the Liberal Studies curriculum] and…to synthesize knowledge in general through enquiry into issues of interest to individual students. It encourages students to appreciate the complexities of the modern world, develop critical thinking skills and make informed decisions" (Curriculum Development Council [CDC], 2007, p. 12).

2. The IES adopts the school-based assessment, which means assessments are administered in schools and marked by the students' own teachers. It will account for 20% of the subject grade, while the remaining 80% is the written assessment. Schools are required to submit to HKEAA IES scores for each student at three stages of the IES work, namely, Project proposal, Data collection, and Product, across the three-year senior secondary schooling (Hong Kong Examinations and Assessment Authority [HKEAA], 2009).

3. The official curriculum aims of Liberal Studies is for students to "explore issues relevant to the human condition in a wide range of contexts," "to understand the contemporary world and its pluralistic nature," "[to] us[e] knowledge and perspectives from other subjects to study contemporary issues, for the purpose of connecting knowledge and concepts, and develop cross-curricular

thinking." The ultimate goal is for students "to construct personal knowledge of immediate relevance to themselves in today's world" (CDC, 2007, p. 2).

4. All names in this chapter are fictitious to protect the privacy of participants.

5. The four key tasks of the Education Bureau's educational reforms are Project Learning, Moral Education and Civic Education, Reading to Learn, and Information Technology for Interactive Learning.

6. The Curriculum Development Council (CDC) is a free-standing advisory body in Hong Kong giving advice to the Government on matters relating to curriculum development for the local school. It was formally known as the Curriculum Development Committee responsible for developing teaching syllabuses and curriculum and assessment guides recommended for use in local primary and secondary schools before reorganization took place in 1988. Despite the name change, the body's scope of duties remained basically the same. Throughout this chapter, it will be referred to as simply the CDC (http://cd1.edb.hkedcity.net/cd/cdc/en/page01.htm).

7. In the old secondary academic structure, students who preferred a university education would continue their studies for two years of matriculation, and take the HKALE at the end of the two-year matriculation process.

REFERENCES

Boal, A. (1995). *The rainbow of desire: The Boal method of theatre and therapy.* London, England: Routledge.

Curriculum Development Committee. (2002). *Personal, social and humanities education: Key learning area curriculum guide (Primary 1–Secondary 3).* Hong Kong: Education Department.

Curriculum Development Council. (2001). *Learning to learn: The way forward in curriculum development* [Web edition]. Hong Kong: Education Department. Retrieved from http://www.edb.gov.hk/index.aspx?langno=1&nodeID=2877

Curriculum Development Council. (2007). *Liberal studies: Curriculum and assessment guide (S4-6).* Hong Kong: Curriculum Development Council.

Curriculum Development Institute. (n.d.). Project Learning. Retrieved December 31, 2007, from http://cd1.edb.hkedcity.net/cd/projectlearning/index_e.html

Freire, P. (2000). *Pedagogy of the oppressed.* New York: Continuum. (Original work published 1970)

Giroux, H. (1981). *Ideology, culture & the process of schooling.* Philadelphia, PA: Temple University Press.

Giroux, H. (1985). Introduction. In P. Freire. *The politics of education: Culture, power, and liberation* (pp. xi–xxv). Westport, CT: Bergin & Garvey.

Ho, L. S. (2005a). Education reform: A socio-economic perspective. In L. S. Ho, P. Morris, & Y. P. Chung (Eds.), *Education reform and the quest for excellence: The Hong Kong story* (pp. 9–22). Hong Kong: Hong Kong University Press.

Ho, L. S. (2005b). Education reform in Hong Kong: What are the lessons? In L. S. Ho, P. Morris, & Y. P. Chung (Eds.), *Education reform and the quest for excellence: The Hong Kong story* (pp. 217–222). Hong Kong: Hong Kong University Press.

Hong Kong Curriculum Development Council. (2007). *Liberal studies: Curriculum and assessment guide (S4-6).* Hong Kong: Curriculum Development Council.

Hong Kong Examinations and Assessment Authority. (2009a). *Hong Kong diploma of secondary education examination 2012: Liberal Studies, school-based assessment teachers' handbook.*

Retrieved May 27, 2010, from http://www.hkeaa.edu.hk/DocLibrary/SBA/HKDSE/SBAha-ndbook-2012-LS-E-300609.pdf

Hong Kong Examinations and Assessment Authority. (2009b). *Hong Kong diploma of secondary education examination regulations and assessment frameworks 2012*. Hong Kong: Hong Kong Examinations and Assessment Authority.

Hong Kong Examinations and Assessment Authority. (2010). School-based Assessment (SBA). Retrieved May 27, 2010, from http://www.hkeaa.edu.hk/en/sba/

Law, M. (2006). *Cultivating identities and differences: A case study of the Hong Kong junior secondary Economic and Public Affairs curriculum* (Unpublished master's thesis). Lingnan University, Hong Kong.

Law, M. (2012). *Drama as method: Recontextualizing project learning for Hong Kong secondary schools* (Unpublished doctoral dissertation). Lingnan University, Hong Kong.

Lewis, T. E. (2009). Education in the realm of the senses: Understanding Paulo Freire's aesthetic unconscious through Jacques Ranciere. *Journal of Philosophy of Education, 43*(2), 285–299.

McCarthy, E. D. (1996). *Knowledge as culture: The new sociology of knowledge*. London, England: Routledge.

Morris, P., & Adamson, B. (2010). *Curriculum, schooling and society in Hong Kong*. Hong Kong: Hong Kong University Press.

Neelands, J., & Goode, T. (2000). *Structuring drama work: A handbook of available forms in theatre and drama*. Cambridge, England: Cambridge University Press.

Ngan, M. Y., & Lee, C. K. J. (Eds.). 顏明仁、李子建編著 (2010).《課程與教學改革：學校文化、教師轉變與發展的觀點》 [Curriculum and teaching reform: From the perspective of school culture, teacher change and development]. (In Chinese) 北京：教育科学出版社。

O'Neill, C. (1995). *Drama worlds: A framework for process drama*. Portsmouth, NH: Heinemann.

Shor, I., & Freire, P. (1987). *A pedagogy for liberation: Dialogues on transforming education*. South Hadley, MA: Bergin & Garvey.

Tse, K. C. T. (2005). Quality education in Hong Kong: The anomalies of managerialism and marketization. In L. S. Ho, P. Morris, & Y. P. Chung (Eds.), *Education reform and the quest for excellence: The Hong Kong story* (pp. 99–123). Hong Kong: Hong Kong University Press.

Williams, R. (1983). Drama in a dramatized society. In R. Williams, *Writing in society* (pp. 11–21). London, England: Verso.

Žižek, S. (1989). *The sublime object of ideology*. London, England: Verso.

CHAPTER THIRTY-ONE

Decolonizing Ways of Knowing: Communion, Conversion, and Conscientization

JON AUSTIN

INTRODUCTION

The struggle to know and name the world is a central aspect of any decolonizing project, and Freire's notion of *conscientização* (conscientization) refers to a form of critical engagement with the realities of the lived experience of the colonized world. It is not enough to know the world; knowledge must be brought to bear on changing the world. This chapter looks to draw together three key ideas from decolonial activists to anchor an exploration of the experiences of the (white) author with indigenous scholars engaged in research work where indigenous ways of knowing have been, in effect, quarantined by those scholars outside the academy. The inability/refusal of these scholars to see and acknowledge the legitimacy of their culturally familiar ways of knowing (Du Bois's [1903] double consciousness) can be seen to be a manifestation of the cultural amputation Fanon (1967) so vehemently resisted. The central concern of this chapter is to draw from the experience of deliberately engaging a process approaching that of conscientization, where shadows of vanguardism and neocolonial maneuvers were (possibly) cast unwittingly across an intent to expose and disrupt colonized ways of knowing, to consider the implications of Freire's (1970/1972b) idea of communion for collaborative decolonial praxis.

The primary aim of the decolonial project is the positive reconstruction of the relationship between the colonized and the colonizer. This, as Paulo Freire explained, is a project of humanizing through liberation, and should be seen as lying at the crux of what he saw as a pedagogy of the oppressed. This chapter looks to explore Freire's view of the colonized-colonizer nexus from three perspectives: one, that of the philosophical and political antecedents, primarily those of Du Bois and Fanon, that locate Freirean thinking clearly within what has come to be seen as decolonial theorizing; the second, that of Freire's notion of communion and conversion and what they have to offer by way of explanatories and guidance; and the third, that of the concrete, lived experience of a member of the colonizer class (in Freirean language) looking to disavow and make amends for the effect of colonization; in effect, to engage in decolonial praxis.

My own professional life began as Freire's ideas were becoming available in and to the West, and one of the advantages of having four decades in which to (irregularly) return to these ideas is that for each of the various stages of my personal-professional development over that time, there was always something in Freirean and related works to provoke, perplex, and advise. I first encountered Freire's *Pedagogy of the Oppressed* during my initial teacher education days in early 1970s Australia. It was a part of a slew of what were then—and probably are seen as more so today—radical but not hopelessly outrageous or overly utopian alternatives for education. We were, after all, still in the slipstream of the Woodstock era and the alternative and countercultural aspirations that had arisen during the late 1960s. In addition to *Pedagogy of the Oppressed* (Freire, 1970/1972b), *Cultural Action for Freedom* (Freire, 1970/1972a) and *Education for Critical Consciousness* (Freire, 1973) formed a compendium of sometimes mysterious but usually inspirational pieces that seem to have impacted my teaching and educative work ever since.

In my early childhood classroom teaching days, I took from these books ideas of genuine student-teacher engagement, the importance of dialogic forms of pedagogy, the political purpose of education being that of social betterment, and the imperative of linking learning to the concrete realities and needs of the learner. Living and working in and with almost exclusively white "First World" environs, contexts, and people, Freire's focus on colonized societies and cultures didn't have particular resonance or relevance for me at that time. As I moved into university teacher education in the late 1980s, the idea of teacher activism and the political nature of schooling drove the work I did there, most frequently with undergraduate students, but increasingly with a growing number of graduate students for whom the prevailing images and assertions of the political neutrality of teaching were perplexing and nonsensical.

As I became more conscious of the multiple forms and expressions of the various privileges I had unthinkingly benefited from and continued to enjoy, and of the consequences for those not so privileged, Freire's work on the project of humanization and the attendant imperative of the simultaneous eradication of both the oppressor and the oppressed classes assumed a greater cogency for me. From my anti-racist curriculum and pedagogy focus in the 1990s to my doctoral project that explored the development of white racial identities in the Australian context to a wider engagement with the implications of adopting a position of mutlilogicality (Kincheloe & Steinberg, 2008), I returned to Freire's central theme: that genuine humanization requires the collaborative and communal development of and commitment to a pedagogy of the oppressed.

Having now moved from teacher education into work with and for Australian Aboriginal people, the concrete realities of this task confront me on an almost daily basis and throw up questions of legitimacy, authority, and neocolonialism: How might I contribute to the enactment of such a pedagogy? What limits or constraints are there upon those on the "colonizer" side of the relationship working to dissolve the binary of oppression? Is it possible for the "colonizer" to want change more than the "colonized"?

TALKING BACK TO THE OPPRESSOR: THREE MOMENTS OF BAFFLEMENT

My lived experience tells me that white Western middle-class males are not somehow universally quarantined from the constraining and dehumanizing effects of economic and political systems of social ordering and alienation. As someone who displays that particular constellation of characteristics, I can be certain that my life has been very much more comfortable, secure, and valued than most of those who don't share these features. However, under systems and circuits of ever-morphing avenues and expressions of exploitation and dominance—a "matrix of oppression," as Patricia Hill Collins (1990) describes this; a "simultaneity" of core social locations (Brewer, 1993, p. 27); or a "multiplex of oppression," in Dei's (2003, p. 222) words—we must keep confronting and challenging the "simple hierarchies that routinely label affluent White men as global oppressors, poor Black women as powerless victims, with other groups arrayed in between" (Collins, 1990, p. 245). That is, while we are all subjected to the vagaries of global economic exploitation, social stratification, and ascribed identity location, we are not equally oppressed, but neither are we equally privileged. As such, as a member of the oppressor or colonizer class in Freirean terms, my life experiences do not preclude an empathetic connection to the oppressions enacted upon those who more visibly constitute the colonized class. It is from within this space of connection—perhaps of communion—that my attempts to generate authentic alliances in the struggle for social justice and the re-humanizing of the species is rooted.

Gayatri Spivak talks about "moments of bafflement," moments that disclose not only the limits but also possibilities for a new politics within the encounter with confusion, the moments that lead to transgression. For Spivak, "[it] is more interesting to enter into texts so that the moments of bafflement can become useful" (Spivak, 1990, p. 55). The most powerful point of focus for deconstructing the nature of the social is through "small things: margins, moments, etc." (Spivak, 1990, p. 136). Herein follow three moments of personal-cultural bafflement that have led me to a serious questioning of the role of the not-quite-as-oppressed ally in the struggle for justice, liberation, and humanization. These are tales—greatly simplified in detail and written to maintain a degree of anonymity for all protagonists save myself—that have individually and collectively unsettled and made problematic work I had done, work I thought had positioned me on the side of Justice and of the Good. In telling these stories previously, I have referred to these events as personal "shudder moments"—moments that went beyond bafflement, and caused an almost-immediate physically unsettling response.

THE FIRST TALE: "WHY HAVE YOU TAKEN SO LONG?"

In 2009, I was visiting a university in Aotearoa New Zealand and spent an unplanned session with a class of mature, female, Pasifika early childhood teacher education students. The conversations and discussions ranged across topics such as bell hooks's work (the focus of that week's tutorial), the importance to these students of returning to home and family upon graduation to give back to and work within their communities, and my personal involvement in anti-racist work. This latter topic seemed to be of considerable interest to the group, particularly my doctoral work on white racial identities. After a period of discussion about the unfamiliar situation (to these students) of whites investigating their whiteness and skin privilege, one of the students who had not spoken at all during the session indicated her desire to speak. As the rest of the group sat in silence, the speaker stood in her place and fixed me with a look of what, in hindsight, was almost desperation. She pointed her extended fingers at me and asked one question: "*Why have you taken so long?*" This wasn't an accusatory comment, but one I took to be a plea for urgency. She then resumed her seat and her silence.

THE SECOND TALE: "I DON'T TRUST YOU"

In September last year, the centre at which I work was visited by a delegation of Native Americans, members of the Cherokee Nation. The delegation included a professor of nursing at a U.S. university (John) and the chief of his tribe (Jim). During the course of the visit (and during a heavy hail storm), a conversation developed between five non-indigenous staff of the centre and the four members of the Cherokee delegation. In this conversation, I asked a question of John with regard to the role that non-indigenous academics might play in the struggle of indigenous peoples for recognition, reparations, and reconciliation. He didn't find a response easy to come by, and turned to Jim for his wisdom. Sitting to one side of the group, Jim waited a while and then spoke. What follows is a verbatim transcript of what Jim said, the conversation having been recorded for future teaching purposes and with the knowledge and consent of all involved.

Jon: *What role do you folks see that we* [non-indigenous activist-academics] *could or should play? How do we contribute to the justice mission? What role could or might I play that is not re-colonizing or re-embedding white Western ways of knowing? How can I contribute my skills without re-colonizing?*

[very long pause]

Jim: *We have our own strengths, we have our own strengths* [pause] *to take care of ourselves. We've been doing that for eons of years. We didn't have to have you guys come in and help us, we didn't have to have your help, but you came in and said, 'Hey, I'm here to help you', and you wound up taking our lands and* [pause] *taking our culture* [pause] *and that's how you help us* [pause] *and today, we don't understand the Western philosophy of help.* [pause] *We've been prodded, we've been poked. We've been loaded on trains and hauled away from our indigenous lands in the name of 'helping you'. So there's a trust factor. I don't trust you.* [long pause] *I don't care how much you say 'I've come to help you', I don't trust you.* [emphasis added] (Courtyard Conversation series, Centre for Australian Indigenous Knowledges, September 26, 2012)

THE THIRD TALE: "IT'S NOT PROPER RESEARCH THOUGH, IS IT?"

Through 2011, I worked with a group of Australian Aboriginal academics on the development of research capacity. This work had commenced with the expectation that the teaching-learning approach would be one of reciprocity: I would explain what I knew about Western approaches to research, particularly in the collection and use of visual (observation) and oral (interview, conversational) research approaches and other participants would do likewise with their personal (Australian Aboriginal) cultural experiences of coming to know—yarning and the like. The reciprocal or two-way learning did not eventuate. The focus remained exclusively on the development of facility with Western ways of knowing. One of the participants, Veronica—a septuagenarian Australian Aboriginal woman—was in the final stages of preparing her doctoral dissertation for examination.

Some months later, after she had had her doctoral award conferred, we met to talk about her methodology, which I knew from conversations with her had involved an extensive use of yarning. She explained in great detail some of the forms, uses, and protocols that attached to yarning (some I could not be permitted to know). She knew this particular way of coming to know was culturally familiar to the Australian Aboriginal participants in her doctoral study. She knew that she had been able to elicit far more authentic insights from the use of this technique than had she worked the non-indigenous vein of research method. She was aware of the power of drawing in and on the silences and the seeming irrelevances that were introduced into the yarns, and of reading the positioning of the body in various ways. She knew yarning was a research method(ology) that had helped her come to understand the focus of her dissertation.

TABLE OF CONTENTS

v

Figure 1. Veronica's dissertation: Table of contents.

So why, I asked, did she not foreground yarning in the methodology chapter of her dissertation? Why had she (very) briefly discussed yarning in her literature review chapter but fail to mention it in her methodology chapter (see Figure 1)?

Her response was to the effect that yarning probably wasn't "real research," it wasn't what "real researchers" did. She appeared quite content to submerge her culturality and the actual ways she had gone about her task as a researcher because of a belief in the inferiority of her people's ways of knowing. How does one respond to a situation such as this? Was this a moment for the provocation of conscientização to emerge?

Captured within the first two tales is, for me, the essential dilemma facing would-be allies of the colonized-oppressed: on the one hand, there is an expectation of urgent action (*What has taken you so long?*) while on the other there is a distrust and suspicion that would seem to work against anything approaching a collaborative or joint front in the struggle against the dehumanization that attends the ongoing colonial project (*I don't trust you*). I did not wish to re-centre the angst of the white Western male in the midst of widespread physical, cultural, emotional, and economic alienation and exploitation suffered by millions around the colonized world, but this is the space wherein I reside, and it is only from this space—this place of my concrete lived experience—that I can launch and continue my contribution to the re-humanizing task. The question became, How do I resolve the decolonial dilemma described in the first two tales in order to see my way clear in approaching the third?

Further, how might I move to reconcile my particular personal characteristics, experiences, and locations to genuinely respond to the concerns raised by almost daily challenges to my "right" to be involved in such struggles in the first place?

By way of illustration, as I was in the process of writing this piece, an indigenous Australian academic colleague at the university at which I work widely distributed a caution in an e-mail (some perceived it as a direct threat or, at the very least, an admonition to stay clear) regarding the terms of reference for the establishment of an Elders and Valued Persons Advisory Board. The board's function is to provide a link between Aboriginal and Torres Strait Islander peoples and their communities and the university. In so doing, the board would be a point of advice to indigenous and non-indigenous researchers and activists looking to work in, with, and for indigenous communities in their multifaceted struggles. The board would also provide entrée to such communities by approving, recommending, and advising individuals and projects. Accordingly, the terms of reference stipulate the composition of the board as being exclusively Aboriginal and Torres Strait Islander peoples. In response to a call for comment on these terms of reference, my Australian Aboriginal academic colleague wrote: "I just hope this committee will have a First Nations voice in its decision making processes and not be overrun by people 'speaking on behalf of' Aboriginal peoples and Torres Strait Islander peoples" (personal communication, November 4, 2012). This particular staff member's indigeneity has only fairly recently become known to her, and there is no clear community acceptance of her claim to belong to a particular mob, but nevertheless, her admonition and warning away of non-indigenous academic-activists presents other layers of complexity. Are there hierarchies of authenticity in the struggle against oppression and for re-humanization? Does the possession of certain characteristics of the oppressed privilege some in the struggle while the lack of some such characteristics excludes or disqualifies others? Should my participation in the struggle be downgraded, made suspect, or shunned entirely because of the fact of my non-indigeneity?

DECOLONIAL PRAXIS: FREIRE, FANON, AND DU BOIS

In looking to come to understand something of the importance of the Veronica episode, Freire's contribution to the field of decolonial theory/praxis is apparent. I'd like to use a couple of key ideas developed by two other decolonial workers—W. E. B. Du Bois and Frantz Fanon—to unravel Veronica's seemingly deliberate and, to her, necessary submersion of her personal cultural ways of knowing in the pursuit of her doctorate. Following this, I return to Freire's ideas of conversion and communion in addressing the question of the ways in which oppressor-class comrades might contribute to as opposed to taking over the struggle for rehumanization.

Veronica's denial of the legitimacy of her culturally familiar ways of knowing was unexpected by me. She had participated in a research development program with me wherein the cultural and epistemological specificity of all research approaches had figured prominently. The program had at the very least opened up the value and appropriateness of the incorporation of ways to collect information, insights, and perspectives other than through the typical Western academic views of what constitutes "valid" research. The program had raised ideas of the value of thinking about how a broader conception of what constitutes the operation of the senses—indeed, even of what the range of the human senses might be—could contribute to the enhancement of the research repertoire of all researchers, and particularly allow indigenous researchers to find cultural comfort and familiarity within the more complex array of ways of knowing. For example, while research theorists such as Sarah Pink exhort researchers to consider ways in which they might draw upon the fuller range of the sensorium to make their ethnographic work more layered and "thick" (Pink, 2009), and arts-based research theorists are impacting on the ways in which researchers are making the presentation of their work more evocative of the human experience (Knowles & Cole, 2008), much of this contemporary work takes a certain sensory, experiential, and epistemological universe for granted.

Other perspectives (typically, the perspectives of the Other) might have us look at a much wider range of sensory possibilities available to both inform our research work and our working with communities to use extant wisdom in pursuit of social betterment ends. As one example, the role of trance in many cultures around the world is well documented (see, for example, Jacobs, 1998), but would typically fall outside "standard" research texts and courses as a means of coming to know in any verifiable, "scientific" way.

Ways of engaging orally through things such as speaking or healing circles (features of many North American indigenous cultures) or the use of yarning in Australian Aboriginal and Torres Strait Islander cultures (Bessarab & Ng'andu, 2010; Carrello, 2009; Power, 2004) present ways similar to but distinctively different from the Western research focus on interviews, focus groups, and even learning conversations as ways of eliciting information or data through oral engagement. Veronica, as an Australian Aboriginal woman, drew upon the cultural familiarity, the knowledge of appropriate protocols held by both her and the Australian Aboriginal participants in her study, and on her faith that such an approach would best elicit the type of insights, opinions, and experiences she needed for her doctoral work. And yet, she declined to accord such a data-gathering approach the status of a research method. How might this peculiarity (to me) be explained and understood, and how might Veronica's legitimatization of the illegitimacy of her cultural ways of knowing be made sense of?

W. E. B. Du Bois, Frantz Fanon, and Paulo Freire each offer their own theoretical positions on this type of phenomenon, but all essentially proffer a similar explanation. Du Bois's notions of the double bind of consciousness and the Veil are the result of some of the earliest Western explorations of what Du Bois saw as the processes at play that led to a racialized society within which both black and white (these were the essentialized racial categories with which he worked, despite warning about the "homogenizing" of the African race) suffered from a loss of completeness. For Du Bois, dominant white ideological practices led to the division and compartmentalization of society along what he termed a (metaphoric) color line: whites on one side, blacks on the other. Marking this line was the Veil, through which inter-racial communication and knowledge of the Other was blurred. Dominant (white) society saw only the black lifeworld in a grossly distorted form that was replicated by the black view of the white world. The difference that hegemonic power makes, though, is that the inhabitants of the black side of the line came to see themselves as they were seen by the white world: as inferior and unworthy of full civic and cultural membership of the community and society.

In *The Souls of Black Folk*, Du Bois argued that the Veil was not necessarily a totally emasculating thing for the black world; that it had the power to obfuscate, blur, and protect as much as to reveal aspects of the Negro (to use Du Bois's term) lifeworld (Du Bois, 1903, p. vii). The relationship between the color line, the Veil and the experience of double-consciousness is an important one for the purposes of this chapter. Reiland Rabaka, a critical theoretical scholar of Du Bois's work, has described this relationship thus:

> Racial oppression, racial exploitation, and racial violence, first, racially divide and socially separate (the color-line); second, distort cultural communications and human relations between those they racially divide along the color-line (the Veil); and, third, as a result of these aforementioned, cause blacks to suffer from a severe inferiority complex that insidiously induces them to constantly view themselves from whites' supposed "superior" points of view (double consciousness). (Rabaka, 2010, pp. 134–135)

Du Bois emphasized the psychic impact of this life of no true self-consciousness:

> It is a peculiar sensation, this double-consciousness, this sense of always looking at one's self through the eyes of others, of measuring one's soul by the tape of a world that looks on in amused contempt and pity. One ever feels this twoness—an American, a Negro; two souls, two thoughts, two unreconciled strivings; two warring ideals in one dark body, whose dogged strength alone keeps it from being torn asunder. The history of the American Negro is the history of this strife…this longing to attain self-conscious manhood, to merge his double self into a better and truer self. (Du Bois, 1903, p. 3)

From a Du Boisian perspective, Veronica's refusal to accord to ways from her side of the Veil the legitimacy she accords to those from the Other side would appear to be a result of the internalization of a sense of Self mired deeply in the mud of self-deprecation, a self-loathing that is almost a by-product of the power of hyper-visible whiteness to embed its ways as superior. Through the process of the development of a double-consciousness, Veronica's position is explicable as one where, while she knows how people like herself use culturally sound ways of knowing, these ways do not accord with what she sees as the superior—and appropriate, proper, and correct—ways of the West.

This is the false consciousness that can only, in Freire's view, be addressed through the development of a critical consciousness, of *conscientização*. The genesis of such false consciousness can be explained through Frantz Fanon's notion of cultural amputation. Here, the colonized-oppressed must effectively cut themselves adrift from their cultural identities if they are to achieve any sense of (faux) self-worth. By constructing blackness as inferior, shameful, and despicable, the non-white colonized-oppressed have little choice but to eschew any connection with traits of that identity, in much the same way as black attempts at passing as white require the erasure of memory, familial and cultural relationships, and sense of (historical) self. It was the development of a resistance to such amputation that drove Fanon's anti-colonial work.

In resonance with Freire, Fanon argued that the colonizer worked most effectively when operating on the psyche or consciousness of the colonized. In a way not dissimilar to Althusser's (2001) distinction between repressive and ideological State apparatuses, Fanon saw the inability or refusal of colonized cultures to acknowledge the veracity of their own ways of knowing as part of the price to be paid to live as imitation colonizers. Fanon saw that "structures of colonialism were designed to amputate the colonized subjects from their history, culture, values, and worldviews till they believe the colonizer is their savior and only source of hope" (Adjei, 2010, pp. 90–91). Such a notion is similar to Freire's idea of adhesion wherein "one pole [the oppressed] aspires not to liberation, but to identification with its opposite pole [the oppressor]" (Freire, 2000, pp. 45–46). With a somewhat broader brush and working through Malcolm X's idea of "psychic conversion," bell hooks exposes the dilemma facing the colonized:

> Assimilation comes with a price, for the dominant culture is also dominator culture. This means that in order to attain material success beyond the boundaries of economic necessity…they usually must collude in supporting the thinking and practice of white supremacy. (hooks, 2012, p. 24)

Both Du Bois and Fanon speak to this core aspect of colonization—and therefore, a prime site for decolonial struggle—that might be seen as a form of cultural and epistemological transvestitism: the adopting of the psychic as well as the material adornments of the dominant/dominator culture by the colonized. Veronica's episode here presents as a likely instance of what Peter McLaren terms "epistemicide" (McLaren, 2012). In this instance, the erasure or destruction of the legitimacy of a culture's way of knowing occurs with the complicity of the carriers and constructors of that culture.

Freire entered into the question of the type of relationship necessary to enable the colonizer and colonized to effect a peace (of sorts) in order to work to ensure the dissolution of their respective subject positions. The mission of the oppressed is clear: "to liberate themselves and their oppressors as well" (Freire, 2000, p. 44) through what becomes a pedagogy of the oppressed. On the role or contribution of the colonizer/oppressor, however, Freire provides far less guidance and greater ambiguity. For Freire, "The oppressor, who is himself dehumanized because he dehumanizes others, is unable to lead this struggle" (2000, p. 47); a pedagogy of the oppressed "cannot be developed or practiced by the oppressors" (p. 54). But while members of the oppressor class cannot lead or practice the humanizing project that is the aim of a pedagogy of the oppressed, "[t]heirs is a fundamental role, and has been throughout the history of this struggle" (p. 60).

The ideas of conversion and communion are important here, as much for the caveats they carry as for their illuminative potential. The conversion process involves members of the colonizer-oppressor class moving to the side of the colonized-oppressed in the pursuit of a just and humane social order. For Freire, such allies, as indicated above, are crucial to the decolonization task, but suffer the effects of psychic colonization as well: "as they cease to be exploiters and move to the side of the exploited, they almost always bring with them the marks of their origin: their prejudices and their deformations, which include a lack of confidence in the people's ability to think, to want, and to know" (Freire, 2000, p. 60). As such, "false charity" and "malefic generosity" are the hallmarks of such attempts to soften the exploitative colonial relationship without actually addressing the structural framework of this relationship.

To effect genuine collaboration, the convert needs, in a Freirean sense, to develop a genuine communion with the colonized-oppressed. Using Che Guevara's experiences in Sierra Maestra as examples, Freire asserts the importance of communion with the oppressed:

> In dialogical theory, at no stage can revolutionary action forgo communion with the people. Communion in turn elicits cooperation, which brings leaders and people to the fusion described by Guevara. This fusion can exist only if revolutionary action is really human, empathetic, loving, communicative, and humble, in order to be liberating. (Freire, 2000, p. 171)

In the problematic situation in which I found (and continue to find) myself—Veronica's story—and at the same time conscious of also being caught between the twin pincers of urgency and mistrust, I am left wondering about the complexities surrounding the convert colonizer-oppressor's relationship with the colonized-oppressed. Is it possible to desire a new relationship more than those most likely to gain from the reconstruction of the relations of inequity? Is patience an essential quality of the convert? How does one provoke *conscientização* without engaging in either vanguardism or neocolonial activities? Freire warns of the dangers of the latter: "to consider oneself the proprietor of revolutionary wisdom—which must then be given to (or imposed on) the people—is to retain the old ways" (Freire, 2000, pp. 60–61). And, of course, the wisdom of Chief Jim and his comments about the centrality of trust is evident throughout Freire's work here: "They talk about the people, but they do not trust them; and trusting the people is the indispensible precondition for revolutionary change" (p. 60).

Freire has centred the importance of developing trust through truly dialogic engagement across the colonizer-colonized divide, but the central and continuing question for me, as a (hopeful) convert or ally in the liberatory struggle remains: Can the oppressor only work on her or his side of the dichotomy in the re-humanizing project? At present, I am left to wonder at the probability of engaging with the colonized in anything approaching a liberatory relationship born of, in Freire's terms, a genuine communion with the oppressed. There is clearly a need not only for the oppressed, but also for members of the oppressor class to seek the solace, wisdom, and inspiration of allies in the pursuit of a genuinely decolonial praxis and world.

REFERENCES

Adjei, P. (2010). Resistance to amputation: Discomforting truth about colonial education in Ghana. In G. J. S. Dei & M. Simmons (Eds.), *Fanan & education: Thinking through pedagogical possibilities* (pp. 78–104). New York, NY: Peter Lang.

Althusser, L. (2001). *Lenin and philosophy and other essays* (B. Brewster, Trans.). New York, NY: Monthly Review Press.

Bessarab, D., & Ng'andu, B. (2010). Yarning about yarning as a legitimate method in indigenous research. *International Journal of Critical Indigenous Studies, 3*(1), 37–50.

Brewer, R. M. (1993). Theorizing race, class and gender: The new scholarship of black feminist intellectuals and black women's labor. In A. P. A. Busia & S. M. James (Eds.), *Theorizing black feminisms: The visionary pragmatism of black women* (pp. 13–30). London, England: Routledge.

Carrello, C. (2009). Yarning—Aboriginal people's way of doing business. *The Journal of Aboriginal Health, 4,* 3.

Collins, P. H. (1990). *Black feminist thought: Knowledge, consciousness, and the politics of empowerment.* London, England: Unwin Hyman.

Dei, G. S. (2003). Why write black? Reclaiming African culture resource knowledges in diasporic contexts. In J. L. Conyers (Ed.), *Afrocentricity and the academy: Essays on theory and practice* (pp. 221–230). Jefferson, NC: McFarland.

Du Bois, W. E. B. (1903). *The souls of black folk: Essays and sketches.* Chicago, IL: A.C. McClurg.

Fanon, F. (1967). *Black skin, white masks.* New York: Grove Weidenfeld.

Freire, P. (1970/1972a). *Cultural action for freedom.* Harmondsworth, Middlesex, England: Penguin.

Freire, P. (1970/1972b). *Pedagogy of the oppressed* (M. B. Ramos, Trans.). Harmondsworth, Middlesex, England: Penguin.

Freire, P. (1973). *Education for critical consciousness.* New York, NY: Seabury.

Freire, P. (2000). *Pedagogy of the oppressed.* New York, NY: Continuum.

hooks, b. (2012). *Writing beyond race: Living theory and practice.* London, England: Routledge.

Jacobs, D. T. (1998). *Primal awareness.* Rochester, VT: Inner Traditions International.

Kincheloe, J., & Steinberg, S. (2008). Indigenous knowledges in education: Complexities, dangers, and profound benefits. In N. K. Denzin, Y. S. Lincoln, & L. T. Smith (Eds.), *Handbook of critical and indigenous methodologies* (pp. 135–156). Los Angeles, CA: Sage.

Knowles, J. G., & Cole, A. L. (Eds.). (2008). *Handbook of the arts in qualitative research: Perspectives, methodologies, examples, and issues.* Los Angeles, CA: Sage.

McLaren, P. (2012). *Occupying critical pedagogy: Reclaiming the legacy of Freire.* Paper presented at Paulo Freire: The Global Legacy conference, Hamilton, Aotearoa/New Zealand.

Pink, S. (2009). *Doing sensory ethnography.* London, England: Sage.

Power, K. M. (2004). Yarning: A responsive research methodology. *Journal of Australian Research in Early Childhood Education, 11*(1), 37–46.

Rabaka, R. (2010). *Against epistemic apartheid: W. E. B. Du Bois and the disciplinary decadence of sociology.* Lanham, MD: Lexington Books.

Spivak, G. C. (1990). *The post-colonial critic: Interviews, strategies, dialogues.* London, England: Routledge.

CHAPTER THIRTY-TWO

Music Education as a "Practice of Freedom"

LINDA M. LOCKE

Much current political educational rhetoric boasts a concern for the raising of standards and the closing of "gaps." A typical example is Minister of Education Hekia Parata's 2012 budget speech entitled *Raising Achievement for All*.

> We are ambitious to see all our children reach their potential and that's why we aim to have 85% of all 18-year-olds having achieved a minimum of Level Two qualifications, NCEA or equivalent for 2016. This is a passport to a better life—because learning is earning… that's why our education plan is focused on raising five out of five of our kids. We want all our learners to realise their potential and we want to create kiwis that can fly. (Parata, 2012)

This empty rhetoric ("Learning is earning") with an apparent concern for matters of equity of opportunity shallowly masks a failure to openly engage with crucial issues related to the nature and purpose of education.

Freirean discourse is deeply concerned with ideals of justice and respect for humanity and invites dialogical engagement with these ideals and how they might be embedded in educational practice. Freirean pedagogy highlights the political nature of education and calls unashamedly for education as "humanisation" to be achieved through "critical dialogical praxis" (Freire, 2011). Critical dialogical praxis calls for the exercise of individual agency in a way that respects and in turn enables the exercise of agency in others.

This chapter will engage with these Freirean notions in relationship to a vision of music education in the twenty-first century. With specific reference to general music education in the Aotearoa New Zealand state primary school context, it will ask: "What might be required for music education to be both conceived and enacted as a practice of freedom?"

> Education either functions as an instrument which is used to facilitate integration of the younger generation into the logic of the present system and bring about conformity or it becomes the practice of freedom, the means by which men and women deal critically and creatively with reality and discover how to participate in the transformation of their world. (Freire, 1993, p. 34)

LEARNING TO ASK THE QUESTION: WHAT DOES IT MEAN TO EDUCATE?

My life as a teacher began when I entered Dunedin Teacher's College as a young and somewhat sheltered 16-year-old adolescent from a small coastal village in East Otago. As a country girl, I had been supported through boarding school by my parents, until my somewhat overdeveloped conscience and an adolescent longing for independence impelled me to free them of their financial responsibility for me. The small wage available to teacher trainees in the 1960s enabled this transition. Barely out of high school and hardly aware of the culture and contours of my own country, I was somewhat bamboozled by the first Education 101 assignment, which asked me to comment on the difference between, and pass opinion on, the relative value of the education systems in the ancient Greek states of Athens and Sparta. Despite my extreme naïvety at the time, this essay aroused my first flicker of interest in the question, "What does it *mean* to *educate?*"

In my life since that time as a classroom teacher and as a classroom-based music teacher, in particular, I have challenged myself to engage with this question at depth in the action reflection cycle of my classroom practice. In more recent times, reading and research activity have enabled me explore this question, specifically in relation to issues in music education, through a number of lenses that can be seen to come under the broad umbrella of the term *critical theory,* which, as Regelski (2005) argues, offers "totally fresh approaches for understanding both the status of music education today and for addressing its many problems as a social project" (p. 2).

In what follows, I will explore this question of what it means to educate musically in relationship to the critical pedagogy of Paulo Freire. Taking on board Freire's consistent challenge to the educator to take up an ethical position in relationship to the act of teaching, I will ask, "What does viewing music education as a practice of freedom in Freirean terms mean?" In addition, I will address the question: "What implications might this have for music education in the context of primary schooling in Aotearoa New Zealand?"

FREIREAN EPISTEMOLOGY

The Freirean dialectical view of reality acknowledges the prevalence of contradictions and asserts that all things—the world of nature, socially created material objects, institutional practices, and so on—are in a state of motion or change (Freire, 1985). It follows that reality can never be known fully. We can come to know more fully, but we cannot ever say that we possess full knowledge.

> Knowledge is always becoming. That is if the act of knowledge has historicity, then today's knowledge about something is not necessarily the same tomorrow. Knowledge is changed to the extent that reality also moves and changes. (Horton, 1990, p. 101)

Emanating from the belief that knowledge is always becoming, so too are we as human beings ever in a process of becoming. Freire (1998) explores the idea that a particular kind of growth characterises human life when he says:

> Growing to us (human beings) is something more than growing to the trees or the animals that unlike us cannot take their own growth as an object of their preoccupation. For us growing is a process in which we can intervene.... We are indisputably programmed beings but we are in no way predetermined.... It is precisely because we become capable of inventing our existence, something more than the life it implies but supplants, that growing to us gradually becomes much more complex and problematic, in the rigorous sense of this adjective, than growing is to trees and animals. (p. 94)

For Freire, the creative process of becoming is also intimately bound up with his ethical ideal of humanisation. It is not a project, which can be completed; rather, it is a process that has at its heart ongoing, creative change, and growth as a result of interaction, communication, and dialogue with others.

TEACHING AS A POLITICAL ACT

For Freire, education *is* never, and *can* never be a neutral activity. Freire's assertion that to teach is to engage in a political act is a call to accountability of a very different kind from that of the extrinsic accountability constructed by neoliberal discourse exercised through the imposition of "standards" against which teachers and students alike are continually measured through wide-ranging forms of bureaucratic surveillance. Teaching as a political act in Freirean terms demands a commitment to intrinsic accountability, in which teachers, through dialogical praxis, hold themselves accountable to a process of action and reflection, which is at the same time an "act of creation" (2011, p. 89). Teaching as a political act takes careful and thoughtful account of the exercise of power.

To engage in critical, dialogical praxis implies a communicative relationship with others and the world. It is the process though which we can come to know and recreate the world. Dialogical praxis allows for the continual interplay of action and reflection, which enables meanings to be changed through action. To engage in true dialogue is to name the world; in naming the world, the world can be transformed (Freire, 1972).

> Men and women are human beings because they are historically constituted as beings of praxis, and in the process they have become capable of transforming the world—of giving it meaning. (Freire, 1985, p. 155)

Being engaged with the world, objectifying oneself, inheriting acquired experience, responding to experience, creating and recreating reality—all these enable human beings to intervene in reality and, as artists, to effectively make and remake history and culture. The essence of living a truly human life involves one in a communicative relationship with the world in which there is a unity of theory and practice, thought and being, and a balance of action and reflection. For Freire, education has a key role to play in the process of humanisation.

THE EXERCISE OF FREEDOM

The exercising of freedom is itself a quest or, in Freirean terms, an ongoing, never-to-be-completed project. For, as Peter Abbs (2003) describes authentic education, the art of teaching is not to prescribe "settled narratives of meaning but to engender a quest of what is not yet known or what may never be known" (p. 15). This quest for both teacher and student depends upon a choice for active engagement with the process of collaborative meaning-making that only ceases when we cease to live.

This view of freedom poses challenges on a personal and professional level. Freedom is available; we are simply challenged *and* ethically obliged to exercise it. From the Freirean point of view, the road (to freedom) is simply made by walking (it) (Horton, 1990).

BANKING EDUCATION VERSUS PROBLEM-POSING EDUCATION

Freire's characterisations of education, one of banking education and the other of problem posing, each imply a particular relationship with knowledge and with the process of humanization. Banking education is inherently oppressive and therefore dehumanising. It regards the teacher as a possessor of knowledge, which is to be bestowed as a "gift" upon passive, voiceless students. Knowledge becomes static and lifeless, and students are regarded as adaptable, manageable beings (Roberts, 1996, p. 126). Discouraging curiosity and creativity, banking education serves to maintain oppressive systems, reinforcing divisions and inequalities.

Pedagogical practices need to be examined for the ways in which power is exercised through unthinking complicity with particular "taken-for-granted" belief systems. Educators need to ask: Whose interests are being served in the ways in which I choose to represent the "world" or "reality" to the students I teach? Music education as the practice of freedom demands that teachers support reversible and fluid power relationships. Reversibility and fluidity will be promoted in teaching situations where the teacher and learner have opportunities for the exchange or negotiation of roles. Students can be encouraged not only to challenge, to question, to disagree, but also to take the lead in situations in which others (including the teacher) position themselves as co-learners. Where curriculum is tightly defined and teachers are appraised on the basis of pupils' attainment of particular learning outcomes, roles are likely to become fixed. Education, as the practice of freedom, however, seeks the engagement of the learner in a collaborative way, where the learner is enabled to make choices and participate willingly. Moreover, it encourages the aforementioned opportunities for role reversal, where the domination or acquiescence to arbitrary authority is resisted and replaced with a genuine empowerment of the learner.

Problem-posing education, which is at the heart of Freire's philosophy, has at its heart the process of dialogical praxis fostering reflection and action. Dialogue becomes the pivotal, pedagogical process (Roberts, 1996). Teachers and students are involved in a non-hierarchical relationship in which they communicate, critically reflect, and come to know. Through this process, knowledge is made and remade together.

CRITICAL DIALOGICAL PRAXIS AND MUSIC EDUCATION IN NEW ZEALAND

In considering the relevance of Freire's approach to freedom, knowledge, and education, with its emphasis on a process of becoming through critical dialogical praxis, to the context of music education in New Zealand, it is useful to note that the subject "Music" in New Zealand state schools has denoted quite different content since the time of its inception in the 1870s (Braatvedt, 2002). There has been, and continues to be, an evolution in the way music as a subject is constructed in the school curriculum. Nevertheless, a subject domain denoted by the word "Music," and now with the additional nomenclature "Sound Arts," continues to be a mandated area as one of four arts disciplines within the Arts curriculum (Ministry of Education, 2007).

There is wide-ranging commentary on the inadequacy of the term "music" to describe a phenomenon that involves a diverse set of socio-cultural practices (e.g., Small, 1998). While music may be a universal human phenomenon, a description of music that implies a kind of universal language is no longer regarded as valid (Shehan Campbell, 1997). As ethnomusicologist Borgo (2013) points out, the plural denotation "music(s)" offers a recognition of the plurality of musical practices that is not necessarily acknowledged in the use of the singular noun.

Small (1998) coined the term "musicking" to make clear the centrality of the doing, or active involvement in a range of individual practices and activities within a social context, be it as listener, performer, mover of instruments, or publicity agent. In using such a term, he was highlighting the socially constructed nature of musical practices.

MULTIPLICITY OF PRACTICES

The Freirean construct of dialogical praxis is highly relevant to a music education pedagogy seeking to be responsive to the multiplicity of musical practices in ways in which the importance and the complexity of the context are recognised and acknowledged. According to Bowman (2005), a praxial philosophy of music education recognises the need for *"mindful doing"* in music education. Such a philosophy emphasises the appropriateness of evaluating any music on its own terms, and acknowledges the situatedness and multiplicity of practice, that is, that musics are "multi-dimensional, fluid, polysemic, and unstable" (p. 71) Bowman suggests that praxialism offers an "heuristic tool to music education philosophy rather than a set of answers" (p. 73). Seeking to engage with moral and political issues, he is concerned not just with what *is* but with what *ought* to be:

> Music education is not just about music, it is about students and it is about teachers and it is about the kind of societies we hope to build together. (2005, p. 75)

He argues that a praxial approach can "commend certain instructional methods for their apparent congruence with a given musical practice but has little to say about whose or which musical practices warrant musical instruction" (p. 71).

TRANSFORMATIVE MUSIC EDUCATION

A Freirean philosophy, when applied to music education, clearly implies a commitment to the view that education ought to be transformative. Regelski (1998) suggests that a praxial music education is governed by an ethical dimension (phronesis) in which right results are judged specifically in terms of the people served. Therefore, one must ask how particular learning experiences are offered, and whether they are transformative in terms of the goal of humanisation. Freirean dialogical praxis cannot, without an internal contradiction, definitively answer the question, "What will I teach?" But it offers, in the way in which negotiated meaning-making and a process of action and reflection are embedded, a rigorously ethical, interactive approach to the process of designing music programmes both at the macro and micro level. Abrahams (2005), drawing on Freirean pedagogy, suggests that critical pedagogues need to ask four questions when planning music instruction: "Who am I? Who are my students? What might they become? What might we become together? These questions offer a starting point for both procedure and content" (p. 63).

The Freirean view emphasises connectedness to others and to the world. According to Roberts (2003), Freire argues that "it is only through intersubjectivity that individual existence makes sense.... For Freire the "we exist" explains the "I exist"" (p. 106). Poet and educator Peter Abbs (2003), in discussing the collaborative nature of teaching and learning, draws attention to the African philosophical view that identity is communally determined when he quotes a famous Swahili saying: "I am because we are" (p. 16).

The praxial approach to music education and Freirean critical dialogical praxis both demand full and active engagement and involvement in learning experiences by all participants in a social situation. All the "players" in any learning "ensemble" must be positioned as capable of making valid choices and contributions. This requires a shift in thinking away from notions of music teaching as the identification and nurturing of special talent, toward the offering of opportunities in which all students can engage in meaningful musical behaviour.

The recent development of informal large-scale community musical festivals for children in, for example, Auckland, Christchurch, and Hamilton, such as the marimba festival and the ukulele festival, are joyful, celebratory community events. These festival ensembles focus on engaged, successful music-making for *all* and cater to a wide range of sophisticated and less sophisticated musical behaviour in which both formal (school-based general music classes and instrumental instruction) and informal learning are reflected. Repertoire for these events typically reflects the wide-ranging musical discourses that are available to students in their everyday life. Such repertoire includes traditional material (Pasifika, Maori, Celtic, and so on), popular music, adaptations of long-held favourites, and recently composed original material, including students' compositions. The development of these festivals can be attributed to the a recognition, on the part of a particular music education community, of the importance of providing music-learning experiences for all children that respond to their everyday lives and enable music-making within appropriately scaffolded musical ensembles that are meaningful in their own terms.

SELF-REFLEXIVITY AND SCEPTICISM

Critical dialogical praxis also calls for the development of critical self-reflexivity in music teachers themselves. First, it asks us to consider the socially and culturally constructed nature of our own knowledge and to bring a healthy scepticism (Jorgensen, 2003) to the positions we have come to inhabit, and in particular to be alert for the need to challenge (within ourselves) "taken-for-granted" or "commonsense" beliefs. Second, it demands that we apply this same scepticism and wariness to educational discourses, which offer "settled narratives" in the form of final answers, and watertight, widely applicable solutions to problems.

Scepticism and its more active form, interrogation, are particularly pertinent to one's approach to curriculum statements and assessment regimes. In the case of the *New Zealand Curriculum* (The Arts: Music) (Ministry of Education, 2007) and its implementation at the primary level, the exercise of freedom means to take responsibility for the making of meaning in our own way, while also taking account of others' interpretations of the four learning strands and their associated achievement objectives. Rather than accepting, or even seeking, absolute definitions from a Ministry of Education or its agents, we ought as professionals to explore and define in our own terms and those relevant to our own students, the very broad umbrella concepts encompassed in such strands as "Understanding music in context."

Similarly, the open-ended achievement objectives associated with each strand need to be interrogated and shaped and reshaped to fit a need and/or an agenda arrived at through a process of critical dialogical praxis. Teachers need to give themselves permission to "play" with interpretations of any curriculum statement in order that learning experiences in relationship to and with particular school communities, who inhabit particular geographical, cultural, and socioeconomic "places" at particular moments in history, may be designed and offered.

PRAXIS VERSUS METHODOLOTRY

Roberts (1996) cautions against the domestication of Freirean pedagogy in ways that simplify his philosophy and reduce it to a few stock phrases. He also cautions against reducing the Freirean approach to a set of fixed techniques or strategies. He argues that, from a Freirean point of view, the first question that must be asked in any situation is: "What human ideals do we wish to promote?" not "What methods should I use?"

In recent years, there has been a resurgence of interest in the Orff Schulwerk approach to music education in New Zealand, particularly in early childhood, primary, and intermediate settings, evidenced in the formation of a national society, Orff New Zealand Aotearoa (ONZA), and increased professional development opportunities for music teachers. There is, of course, a propensity for music education to become captured by particular approaches that become fads and that are susceptible to becoming prescriptive methods (Mills, 2005; Regelski, 2002). This propensity often reflects the dubious comfort teachers can find in the seemingly fixed meanings that are provided by tight prescriptions and "how to" manuals. Regelski coined the term *methodolotry* for this (2002). Methodolotry is the antithesis of a critical pedagogy.

In the case of the Schulwerk, however, in-depth examination of the principles and processes outlined in the original documentation of the work of Carl Orff and Gunild Keetman reveal the centrality of improvisation and composition, and the need for responsiveness to temporal, cultural, and geographical contexts (Dunbar-Hall, 2000; Haselbach, 2011; Keetman, 1970; Orff, 2011). Such principles are compatible with a dialogical approach and, I would argue, a critical pedagogy.

Applications of the Orff Schulwerk approach in some New Zealand primary, intermediate, and secondary contexts have resulted in opportunities for students to participate equitably in musical ensembles composed of authentic (as opposed to "toy") instruments that do not require highly developed technical or music-reading skills (Locke & Locke, 2011) Critical dialogical praxis in sound could be said to exist when students are enabled to engage in holistic music-making, that is, music-making that involves listening, playing, moving, improvising, conducting, and so on, which draws on the autobiographies of learning (Burnard, 2005, p. 267) that the students bring to the classroom.

What is called for, in critical pedagogy, is an engagement with "ideas," contemporary or less so, which recognises the situatedness of all pedagogical theory and an accompanying interrogative approach that examines the degree to which theory may yield approaches and practices that are able to contribute, to a greater or lesser degree, to the process of transformation.

New Zealand music educators who engage with the ideas of Orff Schulwerk, or any ideas deemed worthy or potentially relevant to a teaching context, *may* discover that they can employ content, strategies, and resources based on these ideas within a critical pedagogy approach to music education, where "they create a rich and varied music programme and encourage learning experiences that are multiple and liberating" (Horton, 1990). Prescribed sequences of learning, lesson, or unit templates may inspire or even scaffold planning, but the relevance and vitality of a music programme depends upon a reflexive exercise of freedom in which a cycle of activity and reflection on activity are finely balanced.

AN EXAMPLE FROM THE CLASSROOM

Burnard (2005) suggests that a praxial view offers much to the teacher of general music education:

> It firmly locates the musical understandings of teachers and learners within our personal autobiographies of learning, so that we find authority in our individual musical experiences. Furthermore, it affirms the complexity of children as reflective music makers and validates listening, performing, improvising, arranging and conducting as interdependent forms of creative doing. (p. 267)

At my own school, what began as a small-group, somewhat spontaneous, compositional activity related to our school's environmental education programme ended up becoming a whole-school, cross-curricular project involving a large number of students, other teachers, local community members, parents, and musicians. A series of haiku had been written by a small group of children, which captured their experience of the local stream to which they were connected through their everyday life and, as well, through their knowledge of Maori mythology of this area (as the home of the local taniwha, Mokoroa). The following example was written by a 10-year-old student:

Criss-cross leaves on tree
Curling ferns fan upwards
Sly singing waters

Drawing on these haiku, students became composers of soundscapes. Becoming conductors, they directed improvised performances of the soundscapes. Becoming musical collaborators, they worked with a local musician to extend the soundscapes into a larger composition. Finally, choosing to become performers, some students performed this composition—the musical suite of pieces, *Opanuku Stream*, of which they felt considerable "ownership"—at a regional music festival with a very large (and appreciative) audience. Retrospectively, it is clear to me that all strands of the curriculum were covered. Formative assessment was embedded into learning process. However, summative assessment was rendered irrelevant and impracticable in such a situation, because of the ineffectiveness of any assessment tool in capturing the richness of these students' multi-dimensional experiences.

CONCLUDING THOUGHTS

In the New Zealand context, the Arts in Years 1 to 10 have so far eluded the crushing imposition of "national standards." Music at these levels has escaped the obsessive concern for the establishment of uniform, measurable outcomes that have become the sacred cow in other areas of the curriculum. Many would argue that this constitutes, or is symptomatic of, the marginalisation of the arts within the schooling enterprise. (It can, of course, be argued that the nature of the whole artistic enterprise is to *be* a voice from the margins.) However, the absence of this heavy, top-down surveillance, in which a one-size-fits-all assessment regime is applied to complex areas of human activity, may be considered an advantage. While a subject such as music evades this normalising gaze, there is a space for music teachers to engage their freedom and, as professionals, to take seriously the opportunity to build their pedagogical practice as a space in which meaning-making is created in a negotiated and dialogical way. If, as in Freire's terms, "to read the word is to read the world" (2011), is not to make music, to sing the world—to play and listen to the world in sound?

This vital interconnection between pedagogy and ethics as the practice of freedom requires a commitment to the process of being the "authors of our own lives" (Garrison, 1997, p. 169). For, as Foucault (1987) said, "What is morality if it is not the practice of liberty, the deliberate practice of liberty?" (p. 4) In a world of givens—the givens of our own biological identity, our life circumstances, and the discourses, which we inhabit and which inhabit us—there is still considerable "room to move."

> In a human being there is always something that only he himself can reveal, in a free act of self-consciousness and discourse, something that does not submit to an externalising second hand definition…. As long as a person is alive he lives by the fact that he is not yet finalized, that he has not yet uttered his ultimate word. (Bahktin, 1984, pp. 58–59)

Freire's approach to knowledge and to life, with its emphasis on a process of becoming, offers opportunities and challenges for the exercise of creative action. Programme design and implementation call into play creative, musical, and intellectual faculties, whereby we take seriously the nature of our own becoming as educators and as musicians. We cannot be mere transmitters of fixed musical knowledge since, consistent with a Freirean view, there is simply no such knowledge. We are teachers learning how to teach and we must acknowledge our status as learners and our students' status as teachers. This involves listening to ourselves and to our colleagues. Crucially, however, it demands the sometimes hard graft of listening to the students we teach. We are challenged to listen to the voices on the margins, but it is necessary to note that those voices we regard as on the margins will differ according to where any of us, at any given time, choose to stand on the page.

As musicians, we need to acknowledge that we have an ever-growing and constantly changing set of skills, beliefs, and attitudes in relation to music. Teachers of music have often been musically educated within musical traditions that have emphasised performance reliant on a high level of technical musical expertise in relation to the interpretation of notated scores rather than improvisatory and inventive musical skills. This poses particular challenges in adapting to musical practices that promote creative musical action through improvisation and composition. It is important that teachers are challenged to engage and develop their own skills in this area, in order to be able to both model confident positive attitudes to musical inventiveness and to provide appropriate scaffolding for students engaging in creative musical activities. We must all be willing to subject ourselves to the risk-taking of art-making.

General music education in Aotearoa can exemplify and amplify critical dialogical praxis, guided by what Regelski (2005) terms phronesis, the concern for right results, through listening to, performing, composing, and improvising music that gives evidence of an authentic connection with the lives and concerns of particular communities. This demands an ongoing commitment to listening and responding to biographies, histories, herstories, and current political-social concerns of all students, colleagues, parents, and caregivers within a particular school community. The music teacher is challenged to be flexible enough to adapt her musicianship, musical interests, preferences, and knowledge to the situation in which she finds herself teaching.

REFERENCES

Abbs, P. (2003). *Against the flow: Education, the arts and postmodern culture*. London, England: Routledge Falmer.

Abrahams, F. (2005). Transforming classroom music instruction with ideas from critical pedagogy. *Music Educators Journal, 92*(1), 62–67. doi:10.2307/3400229

Bahktin, M. (1984). The hero and the position of the author with regard to the hero in Dostoyevsky's Art (C. Emerson, Trans.). In C. Emerson (Ed.), *Problems of Dostoyevsky's poetics* (pp. 58–59). Minneapolis: University of Minnesota Press.

Benedict, C. (2010). Methods and approaches. In H. F. Abeles & L. A. Custodero, *Critical issues in music education: Contemporary theory and practice* (pp. 194–214). New York, NY: Oxford University Press.

Borgo, D. (2013). *What does it mean to be musical?* San Diego, CA: uctv. Retrieved from http://www.youtube.com/watch?feature=player_embedded&v=wVP8tWg7SQY

Bowman, W. (2005). The limits and grounds of musical praxialism. In D. J. Elliott (Ed.), *Praxial music education: Reflections and dialogues* (pp. 52–78). Oxford, England: Oxford University Press.

Braatvedt, S. (2002). *A history of music education in New Zealand state primary and intermediate schools* (Unpublished doctoral dissertation). University of Canterbury, Christchurch, New Zealand.

Burnard, P. (2005). What matters in general music? In D. J. Elliott (Ed.), *Praxial music education: Reflections and dialogues* (pp. 267–280). Oxford, England: Oxford University Press.

Dunbar-Hall, P. (2000). World music, creativity and Orff pedagogy. In A. de Quadros (Ed.), *Many seeds, different flowers: The music education legacy of Carl Orff* (pp. 58–66). Perth, Western Australia: Callaway International Resource Centre for Music Education.

Foucault, M. (1987). The ethic of care for the self as a practice of freedom: An interview with Michel Foucault on January 20, 1984 (J. Gauthier, Trans.). In J. Bernauer & D. Rasmussen (Eds.), *The final Foucault* (pp. 1-20). Cambridge, MA: MIT Press.

Freire, P. (1972). *Pedagogy of the oppressed*. New York: Continuum.

Freire, P. (1985). *The politics of education*. London, England: Macmillan.

Freire, P. (1993). *Pedagogy of the oppressed, 20th anniversary edition*. New York, NY: Continuum.

Freire, P. (1998). *Pedagogy of freedom: Ethics, democracy, and civic courage*. Lanham, MD: Rowman & Littlefield.

Freire, P. (2011). *Pedagogy of the oppressed, 30th anniversary edition*. New York, NY: Continuum.

Garrison, J. (1997). *Wisdom and desire in the art of teaching*. New York, NY: Teachers College Press.

Haselbach, B. (Ed.). (2011). *Basic texts on theory and practice of Orff Schulwek* (Vol. 1). Mainz, Germany: Schott.

Horton, M. (1990). *We make the road by walking: Conversations on education and social change*. Philadelphia, PA: Temple University Press.

Jorgensen, E. (2003). *Transforming music education*. Bloomington: Indiana University Press.

Keetman, G. (1970). *Elementaria* (M. Murray, Trans.). London, England: Schott.

Locke, L., & Locke, T. (2011). Sounds of Waitakere: Using practitioner research to explore how year 6 recorder players compose responses to visual representations of a natural environment. *British Journal of Music Education*, 28(3), 263–284.

MENC, the National Association for Music Education (U.S.). (2010). *Alternative approaches in music education: Case studies from the field*. Lanham, MD: Rowman & Littlefield Education.

Mills, J. (2005). *Music in the school*. Oxford, England: Oxford University Press.

Ministry of Education. (2007). *The New Zealand Curriculum*. Wellington, New Zealand: Learning Media.

Orff, C. (2011). Orff Schulwerk: Past and future (1963). In B. Haselbach (Ed.), *Texts on theory and practice of Orff-Schulwerk* (pp. 134–159). Mainz, Germany: Schott.

Parata, H. (2012, May 16). *Speech notes: Raising achievement for all*. Presented at the Budget 2012 meeting, Wellington, New Zealand. Retrieved from http://www.scoop.co.nz/stories/PA1205/S00262/hekia-parata-raising-achievement-for-all-in-budget-2012.htm

Regelski, T. (1998). The Aristotelian bases for music and music education as praxis. *Philosophy of Music Education Review, 6*(1), 22–59.

Regelski, T. (2002). On "methodolatry" and music teaching as critical and reflexive praxis. *Philosophy of Music Education Review, 10*(2), 102–123.

Regelski, T. (2005). Critical theory as a foundation for critical thinking in music education. *Visions of Research in Music Education, 6*. Retrieved from http://www-usr.rider.edu/~vrme/v6n1/visions/Regelski%20Critical%20Theory%20as%20a%20Foundation.pdf

Roberts, P. (1996). Structure, direction and rigour in liberating education. *Oxford Review of Education, 22*(3), 295–316.

Shehan Campbell, P. (1997). Music, the universal language: Fact or fallacy. *International Journal of Music Education, 29*(2), 32–39.

Small, C. (1998). *Musicking*. Hanover, NH: University Press of New England.

CHAPTER THIRTY-THREE

Activism, Reflection, and Paulo Freire—an Embodied Pedagogy

TRACEY OLLIS

INTRODUCTION

This chapter explores the critical pedagogy of activists as they participate in activism on some of the most important human rights issues of our time. I argue that the pedagogy of activism is critically cognitive and embodied in a practice that is inherently social. The chapter commences with some writing on what I claim is Freire's own activism, always working toward a struggle for social justice and social change. His educational practices were never removed from sites and movements of struggle and resistance and he encouraged teachers to be political, that their teaching should never be disassociated from a critique of the political and social realities that impact on and create impediments to a democratic education.

The chapter then outlines empirical research on the learning dimensions of activists conducted in Australia and draws on some of their personal narratives. I explore the reflexivity of activists as they work within and against the state, on issues of indigenous self-determination, racism, religion, homophobia, urban development, climate change, civil liberties, economic inequality, and other topics of concern. I argue for a critically reflexive pedagogy, as Paulo Freire reminds us, activism without purposeful reflection has the potential to become what he termed "naïve activism." That is, a focus on the theory and philosophical underpinnings of activism, and the tactics and strategies necessary to instigate social change, can create a pedagogy that is wanting in praxis. Yet the urgency of activism and the desire for significant social change often prevents a critical space for reflection to occur.

The chapter concludes with some suggestions for how Freire's writing on praxis can improve activists' important practices.

METHODOLOGY AND CONTEXT OF THE CHAPTER

This chapter focuses on the critical reflection of activists, and reveals through their narratives their critical engagement with the world around them.[1] Using empirical research conducted in Australia, the findings of this research revealed that activists' learning is cognitive, embodied, and situated in practice (Ollis, 2008, 2011, 2012). The research cited here is extrapolated from in-depth interviews conducted with activists to uncover their important pedagogy. The initial research explored the learning dimensions of two groups of activists: "lifelong activists," who have generally been involved in student politics and have participated in activism over many years, and the learning of "circumstantial activists," who become involved in protest as a result of a series of life circumstances. The research found that while both groups' learning is social and informal, lifelong activists tend to develop their skills incrementally by being involved in the fertile site of student politics. Conversely, circumstantial activists, not having had the benefit of early immersion in a community of practice, are rapid learners. They are frequently taken out of their comfort zone as activists and need to acquire new knowledge and skills urgently in order to practice effectively. Some circumstantial activists remain on the periphery of activism and never fully immerse themselves in the practices of activism (Ollis, 2012).

FREIRE'S ACTIVISM

Activism is a dynamic, engaged and embodied practice, one which provides us with a rich opportunity to understand adult learning (Foley, 1999; Ollis, 2008). My own recent research has focused on the embodied pedagogy of adult activists as they go about their important social change work, not always recognised as real adult education, but education nonetheless. It is fair to say that the pedagogy of activism is still in its infancy around the world (Branagan & Boughton, 2003; Crossley, 2002; Jasper & Goodwin, 2004; Whelan, 2002).

Although Paulo Freire never spoke of himself as an activist, it is clear that his actions were those of a person who was deeply committed to social justice and a democratic education for all. His commitment to educators and to those who teach was embodied in his writing, work, and actions. He firmly believed that education is political and that education cannot be removed from the current context of our social and political realities (Freire, 1972b, 1998, 2005b).

He also believed that educators should never remain politically neutral (Freire, 1998). For Freire, education was never and would never be without politics (Freire, 1998). He believed it was important for educators to state their political position on issues that concerned them and stake a claim for a just education system. This is expressed beautifully by Freire in his book *Pedagogy of Freedom*, in which he writes on education as a form of intervention in the world. "Education never was, is not and never can be neutral or indifferent in regard to the reproduction of the dominant ideology or the interrogation of it" (1998, p. 91). Freire had faith that students were able to form their own views, to challenge, to speak, to disturb, and to interrogate the ideas of their teachers; he knew that students would be able to find their own perspective on an issue even when a teacher expressed a political position of his or her own:

> I cannot deny or hide my posture, but I also cannot deny others the right to reject it. In the name of respect I should have towards my students, I do not see why I should omit or hide my political stance by proclaiming a neutral position that doesn't exist. On the contrary, my role as a teacher is to assent the student's right to compare, to choose, to rupture, to decide. (Freire, 1998, p. 68)

In *Teachers as Cultural Workers: Letters to Those Who Dare to Teach*, Freire's own activism is never clearer than in his argument for teachers to fight for justice in education. He claimed that although teaching required passion and a great thirst for knowledge, it also required teachers to fight for social justice in their everyday practise:

> It is for this reason that I stress that those wanting to teach must be able to dare, that is, to have the predisposition to fight for justice and to be lucid in defence of the need to create conditions conducive to pedagogy in schools. (Freire, 2005b, pp. 7–8)

Furthermore, Freire believed the struggle for democracy was not an individual effort and would only remain strong through teachers working collectively to push back against the state's imposition of policy that impacts on teachers' progressive pedagogy and practices:

> The project of democracy must never be transformed into or understood as a singular and individual struggle, even, as often happens, in the face of cheap persecution against this or that teacher for reasons that are purely personal. Furthermore, teachers should always stick together as they challenge the system so that their struggle is effective. (Freire, 2005b, p. 12)

Freire's theory of education brings together "radical critical theory and the imperatives of radical commitment and struggle" (Giroux, 1985, p. xii). An example of his solidarity with social movements is demonstrated when Freire was questioned by a student about why he supported the landless peasant movements in Brazil, whom the student perceived to be "troublemakers." He responded with the following:

> You do have some troublemakers among the landless peasants, but their struggle against oppression is both legitimate and ethical. The so-called troublemakers represent a form of resistance against those who aggressively oppose the agrarian reform. For me, the immorality and the lack of ethics lay with those who want to maintain an unjust order. (Freire, 1998, p. 68)

Freire's love of humanity was oftentimes shown in his rage about the impact of neoliberalism and its costs to those who were most disadvantaged: "My abhorrence of neo-liberalism helps to explain my legitimate anger when I speak of the injustices to which the rag pickers among humanity are condemned" (1998, p. 22).

Freire's lasting legacy is not only his seminal critique of rationalism and a dominant "banking system of education" and his encouragement for people's consciousness to be raised, but also his exhortation for them to act on their convictions; his lifelong belief that there was no teaching without learning; his passion, love, and commitment to his students, teaching, and teachers; and his clear and profound commitment to a democratic education. This legacy still influences new teachers today, and resonates strongly when they realise they have entered a profession that is inherently conservative, and they need to find a way not to have their newly found aspirations quashed by an education system that values performativity and instrumentalism, rather than their efforts to be creative and inspirational teachers. On this note, Freire (1998) encouraged teachers to stand strongly in an "armed love" of resistance against the impact of neoliberalism on teaching and teachers' practice, on the demands from bureaucracies and schools that prevent creative and imaginative work with students. He encouraged teachers to stand in solidarity with their colleagues to resist any changes to progressive pedagogy. "It is indeed necessary, however, that this love be an armed love of those convinced of the right and duty to fight, to denounce, and to announce. It is this form of love that is indispensable to the progressive educator and that we must all learn" (1998, p. 74).

More important, we see the influence of Freire's work in many of the popular education movements around the world. We can see his ideas resonate in the worker and peasant movements in Latin America, in the work of the Chiapas indigenous people in Mexico, the migrants in Western Europe, the popular education movements in Burma and the indigenous struggles for self-determination around the globe. With these popular education movements, Freire's language of conscientisation has flourished. More recently, we can see his ideas about consciousness: power and culture in the global occupy movements resisting the greed of corporate excess that has seen the global financial systems collapse. As they cry, "We are the 99%," no doubt they push back, resisting the global dominance of the way big business and global financial markets tend to dominate much of our lives.

THE LANGUAGE OF POSSIBILITY

Freire's extensive writing and theorising on conscientisation has taught us about the language of possibility, and his language of possibility comes through the power of education to transform people's lives. Freire's humanising pedagogy was influenced by Marx's historical materialism. His theory of conscientisation aligns with Marx's notion of thinking dialectically—to think in a way that allows us to truly see the world in its social historical and material contexts. This is not some watered-down form of critical thinking so popular in education circles today. His conscientisation was an embodied notion of self, world, and other, able to connect discourses and forms of oppression with his own life and others. His philosophy of education was an obstruction to rationalism and the objectification of knowledge, so readily seen as "real" knowledge by policy makers and governments. Freire knew that thinking, intelligence, emotions, and his own subjective experience were all important ways of knowing.

> We must dare in order to say scientifically and not as mere blah-blah-blah, that we study, we learn, we teach, we know with our entire body. We do all of these things with feeling, with emotion, with wishes, with fear, with doubts, with passion and also with critical reasoning. (Freire, 2005, p. 5)

Through thinking dialectically, we are no longer objects of oppression but active agents, able to construct and challenge inequality around us. We become empowered with this knowledge and reach a stage of conscientisation.

> True dialogue cannot exist unless it involves critical thinking—thinking which discerns an indivisible solidarity between the world and men admitting no dichotomy between them—thinking which perceives reality as process and transformation, rather than as a static entity—thinking which does not separate himself from action, but constantly emerges itself in temporality without fear of the risks involved. (1972, pp. 64–65)

Freire's conscientisation has so often been misunderstood; it is not a state of mind with a focus on the self or individual empowerment so readily constructed in twenty-first-century discourses about ideas of self-help or self-empowerment (Darder, 2012). His conscientisation is one that is constructed as a positive force for change when critically conscious people come together to change the world for the common good. It was an important part of his own activist work in Brazil among the peasants on literacy education, and continues to be a focus of his work today as new educators come to understand and know his humanising education. Freire always linked the language of possibility to the empowerment of the people and his own work as an educator. Of course, this was challenging to the government of the time and he was exiled for it. Nevertheless, this legacy continues and is crucial to what he imagined would be the role of the educator as cultural worker.

ACTION, REFLECTION, AND PRAXIS

Freire argued for a reflective practice, one that was deeply engaged with an epistemology of historical materialism. Like Marx before him, he knew that the impact
of colonisation and capitalism would inevitably impact those who were most disadvantaged and alienated. Freire's humanising education was revolutionary, but he
was cautious about activism that was not a well-thought-out practice. Without a
dialectical engagement with inequality, culture, and power, Freire believed activism
could become easily split off from practice (Freire, 1972). As Antonia Darder reminds us, it is easy in the heat of the moment for activists to pursue action against
the state without reflection. The work is urgent; there is much to be done and
changed, but well-intentioned social action can become misguided (Darder, as
cited in Ollis, 2012). Activism devoid of praxis is what Freire referred to as "naïve
activism," purposeless action split off from reflection and praxis (Freire, 1972).
Moreover, his pedagogy was one that was embodied; he connected the importance
of epistemology to emotions and action, in which theory should never become
devoid or split from practice. When these two phenomena were connected—we
needed theory and we also needed practice—through reflection and action, we
achieved praxis. This in effect would become an evolving ontology, informed
by the daily experience of being-in-the world as educators. As Freire (1972) so
importantly reminds us:

> For apart from inquiry, apart from the praxis, individuals cannot be truly human. Knowl-
> edge emerges only through invention and re-invention, through the restless, impatient,
> continuing, hopeful inquiry human beings pursue in the world, with the world, and with
> each other. (Freire, 1972)

Freire also warned that practice is not a theory in itself; theory and reflection
belong together.

> There is no way to reduce one to the other, in a necessary dialectical or contradictory
> relationship. In itself, inverse in its refusal of theoretical reflection, practice in spite of its
> importance, is not sufficient to offer me a knowledge that explains the raison d'être of
> relations among objects. Practice does not itself represent a theory of itself. But, without
> practice, theory runs the risk of wasting time of diminishing its own validity as well as the
> possibility of remaking itself. In the final analysis, theory and practice, in their relationship
> become necessary as they complement each other (1992, p. 101).

The conversations of the activists listed below show their agency, drive, and passion.
It reveals their thoughtful reflection on their own practice and their commitment
to social issues that concern them. The second part of this chapter commences by
showing the agency of activists and their desire to make the world a better place
as they learn to change it.

A LIVING PEDAGOGY OF ACTIVISM

As previously stated, my recent research showed the critically reflexive practice of activists often engaged on some of the most important social justice issues of our time. The dialogue below outlines activists' passion and commitment to their social change work.

When they were asked what drove their activism, they responded with the following:

Jane[2] says: *I mean the argument really is if there's any social justice in the world, if there is any conflict around the human rights movement, everyone is affected— which is the same argument about why people should not support war and they should free the refugees.... Because it doesn't matter whether it affects you in your day-to-day life, any kind of infringement on human rights or social justice affects everybody.*

Jack[3] says: *I just think everyone should have the right to basic stuff, you know, food and shelter and water and we should do that without burning us off the planet. They're just inalienable truths as far as I can see, and yet both of those things are not happening so the question is will I do something about it or do I ignore it or do I complain about it?*

Kerry[4] says: *I think it's just being passionate, and if you're passionate enough to share what you know then you share it in a way that people feel it coming from your heart and coming from your soul; they get to understand those things.*

Hugo[5] says: *...You know, as children we spent our childhood sitting around the kitchen table listening to our parents talk politics. I think this is interesting because what they've told us wasn't pedagogical; it was really about their stories that were heartfelt and sad and bitter.... It's not like we were taking in Marx or anything like that directly; it was mainly emotions and how we were affected by those stories. I mean, psychologically speaking, it is quite amazing a lot of us were obviously the average kid who wanted to do something for their parents. Well, for us it became a political thing like that, finishing a journey they could not complete.*

Activists need a high level of knowledge to equip them in their practice. The narratives reflected above reveal that activists are frequently emotionally connected to an issue. Their passion and desire for changes drive them forward to change the world. Hugo's emotional connection to his family, their persecution in Chile and subsequent exile to Australia as refugees developed a political awakening. Jack's passion for the environment has sustained his many years of campaigning. Jane links her commitment to gay and lesbian rights to all other issues of justice and inequality in the world.

Activism can push people into disconcerting moments; they are frequently out of their "comfort zone" and often learning a great deal. Yet, it is these disconcerting moments, these edgy moments of tension that occur through praxis, that provide opportunity and produce an agency to learn. It is through reflection and action that real meaning is produced. Once you leave the dynamics of the social space, you are left with the resonance of what actually occurred. Freire (1972) argues critical reflection was all important to the process of learning; he believed that critical awareness is raised through reflection. Through careful reflection, activists revise and remake their practices. Activists often ask themselves questions: What worked well? What did not work? How can I better engage this individual? They reflect on moments of difficulty as well as moments of triumph. They revise and review judgments they have made in the heat of action.

When I asked the activists whether they were thoughtful and reflective about their practices, they responded with the following:

Hugo says:	*You have probably caught me at a time when I am particularly reflective about this in fact; I'm waking up at night sometimes thinking about this.... I remember when first reading Descartes [thinking] at least this guy's got one thing right—if you keep asking questions you will get there.*
Kerry says:	*Sometimes it takes me a while to be reflective. Normally I come out and think 'Bloody bastards, they're still not listening to me!'...And you go round to the other mob and think 'We went there and we tried this and they said this'.... Then probably a day or two later without realising I've thought about it, I just do [this] subconsciously now—I think, 'Oh, need to put it in that format, need to talk about it in this way, need to link it to that'.*
Catherine[6] says:	*You've got to move on to the next phase. Okay, you have the awareness, some people are aware, some people are disquieted, and so what are you going to do with that? How will you take it to the next stage which is to change the legislation, to get the release of people? To diminish the pain of those suffering from the policy and that is around approaching the government, getting people to sign petitions, creating a wave of resistance but at a different level.*

Reflexivity or the meta-cognition of Hugo is skilful reflection on his own practices as an activist; he is being kept awake through his own reflection, and he is revising and renewing his practice. Like Hugo, Kerry uses critical reflection as a tool to improve her practice. Catherine has moved from her initial direct-action phase to becoming more strategic about how she can manage to influence government policy on refugees.

FREIRE AND "NAÏVE" ACTIVISM

While Freire was supportive of resistance and struggle, he was cautious about what he called "naïve" activism, activism that had become split off from practice and was devoid of reflection. In *Pedagogy of the Oppressed*, he stakes a strong claim for the combination of critical reflection and activism—forming praxis. "This discovery cannot be purely intellectual but must involve action; nor can it be limited to mere activism, but must include serious reflection: only then will it be a praxis" (1972b, p. 1).

Freire believed that we must involve the oppressed in every form of the process and dialogue; without this, our actions could be an act of oppression in itself and could possibly be a form of manipulation. He argues strongly that we should trust in the ability of oppressed people to be able to reason and become active agents constructing their own liberation. "Political action on the side of the oppressed must be pedagogical action in the authentic sense of the word, hence action with the oppressed" (1972, p. 42).

This conundrum of the need for critical reflection with practice, strategy, and planning in activism can at times be wanting, even when the most well-intentioned campaign is planned. When protest, emotions, anger, and passion drive action on some of the most important social issues of our time, the need for action and reflection becomes crucial. An example is shown here in the dialogue below, from refugee activist Catherine; she reflects on a crisis that occurred in the middle of a campaign, when a protest at a refugee camp at a detention centre in Woomera, South Australia, went eerily wrong. In the heat of the moment when both the police and activists clashed, the fence was torn down and the refugees were released into the central Australian desert.

> *I arrived the day after the escapes and what I saw was a very traumatised community. The activists were in shock, many of them had spent the night in tents sitting and listening to the stories of the refugees. Many of the refugees were still there, the police were clomping around in their heavy boots, batons and shields, and it was surreal really. People were just quietly going on around these things. We knew that some of the people who had escaped had gone back in, but some hadn't. We did not know where they were and of course there was a huge roadblock. There was one way in there and one way out. They [the police] were searching the cars; in the middle of the desert*—Catherine.

The example above highlights the dynamic, embodied, and engaged practice that is activism. It also shows the importance of reflective practice being central to the judgments activists make. In the heated action of protest, in the heat of the moment, a campaign can easily change from its initial intent. Catherine's reflection shows us that even the most well-intentioned activism without careful reflection can go dangerously wrong. Freire's reminder to those who "dare to teach"—is there is "no teaching without learning" (1998, p. 32). Even when activists are teaching the world about the oppression of refugees in Australia, they are learning about how to improve their own practices.

CONCLUSION

This chapter commenced by uncovering Paulo Freire's commitment to education, social justice, and activism. There is little wonder that Freire's writing is a beacon for educators around the world in its promise of education being more than what occurs in the classroom or teaching space, instead being about "reading the world" beyond those boundaries. Freire's actions were those of a man who was deeply committed to education and social justice. He argued for a critically reflexive ontology that would inform our practice as activist educators. There is much to learn in Freire's writing on reflection and action for educator activists, solidarity groups, and popular education movements around the world.

The activists' narratives revealed here in this chapter show the deep level of commitment to their own pedagogy and practice. Their agency to act and their desire to create a more just world and planet for future generations is driven by a deep passion. It is not surprising, given the urgency of the work and the demands and dynamics of activism, that there is limited time for critical reflection. Thus, theory can easily become split off from practice in the way that Freire predicted.

Freire's notion of naïve activism and his call for a reflexive praxis, first introduced in his seminal text *Pedagogy of the Oppressed* some 40 years ago, provides a way forward for activists to improve their practices. The nexus of theory, reflection, and action provides a basis for an evolving pedagogy of activism, constantly developing, adapting and changing, enabling activists to renew and remake their practice. Freire's language of possibility continues to resonate in their important work.

NOTES

1. This research was granted ethics approval by the Victoria University Research Ethics Committee. In the research narratives cited here, pseudonyms are used to protect the identity of the research participants.
2. Jane became involved in activism in student politics. Her more recent activism has focused on working toward fertility rights for lesbians.

3. Jack has been involved in environmental campaigns since his early 20s; he is a campaign coordinator and has campaigned on dozens of issues, from forests, toxic waste and indigenous affairs, to sustainability and climate change.
4. Kerry has been involved in indigenous politics since her early 20s.
5. Hugo has been an activist from an early age; he is involved in Latin American politics and the anti-corporate globalization movements, among others.
6. Catherine became involved in activism in middle age. She is at present involved in campaigns in Australia for the rights of refugees.

REFERENCES

Branagan, M., & Boughton, B. (2003). How do you learn to change the world? Learning and teaching in Australian protest movements. *Australian Journal of Adult Learning, 43*(3), 346–360. Retrieved from http://www.ajal.net.au/

Crossley, Nick. (2002). *Making sense of social movements*. Buckingham: Open University Press.

Darder, A. (2003). Teaching as an act of love: Reflections on Paulo Freire and his contributions to our lives and our work. In A. Darder, M. Baltodano, & R. Torres (Eds.), *The critical pedagogy reader* (pp. 497–510). New York, NY: RoutledgeFalmer.

Darder, A. (2012). Preface. In T. Ollis, *A critical pedagogy of embodied education: Learning to become an activist*. New York, NY: Palgrave Macmillan.

Foley, G. (1999). *Learning in social action: A contribution to understanding informal education*. New York, NY: Zed Books.

Freire, P. (1972a). *Cultural action for freedom*. Harmondsworth, England: Penguin.

Freire, P. (1972b). *Pedagogy of the oppressed*. Harmondsworth, England: Penguin.

Freire, P. (1974). *Education for critical consciousness*. London, England: Sheed & Ward.

Freire, P. (1992). *Pedagogy of hope*. New York, NY: Continuum.

Freire, P. (1998). *Pedagogy of freedom: Ethics, democracy, and civic courage*. Lanhan, MD: Rowman & Littlefield.

Freire, P. (2005a). *Education for critical consciousness*. New York, NY: Continuum.

Freire, P. (2005b). *Teachers as cultural workers: Letters to those who dare to teach* (Rev. ed.). Boulder, CO: Westview.

Freire, P., & Freire, A. M. A. (1997). *Pedagogy of the heart*. New York, NY: Continuum.

Giroux, Henry. (1985). *Introduction in Paulo Freire. The Politics of Education, Culture, Power, Liberation* (D. Macedo, Trans.). South Hadley, MA: Bergin & Garvey.

Jasper, J., & Goodwin, J. (2004). *Rethinking social movements : structure, meaning, and emotion*. Lanham, MD: Rowman & Littlefield.

Ollis, T. (2008). The accidental activist: Learning, embodiment and action. *Australian Journal of Adult Learning, 48*(2), 316–335. Retrieved from http://www.ajal.net.au/

Ollis, T. (2011). Learning in social action: The informal and social learning dimensions of circumstantial and lifelong activists. *Australian Journal of Adult Learning, 51*(2), 249–268. Retrieved from http://www.ajal.net.au/

Ollis, T. (2012). *A critical pedagogy of embodied education: Learning to become an activist*. New York, NY: Palgrave Macmillan.

Whelan, J. (2002). *Education and training for effective environmental advocacy* (Unpublished doctoral dissertation). Griffith University, Nathan, Australia.

CHAPTER THIRTY-FOUR

Entwining Three Threads: Working Within and Through a Culturally Responsive Pedagogy of Relations

ITI JOYCE AND DAWN LAWRENCE

Kotahi te kōhao o te ngira e kuhuna ai te miro mā, te miro pango, te miro whero.

There is but one eye of the needle through which passes the white thread, the black thread, the red thread.

INTRODUCTION

Historical failures to address disparities between the academic achievement of Māori and Pākehā (non-Māori) students have had devastating outcomes for Māori in the wider context of New Zealand society. These educational disparities have resulted in generations of Māori being over-represented in negative indices including incarceration, unemployment, and poor health—symptoms of an oppressed people. However, Māori communities are no longer willing to accept that simply being Māori equates to failure and expect schools to be contexts where Māori students can enjoy and achieve education success as Māori. Our stories sit within this context; that of two women, both of whom are graduates of the New Zealand education system, both mothers, teachers and members of the Te Kotahitanga professional development team, but both with different cultural identities: one English and one Māori. For us, the whakataukī (proverb) used above at the opening of this chapter speaks of the way in which Pākehā (te miro mā) and Māori (te miro pango) can come together in a non-dominating relationship of interdependence (te miro whero). All three threads may intertwine but each remains distinct from the others (Berryman, 2008), thus challenging the hitherto mono-cultural responses to the educational disparities for Māori.

HISTORICAL CONTEXT

Epistemological racism, as explained by Scheurich and Young (1997), is embedded within the dominant Pākehā discourse within New Zealand (Bishop & Glynn, 1999). It is a racism that has developed since the 1840 Treaty of Waitangi. Māori saw the treaty as a "charter for power sharing between Māori and the Crown" (Berryman, 2008, p. 16), enabling them to participate as self-determining individuals in future decision making. But from its very first moments, there were "difficulties of interpretation" (Orange, 1987, p. 1). If Crown officials were aware of Māori understandings, they chose to ignore them and proceeded by addressing perceived Māori inadequacies through an education system developed within colonial epistemologies.

Educational discrepancies between Māori and Pākehā were first statistically documented in the Hunn Report in 1960. The subsequent Currie Report that followed in 1962 emphasised Māori underachievement as a central priority. The response from the government was to initiate a range of remedial and culturalist programmes, such as Taha Māori in the 1980s. Taha Māori, which literally means "the Māori side," used Māori knowledge to support Pākehā teachers to develop understandings of Māori culture and practices. However, the programme was developed within the dominant Pākehā discourse that pathologised Māori students (Shields, Bishop, & Mazawi, 2005) as remedial and failed to address the educational disparities between Māori and Pākehā.

CURRENT NEW ZEALAND CONTEXT

Contemporary Māori resistance to mainstream discourses have had little impact on the way Māori are viewed and represented in New Zealand society. There are still disparities between Māori and Pākehā within a range of social indicators. Māori are being imprisoned well in excess of any other cultural group in New Zealand. Similarly, disparities between Māori and Pākehā exist within our mainstream education settings, particularly at the secondary level. Interestingly, achievements of Māori students in Māori-medium schools indicate that they have a greater likelihood of achieving education success here, than their counterparts do in mainstream settings. Evidence in Ngā Haeata Mātauranga (Ministry of Education, 2010) demonstrates that Year 11 to 13 students in Māori-medium were more likely to gain a typical level or higher NCEA qualification and "the proportion of students who leave school qualified to attend university is much higher than the number of Māori students in English-medium schools and comparable with the proportion of non-Māori in English-medium schools" (Ministry of Education, 2010, p. 13). Figure 1 shows the comparison of Māori students leaving Māori-medium schools and those leaving mainstream schools with NCEA Level 2 or above, between 2002 and 2010.

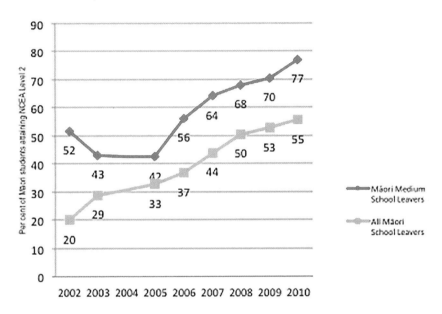

Figure 1. Percentage of Māori-medium Māori school leavers and all Māori school leavers with NCEA Level 2 or above (2002–2010).

The data show that Māori students are more successful in Māori-medium settings than in mainstream settings. The reason for this is often reported as a culturally appropriate curriculum and pedagogical practices.

Te Kotahitanga, a kaupapa Māori education reform, aims to improve the educational achievement of Māori students within mainstream secondary education settings by supporting teachers to work within both a culturally appropriate and responsive pedagogy of relations (Bishop & Berryman, 2006; Bishop, Berryman, Cavanagh, & Teddy, 2007; Bishop, Berryman, Tiakiwai, & Richardson, 2003).

TE KOTAHITANGA: A KAUPAPA MĀORI RESPONSE WITHIN A MAINSTREAM SETTING

The Te Kotahitanga narratives of experience (Bishop & Berryman, 2006) showed that teachers typically explained Māori underachievement by apportioning blame to an array of factors outside of their sphere of influence, or agency, thus providing few, if any, solutions and perpetuating the disparities for Māori in mainstream education. However, Māori students within these narratives were clearly positioned within a relational discourse where numerous solutions were evident. They explained the importance of a relationship that allowed them to bring who they are into the classroom, thus giving them a voice within their learning. This formed the basis of what has been termed a culturally responsive pedagogy of relations (Bishop et al., 2007).

POSITIONING OUR NARRATIVES

Next we present our stories and experiences of working within and through a culturally responsive pedagogy of relations. Being teina (younger sibling/learner) as we listen to our tuakana (older sibling/teacher), we learn other ways to make sense of our experiences and new words with which to name our world. This learning becomes part of our shared experience and it is this that we share here. It is not our intention to provide a generalised picture that speaks for all; rather, we invite readers to connect in ways that they may reflect and learn from the particularities of their own stories.

TE MIRO PANGO : ITI'S STORY

> Ko Whakarongorua toku maunga
> Ko Hokianga toku moana
> Ko Mataitaua toku marae
> Ko Ngāpuhi toku iwi
> Ko Iti Joyce toku ingoa

I was brought up in South Auckland with my four sisters and one brother. The majority of my schooling was based in South Auckland. I was aware that I was Māori at primary school. I was also aware of who was Pākehā. I was aware that we were treated differently to Pākehā.

I failed secondary school, as did others in my family. I was pretty quiet in my classes, didn't play up, was never in trouble, but found difficulty in understanding anything that was supposedly being taught and I knew absolutely nothing about my teachers. They operated at some other level that I found was foreign. Everything about them was a secret. The failure that I had experienced at school was a regular occurrence with cousins and family friends. These experiences were familiar across whānau (family) and across generations. Some of my siblings were in the top streamed classes. Why did they fail?

I was fortunate enough to be pretty good at sport. This was a place where I could succeed and do really well. I was confident in who I was and how I interacted with others. I identified myself as successful in this domain. I had excellent coaches and we learnt together through trial and error. Sport and my whānau were my teachers. The most significant thing I learnt was how important relationships are. The most successful teams I have been in are the ones where we gel on the court and gel off the court. Our relationships were built on whanaungatanga (familial-like relationships) so that we interacted with each other effectively. In sport, there was a level playing ground where no one dominated the other and the kaupapa (collective vision, philosophy) was the vehicle that ensured that we worked together collectively. The same practices my whānau exhibits.

After becoming a young mother and holding down three jobs in order to pay the bills, I grew frustrated. I found out that as a mature student you could enroll at University. I enrolled into a sports degree and then applied for a teaching diploma. While doing my diploma, I applied for a teaching position and was successful in securing my first teaching position. My daughter was in her last year of secondary school and my son was in Year 6. I watched my daughter go through secondary school with angst. It seemed like déjà vu to me. In Year 7, my son started at the school where I was teaching. His results in the first two years at the school were in the average pass range. While results in the average range don't normally ring alarm bells, they did for me. It was my story and my daughter's.

At the same time, I was assigned my Year 10 homeroom class for the year. When other teachers saw the list of names on my class list, they chuckled and informed me that I would have a challenging year. My first two months were challenging. When I am confronted with challenging situations, I refer back to how I would handle it in sport or within whānau situations, because that is what I know best. As I started to get to know my students, things started to change. They were also interested in getting to know me. One thing I had learnt from my own experiences was that relationships matter. A significant point at this time is that some of my Māori students in my class were getting suspended or stood down. I was getting frustrated and would talk to the teachers concerned, trying to understand why this was happening. I knew we had a huge problem; what I didn't know was how to address the issue. I was starting to become conscious of the inequity and injustices within our school.

The following year, Te Kotahitanga was introduced into our school and I became one of the facilitators. I found the job very challenging and uncomfortable at times, but I also found that I thrived in this situation. I was a Māori mother and teacher and I connected to the kaupapa. I read *Culture Speaks* (Bishop & Berryman, 2006), the narratives of Māori student experiences at secondary school. They were telling my story. It was so identical and familiar that it was scary. I gave my friends and members of my family the narratives to read. We made connections all the way through. At the same time, *Culture Speaks* was introduced to teachers participating in Te Kotahitanga. I remember sitting with a group of teachers who had middle-management and senior management roles and responsibilities in our school. They talked about how these narratives were a tragedy, but fortunately for us they weren't happening in our school. They were unconscious of what was happening in front of them.

TE MIRO MĀ: DAWN'S STORY

I am an English-born immigrant. We initially settled in Mangere, a suburb of South Auckland with a high percentage of Māori and Polynesian families. Being age five, I was immediately enrolled at the local primary school and found myself immersed in a cultural context in which I was the minority. I recall feeling isolated, self-conscious, and very aware of difference. Six months later, however, my family moved to a new suburban development within West Auckland, largely populated by British immigrants and Pākehā New Zealanders, and once again I was part of the majority. It was within this cultural context that I went through school.

In my fifth form year at secondary school I was put into a top stream class. No one told me why; all I knew was that the work was harder and there was more of it. Our pathways were seemingly predetermined. I became aware of this when I asked to take beginner's typing in my sixth form year, and was politely informed that I would not need to type as I was destined for university. At school, I didn't know whether my friends were Māori, Pacifika, or of any other cultural heritage, for that matter. We were all the same. It never crossed my mind that other people may not experience the world the same way I did. The way in which we were all channelled through the same textbooks, tasks, and tests at school never suggested anything different. My experience of Māori culture was basically limited to the social studies projects about the arrival of Māori on "seven great canoes from the mythical Hawaiki," the bringing of civilisation to New Zealand by the missionaries, and the signing of the Treaty of Waitangi in 1840, all of which were filtered through the dominant Pākehā discourse of my teachers.

In 1994, I trained as a secondary teacher. Although it says in my record of learning that, within that year, I completed a total of 45 hours of "Māori Studies," I learnt nothing of how to work alongside Māori students. No one ever suggested to me that it might be useful to know the cultural identity of my students. As a young teacher, I was getting ticks on my appraisal form and that was enough for me. But then I returned to England and took up a teaching position in the East End of London. Once again, I found myself in the cultural minority. Most of the students were refugees or immigrants from the Middle East, Pakistan, and parts of Africa. I vividly recall one particular boy. Two days before I met him he had been in the midst of a civil war–ravaged area of Africa, he spoke no English and panicked at every loud noise. I was teaching Shakespeare, as required, at the time. As I sat on the floor, underneath a desk trying my best to comfort this boy, the absurdity of the education system I was a part of became all too apparent. I began to I experiment with what I now understand as responsive learning. I developed something of a passion for taking teaching strategies and playing with them to ensure high levels of engagement and generally positive outcomes for students. Back in New Zealand, I was determined to continue in this vein, for I was pretty convinced that I had developed a more effective way of teaching.

Through a series of Te Kotahitanga observations and feedback sessions, I came to understand that all my fancy teaching strategies were worth little to Māori students if I did not recognise and address my deficit positioning, establish relationships not based on power differentials, and begin to understand myself as a learner alongside others. In 2006, I took on the role of an in-school Te Kotahitanga professional development facilitator and gave birth to my first child. My daughter's arrival unceremoniously repositioned me as a learner. I also became acutely aware that I was part of a system that, whatever the rhetoric stated, worked to limit and dehumanise people. From that point, I began looking for a way to make education more human. At that stage, I was focused on ensuring a better system of education for my daughter and it was not until two years later, having taken up my current position as a Te Kotahitanga Regional Coordinator, and writing a paper on the notion of educational debt (Ladson-Billings, 2006), did I begin to understand the role I might also play in responding to the disparities for Māori in education.

TE MIRO WHERO: WORKING WITHIN A RELATIONALLY AUTONOMOUS PARTNERSHIP

The challenge for us has always been to develop a relational autonomy that utilises the strength of our combined cultural identities in such a way that neither dominates. It is our suggestion this has developed through our work within a culturally responsive pedagogy of relations beginning with whanaungatanga.

When working within a culturally responsive pedagogy of relations, the relational space created is perhaps best understood through the Māori metaphor, whanaungatanga. We experience whanaungatanga as a collaborative partnership within a mutually respectful and reciprocal experience. This moves beyond the Western view of professional relationships to encompass both an emotional and spiritual connection. It is perhaps what Freire (1986) means when he says, "Founding itself on love, humility and faith, dialogue becomes a horizontal relationship of which mutual trust between the participants is the logical consequence" (p. 64). As in the whakataukī that opened this chapter, we believe the real strength within such a relationship comes from the aspects of self that make us different.

Iti: *My understanding of whanaungatanga is grounded by my experiences of being Māori and my relationships with my whānau, friends and relations. These relationships range from smooth, easy-going reciprocal understandings to tense, uncomfortable frustrating interactions. The relationship of whanaungatanga grounds us in the way we communicate and act. Whatever the kaupapa, the outcome is always, we're still whānau and we still have our responsibilities and commitment to each other, which can be really hōhā (annoying) at times.*

    The links that I make through my understandings of whanaungatanga have helped me through our kaupapa. If our relationships are based on whanaungatanga, all else will fall into place, as it does with our own whānau members. It is not always smooth and can be really uncomfortable at times, but through our shared responsibility and commitment to each other, we can work through things collectively toward our shared common goal. That's how it works in my whānau relationships and that's how it can work in the relationships we develop through our mahi (work).

Dawn: *My experience of relationships has been one of compartmentalisation. The relationship I have with family members was separate and different to those I have with friends or work colleagues. Each type of relationship had different rules of engagement. To engage appropriately, I developed a number of versions of myself. A priority for me, as I began to understand whanaungatanga and work within a relational space, was to reconnect all the pieces of myself so that I could authentically connect to those around me.*

The relational space within which we work is shaped by the now reified definition that asserts that a culturally responsive pedagogy of relations exists:

> …where power is shared between self-determining individuals within non-dominating relations of interdependence; where culture counts; learning is interactive, dialogic and spirals; participants are connected and committed to one another through the establishment of a common vision for what constitutes excellence in educational outcomes. (Bishop et al., 2007, p. 15)

While unravelling the red thread, and looking to step beyond the metaphors within the colonised discourses of the English language, we found ourselves grappling with Māori metaphors to express our ideas. What we present below is our current understanding of each entwined aspect of a culturally responsive pedagogy of relations in this moment of our "unfinishedness" (Freire, 1998). Lifting each aspect of the statement directly from the definition, we have discussed each alongside a related Māori metaphor entwined with our shared and individual understanding and experience.

POWER IS SHARED WITHIN NON-DOMINATING RELATIONSHIPS OF INTERDEPENDENCE: TINO RANGATIRATANGA

The literal meaning of *rangatiratanga* is chiefly "control," but it is understood here as a metaphor for self-determination and relational autonomy. Self-determination within Māori epistemology is the right to create your own vision for the future and determine how that vision may be realised in relation to others. As Bishop et al. (2007) explain, this means that the mana (power) and tapu (potential) of all participants in a relationship are acknowledged. It is this that keeps the colour of the three threads unique but ensures their collective strength.

Iti: *Tino rangatiratanga has challenged me in understanding who I am, what I want to be and how I act in order for me to have effective relationships with others. Addressing my own discourses, beliefs and practices has been part of this journey. I have had to make adjustments, and I continue to do so. Knowing oneself provides the opportunity to see and act in relation to others, especially when there are disagreements.*

The importance of tino rangatiratanga is the ultimate intended outcome. Māori voices need to be validated and legitimated in order for this to occur, where genuine wānanga occur within relationships of whanaungatanga. The importance of listening and not talking past each other is critical in order for listening and learning from each other to occur.

Dawn: *Joining the Te Kotahitanga Professional Development Team, I immediately recognised I was working in a space determined largely by Māori epistemologies. The first thing that struck me was the non-hierarchical relationships; people held positions of responsibility but there was a reciprocity that was unfamiliar to me. It was a space that challenged me because I wasn't sure of the terms of engagement. I saw a group of people for whom tino rangatiratanga (the right to self-determination) wasn't simply words in vision statements and charter documents; it was what defined the space. What challenged me further was that it was a space determined by Māori, defined within a Māori cultural framework of which I had no inherent understanding of, or power within.*

It is not always an easy space to work in. It often highlights ways in which simply being Pākehā in New Zealand brings with it inherent privileges. It challenges me to better understand myself, what has shaped my life and my discursive positioning. To meet this challenge, I have had to learn to listen, both to myself and to others. I constantly examine my beliefs and whose interests they serve. I am engaged in a constantly spiraling learning process, looking to unlearn the colonial discourses of relationships that have perpetuated the power imbalances and marginalisation of Māori within the dominant Pākehā culture. In short, I am learning to centre myself within a relational autonomy.

CULTURE COUNTS: WHAKAPAPA

For us, culture is:

> …what holds a community together, giving a common framework of meaning. It includes how people communicate with each other, how we make decisions, how we structure our families and who we think are important. It expresses our values towards land and time and our attitudes towards work and play, good and evil, reward and punishment.

> Culture is preserved in language, symbols and customs and celebrated in art, music, drama, literature, religion and social gatherings. It constitutes the collective heritage, which will be handed down to future generations. (Quest Rapuara, 1992, p. 7)

Working within a culturally responsive pedagogy of relations, we understand that neither of us are culturally neutral and that each is unique in the way we determine who we are and how we understand the world. This works to counter the "essentialisation" of both Māori and Pākehā within the contemporary discourse of "New Zealanders as one people." It locates power with Māori rather than the dominant Pākehā culture, "sharing" the power it currently monopolises. In this way, it works to establish tino rangatiratanga (the right of self-determination) and guides us in seeking relational autonomy.

Iti: *At school, I remember being taught about Mao Tse Tung's little red book, the Boer War and the living conditions in the slums in London. What stands out for me is how totally uninterested I was about all those topics. I couldn't and didn't connect to anything. The history and culture of my own people seemed not to matter. I don't remember the Treaty of Waitangi being brought up in any lesson. I don't think my teachers knew about it. This experience has taught me how important culture is, and if it is ignored and excluded, the detrimental effects it has down the line.*

Dawn: *The discourse of cultural neutrality is one that has saturated my experiences. I have grown up with two pervasive discourses around culture. The first is that culture is something rich, powerful people have—it is opera, art, ballet and haute cuisine. The second discourse explains culture as difference—the traditions and customs of people from other lands. So pervasive was this discourse that even my experiences of being in the physical minority did little to challenge it. It took the cognitive dissonance of being immersed in a space determined by a Māori worldview, and my efforts to make sense of it, that afforded me the opportunity to begin to understand my own cultural identity.*

LEARNING IS INTERACTIVE, DIALOGIC, AND SPIRALING: WĀNANGA

We have a well-worn phrase that says "the learning is in the conversation." Akin to what Freire (1986) terms "dialogue," learning conversations bring together our individual reflections and understandings in order to co-construct our shared future actions. We understand this type of dialogue as wānanga (the process of sharing and reshaping knowledge). The koringoringo (double spiral) symbolises this. At its centre is a space that represents the connection between the active and quiescent elements present within a learning conversation, from which new knowledge is constructed and change brought about (Berryman, 2008).

All knowledge and experience have legitimacy within this space and, as Freire explains (1986), "At the point of encounter there are neither utter ignoramuses nor perfect sages; there are only men [and women] who are attempting, together, to learn more than they now know" (p. 63). Metaphorically, it is perhaps these learning conversations that work to entwine the black and white threads alongside the red.

Underpinning our conversations is the shared understanding of ourselves as learners, "beings in the process of *becoming*—as unfinished, uncompleted beings in and with a likewise unfinished reality" (Freire, 1986, p. 57). Ako (reciprocity within the teaching and learning relationship), a metaphor from within Māori epistemologies, guides us in this process. Ako encompasses the idea that there is no singular and fixed truth, and that the acquisition of knowledge comes from within a process of sharing and reflecting on prior experiences and understandings in order to co-construct new knowledge in response to the current context. As a process, ako counters power differentials; as the prior learning and experiences of each learner within the relationship are legitimate and valid within the co-construction of new knowledge, there are neither spectators nor objects within the relationship that this creates.

Iti: *I remember different types of wānanga happening often at our house. They would start with a karakia (prayer) and waiata (song), then issues or concerns would be discussed. There would be laughter, heated discussions, listening, deep conversations that linked to whakatauki or Māori metaphor, then more laughter. They would conclude with another waiata and another karakia. There were whānau, church, community, marae and iwi related wānanga. What I remember mostly about them are the relationships of trust and respect, the laughter and the big meals we would have afterward. Everyone had a voice. I remember being asked whether I wanted to add anything in some of these gatherings. There was always an active ingredient to these gatherings, where new learnings would initiate action. My parents still have wānanga in their home.*

I understand how important our relationships are in the different types of wānanga we participate in through our work. These relationships are fundamental in order for us to disrupt the status quo for us to be able to discuss issues and concerns that initiate new learning and actions toward our common goal.

Dawn: *Initially, I found the notion of wānanga really challenging. My experiences of learning had been that you read, listened, digested and regurgitated the singular truths transmitted by more knowledgeable others. I believe my repositioning occurred largely by virtue that those around me constantly engaged in such conversations and I was slowly drawn in.*

A VISION IS SHARED: KOTAHITANGA

The word *kotahi* means "one"; thus, we have come to understand kotahitanga to mean unity, but as a process, not an object. Our experience of kotahitanga is that it pulls all the other metaphors together. It is difficult to write about each metaphor as a discreet entity, for they work within a relational autonomy where each is less than itself when not entwined with the others. It is that active process of connectedness, within a non-dominating relationship of interdependence, discursively positioned within a culturally responsive pedagogy of relations that enables us to work critically to address the educational disparities for Māori within the mainstream setting.

Iti: *Within my own whānau, if one of us succeeds in any forum, we all succeed; if one fails, it is our whānau responsibility to ensure that we do something about it so that it doesn't happen again. We all celebrate or commiserate and work together as one big machine. We understand how these different and yet similar metaphors work within our whānau and how they interrelate with each other.*

           The ways in which we operate within the work we do have the same elements. Our understandings of these metaphors all intertwine with each other, in order that we work collectively toward a shared vision of ensuring positive outcomes for Māori students, as we would our own whānau members.

Dawn: *The idea of a shared vision within a unifying process is one that sits heavily alongside the notion of individual meritocracy that is woven deep into my being. The question 'What's in it for me?' has not gone but my response has changed.*

CONCLUSION

It is not scholarly papers, symposia, or published works that will make a difference to the educational disparities for Māori within mainstream settings. While expressed here in the written word, the intertwining of the white, black, and red threads is a transformational action that calls on both Māori and Pākehā to roll up their sleeves. The success of Māori within Māori-medium settings shows us that it can be done despite many previous attempts—attempts, however, determined within the dominant Pākehā discourse. It is to kaupapa Māori that we must then look, as we consider the nature of that action. It is this that we have tried to do in this chapter and, more important, in our work—challenging the colonising discourses through the use of Māori metaphor to express and live our understanding of a culturally responsive pedagogy of relations.

REFERENCES

Berryman, M. (2008). *Repositioning within indigenous discourses of transformation and self-determination.* (Unpublished doctoral dissertation) University of Waikato, Hamilton, New Zealand. Retrieved from http://researchcommons.waikato.ac.nz/handle/10289/2565

Bishop, R., & Berryman, M. (2006). *Culture speaks: Cultural relationships and classroom learning.* Wellington, New Zealand: Huia.

Bishop, R., Berryman, M., Cavanagh, T., & Teddy, L. (2007). *Te Kotahitanga phase 3 Whānaungatanga: Establishing a culturally responsive pedagogy of relations in mainstream secondary school classrooms.* Wellington, New Zealand: Ministry of Education.

Bishop, R., Berryman, M., Tiakiwai, S., & Richardson, C. (2003). *Te Kōtahitanga: The experiences of year 9 and 10 Māori students in mainstream classrooms.* Wellington, New Zealand: Ministry of Education.

Bishop, R., & Glynn, T. (1999). *Culture counts: Changing power relations in education.* Palmerston North, New Zealand: Dunmore Press.

Commission on Education in New Zealand (Currie Commission). (1962). *Report of the Commission on Education in New Zealand.* Wellington, New Zealand: Government Printer.

Education Review Office. (2002). *The performance of Kura Kaupapa Māori June 2002.* Wellington, New Zealand: Author.

Freire, P. (1986). *Pedagogy of the oppressed.* Middlesex, England: Penguin.

Freire, P. (1998). *Pedagogy of freedom: Ethics, democracy, and civic courage.* Lanham, MD: Rowman & Littlefield.

Hunn, J. K. (1960). *Report on the department of Māori affairs.* Wellington, New Zealand: Government Printer.

Ladson-Billings, G. (2006). From the achievement gap to the education debt: Understanding achievement in U.S. schools. *Educational Researcher, 35*(7), 3-12. Retrieved from http://ezproxy.auckland.ac.nz/login?url=http://search.proquest.com/docview/216898326?accountid=8424

Ministry of Education. (2010). *Ngā Haeata Mātauranga—The annual report on Māori education, 2007/08.* Wellington, New Zealand: Ministry of Education.

Murray, S. (2005). *Māori achievement and achievement at Māori immersion and bilingual schools. January 2005.* Demographic and Statistical Analysis Unit. Wellington, New Zealand: Ministry of Education.

Murray, S. (2007, April). *Māori achievement and achievement at Māori immersion and bilingual schools. April 2007.* Demographic and Statistical Analysis Unit. Wellington, New Zealand: Ministry of Education.

Orange, C. (1987). *The Treaty of Waitangi.* Wellington, New Zealand: Allen & Unwin New Zealand.

Quest Rapuara. (1992). *Cultural identity, Whakamana tangata: A resource for educators* (3rd ed.). Wellington, New Zealand: Quest Rapuara, the Career Development and Transition Education Service.

Scheurich, J., & Young, M. (1997). Colouring epistemologies: Are our research epistemologies racially based? *Educational Review, 26*(4), 4–16.

Shields, C., Bishop, R., & Mazawi, A. (2005). *Pathologizing practices: The impact of deficit thinking on education.* New York, NY: Peter Lang.

CHAPTER THIRTY-FIVE

Freire's Theory as a Reference to Teaching Practice in Adult Education

SONIA MARIA CHAVES HARACEMIV AND VERONICA BRANCO

INTRODUCTION

This chapter presents our experience in pedagogy at Universidade Federal do Paraná (UFPR) in the formation of adult and young adult teachers/educators, and formulations based on the ideas of Paulo Freire, in an attempt to extract elements from their journey to enlighten and contribute to the construction of our own methods. We seek to develop a practice consistent with the statements of the master, who recommended that the educator recognize and use the knowledge and the life experiences of the learners themselves, to leverage their critical thinking and social background, providing experiences that can sharpen the investigative capacity and commitment to popular groups. The method used in this work is critical-investigative, aiming to reveal reflective practices, where in each one is recognized as autonomous, with a broader view beyond the individual and the world becoming a collective project, in the hope of a better world, more fair and egalitarian.

> Those who put into practice my thoughts, strive to recreate it, also rethinking it. And after doing so, have in mind that no educational practice takes place in the abstract, but in a concrete, historical, social, cultural, economic, political context, which not necessarily is identical to another context. (Freire, 1976)

The speech of the master guided us into the incursion of the reality of public schools on the development of Educational Practice in Adult Education, phase

I, literacy. All the main individuals responsible for teacher training sought to base their ideas on the propositions of Paulo Freire, accepting the challenge, in group work that required intellectual disposition to read, search, listen, discuss, teach, and continuously learn. This meant a collective effort to understand and extract, from the experience in the classroom, elements that could extend the understanding in relation to adult literacy and initial literacy teacher training of Pedagogy UFPR students.

The experiences during Teaching Practice and Supervised Internship played a key role in the training of professional educators in Adult Education; thus, we made a collective commitment to create and recreate, from previous experiences, a qualified and more systematic practice, in order to allow a better explanation of the pedagogical intervention project to establish a more effective dialogic relationship between the university and the public schools involved in this process. In the course and construction of theoretical and practical contexts, we sought the appropriation/recreation of facts, which implied understanding the essence and relations of the academic reality and the school, which was removed from us (Freire, 1996).

Our hope is that this dialectical movement theory and practice would permit the link of the particular and the general, integrating in an organized and articulated way the scientific and technical understanding of the social meaning of education of adults and young adults in the literacy process (Freire, 1988).

The time spent in school is always a moment of possibilities; therefore, we consider as the basic lines of teaching practice, the time spent as a demarcation in the historical construction of the literacy context in Adult Education (Freire & Macedo, 1990). Everything was developed considering that our school was historically composed of professionals who have been acting in it, and that in its space other professionals are formed. We also made an educational contract where UFPR teachers, responsible for training new teachers, would observe the students in the same space and at the same time, continually rethinking the educational process in the educational context of literacy.

Thus, seeking to form a professional who is more qualified, autonomous, able to understand and act more effectively upon cultural diversity, we, Federal University of Paraná teachers, consider the principles of the Political Pedagogical Project of the Pedagogy Course, which considers human formation a rather broad process, and should require that the teacher and the school have greater knowledge inherent in didactic pedagogical knowledge.

Pedagogical action, from the perspective of teaching as the professional identity of the teacher, makes scientific and philosophical knowledge the concrete educational reality, and makes school the space for teacher training at any of its levels, developed as a theoretical and practical political-social activity. (Freire, 1996)

In this chapter, we aim to describe an effective learning experience of the literacy teacher training, using Freire as theoretical mentor in the context of Adults and Young Adults Literacy, explaining each step of this practice, rethinking it collectively, where students and educators under the guidance of UFPR teacher trainers study the analysis of Freire's methodological propositions. Freire recommends acting with respect, as well as reviewing and updating. He also recommends paying attention to the theoretical misunderstandings and misconceptions observed in literacy practices, based on the reflective observation and diagnosis, considering the aspect of the theory-practice relationship and the situations and needs identified within the school (Freire, as cited in Beisiegel, 1989).

TEACHING PRACTICE BY FREIRE: ADULT EDUCATION TEACHER TRAINING AND THE INCURSION INTO THE SCHOOL

> …an approach to the concrete…should allow the arise of multiple relationships, . . .taking the daily life as the basis of real knowledge, that comes from reality, which generates concrete facts (language, concepts, conflicts, anxieties, hopes) that transits to the theoretical context, in the sense that there is an appropriation/recreation of these facts that arise from knowledge, which involves better understanding of the essence and of its relations with the reality. (Freire, 1996)

The work in Teaching Practice makes incursion into the reality of the public school in trying to understand, learn and teach together with the Adult and Young Adult Literacy students, under the supervision of all main participants responsible for teacher training. The incursion into the reality of the school allows the initial and continuing training of the teacher researcher, which we consider to be

> …parts of the nature of the teaching practice are inquiry, search, research. What is needed is that, in their continuing education, teachers realize themselves and come out.…From the point of view of the teacher, it is implied both the respect for common sense in the process of their overcome as well as the respect and the motivation to the student's creative capacity. It implies the commitment of educators with the student's critical awareness. His/hers "promotion" of naivety is not done automatically. (Freire, 1996)

In this journey of teacher training in Adult Education, in Teaching Practice of the early years of Elementary school—Supervised Internship—Federal University of Paraná teachers went from the already known, i.e., the internship orientation, in which they observe the *in locus* trainee of the school, during the daytime. This made the Children Education teacher's daily routine less thoughtful, less understood, and very complex. This also made the orientation in teaching and adult learning, to the real world of Adult Education schools—establishing relationships with different communities—more difficult.

In the course of Teaching Practice and Supervised Internship, it was accepted that commitment to a qualified, more systematic contribution explicit to the project of human emancipation would be effected in order to seek and establish a more effective dialogic relationship between the university and the public schools involved in this process. This dialectical movement theory/practice is possible from the articulation of both the particular and general, integrating scientific and technical understanding of the social significance of education (Freire, 1988). We assume that ". . .the incursion into reality allows an approach to the concrete to unveil it, taking practice as the basis of real knowledge that comes from reality, that generates facts as language, conceptualization, conflicts, anxieties, hopes." (Freire, 1996).

For the effective qualification of the Adults Literacy teacher, in the sense that the trainee learns in the specific context of the school, the understanding has been that everybody must collectively rethink the concreteness of reality learners, educators, class conductors and trainees, pedagogical team and UFPR teachers.

Thinking about teacher training requires thinking about the design of illiteracy, which according to Freire cannot be attributed to problems related to the illiterate, subject to limitations, incapacities, and "laziness," but as people whose objective conditions of their reality have been denied the right to read (Freire, 1976).

Freire provides us with the elements to evaluate the teaching practices that shaped the children who are now adults, practices called "mechanistic" or "banking," in which our Pedagogy graduates were educated, so they do not reproduce the same with adults. Very often teachers do not realize that they are at the service of the ruling class, and use the same practices of domination, which is to stay quiet, copying meaningless texts, speeches and "politicized" speeches, according to the conception of the literacy teacher. In fact, educators are possessed of a messianic vision that to save the illiterate, young adults and adults, it is necessary that they dominate reading and writing, domesticating them, making them alienated, because the practices developed have nothing to do with the existential experiences of the literacy students; childlike practices having nothing to do with their everyday lives (Freire, 1976).

Practices should be characterized in terms of the school routine—dialogical, with political meaning—by placing as initially "equals" those who were previously considered "objects of civilization, i.e., what should be civilized and thus integrate them into society" as a deeply counter-hegemonic practice and, from there, essentially (Freire, 1993).

So, his pedagogical proposition regarding the Literacy Teachers training is that it is based on a critical and transformative view, which opposes the alienating conception of men and education, and must be considered from a pedagogy of men engaged in the fight for liberation, a pedagogy that has to provide the oppressed with the knowledge to critically start knowing what oppresses them and the subjects that oppress them (Freire, 1982).

"Critical reflection about practice becomes a requirement of the relation theory/practice without which, the theory can turn into a pointless conversation and the practice, activism," considering the recommendation of the author on the practice of literacy in Adult Education, it was necessary to "outline and discuss some fundamental knowledge on the educational-critical practice" rethinking the "required content" already worked into the subjects of the course "to the programmatic organization of teacher education" (Freire, 1996).

THE ORGANIZATION OF TEACHING PRACTICE IN ADULT EDUCATION STUDIES

The goal of Teaching Practice Supervised Internship is the teacher-trainee formation, experiencing the pedagogical routine of the public school and the teaching practice carried out in it, so that they will develop their pedagogical intervention as practice acquired in the classroom, along with students, schoolteachers, and the pedagogical team, under the guidance of the schoolteachers and UFPR teachers.

The total workload of the course is 120 hours, with collective meetings on the premises of UFPR, making a total of twenty-four hours, divided into six meetings with UFPR training professors and schoolteachers from the schools/internship field.

The program of the course consists of six units, the first of which deals with the Legalization of Supervised Internship, in the sense that there is a legal commitment with four copies of documents signed by all parties and delivered to UFPR. The Coordination of Internship Orientation—COE, consisting of teachers who work in the course and the General Coordination of Internship of the Dean of Undergraduate studies, co-validate and return three copies, one for the Coordination, one for the student, and another for the school/internship field.

This unit presents to the student all the legislation on internship. The intention is to make clear, from the beginning, to everyone involved in this course, the importance of legislation so that everyone has equal rights. There are many main characters acting in different times and spaces.

> It is for these reasons that law's importance is not identified and recognized as a mechanical or linear tool for social rights practice. It follows the contextualized development of citizenship....Its importance arises from the contradictory character that comes with it: there always lies a dimension of struggle. Struggle for more democratic enrolments, and for more realistic efetivations. (Freire as cited in Cury, 2002)

It is known that the laws made by men, from social demands, set limits, but recognize the rights of all to exercise citizenship, so there is a huge impact on people's lives; even if they are not always aware that all implications and consequences are a recognized right, it is necessary that they are guaranteed. Therefore, the first guarantee is that they are registered in national law character (Freire, as cited in Cury, 2002).

In the second unit the discussion focuses on the Theoretical Foundation, necessary for critical reading of the school space, based on a critical study of the dynamics of the educational process in the school, observation of the classroom routine and participatory planning of action, necessary for the production, development, and evaluation of an intervention project.

Taking Freire as reference, in this unit it is proposed to expose learners to the cognizable objects, constructed by theorists from the pedagogical everyday life they have experienced, to achieve the construction of new knowledge through educational intervention, seeking to elucidate the social, economic, political, scientific, and educational reality of the school and internship site, aiming at the education of the individual. The individual is the one who produces knowledge committed to the theory and real practice, becoming a producer of new knowledge, as there are differences between what is experienced and what is produced by different individuals. "The students should assume the subject's role of their world's intelligence development...recognize themselves as the architects of their own cognitive practice" (Freire, 1996).

The third unit is trainee orientation in order to learn to observe, diagnose, and become more able to support the planning of educational intervention. They must be aware of the educational environment that will develop their teaching practice, seeking to situate themselves and learn about pedagogical and didactically significant aspects. Thus, trainees need to experience the space of the institution/school, mainly the routine of the professional group, involving other agents that are to live in the school community, and that somehow interfere with the development of the teaching profession.

> There is an undeniable pedagogicity on space's materiality. Knowing is not actually guessing, but it has something to do with...the understanding of value of feelings, emotions, desire, and insecurity to be overcome by security.... A teacher's training indifferent to the decency and prettiness is also not possible...there is no educational practice that is not an aesthetic and ethical essay itself. (Freire, 1996)

The fourth unit refers to the planning of teaching activities, and the development of the teaching plan. This unit begins when the trainees plan their activities, based on the data collected during the observation phase and diagnosis of the school. Only then do trainees develop the activities and evaluate the methodological processes and outcomes of their work as teachers. During the development of the design of the Teaching practice and pedagogical intervention, all participants have assignments on reflecting, observing, diagnosing, recording, analyzing, planning, intervening, and evaluating, seeking to make the students revise the theories that underlie the areas of education, so that in this way, it is possible to establish connections among the teaching knowledge required for learning to teach (Freire, 1996).

The pedagogical intervention at school was described in unit five. This phase of work is idealized by everybody involved in the training process. At this point the teacher in training acts as a literacy class teacher. The intervention takes place to the extent that there is interaction among those involved. They act collectively and reconsider the action, in search of the transformation of the process and individuals. In the Freirean concept, "for these practices to be developed, it is necessary to take into account the teacher's knowledge of the individuals involved, and how the relationship between them should be, being the human possibility of existing more important than living. This makes men eminently relational beings.... this is a dynamic position they occupy in their own circumstances" (Freire, 1987).

The intervention was based on readings, observations, records, and plans constructed during this period of time, with professionals who have autonomy, discernment, methodical rigor, and the knowledge necessary for educational practices (Freire, 1997).

The relationship among the trainees, the literacy conductor, and literacy students is fundamental and complex, sometimes difficult, requiring a constant rethinking about the origins of the difficulties that arise and the changes in the forms of planning and developing pedagogical practice. Thus, "the educator is not only the one who teaches, but the one who also learns while education is taught through dialogue with the apprentice. Educator and learner grow together to become subjects of the process,...that support the pedagogical relation" (Freire, 1982).

The evaluation of the pedagogical intervention action, the sixth unit of study, is initiated when the trainee-student should be able to present the possibilities that the process, experienced within the school, effectively provided training and human learning. Freire points out, at this point, theoretical and practical constructs in three fields of knowledge, namely:

> ...the political nature about the very essence of being the subject, of their being in the world and with the world, and the understanding of the world itself and its influences on the subject...The educational activity nature, the pedagogical practice, the constituent elements of this action...are a specific science that will provide teachers and students activities. (Freire, 1996)

To evaluate the educational intervention, each trainee was instructed to analyze the contexts in order to approach the proposed activities in the classroom and to adjust him- or herself to the content. Moreover, it was necessary to analyze the adjustments, the degrees of complexity and difficulty of the students, to indicate the assessment criteria, so that learners and educators knew what was being proposed. The evaluation was not isolated from the social and institutional context in which the trainee participated, employing instruments and procedures of assessment.

Throughout the work each trainee evaluated the educational process in the following aspects: the meaning of the internship for vocational training, the most meaningful learnings, the aspects that favored the development of literacy teaching practice and those that made it difficult, as well as making suggestions to teachers and supervisors of the internship and to students who will take Teaching Practice the next school year. This evaluation practice is recommended by Freire (1996), who states. "Those who read my papers to seek the addition of their suggestions on the knowledge that is needed on how 'to teach rightly' and consequently to the performance of the literacy practice, other knowledge he could not identify" (Freire, 1982).

The last unit focuses on the organization of the Educational Practice report. The report should record the complete course of the process, in a detailed and reflective way, and include space where the graduate students portray their experiences at school, reporting and evaluating teaching resources created or suggested by those involved in the course. Similar to Freire (1996), we consider this process incomplete and unfinished, but it points out limits and possibilities to the pedagogical work in literacy teacher training. This incompleteness opens spaces for us to continually seek new formulations, practices, and pedagogies.

STRATEGIES FOR DIDACTIC-PEDAGOGICAL ORIENTATION

Each pedagogical step was organized into three phases, the first being the theoretical foundation, the conceptual support that helped the realization of educational activities, which the trainee developed in the school. This step presented a script of readings for reflection, which were deepened by practical activities, such as interpretation, analysis, and application of the concepts discussed in the basic texts, with examples to illustrate the mechanisms of reading, writing, and calculation— contents worked out in the literacy class. Designing the process of Adult Literacy as a broad process in which the dialogue about readings and critical unveiling and awareness of the world, in which they are somehow placed, allows those involved to come to the reading and writing production of the world (Freire, 1976).

The second step in research activities encourages creative thinking in the writing of the diagnostic research project, aiming to characterize the space of the school, as well as teaching practices and personal relationships that develop. In addition to subsidizing the development of research tools and further analysis in the light of the concepts discussed in the text referenced, the drafting of the Research Project and subsequent intervention in the classroom, are main objects of this course. Therefore, research guides were presented to trainees who, guided by class conductors, proposed new texts according to the demands and interests of the school community in order to expand the repertoire of conceptual tools.

During the third step, Practical Activity, proposed as the activity of each unit, students built a text by creatively applying textual mechanisms studied in the unit.

STRATEGIES FOR PEDAGOGICAL MEDIATION IN THE TEACHING PRACTICE OF LITERACY

The real classroom, at the school, the space of formation, was where teaching activities were taught collectively based on the readings of the texts, as well as on other study materials. Therefore, discussions and comments occurred in the school where students developed the Educational Practice activities, as well as spaces of collective interaction with the class teacher of the school/training field, and with their classmates.

Suggestions were made for readings of texts, for deepening the theoretical-practical, aimed at facilitating the understanding of issues related to the pedagogical action in the school. Other study materials, such as videos, music, and images, were available on the Internet and were considered important for the process of initial teacher training and continuing teacher education in the school. The activities required in each unit were followed by more specific information about the realization of the teaching activity in the Adult Education classroom, and were evaluated.

When preparing the Field Journal, knowledge productions were expressed. By having an open space for the communication of the results, students all began to consider themselves as idea builders, listeners, and processors of ideas in order to develop self-confidence and autonomy in the group (Freire, 1996). This form of assessment was emancipating.

FINAL THOUGHTS

From the Teaching Practice that we had knowledge of, to the Teaching Practice built based on Freire, which guides us on how one should learn to live, it was possible to dream to the extent that new paths and directions allowed envisioning a university of quality committed to its basic principles.

This learning was progressive, trying to deal with everyone and everything referred to as school. And as Freire says, metaphorizing the pedagogical practice with

> ...The practice of sailing, which requires basic knowledge, such as the mastery of the boat, of its components and their function, as well as knowledge of winds, their strength, direction, winds and sails, the position of the boat, the role of the engine and the combination of motor and sails. In the sailing practice, these powers are confirmed, modified or extended. (Freire, 1996)

Having the Pedagogical Policy and Expectation of the course, the navigation letter, it was possible to know where we were aiming, the harbor, the literacy teacher education. Many factors were involved at this time: the route, the course, had to be problematized, i.e., diagnosed, studied, and treated case by case, together with the main characters of the process because "no one walks without learning to walk—without learning to walk by walking, without learning to remake, to retouch, the dream for whose cause the walkers have set off down the road" (Freire, 1996, p. 155).

This work with the Teaching Practice allowed the rearrangement of ways of coexisting and pointed out changes based on reinterpretation of school contexts. It was necessary to change pedagogical attitudes when facing these challenges, because "change implies the dialectic between exposing the situation to the announcement of its overcoming deep down, our dream" (Freire, 1996).

The practice of this walking meant redesigning, organizing, developing, implementing, evaluating, and recreating the daily life of the university on its own course of professional training, by monitoring trainees, directors, educators, and teachers at the schools.

Each step of this journey helped in determining the responses that were spelled out in the final reports submitted in the Thematic Seminars, a humanizing activity, constructed from a collective practice of creating people committed to learning to teach, to form educators in the movement of consubstantiating theory into practice and doing through the word.

REFERENCES

Beisiegel, R. C. (1989). *Política e educação popular (teoria e a prática de Paulo Freire no Brasil)*. São Paulo, Brazil: Ed. Ática.

Cury, C. R. J. (2002). *Democracia e construção do público no pensamento educacional Brasileiro/* Organizado por Osmar Fávero, Giovani Semeraro. Petrópolis. RJ, Brazil: Vozes.

Freire, P. (1982). *A importância do ato de ler*. São Paulo, Brazil: Cortez.

Freire, P. (1987). *Ação cultural para a liberdade e outros escritos*. (8a ed.). Rio de Janeiro, Brazil: Paz & Terra.

Freire, P. (1988). *Educação e mudança*. São Paulo, Brazil: Paz & Terra.

Freire, P. (1988). *Pedagogia do oprimido*. Rio de Janeiro, Brazil: Paz & Terra.

Freire, P. (1993). *Política e educação*. São Paulo, Brazil: Cortez.

Freire, P. (1996). *Pedagogia da autonomia: Saberes necessários à prática educativa*. São Paulo, Brazil: Paz & Terra.

Freire, P., & Macedo, D. (1990). *Alfabetização: Leitura do mundo, leitura da palavra*. (3a ed.). Rio de Janeiro, Brazil: Paz & Terra.

CHAPTER THIRTY-SIX

Freire and Skinner: Is There Space for a Dialogue on Education?

DENISE BACHEGA AND JOÃO DOS SANTOS CARMO

INTRODUCTION

Although there is extensive academic production of behavior analyses focused on education, some studies suggest that in the Brazilian educational context there are many misconceptions and poorly founded criticisms regarding the value of their contributions to education. In contrast, Freire's liberating education has had great impact and acceptance in the global educational community. Freire and Skinner lived and worked in quite different cultural milieus and historical eras, and they have influenced educational practice in several respects. Considering that the origins of the relevant educational contributions of these authors arose from radically different epistemological fields and theoretical traditions, the following question arises: What are the main concordant and conflicting aspects between their two ways of approaching education? The aim of this chapter is to identify contributions of Freire's and Skinner's propositions regarding academic teaching and learning. In view of the misunderstandings prevalent among educational theorists, the proposed comparison seems relevant to clarifying for education professionals the educational propositions derived from Skinner's psychological approach and to providing behavioral analysts with cogent examples, questions, and reflections on ways of thinking about and implementing education. Therefore, the considerations in this chapter represent the opening of an ongoing dialogue expected to be enriching and productive.

FREIRE AND SKINNER: IS THERE SPACE FOR
A DIALOGUE ON EDUCATION?

By its nature, education is a polysemous phenomenon with different languages, dimensions, and ways of seeing interactions among people and the world. Therefore, the coexistence of different approaches, languages, and methodologies is not always harmonious. It is possible to look at education through broad dimensions, such as the political and the ideological, and, in this sense, to understand it as a determinant of behaviors and ways of being in society. It is also possible to look at aspects related to methodology in specific learning environments such as school. Among all dimensions, it is possible to identify a continuum of possible analyses.

Through whatever lens one uses, subject/subject and subject/world interactions are perceived. Accordingly, one can take a risk and state that all approaches to education see it as a human enterprise with a twofold goal: to teach individuals to act in a certain way and to bring about conditions that advance humanity's survival.

Based on these assumptions, this chapter is an initial examination of the possibilities of dialogue between two influential thinkers who, each in his own way, have deeply influenced relevant fields of human knowledge and action. At first glance, Paulo Freire and Burrhus Frederic (B. F.) Skinner appear to represent positions that are markedly antagonistic or, at least, nonconvergent. Our review does not intend to examine all dimensions of Freire's and Skinner's thoughts and works or to attain a theoretical, epistemological, or political conciliation. Strictly speaking, the aim is to identify contributions of these two thinkers, cast a critical eye on some of Skinner's propositions regarding academic teaching and learning, and identify how behavior analysts could benefit from methodological systematization derived from Freire's work. In view of space limitations, it is possible to offer only some preliminary reflections in these pages.

There is no doubt the present text is likely to startle some educators and behavior analysts who are applying the theories of Freire and Skinner, respectively. As this is a preliminary study, comments, critiques, and recommendations for further research are welcome.

As noted, our primary focus is the work of Freire and Skinner related to education. The chapter constitutes a preliminary version of theoretical research to be presented more fully in Bachega's master's thesis. In this chapter, we first present some pertinent propositions of Freire and Skinner and proceed to examine their principal complementarities and incompatibilities.

BACKGROUND

Since the onset of behavioral analysis, its researchers have produced various educational works, including in Brazil (Hübner, 1987; Luna, 2000; Neri, 1980; Zanotto, 2000). Skinner published twenty-five articles or book chapters on education during a thirty-year period (Skinner, 1989/1991). The concepts and discussions present in his proposals are crucial for studying human behavior and its interaction with physical and social environments. While the contributions of Skinner's work are not restricted to psychology, the understanding of these works outside their original field is problematic in Brazil as a result of misconceptions and poorly founded criticisms regarding the value of their contributions to education (Rodrigues, 2006; Rodrigues & Moroz, 2008). Accordingly, this chapter highlights some of Skinner's contributions to educational practice.

In contrast to the dearth of clear understanding and broad acceptance of Skinner's proposals, Freire's liberating education has had great impact and acceptance in the global educational community. Freire can rightly be considered one of the greatest and most significant educators of the twentieth century with contributions and repercussions that persist to this day. He has made significant criticisms of Brazilian education and proposed radical revisions in executing the responsibilities of Brazil's educative process. Indeed, his educational proposals are considered revolutionary for Brazilian and worldwide educational praxis (Gadotti, 1989).

Freire and Skinner lived and worked in quite different cultural milieus and historical eras, and they have influenced educational practice in several respects. Considering that the origins of the relevant educational contributions of these authors arose from radically different epistemological fields and theoretical traditions, the following question naturally arises: What are the main concordant and conflicting aspects between their two ways of approaching education?

In view of the misunderstandings prevalent among educational theorists and behavioral analysts in Brazil (Gioia, 2001; Rodrigues, 2006; Rodrigues & Moroz, 2008) and the broad acceptance of Freire's theories, the proposed comparison seems relevant to clarifying for education professionals the educational propositions derived from Skinner's psychological approach and to providing behavioral analysts with cogent examples, questions, and reflections on ways of thinking about and implementing education.

According to Bittencourt (2004), interdisciplinary research is essential to increasing public awareness of diverse theoretical and methodological frameworks. Moreover, as Miranda and Cirino (2007) point out, these studies also enable greater sophistication in fields and perspectives related to their subjects. Thus, the chapter seeks to contribute to methodological enrichment and the generation of better communication and understanding among scholars in these two theoretical fields—education and behavioral analysis. The postulates of Freire and

Skinner that follow concern three topics—education, knowledge, and the role of the teacher—and afford initial components to construct our proposed comparison.

PAULO REGLUS NEVES FREIRE (1921–1997)

In the opening chapter of *Education, the Practice of Freedom*, Freire states that there is no education outside human society and no man exists in the void (Freire, 2011). The statement points out two fundamental aspects of his educational proposals, the consideration that humans live in society and education is a typically human task. As cited in the same work, Weffort affirms that in Freire's problem-posing education, words should never be taken as givens or grants from the educator to the student, since words do not exist apart from their significance in reference to life (Weffort, 2011).

EDUCATION

According to Freire, education is eminently a human action deliberated in the community in which it occurs. The author quotes a passage from the Hungarian sociologist Karl Mannheim, who states that we live in societies where the most important changes are decided collectively and revaluation must be based on acceptance and intellectual comprehension. One of the main questions the author addresses is the possibility that educational practice serves both to maintain and transform the dichotomous conditions of both oppressors and oppressed, which mark the vast majority of societies (Freire, 2005).

In Freire's proposals, education has to be forged with oppressed individuals and not for them in the constant struggle to recover their humanity. Such struggle is necessary to make a person the subject of her or his historical moment; in other words, a person is able to reflect on one's self, time, responsibilities, and role in the cultural moment. That is, people should be able to identify the conditions of their reality and act to transform, rather than merely accept and reproduce without thinking or questioning, the conditions of inequality and injustice imposed on them.

Taking education as a necessary, but inadequate, condition for the construction of a more just and egalitarian society, Freire states that education should provide people with the conviction that they can be part of social change because this conviction is a prerequisite to the development of democracy (Freire, 2011). To produce social change, however, education must be linked to the reality of one's daily life and should not use authoritarian and antidialogical means. It is impossible to build a more human reality through education that ignores students' reality.

Furthermore, one can build genuine democracy only through dialogic means, since democratic knowledge is only internalized through existential experience (Freire, 2011).

KNOWLEDGE

The proposal of a problem-posing education is contrary to the concept of teachers as transmitters of knowledge and students as nothing more than receptacles. In this banking model of education, teachers are more comfortable when their students conform to, rather than criticize, the status quo. The model criticized by Freire is analogous to Sartre's concept in which knowledge is compared to food, that is, the educator feeds students as if they needed to be fattened (Freire, 2005). Similarly, students are filled with snippets of meaningless content disconnected from the reality of their oppression.

In problem-posing education, knowledge is seen as a process of inquiry, a restless, impatient, and continuing search performed in the world, with the world, and with the others and exists only when it is created within the context of a new reality (Freire, 2005).

THE ROLE OF THE TEACHER

In education for liberty, the teacher's role should not be to wait passively for students eventually to recognize the contradictions of their oppression and banking education, but to identify with the students and orient education toward their mutual humanization. The educator sees knowledge not as a gift to be delivered, but rather, as one believing in humanity and in its creative power, one that requires maintaining an egalitarian relationship with learners. Freire states that in problem-posing educations,

> the teacher is no longer merely the-one-who-teaches, but one who is himself taught in dialogue with the students, who in turn while being taught also teach. They become jointly responsible for a process in which all grow. In this process, arguments based on "authority" are no longer valid; in order to function, authority must be *on the side of* freedom, not *against* it. Here, no one teaches another, nor is anyone self-taught. People teach each other, mediated by the world, by the cognizable objects which in banking education are "owned" by the teacher. (Freire, 2005, p. 80, emphasis in original)

BURRHUS FREDERIC SKINNER (1904–1989)

The first explanation necessary to understanding Skinner's educational propositions concerns his concept of behavior. To the author, behavior refers not only to one's actions, but also to their interaction with the physical, biological, social, and cultural environment in which they occur. Any action, even internal, might be taken by behavioral analysis as behavior. Some of them may be more easily observed and described, but this does not mean that behaviors that are not directly observable should be excluded or underestimated. In other words, thoughts, intentions, and emotions are also considered and studied in behavioral analysis.

Furthermore, Skinner proposes that the explanation of behavior should consider three levels of origin and development: that of the species (phylogenesis), of the individual (ontogenesis), and specific modes of interaction of individuals within specific groups (culture). He designated a particular type of behavior as operant. This concept is crucial to understanding why individuals act the way they do and why our species has a great capacity to change ourselves and the world. As Skinner describes it, "Men act upon the world, and change it, and are changed in turn by the consequences of their action" (Skinner, 1957, p. 1).

EDUCATION

Skinner (1969, p. 48) states, "A species has no existence apart from its members or a culture apart from the people who practice it" and makes varied analyses about education: sometimes, he analyzes it from a macro-viewpoint and considers it as a behavior control agent, along with the government, religion, economy, and psychotherapy. Skinner also observes that the primary function of these agencies has been to regulate individual and group behavior.

In describing the functioning of such control agencies, Skinner expresses concern with the inefficiency and harm caused by the means of implementation and "especially with certain kinds of power over variables which affect human behavior and with the controlling practices which can be employed because of this power" (Skinner, 1953, p. 334ff.). Nonetheless, he offers no concrete proposals to address these concerns. While favoring an ethic that promotes the good of the community and is critical of the use of coercive control, Skinner is unclear in explaining, much less defending, a political position or propositions about the phenomena that he observes and describes. His argument is to the effect that science, particularly the science of human behavior, will itself make the major contributions to solving social problems.

From an analysis of the interactions between people in social environments, such as groups, Skinner depicts education as a cultural enterprise that aims to ensure the survival of our species. The author says that education is "the establishing of behavior which will be of advantage to the individual and to others at some future time" (Skinner, 1953, p. 402). In the context he intends, preparing for the future, both individual and collective, is a fundamental necessity that justifies educational activity. At the same time, it is critical that this future cover both long- and short-term aspects. In isolation, preparation for either the long or near term is disadvantageous. For example, the latter may disregard conditions that could arise in the distant future, while, as Skinner notes, the former prepares students for a world that is too remote.

Skinner refers critics to the traditional school's teaching methodology and its discouraging results. He indicates that predominantly verbal and descriptive teaching methods can be disadvantageous, for example, when students are taught about what can be done and the consequences. To the contrary, for learning to be advantageous, students must eventually acquire knowledge through understanding that their behavior has direct reinforcing consequences. Generally, however, this only occurs later in life (Skinner, 1989/1991).

In this regard, Skinner notes that one of the most important institutions in society, the school, is not properly meeting its educational responsibilities since much of teaching is limited to a verbal mode. "Most knowledge acquired in education is verbal" (Skinner, 1953, p. 408). This thought permeates his criticism of the way the public school addresses its role:

> Public school was invented to offer the services of a private tutor to more than one student at a time. As the number of students increased, each one necessarily started to receive less attention. By the time the number had reached 25 or 30, personal attention became sporadic. Textbooks were invented to take over some of the work of the tutor, but two problems remained unsolved. What is done simultaneously by every member of a large group cannot be evaluated immediately, and what is taught to a large group cannot be precisely what each student is ready just at that moment to learn. (Skinner, 1986, p. 103)

Skinner's perspective begins with a critique of the teaching conditions commonly seen in school. Furthermore, he is highly critical of the way schools usually teach, that is, the common and widespread use of "aversive control." By aversive control, Skinner means the threat and application of punishment. As such, he proposes that the real reason—rarely admitted—that students pay attention to teachers and read books assigned them is that, one way or the other, they were punished when they fail to do so. If they could, students would flee to hockey games or go to sleep, and even counter-attack by vandalizing and assaulting schoolteachers (Skinner, 1989/1991).

Skinner also indicates that punitive control over students has moved from direct ways, such as corporal punishment, to more subtle ways, though as harmful as the first.

KNOWLEDGE

On different occasions, Skinner proposes that knowledge can be divided into *descriptive knowledge*, related to what he calls *rule-governed behavior*, and *knowledge by understanding*, related to *shaped behavior contingency*. Although both types of knowledge are relevant and important, schools have traditionally overemphasized descriptive knowledge, making learning pedantic, innocuous, and insignificant. Instead, it could foster knowledge by enhancing understanding through direct exposure to relevant contingencies. In other words, in the first case, we would learn from verbal descriptions and in the second, by *learning by doing*, which often provides more meaningful learning (Skinner, 1969).

For teaching to enable knowledge by understanding, on the one hand "it is important to emphasize that a student does not passively absorb knowledge from the world around him but must play an active role, and also that action is not simply talking" (Skinner, 2003, p. 5). On the other hand, while Skinner agrees that "to know is to act effectively, both verbally and nonverbally" (Skinner, 2003, p. 5), he recognizes that "a student does not learn simply by doing" (p. 5), as this would reduce the acquisition of knowledge solely to acting and lead to the misunderstanding that simply inserting students in situations in which they must act would cause them to acquire knowledge. In this sense, Skinner warns that it is more effective to plan and schedule academic learning so that the student does not see himself or herself submitted to trial and error, that is, exposed to situations in which one lacks resources to solve problems and move ahead in a more autonomous manner. At the same time, it does not mean that all students should follow the same plan and schedule.

Accordingly, if it is true that the "student is to learn about the world in which he lives and must be brought into contact with it" (Skinner, 2003, p. 6), it is equally clear that "from experience alone a student probably learns nothing. He will not even perceive the environment simply by being in contact with it" (Skinner, 2003, p. 6). Thus, we see that Skinner's approach is not spontaneist in the sense that all we need to acquire knowledge is simply contact with the world; rather, knowledge by understanding occurs in conditions of teaching and programmed situations, that is, shaped behavior contingencies. Hence, the importance is given to the essential role of the teacher.

THE ROLE OF THE TEACHER

Skinner first observes that teachers are generally helpless in regard to their formal preparation for teaching. In addition, as noted previously, he suggests that schools still use coercive methods and generate inappropriate conditions for educational work. Therefore, in observing that academia has generated a significant amount of knowledge about learning and conditions that facilitate it, Skinner denounces the existence of a gap between the knowledge that the science of learning produces and its access by teachers, so that "from this exciting prospect of an advancing science of learning, it is a great shock to turn to that branch of technology which is most directly concerned to the learning process—education" (Skinner, 2003, p. 14).

The working conditions in the classroom are extremely unfavorable for both teachers and students, but the question remains: What characterizes the role of the teacher? Among varied proposals, ranging from nondirective to directive, Skinner proposes that the primary role of the teacher is to teach and "teaching is the expediting of learning; a person who is taught learns more quickly than the one who is not" (Skinner, 2003, p. 5). This proposition indicates an active role for teachers, but not necessarily a set of actions that burden them with the entire responsibility for learning outcomes. For this reason, Skinner proposes that "teaching is simply the arrangement of contingencies of reinforcement" (Skinner, 2003, p. 5). In other words, it is necessary to establish conditions of teaching that guarantee the presence of natural and social reinforcers during learning. He proceeds to observe that "the school of experience is no school at all, not because no one learns in it, but because no one teaches" (Skinner, 2003, p. 5).

> If we must have a metaphor to represent teaching, *instruction* (or better, the cognate *construction*) will serve. In this sense we say that the teacher *informs* the student, in the sense that his behavior is given form or shape. To teach is edifying in the sense of built. It is possible, of course, to say that the teacher builds precursors such as knowledge, habits or interests, but the metaphor of construction does not demand this because the *behavior* of the student can in a very real sense be constructed. (Skinner, 2003, p. 4, emphasis in original)

Skinner proposes that the teacher's working conditions should change from issues related to better wages to concrete conditions in the classroom, for example, the number of students. Therefore, we conclude this section with Skinner's idea that education is "a utopian dream" in which teachers will have more time to talk with their students, counsel them, and get to know them better, perhaps even staying in contact with them. Accordingly, teachers would be more capable of helping students select their fields of study. Instead of teaching subjects inefficiently under current conditions, they will have the satisfaction of taking part in a system that teaches all students effectively. In return for increased productivity, teaching will be well paid and satisfying (Skinner, 1989/1991).

COMPARISONS BETWEEN FREIRE'S AND SKINNER'S PROPOSALS

Both Freire's and Skinner's works focus on education as a typically human activity strongly influenced by the culture in which it operates and having significant impact on constructing social practices. Freire emphasizes the political nature of education and its role as a fundamental condition in building a truly democratic society. Although Skinner highlights the importance of social interaction for building societies and the political role of education as an agency for social control, his proposals do not indicate a specific political position and are focused on describing and understanding the behaviors involved in teaching and learning.

While a behavioral, analytical understanding of teaching as affecting behavioral change could encompass teaching by antidialogical means in which the teacher is the keeper of knowledge that students merely receive and replicate, a more comprehensive assessment of Skinner's proposals enables us to see that Skinner delineates teaching methods that promote changes in students' behavior that are open to other means. His clear and cogent criticisms of the use of coercive methods and predominantly verbal instruction are telling examples. Furthermore, the same behavioral vision equips one to understand that an antidialogical practice of teaching that seeks only to alter behaviors by reproducing content without promoting intellectual autonomy and creativity is unlikely to be advantageous for either the individual or the community.

Skinner's concept of knowledge is incompatible with Freire's description of banking education, since Skinner describes teaching as intrinsically linked to acting and the view that behavioral change is something provided by the school to be built from the relations and interactions offered by the teacher. What should be taught, according to Skinner, are ways of acting in society and thus a better metaphor would be building behaviors rather than transferring knowledge.

INITIAL REFLECTIONS

The considerations in this chapter represent the opening of an ongoing dialogue expected to be enriching and productive. Hence the title of this section alludes to "initial reflections," as it is an invitation for us to leave the comfort zone of our own ideas and engage in a unique—even provocative—dialogue, which will challenge our preconceptions and likely modify them.

As behavioral analysis arises from a pragmatic tradition culturally linked to a particular mode of education, it is not surprising that Skinner's concepts of education reflect significant epistemological and philosophical differences from those of Freire. Nevertheless, behavioral analysis affords educators the opportunity to explore its significant contributions to a critical and long overdue dialogue on education reform.

At the same time, behavior analysts would benefit from considering Freire's radical critique of traditional education and advocacy of liberating education that promotes social change. Indeed, it is time to ask the natural question that arises from a shared consensus of the deficiencies of the present educational system: For whom is the educational system designed and implemented?

REFERENCES

Bittencourt, T. (2004). Aviso ao leitor [Note for the reader]. In M. L. Passos, *Bloomfield e Skinner: Língua e comportamento verbal* [Bloomfield and Skinner: Language and verbal behavior]. Rio de Janeiro, Brazil: NAU.

Freire, P. (2005). *Pedagogy of the oppressed, 30th anniversary edition* (M. B. Ramos, Trans.). New York, NY: Continuum.

Freire, P. (2011). *Educação como prática da liberdade* [Education, the practice of freedom] (14ª ed.). Rio de Janeiro, Brazil: Paz e Terra.

Gadotti, M. (1989). *Convite à leitura de Paulo Freire* [Invitation to Paulo Freire's reading]. São Paulo, Brazil: Scipione.

Gioia, P. S. (2001). *Abordagem behaviorista transmitida pelo livro de psicologia direcionado à formação de professores* [Behaviorist approach transmitted through the psychology book directed to teachers]. Tese de Doutorado em Psicologia da Educação. Pontifícia Universidade Católica de São Paulo, São Paulo, SP.

Hübner, M. M. C. (1987). *Analisando a relação professor-aluno: Do planejamento à sala de aula* [Analyzing the teacher-student relation: From planning to the classroom]. São Paulo, Brazil: CLR-Balieiros.

Luna, S. V. (2000). Contribuições de Skinner para a educação [Skinner's contribution to the education]. In V. M. N. de S Placco (Org.), *Psicologia & educação: Revendo contribuições* (pp. 145–179). São Paulo, Brazil: Educ.

Miranda, R. L., & Cirino, S. D. (2007). Resenha língua e comportamento verbal: Diálogos entre a linguística e a análise do comportamento [Review languages and verbal behavior: Dialogues between linguistics and behavior analysis]. *Revista Brasileira de Terapia Comportamental e Cognitiva, 9*(2), 375–379.

Neri, A. L. (1980). O modelo comportamental aplicado ao ensino [The behavioral model applied to teaching]. In W. M. A. Penteado (Org.), *Psicologia e ensino* (pp. 118–133). São Paulo, Brazil: Papelivros.

Rodrigues, M. E. (2006). Behaviorismo: Mitos, discordâncias, conceitos e preconceitos [Behaviorism: Myths, disagreements, concepts and prejudices]. *Educere et Educere Revista de Educação, 1*(2), 141–164.

Rodrigues, M. E., & Moroz, M. (2008). Formação de professores e análise do comportamento: A produção da pós-graduação nas áreas de Psicologia e Educação [Teacher formation and behavior analysis: The graduation production in the fields of Psychology and Education]. *Acta Comportamentalia, 16*(3), 347–378.

Skinner, B. F. (1953). *Science and human behavior.* New York, NY: Macmillan.

Skinner, B. F. (1957). *Verbal behavior.* New York, NY: Appleton-Century-Crofts.

Skinner, B. F. (1969). *Contingencies of reinforcement: A theoretical analysis.* New York, NY: Appleton-Century-Crofts.

Skinner, B. F. (1986). Programmed instruction revisited. *Phi Delta Kappan, 68*, 103–110.

Skinner, B. F. (1991). *Questões recentes na análise comportamental* [Recent issues in behavioral analysis] (L. Neri, Trans.) Campinas, SP, Brazil: Papirus. (Original work published 1989)

Skinner, B. F. (2003). *The technology of teaching.* Acton, MA: Copley.

Weffort, F. C. (2011). Educação e política: Reflexões sociológicas sobre uma pedagogia da liberdade. [Education and politics: Sociological reflections on a pedagogy of freedom] In P. Freire, *Educação como prática da liberdade* (pp. 7–39). Rio de Janeiro, Brazil: Paz e Terra.

Zanotto, M. L. B. (2000). *Formação de professores: A contribuição da Análise do Comportamento* [Teachers' formation: The contribution of behavior analysis]. São Paulo, Brazil: EDUC.

CHAPTER THIRTY-SEVEN

Appropriate/Critical Educational Technology Within Freire's Framework, Toward Overcoming Social Exclusion

BEATRIZ LIDIA FAINHOLC

INTRODUCTION

The intent of the socio-cultural-educational approach for public policies is to strengthen social inclusion—an alternative to the existing lines. In general, this characterizes Latin American education. This approach provides a comprehensive framework and the cross perspective in face-to-face and virtual educational programs applying Freire's Pedagogy and Cultural and Social Studies. This gives us inputs to contribute—under the umbrella of the Appropriate and Critical Education and Technology approaches—to the construction of a substantive equity and conviviality, by the concise application of ICT networks and derivative devices, articulated with its collaborative, dialogic, and participatory Freirean methodologies.

The combination with other pedagogical issues, such as problem-based learning methodology, self/peer evaluation, community designs of programs, learning centered in the students, should be the pillars of the decision makers of public policies, managers, professors, and tutors. These decision makers, by training, will recognize critical alternatives to the linear model of understanding the reality to replace them with situated and distributed, systemic-holistic and socio-technological approaches.

These interpretations are the result of experiences in Argentinean training of future professors, stressing the conditions of production and use of knowledge, more and more mediated by ICT, to improve the inclusion and use of emancipator proposals.

The teaching and learning in the digital culture are run by technological mediations and virtual networks beyond schools and universities. The communities, families, informal groups' interaction, social media, and network socialization are more important than formal training. Many times this is anachronized for the twenty-first century and for emancipatory and democratic ideas. Paulo Freire's framework seems to have more pertinence than ever.

The awareness works—beyond its limitations, because there is no panaceic method as complex in today's world. With exclusions and inequities this requires critical and reflective vision and practice.

The entire actual global situation, especially for Latin America, as represented by extensive research and existing literature in this regard, is not included in this chapter owing to limitations of space. But, despite everything written, Latin America has not overcome the stage of inequity.

The configuration of settings of social inclusion considers all forms for every user (students, groups, communities, etc.) and includes the tools for the practice, in our case, of digital skills in order to perform, with relevance and prudence, proactively and responsibly, a (cyber) citizenry. These tools are important for valuable, productive and valid behaviour that meets the needs of life.

Articulated to this context, the reality was transformed by socio-cultural and political representative means, basically by Internet, ICT and virtual networks that mutate each social process, relationships, and so on. These are exhibited daily in behaviors and reformulated values. It brings other opportunities, ways and technological formats to build knowledge, in more horizontal and participative proposals based on the interests and real needs of people, groups and local organizations. The approach does not fail to recognize other types of challenges in theoretic-practical, conceptual, and methodological areas, to which Freire contributed in a very valuable epistemic approach toward the concepts and performance of face-to-face and virtual education programs.

OBJECTIVES

In that context, this chapter hopes to:

1. Provide a necessary new conceptual meaning and useful methodological articulation applying Freire's framework to educational issues

2. Propose a few lines of inquiry focused on the socio-ethic, practical, and political educational approach, as related to the electronic socio-educational programs toward social inclusion

3. Imagine a possible anticipation of sustainable and feasible actions, related to electronic socio-educational programs for informed educational efforts. This should aim toward a new critical reconstruction of the local praxis inserted in the global/local world.

WHERE ARE WE?

The people of the twenty-first century—within a hyper-capitalism that still is surviving—are step by step organizing the world in a fantastic network of contradictory effects. Post-industrial products from advanced countries arrive not only at the periphery of poor countries through the Internet, ICT and their different software but also in many regions of the internalized world—where, despite opening vast new possibilities for human communication, only the hegemonic-commercial spirit prevails.

Social relationships and processes (which are generated by ICT networks with decentralized access, but with management and centralized organization) are very fragile, with an emotional empathy and a large number of popular followers (celebrities) with great communicative power.

But they do not think that an equity exists among the same protagonists in this digital network civilization. Although Google and others contain the highest quantity of information and answers, Google, with its reach algorithms (Baricco, 2008), offers a large quantity of connected sites, many of them in camouflaged locations. So, the mechanisms of e-exclusion continue.

This is also true owing to the fact that the property software and its design, the interfaces for navigation, are defined by other users rather than being defined and designed by the protagonists from specific scenarios with special needs. Thus, there is the need for a continuous re-reading/re-negotiation of meanings, in terms of removing false consciousness or bias underlying political representations and concepts. Therefore it is important to be aware of the subjacent communications models. These are crucial toward a knowledgeable implementation of teaching strategies, if the goal is to reach open, flexible, and democratic social representations, with constant alternative revisions of the status quo.

FREIRE'S FRAMEWORK APPLIED TO VIRTUAL EDUCATION

Paulo Freire's framework is pertinent inside of and outside of Latin America, because of its historical legacy of the democratic tradition. It constitutes authentic and original contributions, taking into account the points of view of the needs and expectations of the users/students/people as central inputs for situated education programs, face-to-face or virtual. It is necessary to turn our attention to several aspects of the issues that are specific to Latin America, in order to include a hybrid inter/trans-disciplinary field of study with such a diversity of socio-cultural contexts and countries. These are inextricably linked to public policies and actions, recognizing critical alternatives to the linear model of technological innovation, to replace it with a systemic-holistic and socio-technological understanding, stressing the particular conditions of production and use of knowledge in this region, with the articulation of ICT, mainly to consolidate open virtual education.

The rescue of the dialogue—mediated by networks or formal training curricula and strong informal socialization—as a fundamental pedagogical resource, is crucial within the concept of praxis toward an awareness/conciseness technologically mediated by process and action. This means a philosophical, epistemological, political, and ethical framework related to a critical, transformative, and social democracy for open and distant projects and training alternatives. The praxis represents the theoretical and practical thoughts and actions as a whole, where the people/students through technological literacy could generate proposals about the world toward an equal transformation by education. Consider that Freire's methodology appears in the mid-twentieth century, when 80% of Brazilian inhabitants were illiterate.

The awareness needs to be in the spirit of the incorporation and enhancement of ICT in social life and educational efforts. Many theorists claim that his ideas are anachronistic or fixed to a specific context.

We could say that Freire's method is a psycho-social and reflective-critical approach, within a horizontal dialogue between teachers and professors, social communicators, distance tutors, administrators, and common people, as a tool for expression. In that educational context, the legacy of Freire is pertinent to the educational programs within the network society (Castells, 2004) of the twenty-first century because it is an adequate environment where the characteristics of the social open networks and OER (Open Educative Resources) could be appropriated to virtual learning and teaching environments, mediated by ICT, within that praxis's approach.

His ideas of educating to know the reality in a demystifying way acts to provide people with an idea to transform the reality. Education is dialogue, and should inspire the ICT spirit and be used in that framework. Internet, ICT, and any kind of network with methodologically rigorous research proposals provide action programs, respectful of students' and everyone's interests and needs, in an ethical way, using examples and models that reflect the socio-pedagogical practices and show the possibilities of assuming the cultural identity to be recreated by the intercultural electronic exchange. This is an opportune time to be involved in thinking about Freire's ideas. The articulation and appropriation of electronic educational technology generate a lot of discussion, especially about what higher education may look like in a few years.

At the same time there is contemporary discourse on how technology can "transform" education concerns, because it is largely guided by techno-enthusiasm, techno-determinism and a desire to improve "efficiency" on models grounded on cutting costs, supported by a technical-instrumental rationality. This is not a new concern: many social scientists have described what current thinking in the educational technology corporate world looks like.

My point of view is that, if it is necessary to improve education and quality of life for all, we have to engage, extend, and apply educational technology artifacts, actions, and minds critically. Engagement means involving decision makers, managers, and educators, among others, in designing innovations and using the existing research from anthropology, sociology, cognitive psychology, linguistics, and appropriate educational technology (Fainholc, 2012a, 2012b) in order to build knowledge. Knowledge is not something that can be limited to a definite time or place, because it is inscribed into an invisible, dynamic, and ubiquitous learning.

This is not contradictory to the several participative designs of programs and social efforts. But this proposal is an attempt to highlight alternative ways of thinking, interacting, and living that are more pertinent for many regions. Alternative perspectives are important because they help us question our assumptions and worldview.

ANALYSIS OF SOME FACTORS TO PROMOTE A SOCIO-TECHNOLOGICAL AND PEDAGOGICAL INCLUSION MEDIATED BY TECHNOLOGIES

It is easy to see who is included and who is not, through the impact produced in the construction of identities, given in turn by the practice of an inter-subjective interaction or communicational interplay (increasingly mediated in a virtual way) of these subjectivities.

Without horizontality, e-inclusion, dialogue, and OER point out ingenious and creative ways in which people become "producers, re-creators and diffusers of knowledge"—by the appropriation (Fainholc, 2012) of any kind of tools, from popular theatre, marionettes, and dances to the Internet and ICT—and not only consumers. Such is the capacity of the situated appropriation of digital tools toward the (re)creation of alternative educational possibilities.

The appropriation process, in our case, of technology, is related to two facets:

1. The cultural relevance and social pertinence of the proposals: strategic plans, programs, materials with their interfaces designs, local languages, and tutors

2. The interactive and participative, socio-constructive and collaborative work to change attitudes, beliefs, deconstruction of knowledge, and bias, such as to work with tacit tactics of learning (mindware, cognitive skills, digital competences, etc.) and teaching strategies such as project planning, case study, learning-based problems (LBP), for virtual environments, to open and distance programs.

WHAT SHOULD WE DO?

An epistemic, methodological, ethical, and political interdisciplinary view for a socio-educational proposal (face-to-face and at a distance), we hope, will be a solution to contrast in specific contexts, facing the new, uncertain, and complex global/local scenarios of work and study, in improving the educational programs and, as a consequence, life quality.

The configuration of the empowerment and practice of citizenry by digital skills today, in a proactive and responsible way, will contribute to a valuable, intercultural and socially productive framework. But it does not refer to the recognition of the contradictions and social tensions, communicational negotiation and practice. It will address the main political task of overcoming diverse world e-exclusions.

Digital technology environments and tools in their horizontal ways to act basically by OER will allow reaching and analyzing new phenomena and objects—many of them cyborgs—in recreational alternative ways, as noted above. The networks—like the work that Freire suggested many years ago—would be used as an open and free space for a democratic, critical reading and a reflexive navigation with the digital artifacts.

The approach means processing information by the "pro-sumer" (producer and consumer), to transform it into knowledge by using the media (ICT, Internet, and its derivates) with strong guidance, toward its application: by the mediated interaction, we do not learn only content but also communicational modes.

In this way, the technological-digital rationality has to give us the conditions of technological freedom to contribute to configure the "collective intelligence" (Levy, 1999) by learning and transforming different environments (not only the digital), because one of the results will be to increase the cognitive-socio-cultural baggage.

From an epistemological and pedagogical point of view, we have to take advantage of cultural situations and historical circumstances, given by open and inter-transdisciplinary conceptions, design and use of the actual digital technologies: wiki tools, blogs, web quests, Twitter, and so on, for different, unique, vulnerable, and exceptional situations with people, groups, organizations, countries, and regions.

MORE THAN PROPOSALS, CONCRETE ACTIONS

Implementation and evaluation of the main and concrete mediated activities within socio-pedagogical digital environments could be (following and recreating Siemens's [2004] lines):

1. *Aggregation.* To design and offer teaching proposals, in order to re-elaborate different content by the students, from local and various experiences and resources taken from articles, magazines, blogs, Twitter, wiki—delicious reservoirs to discuss posts, ads, photos, and newsletters in their content and format, to be re-read in a critical (Fainholc, 2004) way, to watch/attend videos and other media, to cultivate and to look forward to dialogue to reconstruct explanations.

2. *Remixing.* To design more than connections, to understand many cognitive and social interrelations of people and groups, by controlling mixed materials or content. We learn by a share/group content combination that people have to confront, evaluate, and adjust in and through practice.

3. *Repurposing.* To repurpose projects and materials, not by repetitions or filtering but by active participation for recreation: this is the more difficult and important part of the process, because not everyone is able to do it.

   The added material, remixed and repurposed online, will be the main issue to configure new thoughts and comprehensions. Second or third readings create new discernments and, as a consequence, knowledge. Teachers, instructors, professors, tutors, and socio-cultural animators are central here with their specific expertise. They will have to use demonstrations, examples, and strategies in an ethical chat and observe community issues or ideas. As a consequence, we can see that it is not a new educational theory, but rather the old "apprenticeship" theory (close to socio-constructivism), in which Freire's proposal of practice as the center of this pedagogical approach is used.

4. *Feeding environment's opportunities forward by a virtual collaborative and shared work done in order to validate it in actions.* Many times, it is difficult to expose one's own errors. It is important to take time, to become aware of and recognize what we are doing, often with the help of others. This could be a way to share proposals aimed at increasing an authentic motivation. *All of these conceptions* are not an abstraction of the complex interactive education process of virtual education, such as the real world,

produced by digital networks and a set of flexible principles and rules. However, respecting all of the differences is difficult to put in practice.

A POSSIBLE ANTICIPATION OF AMBITIOUS AND FEASIBLE THOUGHTS IN FREIRE'S FRAMEWORK

Electronic education programs and ICT in education do not guarantee social inclusion and equity, nor do they guarantee educational quality and innovations. These do not belong to the world of machines but to attitudes and public policy approaches to technology management. They generate, in the close interdependence of multiple factors, the production of local scientific and technological knowledge, anchored in specific socio-economic and cultural contexts.

So, sustainable and self-sustaining development of the regional and national units will not take place only through the introduction of ICT. Nevertheless, without the Internet connectivity and support, little can be accomplished and expanded upon today. Technological support is essential for educational development, but it cannot be the only component of the process.

The public policy approach for the management of local education (including scientific and technological innovations) should consider in a systemic and coordinated way, the following contrasting lines of thought and action:

1. Renewing the educational paradigm with teachers trained in digital competences.
2. Strengthening the research system in basic centers to prepare researchers and professionals, professors and faculty, in coordinated actions with schools, universities, industries, businesses, etc.
3. A strong and sustained investment in infrastructure: to build poles of technological development requires a basic network with electricity services, transportation, communications, that is in tune with technology, without which exclusion and the various gaps will continue to grow in Latin America.

Thus, we cannot fail to consider the issue of social exclusion, which is what leads us to understand the articulated incorporation of cutting-edge technology, in the production of knowledge in the digital age. In other words, there cannot be a model of sustainable human development nor is conviviality possible without the achievement of social inclusion, given by an education for all, where today, ICT contributes to this. Although this historical time is different, we would say that they are in line with Freire's ideas, but "revisited" to this digital culture.

Therefore, we understand that with the inclusion of ICT in everyday use—in general, an instrumental approach—a new conviviality will not take place automatically, but without them and without distance education programs, little will be achieved in terms of a new coexistence. That is, a society that produces and distributes productive and valuable knowledge through ICT to be shared and recreated by all is what is needed.

To produce inclusion, we will have to work hard to carry out tasks, such as:

- Removing perceptions and thoughts, prejudices and habits after conducting serious diagnoses of the current situation of what exists in terms of education, culture, science, technology, and innovation that guide us (or not) in a grounded way in a reformulation of the exclusionary situations;
- Assessing the "technological flexibility" that arises, as we abandon the (erroneous) beliefs held, as we acknowledge other social uses of ICTs (via respect for cultural diversity) and enhance the capacity of users to meet their demands for information, communication, and recreation of knowledge, which contributes to their sustainability;
- Agreeing on public policy to integrate ICT in education in a prudent way, from a substantive educational technology focus, with innovative teaching training. It takes full advantage of all the spaces for learning: we understand this is ubiquitous, collaborative, and lifelong, and should be for advancement toward *e-maturity* for a significant and relevant adoption of ICT, and including *e-awareness*, or electronic consciousness toward genuine democratic citizen participation. This will overcome the socio-cognitive former and current deficit of a mere instrumental conception of technology;
- Planning in a decentralized way with regional and local policies, of translation of demands according to cultural patterns to be distributed in a customized way by strengthening the power of knowledge;
- Developing and building *new capacities for power*, that is, to lead and empower ourselves in a representative and shared way in the usage of ICTs within the socio-reticular spaces. These contexts are optimal to the design and development of sustained environments by reflective political decisions on technology to reconcile various apparently conflicting theories of thoughts by doing some synthesis.

This proposal might produce social equity, e-inclusion, and a new conviviality. In other words, the experience of collaborative, distributed, contextual, and interaction processes of material and symbolic products, goods, and services, presupposes two types of learning:

1. One approach: referred to the historical idea that reflection takes place by anchoring the new information in past experiences.
2. The other approach: to focus on "future emergents" through the practice of insights (or visionary or intuitive findings), where a surprising or sudden clarity about what to do is produced.

As a result, ranks of freedom are earned from the constraints and the way of seeing and thinking is changed.

It is also necessary to practice:

1. *New literalism to develop skills in the form of e-skills* that refer to digital media literacy, with the appropriate use of technologies for communication and expression with the resources of the social Web 2.0 and networks for an e-training (e-learning, blended learning, etc.), and e-working. This implies not only access to telematic resources, but also to practice an essential reading and strategic writing on the Internet to reach a self-regulatory protagonist in the virtual environment. Also, the sustainable technologies from the user's perspective by a student-centered learning, community, and families, lead to diversity. Literacy, deconstruction, and awareness are the processes that characterize and consider the various types of social inclusion in general, and especially digital, as Freire would have said. It means seeing how ICT and networks help (or not) to overcome exclusion. They constitute unavoidable steps to begin training and appropriating symbolic languages and tools, to acquire digital skills. That is so, because only concepts and procedures are really understood when the artifactual devices correspond to the required processes and products.
2. Social and e-inclusion in the umbrella of the above mentioned frameworks link the *relevant principles of precaution, sustainability, prudence, and ethics.* They should be standards for open development strategies that have originated from the paradigm pillars named above, which drive the creative potential of context and users. It means recognizing their economy and culture, transforming the negative aspects (lack of infrastructure, shortage of strategies of abstract thinking, and reduced resources for production) into positive processes and products of relevant socio-cultural and technological innovation.

The more meaningful principles of socio-technological-educational inclusion could be:

1. *Precaution.* Its meaning etimologically: the prefix *pre-* means before, and *caution* means carefulness in the face of danger. A fire drill is a precaution so that you know what to do in case of a real fire.

2. *Sustainability.* Although everything that we need for our survival and well-being depends, either directly or indirectly, on our natural environment, the sustainability criterion creates and maintains the conditions under which humans and nature can exist in productive harmony, in ways that permit fulfilling the society and economy, and other requirements of present and future generations. In the case of virtual educational sustainable programs, it is important to take into account the multidimensional evaluation model, to make sure that the virtual program is satisfying and will continue satisfying needs, hopes, and expectations for more productivity, equality, and democracy of the educational proposals.

3. *Ethics.* Ethics are referred to as a product of society. They form a set or system of moral ideals, sometimes linked to diverse ideologies. Many ethical issues deal with the relationship between the individual and groups, in which changes occur very fast and with ambiguity. Ethics are also related (and commonly confused perhaps, because of their inherent overlap) to other concepts such as *morality* and *values*.

- *Morality.* This is the personal or/and group perception of what is right and wrong, good and bad. In general, the perception of morality is modulated more or less directly by the electronic media. Nobody knows how the media affect other people—in their attitudes and wills—with their diverse influences.
- *Values.* These are the qualities or ideas each person or group cares about and considers important. They can be morally or ethically based, or simply based on natural hopes and/or needs. They can be good or bad, reasonable or unreasonable. Values are the elements on which people base future actions.

4. *Prudence.* This is related to wisdom in handling practical issues such as selection and combination of technologies, which need professional insight in exercising good judgment (and many times taking into account common sense). It is often associated with virtue, knowledge, wisdom, and so on. It is the ability to judge situations with regard to appropriate mediated actions by the Internet and ICT, at a given time and place.

It is the state's role to assume and promote an economic/financial/cultural agenda that corresponds to the training of people in general, and using multidirectional virtual networks to enhance communications and install viable innovation. This in turn is feasible for educational programs in Latin American countries—and other peripheral countries—as leaders, who assume, design, and protect—with "designs for all"—educational and technological strategies and policies of digital inclusion.

However, we still see that, despite the huge presence of explicit statements such as this, there are curious paradoxes and little realization, given, for example, by some good economic indicators. But these indicators do not comply with the achievement levels that the information society should achieve, not only to create knowledge, but also to apply it to reduce material poverty and increase symbolic production for the greatest social benefit.

No breakthroughs have been found in the concepts and their significant practical applications, viewed on a generalization of integrating into society the advanced technological apparatus to promote skill development (i.e., full liberties) as opportunities for all. In other words, the hegemony of "official" knowledge still abounds, supported by socio-economic, political, and cultural inequality, which adopt new clothes, evidences.

SOME OPEN RECOMMENDATIONS

Making recommendations for consolidating e-democratic inclusion by training people in representative ways is an educational task par excellence, which guarantees minimum conditions of quality of life and global social peace through socio-educational interaction mechanisms. These mechanisms are increasingly mediated by technology today, and are included within Freire's framework of ideas, values, and attitudes based on consensus of civic responsibility, inter-subjective empathy, intercultural respect, and recognition of contradictions and tensions, among others. It involves several theoretical, methodological, and practical tasks of negotiation, as an alternative for overcoming various exclusions. So concurrently and through successive approximations, we propose a deepening not only of the new sociology of science and technology, but also different lines of inquiry. These will affect the electronic distance education programs that are characterized today by a consumerist scientific-technological boom, with global controversy, disparities, and adversity.

The practice of a substantive reflexivity will give not only a new meaning to the concept of social inclusion for a new conviviality within global social systems traversed by ICT, but also the analysis of public policy proposals that would overcome socio-educational and technological exclusion.

The lines of inquiry (related to electronic mediated education, social, and e-inclusion, for a new cultural and educational paradigm, with the use of ICT and virtual network) might be:

1. An *epistemological line* that identifies and encodes the features of the situated production of knowledge for a socially useful, pertinent, and prudent use to counter the techno-scientific effects of risk;

2. A *socio-cultural line* that leads us to think collectively and reflectively (with special emphasis placed in the communities of virtual learning, practice, knowledge production, and research) on aims and content of a necessary training, as well as of the role of knowledge and its social legitimization produced in the peripheral societies or emerging countries, and which would be distributed (equally) by ICT;

3. A *historical-political line* represented by interpellations throughout time: one provoked "from the outside" to stimulate the creation and implementation of policies and instruments of socio-structural change; and one viewed "from the inside," given by the greater active participation of social actors that require not only knowing more but also developing the skills to perform in the knowledge society, and who are "clients" of higher electronic distance education;

4. A *pedagogical and technological-educational line* that strays from—after revealing the educational non-contextualized standardization produced by lineal and senseless electronic learning—the features that the *online education training programs and materials should possess, taking advantage of the potentialities* of human interaction/communication in telematic networks with strong socio-cultural grounding, mediated by Internet. In turn, they announce and propose an equitable distribution and collaboration through a "humanizing" configuration of electronic systems: a design alternative, opportunities, and ways to communicate are multiplied, as an aid to human development and the *online* community.

REFERENCES

Baricco, A. (2008). *Los bárbaros. Ensayo sobre la mutación*. Barcelona, Spain: Anagrama.

Castells, M. (2004). *The network society: A cross-cultural perspective*. Northampton, MA: Edward Elgar.

Dowens, S. (2011). Connectives and connective knowledge. *Education: The Internet Newspaper*. Retrieved October 20, 2013, from http://www.huffingtonpost.com/stephen-downes/connectivism-and-connecti_b_804653.html

Fainholc, B. (2004). Lectura critica en Internet. Homo Sapiens, Argentina. Retrieved October 20, 2013, from http://www.lecturayvida.fahce.unlp.edu.ar/numeros/a26n2/26_02_Fainholc.pdf

Fainholc, B. (2008). *Programas, profesores y estudiantes virtuales: Una sociología de la educación a distancia*. Buenos Aires, Argentina: Santillana.

Fainholc, B. (2010). *Flexible and open educational programs*. New York, NY: Nova Science.

Fainholc, B. (2012a). *Appropriate and critical educational technology. New concepts* [E-book; ISBN 978-3-659-06227-8]. Retrieved from www.morebooks.es

Fainholc, B. (2012b). *Una tecnología educativa apropiada y critica: Nuevos enfoques*. Buenos Aires, Argentina: Humanitas-Lumen.

Levy, P. (1999). *Collective intelligence: Mankind's emerging world in cyberspace*. New York: Basic.

Siemens, G. (2004). Connectiveness: A learning theory for the digital age. *Elearnspace: Everything elearning.* Retrieved October 10, 2013, from http://www.elearnspace.org/Articles/connectivism. htm

Siemens, G. (2006). Connectivism: Learning theory or pastime of the self-amused? *Elearnspace: Everything elearning.* Retrieved October 10, 2013, from http://www.elearnspace.org/Articles/connectivism_self-amused.htm

Contributors

Yasmeen Ali graduated from University of Central Lancashire in 2003. She has a keen interest in working with young people from marginalised groups, acting as an advocate for young people in care as well as gaining qualifications in mentoring young offenders. She currently coordinates the Global Youth Solutions Programme which aims to help young people to take a lead in identifying and actively planning solutions to community issues in countries such as Turkey and Pakistan.

Jon Austin is an Associate Professor and Director of Research at the Centre for Australian Indigenous Knowledges at the University of Southern Queensland. His doctorate explored the development of white racial identities and he has published widely in the areas of critical pedagogies, whiteness and identity studies, critical and indigenous research methodologies, and anti-racist education.

Denise Bachega, a psychologist, gained a master's degree in Psychology at Federal University of São Carlos (UFSCar), Brazil. She has a particular interest in research about Paulo Freire's theories and on the fields of Education and Psychology of Education.

Renee Baynes is a lecturer in Indigenous Studies with the Centre for Australian Indigenous Knowledges at the University of Southern Queensland (USQ).

Currently a doctoral student with USQ, Renee has also completed an MPhil, Grad Dip (Learn and Teach), and a BApp.Sc.

Leon Benade has an EdD and is a senior Lecturer and Director of Research in the School of Education at Auckland University of Technology, New Zealand. His research activity focuses on the purposes of the New Zealand Curriculum, the ethical nature of teachers' work and the role of critical and reflective activity in schools. Leon is on the Executive Committee of the Philosophy of Education Society of Australasia (PESA).

Tina Besley is Professor of Education and Director of the Centre for Global Studies in Education, University of Waikato. She has held academic posts at the University of Glasgow, California State University–San Bernardino, and the University of Illinois at Urbana-Champaign, where she remains Adjunct Professor. Tina's research interests encompass philosophy of education, school counseling, educational policy, subjectivity, youth studies, interculturalism, and global knowledge economy. Tina has written some 10 books and monographs and is associate editor of *Educational Philosophy and Theory* (EPAT), co-editor of *E-Learning and Digital Media* and sits on many editorial boards. Tina is vice-president of the Philosophy of Education Society of Australasia (PESA), a long-standing member of the New Zealand Association of Counsellors (MNZAC). Her recent books include *Intercul-turalism, Education and Dialogue* (2012), *The Creative University* (2013), and *Re-imagining the Creative University in the 21st Century* (2013).

Russell Bishop was the Foundation Professor for Māori Education, Faculty of Education, University of Waikato, New Zealand. Russell has made substantial contributions to educational research in both national and international settings with much being grounded in kaupapa Māori research, the methodology by which he undertook both his master's degree and doctoral study. From these studies, his hypotheses, examinations, and theorising about the importance of Māori metaphors and the place power plays in research when it is being undertaken in Māori communities have paved the way for his ongoing research and for developing scholars around the world. From this work, Russell has an impressive list of publications, keynotes, and awards for excellence in research both nationally and internationally.

Veronica Branco is a teacher of the Department of Theory and Practice of Education of the Federal University of Paraná, Teaching Practice of Adult Education. She is Project Coordinator for Human Rights Education in Technology and Human Dignity in the Criminal System of Paraná, sub-project Environmental Education: systemic look at Penal Unit of Paraná,

Strengthening Management Practices of the Committees for Human Rights Education: social and collective commitment and Educational Activities of musicalization. She is also Coordinator of Research Voices from Prison, partnership with the State Department of Justice, Citizenship and Human Rights of Paraná.

Tim Budge is a PhD candidate at Deakin University, Australia. His diverse professional background includes secondary and adult education, community development, human rights, and international development. From 2005 to 2013, he worked in Timor-Leste and Zambia as Country Director for Plan International.

João dos Santos Carmo is Professor in the Department of Psychology at Federal University of São Carlos (UFSCar), Brazil. He is Researcher at the National Institute of Science and Technology on Behavior, Cognition and Teaching (INCT-ECCE)–Brazil.

Lea Campbell coordinates internships for the School of Social and Political Sciences at University of Melbourne. Her PhD pursued social theory linking social policy with drug policy. She become a research coordinator for a digital storytelling project, "I just want to go to school." Always involved in research, partnership, and policy work, her passion lies in addressing educational inequities. She is currently involved in Our Children, Our Schools to help mobilise parents for the planned and "apolitical" provision of public schools in Victoria, Australia.

Antonia Darder is a distinguished international Freirean scholar. She holds the Leavey Presidential Endowed Chair of Ethics and Moral Leadership at Loyola Marymount University, Los Angeles, and is Professor Emerita of Education Policy, Organization, and Leadership at the University of Illinois at Urbana-Champaign. Her scholarship focuses on issues of racism, political economy, social justice and education, critical pedagogy, and Latino education. She has published widely and is an activist and visual artist, participating in a variety of grassroots efforts tied to educational rights, worker's rights, bilingual education, women's issues, environmental justice, and immigrant rights.

Júlio Emílio Diniz-Pereira is a Professor at Federal University of Minas Gerais (UFMG), Brazil. He received his PhD in 2004 from the University of Wisconsin–Madison in Curriculum and Instruction. Author of the book *How the Dreamers Are Born: Struggles for Social Justice in Brazil and the Identity Construction of Activist Educators* (Peter Lang, 2013), Professor Diniz-Pereira has been a Short-Term Scholar at UW–Madison, where since 2004 he has taught a summer course entitled "Paulo Freire and Education for Social Justice."

Susila Kumari Embekke obtained her PhD from the University of Peradeniya, Sri Lanka, and Master of Philosophy degree in Education from the University of Peradeniya. She is currently teaching at the University of Peradeniya, Department of Education, Sri Lanka.

Beatriz Fainholc is General Director of CEDIPROE Center, Titular Professor and Researcher in Educational Technology and Distance Learning (E- and blended learning) at degree and post-studies levels in national and international universities (University del Salvador, Tecnologica Nacional De Buenos Aires) in Mexico, Spain, and Uruguay. She works in the Education Sciences Department at National University of La Plata, Buenos Aires, Argentina.

Ana Maria Araujo Freire (Nita Freire) holds a master's and a PhD in Education from the Catholic University of São Paulo (PUC-SP). Since 1997, as Paulo Freire's widow, she has been the legal successor of his work. Nita Freire speaks at conferences and seminars around the world, especially on the theory and praxis of Paulo Freire as well as on the history of Brazilian education, with emphasis on illiteracy in Brazil. Nita Freire was twice the recipient of the Jabuti Award, the most important literary prize in Brazil—the first time with Paulo Freire (*Pedagogia da Tolerância*, 2006), and in 2007, for her rigorous work, *Paulo Freire: Uma História de Vida*. She is also the recipient of the Commendation of Educational Merit Paulo Freire, granted by the Board of Education of Pernambuco, Brazil (1998). In 2009, she was awarded the Sixty Years UNESCO Medal, granted by UNESCO, and the Key of Wisdom Trophy, granted by the Brazilian Ministry of Education. Some of her publications are: *Nós Dois—Nita e Paulo Freire* (2013); *Chronicles of Love: My Life With Paulo Freire* (2001); *Analfabetismo no Brasil*, (1989); *Centenário de Nascimento de Aluízio Pessoa de Araújo* (1997); *Centenário de Nascimento de Francisca de Albuquerque Araújo—Genove* (2002); *A Pedagogia da Libertação em Paulo Freire* (org. 1999); *Pedagogia dos Sonhos Possíveis* (org. 2001); and *Pedagogia da Solidariedade* with Paulo Freire and Walter de Oliveira (2009).

Bradley Hannigan holds a BA, BA (Hons.), MA, and PhD from Victoria University in Wellington, New Zealand. He works as a Senior Education Advisor for Nelson Tasman Kindergartens, where he is responsible for the education programme throughout the Association.

Anne Harris, PhD is currently an Australian Research Council Early Career Research Award (DECRA) Fellow 2014-2016 researching the commodification of creativity. She is a Senior Lecturer in Education at Monash

University (Melbourne), and an interdisciplinary researcher in the areas of creative arts and pedagogy, culture, diversity, and digital media. She is a native New Yorker and has worked professionally as a playwright, teaching artist, and journalist in the USA and Australia. She has published over 50 articles and 6 books in this area, her latest being *Queer Teachers, Identity and Performativity* (2014, Palgrave).

Liz Jackson holds a doctorate from the University of Illinois at Urbana-Champaign. Liz is Assistant Professor of Education at the University of Hong Kong. She has also worked in South Africa and the United Arab Emirates in educational policy. Her research areas include multicultural and international education. Her book *Muslims and Islam in U.S. Education: Reconsidering Multiculturalism* (2014, Routledge) has been well received.

Asoka Jayasena obtained her PhD from Monash University, Australia, and two master's degrees from Teachers College, Columbia University, New York, and the University of Colombo, Sri Lanka. She was the Professor of Education at the University of Peradeniya, Sri Lanka, and is currently professor at Walden University, United States.

Jorge Jorquera is a long time educator and community activist. He has taught in education, sociology, and politics at various universities and TAFE Institutes, as well as having developed and taught a wide range of advocacy and campaign skills courses for many NGOs.

Iti Joyce is a member of the Te Kotahitanga research and professional development team at the University of Waikato, New Zealand. She has a master's degree in Educational Leadership and has worked within the Te Kotahitanga project as a teacher and in-school professional development facilitator.

Débora Barbosa Agra Junker is Brazilian and currently Assistant Professor of Christian Education and Director of the Master of Arts Degree in Multicultural Christian Education at Christian Theological Seminary in Indianapolis, Indiana. She holds a PhD in Education and Congregational Studies from Garrett-Evangelical Theological Seminary, Illinois, a Master of Arts in Christian Education from Christian Theological Seminary and a Master in Practical Theology from the Methodist University of São Paulo, Brazil.

Rosetta Khalideen is currently Dean of the Faculty of Professional Studies at the University of the Fraser Valley, British Columbia, Canada. Her background is in Education with a focus on Adult Education. Her research areas include the internationalization of higher education, critical Adult Education, Prior Learning Assessment and Recognition, and the teaching of English as a Second Language.

Wajid Khan graduated in Law from University of Central Lancashire in 2002. He then worked in the voluntary sector with young offenders, gaining qualifications in advice and guidance as well as mentoring, and teaching homeless young people numeracy and literacy. In 2004, he completed a master's degree in European Law. Inspired by the 2001 race riots in Burnley, UK, he initiated several projects involving community cohesion, including the Corrymeela project, through which his role gained him a HEACF Volunteering Award in 2004.

Althea Lambert gained her PhD from Auckland University of Technology in 2011. She is a teacher and (social) scientist, who spent fourteen years as a wool biologist (with 50+ publications). She describes herself as a critical irritant, voice-raising activist for women who imbibed "resistance" during time in the Chiapas highlands documenting indigenous ways of knowing with Tzotzil women and their sheep. She has ten years of teaching experience (prisons, tertiary, community). Her current focus is on critical pedagogy, young women's health, and "love" methodologies.

Muriel Yuen-fun Law obtained her PhD (Cultural Studies) at Lingnan University, Hong Kong. Muriel is an independent researcher, specializing in cultural research, and research in arts and drama education. She teaches applied drama/theatre at Hong Kong Art School and publishes in local and overseas academic journals in cultural studies and drama education. She now serves as the editor of DaTEAsia (an academic journal published by TEFO).

Dawn Lawrence is a postgraduate student at the University of Waikato, New Zealand. Previously a teacher and Te Kotahitanga in-school professional development facilitator, she is currently a member of the Te Kotahitanga research and professional development team in the Faculty of Education, University of Waikato.

Linda M. Locke has been a primary school music specialist for more than twenty years. Her MEd thesis investigated philosophically the claim that teaching is an art, especially in relation to music education. Her classroom-based research has appeared in the *British Journal of Music Education* and *Thinking Skills and Creativity*. She is currently undertaking doctoral research investigating the application of the Orff Schulwerk approach in New Zealand contexts.

Peter McLaren, Distinguished Fellow in Critical Studies, Chapman University, was formerly Professor in the Division of Urban Schooling, Graduate School of Education and Information Studies, University of California, Los

Angeles. Peter is a dual Canadian-U.S. citizen, the author and editor of approximately 50 books with research interests in critical pedagogy, critical ethnography, political sociology of education, critical theory, Marxist theory, revolutionary social movements, critical race theory, and social justice education. Five of his books have won the Critic's Choice Award of the American Educational Studies Association. His critically acclaimed book *Life in Schools: An Introduction to Critical Pedagogy in the Foundations of Education* (Allyn & Bacon) is now in its sixth edition, now with Paradigm Press.

Alethea Melling holds a PhD and is Director of the Centre for Volunteering and Community Leadership, University of Central Lancashire. She has spent more than twenty-five years working with young people in various contexts. She is responsible for the development and delivery of major volunteering and community cohesion projects across Lancashire, Cumbria, and internationally. Her Community Cohesion projects in East Lancashire have been recognised at the governmental level as examples of good practice and she has been honoured with MBE.

Jacob Neumann is Assistant Professor in Curriculum & Instruction at the University of Texas–Pan American. He holds an Ed.D in Social Education from the University of Houston. His work has recently been published in *Teachers College Record*, *The Urban Review*, and *The Educational Forum*.

Holger Nord received his PhD in 2005 from the University of Melbourne (Australia), looking at language policies and neocolonial structures infiltrating the classroom. His MA thesis looked at advertisements as historical documents. He has worked at tertiary and secondary institutions in Australia and overseas. He is currently an area manager for the Victorian Schools of Languages in Melbourne.

Tracey Ollis is a lecturer and Course Director of the Graduate Diploma of Applied Learning in the Education school at Deakin University. Tracey uses critical pedagogy and the writing of the renowned educational philosopher Paulo Freire to examine the informal learning dimensions of adults, activists, communities, and social movements. Her recent book, *A Critical Pedagogy of Embodied Education: Learning to Become an Activist* (Palgrave), examines the informal learning of circumstantial and lifelong activists.

Glen Parkes is a lecturer and doctoral student within the Centre for Australia Indigenous Knowledges, University of Southern Queensland, Australia. His interests involve looking to critically engage and participate in the decolonial project through locating multiple ways of viewing and researching our worlds. Charlie and Donna inspire him daily to undertake this journey.

Kura Paul-Burke is the Manager of Environment and Research at Te Mana o Ngāti Rangitihi Trust (Māori Tribal Authority) based in Matatā, Aotearoa/ New Zealand. Kura was formerly Education Lecturer, University of Waikato and Te Whare Wānanga o Awanuiārangi. She has worked on advisory panels for the Ministry of Education (ECE), Teacher Education Degree Accreditation Panels (New Zealand Teachers Council), Kaupapa Māori Assessment Advisory Panels and was one of five writers to develop, research and write a Māori Centred Teaching Degree Program that was successfully accredited and rolled out across New Zealand in 2011. Kura's PhD research focuses on mātauranga Māori (Māori knowledge) and Western science, informing the sustainable management of traditional customary marine resources.

Michael A. Peters is currently Professor of Education, WMIER, University of Waikato. He held a Personal Chair at the University of Auckland, was Professor at the University of Glasgow and the University of Illinois at Urbana-Champaign (now Emeritus Professor). Michael is an international scholar with interests in education, philosophy, and social policy, who has published more than 65 books and is editor-in chief of *Educational Philosophy and Theory* (EPAT) as well as editor of *Policy Futures in Education* and *E-Learning and Digital Media*. Some recent books: *Education Philosophy and Politics: Selected Works of Michael A. Peters* (2011); *Education, Cognitive Capitalism and Digital Labour* (2011), with Ergin Bulut; *Neoliberalism and After? Education, Social Policy and the Crisis of Capitalism* (2011); *The Last Book of Postmodernism: Apocalyptic Thinking, Philosophy and Education in the Twenty-First Century (2011); The Virtues of Openness: Education, Science and Scholarship in a Digital Age* (2011), with Peter Roberts; *Education in the Creative Economy* (2010), with D. Araya; a trilogy on Creativity, all with Simon Marginson and Peter Murphy (2009–2010); *Subjectivity and Truth: Foucault, Education and the Culture of the Self* (2008) (AESA Critics Book Award 2009); and *Building Knowledge Cultures: Educational and Development in the Age of Knowledge Capitalism* (2006), *The Creative University, Re-imagining the Creative University in 21st Century* (2013), with Tina Besley.

Lesley Rameka is a Senior Lecturer at the School of Educational Psychology and Pedagogy, Faculty of Education, Victoria University of Wellington. She has a background in te *kōhanga* reo and professional development. Lesley's interest in assessment led to her working as a coordinator on the Kei Tua o te Pae: early childhood exemplars project and as Project Director for the Te Whatu Pōkeka: Kaupapa Māori Assessment for Learning: Early Childhood

Exemplars project. Lesley's current interests include: Māori early childhood education, Assessment and Curriculum and Māori perspectives of Infants and Toddlers.

Peter Roberts is Professor of Education at the University of Canterbury in New Zealand. His research interests include philosophy of education, the ethics and politics of education, literature and education, the pedagogy of Paulo Freire, and tertiary education policy. His most recent book is *Better Worlds: Education, Art, and Utopia*, with John Freeman-Moir (2013). In 2010, he was a Canterbury Fellow at the University of Oxford, and in 2012 he was an inaugural Rutherford Visiting Scholar at Trinity College, Cambridge. He is current President of the Philosophy of Education Society of Australasia (PESA).

Charlotte Sexton completed a master's degree in Visual Arts at Monash University. Working as a visual artist, writer, academic, and curator, her work was featured in a number of Australian and international magazines, books, galleries, and museums. She has a Diploma in Government, which enabled her to work in the NSW and Commonwealth Public Service. She has commenced a Bachelor of Business/Bachelor of Law at the University of New England in Armidale, NSW.

Graham Smith is an internationally renowned Māori educationalist who has been at the forefront of the alternative Māori education initiatives contributing significantly to the political, social, economic, and cultural advancement of Māori communities. He has also worked extensively with other indigenous/First Nations peoples across the world, including Canada, Hawaii, US mainland, Taiwan, Chile, Australia, and the Pacific nations, contributing to national forums on indigenous issues. His academic background is within the disciplines of education, social anthropology, and cultural and policy studies, with recent academic work centred on developing theoretically informed transformative strategies for intervening in Māori cultural, political, social, educational, and economic crises. His other specialist interest is in institutional transformations in order to deliver more effectively to, and for the interests of, indigenous students, faculty, and communities. He has published widely and is in demand as a commentator on national and international indigenous matters.

M. J. Stuart holds a doctorate from Auckland University of Technology in early childhood education. She has an educational interest in social justice in education. She works for Te Tari Puna Ora o Aotearoa, NZ Childcare association.

Si Belkacem Taieb is an Amazigh/Berber from Algeria. He is working as an associate researcher with Pr Ratna Ghosh from McGill University, Montreal, Canada. He received a PhD in Education from Te Kura Māori, Victoria University of Wellington, New Zealand. Si Belkacem is currently working on a postdoctoral project that integrates the cultural in the writing of an Amazigh philosophy of education for an educational curriculum and pedagogy.

Glenn Toh completed his BA (Honors) at Victoria University of Wellington. He then went on to complete a master's in Educational Studies and PhD at Northern Territory University and Curtin University, respectively. He teaches at Tamagawa University in Tokyo and keeps a keen watch over developments in pedagogy and power.

Eric D. Torres is an Assistant Professor of Education at the University of Wisconsin, Eau Claire. He earned a PhD. in Curriculum and Teaching with a specialization in Cultural Studies from the University of North Carolina at Greensboro, where he was a Franklin/Houston Scholar, and a JD from the Pontificia Universidad Católica del Perú.

Mauro Torres Siqueira has a BA in History and master's degree in Social Work, has twelve years of experience in teaching and research, and as a teacher worked with adult literacy projects as well as high school. In the MSW he developed research on Representations of Traditional Teaching for literacy teachers in public school (2005). Part of this study was later published in conference proceedings. Currently he is pursuing a PhD in Educational Psychology FE-USP/São Paulo, with research thoughts, feelings, and prejudices among young people in the periphery of São Paulo and has recently published works in the field of prejudice and racism.

Rob Townsend is Associate Dean of Engagement and a senior lecturer in social work with the Faculty of Education and Arts at Federation University Australia. Rob's areas of research include adult transitions and well-being, particularly how human and social capital is developed in diverse 21st century communities via formal and informal learning processes. Rob's recent research has been around peer learning and mature age transitions that facilitate access to tertiary education.

E. Jayne White is Senior Lecturer in the Faculty of Education at University of Waikato. Her work focuses on early years pedagogy and philosophy of education, on the complex processes and practices of meaning-making in contemporary society. At the heart of her practice lies a strong emphasis on dialogic pedagogy, and the ways in which teachers can best engage within complex learning relationships—regardless of the age of the learner. She has published books and recently organized an international conference on Bakhtin. Jayne is Secretary of the Philosophy of Education Society of Australasia (PESA).

Jo Williams is a former secondary school music and drama teacher, now teacher educator in the College of Education, Victoria University, Melbourne. Her research interests include critical pedagogy, teacher education, comparative education, and Latin American education systems. Her current PhD research focuses on a critical model of educational partnerships for social justice in an era of neoliberal crisis.

Name Index

Studies in the Postmodern Theory of Education

General Editor
Shirley R. Steinberg

Counterpoints publishes the most compelling and imaginative books being written in education today. Grounded on the theoretical advances in criticalism, feminism, and postmodernism in the last two decades of the twentieth century, Counterpoints engages the meaning of these innovations in various forms of educational expression. Committed to the proposition that theoretical literature should be accessible to a variety of audiences, the series insists that its authors avoid esoteric and jargonistic languages that transform educational scholarship into an elite discourse for the initiated. Scholarly work matters only to the degree it affects consciousness and practice at multiple sites. Counterpoints' editorial policy is based on these principles and the ability of scholars to break new ground, to open new conversations, to go where educators have never gone before.

For additional information about this series or for the submission of manuscripts, please contact:

Shirley R. Steinberg
c/o Peter Lang Publishing, Inc.
29 Broadway, 18th floor
New York, New York 10006

To order other books in this series, please contact our Customer Service Department:

(800) 770-LANG (within the U.S.)
(212) 647-7706 (outside the U.S.)
(212) 647-7707 FAX

Or browse online by series:
www.peterlang.com